# BUSINESS
# **CHINESE**
# DICTIONARY

# BUSINESS
# **CHINESE**
# DICTIONARY

## English-Chinese

**Editorial Team**
P.H.Collin
Chen Qingbai
Jiang Yan
Jin Shuyu
Song Xinguo
Wang Xian
Zhou Lijuan

# 英 汉 双 解 商 业 词 典

PETER COLLIN PUBLISHING
BEIJING WORLD PUBLISHING CORPORATION

First published in Great Britain 1995
by Peter Collin Publishing Ltd
1 Cambridge Road, Teddington, Middlesex, TW11 8DT

©Copyright PCP Ltd 1995
© English Text copyright P.H.Collin 1986, 1995

Published in China
by Beijing World Publishing Corporation

©Chinese text copyright Beijing World Publishing Corporation 1994

British Library Cataloguing in Publication Data

A Catalogue record for this book is available from the British Library
ISBN 0-948549-63-7

# 英汉双解商业词典

(English – Chinese Business Dictionary)

[英]P.H. 科林 编著

王献 陈庆柏 宋新国 金淑玉 周丽娟 姜燕 译

周丽娟 陈庆柏 审订

责任编辑 西世良

世界图书出版公司北京公司出版

北京朝阳门内大街 137 号

北京中西印刷厂印刷

新华书店北京发行所发行 各地新华书店及外文书店经销

Printed in Great Britain by
Antony Rowe Ltd, Chippenham, Wiltshire

# PREFACE

The aim of this dictionary is to give the user the essential English business vocabulary with translations in Chinese.

The entries cover the main areas of day-to-day business usage, including office practice, sales and purchases, shops, banking, insurance, taxation, commercial law, international trade and business travel. In addition, terms used in marketing, distribution, company finance and the stock exchange are also included. The differences between British and American usage are also covered.

Translations are given not only for the main words and their derived forms, but also for examples, with long example sentences showing how the words can be used and translated in context.

We particularly wish to acknowledge the work of the translators, and expecially Professor Chen Qingbai and Professor Zhou Lijuan, who edited the final text.

## 内 容 简 介

本书按英文字母顺序排列，收入有关商业、财会、金融、保险、税收、商法、企业管理及经济贸易等专业的 4500 词条；对每一词条提供了全面、简洁的定义及解释，并附有例句及英中文对照。此外，还对一些词汇作了简明语法注释；说明英美两国对某些词汇的不同用法等。

本书可供经济学和商学专业人员及有关大专院校师生使用。

# Aa

**AAA** letters indicating that a share or bond or bank is very reliable ; A³ (指股票、债券、银行是十分可靠的) : These bonds have an AAA rating 这些债券的信用程度是3A级的(十分可靠的)。
NOTE: you say 'triple A'

**"A" shares** pl. n. ordinary shares with limited voting rights A 种股票(表决权有限的普通股票)。

**A1** a. (a) best 最好的 : We sell only goods in A1 condition. 我们只出售最佳的商品。(b) ship which is A1 at Lloyd's = ship which is in best condition according to Lloyd's Register. 劳合船级社最好的船

◇**A1, A2, A3, A4, A5** n. standard international sizes of paper 纸张的国际标准型号 : You must photocopy the spreadsheet on A3 paper. 你应当在 A3 型纸上复制棋盘式对照表。We must order some more A4 headed notepaper. 我们应当订购一些 A4 型有抬头的便笺纸。

**abandon** v. (a) to give up or not to continue ; 放弃 : We abandoned the idea of setting up a New York office. 我们放弃了设立纽约办事处的打算。The development programme had to be abandoned when the company ran out of cash. 公司的资金全部用完, 不得不放弃其发展计划。to abandon an action = to give up a court case 放弃诉讼 (b) to leave (something) 离弃 : The crew abandoned the sinking ship. 全体船员离弃了正在下沉的轮船。

◇**abandonment** n. act of giving something up 放弃 : abandonment of a ship = giving up a ship and cargo to the underwriters against payment for total loss 船舶的放弃;弃船

**abatement** n. act of reducing 折扣;降低 : tax abatement = reduction of tax 减税

**abroad** adverb to or in another country 到国外;在国外 : The consignment of cars was shipped abroad last week. 寄售的小汽车于上周装船运往国外。The chairman is abroad on business. 董事长因公出国。Half of our profit comes from sales abroad. 我们的一半利润来自国外的销售额。

**absence** n. not being at work or at a meeting 缺席;缺勤 : in the absence of = when someone is not there 当…缺席 : In the absence of the chairman, his deputy took the chair. 董事长不在时, 由他的副职主持会议。leave of absence = being allowed to be absent from work 准某人假 : He asked for leave of absence to visit his mother in hospital. 他请假去探望住院的母亲。
NOTE: no plural

◇**absent** a. not at work or not at a meeting 缺勤的;缺席的 : Ten of the workers are absent with flu. 十名工人因患流感而缺勤。The chairman is absent in Holland on business. 董事长因公在荷兰。

◇**absentee** n. worker who stays away from work for no good reason 旷工者

◇**absenteeism** n. staying away from work for no good reason 旷工 : Absenteeism is high in the week before Christmas. 圣诞节前的一周，旷工是司空见惯的事。 The rate of absenteeism or the absenteeism rate always increases in fine weather. 天气好时，旷工率总是升高。

NOTE: no plural

**absolute** a. complete or total 完全的；绝对的；总的：absolute monopoly = situation where only one producer or supplier produces or supplies something 完全垄断: The company has an absolute monopoly of imports of French wine. 该公司完全垄断了法国酒的进口。 ◇ **absolutely** ad. completely 完全地: We are absolutely tied to our suppliers' schedules. 我们完全被供应方的议事日程所束缚。

**absorb** v. (a) to take in a small item so as to form part of a larger one 并吞；兼并：to absorb a surplus = to take back surplus stock so that it does not affect a business 收回盈余：Overheads have absorbed all our profits. = All our profits have gone in paying overhead expenses. 管理费用去我们全部的利润。 to absorb a loss by a subsidiary = to write a subsidiary company's loss into the main accounts 承担子公司的损失 (b) business which has been absorbed by a competitor = a small business which has been made part of a larger one 被一个竞争对手所兼并的企业 ◇ **absorption** n. making a smaller business part of a larger one 兼并（使较小的企业成为较大企业的一部分）

NOTE: no plural

**abstract** n. short form of a report or document 摘要；概括：to make an abstract of the company accounts 作一份该公司的帐目摘要

**a/c** or **acc** = ACCOUNT

**accelerated** a. made faster 加速的：accelerated depreciation = system of de-preciation which reduces the value of assets at a high rate in the early years to encourage companies, because of tax advantages, to invest in new equipment 加速折旧。

**accept** v. (a) to take something which is being offered 接受：to accept a bill = to sign a bill of exchange to indicate that you promise to pay it 承兑票据；to accept delivery of a shipment = to take goods into the warehouse officially when they are delivered 接受发运货物 (b) to say "yes" or to agree to something 认可；同意：She accepted the offer of a job in Australia. 她已同意那份在澳大利亚的工作。 He accepted £200 for the car. 他同意花 200 英镑购买这辆小汽车。 ◇ **acceptable** a. which can be accepted 可接受的：The offer is not acceptable to both parties. 该发价双方都不接受。 ◇ **acceptance** n. (a) signing a bill of exchange to show that you agree to pay it 承兑；认付：to present a bill for acceptance = for payment by the person who has accepted it 提示承兑票据；acceptance house or US acceptance bank = ACCEPTING HOUSE 承兑银行 (b) acceptance of an offer = agreeing to an offer 接受发价；接受发盘；to give an offer a conditional acceptance = to accept provided that certain things happen or that certain terms apply 对发价或要约进行有条件的接受：We have his letter of acceptance. = We have received a letter from him accepting the offer. 我们收到了他对发价的承诺函。 acceptance sampling = testing a small part of a batch to see if the whole batch is good enough 验收抽样认可（抽样检收） ◇ **accepting house** n. firm which accepts bills of exchange (i. e. promises to pay them) and is paid a commission for this 承兑银行（从事承兑汇票业务银行，收取手续费）

**access 1** n. to have access to something = to be able to obtain or reach something 能获得；能接近：He has access to large amounts of venture capital. 他获得了一大笔风险投资的款项。access time = time taken by a computer to find data stored in it 存取(数据)时间
NOTE: no plural
**2.** v. to call up (data) which is stored in a computer 调出数据(指贮存在计算机内的数据)：She accessed the address file on the computer. 她通过计算机获取地址资料。

**accident** n. something unpleasant which happens by chance (such as the crash of a plane)事故：industrial accident = accident which takes place at work 工伤事故；accident insurance = insurance which will pay when an accident takes place 事故保险

**accommodation** n. (a) money lent for a short time 通融；贷款 (b) to reach an accommodation with creditors = to agree terms for settlement 与债权人达成一项通融(协议) (c) accommodation bill = bill of exchange where the person signing is helping someone to raise a loan 通融票据；欠单 (d) place to live 住处：Visitors have difficulty in finding hotel accommodation during the summer. 夏季游客们很难在旅馆找到膳宿。They are living in furnished accommodation. 他们的住处家俱齐全。accommodation address = address used for receiving messages but which is not the real address of the company 通讯地址；收取文件地址(不是该公司真正的地址)
NOTE: no plural in GB English, but US English can have accommodations for meaning (d)

**accompany** v. to go with 伴随；陪同：The chairman came to the meeting accompanied by the finance director. 董事长赴会，财务主任陪同。They sent a formal letter of complaint, accompanied by an invoice for damage. 他们寄出了一封正式投诉信，并附上一份发票，要求赔偿损失。
NOTE: accompanied by something

**accordance** n. in accordance with = in agreement with or according to 与…一致；依据：In accordance with your instructions we have deposited the money in your current account. 遵照你的指示，我们已把钱存入你的活期存款帐户里。I am submitting the claim for damages in accordance with the advice of our legal advisers. 依照法律顾问的建议，我提出获得损失赔偿金的要求。

◇ **according to** prep. as someone says or writes 根据…所说或所写的：The computer was installed according to the manufacturer's instructions. 计算机是按照生产厂家的说明书安装的。

◇ **accordingly** ad. in agreement with what has been decided 按照：We have received your letter and have altered the contract accordingly. 我们收到你的来信之后，对合同做了相应的修改。

**account 1.** n. (a) record of money paid or owed 帐；帐目：Please send me your account or a detailed or an itemized account. 请把你的帐目或明细帐目交给我。expense account = money which a businessman is allowed by his company to spend on travelling and entertaining clients in connection with his business 费用帐户；营业费帐：He charged his hotel bill to his expense account. 他将其旅馆费用记入他的费用帐户上。(b) (in a shop) arrangement which a customer has to buy goods and pay for them at a later date (usually the end of the month) 帐单(商店用)；to have an account or a charge account or a credit account with Harrods 设立帐户或信贷帐户；在哈罗德商店赊帐；Put it on my account or charge it to my account. 把这记到我的

帐户上。(of a customer) to open an account= to ask a shop to supply goods which you will pay for at a later date(顾客用)开立信贷帐户;(of a shop) to open an account or to close an account = to start or to stop supplying a customer on credit(商店用)给…赊帐或停止赊帐; to settle an account = to pay all the money owed on an account 付讫;结帐; to stop an account = to stop supplying a customer until he has paid what he owes 停止赊帐;止赊; on account = as part of a total bill 记帐;赊帐: to pay money on account = to pay to settle part of a bill 先付一部分记帐的钱; advance on account = money paid as a part payment 预付部分记帐的钱;(c) customer who does a large amount of business with a firm and has an account 预付部分记帐的钱; 客户;户头: He is one of our largest accounts. 他是我们最大客户中的一个。Our salesmen call on their best accounts twice a month. 我们的销售人员每月访问最好的客户两次。account executive = employee who looks after certain customers or who is the link between certain customers and his company 客户执行人,营业经理 (d) the accounts of a business or a company's accounts = detailed record of a company's financial affairs 企业帐目或公司帐目: to keep the accounts = to write each sum of money in the account book 记帐;登帐; The accountant's job is to enter all the money received in the accounts. 会计工作是将全部收讫的钱入帐。annual accounts = accounts prepared at the end of a financial year 年度总帐; management accounts = financial information (sales, expenditure, credit, and profitability) prepared for a manager so that he can take decisions 管理帐目; profit and loss account = accounts for a company with expenditure and income balanced to show a final profit or loss 损益帐户; accounts department = dep artment in a company which deals with money paid, received, borrowed or owed 会计部门;会计处; accounts manager = manager of an accounts department 会计部门主任(经理); accounts payable = money owed by a company 应付帐款; accounts receivable = money owed to a company 应收帐款 (e) bank account or US banking account = arrangement to keep money in a bank 银行往来帐户或美国银行帐户; building society account 建筑房屋互助协会帐户; savings bank account 储蓄银行帐户; Girobank account 直接转帐银行帐户; Lloyds account 劳合社帐户: He has an account with Lloyds. 他在劳合社有帐户。I have an account with the Halifax Building Society. 我在哈利法克斯建筑房屋互助协会设有帐户。to put money in(to) your account 将钱存入你的帐户; to take money out of your account or to withdraw money from your account 从你的帐户中取钱; budget account = bank account where you plan income and expenditure to allow for periods when expenditure is high 预算帐户 (在考虑到支出很高时,计划内所允许的收入与支出的银行帐户); current account or cheque account or US checking account = account which pays no interest but from which the customer can withdraw money when he wants by writing cheques 往来帐户;活期存款; deposit account = account which pays interest but on which notice usually has to be given to withdraw money 存款帐户 (一种支付利息的银行帐户,支取时需提前一定的时间发出通知); external account = account in a British bank of someone who is living in anothercountry 对外帐户; frozen account = account where the money cannot be used or moved because of acourt order 冻结帐户; joint account = account for two people 共同帐户;联合帐户; Most married people have joint accounts so that they caneach take money out when they want it. 大多数的已婚者都在银行立了共同帐户, 以备必要时可各自取款。 overdrawn account = account where you have taken out more money than you have put in (i. e. where the bank is lending you money)透支帐户(支取的钱超过存款); savings account = account where you put money in regularly and which pays interest, often at a higher rate than a deposit account 储蓄帐户; to open an account = to start an account by putting money in 开立帐户; She opened an account with the Halifax Building Society. 她在哈利法克斯建筑房屋互助协会开立了帐户。 to close an account = to take. all money out of a bank account and stop the account 停止或关闭帐户(将钱从银行帐户中全部提取, 中止银行帐户); He closed his account with Lloyds. 他已停止使用其劳合社的帐户。(f)(Stock Exchange) period of credit (usually fourteen days at the end of which you must pay for shares bought)赊帐期(在证券交易所, 通常十四天内需付所买的股票): account day = day on which shares which have been bought must be paid for 结算日(须付清所买股票款项的日期); Share prices rose at the end of the account or the account end. 股票价格在结算日期末上扬。(g) notice 注意到: to take account of inflation or to take inflation into account = to assume that there will be a certain percentage inflationwhen making calculations 注意(考虑)到通货膨胀 2. v. to account for = to explain and record a money deal 说明(有关钱的事): to account for a loss or a discrepancy 说明亏损或发生差异的原因; The reps have to account for all their expenses to the sales manager. 推销人员必须向销售经理说明其全部开支。

◇**accountancy** n. work of an accountant 会计工作; 会计学: He is studying accountancy or He is an accountancy student. 他正学习会计学或他是一名会计专业的学生。

NOTE: no plural

◇ **accountant** n. person who keeps a company's accounts or person who advises acompany on its finances or person who examines accounts 会计师: the chief accountant of a manufacturing group 一个制造业集团的总会计师; I send all my income tax queries to my accountant. 我把所有有关所得税的疑问送交会计师。 certified accountant = accountant who has passed the professional examinations and is a member of the Association of Certified Accountants 注册会计师; 执业会计师; US certified public accountant = accountant who has passed professional examinations 美国执业会计师(通过专业考试的会计师); chartered accountant = accountant who has passed the professional examinations and is a member of the Institute of Chartered Accountants 执业会计师; 特许会计师(特许会计师学会成员): cost accountant = accountant who gives managers information about their business costs 成本会计师; management accountant = accountant who prepares financial information for managers sothat they can take decisions 管理会计人员

◇**accounting** n. work of recording money paid, received, borrowed or owed 会计; 会计学: accounting machine 会计计算机; accounting methods or accounting procedures 会计方法或会计程序; accounting system 会计制度; accounting period = period usually covered by a firm's accounts 会计结算期; 会计年度; cost accounting = preparing special accounts of manufacturing and sales costs 成本会计(制定与核算专门生产与销售费用的会计); current cost accounting = method of accounting which notes the cost of replacing assets at current prices, rather than valuing assets at their original cost 现行成本会计

NOTE: no plural

**accredited** a. (agent) who is appointed by a company to act on its behalfpuhc 委任的;任命的;执有委任状的

**accrual** n. gradual increase by addition 应计额;增值加额:accrual of interest = automatic addition of interest to capital 应计利息的累积

**accrue** v. to increase and be due for payment at a later date 自然增值:Interest accrues from the beginning of the month. 利息从月初开始自然增殖. Accrued interest is added quarterly 按季累积利息。accrued dividend = dividend earned since the last dividend was paid 累计股利(红利)

**acct** = ACCOUNT

**accumulate** v. to grow larger by adding 积累:to allow dividends to accumulate 使股利得以积累 accumulated profit = profit which is not paid as dividend but is taken over into the accounts of the following year 累计利润;累积盈利。

**accurate** a. correct 准确的:The sales department made an accurate forecast of sales. 销售部门做了一项准确的销售预测。The designers produced an accurate copy of the plan. 设计人员制作了一份准确的计划本。

◇**accurately** ad. correctly 准确地:The second quarter's drop in sales was accurately forecast by the computer. 电子计算机准确地预测了第二季度销售额下降。

**accuse** v. to say that someone has committed a crime 控告:She was accused of stealing from the petty cash box. 她被指控从小额备用金柜中偷钱。He was accused of industrial espionage. 他被指控从事工业间谍活动。

NOTE: you accuse someone of a crime

or of doing something

**achieve** v. to succeed in doing something or to do something successfully 完成;达到;实现:The company has achieved great success in the Far East. 该公司在远东已取得很大的成就。We achieved all our objectives in 1985. 我们实现了 1985 年全部目标。

**acknowledge** v. to tell a sender that a letter or package or shipment has arrived 承认;确认(说明已收到信件或包裹或装运的货物):He has still not acknowledged my letter of the 24th. 他仍未确认收到我 24 日的信件。We acknowledge receipt of your letter of June 14th 我们确认收到你六月十四日的来信。

◇ **acknowledgement** n. act of acknowledging 承认;签谢:She sent an acknowledgement of receipt. 她寄出一张回执(收到收据的通知)。They sent a letter of acknowledgement. 他们发出一封感谢信。

**acquire** v. to buy 买:to acquire a company 买下一个公司

◇ **acquirer** n. person or company which buys something 购置某物的人或公司

◇ **acquisition** n. thing bought; act of getting or buying something 买得;获得:The chocolate factory is his latest acquisition. 该巧克力工厂是他最近购买的。data acquisition or acquisition of data = obtaining and classifying data 数据收集或分类。

**acre** n. measure of the area of land ( = 0.45 hectares)英亩(英 1 亩 = 0.45 公顷)

NOTE: the plural is used with figures, except before a noun: He has bought a farm of 250 acres or He has bought a 250 acre farm. 他已购置了一个 250 英亩的农场。

**across – the – board** a. applying to everything or everyone 全面的;一致的:

an across – the – board price increase 全面提价；全面涨价

**act 1**n. (a) law passed by a parliament which must be obeyed by the people 条例；法令；法案：GB Companies Act = Act which rules how companies should do their business （英）公司法；Health and Safety at Work Act = Act which rules how the health of workers should be protectedby the companies they work for 卫生与安全工作法；Finance Act = annual Act of Parliament which gives the government power to raise taxes as proposed in the budget 财政法案 (b) act of God = something you do not expect to happen, and which cannot be avoided (such as storms or floods) 天灾；不可抗拒的事情 2. v. (a) to work 做事：充任：to act as an agent for an American company 任一家美国公司的代理（商）；to act for someone or to act on someone's behalf 代理某人 (b) to do something 做某事：The board will have to act quickly if the company's losses are going to be reduced.若要降低公司的亏损，那么董事会应加快行动。The lawyers are acting on our instructions. 律师正按我们的指示行事。to act on a letter – to do what a letter asks to be done 按信意行事

◇ **acting** a. working in place of someone for a short time 代理的：acting manager 代经理；the Acting Chairman 代主席；代理董事长

◇**action** n. (a) thing which has been done 行动；活动：to take action = to do something 采取行动；做某事；You must take action if you want to stop people cheating you . 你若防止上当受骗，必须采取行动。(b) direct action = strike or go – slow by the workforce 罢工；to take industrial action = to do something (usually to go on strike) to show that you are not happy with conditions at work 采取工业行动；罢工 (c) case in a

law court where a person or company sues another person or company 诉讼：to take legal action = to sue someone 起诉；action for damages 赔偿金诉讼；action for libel or libel action 诽谤罪诉讼；to bring an action for damages against someone 要求获得损失赔偿金向某人起诉；civil action = case brought by a person or company against someone who has done them wrong 民事诉讼；criminal action = case brought by the state against someone who is charged with a crime 刑事诉讼

◇**active** a. busy 积极的；繁忙的；active partner = partner who works in the company 任职合伙人；an active demand for oil shares 石油股票畅销；Oil shares are very active.石油股票十分抢手。an active day on the Stock Exchange 证券交易所繁忙的一天 Business is active. 业务繁忙。

◇ **actively** ad. in a busy way 繁忙地：The company is actively recruiting new personnel.公司正忙于补充新职工。

◇**activity** n. being active or busy 活跃；活动：a low level of business activity 低水准的经营活动；There was a lot of activityon the Stock Exchange . 证券交易所买卖活动繁忙。activity chart = plan showing work which has been done so that it can be compared to the plan of work to be done 生产情况示意图：monthly activity report = report by a department on what has been done during the past month 月活动报表
NOTE: no plural

**actual 1** a. real or correct 实际的；真实的：What is the actual cost of one unit? 一个单位的实际成本是多少？The actual figures for directors' expenses are not shown to the shareholders. 经理开支的确切数字尚未告知股东们。2 plural n. real figures 实数：These figures are the actuals for 1984. 一九八四年的这些

数字属实。

**actuary** n. person employed by an insurance company to calculate premiums 保险公司统计员(计算保险费)

◇**actuarial** a. calculated by an actuary 保险统计员计算的：The premiums are worked out according to actuarial calculations. 保险费是依据保险统计员的计算出来。actuarial tables = lists showing how long people of certain ages are likely to live, used to calculate life assurance premiums 保险公司统计项目表(指计算人寿保险金)

**ad** n. = ADVERTISEMENT

**add** v. (a) to put figures together to make a total 加：to add interest to the capital 利息加到本金上；Interest is added monthly. 按月加息。(b) to put things together to make a large group 增加：We are adding to the sales force. 我们正在增加销售人员。They have added two new products to their range. 他们给产品系列增添了两个新产品。This all adds to the company's costs. = This makes the company's costs higher. 这一切加大公司的成本。

◇ **add up** v. to put several figures together to make a total 合计：to add up a column of figures 将一栏的数字加在一起；The figures do not add up. = The total given is not correct. 这些数字总计不对。

◇ **add up to** v. to make a total 合计达：The total expenditure adds up to more than £1,000. 总支出合计超过1.000英磅。

◇**adding** n. which adds or which makes additions 加：an adding machine 加法器；加算机

◇ **addition** n. (a) thing or person added 增加人或物：The management has stopped all additions to the staff. 管理部门不再增加职工。We are exhibiting several additions to our product line. 我们正在展览生产线上增加的几种新产品。The marketing director is the latest addition to the board. 董事会中最新增加的成员是销售经理。(b) in addition to = added to or as well as 除…之外, 加于…上：There are twelve registered letters to be sent in addition to this packet. 除了该包裹外, 还有12封挂号信需邮寄。(c) putting numbers together 加：You don't need a calculator to do simple addition. 你不必使用计算器去做简单的加法。

**additional** a. extra which is added 附加的；追加的：additional costs 附加成本；·追加成本；额外费用；additional charges 附加费用；additional clauses to a contract 合同的附加条款；Additional duty will have to be paid. 附加税必须付清。

**address** 1. n. details of number, street and town where an office is or a person lives 地址：My business address and phone number are printed on the card. 名片上印着我的企业地址和电话号码。accommodation address = address used for receiving messages but which is not the real address of the company 通讯地址；收取信件的地址；cable address = short address for sending cables 电报挂号；forwarding address = address to which a person's mail can be sent on 转交信件的地址；home address = address of a house or flat where someone lives 家庭住址；Please send the documents to my home address. 请把文件送到我家. address list = list of addresses 地址一览表；We keep an address list of two thousand addresses in Europe. 我们持有一份欧洲2000个通讯地址一览表。2. v. (a) to write the details of an address on an envelope, etc. (在信封上)写地址：to address a letter or a parcel 在信上或包裹上写地址；Please address your enquiries to the manager. 请将你的询价呈交给经理。a letter addressed to the managing director 致函总经理；an incorrectly addressed package 地址有误的包裹(b) to speak 向…讲话: to address a meeting 在会议上发言

◇ **addressee** n. person to whom a letter or package is addressed 收件人

◇ **addressing machine** n. machine which puts addresses on envelopes automatically 姓名住址印刷机

**adequate** a. (a) large enough 充分的; 足够的: to operate without adequate cover = to act without being completely protected by insurance 未充分投保就经营

**adjourn** v. to stop a meeting for a period 休会: to adjourn a meeting 休会; The chairman adjourned the meeting until three o'clock. 董事长宣布休会到三点钟。The meeting adjourned at midday. 在正午休会。

◇ **adjournment** n. act of adjourning 休会;闭会: He proposed the adjournment of the meeting. 他提议休会。

**adjudicate** v. to give a judgement between two parties in law; to decide a legal problem 判决;裁定: to adjudicate a claim 裁决一起索赔案; to adjudicate in a dispute 在一项辩论中作裁决; He was adjudicated bankrupt. = He was declared legally bankrupt. 他被裁定为破产者。

◇ **adjudication** n. act of giving a judgement or of deciding a legal problem 判决;裁定; adjudication order or adjudication of bankruptcy = order by a court making someone bankrupt 宣判破产令或宣告破产; adjudication tribunal = group which adjudicates in industrial disputes 审判庭(裁决劳资争端)

◇ **adjudicator** n. person who gives a decision on a problem 裁决者;评判员: an adjudicator in an industrial dispute 工业(劳资)纠纷的裁决者

**adjust** v. to change something to fit new conditions 调节;调整: to adjust prices to

take account of inflation 考虑到通货膨胀而调整价格; Prices are adjusted for inflation. 因通货膨胀而调整价格;

◇ **adjuster** n. person who calculates losses for an insurance company 海损细算人;保险业中的理算员; average adjuster = person who calculates how much of an insurance is to be paid 海损理算员

◇ **adjustment** n. act of adjusting; slight change 调节;调整: tax adjustment 税收调节; wage adjustment 工资调整; to make an adjustment to salaries 调整工资; adjustment of prices to take account of rising costs 考虑到成本提高而调整价格格; average adjustment = calculation of the share of cost of damage or loss of a ship 海损理算

◇ **adjustor** n. = ADJUSTER

**adman** n. infml. man who works in advertising 广告员: The admen are using balloons as promotional material. 广告员正在把气球做为促销材料。

**admin** n. infml. (a) work of administration, especially paperwork 行政管理工作(特指文秘工作): All this admin work takes a lot of my time. 所有这些行政管理工作占用了我许多时间。There is too much admin in this job. 在这项工作中,行政管理工作占有相当大的比重。Admin costs seem to be rising each quarter. 行政管理费似乎每季都有所增加。The admin people have sent the report back. 行政管理人员已发还了这项报告。(b) administration staff 行政管理工作人员: Admin say they need the report immediately. 行政管理工作人员说他们急需这份报告。

NOTE: no plural; as a group of people it can have a plural verb

◇ **administer** v. to organize or to manage 管理: He administers a large pension fund. 他管理一笔巨额退休金。US administered price = price fixed by a manufacturer which cannot be varied by aretailer(美)限价；厂方订价（不受零售的影响）

◇ **administration** n. organization or control or management of a company 管理机构；the expenses of the administration or administration expenses = costs of management, not including production, marketing or distribution costs 管理费；行政费；letters of administration = letter given by a court to allow someone to deal with the estate of a person who has died 遗产管理委任状

◇ **administrative** a. referring to administration 管理的；行政的：administrative details 管理细则；administrative expenses 行政费；管理费

◇ **administrator** n. (a) person who directs the work of other employees in a business 行政管理人员 (b) person appointed by a court to manage the affairs of someone who dies without leaving a will 遗产管理人

**admission** n. (a) allowing someone to go in 允许进入；允许加入：There is a £1 admission charge 入场费为£1. Admission is free on presentation of this card. 出示此卡，方可免费入场。free admission on Sundays 星期日免费入场 (b) saying that something really happened 承认：He had to resign after his admission that he had passed information to the rival company. 当他承认将信息透露公司的对手后，他被迫辞职。

**admit** v. (a) to allow someone to go in 允许进入：Children are not admitted to the bank. 儿童勿入银行。Old age pensioners are admitted at half price. 领取养老金老人可享受半价。(b) to say that something is correct or to say that something really happened 承认：The chairman admitted he had taken the cash from the company's safe. 董事长承认他从公司的保险柜里拿了现金。

NOTE: admitting – admitted

◇ **admittance** n. allowing someone to go in 允许进入：no admittance except on business 非公莫入 NOTE: no plural

**adopt** v. to agree to (something) or to accept (something)通过；采纳：to adopt a resolution 通过一项决议；The proposals were adopted unanimously. 这些建议一致通过。

**ad valorem** phrase showing that a tax is calculated according to the value of the goods taxed 从价(根据已上税的货物价值来计算税) ad valorem duty 从价关税；ad valorem tax 从价税

**advance** 1. n. (a) money paid as a loan or as a part of a payment to be made later 贷款；预付：bank advance 银行贷(放)款；a cash advance 预付现金；to receive an advance from the bank 接受银行一笔贷款；an advance on account 记帐预付；to make an advance of £100 to someone 给某人 100 英镑的预付款；to pay someone an advance against a security 给某人支付一笔担保贷款；Can I have an advance of £50 against next month's salary? 我能以下月工资中预支 50 英磅吗? (b) in advance = early or before something happens 预先：to pay in advance 预付；freight payable in advance 预付运费；price fixed in advance 预订价格 (c) early 提前：advance booking 预订；advane payment 预付款项；You must give seven days' advance motice of withdrawals from the account. 若从帐户中提款，则必须提前七天通知。(d) increase 增加：advance in trade 贸易额增加；advance in prices 涨价；2. v. (a) to lend：借给；The bank advanced him £10,000 against the security of his house. 以他的住宅为抵押，银行贷给他 10,000 英磅。(b) to increase 增加：Prices generally advanced on the stock market. 证券市场的股票价格普遍地上涨。(c) to make something happen earlier 提前：The date of the AGM has been advanced to May 10th. 年度股东大会的日期提前到五月十日。 The meeting with the German distributors has been advanced from 11. 00 to 09.30. 与德国销售人员的会晤由 11：00 提前到 9：30。

**advantage** n. something useful which may help you to be successful 优势；有利条件：Fast typing is an advantage in a secretary. 打字快是秘书的一个优势。 Knowledge of two foreign languages is an advantage. 具有两门外语知识是一种优势。 There is no advantage in arriving at the exhibition before it opens. 没有好处在展览会开展前就到达。 to take advantage of something = to use something which helps you 利用（某物）

**adverse** a. bad or not helpful 不利的：adverse balance of trade = situation when a country imports more than it exports 贸易逆差；入超；adverse trading conditions = bad conditions for trade 不利的贸易条件

**advertise** v. to announce that something is for sale or that a job is vacant or that a service is offered 登广告：to advertise a vacancy 招聘启事；to advertise for a secretary 登广告招聘一位秘书；to advertise a new product 为新产品登广告

◇ **ad** n. infml. = ADVERTISEMENT We put an ad in the paper. 我们在报纸上登了一则广告。 She answered an ad in the paper. 她在报纸上对广告作了答复。 He found his job through an ad in the paper. 他通过报纸上的广告找到一份工作。 classified ads or small ads or want ads = advertisements listed in a newspaper under special headings (like "property for sale", "jobs wanted") 分类广告；小型广告或招聘广告；Look in the small ads to see if anyone has a computer for sale. 看一下小型广告，是否有人出售电子计算机。 coupon ad = advertisement with a form attached, which

is to be cut out and returned to the advertiser with your name and address for further information 带赠券广告；display ad = advertisement which is well designed to attract attention 醒目的广告

◇ **advert** n. GB infml. = ADVERTISEMENT (英国非正式的用语)：to put an advert in the paper 在报上刊登广告；to answer an advert in the paper 在报纸上对广告作肯定答复；classified adverts 分类广告 display advert 醒目的广告

◇ **advertisement** n. notice which shows that something is for sale or that a service is offered or that someone wants something or that a job is vacant, etc. 广告：to put an advertisement in the paper 在报纸上登广告；to answer an advertisement in the paper 在报上对广告作肯定答复；classified advertisements = advertisements listed in a newspaper under special headings (such as "property for sale" or "jobs wanted") 分类广告；display advertisement = advertisement which is well designed to attract attention 醒目的广告；advertisement manager = manager in charge of the advertisement section of a newspaper 广告部经理

◇ **advertiser** n. person or company which advertises 登广告的人或公司：The catalogue gives a list of advertisers. 该目录列出广告客户的名单。

◇ **advertising** n. business of announcing that something is for sale or of trying to persuade customers to buy a product or service 广告；广告业：She works in advertising. 她在广告业工作。 He has a job in advertising; 他从事广告工作。 advertising agent 广告代理人；advertising budget 广告费预算；advertising campaign 广告运动；advertising agency = office which plans, designs and manages advertising for other companies 广告代理；advertising manager = manager in charge of advertising a company's products广告经理; advertising rates = amount of money charged for advertising space in a newspaper or advertising time on TV 广告费; advertising space = space in a newspaper set aside for advertisements 广告版面; to take advertising space in a paper = to put an advertisement in a newspaper 在一张报上登广告 NOTE: no plural

**advice** n. (a) advice note = written notice to a customer giving details of goods ordered and shipped but not yet delivered 装货通知单; as per advice = according to what is written on the advice note 根据通知单 (b) opinion as to what action to take 忠告; 劝告; to take legal advice = to ask a lawyer to say what should be done 获得法律咨询; The accountant's advice was to send the documents to the police.这位会计的意见是把这些票据送给警方。We sent the documents to the police on the advice of the accountant or We took the accountant's advice and sent the documents to the police.我们根据这位会计的意见将这些票据送给警方。我们接受会计的意见并把这些票据送给了警方。

NOTE: no plural

**advise** v. (a) to tell someone what has happened 告知; 通知: We are advised that the shipment will arrive next week.我们接到通知, 装运的货物将于下周抵达。(b) to suggest to someone what should be done 建议; 劝告: We are advised to take the shipping company to court.有人建议我们控告船舶公司。The accountant advised us to send the documents to the police. 会计建议我们将这些票据送给警方。

◇ **advise against** v. to suggest that something should not be done 劝···当心; 劝告···不要(做某事); 建议···不···: The bank manager advised against closing the account. 银行经理建议不要关

闭帐户。My stockbroker has advised against buying those shares. 我的股票经纪人告诫我不要购买那些股票。

◇ **adviser or advisor** n. person who suggests what should be done 劝告者; 顾问: He is consulting the company's legal adviser. 他正在向公司的法律顾问咨询。financial adviser = person or company which gives advice on financial problems for a fee 财务顾问

◇ **advisory** a. as an adviser 咨询的; 顾问的: He is acting in an advisory capacity. 他正以顾问的身份从事。an advisory board = a group of advisers 咨询委员会; 顾问委员会

**affair** n. business or dealings 事务; 业务; 生意: Are you involved in the copyright affair? 你参与著作权的事务了吗? His affairs were so difficult to understand that the lawyers had to ask accountants for advice. 他的事务是十分费解, 于是律师们只好征求会计们的意见。

**affect** v. to change or to have a bad effect on (something)影响: The new government regulations do not affect us. 我们并未受到新政府的规定的影响。The company's sales in the Far East were seriously affected by the embargo. 公司在远东的销售额受到禁运的严重影响。

**affiliated** a. connected with or owned by another company 联营的; 联号的附属的: one of our affiliated companies 我们的联营公司之一。

**affirmative** a. meaning "yes"肯定的: The answer was in the affirmative. = The answer was yes. 答复是肯定的。US affirmative action program = programme to avoid discrimination in employment(美)废除就业歧视的纲领。NOTE: the GB equivalent is "equal opportunities"

**affluent** a. very rich 富裕的; 富足的: We live in an affluent society. 我们生活

在一个富裕的社会中。

**afford** v. to be able to pay or buy 买得起：We could not afford the cost of two telephones. 我们无力买两部电话（我们负担不起两部电话的费用）。The company cannot afford the time to train new staff. 公司花不起时间培训新职工。
NOTE: only used after can, cannot, could, could not, able to

**AFL — CIO** = AMERICAN FEDERATION OF LABOR — CONGRESS OF INDUSTRIAL ORGANIZATIONS
an organization linking US trade unions 劳联—产联（美国联邦政府的产业劳动者联合会）

**afraid** a. sorry, because something has happened 抱歉；表示歉意：I am afraid there are no seats left on the flight to Amsterdam. 真抱歉，飞往阿姆期特丹的班机已无空座。We are afraid your order has been lost in the post. 真抱歉，你的订货单在邮寄过程中丢失了。
NOTE: only used after to be

**after — hours** a. after — hours buying or selling or dealing = buying or selling or dealing in shares after the Stock Exchange has officially closed for the day 股市闭市后进行的股票交易或买卖。

◇ **after — sales service** n. service of a machine carried out by the seller for some time after the machine has been bought 售后服务

◇ **after — tax profit** n. profit after tax has been deducted 税后利润

**against** prep. relating to or part of 用…抵付：作为…部分 to pay an advance against a security 支付一笔担保贷款；Can I have an advance against next month's salary? 我能从下月工资中预支一部分款项吗？The bank advanced him £10,000 against the security of his house. 以他的住宅为抵押，银行给他10,000英磅的贷款。

**agency** n. (a) office or job of representing another company in an area 代理处；代理事务：They signed an agency agreement or an agency contract. 他们签署了一份代理的协议或一份代理合同。
sole agency = agreement to be the only person to represent a company or to sell a product in a certain area 独家代理：He has the sole agency for Ford cars. 他是福特小汽车的独家代理。(b) office or business which arranges things for other companies 代理机构；advertising agency = office which plans or designs and manages advertising forcompanies 广告公司；employment agency = office which finds jobs for staff 职业介绍所；estate agency = office which arranges for the sale of properties 房地产公司；news agency = office which distributes news to newspapers and television stations 通讯社；travel agency = office which arranges travel for customers 旅行社
NOTE: plural is agencies

**agenda** n. list of things to be discussed at a meeting 议事日程：the conference agenda or the agenda of the conference 会议日程；After two hours we were still discussing the first item on the agenda. 两小时之后，我们仍在讨论第一项议程。The secretary put finance at the top of the agenda. 秘书将财政问题放在本次议事日程的首位。The chairman wants two items removed from or taken off the agenda. 董事长打算从本次议事日程中去掉两个议事项目。

**agent** n. (a) person who represents a company or another person in an area 代理人：to be the agent for IBM 国际商业机器公司的代理人；sole agent = person who has the sole agency for a company in an area 独家代理商；独家代理人：He is the sole agent for Ford cars. 他是一位福特小汽车的独家代理商。agent's commission = money (often a percentage of sales) paid to an agent 代理人的

佣金。(b) person in charge of an agency 代理商;代理机构负责人 advertising agent 广告代理商; estate agent 房地产经纪人; travel agent 旅行社的老板或职员 commission agent = agent who is paid by commission, not by fee 佣金代办商; forwarding agent = person or company which arranges shipping and customs documents 货运承揽商;运输行; insurance agent = person who arranges insurance for clients 保险代理商; land agent = person who runs a farm or a large area of land for the owner 土地经营者;地产经纪人;(c) US (business) agent = chief local official of a trade union(美)工会的主要地方官员

**aggregate** a. total or with everything added together aggregate output 总的

**agio** n. charge made for changing money of one currency into another 贴水;银行手续费在兑换货币收取的费用)

## AGM n. = ANNUAL GENERAL MEETING

**agree** v. (a) to say yes or to accept 同意;赞成: After some discussion he agreed to our plan. 经过一番讨论,他同意了我们的计划。We all agreed on the plan. 我们一致同意这项计划。We have agreed to the budgets for next year. 我们已同意下个年度的预算。(b) agree to do something = to say that you will do something 同意(做某事):She agreed to be a chairman. 她同意当董事长。Will the finance director agree to resign? 财务主任同意辞职吗? The bank will never agree to lend the company £250,000. 银行永远不会同意贷给该公司 250,000 英磅。(C)nonstandard to accept 同意;认可:The auditors have agreed the accounts. 审计人员认为帐目正确无误。The figures were agreed between the two parties. 这些数字双方都同意。Terms of the eontract are still to be agreed. 该合同仍还需商定。He has

agreed your prices. 他接受了你的价格。 If has been agreed that the lease will run for 25 years. 同意该租赁期限为 25 五年。

◇ **agree with** v. (a) to say that your opinions are the same as someone else's 同意(某人的意见): I agree with the chairman that the figures are lower than normal. 我同意董事长的看法,这些数字低于正常值。(b) to be the same as 与…一致: The auditors' figures do not agree with those of the accounts department. 审计员给出的数字与会计部门的不一致。

◇ **agreed** a. which has been accepted by everyone 一致接受的的;商定的: an agreed amount 商定的数额;on agreed terms 按商定的条款。

◇ **agreement** n. contract between two parties which explains how they will act 协定;契约;协议: written agreement. 书面协议; unwritten or verbal agreement. 非书面的或口头的协议; to draw up or to draft an agreement 起草或草拟协议; to break an agreement. 违反协议;to sign an agreement. 签署协议;to witness an agreement 为一项协议作证; 做协议的中人;An agreement has been reached or concluded or come to. 协议已经达成或协议已经签订。to reach an agreement or to come to an agreement on prices or salaries 达成一项有关价格或工资的协议; an international agreement on trade 国际贸易协定; collective wage agreement 集体(指劳资双方的)工资协议; an agency agreement 一个代理协议; a marketing agreement 一个销售协议; blanket agreement = agreement which covers many different items 一揽子协议; exclusive agreement = agreement where a company is appointed sole agent for a product in a market 独家代理的协议; gentleman's agreement = verbal agreement between two parties who trust each other. 君子协定

**agribusiness** n. farming, and making productsused by farmers 农业综合经营（其业务包括农业及制造供农夫使用的产品）
NOTE: no plural

**agriculture** n. use of land for growing crops or raising animals 农业
NOTE: no plural

◇ **agricultural** a. referring to agriculture or referring to farms 农业的：agricultural co - operative = farm run by groups of workers who are the owners and share the profits 农业合作社；agricultural economist = person who specializes in the study of finance and investment in agriculture 农业经济学家；Common Agricultural Policy = agreement between members of the EEC to protect farmers by paying subsidies to fix prices of farm produce 共同农业政策（欧共体的）

**ahead** ad. in front of or better than 在前；超过：We are already ahead of our sales forecast. 我们的销售额已突破了预测的数字。The company has a lot of work ahead of it if it wants to increase its market share. 如果公司想增加其市场份额，那么，在此之前公司将有大量工作要做。

**aim** 1. n. something which you try to do 目标；目的：One of our aims is to increase the quality of our products. 我们的目标之一是提高产品质量。The company has achieved all its aims. = The company has done all the things it had hoped to do. 该公司业已实现全部目标。2. v. to try to do something 打算；以…目标：We aim to be No. 1 in the market in two years' time. 我们的目标是两年之内在市场上夺魁。Each salesman must aim to double his previous year's sales. 每位销售员都应把上一年的销售额翻一翻为目标。

**air** 1. n. method of travelling or sending goods using aircraft 航空；空运：to send a letter or a shipment by air 发航空信或空运发货；air carrier = company which sends cargo or passengers by air 航空公司；air forwarding = arranging for goods to be shipped by air 航空转运；air letter = special sheet of thin blue paper which when folded can besent by air mail without an envelope 航空信 2. v. to air a grievance = to talk about or to discuss a grievance 发牢骚：The management committee is useful because it allows the workers' representatives to air their grievances. 管理委员会是有用的，因为它允许工人代表提意见。

◇ **air cargo** n. goods sent by air 空运货物

◇ **aircraft** n. machine which flies in the air, carrying passengers or cargo 飞行器；飞机：The airline has a fleet of ten commercial aircraft. 航空公司拥有一个由十架商业运输机组成的机队。The company is one of the most important American aircraft manufacturers. 该公司是美国最为重要的飞机制造公司之一。to charter an aircraft = to hire an aircraft for a special purpose 租机，包机
NOTE: no plural: one aircraft, two aircraft

◇ **air freight** n. method of shipping goods in an aircraft 空中货运：to send a shipment by air freight 由空运发货；air freight charges or rates 空运费用或价格

◇ **airfreight** v. to send goods by air 空运货物：to airfreight a consignment to Mexico 空运一批货物到墨西哥；We airfreighted the shipment because our agent ran out of stock. 我们空运了这批货物，是因为我们的代理商已无库存了。

◇ **airline** n. company which carries passengers or cargo by air 航空公司

◇ **airmail** 1. n. way of sending letters or parcels by air 航空邮件；航空邮政：

to send a package by airmail 由航空寄包裹；Airmail charges have risen by15％. 航空邮寄费上涨了 15％。airmail envelope = very light envelope for sending airmail letters 航空信封；airmail sticker = blue sticker with the words "by air mail" which can be stuck to an envelope or packet to show it is being sent by air 航空信标签

NOTE: no plural

2. v. to send letters or parcels by air 航空邮寄：to airmail a document to New York 把一个文件航空寄到纽约。

◇**airport** n. place where planes land and take off 机场；航空港：We leave from London Airport at 10.00. 我们十点钟离开伦敦机场。O'Hare Airport is the main airport for Chicago. 奥黑尔机场是芝加哥的主要机场。airport bus = bus which takes passengers to and from an airport 机场通勤车(大巴)；airport tax = tax added to the price of the air ticket to cover the cost of running an airport 机场税；airport terminal = main building at an airport where passengers arrive and depart 机场候机楼

◇ **air terminal** n. building in a town where passengers meet to be taken by bus to an airport outside the town 机场大厦；终点航站；航空集散站

◇ **airtight** a. which does not allow air to get in 不漏气的；密封的：The goods are packed in airtight containers. 这些货物装在密封的集装箱里。

◇ **airworthiness** n. being able and safe to fly 适航性；飞行性能：certificate of airworthiness = certificate to show that an aircraft is safe to fly 准飞证；适合空中航行证

NOTE: no plural

**all** a. & pron. everything or everyone 全部的；所有的：All (of) the managers attended the meeting. 所有的经理都出席了会议。The salesman should know the prices of all the products he is selling. 售货员应知他所销售的每一件商品的价格。

◇ **all‐in** a. including everything 全部的；全包的：all‐in price or rate = price which covers all items in a purchase (goods, delivery, tax, insurance)包括各种费用的价格。

**allocate** v. to divide (a sum of money) in various ways and share it out 分配；配给：We allocate 10％ of revenue to publicity. 我们拨出 10％ 的收入做广告。$2,500 was allocated to office furniture. 划拨 2,500 美元购置办公室家俱。

◇ **allocation** n. (a) dividing a sum of money in various ways 分配；配给：allocation of capital 资金分配；allocation of funds to a project 项目资金的划拨 (b) share allocation or allocation of shares = spreading a small number of shares among a large number of people who have applied for them 股票分配；股份分配

**allot** v. to share out 分配；配给：to allot shares = to give a certain number of shares to people who have appliedfor them 分配股票

NOTE: allotting ‐ allotted

◇ **allotment** n. (a) sharing out funds by giving money to various departments 拨款分配：allotment of funds to a project 项目资金的划拨 (b) giving some shares in a new company to people who have applied for them 分配额：share allotment 股票分配；payment in full on allotment 按分配的股票一次付清；按分配的股票全部付讫；letter of allotment or allotment letter = letter which tells someone who has applied for shares in anew company how many shares he has been allotted 核定认股书

**all‐out** a. complete or very serious 完全的；彻底的：The union called for an all‐out strike. 工会号召总罢工。The personnel manager has launched an all - outcampaign to get the staff to work on Friday afternoons. 人事经理发起了一个全面性的运动,使工作人员星期五下午都上班。

**allow** v. (a) to say that someone can do something 允许;准许: Junior members of staff are not allowed to use the chairman's lift. 下级职员不允许使用董事长的电梯。The company allows all members of staff to take six days' holiday at Christmas. 公司批准全体职工圣诞节放六天假。(b) to give 给予: to allow someone a discount 给予某人折扣; to allow 5% discount to members of staff 给全体职员 5% 的折扣; to allow 10% interest on large sums of money 对巨额款项给予 10% 的利息. (c) to agree or to accept legally(法)同意或接受: to allow a claim or an appeal 同意赔偿或上诉

◇ **allow for** v. to give a discount for or to add an extra sum to cover something 考虑给…折扣;给…加附加额: to allow for money paid in advance 考虑预付款项; to allow 10% for packing 考虑 10% 的包装费; Delivery is not allowed for. = Delivery charges are not included. 运费未考虑在内。allow 28 days for delivery = calculate that delivery will take at least 28 days 允许 28 天交货期。

◇ **allowable** a. legally accepted 可允许的;正当的: allowable expenses = expenses which can be claimed against tax 可列支的费用;可被允许的开支

◇ **allowance** n. (a) money which is given for a special reason 津贴: travel allowance or travelling allowance 旅行(差)补助费; foreign currency allowance 外币津贴; cost - of - living allowance = addition to normal salary to cover increases in the cost ofliving 生活费津贴; entertainment allowance = money which a manager is allowed to spend each month on mealswith visitors 招待费(b) part of an income which is not taxed 补贴: allowances against tax or tax allowances 减免税;税款补贴费; personal allowances 个人补贴; wife's earned income allowance = tax allowance ω be set against money earned by the wife of the main taxpayer 夫人所得税补贴(c) money removed in the form of a discount 折扣: allowance for depreciation 备抵折旧;折旧提存; allowance for exchange loss 汇兑损失备抵

◇ **allowed time** n. paid time which the management agrees a worker can spend on rest or cleaning or meals, not working 容许的时间;放宽的时间(允许吃饭休息不工作的时间)

**all - risks policy** n. insurance policy which covers risks of any kind, with no exclusions 全险保险单;综合险保险单(指包括了各种类型风险的保险单,无保险契约范围的限制)

**all - time** a. 空前的;前所未闻的: all - time high or all - time low = highest or lowest point ever reached 空前的高或空前的低: Sales have fallen from their all - time high of last year. 销售额从去年最高的销售额往下降。

**alphabet** n. the 26 letters used to make words 字母

◇ **alphabetical order** n. arrangement of records (such as files, index cards) in the order of the letters of the alphabet (A, B, C, D, etc.)按字母的顺序

**alter** v. to change 修改;改变;变动: to alter the terms of a contract 变更合同的条款;修改合同的条款

◇ **alteration** n. change which has been made 变更;更换: He made some alterations to the terms of a contract. 他对合同的条款做了某些修改。The agreement was signed without any alterations. 协议业已签署,未做任何改动。

**alternative** 1. n. thing which can be

done instead of another 替换物；两者挑一：What is the alternative to firing half the staff? 除了解雇一半的职员外，还有什么别的选择？ We have no alternative. = There is nothing else we can do. 我们没有选择的余地。2. a. other or which can take the place of something 选择的；可供选择的；两者挑一的；可供替代的：to find someone alternative employment = to find someone another job 替某人找另一件工作

**altogether** ad. putting everything together 全部地；总计：The staff of the three companies in the group come to 2,500 altogether. 该集团三个公司的职员加起来总共达到 2500 人。The company lost £2m last year and £4m this year, making £6m altogether for the two years. 该公司去年损失了£2m，今年为£4m 千英镑，两年合计达到£6m。

**a.m.** ad. in the morning or before 12 midday 午前；正午前：The flight leaves at 9.20 a.m. 飞机于上午 9:20 起飞。Telephone calls before 6 a. m. are charged at the cheap rate. 六点钟之前打电话，电话费便宜。

**amend** v. to change and make more correct or acceptable 改正；修必，修正：Please amend your copy of the contract accordingly. 请你相应地修改合同的文本。请对你的合同文本作相应修正。

◇ **amendment** n. change to a document 修正案；修改；修正；to propose an amendment to the constitution 提议修正宪法；to make amendments to a contract 修订合同

**Amex** n. infml. = AMERICAN STOCK EXCHANGE 美国证券交易所 AMERICAN EXPRESS 美国运通信用卡

**amortize** v. to pay off (a debt) by putting money aside regularly over a period of time 分期偿还；摊还：The capital

cost is amortized over five years. 资本费用在五年中分期偿还。

◇ **amortizable** a. which can be amortized 可分期偿还的：The capital cost is amortizable over a period of ten years. 资本费用可在十年之内分期偿还。

◇ **amortization** n. act of amortizing 摊还；分期偿付：amortization of a debt 分期偿付一笔债务

**amount** 1. n. quantity of money 金额；总额 amount paid 支付额；支出额；amount deducted 扣除金额；扣除款项；amount owing 未付金额；所欠金额；amount written off 注销金额；What is the amount outstanding? 未偿付金额为多少？A small amount invested in gilt - edged stock. 对金边债券投资了一小笔资金。2. v. to amount to = to make a total of 总计，合计：Their debts amount to over £1m. 他们负债总计一百万英镑以上。

**analog computer** n. computer which works on the basis of electrical impulses representing numbers 模拟计算机（以脉冲代替数字的运行计算机）

**analyse or analyze** v. to examine in detail 分析：to analyse a statement of account 分析帐单表；to analyse the market potential 分析市场潜力

◇ **analysis** n. detailed examination and report 分析：job analysis 工作分析；market analysis 市场分析；sales analysis 销售（额）分析；to carry out an analysis of the market potential 进行市场潜力分析；to write an analysis of the sales position 写出销售情况的分析报告；cost analysis = examination in advance of the costs of a new product 成本分析；systems analysis = using a computer to suggest how a company can work more efficiently by analysing the way in which it works at present 系统分析
NOTE: plural is analyses

◇ **analyst** n. person who analyses 分析

人员：market analyst 市场分析人员；
systemsanalyst 系统分析人员

**announce** v. to tell something to the public 发表；宣布；宣告：to announce the results for 1984 宣布 1984 年的结果；to announce a programme of investment 公布投资方案

◇ **announcement** n. telling something in public 发表；宣布；通告：announcement of a cutback in expenditure 削减经费的通知；announcement of the appointment of a new managing director 新总经理的任命通知；The managing director made an announcement to the staff. 总经理通知了全体职员。

**annual** a. for one year 每年的；年度的：annual statement of income 年度收益表；He has six weeks' annual leave. 他每年有六周的假。the annual accounts 年度帐；annual growth of 5% 年增长率为 5%；annual report = report of a company's financial situation at the end of ayear, sent to all the shareholders 年度财务报告(在年末必须提交给所有股东的关于公司财务情况的报告)；on an annual basis = each year 按年度计算；The figures are revised on an annual basis. 这些数字每年都加以修改的；这些数字每年修改。

◇ **annual general meeting** n. meeting of all the shareholders, when the company's financial situation is discussed with the directors 年度股东大会

◇ **annualized** a. shown on an annual basis 按年度的：annualized percentage rate = rate of interest (such as on a hire - purchase agreement) shown on an annual compound basis 按年计算利率

◇ **annually** ad. 年度地；每年地：Each year the figures are updated annually. 这些数字每年更新。

**annuity** n. money paid each year to a retired person, usually in returnfor a lump - sum payment 年金；养老金(每年给退休人员一次整笔的款项)：He has a government annuity or an annuity from the government. 他享受政府发放的年退休金。to buy or to take out an annuity 购买养老金或领取年退休金；annuity for life or life annuity = annual payments made to someone as long as he is alive 终身养老年金或终身年退休金；reversionary annuity = annuity paid to someone on the death of another person 可继承的年金。

NOTE: plural is annuities

◇ **annuitant** n. person who receives an annuity 领取养老年金的人

**annul** v. to cancel or to stop something being legal 废除；取消；无效：The contract was annulled by the court. 法庭宣布该项合同无效。

NOTE: annulling – annulled

◇ **annullable** a. which can be cancelled 能够废除的

◇ **annulling** 1. a. which cancels 取消的：annulling clause 可取消条款：2. n. act of cancelling 废除；取消：the annulling of a contract 取消一个合同

◇ **annulment** n. act of cancelling 废除；取消：annulment of a contract 废除合同；取消合同

**answer** 1. n. reply or letter or conversation coming after someone has written or spoken 回答；答复；回复：I am writing in answer to your letter of October 6th. 我正在就你 10 月 6 日的来信写回信。My letter got no answer or there was no answer to my letter. 我的信没有回音。I tried to phone his office but there was no answer. 我试着给他的办公室打电话，但是没有人接。2. v. to speak or write after someone has spoken or written to you 回答；答复：to answer a letter = to write a letter in reply to a letter which you havereceived 回信；复函；to answer the telephone = to lift the telephone when it rings and listen to what the caller is saying 听电话;接电话

◇ **answering** n. answering machine = machine which answers the telephone automatically when someone is not in the office 录音电话;自动接话机;answering service = office which answers the telephone and takes messages for someone or for a company 代接电话服务站

**antedate** v. to put an earlier date on a document(在信、文件等上)填上较早的日期;倒填日期:The invoice was antedated to January 1st. 将该发票日期填早到 1 月 1 日。

**anti** - prefix against 对;反;排斥

◇ **anti** - **dumping** a. which protects a country against dumping 反倾销的:anti - dumping legislation 反倾销法

◇ **anti** - **inflationary** a. which tries to restrict inflation 反通货膨胀的:anti - inflationary measures 反通货膨胀的措施

◇ **anti** - **trust** a. which attacks monopolies and encourages competition 反托拉斯的(反对垄断鼓励竞争):anti - trust laws or legislation 反托拉斯法

**AOB = ANY OTHER BUSINESS** item at the end of an agenda, where any matter can be raised(议事日程结尾处可提出的任何事项)任何其它事项。

**aperture** n. hole 孔;隙;窄的缺口:aperture envelope = envelope with a hole in it so that the address on the letterinside can be seen 有标准孔径的信封

**apologize** v. to say you are sorry 道歉;认错:to apologize for the delay in answering 迟复为歉;She apologized for being late. 她因迟到而表示歉意。

◇ **apology** n. saying you are sorry 道歉;认错:to write a letter of apology 致歉信(函)I enclose a cheque for £10 with apologies for the delay in answering your letter. 我对延迟复信深表歉意,兹附上十英镑的支票一张。

**appeal** 1. n. (a) being attractive 吸引力;感染力:customer appeal = being attractive to customers 顾客吸引力;sales appeal = quality which makes customers want to buy 销售感染力(b) asking a court or a government department to change its decision 上诉:The appeal against the planning decision will be heard next month. 对该计划决策的上诉,将于下个月审理。He lost his appeal for damages against the company. 他提起上诉向该公司索赔,但败诉了。She won her case on appeal. = Her case was lost in the first court, but the appeal court said that she was right. 她上诉成功。

NOTE: no plural for (a) 2. v. (a) to attract 吸引;投人所好:This record appeals to the under - 25 market. 这张唱片对 25 岁以下的顾客有吸引力。The idea ofworking in Australia for six months appealed to her. 在澳大利亚工作六个月的想法,令她神往。(b) to ask a government department or a law court to alter its decision 上诉;The company appealed against the decision of the planning officers. 对计划人员的裁决,该公司已提出上诉。

NOTE: you appeal to a court or a person against a decision

**appear** v. to seem 似乎;好象:The company appeared to be doing well.该公司经营状况似乎不错。The managing director appears to be in control. 总经理似乎(大权在握)能控制住局面。

**apply** v. (a) to ask for something, usually in writing 申请:to apply for a job 申请工作;to apply for shares 申请买股票;to apply in writing 书面申请;to apply in person 亲自申请(b) to affect or to touch 适用;与…有关:This clause applies only to deals outside the EEC. 这一条款只适用于欧洲共同体以外的事务。

◇ **applicant** n. person who applies for something 申请人:applicant for a job or job applicant 就业申请人或工作申请人；There were thousands of applicants for shares in the new company. 有成千上万的人申请购买该新公司的股票。

◇ **application** n. asking for something, usually in writing 申请；请求：application for shares 股份申请；认股书；shares payable on application 在申请时立即应付的股票（份）Attach the cheque to the share application form. 将支票附在股份申请表上。application for a job or job application 申请就业或工作申请；application form = form to be filled in when applying 申请表；to fill in an application（form）for a job or a job application（form）填写就业申请表或工作申请表；letter of application = letter in which someone applies for a job 申请书；求职信

**appoint** v. to choose someone for a job 任命；委任：to appoint James Smith（to the post of）manager 任命詹姆斯·史密斯为经理；We have appointed a new distribution manager. 我们已任命了一位新的销售经理。

NOTE: you appoint a person to a job

◇ **appointee** n. person who is appointed to a job 被任命的人

◇ **appointment** n. (a) arrangement to meet 约会：to make or to fix an appointment for two o'clock 约会时间为两点；to make an appointment with someone for two o'clock 与某人在 2:00 约会；He was late for his appointment. 他赴约迟到了。She had to cancel her appointment. 她只能取消约会。appointments book = desk diary in which appointments are noted 约见簿 (b) being appointed to a job 任职：on his appointment as manager = when he was made manager 他被任命为经理时；letter of appointment = letter in which someone is appointed to a job 任命书；委任书 (c) job 职业；职位；staff appoint-

ment = job on the staff 工作人员的工作岗位；appointments vacant = list（in a newspaper）of jobs which are available 职位空缺

**apportion** v. to share out（costs）分摊；分配：Costs are apportioned according to projected revenue. 按预计收益分摊费用。

◇ **apportionment** n. sharing out of（costs）分配；分摊

**appraise** v. to assess or to calculate the value of something 估价；对…进行估价

◇ **appraisal** n. calculation of the value of someone or something 评定；估价：staff appraisals = reports on how well each member of staff is working 人事鉴定；对工作人员的评估

**appreciate** v. (a) to notice how good something is 鉴赏；赏识：The customer always appreciates efficient service. 顾客总是欣赏高效率的服务。Tourists do not appreciate long delays at banks. 旅游者不喜欢在银行里耽误过多的时间。 (b) to increase in value 涨价；增值：The dollar has appreciated in terms of the yen. 美元以日元折合升值了。These shares have appreciated by 5%. 这些股票升值了 5%。

◇ **appreciation** n. (a) increase in value 升值；增值；涨价：These shares show an appreciation of 10%. 这些股票增值 10%。the appreciation of the dollar against the peseta 与比塞塔（西班牙货币单位）相比美元升值。 (b) valuing something highly 评价；鉴赏：He was given a rise in appreciation of his excellent work. 由于欣赏他的工作出色而给他提薪。

NOTE: no plural

**apprentice** 1. n. young person who works under contract with a skilled workman to learn from him 学徒；徒弟：2. v. to be apprenticed to someone = to work with a skilled workman to learn from him 给某人做学徒；当某人的徒弟

◇ **apprenticeship** n. time spent learning a skilled trade 学徒年限：He served a six – year apprenticeship in the steel works. 他在钢铁厂，当了六年学徒。

**appro** n. = APPROVAL to buy something on appro = to buy something which you will only pay for if it is satisfactory 购买包退包换的商品

**approach** 1. n. getting in touch with someone with a proposal 打交道；接近：The company made an approach to the supermarket chain. 该公司已与超级市场的联营店接洽。The board turned down all approaches on the subject of mergers. 董事会拒绝了有关合并事宜的任何协商。We have had an approach from a Japanese company to buy our car division. 一家日本公司已与我们接洽，以购买我们的汽车分部。2. v. to get in touch with someone with a proposal 与…打交道；接洽；商谈：He approached the bank with a request for a loan. 他与银行洽谈申请贷款事宜。The company was approached by an American publisher with the suggestion of a merger. 一家美国出版商与该公司商谈有关合并的事宜。We have been approached several times but have turned down all offers. 虽经数次洽谈，但我们拒绝了所有提议。

**appropriate** v. to put a sum of money aside for a special purpose 拨款：to appropriate a sum of money for a capital project 拨款用于基本建设项目。

◇ **appropriation** n. act of putting money aside for a special purpose 拨款：appropriation of funds to the reserve 拨款给储备基金；appropriation account = part of a profit and loss account which shows how the profit has been dealt with (i. e. how much has been given to the shareholders as dividends, how much is being put into the reserves, etc.) 利润分配帐户；拨款帐户

NOTE: no plural

**approve** v. (a) to approve of = to think something is good 满意；赞成：The chairman approves of the new company letter heading. 董事长同意新公司信笺上的笺眉。The sales staff do not approve of interference from the accounts division. 销售人员对会计部门的干预很不赞同。(b) to agree to something officially 批准：to approve the terms of a contract 批准合同条款；The proposal was approved by the board. 董事会批准了这项建议。

◇ **approval** n. (a) agreement 同意：to submit a budget for approval 提交预算以求批准；certificate of approval = document showing that an item has been approved officially 核准证书 (b) on approval = sale where the buyer only pays for goods if they are satisfactory 包退包换的；to buy a photocopier on approval 买一台包退包换的影印机（复印机）

NOTE: no plural

**approximate** a. not exact, but almost correct 大约的；近似的：The sales division has made an approximate forecast of expenditure. 销售部门做了一项经费开支的粗略预测。

◇ **approximately** ad. almost correctly 大约地；近似地：Expenditure is approximately 10% down on the previous quarter. 与前个季度相比，经费大约削减 10% 。

◇ **approximation** n. rough calculation 略计；近似值：approximation of expenditure 经费的概算；The final figure is only an approximation. 最后的数字只是一个近似值。

**APR = ANNUALIZED PERCENTAGE RATE** 年百分率

**arbitrage** n. selling on one market and buying on another at almost the same time to profit from different exchange rates; buying shares in companies which are likely to be taken over and so rise in price套汇；套利：(根据不同汇率，在一地购入几乎同时在别一处卖出以谋取利润；购买有可能被兼并的公司的股票，以谋求股票的增值）：arbitrage syndicate = group of people formed to raise the capital to invest in arbitrage deals 套汇集团(辛迪加）

◇**arbitrager or arbitrageur** n. person whose business is arbitrage 套利者或套汇人

**arbitrate** v. (of an outside party) to be chosen by both sides to try to settle an industrialdispute 仲裁；公断：to arbitrate in a dispute 对争端进行仲裁

◇ **arbitration** n. settling of a dispute by an outside person, chosen by bothsides 仲裁；公断：to submit a dispute to arbitration 将争议提交仲裁；to refer a question to arbitration 把问题提交仲裁；to take a dispute to arbitration 诉诸仲裁；to go to arbitration 诉诸(进行)仲裁 arbitration board or arbitration tribunal = group which arbitrates 仲裁委员会或仲裁法庭；industrial arbitration tribunal = court which decides in industrial disputes 工业劳资纠纷仲裁法庭；to accept the ruling of the arbitration board 接受仲裁委员会的裁决
NOTE: no plural

◇ **arbitrator** n. person not concerned with a dispute who is chosen by both sides to try to settle it 仲裁人；公断者；industrial arbitrator(劳资纠纷)仲裁人；to accept or to reject the arbitrator's ruling 接受或拒绝仲裁人的裁决

**area** n. (a) measurement of the space taken up by something (calculated by multiplying the length by the width) 面积：The area of this office is 3,400 square feet. 这个办事处的面积为3400平方英尺。We are looking for a shop with a sales area of about 100 square metres. 我们正在寻找一个营业面积大

约为 100 平方米的商店。(b) region of the world free trade area = group of countries practising free trade 自由贸易区；dollar area or sterling area = areas of the world where the dollar or the pound is the maintrading currency 美元区或英镑区 (c) subject 学科；领域：a problem area or an area for concern 一个有问题的领域(地方)或令人关注的地方 (d) district or part of a town 区；市区：The office is in the commercial area of the town. 该办事处位于城市的商业区。Their factory is in a very good area for getting to the motorways and airports. 他们的工厂位于很好的地区，去机场和上高速公路相当便利。(e) part of a country, a division for commercial purposes 地区；商业区域：His sales area is the North–West. 他的销售地区是西北部。He finds it difficult to cover all his area in a week. 他发觉一周之内要走遍他要去的商业区域是很困难的。

◇ **area code** n. special telephone number which is given to a particular area 电话区号：The area code for London is 01. 伦敦的电话区号为01。

◇ **area manager** n. manager who is responsible for a part of the country 地区管理人员

**argue** v. to discuss something about which you do not agree 争论；辩论：They argued over or about the price. 他们就有关价格问题进行了争论。We spent hours arguing with the managing director about the site for the new factory. 就新厂的厂址问题，我们与总经理争论了几个小时。The union officials argued among themselves over the best way to deal with the ultimatum from the management. 工会的官员们彼此就如何寻求最佳途径来对付管理部门的最后通谍而争论不休。
NOTE: you argue with someone about or over something

◇ **argument** n. discussing something

without agreeing 争论；辩论：They got intoan argument with the customs officials over the documents. 他们与海关官员就这些文件展开了争论。He was sacked after an argument with the managing director. 在和总经理争论之后，他被解雇了。

**around** prep. approximately 大约；近似：The office costs around £2,000 a year to heat. 办公室的取暖费用一年大约 2000 英镑。His salary is around £85,000. 他的年薪大约为 85,000 英磅。

**arrange** v. (a) to put in order 排列；分类整理：The office is arranged as an open‐plan area with small separate rooms for meetings. 这个办公室按开敞式平面布置，但有几个被隔开的会议室。The files are arranged in alphabetical order. 这些档案是按字母的顺序排列的。arrange the invoices in order of their dates 按日期顺序排列发票（b）to organize 组织；安排：We arranged to have the meeting in their offices. 我们将会议安排在他们的办公室。She arranged for a car to meet him at the airport. 她安排了一辆小汽车到机场去接他。NOTE: you arrange for someone to do something; you arrange for something to be done; or you arrange to do something

◇ **arrangement** n. (a) way in which something is organized 安排：The company secretary is making all the arrangements for the AGM. 该公司秘书正在为年度股东大会做好所有的安排。(b) settling of a financial dispute（财务纠纷）协调；调解：to come to an arrangement with the creditors 与债权人达成解决纠纷协议

**arrears** pl. n. money which is owed, but which has not been paid at the righttime 过期未付的欠款；欠款；arrears of interest 拖欠利息；to allow the pay-

ments to fall into arrears 允许支付款转为欠款；salary with arrears effective from January 1st 拖欠的工资于 1 月 1 日生效；in arrears = owing money which should have been paid earlier 拖欠（债）；The payments are six months in arrears. 付款已拖欠 6 个月了。He is six weeks inarrears with his rent. 他拖欠了六个星期的租金。

**arrive** n. (a) to reach a place 到达：The consignment has still not arrived. 托运物品仍未到达。The shipment arrived without any documentation. 运抵的货物无任何凭证（装运货物到达时无任何单据）。The plane arrives in Sydney at 04.00. 飞机于凌晨四点钟抵达悉尼。The train leaves Paris at 09.20 and arrives at Bordeaux two hours later. 列车于 9:20 离开巴黎，2 小时后抵达波尔多市。NOTE: you arrive at or in a place or town, but only in a country

(b) to arrive at = to calculate and agree 达成（协议）；to arrive at a price 达成一项价格协议；After some discussion we arrived at a compromise. 经过一番讨论之后，我们达成一项折衷方案。

◇ **arrival** n. reaching a place 抵达；到达：We are waiting for the arrival of a consignment of spare parts. 我们正在等候着托运备件的到达。"to await arrival" = note written on an envelope to ask for it to be kept safeuntil the person it is addressed to arrives（在信封上注明的）待领的标记；arrivals = part of an airport dealing with passengers who are arriving 到站出站口

**article** n. (a) product or thing for sale 商品；物品：to launch a new article on the market 市场上投放一种新商品；a black market in luxury articles 一个奢侈品的黑市（b）section of a legal agreement 条款（法律协定中的一部分）：see article 8 of the contract 见合同的第八条。(c) articles of association or US articles of incorporation = document which setsup a company and says what work it will do 公司章程或美国公司组织大纲：director appointed under the articles of the company 按公司章程委任的经理；This procedure is not allowed under the articles of association of the company. 按公司章程，这种程序是不允许的。

◇ **articled** a. articled clerk = clerk who is bound by contract to work in a lawyer's officefor some years to learn the law 签约受雇于律师事务所的见习职员

**articulated lorry or articulated vehicle** n. large lorry formed of two parts, the second pulled by the first 有拖斗的载重卡车或机动车.

**asap** = AS SOON AS POSSIBLE

**aside** ad. to one side or out of the way 放在一边；撇开；to put aside or to set aside = to save (money) 储蓄(钱)；He is putting £50 aside each week to pay for his car. 为付车款他每周存50英镑。

**ask** v. (a) to put a question to someone 询问；请教；问：He asked the information office for details of companies exhibiting at the motor show. 他向信息处询问了有关汽车博览会方面各公司参展的详情。Ask the salesgirl if the bill includes VAT. 问售货员小姐，发票是否包括增值税。(b) to tell someone to do something 请求：He asked the switchboard operator to get him a number in Germany. 他请电话总机接线员给他接通德国的一个电话号码。She asked her secretary to fetch a file from the managing director's office. 她请秘书从总经理办公室取一份档案。The customs officials asked him to open his case. 海关人员请他打开手提箱。

◇ **ask for** v. (a) to say that you want or need something 向…要；请求：He asked for the file on 1984 debtors. 他要有关一九八四年债务人的案卷。They

asked for more time to repay the loan. 他们请求有更多的时间来偿还贷款。There is a man in reception asking for Mr Smith. 在接待处有人要求见史密斯先生。(b) to put a price on something for sale 要价；索价：They are asking £24,000 for the car. 这辆小汽车他们要价24,000英镑。

◇ **asking price** n. price which the seller asks for the goods being sold (卖方) 要价或索价：The asking price is £24,000. (卖方) 索价为2.4万英镑。

**assay mark** n. mark put on gold or silver items to show that the metal is of the correct quality 标明金银成色检验的标记

**assemble** v. to put a product together from various parts 组装；装配：The engines are made in Japan and the bodies in Scotland, and the cars are assembled in France. 发动机由日本制造，车身由苏格兰生产，而小汽车在法国装配。

◇ **assembly** n. (a) putting an item together from various parts 装配：There are no assembly instructions to show you how to put the computer together. 没有装配说明书，你如何把这台计算机装配起来。car assembly plant = factory where cars are put together from parts made in otherfactories 轿车装配厂
NOTE: no plural (b) meeting 集会
NOTE: plural is assemblies

◇ **assembly line** n. production system where the product (such as a car) moves slowly through the factory with new sections added to it as it goes along 装配线：He works on an assembly line or He is an assembly line worker. 他在一条装配线上工作或他是一名装配线上的工人。

**assess** v. to calculate the value of something 评估价值：to assess damages at £1,000 确定损失赔偿金达1,000英镑；to assess a property for the purposes of insurance 估价资产进行保险

◇ **assessment** n. calculation of value 评估；确定金额：assessment of damages 赔偿金的评估；assessment of property 资产评估；tax assessment 税收查定；估税；确定税款金额；staff assessments = reports on how well members of staff are working 职工工作评估

**asset** n. thing which belongs to company or person, and which has a value 资产；财产：He has an excess of assets over liabilities. 他的资产大于其负债。Her assets are only £ 640 as against liabilities of £ 24,000. 她的资产总额仅为 640 英磅，而她的负债总额为 24,000。capital assets or fixed assets = property or machinery which a company owns and uses 资本资产或固定资产；current assets = assets used by a company in its ordinary work (such as materials, finished goods, cash)流动资产；frozen assets = assets of a company which cannot be sold because someone has a claim against them 冻结资产；intangible assets = assets which have a value, but which cannot be seen (such as goodwill. or a patent, or a trademark) 无形资产；liquid assets = cash, or bills which can be quickly converted into cash 流动资产；变现资产：personal assets = moveable assets which belong to a person 动产；个人财产；tangible assets = assets which are solid (such as furniture or jewels or cash)有形资产；asset value = value of a company calculated by adding together all its assets 资产总价值；asset stripper = person who buys a company to sell its assets 资产倒卖者；asset stripping = buying a company to sell its assets 资产剥夺(倒卖)。

**assign** v. (a) to give legally 过户；转让：to assign a right to someone 将权利转让给某人；to assign shares to someone 把股票过户给某人(b) to give someone a job of work 指派；选派：He was assigned the job of checking the sales figures. 分配他去做核对销售额的工作。

◇ **assignation** n. legal transfer 过户；转让：assignation of shares to someone 将股票过户给某人；assignation of a patent 转让专利权

◇ **assignee** n. person who receives something which has been assigned 受让人

◇ **assignment** n. (a) legal transfer of a property or of a right(法律上)转让(财产，权力)：assignment of a patent or of a copyright 转让专利权或转让版权(著作权)；to sign a deed of assignment 签署转让契约(b) particular job of work (派定的)职位或工作：He was appointed managing director with the assignment to improve the company's profits. 他被任命为总经理，负责提高公司利润的工作。The oil team is on an assignment in the North Sea. 该石油勘探队分配到北海油田工作。

◇ **assignor** n. person who assigns something to someone 转让人；委派者

**assist** v. to help 帮助，援助：Can you assist the stock controller in counting the stock? 你能帮助库存管理员清点存货吗？He assists me with my income tax returns. 他帮助我填写所得税申报单。NOTE: you assist someone in doing something or with something

◇ **assistance** n. help 帮助；援助：financial assistance = help in the form of money 财政援助
NOTE: no plural

◇ **assistant** n. person who helps or a clerical employee 助手；助理：personal assistant = secretary who also helps the boss in various ways 私人助理；shop assistant = person who serves the customers in a shop 售货员；店员；assistant manager = person who helps a manager 副经理；协理

**associate** 1. a. linked 联结的；合伙的：

associate company = company which is partlyowned by another 联号;联营公司: associate director = director who attends board meetings, but has not been elected by the shareholders 助理董事;副董事 2. n. person who works in the same business as someone 同事;伙伴: She is a business associate of mine. 她是我生意上的伙伴。

◇ **associated** a. linked 联系的: Smith Ltd and its associated company, Jones Brothers 史密斯股份有限公司和它的琼斯兄弟联营公司

◇ **association** n. (a) group of people or of companies with the same interest 社团;协会: trade association 同业公会; employers' association 雇主联合会; manufacturers' association 制造商协会 (b) articles of association = document which sets up a company and says what work it will do 公司章程

**assume** v. to take 承担;担任: to assume all risks 承担全部风险; He has assumed responsibility for marketing. 他负责销售。

◇ **assumption** n. taking 承担;担任: assumption of risks 承担风险。

**assure** v. to insure or to have a contract with a company where if regular payments are made, the company will pay compensation if you die 保险: to assure someone's life 对某人的生命投保;人寿保险: He has paid the premiums to have his wife's life assured. 他已为妻子投了人寿保险,并支付了保险费。the life assured = the person whose life has been covered by the life assurance 人寿保险

◇ **assurance** n. insurance or agreement that in return for regular payments, a-company will pay compensation for loss of life 人寿保险 assurance company 人寿保险公司; assurance policy 人寿保险单; life assurance = insurance which pays a sum of money when someone dies 人寿保险

◇ **assurer or assuror** n. insurer or company which insures 人寿保险公司 NOTE: assure and assurance are used in Britain for insurance policies relating to something which will certainly happen (such as death); for other types of policy use insure and insurance

**at best** phrase sell at best = instruction to stockbroker to sell shares at the best price possible 尽可能以最好价格售出

**at par** phrase share at par = share whose value on the stock market is the same as its face value 平价股票;按票面价出售的股票

**ATM** n. = AUTOMATIC TELLING MACHINE 自动出纳机

**attach** v. to fasten or to link 连结;系: I am attaching a copy of my previous letter. 我将附上一份过去信函的副本。Please find attached a copy of my letter of June 24th. 兹附上一份我的 6 月 24 日信件的副件。The machine is attached to the floor so it cannot be moved. 这台机器连在地面上,因此不能移动。The bank attaches great importance to the deal. 该银行很重视这笔交易。

◇ **attach** n. junior diplomat who does special work 外交使节随员;使馆随员: commercial attache = diplomat whose job is to promote the commercial interests of his country 商务专员; attache case = small case for carrying papers and documents 小型手提公文箱

◇ **attachment** n. holding a debtor's property to prevent it being sold until debts are paid 查封(控制债务人的财产,以防变卖,至付清债务为止);扣押

**attempt** 1. n. trying to do something 尝试;试图: The company made an attempt to break into the American market. 该公司试图打入美国市场。The takeover attempt was turned down by the board. 收购兼并的企图遭到了董事会的拒绝. All his attempts to get a job have failed. 他找工作的全部尝试均已落空。2. v. to try 企图；试图：The company is attempting to get into the tourist market. 该公司正力图挤入旅游市场. We are attempting the takeover of a manufacturing company. 我们正试图兼并一个制造业公司. He attempted to have the sales director sacked. 他图谋解雇销售经理。

**attend** v. to be present at 出席；参加：The chairman has asked all managers to attend the meeting. 董事长已邀请了所有经理参加会议. None of the shareholders attended the AGM. 没有一个股东出席年度股东大会。

◇ **attend to** v. to give careful thought to (something) and deal with it 照料；料理：The managing director will attend to your complaint personally. 总经理将亲自处理你们的申诉. We have brought in experts to attend to the problem of installing the new computer. 我们请专家来处理安装新型计算机所遇到的问题。

◇ **attention** n. giving careful thought 注意；照顾：for the attention of the Managing Director 由总经理办理；Your orders will have our best attention. 我们会很重视你的订货单。

**attorney** n. (a) person who is legally allowed to act on behalf of someoneelse 代理人(指法律事务)；power of attorney = legal document giving someone the right to act on someone's behalf in legal matters 委托书；授权书：His solicitor was granted power of attorney. 给他的律师(初级的)授予委托书。(b) US lawyer(美)律师

**attract** v. to make something or someone join or come in 吸引；诱惑；引起：The company is offering free holidays in Spain to attract buyers. 该公司以提供到西班牙免费度假来吸引买主. We have

difficulty in attracting skilled staff to this part of the country. 要吸引熟练工作人员到该国这个地区来，我们确有难处。

◇ **attractive** a. which attracts 有吸引力的；有诱惑力的：attractive prices = prices which are cheap enough to make buyers want to buy 相当便宜的价格；有吸引力的价格；attractive salary = good salary to make high - quality applicants apply for the job 高薪；有吸引力的薪水

**attributable** a. attributable profits = profits which can be shown to come from a particular area 有归属的利润

**auction** 1. n. selling of goods where people offer bids, and the item issold to the person who makes the highest offer 拍卖；出售 sale by auction 拍卖 auction rooms 拍卖行(店) to sell goods by auction or US at auction 由拍卖出售商品；to put something up for auction = to offer an item for sale at an auction 把某物进行拍卖；Dutch auction = auction where the auctioneer offers an item for sale at a high price and gradually reduces the price until someone makes a bid 荷兰方式拍卖；价格逐渐下降的拍卖；2. v. to sell at an auction 拍卖：The factory was closed and the machinery was auctioned off. 工厂倒闭，机器被拍卖掉。

◇ **auctioneer** n. person who conducts an auction 拍卖商；拍卖人

**audio - typing** n. typing to dictation from a recording 听录音打字；按…的口授打字；听写打字

NOTE: no plural

◇ **audio - typist** n. typist who types to dictation from a recording on a dictating machine 听写或听录音打字的打字员

**audit** 1. n. examination of the books and accounts of a company 审计；稽核：to carry out the annual audit 进行年度审计；进行年度查帐；external audit or independent audit = audit carried out by anindependent auditor 外部审计或独立审计; internal audit = audit carried out by a department inside the company 内部审计; He is the manager of the internal audit department. 他是内部审计部门的管理人员. 2. v. to examine the books and accounts of a company 审计; 稽核: to audit the accounts 审计帐户; 查帐 The books have not yet been audited. 该帐簿尚未审计.

◇ **auditing** n. action of examining the books and accounts 审计; 查帐

◇ **auditor** n. person who audits 审计员: The AGM appoints the company's auditors. 年度股东大会任命公司的审计员. external auditor = independent person who audits the company's accounts 外部审计员; internal auditor = member of staff who audits a company's accounts 内部审计员

**authenticate** v. to say that something is true 证实; 鉴定; 认证

**authority** n. (a) power to do something 权力: He has no authority to act on our behalf. 他无权代表我们行事. (b) local authority = elected section of government which runs a small area of acountry 地方权力机构; the authorities = the government or the people in control 当局; 权威人士; 当权者
NOTE: no plural for (a)

**authorize** v. (a) to give permission for something to be done 允许: 授权 to authorize payment of £10,000 授权支付10,000英磅 (b) to give someone the authority to do something 授权; 委任: to authorize someone to act on the company's behalf 授权某人代表公司行事

◇ **authorization** n. permission or power to do something 认可; 授权: Do you have authorization for this expenditure? 你有权处理这笔开支吗?

He has no authorization to act on our behalf. 他无权代表我们行事.
NOTE: no plural

◇ **authorized** a. permitted 允许的; 批准的: authorized capital = amount of capital which a company is allowed to have, as stated in the articles of association 额定资本; 核定资本; authorized dealer = person or company (such as a bank) which is allowed to buy andsell foreign currency 特许的经纪人; 授权交易商(买卖外币)

**automated** a. worked automatically by machines 自动的; 自动化的: fully automated car assembly plant 完全自动化的小轿车装配厂

◇ **automation** n. use of machines to do work with very little supervision bypeople 自动; 自动化
NOTE: no plural

**automatic** a. which works or takes place without any person making it happen 自动的; 自动化的: There is an automatic increase in salaries on January 1st. 1月1日自动加薪. automatic data processing = data processing done by a computer 自动化的数据处理; automatic telling machine US automatic teller machine = machine which gives out money when a special card is inserted and special instructions given 自动出纳机; automatic vending machine = machine which provides drinks, cigarettes, etc. when a coin is put in 自动售货机.

◇ **automatically** ad. working without a person giving instructions 自动地; 自动化地: The invoices are sent out automatically. 发票自动地输出. Addresses are typed in automatically. 自动地打印地址. A demand note is sent automatically when the invoice is overdue. 若发票愈期未付, 一张即期票据(交费通知单)便自动输出.

**available** a. which can be obtained or

bought 可得到的；可购到的：available inall branches 可在所有子公司中购得；item no longer available 不再能购到的商品；items available to order only 只有定货，才能购买的商品；funds which are made available for investment in small businesses 可用于小型企业投资的资金；available capital = capital which is ready to be used 可动用的资本；可用资金

◇ **availability** n. being easily obtained 可得性；可用性：offer subject to availability = the offer is valid only if the goods are available 有效的报盘（以有货为准）。

NOTE: no plural

**average** 1. n. (a) number calculated by adding together several figures and dividing by the number of figures added 平均；平均数：the average for the last three months or the last three months' average 最后三个月的平均数或第四季度的平均数；sales average or average of sales 平均销售额；weighted average = average which is calculated taking several factors into account, giving some more value than others 加权平均数（综合考虑几种因素而计算出的平均数，比其他指标更具有参考价值）on an average = in general 按平均数计算；On an average, £15 worth of goods are stolen every day. 平均每天被窃取的货物价值为 15 英镑。(b) sharing of the cost of damage or loss of a ship between the insurers and the owners 海损(指船舶的损失在保险商与船主之间分摊的价值)；average adjuster = person who calculates how much of an insurance is to be paid 海损理算人；海损理算师；general average = sharing of the cost of the lost goods by all parties to an insurance 共同海损；公共海损；particular average = situation where part of a shipment is lost or damaged and the insurance costs are borne by the owner of the lost goods and

not shared among all the owners of the shipment 单独海损 2. a. (a) middle (figure) 平均的；折中的；当中的（数字）；average cost per unit 单位平均成本；average price 平均价格；average sales per representative 人均销售额；the average figures for the last three months 第四季度的平均数字；the average increase in prices 价格的平均增长 (b) not very good 平常的；普通的：The company's performance has been only average. 该公司的业绩平平常常。He is an average worker. 他是一名普通的工人。3. v. to produce as an average figure 从…得出平均数；求平均数：Price increases have averaged 10% per annum. 每年价格平均上涨 10%。Days lost through sickness have averaged twenty-two over the last four years. 疾病会使寿命缩短，过去四年缩短的平均数为 22 天。

◇ **average due date** n. date when several payments（due at different dates）are settled in one payment 平均到期日（指对在不同到期日应付的款项，择定一个折中日期进行全部支付）

◇ **average out** v. to come to a figure as an average 达到平均数；扯平：It averages out at 10% per annum. 它每年达到 10% 的平均数。Sales increases have averaged out at 15%. 销售额增长率平均达到 15%。

◇ **averager** n. person who buys the same share at various times and at various prices to give an average price 理算人（按不同的时间和不同的价格以获得它们平均价格的人）

◇ **average-sized** a. not large or small 普通尺码的；中型的：They are an average-sized company. 他们拥有一个中等规模的公司。He has an average-sized office. 他有一间不大不小的办公室。

◇ **averaging** n. buying shares at different times and at different prices to

give an average price 以平均值收购买股
票(在不同的时间和以不同的价格的股
票在购买时均按平均价格支付)
NOTE: no plural

**avoid** v. to try not to do something 回
避;避免: The company is trying to
avoid bankruptcy. 该公司正力图避免破
产。My aim is to avoid paying too much
tax. 我的目的在于避免支付太多的税
款。We want to avoid direct competition
with Smith Ltd. 我们想避免与史密斯
公司直接竞争。
NOTE: you avoid something or avoid
doing something

◇ **avoidance** n. trying not to do something 避免;撤消: avoidance of an agreement or of a contract 合同的撤销; tax
avoidance = trying (legally) to pay as
little tax as possible 逃税
NOTE: no plural

**avoirdupois** n. old system of weights
used in Britain, shown in pounds,
ounces, etc. 常衡(英国用的老的计重
制,以磅盎斯为单位); one ounce
avoirdupois 一盎司常衡

**await** v. to wait for 等候;等待: We are
awaiting the decision of the planning
department. 我们正等待着计划部门的
决定。They are awaiting a decision of
the court. 他们正等候着法院的裁决。
The agent is awaiting our instructions. 代
理商正等待着我们的指示。

**award** 1. n. decision which settles a
dispute 裁决;裁定: an award by an industrial tribunal 由劳资法庭的一项裁
决; The arbitrator's award was set aside
on appeal. 在上诉时,仲裁人裁决被驳
回。2. v. to decide the amount of money
to be given to someone 公断赔偿;判决:
to award someone a salary increase 裁定
给某人增加工资; to award damages 裁
定给予损失赔偿; The judge awarded
costs to the defendant. 法官判被告付诉
讼费。to award a contract to someone =

to decide that someone will have the contract to do work 裁决给某人一份契约

**away** ad. not here or somewhere else 离
开;远离: The managing director is away
on business. 总经理出差了。My secretary isaway sick. 我的秘书因病离开。
The company is moving away from its
down - market image. 公司正在摆脱它
的低挡品市场的形象。

**awkward** a. difficult to deal with 难处
理的;难应付的: The board is trying to
solve the awkward problem of the managing director's son. 董事会正试图解决
总经理儿子的棘手问题。When he
asked for the loan the bank started to ask
some very awkward questions. 当他申请
贷款的时候,银行开始提出一些令人难
以回答的问题。He is being very awk-
ward about giving us further credit. 他为
给我们进一步地增加贷款而为难。

**axe** 1. n. The project got the axe. =
The project was stopped. 项目已下马。
工程已停止。2. v. to cut or to stop 削
减;停止: to axe expenditure 削减经费;
Several thousand jobs are to be axed. 几
千人就业被削减了

# Bb

**"B" shares** pl. n. ordinary shares with
special voting rights (often owned by the
founder of a company and his family)B
种股票(具有特殊表决权的普通股票,
通常是公司创建人及其家庭所有)

**baby bonds** pl. n. US bonds in small
denominations (i. e. $100) which the
small investor can afford to buy 小额债
券(例如面额为 100 美元小本投资者买
得起)

**back** 1 n. opposite side to the front 背面;反面: Write your address on the back of the envelope. 在信封的背面写上你的地址。The conditions of sale are printed on the back of the invoice. 销售条件印在发票的背面。Please endorse the cheque on the back. 请在支票的背面签名或背书 2 a. referring to the past 过期的;拖欠的: back interest = interest not yet paid 欠息;拖欠过期的利息; back orders = orders received in the past and not fulfilled ( usually because the item is out of stock) 拖欠订货;延期交货: After the strike it took the factory six weeks to clear all the accumulated back orders. 罢工之后,该厂用了六周的时间把全部积压的订货发出。back pay = salary which has not been paid 欠付的工资; I am owed £ 500 in back pay. 欠我五百英镑的工资。back payment = paying money which is owed 欠付款项; The salesmen are claiming for back payment of unpaid commission. 销售人员正在提出索取尚未支付的佣金的要求。back payments = payments which are due 到期付款额; back rent = rent owed 欠租; The company owes £ 100,000 in back rent 该公司拖欠十万英镑租金。3. ad. as things were before 原处;原状: He will pay back the money in monthly instalments. 他将按月分期付款的方式偿还。The store sent back the cheque because the date was wrong. 百货商店送还支票,因为日期有误。The company went back on its agreement to supply at £ 1.50 a unit. 该公司违背了按单价 1.50 英镑供货的协议。4. v. (a) to back someone = to help someone financially 资助: The bank is backing him to the tune of £ 10,000. 银行资助他总额达 10,000 英磅。He is looking for someone to back his project. 他正在找人资助他的项目。(b) to back a bill = to sign a bill promising to pay it if the person it is addressed to is not able to do

so 在票背签字;在支票上背书

◇ **backdate** v. to put an earlier date on a cheque or an invoice 回溯;倒填日期(支票或发票); Backdate your invoice to April 1st. 你的发票日期应倒填到 4 月 1 日算起。The pay increase is backdated to January 1st. 工资增加是从 1 月 1 日算起。

◇ **backer** n. (a) person who backs someone 支持者;赞助者: He has an Australian backer. 他有一位澳大利亚赞助者。One of the company's backers has withdrawn. 公司的赞助人之一已经退出。(b) backer of a bill = person who backs a bill 负责兑付票据的人;票据背书人

◇ **background** n. (a) past work or experience 经历;履历: His background is in the steel industry. 他有过一段在钢铁工业部门工作的经历。The company is looking for someone with a background of success in the electronics industry. 该公司正在招聘一位在电子工业方面有成就的人。She has a publishing background. 她有在出版业工作的经历。What is his background or do you know anything about his background? 他有哪些经历或你知道他的经历吗?(b) past details 背景情况: He explained the background of the claim. 他阐明了索赔的背景。I know the contractual situation as it stands now, but can you fill in the background details? 我只知道合同的现状,但你能告诉我该合同的背景详情吗?

◇ **backhander** n. infml. bribe or money given to someone to get him to help you 贿赂,黑钱

◇ **backing** n. (a) financial support 担保;资助: He has the backing of an Australian bank. 他得到一家澳大利亚银行的资助。The company will succeed only if it has sufficient backing. 只有当该公司获得足够的资助,它才会成功。Who is providing the backing for the project or Where does the backing for the project come from? 该项目有谁资助? 或该项目的资助出自何方?(b) currency backing = gold or government securities which maintain the strength of a currency 货币担保(支撑)

NOTE: no plural

◇ **backlog** n. work (such as orders or letters) which has piled up waiting to be done 积压;积压而未交的订货(这里指积压的订单,订货或信件): The warehouse is trying to cope with a backlog of orders. 仓库正试图处理积压下来的订货。My secretary can't cope with the backlog of paperwork. 我的秘书无力处理积压下来的文书工作。

NOTE: no plural

◇ **back out** v. to stop being part of a deal or an agreement 终止;不履行: The bank backed out of the contract. 银行终止该项合同。We had to cancel the project when our German partners backed out. 德国合伙人退出了,我们只好取消该项目。

◇ **back up** v. to support or to help 支持;帮助: He brought along a file of documents to back up his claim. 他随身携带一卷宗文件以便证实索赔要求。The finance director said the managing director had refused to back him up in his argument with the VAT office. 财务主任说总经理已拒绝支持他与增值税办公室的辨论。

◇ **backup** a. supporting or helping 支持的;帮助的: We offer a free backup service to customers. 对顾客我们提供免费配套服务。After a series of sales tours by representatives, the sales director sends backup letters to all the contacts. 销售人员做了一系列巡回销售之后,销售主任向所有有业务接触的客户发出了成交证实信函。backup copy = copy of a computer disk to be kept in case the original disk is damaged 备查软盘本;备用软盘

◇ **backwardation** n. penalty paid by the seller when postponing delivery of shares to the buyer 证券交割延期费(不能按期将证券交付买方,则卖方要付罚金)

**bad** a. not good 坏的;低劣的: bad bargain = item which is not worth the price asked 亏本交易; bad buy = thing bought which is not worth the money paid for it 赔本购买的东西; bad debt = debt which will not be paid 呆帐,death: The company has written off £30,000 in bad debts. 该公司已注销了三万英镑的呆帐。

**bag** n. thing made of paper, cloth, or plastic for carrying items 袋,包(一般由纸,布或塑料制成): He brought his files in a Harrods bag. 他把文件装在哈罗德牌号的包中。We gave away 5,000 plastic bags at the exhibition. 在展览会上,我们赠送了五千只塑料袋(包)。shopping bag = bag used for carrying shopping 购物袋;商品袋

**baggage** n. suitcases or bags for carrying clothes when travelling 行李: free baggage allowance = amount of baggage which a passenger can take with him free on a plane 免费携带行李的重量; US baggage room = room where cases can be left while passengers are waiting for a plane or train(美)行李房;小件行李寄存处

NOTE: no plural; to show one suitcase, etc., you can say a piece of baggage

**bail** n. payment made to a court as guarantee that a prisoner will return after being released 保释金: to stand bail of £3,000 for someone 为某人支付3000英镑的保释金; He was released on bail of £3,000. or He was released on payment of £3,000 bail. 支付3000美元他被保释或他被保释支付了3,000美元。

to jump bail = not to appear in court af-
terhaving been released on bail 在保释中
逃跑
NOTE: no plural

◇ **bail out** v. (a) to rescue a company
which is in financial difficulties 帮助…摆
脱财政困境 (b) to bail someone out =
to pay money to a court as a guarantee
that someone will return to face charges
保释出(某人): She paid $3,000 to
bail him out. 她支付了3,000美元把他
保释出来。

◇ **bail - out** n. rescue of a company in
financial difficulties 帮助摆脱困境(财政
方面)

**balance** 1. n. (a) amount in an account
which makes the total debits and credits
equal 平衡(指帐户上借方与贷方资金
总额相等); credit balance = balance in
an account showing that more money has
been received than is owed 贷方余额;
debit balance = balance in an account
showing that more money is owed than
has been received 借方余额; The account has a credit balance of £100;该帐
户有100英磅的贷方余额。Because of
large payments to suppliers, the account
has a debit balance of £1,000. 由于支
付大量金额给供应商,帐目上有1,000
英磅的借方余额; balance in hand =
cash held to pay small debts 手头余额
(手头所掌握的现金,用以支付小额的
债务); balance brought down = amount
entered in an account at the end of a period to balance income and expenditure
承转余额,余额移后: balance brought
forward or balance carried forward =
amount entered in an account at the end
of a period tobalance the expenditure and
income which is then taken forward
tostart the new period 余额承前 (b)
rest of an amount owed 所欠金额的余
额: You can pay £100 deposit and the
balance within 60 days 你可先支付100
英磅的保证金而其余款项可在60天之

内支付。balance due to us = amount
owed to us which is due to be paid 欠我
们的钱数 (c) balance of payments =
the international financial position of a
country, including invisible as well as
visible trade 国际收支; balance of trade
or trade balance = international trading
position of a country, excluding invisible
trade 贸易差额; adverse or unfavourable
balance of trade = situation where a
country imports more than it exports 贸
易逆差; favourable trade balance = situation where a country exports more
than it imports 贸易顺差; The country
has had an adverse balance of trade for
the second month running. 该国家已连
续两个月出现贸易逆差。(d) bank bal-
ance = state of an account at a bank at a
particular time 银行往来余额;银行存
款余额
NOTE: no plural
2. v. (a) to calculate the amount needed
to make the two sides of an account equal
使…平衡(指一个帐目上借与贷两边相
等); I have finished balancing the accounts for March. 我三月份的帐目收支
实现了平衡。The February accounts do
not balance. = The two sides are not
equal. 二月份帐目收支不等。(b) to
plan a budget so that expenditure and income are equal 使…相抵;使预算收支
平衡: The president is planning for a
balanced budget. 总经理正计划平衡预
算。

◇ **balance sheet** n. statement of the
financial position of a company at a particular time, such as the end of the financial year or the end of a quarter 资产负
债表(指一个公司在一个特定日期如财
政年度末或季度末其财务状况的报
表): The company balance sheet for
1984 shows a substantial loss. 该公司
1984年的资产负债表说明亏损额很
大。The accountant has prepared the
balance sheet for the first half year. 会计

已准备出上半年的资产负债表。

**bale** 1. n. large pack of wool or paper or cotton, etc. 大包；大捆（羊毛、纸或棉花等）；a bale of cotton 一大包棉花；2, 520 bales of wool were destroyed in the fire. 2,520 包羊毛在大火中烧毁。2. v to tie wool or paper or cotton to make a bale 把…打包（捆）

**ballot** 1. n. (a) election where people vote for someone by marking a cross on a paper with a list of names 投票选举：ballot paper = paper on which the voter marks a cross to show who he wants to vote for 选票 ballot box = sealed box into which ballot papers are put 选举箱；投票箱；postal ballot = election where the voters send their ballot papers by post 邮政投票选举；secret ballot = election where the voters vote in secret 无记名投票选举；（b）selecting by taking papers at random out of a box 抽签；The share issue was oversubscribed, so there was a ballot for the shares. 由于股票超额认购,所以用抽签办法购买股票。2. v. to take a vote by ballot 投票：The union is balloting for the post of president. 工会正在投票选举主席的职位。

◇ **ballot - rigging** n. illegal arranging of the votes in a ballot, so that a particular candidate or party wins 控制选票；操纵选举

NOTE: no plural

**ban** 1. n. order which forbids someone from doing something 禁止；禁令：a government ban on the import of weapons 一项有关进口武器的政府禁令；a ban on the export of computer software 一个有关计算机软件出口的禁令；overtime ban = order by a trade union which forbids overtime work by itsmembers 禁止加班令；to impose a ban on smoking = to make an order which forbids smoking 实施禁烟令；to lift the ban on smoking = to allow peo-

ple to smoke 解除禁烟令；to beat the ban on something = to do something which is forbidden – usually by doing it rapidly before a ban is imposed, or by finding a legal way to avoid a ban 设法逃避禁令（在禁令前做或以合法手段逃避禁令）2. v. to forbid something or to make something illegal 禁止；取缔；The government has banned the sale of alcohol. 政府已取缔了酒的销售。

NOTE: banning – banned

**band** n. rubber band = thin ring of rubber for attaching things together 橡皮筋（圈）；Put a band round the filing cards to stop them falling on the floor. 用一条带子把档案卡捆起来, 以免其散落到地上。

**bank** 1. n. (a) business which holds money for its clients, which lends money at interest, and trades generally in money 银行：Lloyds Bank 劳埃德银行；The First National Bank 第一国家银行；The Royal Bank of Scotland 苏格兰皇家银行；He put all his earnings into his bank. 他将其全部所得存入银行。I have had a letter from my bank telling me my account is overdrawn. 我接到开户行的函件,通知我的帐户透支了。bank loan or bank advance = loan from a bank 银行贷款；He asked for a bank loan to start his business. 他为开业向银行申请一笔贷款。bank borrowing = money borrowed from a bank 银行借款；The new factory was financed by bank borrowing. 新建的工厂所需经费由银行贷（借）款。Bank borrowings have increased. = Loans given by banks have increased. 增加银行贷款。bank deposits = all money placed in banks 银行存款 (b) central bank = main government – controlled bank in a country, which controls the financial affairs of the country by fixing main interest rates, issuing currency and controlling the foreign exchange rate 中央银行；the Bank of England = central

British bank, owned by the state, which, together with the Treasury, regulates the nation's finances 英格兰银行; the Federal Reserve Banks = central banks in the USA which are owned by the state, and directed by the Federal Reserve Board 美国联邦储备银行(美国中央银行); the World Bank = central bank, controlled by the United Nations, whose funds come from the member states of the UN and which lends money to member states 世界银行; (c) savings bank = bank where you can deposit money and receive interest on it 储蓄银行; merchant bank = bank which lends money to companies and deals ininternational finance 商业银行;商人银行; the High Street banks = main British banks which accept deposits from and allow withdrawals by individuals(英)大银行; (d) data bank = store of information in a computer 数据库 2. v. to deposit money into a bank or to have an account with a bank 把钱存入银行或在银行开设存款帐户: He banked the cheque as soon as he received it. 他一收到支票就把它存入银行。Where do you bank? = Where do you have a bank account? 你在那个银行存钱? I bank or with Barclays 我在巴克利有户头。

◇ **bankable** a. which a bank will accept as security for a loan 银行可承兑的或可贴现的; a bankable paper 可承兑的票据;可贴现的票据

◇ **bank account** n. account which a customer has with a bank, where the customercan deposit and withdraw money 银行往来帐户;活期存款帐户(储户在银行开设的存款帐户并可存、取): to open a bank account 开立银行帐户; to close a bank account;结束银行帐户; How much money do you have in your bank account? 你在银行帐户中存了多少钱? She has £100 in her savings bank account. 她在储蓄银行帐户中存

了100英磅。If you let the balance in your bank account fall below £100, you have to pay bank charges. 如果你使银行帐户中的存款低于 100 英磅的话,那么你必须向银行支付手续费。

◇ **bank balance** n. state of a bank account at any particular time 银行存款余额;银行往来余额(指在任何特定时期银行帐户的状况): Our bank balance went into the red last month. 上个月,我们的银行存款余额已出现了赤字。

◇ **bank bill** n. (a) GB order by one bank telling another bank (usually in anothercountry) to pay money to someone 银行票据, 银行汇票(英)(指银行要求国外银行凭票付款给某人) (b) US piece of printed paper money(美)钞票

◇ **bank book** n. book, given by a bank, which shows money which you deposit orwithdraw from your savings account 银行存折

◇ **bank charges** pl. n. charges which a bank makes for carrying out work for acustomer 银行手续费(银行向顾客提供劳务所收的费用)

◇ **bank clerk** n. person who works in a bank, but not a manager 银行职员(在银行工作,但不是管理人员)

◇ **bank draft** n. order by one bank telling another bank (usually in another country) to pay money to someone 银行汇票(指银行要求国外银行凭票付款给某人)

◇ **banker** n. (a) person who is in an important position in a bank 银行家(指在银行中身居要职的人); merchant banker = person who has a high position in a merchant bank 商业银行家 (b) generally, a bank 银行; banker's bill = order by one bank telling another bank (usually in anothercountry) to pay money to someone 银行汇票; banker's order = order written by a customer asking a bank to make a regularpayment 银行本票；He pays his subscription by banker's order 他用银行本票支付其认购款。

◇ **bank giro** n. GB method used by clearing banks to transfer money rapidly from one account to another(英)银行直接转帐制(很快地将钱从一个帐户中转到另一个帐户中所使用的方法)

◇ **bank holiday** n. a weekday which is a public holiday when the banks are closed 银行节假日：New Year's Day is a bank holiday. 新年是银行的节假日。

◇ **banking** n. the business of banks 银行业务：He is studying banking. 他正学习银行业务。She has gone into banking. 她已从事银行业。US banking account = account which a customer has with a bank(美)银行帐户；a banking crisis = crisis affecting the banks 银行业危机；banking hours = hours when a bank is open for its customers 银行营业时间；You cannot get money out of the bank after banking hours. 在银行营业时间过后,你不能从银行取钱了。NOTE: no plural

◇ **bank manager** n. person in charge of a branch of a bank 银行经理：He asked his bank manager for a loan. 他向银行的经理申请一笔贷款。

◇ **bank note or banknote** n. piece of printed paper money 钞票：He pulled out a pile of used bank notes. 他掏出一叠旧钞票。

◇ **bank on** v. to do something because you are sure something will happen 指望；信赖：He is banking on getting a loan from his father to set up in business. 他正期待着从他父亲那里得到一笔贷款,以便从商。Do not bank on the sale of your house. 不要指望出售你的住宅。

◇**bankroll** v. infml. to pay for or to finance (a project)资助；提供资金(项目)

◇ **bank statement** n. written statement from a bank showing the balance of an account 银行对帐单；银行结单(说明该帐户的收支平衡状况)

**bankrupt** 1. a. & n. ( person or company) which has been declared by a court not to be capable of paying its debts and whose affairs are put into the hands of a receiver 破产的；破产者(由法院宣布个人或公司无力偿还债务,其事务由破产事务官管理)：He was adjudicated or declared bankrupt. 他被宣告破产。a bankrupt property developer 一位破了产的房地产开发者：He went bankrupt after two years in business 经商两年后,他破产了。certificated bankrupt = bankrupt who has been discharged from bankruptcy with a certificate to show he was not at fault 有证书的破产者；discharged bankrupt = person who has been released from being bankrupt because he has paid his debts 已解除债务的破产者；undischarged bankrupt = person who has been declared bankrupt and has not been released from that state 未被解除债务的破产者 2. v. to make someone become bankrupt 使…破产：The recession bankrupted my father. 经济衰退使我的父亲破产了。

◇ **bankruptcy** n. state of being bankrupt 破产：The recession has caused thousands of bankruptcies. 经济衰退造成了成千上万的人破产。adjudication of bankruptcy or declaration of bankruptcy = legal order making someone bankrupt 宣告破产；discharge in bankruptcy = being released from bankruptcy after paying debts 解除破产者债务；to file a petition in bankruptcy = to apply officially to be made bankrupt or to ask officially for someone else to be made bankrupt 正式申请破产

**bar** n. (a) place where you can buy and drink alcohol 酒吧：The sales reps met in the bar of the hotel. 销售员们在旅馆的酒吧间见面。(b) small shop 小店铺: sandwich bar = small shop where you can buy sandwiches to take away 三明治店; snack bar = small restaurant where you can get simple meals 快餐店; 小吃店; (c) thing which stops you doing something 阻碍物; Government legislation is a bar to foreign trade. 政府的立法阻碍了对外贸易。(d) GB the profession of barrister(英)律师(大律师); to be called to the bar = to become a barrister 成为一位大律师。

◇ **bar chart** n. chart where values or quantities are shown as thick columns of different heights 柱形图表(以不同高度的柱形表示数值的图表)

◇ **bar code** n. system of lines printed on a product which when read by a computer give a reference number or price 条纹码(该产品上的线条系统, 由计算机阅读则显示相应的号码与价格)

**bareboat charter** n. system of chartering a ship where the owner provides only the ship, but not the crew, fuel or insurance 空船租赁合同(指船主仅提供船而不提供船员、燃料、保险的一种租赁船舶的方式)

**barely** ad. almost not 几乎没有: There is barely enough money left to pay the staff. 剩下的钱难以支付职工的工资。She barely had time to call her lawyer. 她几乎没有时间去请律师。

**bargain** 1 n. (a) agreement on the price of something 讲价; 交易: to make a bargain 达成协议; to drive a hard bargain = to be a difficult negotiator 狠狠杀价; to strike a hard bargain = to agree a deal which is favourable to you 达成对自己极有利的协议; It is a bad bargain. = it is not worth the price. 这东西买贵了(这是一笔亏本生意)。(b) thing which is cheaper than usual 便宜货; 廉价物: That car is a (real) bargain at £500. 那

辆小汽车确实是便宜货, 才花了500英磅。bargain hunter = person who looks for cheap deals 买便宜货的人 (c) sale of one lot of shares on the Stock Exchange(在证券交易所成批)股票出售; bargains done = number of deals made on the Stock Exchange during a day(证券交易所一天之内)出售的数量 2. v. to discuss a price for something 议价; 讨价还价: You will have to bargain with the dealer if you want a discount. 如果你想打些折扣的话, 你必须与商贩讨价还价。They spent two hours bargaining about or over the price. 他们花费了两个小时讨价还价。NOTE: you bargain with someone over or about or for something

◇ **bargain basement** n. basement floor in a shop where goods are sold cheaply 廉价部(销售廉价商品的地方, 通常设在商店的地下室): I'm selling this at a bargain basement price. = I'm selling this very cheaply. 我以低价将此出售。

◇ **bargain counter** n. counter in a shop where goods are sold cheaply 廉价货品柜台; 廉价部

◇ **bargain offer** n. sale of a particular type of goods at a cheap price 廉价销售(以便宜价格销售某特别种类商品): This week's bargain offer - 30% off all carpet prices. 本周出售的地毯价格均优惠30%。

◇ **bargain price** n. cheap price 廉价: These carpets are for sale at a bargain price. 这些地毯廉价出售。

◇ **bargain sale** n. sale of all goods in a store at cheap prices 大廉价; 大甩卖

◇ **bargaining** n. act of discussing a price, usually wage increases for workers 商议; 谈判(通常为工人增加工资所进行的): (free) collective bargaining = negotiations between employers and workers' representatives over wage in-

creases and conditions 集体谈判；bar-
gainingpower = strength of one person
or group when discussing prices or wage
settlements 谈判的能力；bargaining position = statement of position by one
group during negotiations 谈判的地位
**barrel** n. (a) large round container for
liquids 大圆桶：He bought twenty - five
barrels of wine. 他买了二十五大桶酒。
to sell wine by the barrel 以桶为单位出
售酒 (b) amount of liquid contained in a
barrel 一桶(一种容量单位)；The price
of oil has reached ＄30 a barrel. 石油的
价格已涨到每桶 30 美元。= **barrier**
n. thing which stops someone doing
something, especially sending goods from
one place to another 关卡，障碍：cus-
toms barriers or tariff barriers = customs duty intended to make trade more
difficult 关税壁垒；to impose trade barriers on certain goods = to restrict the
import of certain goods by charging high
duty 对某些商品实行贸易壁垒；The
unions have asked the government to impose trade barriers on foreign cars. 这些
协会要求政府对进口小汽车采取贸易
壁垒。to lift trade barriers from imports
= to remove restrictions on imports 解
除进口贸易壁垒；The government has
lifted trade barriers on foreign cars. 政府
已解除了对进口小汽车的贸易壁垒。
**barrister** n. GB lawyer (especially in
England) who can speak or argue a case
in one of the higher courts(英)(在英国
有资格出席高等法庭的)律师；大律师
**barter** 1. n. system where goods are
exchanged for other goods and not sold
for money 易货贸易；易货交易(以货易
货,商品是用来交换别的商品而不卖
钱)：barter agreement or barter arrangement or barter deal = agreement to exchange goods by barter 易货协定；The
company has agreed a barter deal with
Bulgaria. 该公司已同意与保加利亚达
成易货贸易的协议。

NOTE：no plural
2. v. to exchange goods for other goods,
but not buy them for money 货物交换；
以货换货：They agreed a deal to barter
tractors for barrels of wine. 他们同意以
拖拉机换大桶酒的交易。
◇ **bartering** n. act of exchanging
goods for other goods and not for money
易货
NOTE：no plural

**base** 1. n. (a) lowest or first position
最低点；起点：Turnover increased by
200％, but starting from a low base. 尽
管营业额以 200％ 的速度增长,但是其
起点很低。base year = first year of an
index, against which later years'
changesare measured 基年；基准年：
bank base rate = basic rate of interest
which a bank charges on loans to its customers 银行基本利率；see DATABASE
(b) place where a company has its main
office or factory or place where a businessman has his office 厂部；总部：The
company has its base in London and
branches in all European countries. 该公
司总部设在伦敦其分公司遍及欧州各
国。He has an office in Madrid which he
uses as a base while he is travelling in
Southern Europe. 在南欧旅行期间,他
将在马德里的办事处做为总部。2. v.
(a) to start to calculate or to negotiate
from a position(以 … 为计算或谈判的)
根据：We based our calculations on the
forecast turnover. 我们的计算是以预测
营业额为根据 based on = calculating
from 基于；以…作为根据；based on last
year's figures；以去年的数字为依据；
based on population forecasts 以人口预
测为依据 (b) to set up a company or a
person in a place 建立在…；安排在…：
the European manager is based in our
London office；这位欧洲经理安排在我
们的伦敦办事处。Our overseas branch
is based in the Bahamas；我们的海外分
部设在巴哈马群岛。a London - based

sales executive 一位安排到伦敦任职的销售总经理

◇ **basement** n. section of a shop which is underground 地下营业区; bargain basement = basement floor in a shop where goods are sold cheaply 地下廉价商品部; I am selling this at a bargain basement price 我正以地下廉价部的价格出售这件商品。(这货我要价够便宜的)。

**basic** 1. adjective (a) normal 基本的; 标准的: basic pay or basic salary or basic wage = normal salary without extra payments 基本工资; 基本收入; basic discount = normal discount without extra percentages 基本折扣; 基准贴现率: Our basic discount is 20%, but we offer 5% extra for rapid settlement 我们的基准贴现率为 20%, 但为快速结帐, 我们另外加付 5%。(b) most important 首要的; 基本的: basic commodities = ordinary farm produce, produced in large quantities (such as corn, rice, sugar, etc.) 基本生活用品: (c) simple or from which everything starts 简单的; 基础的: he has a basic knowledge of the market. 他具有市场方面的基本知识。To work at the cash desk, you need a basic qualification in maths. 为了能在出纳台工作, 你需持有数学合格证。

◇ **basics** pl. n. simple and important facts 要点; 基础: He has studied the basics of foreign exchange dealing. 他已学习了外汇交易的基础知识。to get back to basics = to consider the basic facts again 回过头来, 考虑一下要点

◇ **basically** ad. seen from the point from which everything starts 基本上; 根本上

◇ **BASIC** n. = BEGINNER'S ALL - PURPOSE SYMBOLIC INSTRUC-TION CODE simple language for computer programming(指用于计算机程序上的)Basic 语言

**basis** n. (a) point or number from which calculations are made 基础; 基准; 根据: we forecast the turnover on the basis of a 6% price increase/ 我们根据价格上涨 60% 来预测营业业额。(b) general terms of agreement 协议的一般条款: on a short - term or long - term basis = for a short or long period 短期或长期; He has been appointed on a short - term basis. 他被短期任用。We have three people working on a freelance basis. 我们有三个授雇于他人的独立工作的人(自由职业者)。

NOTE: the plural is bases

**basket** n. (a) container made of thin pieces of wood or metal or plastic 篮子; 盒子; 筐子: a basket of apples 一筐苹果; filing basket = container kept on a desk for documents which have to be filed 文件筐 shopping basket = basket used for carrying shopping 购物筐 waste paper basket = container into which paper or pieces of rubbish can be thrown 废纸篓 (b) group of prices or currencies taken as a standard 一揽子作为标准的货币; The pound has fallen against a basket of European currencies. 与一揽子欧洲货币相比英镑已下跌。The price of the average shopping basket or US the market basket has risen by 6%. 一揽子价格或(美)市场一揽子价格上升 6%。

**batch** 1. n. (a) group of items which are made at one time 一批; 一组: This batch of shoes has the serial number 25 - 02。这批鞋系列号码为 25—02 (b) group of documents which are processed at the same time 批; 批量; 成批处理(文件) a batch of invoices 一批发票; today's batch of orders 今天的一批订单; The accountant signed a batch of cheques. 会计签发的一批支票。We deal with the orders in batches of fifty. 我们以 50 张为一批来处理订单。batch processing = system of data processing where information is collected into batches before being loaded into the computer 成批处理；成批分理 2 v. to put items together in groups to batch invoices or cheques 成批处理发票或支票

◇ **batch number** n. number attached to a batch 批号；When making a complaint always quote the batch number on the packet. 投拆时时常引用该包装袋上的批号。

**battery** n. small object for storing electric power 电池：The calculator needs a new battery. 计算器需换新电池。a battery - powered calculator 一种以电池供电的计算器

**battle** n. fight 战斗：boardroom battles = arguments between directors 董事会在会议室的辨论战；circulation battle = fight between two newspapers to sell more copies in the same section of the market(报纸)发行竞争；发行大战

**bay** n. loading bay = section of road in a warehouse, where lorries can drive in to load or unload 装卸场道

**b/d** = BARRELS PER DAY(石油日产量的计算单位)桶

**bear** 1. n. (a) large wild animal covered in fur 熊：Their advertising symbol is a bear. 他们的广告标志是一只熊。(b) (Stock Exchange) dealer who sells shares because he thinks the price will fall and he will be able to buy them again more cheaply later 空头(指证券所交易商，估计证券有跌价的趋势时，先售出，待跌价后再买进，借以获利)；bear market = period when Stock Exchange prices fall because shareholders are selling 熊市；空头市场；看跌市场：see BULL 2. v. (a) to give interest 付息；生息：government bonds which bear 5% interest 利息为5%的政府债券 (b) to have (a name) or to have something written on it 具有；带有：The cheque bears the signature of the company secretary. 该支票有公司秘书的签字。envelope which

bears a London postmark 盖有伦敦邮戳的信封；a letter bearing yesterday's date 注有昨日日期的一封信；The share certificate bears his name。该股票有他的名字。(c) to pay costs 支付；承担(费用) The costs of the exhibition will be borne by the company. 展览会的费用将由该公司承担。The company bore the legal costs of both parties. 公司承担双方的诉讼费用。

NOTE: bearing - bore - has borne

◇ **bearer** n. person who holds a cheque or certificate 持票人：The cheque is payable to bearer. = is paid to the person who holds it, not to any particular name written on it 该支票应支付给持票人。

◇ **bearer bond** n. bond which is payable to the bearer and does not have a name written on it 无记名债券

◇ **bearing** a. which bears or which produces 负担的；产生的：certificate bearing interest at 5% 利息为5%的单据；interest - bearing deposits 附息存款

**beat** v. (a) to win in a fight against someone 战胜：They have beaten their rivals into second place in the computer market. 他们在计算机市场上击败了对手使其居第二位。(b) to beat a ban = to do something which is forbidden by doing it rapidly before the ban is enforced 设法躲过一项禁令

NOTE: beating - beat - has beaten

**become** v. to change into something different 变为；成为：The export market has become very difficult since the rise in the dollar. 自美元升值以来，出口市场已变得非常困难。The company became very profitable in a short time. 在短期内，该公司变得十分有利可图。

NOTE: becoming - became - has become

**bed - and - breakfast deal** n. arrangement where shares are sold one day and bought back the following day, in order to establish a profit or loss for tax declaration 暮售朝购的股票交易(安排一天的股票销售,同时第二天又将其购回以便为纳税申报确定盈亏)

**begin** v. to start 开始: The company began to lose its market share. 该公司开始丧失它的所占有市场份额。He began the report which the shareholders had asked for. 他开始做股东所要求的报告。The auditors' report began with a description of the general principles adopted. 审计员的报告是从阐述审计工作所应采用的一般原则开始的。NOTE: you begin something or begin to do something or begin with something. Note also: beginning – began – has begun

◇ **beginning** n. first part 开始;起点: The beginning of the report is a list of the directors and their shareholdings. 报告的开头列了董事与他们持有股份的情况。

**behalf** n. on behalf of = acting for (someone or a company) 作为…的代表;代表(某人或某公司): I am writing on behalf of the minority shareholders. 我正以少数股东的名义写一份材料。She is acting on my behalf. 她是代表我行事。solicitors acting on behalf of the American company 代表美国公司行事的小律师

**behind** 1. prep. at the back or after 在…后面: The company is No. 2 in the market, about £4m behind their rivals. 该公司在市场中名列第二,约相差 400 万英磅而居于他们的竞争对手之后。2. ad. after 在后: We have fallen behind our rivals. = We have fewer sales or make less profit than our rivals. 我们已落在竞争对手后面。The company has fallen behind with its deliveries. = It is late with its deliveries. 该公司已延缓交货。

**believe** v. to think that something is true 相信,信任: We believe he has offered to buy 25% of the shares. 我们确信,他已提出购买 25% 的股票。The chairman is believed to be in South America on business. 确信董事长因公在南美出差。

**belong** v. (a) to belong to = to be the property of 属于;列入: The company belongs to an old American banking family. 该公司属于一个历史悠久的美国银行业家族。The patent belongs to the inventor's son. 此项专利属于发明者的儿子。(b) to belong with = to be in the correct place with 适用;归入: Those documents belong with the sales reports. 那些文件归入销售报告。

**below** prep. lower (down) than or less than 在…下面;低于: We sold the property at below the market price. 我们以低于市场的价格售出该财产。You can get a ticket for New York at below £150 from a bucket shop. 你能够以低于 150 英磅的价格从出售低价机票的小旅行社那里买到一张去纽约的票。

◇ **below – the – line** a. below – the – line expenditure = exceptional payments which are separated from a company's normal accounts 线下项目支出;例外支出

**benchmark** n. point in an index which is important, and can be used to compare with other figures 基准点(指用来与其它数值相比较的一个很重要的指数)

**beneficial** a. beneficial occupier = person who occupies a property but does not own it fully 有使用权的占有者;受益占有人: beneficial interest = interest which allows someone to occupy or receive rent from a property, but not to own it 受惠权益;有权益的利息

◇ **beneficiary** n. person who gains money from something 受益者: the beneficiaries of a will 遗嘱继承人;遗嘱受

益人

**benefit** 1. n. (a) payments which are made to someone under a national or private insurance scheme 救济金;抚恤金;保险赔偿费 She receives £20 a week as unemployment benefit. 她每周领 20 英磅的失业救济金。The sickness benefit is paid monthly. 疾病救济金按月支付。The insurance office sends out benefit cheques each week. 保险公司每周汇出保险赔偿费的支票。death benefit = money paid to the family of someone who dies in an accident at work 死亡抚恤金 (b) fringe benefits = extra items given by a company to workers in addition to their salaries (such as company cars, private health insurance) 附加福利 2.. v. (a) to make better or to improve 有利于;改善: A fall in inflation benefits the exchange rate. 通货膨胀的下降对汇率有利。(b) to benefit from or by something = to be improved by something or to gain more money because of something 受益;得益于…: Exports have benefited from the fall in the exchange rate. 汇率的下跌使出口受益。The employees have benefited from the profit – sharing scheme. 雇员们从利润分享的计划中受益。

**bequest** n. property, money, etc., given to someone in a will 遗产;遗赠: He made several bequests to his staff. 他给其职工留下几件遗物。

**berth** 1. n. place in a harbour where a ship can tie up 泊位: 2. v. to tie up at a berth 停泊;使停泊; The ship will berth at Rotterdam on Wednesday. 该轮将于星期三停泊在鹿特丹港。

**BES = BUSINESS EXPANSION SCHEME** 商业发展规划

**best** 1. a. very good or better than all others 最好的: His best price is still higher than all the other suppliers. 他最好的价格仍高于其他供应商的价格。

1985 was the company's best year ever. 1985 年是该公司最景气的一年。2. n. very good effort 最佳表现;最大的努力: The salesmen are doing their best, but the stock simply will not sell at that price. 售货员竭尽全力,但存货完全不会按这样的价格出售。

◇ **best – seller** n. item (especially a book) which sells very well 畅销物(品)(尤其是书)

◇ **best – selling** a. which sells very well 畅销的: These computer disks are our best – selling line. 这些计算机磁盘是我们的畅销货。

**bet** 1. n. amount deposited when you risk money on the result of a race or of a game 打赌;赌注: 2. v. to risk money on the result of something 打赌: He bet £100 on the result of the election. 他在选举结果上下了一百英镑的赌注。I bet you £25 the dollar will rise against the pound. 我认为美元比英镑升值的可能性大,不信咱俩打 25 英磅的赌。betting tax = tax levied on betting on horses or dogs, etc. (在赛马,赛狗…上的)打赌税

NOTE: betting – bet – has bet

**better** a. very good compared with something else 较好的; This year's results are better than last year's. 今年的成绩胜过去年。We will shop around to see if we can get a better price. 我们到各商店去转转,看看是否能买到价格更好的东西。

**beware** v. to be careful 当心;谨防; beware of imitations = be careful not to buy cheap low – quality items which are made to look like more expensive items 谨防假冒伪劣的赝品

**bi –** prefix twice 两次: bi – monthly = twice a month 一月两次或半月一次; bi – annually = twice a year 一年两次或半年一次

**bid** 1. n. (a) offer to buy something at

a certain price 出价；to make a bid for something = to offer to buy something 出价购买 … He made a bid for the house. 他出价购买房子。 The company made a bid for its rival. 本公司出价购买其竞争者的公司。 to make a cash bid = to offer to pay cash for something 以现金开价；to put in a bid for something or to enter a bid for something = to offer (usually in writing) to buy something 为购某物提出价钱；(at an auction) opening bid = first bid 第一次出价(指在拍卖中) closing bid = last bid at an auction or the bid which is successful 拍卖中最后的出价；收盘出价 (b) offer to do some work at a certain price 要价；投标：He made the lowest bid for the job. 为了得到这份工作，他要价最低。 US offer to sell something at a certain price (美)发盘价；出价；They asked for bids for the supply of spare parts. 他们要求对方就备件供应出价。 (c) takeover bid = offer to buy all or a majority of shares in a company so as to control it 兼并出价；合并递价：to make a takeover bid for a company 为兼并一个公司(递价)；to withdraw a takeover bid 撤消兼并出价；The company rejected the takeover bid. = The directors recommended that the shareholders should not accept it. 该公司不接受兼并出价 2. v. (at an auction) to offer to buy something = to offer to buy something(在拍卖行)出价：He bid £1,000 for the jewels. = He offered to pay £1,000 for the jewels. 他出价£1,000 英磅购买这些宝石。
NOTE: bidding – bid – has bid

◇ **bidder** n. person who makes a bid (usually at an auction)出价人(通常用于拍卖时)：Several bidders made offers for the house. 几个竞买人为该房子出价。 The property was sold to the highest bidder. = to the person who had made the highest bid or who offered the most money 该项财产拍卖给出价最高的人。

The tender will go to the lowest bidder. = to the person who offers the best terms or the lowest price for services. 要价最低的人将中标。

◇ **bidding** n. action of making offers to buy (usually at an auction)出价：The bidding started at £1,000. = The first and lowest bid was £1,000. 起价为1,000 英磅。 The bidding stopped at £250,000. = The last bid (and the successful bid) was for £250,000. 最后的成交价为250,000 英磅。 The auctioneer started the bidding at £100. = He suggested that the first bid should be £100. 拍卖商以100 英磅为起点价。
NOTE: no plural

**Big Board** n. US infml. = NEW YORK STOCK EXCHANGE 纽约证券交易所

**bilateral** a. between two parties or countries 双边的(指两个当事人或两个国家间的事)：The minister signed a bilateral trade agreement. 部长已签署了一项双边贸易协定。

**bill** 1. n. (a) written list of charges to be paid 票据；发票；帐单：The salesman wrote out the bill. 售货员开了发票。 Does the bill include VAT? 请问发票包括增值税吗？ The bill is made out to Smith Ltd. 帐单是开给史密斯有限公司的。 The builder sent in his bill. 这个建筑工人交上他的帐单。 He left the country without paying his bills. 他没有付帐就离开了该国。 to foot the bill = to pay the costs 付帐 (b) list of charges in a restaurant(用于饭店帐单：Can I have the bill please? 请给我帐单，好吗？ (即请给我结帐)。 The bill comes to £20 including service. 帐单包括服务费共计20 英磅。 Does the bill include service? 这份帐单包括服务费了吗？ The waiter has added 10% to the bill for service. 服务员在帐单中加了10% 的服务费。 (c) written paper promising to pay money 汇票；支票；bill of exchange = document which tells a bank to pay a person (usually used in payments in foreign currency) 汇票：accommodation bill = bill of exchange where the person signing is helping someone else to raise a loan 通融票据；bank bill = bill of exchange endorsed by a bank 银行汇票；demand bill = bill of exchange which must be paid when payment is asked for 即期汇票；to accept a bill = to sign a bill of exchange to show that you promise to pay it 承兑汇票；to discount a bill = to buy a bill of exchange at a lower price than that written on it in order to cash it later 贴现汇票；bills payable = bills which a debtor will have to pay 应付票据；bills receivable = bills which a creditor will receive in the end 应收票据；(d) bill of lading = list of goods being shipped, which the transporter gives to the person sending the goods to show that the goods have been loaded 提货单 (e) US piece of paper money(美)纸币；a $5 bill 一张五美元美钞；(f) bill of sale = document which the seller gives to the buyer to show that the sale has taken place 出货单，销售契约；卖据：(g) draft of a new law which will be discussed in Parliament 议案；法案 2. v. to present a bill to someone so that it can be paid 开帐单：The builders billed him for the repairs to his neighbour's house. 营造商给他开了一张修理邻居住宅的帐单。

◇ **billing** n. US writing of invoices or bills 开票(发票,帐单)
NOTE: no plural

**billion** number one thousand million or one million million 十亿或万亿

**bin** n. large container 大箱子；separate section of shelves in a warehouse 仓库分格架；dump bin = display container like a large round box, filled with goods for sale 圆形的货品陈列箱

**bind** v. to tie or to attach 使受…约束：The company is bound by its articles of association. 该公司受公司章程约束。He does not consider himself bound by the agreement which was signed by his predecessor. 他不认为自己受前任所签署协议的约束。
NOTE: binding – bound

◇ **binder** n. (a) stiff cardboard cover for papers(活页)封面：ring binder = cover with rings in it which fit into special holes made insheets of paper 四眼活页夹 (b) US temporary agreement for insurance sent before the insurance policy is issued(美)暂保单；临时契约(指正式保险单未签发前而发出的临时保险单)
NOTE: the GB English for this is cover note

◇ **binding** a. which legally forces someone to do something 有拘束力的：a binding contract 有约束力的合同；This document is not legally binding 这份文件在法律上无拘束力。The agreement is binding on all parties. = All parties signing it must do what is agreed. 该协议对所有各方均有拘束力。

**black** 1. a. (a) black market = buying and selling goods in a way which is not allowed by law (as in a time of rationing) 黑市：There is a flourishing black market in spare parts for cars. 小汽车备件的黑市生意兴隆。You can buy gold coins on the black market. 你可在黑市上购到金币。to pay black market prices = to pay high prices to get items which are not easily available 支付黑市价格或高价购买紧俏货。(b) black economy = work which is paid for in cash, and therefore not declared for tax 非法经济活动(现金工资不报税的工作) (c) in the black = in credit 有盈利：The company has moved into the black. 该公司业已开始盈利。My bank account is still in the black. 我的银行帐户仍有盈余。2.

v. to forbid trading in certain goods or withcertain suppliers 限制；禁止(经营某商品)：Three firms were blacked by the government. 政府让三家公司停业。The union has blacked a trucking firm. 工会让一家货车运输行停业(指汽车运输公司的运营)

◇ **blackleg** n. worker who goes on working when there is a strike 工贼；罢工破坏者

◇ **black list** n. list of goods or people or companies which have been blacked 黑名单(指列入被停止交易的货物、公司或人)

◇ **blacklist** v. to put goods or people or a company on a black list…列入黑名单：His firm was blacklisted by the government. 政府将他的公司列入黑名单。

**blame** 1. n. saying that someone has done something wrong or that someone is responsible 责备；责怪：The sales staff got the blame for the poor sales figures. 销售人员因销售数字不佳而受到责怪。2. v. to say that someone has done something wrong or is responsible for a mistake 责备；责怪；谴责：The managing director blamed the chief accountant for not warning him of the loss. 经理责怪总会计师没有将损亏的情况预先通知他。The union is blaming the management for poor industrial relations. 工会因劳资关系不好正责备管理部门。

**blank** 1. a. with nothing written 空白的；空着的：a blank cheque = a cheque with no amount of money or name written on it, but signed by the drawer 一张空白支票 2. n. space on a form which has to be completed 空白表格：Fill in the blanks and return the form to your local office. 填写这份空白表格并把此表呈交到地办事处。

**blanket** n. thick woollen cover for a bed 毛毯：blanket agreement = agreement

which covers many items 一揽子协议：blanket insurance = insurance which covers various items (such as a house and its contents) 统保；综合保险；blanket refusal = refusal to accept many different items 概不接受；一揽子谢绝

**blister pack** n. type of packing where the item for sale is covered with a stiff plastic sheet sealed to a card backing 薄膜包装；透明塑料罩

**block** 1. n. (a) series of items grouped together 一宗；一批；一套：He bought a block of 6,000 shares. 他已购买一宗6,000份股票。block booking = booking of several seats or rooms at the same time 整批预订(坐位或房间)；The company has a block booking for twenty seats on the plane or for ten rooms at the hotel. 该公司整批预订了飞机上20个座位或旅馆的10个房间。block vote = voting of a large number of votes at the same time (such as those of a trade union delegation)集体投票 (b) series of buildings forming a square with streets on all sides 地段；街区：They want to redevelop a block in the centre of the town. 他们想在市中心再开发一个街区。a block of offices or an office block = a large building which only contains offices 办公大楼 (c) block capitals or block letters = capital letters (as A,B,C)大写字母；Write your name and address in block letters. 用大写字母书写你的姓名与地址。2. v. to stop something taking place 阻拦；阻挠：He used his casting vote to block the motion. 他运用投票的方式来阻止该项提议。The planning-committee blocked the redevelopment plan. 计划委员会阻挠重振计划。blocked currency = currency which cannot be taken out of a country because of exchange controls 封锁通货；冻结货币；The company has a large account in blocked roubles. 公司有大量的卢布被冻结在帐户上。

**blue** a. blue – chip investments or blue – chip shares or blue chips = risk – free shares in good companies 热门股票；无风险股票；blue – collar worker = manual worker in a factory 兰领工人；blue – collar union = trade union formed mainly of blue – collar workers 兰领工人工会

**blurb** n. piece of advertising，especially an advertisement written by a publisher for a book 特指出版商为介绍一本书所做的广告

**bn** = BILLION 十亿；万亿

**board** 1. n. (a) GB board of directors = group of directors elected by the shareholders to run acompany（英）董事会：The bank has two representatives on the board. 在董事会里，该银行有两位代表。He sits on theboard as a representative of the bank. 他作为一个银行代表参加董事会。Two directors were removed from the board at the AGM. 在年度股东大会上将两位董事免职。She was asked to join the board. = She was asked to become a director. 她应邀参加董事会。board meeting = meeting of the directors of a company 董事会议 (b) US board of directors = group of people elected by the shareholders to draw up company policy and to appoint the president and other executive officers who are responsible for managing the company（美）董事会
NOTE：the board of an American company may be made up of a large number of non – executive directors and only one or two executive officers；a British board has more executive directors (c) group of people who run a trust or a society 委员会：advisory board = group of advisors 咨询委员会；editorial board = group of editors 编辑委员会 (d) on board = on a ship or plane or train 登上（船、飞机、火车）：free on board（f.o.b.）= price

includes all the seller's costs until the goods are on the ship for transportation 离岸价格；船上交货价格
2．v. to go on to a ship or plane or train 登上… Customs officials boarded the ship in the harbour. 海关官员在港口登上这条船。

◇ **boarding card or boarding pass** n. card given to passengers who have checked in for a flight to allow them to board the plane 登机证（允许旅客登机的卡片）

◇ **boardroom** n. room where the directors of a company meet 董事会的会议室：boardroom battles = arguments between directors 董事会之间争论

**boat** n. ship 小船：cargo boat 货船；passenger boat 客轮；We took the night boat to Belgium. 我们乘晚班航轮开往比利时。Boats for Greece leave every morning. 每天早晨有客轮去希腊。

**bona fide** a. trustworthy or which can be trusted 真正的；诚实的：a bona fide offer = an offer which is made honestly 诚实的发盘（要约）

**bonanza** n. great wealth；very profitable business 高利润企业；The oil well was a bonanza for the company. 该油井是这个公司的巨大财源。1984 was a bonanza year for the computer industry. 1984 年是计算机工业获得厚利的年份。

**bond** n. (a) contract document promising to repay money borrowed by a company or by the governmen 债券（公司或政府机构对借款承担偿还的凭证）；government bonds or treasury bonds 公债；国库券；municipal bond or local authority bond = bond issued by a town or district 市政公债；市政债券 (b) contract document promising to repay money borrowed by a person 还款契约或保证书：bearer bond = bond which is payable to the bearer and does not have a name written on it 无记名债券 debenturebond = certificate showing that a debenture has been issued 公司债券; mortgage bond = certificate showing that a mortgage exists and that propertyis security for it 抵押债券; GB premium bond = government bond, part of the National Savings scheme, which pays no interest, but gives the owner the chance to win a weekly or monthly prize (英)无息有奖债券 (c) goods (held) in bond = goods held by the customs until duty has been paid 保税货物;关税保税的货物; entry of goods under bond = bringing goods into a country in bond 将货物存于海关保税仓库中; to take goods out of bond = to pay duty on goods so that they can be released by the customs(纳税后)自保税仓库中提出货物

◇ **bonded** a. held in bond 关栈保税的;有担保的: bonded warehouse = warehouse where goods are stored in bond until duty is paid 保税仓库

◇ **bondholder** n. person who holds government bonds 债券持有者

◇ **bond – washing** n. selling American Treasury bonds with the interest coupon, and buying them back ex coupon, so as to reduce tax 债券洗售(高价出售有红利的国库券,同时以低价将其买进不付红利以便减税款)

**bonus** n. extra payment 奖金;额外津贴: capital bonus = extra payment by an insurance company which is produced by capital gain(保险公司所付)资本红利; cost – of – living bonus = money paid to meet the increase in the cost of living 生活费津贴; Christmas bonus = extra payment made to staff at Christmas 圣诞节津贴; incentive bonus = extra pay offered to a worker to encourage him to work harder 奖金; productivity bonus = extra payment made because of in-creased productivity 超产奖金; bonus share = extra share given to an existing shareholder 红利股; no – claims bonus = reduction of premiums on an insurance because no claims have been made (因无索赔减收应缴保险费)无索赔奖金

NOTE: plural is bonuses

**book** 1. n. (a) set of sheets of paper attached together 帐本;帐簿: a company's books = the financial records of a company 公司的帐簿; account book = book which records sales and purchases(记载售出购进的)帐册;帐簿; cash book = record of cash 现金出纳簿; order book = record of orders 订货簿; The company has a full order book. = It has sufficient orders to keep the workforce occupied. 公司有足够的订单或因订单不断,公司买卖兴隆。purchase book = records of purchases 采购簿; sales book = records of sales 销售簿; book sales = sales as recorded in the sales book 帐面销售额; book value = value as recorded in the company's books 帐面价值 (b) bank book = book which shows money which you have deposited or withdrawn from a bank account 银行存折; cheque book = book of new cheques 支票本(簿) phone book or telephone book = book which lists names of people or companies with their addresses and telephone numbers 电话号码簿 2. v. to order or to reserve something 预定;定货; to book a room in a hotel or a table at a restaurant or a ticket on a plane 在旅馆预定一个房间或在饭店定一桌酒席或预定一张飞机票; I booked a table for 7.45. 我预定好七点四十五分用餐桌。He booked a ticket through to Cairo. 他预定了一张直达开罗的飞机票。to book someone into a hotel or onto a flight = to order a room or a plane ticket for someone 为某人在旅馆订房间或订机票; He was booked on the 09.00 flight to Zurich. 已帮他订了一张九点飞往苏黎世的机票。The hotel or the flight is fully booked or is booked up. = All the rooms or seats are reserved. 旅馆客房预定一空或机票已全部预售完。The restaurant is booked up over the Christmas period. 圣诞节期间饭店预订一空。

◇ **booking** n. act of ordering a room or a seat 预定。Hotel bookings have fallen since the end of the tourist season. 自旅游季节结束以来，旅馆客房的预定下降。booking clerk = person who sells tickets in a booking office 售票员；booking office = office where you can book seats at a theatre or tickets for the railway 售票处；block booking = booking of several seats or rooms at the same time 整批预订；to confirm a booking = say that a booking is certain 预定确认；证实订妥；double booking = booking by mistake of two people into the same hotel room or the same seat on a plane 订重或重复预订

◇ **bookkeeper** n. person who keeps the financial records of a company 簿记员；记帐员（记录财务事务的人员）

◇ **bookkeeping** n. keeping of the financial records of a company or an organization 记帐簿记；簿记学：single - entry bookkeeping = noting a deal with only one entry 单式簿记；double - entry bookkeeping = noting of both credit and debit sides of an account 复式簿记
NOTE: no plural

◇ **booklet** n. small book with a paper cover 小册子

◇ **bookseller** n. person who sells books 书商

◇ **bookshop** n. shop which sells books 书店

◇ **bookstall** n. small open bookshop (as in a railway station) 书亭；书摊（如在车站）

◇ **bookstore** n. US bookshop（美）书店

◇ **bookwork** n. keeping of financial records 财务帐簿的保管
NOTE: no plural

**boom** 1. n. time when sales or production or business activity are increasing 畅销期；繁荣期：a period of economic boom 经济繁荣时期；the boom of the 1970s 二十世纪七十年代的昌盛时期；boom industry = industry which is expanding rapidly 迅速繁荣的工(产)业；a boom share = share in a company which is expanding 畅销股票；the boom years = years when there is an economic boom(经济繁荣)景气年份：2. v. to expand or to become prosperous 迅速发展；使繁荣：Business is booming. 生意兴隆。Sales are booming. 销售额激增。

◇ **booming** a. which is expanding or becoming prosperous 繁荣的；激增的；a booming industry or company 迅速繁荣的工业或公司；Technology is a booming sector of the economy. 技术是一个迅速发展的国民经济部门。

**boost** 1 n. help to increase 提高；增加；This publicity will give sales a boost. 这种宣传将促使销售额提高。The government hopes to give a boost to industrial development. 政府希望促进工业发展。2 v. to make something increase 使提高；增加：We expect our publicity campaign to boost sales by 25%. 我们期望我们的促销宣传运动能提高 25% 的销售额。The company hopes to boost its market share. 公司希望提高其市场份额。Incentive schemes are boosting production. 奖励的计划正在促进生产。

**booth** n. (a) small place for one person to stand or sit(仅容一人站或坐的地方)摊位：telephone booth = public box with a telephone(公用)电话亭；ticket booth = place outdoors where a person sells tickets 售票亭 (b) US section of a commercial fair where a company ex-

hibits its products or services(美)(公司在商品交易会展出其产品或劳务的)参展台;商展摊位
NOTE: the GB English for this is stand

**borrow** v. to take money from someone for a time, possibly paying interest for it, and repaying it at the end of the period 借钱;借贷: He borrowed £1,000 from the bank. 他从银行借了 1,000 英磅。The company had to borrow heavily to repay its debts. 公司必须借入大量的贷款以偿还其债务。They borrowed £25,000 against the security of the factory. 他们以工厂作抵押借入 25,000 英磅。to borrow short or long = to borrow for a short or long period 短期借贷(款)或长期借贷(款)

◇ **borrower** n. person who borrows 借款人;债户: Borrowers from the bank pay 12% interest. 银行债户需支付 12% 的贷款利息。

◇ **borrowing** n. (a) action of borrowing money 贷款;借款: The new factory was financed by bank borrowing. 建新工厂用银行贷款来筹措资金。borrowing power = amount of money which a company can borrow 借款(举债)能力 (b) borrowings = money borrowed 借款额;贷款额: The company's borrowings have doubled. 公司的贷款额已增加一倍。bank borrowings = loans made by banks 银行贷款

**boss** n. infml. employer or person in charge of a company or an office 老板;上司: If you want a pay rise, go and talk to your boss。如果你想加薪,应找你的老板谈谈。He became a director when he married the boss's daughter. 他和老板的女儿结婚以后,他已被提升为主任(或董事)。

**bottleneck** n. position when business activity is slowed down because one section of the operation cannot cope with the amount of work 瓶颈;防碍生产的卡脖子环节: a bottleneck in the supply system 在供给系统上的卡脖子环节(瓶颈处)。There are serious bottlenecks in the production line. 在生产流水线上,存在着严重的瓶颈环节。

**bottom** 1 n. lowest part or point 底;最低点: Sales have reached rock bottom. = the very lowest point of all 销售额已达到最低点。The bottom has fallen out of the market = Sales have fallen below what previously seemed to be the lowest point. 销售额跌幅比预想的最低点还低。bottom price = lowest price 最低价格;最低限价: rock - bottom price = lowest price of all(全部)最低价格; bottom line = last line on a balance sheet indicating profit or loss(资产负债表上体现盈亏)末行数字; The boss is interested only in the bottom line. = He is only interested in the final profit. 老板仅对末行数字(盈利)感兴趣。2 v. to bottom (out) = to reach the lowest point 至最低点: The market has bottomed out. = has reached the lowest point and does not seem likely to fall further 市场价已跌至最低点。

**bottomry** n. mortgage of a ship to pay for repairs 押船借款(以船作抵押付修理费)

**bought** see BUY bought ledger = book in which expenditure is noted 进货分类帐: bought ledger clerk = office worker who deals with the bought ledger 处理进货分类帐的办事员。

**bounce** v. (of a cheque) to be returned to the person who has tried to cash it, because there is not enough money in the payer's account to pay it 未兑现支票;支票拒付退回出票人(原票退还开票人,因帐户中没有足够的钱支付): He paid for the car with a cheque that bounced. 他用一张被拒付支票支付小汽车货款。

**bounty** n. government subsidy made to

help an industry 津贴；补贴（指政府用于帮助工业）

**boutique** n. small specialized shop, especially for up‐to‐date clothes 时装精品店；section of a department store selling up‐to‐date clothes a jeans boutique 牛仔精品店；a ski boutique 滑雪用品店

**box** n. (a) cardboard or wood or plastic container 箱；盒（硬纸板或木制或塑料制）：The goods were sent in thin cardboard boxes. 商品装在很薄的硬纸箱中发出。The watches are prepacked in plastic display boxes. 手表预先包装在塑料陈列盒中。Paperclips come in boxes of two hundred. = packed two hundred to a box 每盒内装回形针二百枚。box file = file (for papers) made like a box 盒式文件夹 (b) box number = reference number used in a post office or an advertisement to avoid giving an address 邮箱号（用于邮政与广告）：Please reply to Box No. 209. 请给 209 号信箱复函。Our address is: P. O. Box 74209, Edinburgh. 我们的地址是爱丁堡 74209 信箱。(c) cash box = metal box for keeping cash 现金箱；letter box or mail box = place where incoming mail is put 信箱；信筒；call box = outdoor telephone kiosk 公用电话亭（间）

◇ **boxed** a. put in a box or sold in a box 盒装的；盒装销售的：boxed set = set of items sold together in a box 盒装销售的系列商品

**boycott** 1 n. refusal to buy or to deal in certain products 联合抵制（拒绝购买或经营某种产品）：The union organized a boycott against or of imported cars. 工会组织联合抵制进口小汽车。2 v. to refuse to buy or to deal in a certain product 联合抵制（拒绝购买或经营某种产品）：We are boycotting all imports from that country. 我们正联合抵制来自那个国家的所有进口商品。The management has boycotted the meeting.

= has refused to attend the meeting 管理部门人员已经联合抵制了这次会议。

**bracket** 1 n. group of items or people taken together 等级；阶层：people in the middle‐income bracket = people with average incomes, not high or low 中等收入阶层的人；He is in the top tax bracket. = He pays the highest level of tax. 他是支付最高税额的人。2 v. to bracket together = to treat several items together in the same way 归为同类：In the sales reports, all the European countries are bracketed together. 在销售报告中，将所有的欧洲国家的均归为同类。

**branch** 1 n. local office of a bank or large business 分行或分公司（指银行的分行，大公司的分公司）；local shop of a large chain of shops（连锁店）分店：The bank or the store has branches in most towns in the south of the country. 该银行（或百货商店）在本国南部地区的大多数城市中设有分行（或分店）。The insurance company has closed its branches in South America. 保险公司已经关闭了其设在南美的分公司。He is the manager of our local branch of Lloyds bank. 他是我们当地劳埃德银行分行的行长。We have decided to open a branch office in Chicago. 我们已决定在芝加哥开设一家分公司。the manager of our branch in Lagos or of our Lagos branch 我们的拉各斯分行行长；branch manager = manager of a branch 分行行长（经理）2 v. to branch out = to start a new (but usually related) type of business 扩大经营范围：From car retailing, the company branched out into car leasing. 公司从小汽车的零售，扩充到小汽车租赁。

**brand** n. make of product, which can be recognized by a name or by a design 商标；牌子：the top‐selling brands of toothpaste 名牌牙膏 The company is launching a new brand of soap. 公司开始投放一种新型的肥皂。brand name =

name of a brand 商标名称；brand image = idea of a product which is associated with the brand name 商标形象；brand loyalty = loyalty by the customer who always buys the same brand 商标信誉；消费者对商标的信任；own brand = name of a store which is used on products which are speciallypacked for that store 自己的商标(店名与商标名相同)

◇ **branded** a. branded goods = goods sold under brand names 有商标的商品

◇ **brand new** a. quite new or very new 崭新的；

**breach** n. failure to carry out the terms of an agreement 违反；不履行：breach of contract = failing to do something which is in a contract 违反合同；毁约；The company is in breach of contract. = It has failed to carry out the duties of the contract. 公司没有履行合同。breach of warranty = supplying goods which do not meet the standards of the warranty applied to them 违反担保

**break** 1 n. short space of time, when you can rest 短时间休息；间隔：She typed for two hours without a break. 她打字两个小时而未休息片刻。coffee break or tea break = rest time during work when the workers can drink coffee or tea 喝咖啡或饮茶休息的时间。2 v. (a) to fail to carry out the duties of a contract 违反；违约：The company has broken the contract or the agreement. 该公司已经违反合同或违反协议。to break an engagement to do something = not to do what has been agreed 违反做某事的保证 (b) to cancel (a contract) 取消；中止(一项合同)：The company is hoping to be able to break the contract. 公司正希望能够撤消该项合同。
NOTE: breaking – broke – has broken

◇ **breakages** pl. n. breaking of items

货物损坏：Customers are expected to pay for breakages. 顾客要支付货物损坏赔偿费。

◇ **break down** v. (a) to stop working because of mechanical failure 出故障：The telex machine has broken down. 电传机已经发生了故障。What do you do when your photocopier breaks down? 当你的复印机出毛病的时候你怎么办？(b) to stop 停止：Negotiations broke down after six hours. 六小时之后谈判破裂。(c) to show all the items in a total list of costs or expenditure 分项列出；分成细目：We broke the expenditure down into fixed and variable costs. 我们把支出分为固定成本和可变成本。Can you break down this invoice into spare parts and labour? 你能将这张发票上的备件费与人工费分列吗？

◇ **breakdown** n. (a) stopping work because of mechanical failure 故障；损坏：We cannot communicate with our Nigerian office because of the breakdown of the telex lines. 由于电传线路的故障，我们不能与尼日利亚的办事处联系。(b) stopping talking(谈判)破裂或停顿：a breakdown in wage negotiations 工资谈判破裂；(c) showing details item by item 分细目；分门别类：Give me a breakdown of investment costs. 给我一份投资费用的细目。

◇ **break even** v. to balance costs and receipts, but not make a profit 不亏不盈；收支相抵：Last year the company only just broke even. 去年，公司恰好不亏不盈(收支相抵)。We broke even in our first two months of trading. 头两个月的交易，我们不亏不盈。

◇ **breakeven point** n. point at which sales cover costs, but do not show a profit 盈亏平衡；收支相抵

◇ **break off** v. to stop 中断；结束：We broke off the discussion at midnight. 我们于午夜结束了讨论。Management broke off negotiations with the union. 管理部门中断了与工会的谈判。

◇ **break up** v. (a) to split something large into small sections 分解；分裂：The company was broken up and separate divisions sold off. 公司分裂又廉价卖掉各个分部。(b) to come to an end 结束：The meeting broke up at 12.30. 会议于 12 点 30 分结束。

**bribe** 1 n. money given to someone in authority to get him to help 贿赂；行贿：The minister was dismissed for taking bribes. 因受贿，该部长被罢免。2 v. to pay someone money to get him to do something for you 行贿；向…行贿：We had to bribe the minister's secretary before she would let us see her boss. 我们必须向这位部长的秘书行贿，她才能让我们见她的老板。

**bridging loan** n. short – term loan to help someone buy a new house when he has not yet sold his old one 过渡贷款；短期贷款；临时性贷款

**brief** v. to explain to someone in detail 作简要的汇报；The salesmen were briefed on the new product. 就新产品给销售人员做简要介绍。The managing director briefed the board on the progress of the negotiations. 总经理就谈判的进程向各位董事作简要汇报。

◇ **briefcase** n. case with a handle for carrying papers and documents 公事包：He put all the files into his briefcase. 他将所有文件档案放入他的公事包内。

◇ **briefing** n. telling someone details 简单介绍情况；简况介绍会：All salesmen have to attend a sales briefing on the newproduct. 所有推销人员必须参加有关新产品情况介绍会。

**bring** v. to come to a place with someone or something 带来：He brought his documents with him. 他随身携带文件。The finance director brought his secretary to take notes of the meeting. 财务主任携其秘书到会，以便做会议记录。to bring a lawsuit against someone = to tell someone to appear in court to settle an argument 对某人进行起诉。

NOTE: bringing – brought

◇ **bring down** v. (a) to reduce 降低：Petrol companies have brought down the price of oil. 石油公司已经降低了油价。(b) to add a figure to an account at the end of a period to balance expenditure and income 转下；结转（在某一个时期未把数字加到一个帐户上，使收入与支出平衡）；Balance brought down：£365.15. 余额移后：365.15 英磅。

◇ **bring forward** v. (a) to make earlier 把…提前：to bring forward the date of repayment 把偿还日期提前；The date of the next meeting has been brought forward to March. 下次会议的日期已被提前至三月份。(b) to take a balance brought down as the starting point for the next period in a balance sheet 结转下期：Balance brought forward：£365.15. 余额承前：365.15 英磅。

◇ **bring in** v. to earn (an interest) 获得（利息）：The shares bring in a small amount. 这些股票获利甚微。

◇ **bring out** v. to produce something new 生产（某种新产品）：They are bringing out a new model of the car for the MotorShow. 为了参加汽车展销会，他们正在生产一种新型小汽车。

◇ **bring up** v. to refer to something for the first time 提出：The chairman brought up the question of redundancy payments. 董事长提出了裁员补贴问题。

**brisk** a. selling actively 生意兴隆的；活跃的：Sales are brisk. 销售十分活跃。The market in oil shares is particularly brisk. 石油股票交易市场特别兴隆。a brisk market in oil shares 生意兴隆的石油股票市场

**broadside** n. US publicity leaflet（美）广告传单；宣传单

**brochure** n. publicity booklet 小册子：We sent off for a brochure about holidays in Greece or about postal services. 我们去信要一本希腊的度假指南或邮政服务指南。

**broke** a. infml. having no money 破产的：The company is broke. 该公司破产了。He cannot pay for the new car because he is broke. 他已无力支付这辆新小汽车的款项，因为他破产了。to go broke = to become bankrupt 破产：The company went broke last month 公司于上月破产。

**broker** n. (a) dealer 经纪人；掮客：foreign exchange broker = person who buys and sells foreign currency on behalf of other people 外汇经纪人；insurance broker = person who sells insurance to clients 保险经纪人；ship broker = person who sells shipping or transport of goods to clients 船舶经纪人 (b) (stock) broker = person who buys or sells shares for clients 股票经纪人

◇ **brokerage or broker's commission** n. payment to a broker for a deal carried out 经纪人佣金

◇ **broking** n. dealing in stocks and shares 经纪业（经营股票与证券的行业） **bubble pack** n. = BLISTER PACK 簿膜包装

**buck** 1 n. US infml. dollar（美俚）美元 2 v. to buck the trend = to go against the trend 与趋势逆行

**bucket shop** n. infml. travel agent selling airline tickets at a discount 小型机票代理处；打折扣出售机票的小型旅行社。

**budget** 1 n. (a) plan of expected spending and income (usually for one year) 预算（通常为某一年收入与支出的计划）：to draw up a budget 制定一项预算；We have agreed the budgets for next year. 我们就下个年度的预算达成一致意见。advertising budget = money planned for spending on advertising 广告费用预算；cash budget = plan of cash income and expenditure 现金预算；overhead budget = plan of probable overhead costs 间接或管理费预算；publicity budget = money allowed for expected expenditure on publicity 宣传费预算；sales budget = plan of probable sales 销售（额）预算 (b) the Budget = the annual plan of taxes and government spending proposed by a finance minister 政府财政预算年度计划：The minister put forward a budget aimed at boosting the economy. 该部长提出一项旨在促进经济增长的预算方案。to balance the budget = to plan income and expenditure so that they balance 使预算平衡；The president is planning for a balanced budget. 总裁正为平衡预算作计划。(c) (in a bank) budget account = bank account where you plan income and expenditure to allow for periods when expenditure is high, by paying a set amount each month（在一个银行）预算帐户 (d) (in shops) cheap（在商店里）廉价的；合算的：budget department = cheaper department 廉价部；budget prices = low prices 廉价；优惠价格；2 v. to plan probable income and expenditure 编制预算；把…编入预算：We are budgeting for £10,000 of sales next year. 我们正在编制明年的销售额为10,000 英磅的预算。

◇ **budgetary** a. referring to a budget 预算的：budgetary policy = policy of planning income and expenditure 预算政策；budgetary control = keeping check on spending 预算控制；budgetary requirements = spending or income required to meet the budget forecasts 预算需要或所需预算经费

◇ **budgeting** n. preparing of budgets to help plan expenditure and income 编制预算

NOTE: no plural

**build** v. to make by putting pieces together 建立；建设 …：to build a sales structure 建立一个销售体系；to build on past experience = to use experience as a base on which to act in the future 建立在以往的经验基础之上

NOTE: building – built

◇ **building** n. house or factory or office block, etc. 建筑物：They have redeveloped the site of the old office building. 他们重新开发了这座旧办公楼的地皮。the Shell Building = the office block where the head office of Shell is 壳牌石油公司总部办公大楼

◇ **building and loan association** n. US = SAVINGS AND LOAN ASSOCIATION(美)建筑信用协会

◇ **building society** n. GB financial institution which accepts and pays interest on deposits and lends money to people who are buying property(英)住宅互助协会(提供购房贷款的组织)：He put his savings into a building society or into a building society account. 他将钱存入住宅互助协会。I have an account with the Halifax Building Society. 我有一个哈利法克斯房屋互助协会户头。I saw the building society manager to ask for a mortgage. 我见了房屋互助协会经理，要求得到一项抵押贷款。

◇ **build into** v. to add something to something being set up 加入；插入：You must build all the forecasts into the budget. 你必须将所有不预测情况(数字)编入预算。We have built 10% for contingencies into our cost forecast. = We have added 10% to our basic forecast to allow for items which may appear suddenly. 我们已把10%的意外开支编入我们成本预算中。

◇ **build up** v. (a) to create something by adding pieces together 建立；建成：He bought several shoe shops and gradually built up a chain. 他买下了几处鞋店，并且逐步建成连锁店。(b) to expand something gradually 增大：to build up a profitable business 发展成为一个有利可图的企业；to build up a team of salesmen 扩大销售人员队伍

◇ **buildup** n. gradual increase 增进；加强 a buildup in sales or a sales buildup 销售上升(增长)；There will be a big publicity buildup before the launch of the new model. 新型号产品打入市场之前，要为其大作广告宣传。

◇ **built – in** a. forming part of the system or of a machine 不可分的；嵌入的：The micro has a built – in clock. 微型计算机有一个固有的小钟。The accounting system has a series of built – in checks. 会计制度包括有一系列核对。

**bulk** n. large quantity of goods 大量：in bulk = in large quantities 大批：大量；to buy rice in bulk 购买大批稻米；bulk buying or bulk purchase = buying large quantities of goods at a lower price(以较低的价格)大量购买；bulk carrier = ship which carries large quantities of loose goods (such as coal)散装货船(运输如煤这种松散的货物)；bulk shipments = shipments of large quantities of goods 大批量装船；散装装运

NOTE: no plural

◇ **bulky** a. large and awkward 庞大的；笨重的：The Post Office does not accept bulky packages. 邮局不受理庞大的邮寄包裹。

**bull** n. Stock Exchange dealer who believes the market will rise, and therefore buys shares to sell at a higher price later (证券交易所的)多头商(指当他认为证券有涨价趋势时，先购进证券，以后再以高价出售)；bull market = period when share prices rise because people are optimistic and buy shares 牛市；涨市

**bullion** n. gold or silver bars 金锭或银锭：gold bullion 金锭；The price of bul-

lion is fixed daily. 每日定金锭的价格。
tofix the bullion price for silver 确定银
锭价格
NOTE: no plural

**bumper** n. very large crop 大丰收；a
bumper crop of corn 玉米大丰收，1984
was a bumper year for computer sales.
= 1984 was an excellent year for sales.
1984 年是计算机销售兴旺年。

**bumping** n. US situation where a senior
employee takes the place of a junior(in a
restaurant or in a job) 或降级；被排挤
(在饭店或在工作中高级职员取代低级
职员)

**bureau** n. office which specializes 局；
司；处：办事处；所 computer bureau =
office which offers to do work on its
computers for companies which do not
own their own computers 计算机所；
employment bureau = office which finds
jobs for people 职业介绍所；information
bureau = office which gives information
信息处；情报局；trade bureau = office
which specializes in commercial enquiries
商务局；贸易局；visitors' bureau = office which deals with visitors' questions
游客问询处；word‐processing bureau
= office which specializes in word‐pro-
cessing 文字处理办公室；We farm out
the office typing to a local bureau。我们
把办公室的打字业务包给当地办事处。
NOTE: the plural is bureaux

◇ **bureau de change** n. office where
you can change foreign currency 外币兑
换处

**burn** v. to destroy by fire 烧毁：The
chief accountant burnt the documents before the police arrived. 在警察到来之
前,总会计师已将文件烧掉。
NOTE: burning‐burnt

◇ **burn down** v. to destroy completely
in a fire 烧光：The warehouse burnt
down and all the stock was destroyed. 仓
库在大火中化为灰烬,所有存货也被付

之一炬。The company records were all
lost when the offices were burnt down.
当办公室被烧毁后,公司的记录也全部
被毁。

**bus** n. motor vehicle for carrying passengers 公共汽车：He goes to work by
bus.他乘公共汽车上班。She took the
bus to go to her office.她乘这辆公共汽
车去办公室上班。bus company = com-
pany which runs the buses in a town 公
共汽车公司

**bushel** n. measure of dry goods, such as
corn ( = 56 pounds)蒲式耳(计量谷物
等的容量单位＝56 磅)

**business** n. (a) work in buying or selling 商业；生意：Business is expanding.
商业在发展。Business is slow. 营业清
淡(商情不景气)。He does a thriving-
business in repairing cars. 他的汽车修理
业办得很红火。What's your line of
business? 你做什么买卖? business call
= visit to talk to someone on business 商
业(调查)访问；business centre = part
of a town where the main banks, shops
and offices arelocated 商业中心；busi-
ness class = type of airline travel which
is less expensive than firstclass and more
comfortable than tourist class 经济舱(飞
机票的种类,其价格比头等舱便宜)；
business college or business school =
place where commercial studies are
taught 商学院或商业学校；business
correspondent = journalist who writes
articles on business news fornewspapers
商业新闻记者；business efficiency exhibition = exhibition which shows products ( computers, word‐processors )
which help a business to be efficient 商业
促效(提高商业效益)展览会；business
letter = letter about commercial matters
商业信函；business lunch = lunch to
discuss business matters 公务午餐；busi-
ness trip = trip to discuss business matters with clients 公务出差；to be in
business = to be in a commercial firm 经

商;从事商业性工作;to go into business = to start a commercial firm 从商; He went into business as a car dealer. 他开始做汽车买卖。to go out of business = to stop trading 退出商界;停止经商; The firm went out of business during the recession. 该公司在萧条期已停止经营。on business = on commercial work 因公;因事(指有关商业方面的): He had to go abroad on business. 他必须因公出国。The chairman is in Holland on business. 董事长因公在荷兰。(b) commercial company 商业公司: He owns a small car repair business. 他拥有一个小型的汽车修理部。she runs a business from her home. 她在家中管理一个企业。He set up in business as an insurance broker. 他开始做保险经纪人的业务。business address = details of number, street and town where a company is located 企业通讯地址; business card = card showing a businessman's name and the name and address of the company he works for 业务(商业)名片; business correspondence = letters concerned with a business 商业函电; business equipment = machines used in an office 办公设备; business expansion scheme = system in Britain where money invested for some years in a new company is free from tax 企业发展计划; business expenses = money spent on running a business, not on stock or assets 营业费用; business hours = time (usually 9 a.m. to 5 p.m.) when a business is open 营业时间; big business = very large commercial firms 大商号;大企业(公司)(c) affairs discussed 讨论的事,事务: The main business of the meeting was finished by 3 p.m. 会议的主要议程,下午3点钟才结束。any other business = item at the end of an agenda, where any matter can be raised 任何其它事项(议事日程上的最后议题)
NOTE: no plural for meanings (a) and

(c); (b) has the plural businesses

◇ **business agent** n. US chief local official of a trade union(美)工会的当地主要官员;企业代理人

◇ **businessman or businesswoman** n. man or woman engaged in business (男或女)商人;实业家: She's a good businesswoman. = She is good at commercial deals. 她是一位好的实业家。a small businessman = man who owns a small business 小商人;小实业家

**bust** a. infml. to go bust = to become bankrupt 破产

**busy** a. occupied in doing something/in working 繁忙的: He is busy preparing the annual accounts. 他正忙于准备年度总帐。The manager is busy at the moment, but he will be free in about fifteen minutes. 此刻经理正忙着,但约十五分钟后他有空。The busiest time of year for stores is the week before Christmas. 商店一年中最忙的时侯是圣诞节前的一个星期。Summer is the busy season for hotels. 夏季是旅馆的旺季。The line is busy. = The telephone line is being used. 电话占线。

**buy** 1 v. to get something by paying money 买;购: He bought 10,000 shares. 他购入 10,000 股股票。The company has been bought by its leading supplier. 该公司由它的主要供应商买下。to buy wholesale and sell retail 批量买进零星售出; to buy for cash 用现金购买; to buy forward = to buy foreign currency before you need it, in order to be sure of the exchange rate 买入期货(外汇)
NOTE: buying – bought
2. n. good buy or bad buy = thing bought which is or is not worth the money paid for it 合算或不合算;值或不值的购买 That watch was a good buy. 那块表买的很上算。This car was a bad buy. 这辆小汽车买亏了。

◇ **buy back** v. to buy something whichyou have sold 买回；回购（买你已卖掉的东西）：He sold the shop last year and is now trying to buy it back. 去年他卖了这个商店，而现在又试图将其买回。

◇ **buyer** n. (a) person who buys 买主；买方：There were no buyers. = No one wanted to buy. 没有买主。a buyers' market = market where products are sold cheaply because there are few buyers 买方市场；impulse buyer = person who buys something when he sees it, not because he was planning to buy it 即兴购物者 (b) person who buys a certain type of goods wholesale, which are then stocked by a large store 采购员；head buyer = most important buyer in a store 头号买主；主要买方：She is the shoe buyer for a London department store. 她是伦敦百货商店鞋的采购员。

◇ **buy in** v. (of a seller at an auction) to buy the thing which you are trying to sell because no one will pay the price you want 买回自己送出拍卖的东西（指在拍卖行）；买进

◇ **buying** n. getting something for money 购买；bulk buying = getting large quantities of goods at low prices（以廉价）大量购买或成批购买；forward buying or buying forward = buying shares or commodities or currency for delivery at a later date 买期货；impulse buying = buying items which you have just seen, not because you had planned to buy them 即兴购物；非计划购买；panic buying = rush to buy something at any price because stocks may run out 抢购（因怕脱销）；buying department = department in a company which buys raw materials or goods for use in the company（原料）采购部；buying power = ability to buy 购买力；The buying power of the pound has fallen over the last years. 过去几年里, 英镑的购买力已经下降。

NOTE: no plural

◇ **buyout** n. management buyout = takeover of a company by a group of employees (usually managers and directors)（由经理和董事）全部买下；全部收买；leveraged buyout = buying all the shares in a company by borrowing money against the security of the shares to be bought 举债全部买下某公司的股票

**by‐product** n. product made as a result of manufacturing a main product 副产品：Soap is a useful by‐product of oil. 肥皂是一种有用的石油副产品。

**byte** n. storage unit in a computer, equal to one character（计算机）二进位组；字节

# Cc

**cabinet** n. piece of furniture for storing records or display 柜；橱：Last year's correspondence is in the bottom drawer of the filing cabinet. 去年往来的信件均放在公文柜最低层的抽屉中。display cabinet = piece of furniture with a glass top or glass doors forshowing goods for sale 陈列柜；展柜

**cable** 1. n. telegram or message sent by telegraph 电报：He sent a cable to his office asking for more money. 他给办事处拍电报要更多的钱。cable address = specially short address for sending cables 电报挂号 2. v. to send a message or money by telegraph 发电报；电汇：He cabled his office to ask them to send more money. 他给公司拍了封电报要求寄更多的钱。The office cabled him ￡1,000 to cover his expenses. 公司电

汇给他 1.000 英磅支付其开支。

◇ **cablegram** n. telegram or message sent by telegraph 电报

**calculate** v. (a) to find the answer to a problem using numbers 计算;核算: The bank clerk calculated the rate of exchange for the dollar. 银行办事员计算了美元的汇率。(b) to estimate 估计;推测: I calculate that we have six months' stock left. 我估计,我们还留有6个月的库存。

◇ **calculating machine** n. machine which calculates 计算器(机)

◇ **calculation** n. answer to a problem in mathematics 计算;核算: rough calculation = approximate answer 概算;估算; I made some rough calculations on the back of an envelope. 在信封的背面,我粗略地计算了一下。According to my calculations, we have six months' stock left. 按我的估计,我们还留有六个月的库存。We are £ 20,000 out in our calculations. = We have £ 20,000 too much or too little. 在计算时,我们出现了 20,000 英磅的差错。

◇ **calculator** n. electronic machine which works out the answers to problems in mathematics(电子)计算机(器): My pocket calculator needs a new battery. 我的袖珍计算器需换一节新电池。He worked out the discount on his calculator. 他用计算器计算出了折扣。

**calendar** n. book or set of sheets of paper showing the days and months in a year, often attached to pictures 挂历;日历: For the New Year the garage sent me a calendar with photographs of old cars 汽车修理厂为贺新年,送给我一本带有老式汽车照片的挂历。calendar month = a whole month as on a calendar, from the 1st to the 30th or 31st 历月; calendar year = year from the 1st January to 31st December 历年;

**call** 1. n. (a) conversation on the tele-phone(用电话)通话: local call = call to a number on the same exchange 本区电话;市内电话: trunk call or long - distance call = call to a number in a different zone or area 长途电话; overseas call or international call = call to another country 国际电话; person - to - person call = call where you ask the operator to connect you with a named person 请接线员接指名受话人电话; transferred charge call or US collect call = call where the person receiving the call agrees to pay for it(美)向受话者收费的电话; to make a call = to dial and speak to someone on the telephone 打电话; to take a call = to answer the telephone 接电话; to log calls = to note all details of telephone calls made 记录电话内容 (b) demand for repayment of a loan by a lender 偿还贷款: money at call or money on call or call money = money loaned for which repayment can be demanded without notice 短期放款;活期借款 (c) Stock Exchange demand to pay for new shares 股款催缴; call option = option to buy shares at a certain price 购买选择权 (d) visit 访问: The salesmen make six calls a day. 售货员一天登门拜访六次。business call = visit to talk to someone on business 业务拜访; cold call = sales visit where the salesman has no appointment and the client is not an established customer 没有事先安排的访问; call rate = number of calls (per day or per week) made by a salesman (一天或一周)访问的次数 2. v. (a) to telephone to someone 打电话: I'll call you at your office tomorrow. 明天我会给你的办公室打电话。(b) to call on someone = to visit 访问: Our salesmen call on their best accounts twice a month. 我们的销售人员一月两次访问他们最好的客户。(c) to ask someone to do something 号召: The union called a strike. = The union told its members to go on strike. 工会号召罢工。

◇ **callable bond** n. bond which must be repaid at notice 通知偿还债券；可赎回的债券

◇ **call – back pay** n. pay given to a worker who has been called back to work after his normal working hours 加班费（支付给工人在法定工作时间以外工作的工资）

◇ **call box** n. outdoor telephone kiosk 公用电话亭(间)

◇ **called up capital** n. share capital in a company which has been paid for 已催缴股本(已经支付的公司股本)

◇ **caller** n. (a) person who telephones 打电话者 (b) person who visits 访问人；来访者

◇ **call in** v. (a) to visit 访问；来访：The sales representative called in twice last week. 推销员上周来访两次。(b) to telephone to make contact 用电话联系：We ask the reps to call in every Friday to report the weeks' sales. 我们要求推销员每星期五用电话汇报每周的销售情况。(c) to ask for a debt to be paid 要求收回(债款)

◇ **call off** v. to ask for something not to take place 放弃；取消：The union has called off the strike. 工会已取消罢工。The deal was called off at the last moment 这笔交易在最后一刻被取消了。

◇ **call up** v. to ask for share capital to be paid 催缴资本；催缴股本

**calm** a. quiet or not excited 平静的：The markets were calmer after the government statement on the exchange rate. 在政府公布了汇率之后，市场更为平静。

**campaign** n. planned method of working 运动：sales campaign = planned work to achieve higher sales 销售运动；竞销活动；publicity campaign or advertising campaign = planned period when publicity takes place 大做广告；广告运动；They are working on a campaign to launch a new brand of soap. 他们正致力于一场旨在向市场推出一种新型肥皂的运动。

**cancel** v. (a) to stop something which has been agreed or planned 停止；取消：to cancel an appointment or a meeting 取消约会或会议；to cancel a contract 撤消合同；The government has cancelled the order for a fleet of buses. 政府已经取消公共汽车队的订货。(b) to cancel a cheque = to stop payment of a cheque which you have signed 取消支票
NOTE: GB English: cancelling – cancelled

◇ **cancellation** n. stopping something which has been agreed or planned 停止；取消；作废：cancellation of an appointment 撤消约会；cancellation of an agreement 取消一项协议；cancellation clause = clause in a contract which states the terms on which the contract may be cancelled 撤消条款

◇ **cancel out** v. to balance and so make invalid or even 抵消；相销：The two clauses cancel each other out. 这两条款相互抵消。Costs have cancelled out the sales revenue 成本与销售收入相抵消。

**candidate** n. person who applies for a job 候选人：There are six candidates for the post of assistant manager. 副经理的职位有六位候选人。

**canvass** v. to visit people to ask them to buy goods or to vote or to say what they think 兜售；游说：He's canvassing for customers for his hairdresser's shop. 他正为其理发店向顾客招揽生意。We have canvassed the staff about raising the prices in the staff restaurant. 我们事先向职工们说明，职工食堂的东西价格要涨。

◇ **canvasser** n. person who canvasses 兜揽生意的人；推销员；游说者

◇ **canvassing** n. action of asking peopleto buy or to vote or to say what they think 推销；兜揽；拉选票：canvassing techniques(兜)推销技术；door - to - door canvassing 挨家挨户地推销(游说)
NOTE: no plural

**CAP = COMMON AGRICULTURAL POLICY** 共同农业政策

**capable** a. (a) capable of = able or clever enough to do something 有能力的：She is capable of very fast typing speeds. 她具有快速打字能力。The sales force must be capable of selling all the stock in the warehouse. 销售人员必须具备把仓库中的全部存货推销出去的能力。(b) efficient 能干的；有能力的：She is a very capable departmental manager. 她是一位非常能干的部门经理。
NOTE: you are capable of something or of doing something

**capacity** n. (a) amount which can be produced or amount of work which can be done 生产量；生产力：industrial or manufacturing or production capacity 工业或制造业生产量(或能力)；to work at full capacity = to do as much work as possible 超(满)负荷工作；to use up spare or excess capacity = to make use of time or space which is not fully used 用完多余的能力；(b) amount of space 容积；容量：storage capacity = space available for storage 库容量；贮藏量；warehouse capacity = space available in a warehouse 库容量 (c) ability 能力：He has a particular capacity for business. 经商是他的专长。earning capacity = amount of money someone is able to earn 盈利能力；收益能力 (d) in a capacity = acting as 以…资格(身份；地位)；in his capacity as chairman 以他的主席(董事长)身份；speaking in an official capacity = speaking officially 以官方资格讲话；代表官方发言

NOTE: no plural for (a), (b) and (c)
**capita** see PER CAPITA
**capital** n. (a) money, property and assets used in a business 资本：company with £10,000 capital or with a capital of £10,000 拥有一万英镑资本的公司；authorized capital = maximum capital which is permitted by a company's articles of association 核定资本；capital account = account of dealings (money invested in the company, or taken out of the company) by the owners of a company 资本帐户；capital assets = property or machines, etc. which a company owns and uses 资本资产；固定资产；capital bonus = bonus payment by an insurance company which is produced by capital gain 资本红利；capital equipment = equipment which a factory or office uses to work 资本设备；固定设备；主要设备 capital expenditure or investment or outlay = money spent on fixed assets (property, machines, furniture) 资本支出；资本投资. 固定资产开支；capital gains = money made by selling a fixed asset or by selling shares 资本收益；capital gains tax = tax paid on capital gains 资本收益税；capital goods = goods used to manufacture other goods (i.e. machinery)资本货物；capital levy = tax on the value of a person's property and possessions 资本税；财产税；capital loss = loss made by selling assets 资本损失，capital reserves = part of share capital which can be used only when a company is wound up 资本准备金；资本储备；capital structure of a company = way in which a company's capital is set up 公司的资本构成；capital transfer tax = tax on gifts or bequests of money or property 资本转让税；circulating capital = capital required in the form of raw materials, finished products and work in progress for a company to carry on its business 流动资本；周转资本；equity capital =

amount of a company's capital which is owned by the shareholders 股本；产权资本；自有资本；fixed capital = capital in the form of buildings and machinery 固定资本；issued capital = amount of capital issued as shares to the shareholders 已发行资本(股本)；paid - up capital = amount of money paid for the issued capital shares 已缴清的资本；实收资本；risk capital or venture capital = capital for investment which may easily be lost in risky projects 风险资本；share capital = value of the assets of a company held as shares, less its debts 股本；股份资本；working capital = capital in cash and stocks needed for a company to be able to work 流动资本；运营资本；周转资金 (b) money for investment 资金；movements of capital = changes of investments from one country to another 资本流动；资金动向；flight of capital = rapid movement of capital out of one country because of lack of confidence in that country's economic future 资本外流；资金抽走；capital market = places where companies can look for investment capital 资本市场 (c) capital letters or block capitals = letters written as A, B, C, D, etc., and not a, b, c, d 大写字母：Write your name in block capitals at the top of the form. 在表格的最上方用大写字母填写你的名字。

NOTE: no plural for (a) and (b)

◇ **capitalism** n. economic system where each person has the right to invest money, to work in business, to buy and sell, with no restriction from the state 资本主义

◇ **capitalist** 1. n. person who invests money in a business 资本家 2. a. working according to the principles of capitalism 资本主义的：a capitalist economy 资本主义经济；the capitalist system 资本主义制度；the capitalist countries or world 资本主义国家或资本主义世界

◇ **capitalize** v. to invest money in a working company 投资于…；提供资本给…：company capitalized at £10,000 = company with a working capital of £10,000 有 10,000 英磅资本流动的公司

◇ **capitalize on** v. to make a profit from 利用：to capitalize on one's market position 利用某人的市场地位

◇ **capitalization** n. market capitalization = value of a company calculated by multiplying the price of its shares on the stock exchange by the number of shares issued 股票资本市值；市场资本总额；company with a £1m capitalization 拥有 100 万英磅的(股票资本市值)的公司；capitalization of reserves = issuing free bonus shares to shareholders 储备金的资本化

**captive market** n. market where one supplier has a monopoly and the buyer has no choice over the product which he must purchase 垄断市场(指供应方垄断市场而买方没有选择的余地必须购买其产品)

**capture** v. to take or to get control of something 夺取；占领：to capture 10% of the market = to sell hard, and so take a 10% market share 占领 10%的市场；to capture 20% of a company's shares = to buy shares in a company rapidly and so own 20% of it 夺得 20%的公司股份

**car** n. small motor vehicle for carrying people 小汽车：company car = car owned by a company and lent to a member of staff to use as if it were his own 公司的小汽车

◇ **car - hire** n. business of lending cars to people for money 小汽车出租业：He runs a car - hire business. 他经营汽车出租公司。**carat** n. (a) measure of the quality of gold (pure gold being 24 carat) 开(K，计算黄金的单位)：a 22 -

carat gold ring 一只 22 开(K)金的戒指 (b) measure of the weight of precious stones 克拉(计算宝石的计量单位); a 5－carat diamond 一块 5 克拉的钻石 NOTE: no plural

**carbon** n. (a) carbon paper 复写纸: You forgot to put a carbon in the typewriter. 你忘了把复写纸放入打字机内。(b) carbon copy 副本;复写本; make a top copy and two carbons 打一份正本和两份副本

◇ **carbon copy** n. copy made with carbon paper(用复写纸)复写的副本: Give me the original, and file the carbon copy. 请给我正本,将复写的副本归档。

◇ **carbonless** a. which makes a copy without using carbon paper 不用复写纸的: Our reps use carbonless order pads. 我们的推销员使用无复写纸的订货本。

◇ **carbon paper** n. sheet of paper with a black material on one side, used in a typewriter to make a copy 复写纸: You put the carbon paper in the wrong way round. 你把复写纸放反了。

**card** n. (a) stiff paper 厚的硬纸: We have printed the instructions on thick white card. 我们已在厚的硬白纸上打印上了这些指示。NOTE: no plural (b) small piece of stiff paper or plastic (用纸或塑料做的)卡;卡片: business card = card showing a businessman's name and the address of the company he works for 业务名片; cash card = plastic card used to obtain money from a cash dispenser 自动提款卡; charge card = plastic card which allows you to buy goods and pay for them later 赊帐卡; cheque (guarantee) card = plastic card from a bank which guarantees payment of a cheque 支票卡; credit card = plastic card which allows you to borrow money or to buy goods without paying for them immediately 信用卡; filing card = card with information written on it, used

to classify information in correct order 档案卡;卷宗卡; index card = card used to make a card index 索引卡;检索卡; punched card = card with holes punched in it which a computer can read(计算机上使用的)穿孔卡片 (c) postcard 明信片; reply paid card = card to be sent back to the sender with a reply on it, the sender having already paid the postage 邮资已付的要求回复的明信片 (d) to get one's cards = to be dismissed 被(开除)解雇

◇ **cardboard** n. thick stiff brown paper 硬纸板;卡纸: cardboard box = box made of cardboard 硬纸板盒(箱) NOTE: no plural

◇ **card index** n. series of cards with information written on them, kept in special order so that the information can be found easily 卡片索引(把信息注在系列卡片上,并以特定的顺序排列,以便读者查找信息); card - index file = information kept on filing cards 索引卡汇订(信息)

◇ **card - index** v. to put information onto a card index 做卡片索引(检索);

◇ **card - indexing** n. putting information onto a card index 卡片索引(检索); No one can understand her card - indexing system. 无人能知晓她的卡片索引系统。

**care of** phr. (in an address) words to show that the person lives at the address, but only as a visitor 请…转交: Herr Schmidt, care of Mr W. Brown 赫尔施米特的信由 W·布朗先生转交。

**career** n. job which you are trained for, and which you expect to do all your life 职业;事业: He made his career in electronics. 他一生从事电子学专业。career woman or girl = woman who is working in business and does not plan to stop working to look after the house or children 职业妇女

**cargo** n. load of goods which are sent in a ship or plane, etc. 货物(指船运或航运)：The ship was taking on cargo = was being loaded with goods 这条船正在装货。to load cargo = to put cargo on a ship 装货(上船)；air cargo = goods sent by air 空运货物；cargo ship or cargo plane = ship or plane which carries only cargo and not passengers 货船或运输机
NOTE: plural is cargoes

**carnet** n. international document which allows dutiable goods to cross several European countries by road without paying duty until the goods reach their final destination 通行证；过境证(指欧洲国家边境区通行所需要的)

**carriage** n. transporting goods from one place to another; cost of transport of goods 运输；运费：to pay for carriage 支付运费；to allow 10% for carriage 允许10%的运费；carriage is15% of the total cost 运费占总费用的15%。carriage free = deal where the customer does not pay for the shipping 运费已付；运费付讫；carriage paid = deal where the seller has paid for the shipping 运费免付；免费运输；carriage forward = deal where the customer will pay for the shipping when the goods arrive 运费由收货人支付；运费交货时付
NOTE: no plural

**carrier** n. (a) company which transports goods 运输公司：We only use reputable carriers. 我们只用声誉好的运输公司。air carrier = company which sends cargo or passengers by air 航运公司 (b) vehicle or ship which transports goods 运输工具(车辆或船舶)：bulk carrier = ship which carries large quantities of loose goods (such as corn) 散装货船

**carry** v. (a) to take from one place to another 运送；运载：to carry goods 运送货物；a tanker carrying oil from the Gulf 从海湾(波斯湾)产油国运载油的油船 The train was carrying a consignment of cars for export. 列车正在运送一批出口小汽车 (b) to vote to approve 表决通过：The motion was carried. = The motion was accepted after a vote. 该提议获得通过。(c) to produce 生息 The bonds carry interest at 10%. 该种债券按10%的利率计算利息。(d) to keep in stock 备有存货(库存品)；备货销售：to carry a line of goods 备有某种货物；We do not carry pens. 我们不供应钢笔。

◇ **carry forward** v. to take a balance brought down as the starting point for the next period or page 结转；将帐目转入下页：balance carried forward = amount entered in an account at the end of a period to balance the income and expenditure which is then taken forward to start the next period 结转下期；余额转下

◇ **carrying** n. transporting from one place to another 运送；运载：carrying charges 置存资产费用；carrying cost 置存成本或费用；资产折旧成本
NOTE: no plural

◇ **carry on** v. to continue or to go on doing something 继续：The staff carried on working in spite of the fire. 尽管失火，职工们仍坚持工作。to carry on a business = to be active in running a business 继续经商

◇ **carry over** v. (a) to carry over a balance = to take a balance from the end of one page or period to the beginning of the next 结转平衡；将帐目转入次栏 (b) to carry over stock = to hold stock from the end of one stocktaking period to the beginning of the next 结转库存；滚存量

**cartage** n. carrying goods by road 货车运货
NOTE: no plural

**cartel** n. group of companies which try

to fix the price or to regulate the supply of a product because they can then profit from this situation 同业联盟；卡特尔（控制价格或调节产品供应，并从中获利）

**carter** n. person who transports goods by road 运货的人

**carton** n. (a) thick cardboard 厚的硬纸板：a folder made of carton 一个用硬纸板做的文件夹 (b) box made of cardboard 硬纸盒(箱)：a carton of cigarettes 一箱香烟
NOTE: no plural for (a)

**case** 1. n. (a) suitcase or box with a handle for carrying clothes and personal belongings when travelling 手提箱：The customs made him open his case. 海关人员让他打开手提箱。She had a small case which she carried onto the plane. 她有一个带上飞机小的手提箱。(b) cardboard or wooden box for packing and carrying goods 包装箱（纸的或木头的）：six cases of wine = six boxes, each containing twelve bottles 六箱酒；a packing case = large wooden box for carrying items which can be easily broken 装货箱；粗木板箱 (c) display case = table or counter with a glass top, used for displaying items for sale 展柜；陈列柜，柜台 (d) court case = legal action or trial 诉讼案：The case is being heard next week. = The case is coming to court. 该案将于下周开庭审理。2. v. to pack in a case 把···装入盒(箱)内

**cash** 1. n. (a) money in coins or notes 现金：cash in hand = money and notes in the till, kept to pay small debts 备用现金；hard cash = money in notes and coins, as opposed to cheques or credit-cards 现金；硬币和纸币 petty cash = small amounts of money 备用金；零用现金；ready cash = money which is immediately available for payment 现款；现钱；cash account = account which

records the money which is received and spent 现金帐户（目）；cash advance = loan in cash against a future payment 预付现金；cash balance = balance in cash, as opposed to amounts owed 现金余额；现款结存；cash book = book in which cash transactions are entered 现金(出纳)簿；现款簿；cash box = metal box for keeping cash 钱柜；现金柜；cash budget = plan of cash income and expenditure 现金预算；cash card = card used to obtain money from a cash dispenser 自动提款卡；cash desk = place in a store where you pay for the goods bought 现金收款台；cash dispenser = machine which gives out money when a special card is inserted and instructions given 付现(金)机；自动提款机；cash float = cash put into the cash box at the beginning of the day or week to allow business to start 现金浮动；cash offer = offer to pay in cash 现金报价；cash payment = payment in cash 现金支付；cash purchases = purchases made in cash 现金购买；cash register or cash till = machine which shows and adds the prices of items bought, with a drawer for keeping the cash received 现金出纳机；现金收入记录机；cash reserves = a company's reserves in cash, deposits or bills, kept in case of urgent need 现金准备金；现金储备；(b) using money in coins or notes 现款：to pay cash down = to pay in cash immediately 即付现款；即期现金付款；cash price or cash terms = lower price or terms which apply if the customer pays cash 现金付款享受低价或付现条件；settlement in cash or cash settlement = paying a bill in cash 现金结算；cash sale or cash transaction = transaction paid for in cash 现金销售或现金交易；Terms: cash with order. = terms of sale showing the payment has to be made in cash when the order is placed(合同)条款：定货付现或认购即付现金。cash on delivery = payment in cash when goods are delivered 货到付现或交货付现; cash discount or discount for cash = discount given for payment in cash 现金折扣

NOTE: no plural

2. v. to cash a cheque = to exchange a cheque for cash 支票兑现；兑付支票

◇ **cashable** a. which can be cashed 可兑现的：A crossed cheque is not cashable at any bank. 划线支票在任何银行都不能兑现。

◇ **cash and carry** n. large store, selling goods at low prices, where the customer pays cash and has to take the goods away himself 现购自运商店；付现自运(大型百货商店廉价销售商品，顾客付现金并必须自行带走商品)；cash and carry warehouse 付现自运仓库

◇ **cash flow** n. cash which comes into a company from sales less the money which goes out in purchases or overhead expenditure 现金流量(公司现金由销售所得减去购物和间接费支出)：cash flow forecast = forecast of when cash will be received or paid out 现金流量预测；cash flow statement = report which shows cash sales and purchases 现金流量报表；net cash flow = difference between the money coming in and the money going out 净现金流量；negative cash flow = situation where more money is going out of a company than is coming in 负现金流量；positive cash flow = situation where more money is coming into a company than is going out 正现金流量；The company is suffering from cash flow problems. = Cash income is not coming in fast enough to pay the expenditure going out. 该公司正为现金流量问题而困扰。

◇ **cashier** n. person who takes money from customers in a shop; person who deals with customers' money in a bank 出纳员；司库(商店里收款的人或银行内负责财务的人)

◇ **cash in** v. to sell (shares) for cash 兑现(变卖股票获得现金)

◇ **cash in on** v. to profit from 靠…盈利；乘机利用：The company is cashing in on the interest in computer games. 该公司靠计算机游戏方面的产权来获利。

◇ **cash up** v. to add up the cash in a shop at the end of the day 点现金(商店在一天营业后对现金进行结算)

**cassette** n. small plastic box with a magnetic tape on which words or information can be recorded 录音盒带：Copy the information from the computer onto a cassette. 将信息从计算机转录到一盘磁带上。

**casting vote** n. vote used by the chairman in the case where the votes for and against a proposal are equal 决定性的一票(赞成票数与反对票数相等时董事长所投的一票)：The chairman has the casting vote. 董事长有关键性的一票。He used his casting vote to block the motion. 他运用其决定性的一票否决了该项提议。

**casual** a. not permanent or not regular 临时的；碰巧的；偶然的：casual labour = workers who are hired for a short period 临时工；casual work = work where the workers are hired for a short period 临时工作；casual labourer or casual worker = worker who can be hired for a short period 临时工

**catalogue** or US **catalog** 1. n. list of items for sale, usually with prices 商品目录(通常标有价格)：an office equipment catalogue 公司设备价目一览表：They sent us a catalogue of their new range of desks. 他们寄给我们一份他们生产的新式系列办公桌的价目表。mail order catalogue = catalogue from which a customer orders items to be sent by mail 邮购价目表；catalogue price =

price as marked in a catalogue 商品目录价格；2. v. to put an item into a catalogue 把…编入价目表

**category** n. type or sort of item 类目；种类：We deal only in the most expensive categories of watches. 我们仅经营最为昂贵类型的手表。

**cater for** v. to deal with or to provide for 迎合；投合：The store caters mainly for overseas customers. 该商店主要是为海外顾客开设的。

◇ **caterer** n. person who supplies food and drink, especially for parties 承办酒席者；提供饮食服务者

◇ **catering** n. (a) supply of food and drink for a party, etc. 公共餐饮业；包餐服务业；the catering trade = food trade, especially supplying food ready to eat 食物供应行业 (b) catering for = which provides for 提供；以…供应；store catering for overseas visitors 为海外游客提供商品的商店
NOTE: no plural

**cause** 1. n. thing which makes something happen 原因；起因；What was the cause of the bank's collapse? 银行倒闭的原因是什么？The police tried to find the cause of the fire. 警察试图找出火灾的起因。2. v. to make something happen 导致；促使发生：The recession caused hundreds of bankruptcies. 经济衰退造成了许许多多的破产者。

**caveat** n. warning 警告：to enter a caveat = to warn legally that you have an interest in a case, and that no steps can be taken without your permission 正式提出警告

◇ **caveat emptor** = LET THE BUYER BEWARE phrase meaning that the buyer is himself responsible for checking that what he buys is in good order 买主当心(一经售出概不负责)

**cc** = COPIES

NOTE: cc is put on a letter to show who has received a copy of it

**ceiling** n. (a) top part which covers a room 天花板：ceiling light = electric light attached to the ceiling 吊灯 (b) highest point 最高点；上限：Output has reached a ceiling. 产量已创最高记录。to fix a ceiling to a budget 限定预算的最高限额；ceiling price or price ceiling = highest price that can be reached 最高价限价

**cent** (a) n. small coin, one hundredth of a dollar(硬币)分：The stores are only a 25 - cent bus ride away. 这些商店仅需付 25 美分即可乘车到达。They sell oranges at 99 cents each. 他们按每只 99 美分出售桔子。NOTE: cent is usually written c in prices: 25c, but not when a dollarprice is mentioned：$ 1.25 (b) see PER CENT

**centimetre** n. measurement of length (one hundredth of a metre)厘米；公分：The paper is fifteen centimetres wide. 这张纸宽度为 15 厘米。
NOTE: centimetre is usually written cm after figures：260cm

**central** a. organized by one main point 中心的；中央的：central bank = main government - controlled bank in a country, which controls the financial affairs of the country by fixing main interest rates, issuing currency and controlling the foreign exchange rate 中央银行；central office = main office which controls all smaller offices 中央机构；central purchasing = purchasing organized by a central office for all branches of a company 集中购物；统一购买

◇ **centralization** n. organization of everything from a central point 使集中；使形成中心
NOTE: no plural

◇ **centralize** v. to organize from a central point 集中；形成中心：All purchasing has been centralized in our main office. 所有购物活动均已集中在我们的总办事处。 Thegroup benefits from a highly centralized organizational structure. 该团体受益于一个高度集中的组织机构。

**centre or** US **center** n. (a) business centre = part of a town where the main banks, shops and offices are 商业中心 (b) important town(某一地区或区域的)中心区: industrial centre 工业中心; 实业中心; manufacturing centre 制造业中心; the centre for the shoe industry 制鞋中心; (c) GB job centre = government office which lists jobs which are vacant(英)职业介绍中心; shopping centre = group of shops linked together with car parks and restaurants 购物中心; (d) group of items in an account 帐户中的项目类别; cost centre = person or group whose costs can be itemized 共同费用汇集;成本中心;成本项目列明; profit centre = person or department which is considered separately for the purposes of calculating a profit 利润中心

**CEO** US = **CHIEF EXECUTIVE OFFICER**

**certain** a. (a) sure 无疑的;确信的: The chairman is certain we will pass last year's total sale. 董事长确信,我们将超过去年的总销售额。(b) a certain = one particular 某些;有些; a certain number or a certain quantity = some 一(某)些数量 **certificate** n. official document which shows that something is true 证书: clearance certificate = document showing that goods have been passed by customs(海关签发的)结关单; savings certificate = document showing you have invested money in a government savings scheme 储蓄存单

share certificate = document proving that you own shares 股票; certificate of airworthiness = document to show that

an aircraft is safe to fly 适航证书;准飞证; certificate of approval = document showing that an item has been officially approved(项目)核准证书; certificate of deposit = document from a bank showing that money has been deposited 存款单; certificate of origin = document showing where goods were made 原产地证书; certificate of registration = document showing that an item has been registered 注册执照;登记证书

◇ **certificated** a. certificated bankrupt = bankrupt who has been discharged from bankruptcy with a certificate to show that he was not at fault 持有破产证书的破产者

**certify** v. to make an official declaration in writing(以书面形式)证明: I certify that this is a true copy. 我证明这件副本是真的。The document is certified as a true copy. 该文件已被证明是真的。certified accountant = accountant who has passed the professional examinations and is a member of the Association of Certified Accountants 执业会计师;注册会计师; certified cheque or US certified check = cheque which a bank says is good and will be paid out of money put aside from the bank account 保付支票

**cession** n. giving up property to someone (especially a creditor)(财产等的)转让;让与 **chain** n. series of stores belonging to the same company 联号;连锁店: a chain of hotels or a hotel chain;联营旅馆; the chairman of a large do-it-yourself chain 一个大型的供业余爱好者学习的联号的董事长; He runs a chain of shoe shops. 他经营一个鞋店的连锁店。She bought several shoe shops and gradually built up a chain. 他已买下几个鞋店并逐渐建立起一个连锁商店。

◇ **chain store** n. one store in a chain 连锁商店;联营商店

**chair** 1. n. position of the chairman,

presiding over a meeting 主席席位（职位）：to be in the chair；（开会时）担任主席；She was voted into the chair. 她当选为主席。Mr Jones took the chair. = Mr Jones presided over the meeting. 琼斯先生任会议主席。to address the chair = in a meeting, to speak to the chairman and not to the rest of the people at the meeting（在会议上）对主席讲话；Please address your remarks to the chair. 请将你的意见告诉主席。2. v. to preside over a meeting 任（会议）主席；主持会议：The meeting was chaired by Mrs Smith. 史密斯先生担任本届会议主席。会议由史密斯先生主持。

◇ **chairman** n. (a) person who is in charge of a meeting 主席：Mr Howard was chairman or acted as chairman. 霍华德先生是主席。Mr Chairman or Madam Chairman = way of speaking to the chairman 主席先生或主席女士（称呼的方式）；(b) person who presides over the board meetings of a company 董事长：the chairman of the board or the company chairman 公司董事长；the chairman's report = annual report from the chairman of a company to theshareholders 董事长的年度报告。

◇ **chairmanship** n. being a chairman 主席（职位或身份）：The committee met under the chairmanship of Mr Jones. （委员会在琼斯先生任主席的情况下开会）委员会在琼斯先生的主持下开会。

◇ **chairperson** n. person who is in charge of a meeting 会议主席；会议主持人

◇ **chairwoman** n. woman who is in charge of a meeting 会议女主持人

NOTE: the plurals are chairmen, chairpersons, chairwomen. Note also that in a US company the president is less important than the chairman of the board

**Chamber of Commerce** n. group of local businessmen who meet to discuss problems which they have in common and to promote commerce in their town 商会（当地的商人开会讨论他们共有的问题以促进该市镇的商业发展）

**chambers** pl. n. office of a judge 法官办公室：The judge heard the case in chambers. = in his private office, and not in court 法官在他的办公室审理本案。

**chance** n. (a) being possible 可能性：The company has a good chance of winning the contract. 该公司获得该项合同的可能性很大。His promotion chances are small. 他晋升的可能性极小。(b) opportunity to do something（做某事的）机会：She is waiting for a chance to see the managing director. 她正在寻机见总经理。He had his chance of promotion when the finance director's assistant resigned. 当财务主任的助理辞职，他便有了晋升的机会。

NOTE: you have a chance of doing something or to do something

**Chancellor of the Exchequer** n. GB chief finance minister in the government （英）财政大臣

**chandler** n. person who deals in goods, especially supplies to ships 杂货零售商（尤指供应船用杂货）：ship chandler 出售船用杂货（如绳索、帆布等的）商人

◇ **chandlery** n. chandler's shop 杂货店

**change** 1. n. (a) money in coins or small notes 辅币；零钱：small change = coins 硬币；to give someone change for £10 = to give someone coins or notes in exchange for a ten pound note 把 10 英镑换成零钱 change machine = machine which gives small change for a larger coin 找零钱（硬币）；(b) money given back by the seller, when the buyer can pay only with a larger note or coin than the amount asked 找回零钱: He gave me thewrong change. 他找错了钱。You paid the £5.75 bill with a £10 note, so you should have £4.25 change. 你用 10 英镑的纸币, 支付 5.75 英镑的帐单, 还应找你 4.25 英镑。keep the change = keep it as a tip (said to waiters, etc.)找头留下当小费 2. v. (a) to change a £10 note = to give change in smaller notes or coins for a £10 note 把一张 10 英镑钞票换成零钱 (b) to give one type of currency for another 以…兑换; to change £1,000 into dollars 将 1,000 英磅兑换成美元;We want to change some traveller's cheques. 我们想兑换一些旅行支票。(c) to change hands = to be sold to a new owner 易主;(买卖)转手: The shop changed hands for £100,000. 该商店以 100,000 英磅转手。

◇ **changer** n. person who changes money 兑换货币者

**channel** n. way in which information or goods are passed from one place to another(消息或货物传播的)途径: to go through the official channels = to deal with government officials ( especially when making a request)通过官方渠道; to open up new channels of communication = to find new ways of communicating with someone 开辟通讯新渠道(方式); distribution channels or channels of distribution = ways of sending goods from the manufacturer for sale by retailers 分配系统;销售渠道。

**charge** 1. n. (a) money which must be paid or price of a service 收费;应付款项; to make no charge for delivery 送货不收费; to make a small charge for rental 支付小额租赁费; There is no charge for service or no charge is made for service. 免费提供服务。

admission charge or entry charge = price to be paid before going into an exhibition, etc. 入场费;门票费; bank charges = charges made by a bank for carrying out work for a customer 银行手续费; handling charge = money to be paid for packing or invoicing or dealing with goods which are being shipped 手续费;经营费; inclusive charge = charge which includes all items 全部费用; interest charges = money paid as interest on a loan 利息费用; scale of charges = list showing various prices 费用表; service charge = charge added to a bill in a restaurant to pay for service 服务费用; A 10% service charge is added. 增加 10%的服务费。Does the bill include a service charge? 帐单包括服务费吗? charge account = arrangement which a customer has with a store to buy goods and to pay for them at a later date, usually when the invoice is sent at the end of the month 记帐;月结赊购帐户; charges forward = charges which will be paid by the customer 费用先付;买方负责费用; A token charge is made for heating. = A small charge is made which does not cover the real costs at all. 对供暖的象征性收费。free of charge = free or with no payment to be made 免费; (b) debit on an account. 记入(帐户的)借方;借入: It appears as a charge on the accounts. 这记在帐户的借方上。(c) being formally accused in a court 控告;指控: He appeared in court on a charge of embezzling or on an embezzlement charge. 因被指控贪污他上了法庭。2. v. (a) to ask someone to pay for services later 收费: to charge the packing to the customer or to charge the customer with the packing = the customer has to pay for packing 向顾客收取包装费。(b) to ask for money to be paid 要求付钱: to charge £5 for delivery 索取 5 英磅的运费;How much does he charge? 他要多少钱? He charges £6 an hour = he asks to be paid £6 for an hour's work. 一小时他要 6 英磅。(c) (in a court) to accuse someone formally of having committed a crime 控告；指控：He was charged with embezzling his clients' money. 他被指控贪污顾客的钱。

◇ **chargeable** a. which can be charged 应付费的：repairs chargeable to the occupier 向拥有者(居住者)收取修理费；sums chargeable to the reserve = sums which can be debited to a company's reserves 记入储备金帐户的金额

◇ **chargee** n. person who has the right to force a debtor to pay 债权人(有权强制负债人付款的人)

◇ **chargehand** n. chief of a group of workers under a foreman 工长；监工，班长

**chart** n. diagram showing information as a series of lines or blocks, etc. 图(表)：bar chart = diagram where quantities and values are shown as thick columns of different heights or lengths 柱形图；flow chart = diagram showing the arrangement of various work processes in a series 流程图；程序图；organization chart = diagram showing how a company or an office is organized 组织系统图；pie chart = diagram where information is shown as a circle cut up into sections of different sizes 圆形分析图；sales chart = diagram showing how sales vary from month to month(月)销售图

**charter** 1. n. (a) bank charter = official government document allowing the establishment of a bank 银行营业执照；(b) hiring transport for a special purpose 包租(运输工具)：charter flight = flight in an aircraft which has been hired for that purpose 包租航班；charter plane = plane which has been chartered 包机；boat on charter to Mr Smith = boat which Mr Smith has hired for a voyage 史密斯先生包租的船。2. v. to hire for a special purpose 包租：to charter a plane or a boat or a bus 包机、包船或包租公

共汽车

◇ **chartered** a. (a) chartered accountant = accountant who has passed the professional examinations and is a member of the Institute of Chartered Accountants 执业会计师；特许会计师 (b) (company) which has been set up by charter, and not registered as a company 特许的(未注册公司) a chartered bank 特许银行 (c) chartered ship or bus or plane = ship or bus or plane which has been hired for a special purpose 包租的(船、汽车、飞机)

◇ **charterer** n. person who hires a ship, etc., for a special purpose 租船人：包租人；

◇ **chartering** n. act of hiring for a special purpose 租；包租

**chartist** n. person who studies stock market trends and forecasts future rises or falls 预测证券交易所股票涨落行情的专家

**chase** v. (a) to run after someone or something to try to catch them 追赶；追捕 (b) to try to speed up work by asking how it is progressing 催；催要：We are trying to chase up the accounts department for the cheque. 我们正试着向会计部门催要那张支票。We will chase your order with the production department. 我们会向生产部门催你们的订货。

◇ **chaser** n. (a) progress chaser = person whose job is to check that work is being carried out on schedule or that orders are fulfilled on time 进度督导人 (b) letter to remind someone of something (especially to remind a customer that an invoice has not been paid)催(款)单；推交货款的信

**chattels** pl. n. goods or moveable property 动产

**cheap** a. & ad. not costing a lot of money or not expensive 便宜的(地)；廉

价的（地）: cheap labour = workforce whichdoes not earn much money 廉价劳动力; We have opened a factory in the Far East because of the cheap labour or because labour is cheap. 我们在远东已开设了一家工厂, 因为那里的劳动力廉价。cheap money = money which can be borrowed at low interest 低息借款; cheap rate = rate which is not expensive 低利率; cheap rate phone calls 低价通（电）话; 优惠价打电话; to buy something cheap = at a low price 廉价购物; He bought two companies cheap and sold them again at a profit. 他廉价买进两个公司, 然后又售出, 从中赚了钱。They work out cheaper by the box. = These items are cheaper per unit if you buy a box of them. 整盒购买价格就便宜。

◇ **cheaply** ad. without paying much money 便宜地; 廉价地: The salesman was living cheaply at home and claiming a high hotel bill on his expenses. 这个销售人员在家中开销低得很, 却以高级饭店的费用报帐。

◇ **cheapness** n. being cheap 便宜; 廉价; 贬值: The cheapness of the pound means that many more tourists will come to London. 英镑贬值意味着更多的游客会到伦敦来。
NOTE: no plural

**cheat** v. to trick someone so that he loses money 哄骗; 骗取（某人钱物）: He cheated the Income Tax out of thousands of pounds. 他骗取所得税当局几千英镑。She was accused of cheating clients who came to ask her for advice. 她被指控欺骗前来向她咨询的顾客。

**check** 1. n. (a) sudden stop 阻止; 抑止: to put a check on imports = to stop some imports 停止进口 (b) check sample = sample to be used to see if a consignment is acceptable 作验货的样品 (c) investigation or examination 核对; 调查; 检查: The auditors carried out

checks on the petty cash book. 审计人员对小额现金出纳簿进行检查。a routine check of the fire equipment 对防火器材的一次常规检查; baggage check = examination of passengers' baggage to see if it containsbombs 行李检查 (d) US (in restaurant) bill（美）餐馆的帐单; (e) US = CHEQUE (f) US mark on paper to show that something is correct（美）核查无误的标记（通常以√表示）; Make a check in the box marked "R". 在标有"R"标记的盒上打"√"。2. v. (a) to stop or to delay 停止; 耽搁: to check the entry of contraband into the country 严禁违禁品进入该国 (b) to examine or to investigate 检查; 调查: to check that an invoice is correct 检验该发票是准确的; to check and sign for goods 对商品进行核对并签字; He checked the computer printout against the invoices. = He examined the printout and the invoices to see if the figures were the same. 他将发票与计算机打印出的数字核对了一遍。(c) US to mark with a sign to show that something is correct（美）打"√"表示已核对: Check the box marked "R". 在标有"R"记号的盒子上打"√"

◇ **check in** v. (a) (at a hotel) to arrive at a hotel and sign for a room（在旅馆）登记: He checked in at 12:15. 他于12点15分旅馆登记。
(b) (at an airport) to give in your ticket to show you are ready to take the flight（在机场）签到; 登记 (c) to check baggage in = to pass your baggage to the airline to put it on the plane for you（向航空公司）交运（行李）; 托运行李

◇ **check – in** n. place where passengers give in their tickets for a flight（登机）检票处: The check – in is on the first floor. 检票处位于一楼。check – in counter = counter where passengers check in 旅客登记处或（验票并领取登机证的柜台）; check – in time = time at which passengers should check in 检票

时间或办理登记的时间

◇ **checking** n. (a) examination or investigation 检查；调查：The inspectors found some defects during their checking of the building. 检查人员在对该建筑物进行检查时发现某些瑕疵。(b) US checking account = bank account on which you can write cheques(美)支票帐户

NOTE: no plural

◇ **checkoff** n. US system where union dues are automatically deducted by the employer from a worker's paycheck(美)工会费由资方从工人工资中自动地代扣的制度

◇ **check out** v. (at a hotel) to leave and pay for a room(在旅馆)结帐离开：We will check out before breakfast. 我们将在早餐前结帐离开旅馆。

◇ **checkout** n. (a) (in a supermarket) place where you pay for the goods you have bought(超级市场的)收款处 (b) (in a hotel) Checkout time is 12.00. = time by which you have to leave your room(旅馆)结帐退房的时间为 12 点。

◇ **checkroom** n. US place where you leave your coat or luggage, etc. (美)衣帽间或行李房(行李寄存处)

**cheque** n. note to a bank asking them to pay money from your account to the account of the person whose name is written on the note 支票(存款人向银行签发的票据，根据帐户中存款，要求银行支付款项的凭证)：a cheque for £10 or a £10 cheque 一张 10 英磅的支票；cheque account = bank account which allows the customer to write cheques 支票帐户；cheque to bearer = cheque with no name written on it, so that the person who holds it can cash it 不记名支票；crossed cheque = cheque with two lines across it showing that it can only be deposited at a bank and not exchanged for cash 划线支票(仅供在银行存款用)；横线支票：open or uncrossed cheque = cheque which can be cashed anywhere 普通支票；未划线支票；blank cheque = cheque with the amount of money and the payee left blank, but signed by the drawer 空白支票；pay cheque or salary cheque = monthly cheque by which an employee is paid 工资支票；traveller's cheques = cheques taken by a traveller, which can be cashed in a foreign country 旅行支票；dud cheque or bouncing cheque or cheque which bounces or US rubber check = cheque which cannot be cashed because the person writing it has not enough money in the account to pay it 作废支票；拒付支票；(美)空头支票 (b) to cash a cheque = to exchange a cheque for cash 兑现支票；to endorse a cheque = to sign a cheque on the back to show that you accept it 背书支票；to make out a cheque to someone = to write someone's name on a cheque 给某人开出一张支票；Who shall I make the cheque out to? 我给谁开支票？ to pay by cheque = to pay by writing a cheque, and not using cash or a creditcard 用支票支付；to pay a cheque into your account = to deposit a cheque 将支票款额划入你的帐户；The bank referred the cheque to drawer. = returned the cheque to the person who wrote it because therewas not enough money in the account to pay it 因帐户余额不足银行将支票转交给开票人。to sign a cheque = to sign on the front of a cheque to show that you authorize the bank to pay the money from your account 开支票；签发支票；to stop a cheque = to ask a bank not to pay a cheque which you have written(让银行)停付你自己开的支票

◇ **cheque book** n. booklet with new cheques 支票薄(本)

◇ **cheque guarantee card** n. plastic card from a bank which guarantees payment of a cheque up to a certain amount, even if there is no money in the account 支票保付卡(银行保证支付某一限定金额,即便帐户上无钱)

**chief** a. most important 首要的;主要的;最重要的: He is the chief accountant of an industrial group. 他是一个工业集团的主会计师。 chief executive or US chief executive officer = executive in charge of a company 主要执事人员;总裁董事长;(美)行政长管

**chip** n. (a) a computer chip = a small piece of silicon able to store data, used incomputers 计算机芯片 (b) blue chip = very safe investment or risk – free share in a good company 热门股票

**chit** n. bill (for food or drink in a club) 帐单;(小额债务的)单据(指在俱乐部购买食品或饮料)

**choice** 1. n. (a) thing which is chosen 选择;抉择: You must give the customer time to make his choice. 你必须给顾客有选择的时间。 (b) range of items to choose from 选择的范围: We have only a limited choice of suppliers. 我们的商品供应渠道很有限。 The shop carries a good choice of paper. = The shop carries many types of paper to choose from. 该商店出售的纸张类型很多。 2. a. specially selected (food)精选的;上等的(食品); choice meat 精选的肉; choice wines 上等的酒类; choice foodstuffs 精选的食品

**choose** v. to decide to do a particular thing or to buy a particular item (as opposed to something else) 选择;挑选: There were several good candidates to choose from. 有几位不错的候选人可供选择。 They chose the only woman applicant as sales director. 他们选择了唯一的女申请人做为销售经理。 You must give the customers plenty of time to choose. 你必须给顾客充分的时间去选择商品。

NOTE: choosing – chose – chosen

**chronic** a. permanently bad 极劣的;可怕的: The company has chronic cash flow problems. 该公司的现金周转问题一直很严重。 We have a chronic shortage of skilled staff. 我们一直缺有技术的职工。 chronic unemployment = being unemployed for more than six months 长期或经常性失业(6 个月以上)

**chronological order** n. arrangement of records (files, invoices, etc.) in order of their dates 按照日期顺序排列

**c. i. f.** = COST, INSURANCE AND FREIGHT 到岸价格;成本 + 保险 + 运费

**circular** 1. a. sent to many people 通告的;流通的: circular letter of credit = letter of credit sent to all branches of the bank which issues it 流通信用证;巡回信用证; 2. n. leaflet or letter sent to many people 通知;通函: They sent out a circular offering a 10% discount. 他们发出一份提供 10% 优惠的通知(通函)。

◇ **circularize** v. to send a circular to 发通知给…: The committee has agreed to circularize the members. 该委员会已同意给会员发通知。 They circularized all their customers with a new list of prices. 他们给所有的顾客发了一张新价目单。

◇ **circulate** v. (a) (of money) to circulate freely = to move about without restriction by the government (货币)自由流通 (b) to send or to give out without restrictions 使自由流通;通用; to circulate money = to issue money or to make money available to the public and industry 发行货币或使货币流通 (c) to send information to 传播;流传: They circulated a new list of prices to all their customers. 他们向所有顾客发了一张新价目表。

◇ **circulating** a. which is moving

about freely 自由流通的；通用的：cir-culatingcapital = capital required in cash, raw materials, finished products and work in progress for a company to carry on its business 流动资本；周转资金

◇ **circulation** n. (a) movement 流通；传播：The company is trying to improve the circulation of information between departments. 公司正试图改进部门间的信息流通。circulation of capital = movement of capital from one investment to another 资本流通；资本循环 (b) to put money into circulation = to issue new notes to business and the public 发行货币：The amount of money in circulation increased more than was expected. 货币发行量增加的比预期的要多。(c) (of newspapers) number of copies sold (报纸的)发行量：The audited circulation of a newspaper. 已审查的报纸发行量。The new editor hopes to improve the circulation. 新编辑希望增加发行量。a circulation battle = competition between two papers to try to sell more copies in the same market 发行量竞争。

NOTE: no plural for (a) and (b)

**city** n. (a) large town 市；城市：The largest cities in Europe are linked by hourly flights 欧洲的最大城市之间平均每小时一次航班。capital city = main town in a country, where the government is located 首都；inter – city = between cities 城市间的；市际的；Inter – city train services are often quicker than going by air. 乘市际之间的火车常比乘飞机要快些。(b) the City = old centre of London, where banks and large companies have their main offices; the British financial centre 伦敦老城(金融中心)：He works in the City or he is in the City 他在伦敦老城上班。City desk = section of a newspaper office which deals with business news(报馆)商业新闻编辑部 City editor = business or fi-nance editor of a British paper(英)商业金融栏目的编辑；They say in the City that the company has been sold. = The business world is saying that the company has been sold. 商界说那个公司已经被出售。

**civil** a. referring to ordinary people 公民的：civil action = court case brought by a person or a company against someone who has done them wrong 民事诉讼；civil law = laws relating to people's rights and agreements between individuals 民法；

◇ **civil service** n. organization and personnel which administer a country 政府中的文职机构；公务员：You have to pass an examination to get a job in the civil service or to get a civil service job. 你必须通过考试才能在政府机构的文职部门中任职。

◇ **civil servant** n. person who works in the civil service 文职人员；公务员

**claim** 1. n. (a) asking for money 索赔：wage claim = asking for an increase in wages(为增加工资而提出来的)工资要求：The union put in a 6% wage claim. = The union asked for a 6% increase in wages for its members. 工会提出一项增加6%的工资的要求。(b) legal claim = statement that you think you own something legally 合法要求；法律上的要求：He has no legal claim to the property. 法律上他无权要这项财产。(c) insurance claim = asking an insurance company to pay for damages or for loss 保险索赔；claims department = department of an insurance company which deals with claims(保险公司的)理赔部；理赔处；claim form = form to be filled in when making an insurance claim 索赔表；索赔申请书；claims manager = manager of a claims department 理赔部门的经理；no claims bonus = lower premium paid because no claims have

been made against the insurance policy 无索赔奖金(减收保险费,因无索赔); to put in a claim = to ask the insurance company officially to pay damages(向保险公司正式)提出索赔; to put in a claim for repairs to the car 为修理小汽车而提出索赔: She put in a claim for £ 250,000 damages against the driver of the other car. 她提出要对方的司机赔偿 250,000 英磅损失赔偿金的要求。 to settle a claim = to agree to pay what is asked for 理赔,清算债务; The insurance company refused to settle his claim for storm damage. 保险公司拒绝解决由暴雨引起的损失赔偿。 (d) small claims court = court which deals with claims for small amounts of money 小额索赔法庭 2. v. (a) to ask for money 要求;索赔; He claimed £ 100,000 against the cleaning firm. 要求清洗公司赔偿 100,000 英磅损失金。 She claimed for repairs to the car against her insurance. 她要求以其保险付小汽车的修理费用。 (b) to say that something is your property 要求承认;认领: He is claiming possession of the house. 他要求拥有此房屋。 No one claimed the umbrella found in my office. 无人前来认领在我办公室里发现的这把雨伞。 (c) to state that something is a fact 声称;主张: He claims he never received the goods. 他声称他从未收到过货物。 She claims that the shares are her property. 她声称股票是属她个人的财产。
◇ **claimant** n. person who claims 债权人;要求者;索赔人: rightful claimant = person who has a legal claim to something 合法索赔者
**claim back** v. to ask for money to be
◇ **claimer** n. = CLAIMANT 债权人;索赔人
◇ **claiming** n. act of making a claim 索赔
**class** n. category or group into which

things are classified according to quality or price(按质量或价格分的)等级;种类: first - class = top quality or most expensive 一级的;头等的;最昂贵的; He is a first - class accountant. 他是一级会计师。 economy class or tourist class = lower quality or less expensive way of travelling(飞机上的)经济舱或(轮船上的)二等舱: I travel economy class because it is cheaper. 我旅行乘坐经济舱因为它比较便宜。 Tourist class travel is less comfortable than first class. 乘经济舱旅行比不上头等舱舒适。 He always travels first class because tourist class is too uncomfortable. 他总是乘坐头等舱旅行,因为乘经济舱十分不舒适。GB first - class mail = more expensive mail service, designed to be faster(英)一类(快速)邮件: A first - class letter should get to Scotland in a day. 一类函件应在一天之内到达苏格兰。 second - class mail = less expensive, slower mail service(英)二类(一般较便宜但比较慢)邮件: The letter took three days to arrive because he sent it second class. 这封信走了三天,因为他用二类(一般)邮件寄出的。

**classify** v. to put into classes or categories 把…分类;把…分出等级; classified advertisements = advertisements listed in a newspaper under special headings (such as "property for sale" or "jobs wanted")(企业)分类广告; classified directory = book which lists businesses grouped under various headings (such as computer shops or newsagents)(企业)分类指南
◇ **classification** n. way of putting into classes 分类法: job classification = describing jobs listed in various groups 职业分类

**clause** n. section of a contract(合同)条款: There are ten clauses in the contract. 本合同有十项条款。According to clause six, payments will not be due until next year. 按合同第六条款,支付款项明年才到期。 exclusion clause = clause in an insurance policy or warranty which says which items are not covered by the policy 除外责任条款(保险单中的) penalty clause = clause which lists the penalties which will happen if the contract is not fulfilled(违约)惩罚条款; termination clause = clause which explains how and when a contract can be terminated 终止条款

**claw back** v. to take back money which has been allocated 收回(款): Income tax claws back 25% of pensions paid out by the government. 政府所发的退休金的25%从所得税中得到弥补。 Of the £1m allocated to the project, the government clawed back £100,000 in taxes. 政府从划拨给项目的100万英磅中收取10万英磅的税。

◇ **clawback** n. money taken back 收回款项

**clear** 1 a. (a) easily understood 易懂的;清楚的;明白的; He made it clear that he wanted the manager to resign. 他说得十分清楚,他想让经理辞职。 You will have to make it clear to the staff that productivity is falling. 你必须把生产率正在下降向全体职工讲清楚。 (b) clear profit = profit after all expenses have been paid 纯利润; We made $6,000 clear profit on the sale. 在销售上,我们获得了6,000美元的纯利润。 (c) free or total period of time 自由的或完整的(一段时间) three clear days = three whole working days(工作的天数为)整三天: Allow three clear days for the cheque to be paid into the bank. 允许三整天时间将支票付入银行。 2. v. (a) to sell cheaply in order to get rid of stock 贱卖; "demonstration models to clear" 贱卖的展品模型 (b) to clear goods through the customs = to have all documentation passed by the customs so that goods can leave the country 报(结)关出

境; (c) to clear 10% or $5,000 on the deal = to make 10% or $5,000 clear profit 这个买卖净赚10% 或5,000美元的纯利; We cleared only our expenses. = The sales revenue only paid for the costs and expenses without making any profit. 我们所得盈利只供成本开支用。 (d) to clear a cheque = to pass a cheque through the banking system, so that the money is transferred from the payer's account to another 兑现支票;清算支票: The cheque took ten days to clear or the bank took ten days to clear the cheque 该银行花了10天时间清算了这张支票。

◇ **clearance** n. (a) customs clearance = passing goods through the customs so that they can enter or leave the country 结关;海关放行; to effect customs clearance = to clear goods through the customs 报(结)关放行; clearance certificate = certificate showing that goods have been passed by the customs(海关签发的)结关单;离港证; (b) clearance sale = sale of items at low prices to get rid of stock 清仓大贱卖; (c) clearance of a cheque = passing of a cheque through the banking system, transferring money from one account to another 清算支票; You should allow six days for cheque clearance. 你应该允许用6天时间结清支票。

◇ **clearing** n. (a) clearing of goods through the customs = passing of goods through the customs 报关(结关)放行 (b) clearing of a debt = paying all of a debt 清算债务 (c) clearing bank = bank which clears cheques, one of the major British HighStreet banks 清算银行;交换银行; clearing house = central office where clearing banks exchange cheques 票据交换所

◇ **clear off** v. to clear off a debt = to pay all of a debt 请偿一笔债务,清算。

**clerical** a. (work) done in an office or

done by a clerk 办公室工作的；文秘工作的；clerical error = mistake made in an office 文书错误；笔误；clerical staff = staff of an office 全体(办事)人员；clerical work = paperwork done in an office 办公室工作；办事员工作；clerical worker = person who works in an office 办公室工作人员；办事员

**clerk** 1. n. (a) person who works in an office 职员；办事员：articled clerk = clerk who is bound by a contract to work in a lawyer's office for some years to learn the trade 见习律师；chief clerk or head clerk = most important clerk 办事员主任；最重要的办事人员；filing clerk = clerk who files documents 档案管理员；invoice clerk = clerk who deals with invoices 发票管理员；shipping clerk = clerk who deals with shipping documents 装运办事员 (b) bank clerk = person who works in a bank 银行职员；银行办事员；booking clerk = person who works in a booking office 售票员；订票员：US sales clerk = person who sells in a store(美)售货员 2. v. US to work as a clerk 当…店员，职员

◇ **clerkess** n. (in Scotland) woman clerk(在苏格兰)女职员

**clever** a. intelligent or able to learn quickly 聪明的；伶俐的；灵巧的：He is very clever at spotting a bargain. 他在发现交易方面很擅长。Clever investors have made a lot of money on the share deal. 聪明的投资者在股票交易中已赚了大笔的钱。

**client** n. person with whom business is done or person who pays for a service 顾客；客户

◇ **clientele** n. all the clients of a business; all the customers of a shop(企业或商店中)顾客；常客
NOTE: no plural

**climb** v. to go up 向上；攀登：The company has climbed to No. 1 position

in the market. 该公司已跃居市场首位。Profits climbed rapidly as the new management cut costs. 利润迅速上升是由于新的管理方法削减了成本。

**clinch** v. to settle (a business deal) or to come to an agreement 成交，达成协议：He offered an extra 5% to clinch the deal. 为了成交，他多加 5%。They need approv alfrom the board before they can clinch the deal. 他们需得到董事会的批准，才能达成这笔交易。

**clipping service** n. service of cutting out references to a client in newspapersor magazines and sending them to him(美)剪报公司；剪报服务社(专替顾客剪辑报纸或杂志上参考资料的服务机构)

**clock** n. machine which shows the time 钟；表：The office clock is fast. 办公室的钟快。The micro has a built – in clock. 这个微型计算机嵌入一个小钟。digital clock = clock which shows the time using numbers (as 12:05)数字表(如 12:05)

◇ **clock card** n. special card which a worker puts into the time clock when clocking on or off 工时卡；上下班记时卡

◇ **clock in or clock on** v. (of worker) to record the time of arriving for work by putting a card into a special timing machine 打卡上班(向特殊的记时计中投卡，以记录上班的时间)

◇ **clock out or clock off** v. (of worker) to record the time of leaving work by putting a card into aspecial timing machine 打卡记录下班时间(向特殊的记时计中投卡以记录下班的时间)

◇ **clocking in or clocking on** n. arriving for work and recording the time on a time – card 打卡上班

◇ **clocking out or clocking off** n. leaving work and recording the time on a time – card 打卡下班

**close** 1. n. end 结束；终止：At the

close of the day's trading the shares had fallen20％. 在(证券交易所)交易日收盘时,股价已下跌了 20％。
NOTE: no plural
2. a. close to = very near or almost 接近于: The company was close to bankruptcy. 该公司已濒临破产。We are close to meeting our sales targets. 我们即将完成销售指标。3. v. to end 终止;结束: (a) to stop doing business for the day 关门;打烊; The office closes at 5.30. 公司 5 点 30 分打烊。We close early on Saturdays. 星期六我们打烊较早。(b) to close the accounts = to come to the end of an accounting period and make up the profit and loss account 结清帐户 (c) to close an account = (i) to stop supplying a customer on credit 停止赊卖 (ii) to take all the money out of a bank account and stop the account 关闭帐户;结束帐户: He closed his building society account. = He took all the money out and stopped using the account. 他已结束了其房屋互助协会的帐户。(d) The shares closed at $15. = At the end of the day's trading the price of the shares was $15. 股票收盘价为 15 美元。

◇ **close company or** US **close(d) corporation** n. privately owned company where the public may own a small number of shares 股份不公开公司(私人所有的公司,公众可能有少量的股票)

◇ **closed** a. (a) shut or not open or not doing business 关闭的;停止营业的: The office is closed on Mondays. 公司星期一不营业。All the banks are closed on the National Day. 国庆节期间所有的银行停业。(b) restricted 受限制的; closed shop = system where a company agrees to employ only union members in certain jobs 不开放工厂或闭锁店;排外性雇佣制企业; a closed shop agreement 一份限雇外部人员(非工会会员)的协议; The union is asking the management to agree to a closed shop. 工会要求管理部门同意雇外部人员的制度。closed market = market where a supplier deals only with one agent or distributor and does not supply any others direct 关闭式市场(供应厂商仅仅与一个代理商或经销商交易并不直接供应其他人的市场): They signed a closed market agreement with an Egyptian company. 他们与一家埃及的公司签署了一项关闭式市场的协议。

◇ **close down** v. to shut a shop or factory for a long period or for ever(工厂、企业、商店)关闭;歇业: The company is closing down its London office. 该公司正在关闭其驻伦敦办事处。The strike closed down the railway system. 罢工使铁路系统陷于瘫痪。

◇ **close - out sale** n. US selling goods cheaply to try to get rid of them(美)甩卖商品

◇ **closing** 1. a. (a) final or coming at the end 最后的;结束的: closing bid = last bid at an auction or the bid which is successful 收盘出价; closing date = last date 截止日期; The closing date for tenders to be received is May 1st. 收到投标的截止日期为 5 月 1 日。closing price = price of a share at the end of a day's trading 收盘价 (b) at the end of an accounting period 会计年度末: closing balance 期终余额;期末差额; closing stock 期末存货 2. n. (a) shutting of a shop or being shut 停止营业: Sunday closing = not opening a shop on Sundays 星期天不营业; closing time = time when a shop or office stops work 下班时间;关店时间

early closing day = weekday (usually Wednesday or Thursday) when many shops close in the afternoon 商店提早关门日;早打烊日 (b) closing of an account = act of stopping supply to a customer on credit 停止向顾客赊销

NOTE: no plural

◇ **closing down** n. closing – down sale = sale of goods when a shop is closing for ever 商店永远停业后的商品出售

◇ **closure** n. act of closing 关闭

**club** n. group of people who have the same interest; place where these people meet 俱乐部: If you want the managing director, you can phone him at his club. 如果你想找总经理可给他俱乐部挂电话。He has applied to join the sports club 他申请加入体育运动俱乐部。club membership = all the members of a club 俱乐部全体成员; club subscription = money paid to belong to a club 入俱乐部会费; staff club = club for the staff of a company, which organizes staff parties, sports and meetings 职工俱乐部

**cm** = CENTIMETRE

**c/o** = CARE OF 转交

**Co.** = COMPANY J. Smith & Co. Ltd

**co –** prefix working or acting together 共同; 相互

◇ **co – creditor** n. person who is a creditor of the same company as you are 共同债权人

◇ **co – director** n. person who is a director of the same company as you 共同董事

◇ **co – insurance** n. insurance policy where the risk is shared among severalinsurers 共同保险(单)

**COD or c. o. d.** = CASH ON DELIVERY 货到付现款

**code** n. (a) system of signs or numbers or letters which mean something 编码; 代码; 电码: area code = numbers which indicate an area for telephoning 电话区号; What is the code for Edinburgh? 爱丁保的电话区号是多少? bar code = system of lines printed on a product which can be read by acomputer to give a reference number or price

条纹码; international dialling code = numbers used for dialling to another country 国际电话号码; machine – readable codes = sets of signs or letters (such as bar codes or post codes) which can be read by computers 电脑可阅读的号码(条纹码与邮政编码); post code or US zip code = letters and numbers used to indicate a town or street in an address on an envelope 邮政编码: stock code = numbers and letters which refer to an item of stock 货号; 库存品编码 (b) set of rules 法规; 法典: code of practice = rules drawn up by an association which the members must follow when doing business 业务规则; 业务规范

◇ **coding** n. act of putting a code on something 编码; 代码; the coding of invoices 发票的编码; 发票的代号

**coin** n. piece of metal money 硬币: He gave me two 10 – franc coins in my change. 他找给我两枚十法郎硬币。I need some 10p coins for the telephone. 我需要一些10便士硬币打电话用。

◇ **coinage** n. system of metal money used in a country(金属)货币制度

NOTE: no plural

**cold** a. (a) not hot 冷的: The machines work badly in cold weather. 机器在冷天气运转不畅。The office was so cold that the staff started complaining. 办公室是如此寒冷, 难怪职员们开始抱怨。The coffee machine also sells cold drinks. 咖啡机同样出售冷饮。(b) without being prepared 无准备的; 冷不防的: cold call = sales call where the salesman has no appointment and the client is not an established customer 销售人员临时给顾客打电话兜售(销): cold start = starting a new business or opening a new shop where there was none before 开设一个首家商店(企业)

**collaborate** v. to work together 合作;

协作: to collaborate with a French firm on a building project 与一家法国公司合作一个建筑工程项目; They collaborated on the new aircraft. 他们合作搞新型飞行器(飞机)。
NOTE: you collaborate with someone on something

◇ **collaboration** n. working together 合作; 协作; Their collaboration on the project was very profitable. 他们在此项目上的合作赚了很多钱。
NOTE: no plural

**collapse** 1. n. (a) sudden fall in price (价格)暴跌: the collapse of the market in silver 市场上的银价暴跌; the collapse of thedollar on the foreign exchange markets 外汇市场上的美元暴跌 (b) sudden failure of a company 倒闭; 破产: Investors lost thousands of pounds in the collapse of the company. 因公司的倒闭, 投资者损失了成千上万的英镑。
2. v. (a) to fall suddenly 崩溃; 倒坍; (价格)暴跌: The market collapsed. 市场价格暴跌。The yen collapsed on the foreign exchange markets. 外汇市场上的日元暴跌。
(b) to fail suddenly 倒闭; 破产: The company collapsed with £25,000 in debts. 该公司因负债 25,000 英磅而破产。

**collar** n. part of a coat or shirt which goes round the neck 衣领: blue - collar worker = manual worker in a factory 兰领工人; white - collar worker = office worker 白领工人; He has a white - collar job. = He works in an office. 他是一位白领工人。

**collateral** a. & n. (security) used to provide a guarantee for a loan(证券)担保的; 担保品; 抵押品:

**collect** 1. v. (a) to make someone pay money which is owed 收帐; 收款: to collect a debt = to go and make someone pay a debt 收回一笔欠款 (b) to take

things away from a place 带走; 领取: We have to collect the stock from the warehouse. 我们必须从仓库取存货。Can you collect my letters from the typing pool? 你能将我的信从打字组取回来吗?; Letters are collected twice a day. = The post office workers take them from the letter box to the post office for dispatch. 信件一天取两次 2. ad. & a. US (phone call) where the person receiving the call agrees to pay for it(美)(通电话)由接电话者付款; 由对方付款: to make a collect call 打一次由对方付款的电话: He called his office collect. 他打一个由公司付款的电话。

◇ **collecting agency** n. agency which collects money owed to other companies for acommission 收款代理商(为别家公司代收欠款而收取佣金的代理商)

◇ **collection** n. (a) getting money together or making someone pay money which is owed 收款; 收帐: tax collection or collection of tax 收税; debt collection = collecting money which is owed 收债; debt collection agency = company which collects debts for other companies for a commission 收债代理商; bills for collection = bills where payment is due 托收票据; 托收汇票 (b) fetching of goods 取货: The stock is in the warehouse awaiting collection. 货是在库房中待领。collection charges or collection rates = charge for collecting something 托收票据手续费; to hand something in for collection = to leave something for someone to come and collect 让某人领取 (c) collections = money which has been collected 收款; 托收款项 (d) taking of letters from a letter box or mail room to the post office for dispatch(信件)收集(交邮局发出) There are six collections a day from the letter box. (邮递员)每天从信箱取六次信件。

◇ **collective** a. working together 共同的; 集体的: free collective bargaining =

negotiations about wage increases and workingconditions between management and trade unions 集体谈判; collective farm = state - owned farm which is run by the workers 集体农在; collective ownership = ownership of a business by the workers who work in it 集体所有制; They signed a collective wage agreement. = An agreement was signed between management and the trade union about wages. 他们签定了一项集体工资协议(工会与资方之间签订)。

◇ **collector** n. person who makes people pay money which is owed 收款员: collector of taxes or tax collector; 税收员; debt collector 收债人

**college** n. place where people can study after they have left full - timeschool 学院; 大学: business college or commercial college = college which teaches general business methods 商学院; secretarial college = college which teaches shorthand, typing and word - processing 文秘学院

**column** n. (a) series of numbers, one under the other 一行数字; 一列数字: to add up a column of figures 将一行(列)数字加起来; Put the total at the bottom of the column 把总数写在栏底; credit column = right - hand side in accounts showing money received 贷方栏(目); debit column = left - hand side in accounts showing money paid or owed 借方栏(目) (b) section of printed words in a newspaper or magazine(指报刊、杂志中的)专栏; column - centimetre = space in centimetres in a newspaper column, used for calculating charges for advertising(广告的)专栏版面

**combine** 1. n. large financial or commercial group 大财团; 商业集团: a German industrial combine 一家德国工业集团 2. v. to join together 联合; 结合: The workforce and management com-

bined to fight the takeover bid. 劳资双方联合对付兼并出价(收购另一公司的出价)。

◇**combination** n. (a) several things which are joined together 联合; 结合: A combination of cash flow problems and difficult trading conditions caused the company's collapse. 资金周转问题又加上恶劣的贸易环境, 共同导致了该公司的破产。(b) series of numbers which open a special lock 号码组合(开号码锁的数目字): I have forgotten the combination of the lock on my briefcase. 我已忘了我的公文皮包上开锁的号码了。The office safe has a combination lock. 办公室保险柜有一个号码锁。

**comfort** n. letter of comfort or comfort letter = letter supporting someone who is trying to get a loan 告慰函; 安慰信(为获得货款向放款而写)

**commerce** n. business or buying and selling of goods and services 商业; 商务: Chamber of Commerce = group of local businessmen who meet to discuss problems whichthey have in common and to promote business in their town 商会

◇ **commercial** 1. a. (a) referring to business 商业的; 商务的: commercial aircraft = aircraft used to carry cargo or passengers for payment 商用飞机; commercial artist = artist who designs advertisements or posters, etc. for payment 商业画家; commercial attach = diplomat who represents and tries to promote his country' sbusiness interests 商务专员; 商务参赞; commercial college = college which teaches business studies 商学院; commercial course = course where business skills are studied 商业课程; He took a commercial course by correspondence. 他学习了商业函授课程。commercial directory = book which lists all the businesses and business people in a town 商业企业指南; commercial district = part of a town where offices andshops are 商业区; commercial law = laws regarding business 商法 commercial load = amount of goods or number of passengers which a bus or train or plane has to carry to make a profit 商业装载量 (飞机、火车、轮船等运输工具为获利润携带的旅客、货物的必需量); commercial port = port which has only goods traffic 商港; commercial traveller = salesman who travels round an area visiting customers onbehalf of his company 旅行推销员; 商业推销员; 销售代表; commercial vehicle = van or truck, etc. used for business purposes 商业车辆(尤指卡车); Sample only - of no commercial value. = not worth anything if sold 无销售价值只是商品货样。(b) profitable 可获利的; not a commercial proposition = not likely to make a profit 不盈利的建议 2. n. advertisement on television 电视商业广告

◇ **commercialization** n. making something into a business proposition 商业化: the commercialization of museums 博物馆的商业化
NOTE: no plural

◇ **commercialize** v. to make something into a business 使商业化: The holiday town has become so commercialized that it is unpleasant. 度假村(城镇)越来越商业化很煞风景。

◇ **commercially** ad. in a business way 商业化地; 商业上地: not commercially viable = not likely to make a profit 商业上不可行的

**commission** n. (a) money paid to a salesman or an agent, usually a percentage of the sales made 佣金(通常以销售的百分比付给销售人员或代理人): She gets 10% commission on everything she sells. 她每推销一件物品得到10%的佣金。He charges 10% commission. = He asks for 10% of sales as his payment. 他收取10%的佣金。commission agent = agent who is paid a percentage of sales 佣金代办商; 销售代理商; commission rep = representative who is not paid a salary, but receives a commission on sales 佣金代理人; commission sale or sale on commission = sale where the salesman is paid a commission 付佣金的委托销售 (b) group of people officially appointed to examine some problem 委员会: The government has appointed a commission of inquiry to look into the problems of small exporters. 政府已任命了一个调查委员会前去调查为数不多的出口商的问题。He is the chairman of the government commission on export subsidies. 他是政府出口补贴委员会的主席。

**commit** v. to carry out (a crime)干;犯(罪)
NOTE: committing - committed

**committee** n. official group of people who organize or plan for a larger group 委员会: to be a member of a committee or to sit on a committee 加入委员会; He was elected to the committee of the staff club. 他当选为职工俱乐部委员会委员。The new plans have to be approved by the committee members. 这项新计划必须经过委员们的批准。to chair a committee = to be the chairman of a committee 当委员会主席; He is the chairman of the planning committee. 他是计划委员会的主席。She is the secretary of the finance committee. 她是财政委员会的秘书。management committee = committee which manages a club or a pension fund, etc. 管理委员会(俱乐部或养老金)

**commodity** n. thing sold in very large quantities, especially raw materials and food such as metals or corn 商品(特别指原料); primary or basic commodities = farm produce grown in large quantities, such as corn, rice, cotton 初级产品; 农

产品；staple commodity = basic food or raw material which is most important in a country's economy 主要商品；大宗产品；commodity market or commodity exchange = place where people buy and sell commodities 商品市场；商品交易所；commodity futures = trading in commodities for delivery at a later date 商品期货交易；Silver rose 5% on the commodity futures market yesterday. 昨天商品期货交易市场上的银价上涨了5%。commodity trader = person whose business is buying and selling commodities 商人；商品(特别是原料)交易商

**common** a. (a) which happens very often 通常的；常见的；一般的：Putting the carbon paper in the wrong way round is a common mistake. 将复写纸反过来用是一种常见的错误。Being caught by the customs is very common these days. 现今被海关逮住是常事。(b) belonging to several different people or to everyone 共同的；大众的；公共的：common carrier = firm which carries goods or passengers, and which anyone can use 公用运输商；公共承运公司；common ownership = ownership of a company or a property by a group of people 共同所有权；common pricing = illegal fixing of prices by several businesses so that they all charge the same price (非法)共同定价；US common stock = ordinary shares in a company, giving shareholders a right to vote at meetings and to receive dividends (美)(有表决权能分红利的)普通股票；Common Agricultural Policy = agreement between members of the EEC to protect farmers by paying subsidies to fix prices of farm produce (欧共体用补贴保护农民的)共同农业政策

◇ **Common Market** n. the European Common Market = the European Economic Community or organization which links several European countries for the purposes of trade 共同市场(即欧洲经济共同体的简称) the Common Market finance ministers = the finance ministers of all the Common Market countries meeting as a group 欧共体各国财政部长

**communicate** v. to pass information to someone 传达；传递；通话；通讯：He finds it impossible to communicate with his staff. 他发现无法与他的职员联络。Communicating with head office has been quicker since we installed the telex. 我们安装了电传机后与总公司的联系更为迅速。

◇ **communication** n. (a) passing of information 传达；传递；通讯；通话：Communication with the head office has been made easier by the telex. 借助电传机与总公司的联系变得容易些。to enter into communication with someone = to start discussing something with someone, usually in writing 与某人开始联系：We have entered into communication with the relevant government department. 我们已经开始与有关的政府部门建立了通信联系。(b) official message 公函：We have had a communication from the local tax inspector. 我们收到一封地方税务稽查员的公函。(c) communications = being able to contact people or to pass messages 通讯：After the flood all communications with the outside world were broken. 洪水过后，与外界联系中断。

**community** n. (a) group of people living or working in the same place 社区；公众；团体：the local business community = the business people living and working in the area 当地的企业界(经济界) (b) the European Economic Community = the Common Market 欧洲经济共同体(即共同市场)；the Community ministers = the ministers of member states of the Common Market 欧共体成员国财政部长

**commute** v. (a) to travel to work from

home each day 经常乘车往返;通勤: He commutes from the country to his office in the centre of town. 他经常乘车往返于郊外和位于市中心的办事处之间上下班。(b) to change a right into cash 用···交换;兑换;折算: He decided to commute part of his pension rights into a lump sum payment. 他决定将部分养老金权变为一次整笔的付款。

◇ **commuter** n. person who commutes to work 月票旅客: He lives in the commuter belt. = area of country where the commuters live round a town 他住在月票旅客地带。commuter train = train which commuters take in the morning and evening 通勤火车;月票旅客火车

**company** n. business or group of people organized to buy, sell or provide a service 公司 (a) to put a company into liquidation = to close a company by selling its assets for cash 使公司停业清算; to set up a company = to start a company legally 开办公司;创建公司; associate company = company which is partly owned by another company 联营公司;附属公司; family company = company where most of the shares are owned by members of a family 家族公司; holding company = company which exists only to own shares in subsidiary companies 控股公司;股权公司; joint - stock company = company whose shares are held by many people 股份公司;合股公司; limited (liability) company = company where a shareholder is responsible for re-paying the company's debts only to the face value of the shares he owns 股份(责任)有限公司; listed company = company whose shares can be bought or sold on the StockExchange(股票)上市公司; parent company = company which owns more than half of another company's shares 母公司; private (limited) company = company with a small number of shareholders, whose shares are not trad-

ed on the Stock Exchange 私营公司;私人(有限)公司; public limited company (plc) = company whose shares can be bought on the Stock Exchange 股票公开上市公司; subsidiary company = company which is owned by a parent company 子公司 (b) finance company = company which provides money for hire - purchase(为租购提供资金的) 金融公司; insurance company = company whose business is insurance 保险公司; shipping company = company whose business is in transporting goods 海运公司;船舶运输公司; a tractor or aircraft or chocolate company = company which makes tractors or aircraft or chocolate 拖拉机制造公司或飞机制造公司或制造巧克力的公司 (c) company car = car which belongs to a company and is lent to an employee touse personally 公司(借给职工用的)小汽车; company doctor = (i) doctor who works for a company and looks after sickworkers 公司的医生 (ii) specialist businessman who rescues companies which are in difficulties 商业专家 (专门解救处于困境的公司的人); company director = person appointed by the shareholders to help run a company 公司董事; company law = laws which refer to the way companies may work 公司法; company secretary = person responsible for the company's legal and financial affairs 公司秘书; GB the Companies Act = Act of Parliament which states the legal limits within which companies may do their business(英)公司法

**compare** v. to look at several things to see how they differ 比较;对照: The finance director compared the figures for the first andsecond quarters. 财务主任将第一与第二季度的数字进行比较。

◇ **compare with** v. to put two things together to see how they differ 与···相比较;与···相对照: How do the sales this year compare with last year's? 今年的

销售额与去年的相比较情况如何？ Comparedwith 1982, last year was a boom year. 与 1982 年相比，去年是繁荣的一年。

◇ **comparable** a. which can be compared 可比较的：The two sets of figures are not comparable. 这两组数字是不可比较的。Which is the nearest company comparable to this one in size? = Which company is of a similar size and can be compared with this one? 哪个是在规模上与这个公司最接近？

◇ **comparability** n. being able to be compared 可比性：pay comparability = similar pay system in two different companies 工资可比性 NOTE: no plural

◇ **comparison** n. way of comparing 比较；对照：Sales are down in comparison with last year. 与去年相比，销售额下降了。There is no comparison between overseas and home sales. = Overseas and home sales are so different they cannot be compared. 国内销售额与国外销售额无法相比。

**compensate** v. to pay for damage done (损坏) 赔偿；补偿：to compensate a manager for loss of commission 补偿经理的佣金损失

NOTE: you compensate someone for something

◇ **compensation** n. (a) compensation for damage = payment for damage done 赔偿金；补偿金：compensation for loss of office = payment to a director who is asked to leave a company before his contract ends 职位丢失补偿金 compensation for loss of earnings = payment to someone who has stopped earning money or who is not able to earn money(失业和退休的)救济金 (b) US salary(美)薪水(金)：salary compensation package = salary, pension and other benefits offered with a job 薪水一揽子津贴(退休金和其它与工作有关的津贴)

**compete** v. to compete with someone or with a company = to try to do better than another person or another company 竞争：We have to compete with cheap imports from the Far East. 我们必须与来自远东的廉价进口货相竞争。They were competing unsuccessfully with local companies on their home territory 在国内他们竞争不过一些地方公司。The two companies are competing for a market share or for a contract. = Each company is trying to win a larger part of the market or to win the contract. 为获得更大市场份额或赢得合同两公司正在展开竞争。

◇ **competing** a. which competes 竞争的：competing firms = firms which compete with each other 相互竞争的公司，competing products = products from different companies which have the same use andare sold in the same markets at similar prices 竞争产品

◇ **competition** n. (a) trying to do better than another supplier 竞争：free competition = being free to compete without government interference 自由竞争；keen competition = strong competition 剧烈竞争；We are facing keen competition from European manufacturers. 我们正面临着来自欧洲制造商的剧烈竞争。(b) the competition = companies which are trying to compete with your product(与你产品进行)竞争的公司：We have lowered our prices to beat the competition. 我们降低了产品价格，以战胜与其竞争的公司。The competition have brought out a new range of products.竞争者(公司)已经推出一系列的新型产品。

NOTE: singular, but can take a plural verb

◇ **competitive** a. which competes fairly 有竞争性的：competitive price = low price aimed to compete with a rival product 有竞争性价格；competitive pricing =putting low prices on goods so as to compete with other products 竞争性定价；competitive products = products made to compete with existing products 竞争性产品

◇ **competitively** ad. competitively priced = sold at a low price which competes with the price of similarproducts from other companies 竞争性定价

◇ **competitiveness** n. being competitive 竞争性

NOTE: no plural

◇ **competitor** n. person or company which competes 竞争者；竞争对手：Two German firms are our main competitors. 两家德国公司是我们的主要竞争对手。

**competence or competency** n. The case falls within the competence of the court. = The court is legally able to deal with the case. 法院有权受理该诉讼件。

◇ **competent** a. (a) able to do something or efficient 有能力的；胜任的：She is a competent secretary or a competent manager 她是一位能干的(称职的)秘书或经理。(b) The court is not competent to deal with this case. = The court is not legally able to deal with the case. 该法院无权受理这桩案件。

**complain** v. to say that something is no good or does not work properly 埋怨；抱怨：The office is so cold the staff have started complaining. 办公室是如此寒冷,难怪工作人员开始发牢骚。She complained about the service. 他对服务不满意。They are complaining that our prices are too high. 他们正在抱怨我们要价太高。If you want to complain, write to the manager. 如果你要投诉,则写信给经理。

◇ **complaint** n. statement that you feel something is wrong 抱怨；申诉：

When making a complaint, always quote the reference number. 当投诉时,一定引用有关数码。She sent her letter of complaint to the managing director. 她将投诉信寄给总经理。to make or lodge a complaint against someone = ᴛo write and send an official complaint to someone's superior 控告…某人；complaints department = department which deals with complaints from customers(处理)投诉部门；complaints procedure = agreed way for workers to make complaints to the managementabout working conditions 投诉程序

**complete** 1. a. whole or with nothing missing 完全的；完整的：The order is complete and ready for sending. 订货已完备正待寄发。The order should be delivered only if it is complete. 只有在订货完备时才可交付。2. v. to finish 完成：The factory completed the order in two weeks.工厂在两周之内完成这批订货。How long will it take you to complete the job? 你完成这项工作需要多久?

◇ **completely** ad. all or totally 完整地；全部地：The cargo was completely ruined by water. 这批货完全被水毁坏了。The warehouse was completely destroyed by fire. 仓库被大火全部烧毁。

◇ **completion** n. act of finishing something 完成；结束：completion date = date when something will be finished 完工日期；completion of a contract = signing of a contract for the sale of a property when the buyer pays and the seller passes ownership to the buyer 买卖合同全部履行

**complex** 1. n. series of large buildings 建筑群体；综合体；综合物；a large industrial complex 大型工业建筑群体

NOTE: plural is complexes

2. a. with many different parts 综合的；复杂的：a complex system of import controls复杂的进口管制制度；The

specifications for the machine are very complex. 该机器的说明书很复杂。

**complimentary** a. complimentary ticket = free ticket, given as a present 免费票；赠票(券)

◇ **compliments slip** n. piece of paper with the name of the company printed on it, sent with documents or gifts, etc. instead of a letter 礼帖；问候便条

**comply** v. to comply with a court order = to obey an order given by a court 依从法院命令

◇ **compliance** n. agreement to do what is ordered 依从；遵守
NOTE: no plural

**component** n. piece of machinery or section which will be put into a final product(机器)部件；成分；组成部分：The assembly line stopped because supply of a component was delayed. 由于某一构件供应的延误，装配线已停工。components factory = factory which makes parts which are used in other factories to make finished products 配件厂

**composition** n. agreement between a debtor and creditors to settle a debt by repaying only part of it 债务和解协议（借贷双方之间在清偿债务问题上，仅偿还部分欠款而了结债务的协议）

**compound** 1. a. compound interest = interest which is added to the capital and then earns interest itself 复利 2. v. to agree with creditors to settle a debt by paying part of what is owed 和解了结债务

**comprehensive** a. which includes everything 综合的；全面的；广泛的：comprehensive insurance = insurance policy which covers you against all risks which are likely to happen 综合保险

**compromise** 1. n. agreement between two sides, where each side gives way a little 妥协；和解：Management offered £5 an hour, the union asked for £9,

and acompromise of £7.50 was reached. 管理部门（资方）同意一小时支付 5 英磅，而工会则要求每小时支付 9 英磅，双方折衷为支付 7.5 英磅。2. v. to reach an agreement by giving way a little 妥协；让步：He asked £15 for it, I offered £7 and we compromised on £10. 他要 15 英磅，而我给价 7 英磅，最后我们相互作了让步支付 10 英磅。

**comptometer** n. machine which counts automatically 自动计量机

**comptroller** n. financial controller 审计员；主管会计

**compulsory** a. which is forced or ordered 强迫的；强制的：compulsory liquidation = liquidation which is ordered by a court 强制性清算

**compute** v. to calculate or to do calculations 计算

◇ **computable** a. which can be calculated 可计算出来的

◇ **computation** n. calculation 计算

◇ **computational** a. computational error = mistake made in calculating 计算上的错误

◇ **computer** n. electronic machine which calculates or stores information andprocesses it automatically 电子计算机；电脑：computer bureau = office which offers to do work on its computers for companies which do not have their own computers 计算机所；computer department = department in a company which manages the company's computers 公司的计算机部；computer error = mistake made by a computer 计算机的错误；computer file = section of information on a computer (such as the payroll, list of addresses, customer accounts)计算机数据存储；计算机文件；computer language = system of signs, letters and words used to instruct a computer 计算机语言；computer listing = printout of a list of items taken from data stored in acomputer 计算机打印输出表; computer manager = person in charge of a computer department 计算机部管理人员;计算机部负责人; computer program = instructions to a computer, telling it to do a particular piece of work 计算机程序; computer programmer = person who writes computer programs 计算机程序编制人员; computer services = work using a computer, done by a computer bureau 计算机服务; computer time = time when a computer is being used (paid for at an hourlyrate)(按小时付费的 )计算机上机时间: Running all those sales reports costs a lot in computer time. 制做所有销售报告耗费许多计算机上机的时间。business computer = powerful small computer which is programmed for special business uses 商用计算机; personal computer or home computer = small computer which can be used in the home 个人或家用计算机(电脑)

◇ **computerize** v. to change from a manual system to one using computers 电脑化;用电脑管理: Our stock control has been completely computerized. 我们存货控制系统已经全部电脑化了。

◇ **computerized** a. worked by computers 电脑化的: a computerized invoicing system 电脑化化开发票系统

◇ **computer - readable** a. which can be read and understood by a computer 计算机认读的 computer - readable codes 计算机认读代码

◇ **computing** n. referring to computers 计算;演算; computing speed = speed at which a computer calculates 计算机计算速度

**con** 1. n. informal trick done to try to get money from someone 骗钱把戏: Trying to get us to pay him for ten hours' overtime was just a con. 企图让我们支付给他十小时的加班费是一种

骗局。2. v. infml. to trick someone to try to get money 骗钱: They conned the bank into lending them £25,000 with no security. 他们没有任何保证金情况下骗取银行给他们 25,000 英磅贷款。He conned the finance company out of £100,000. 他骗走了金融公司 100,000 英磅。

NOTE: con - conning - conned

**concealment** n. hiding for criminal purposes 隐藏;隐瞒(指犯罪): concealment of assets = hiding assets so that creditors do not know they exist 隐瞒资产

**concern** 1 n. (a) business or company 公司;企业;康采恩: His business is a going concern. = The company is working (and making a profit). 他的企业办得蒸蒸日上的公司。sold as a going concern = sold as an actively trading company 作为一个正常营业的企业被出售 (b) being worried about a problem 关心;关怀;牵挂: The management showed no concern at all for the workers' safety. 管理部门完全不关心工人的安全。2. v. to deal with or to be connected with 涉及;与…有关系: The sales staff are not concerned with the cleaning of the store. 销售人员不用管商店的卫生清洁工作。He filled in a questionnaire concerning computer utilization. 他已填写了一张有关计算机利用的征求意见表。

**concession** n. (a) right to use someone else's property for business purposes 核准;许可(权): mining concession = right to dig a mine on a piece of land 矿山开采权 (b) right to be the only seller of a product in a place 独家销售特许权: She runs a jewellery concession in a department store. 她获得了在一家百货商店独家经营珠宝买卖的特许权。(c) allowance tax concession = allowing less tax to be paid 允许税收减让

◇ **concessionnaire** n. person who has

the right to be the only seller of a productina place 独家经营者;特许权获得者:(尤指获准在某地的一种产品的销售权)

◇ **concessionary** a. concessionary fare = reduced fare for certain types of passenger (such as employees of the transport company)优惠性交通费

**conciliation** n. bringing together the parties in a dispute so that the dispute can be settled 调解;和解

**conclude** v. (a) to complete successfully 结束;完毕: to conclude an agreement with someone 与某人达成一项协议 (b) to believe from evidence 推论;断定: The police concluded that the thief had got into the building through the main entrance.警方断定小偷通过主要的入口处进入了这座大楼.

**condition** n. (a) term of a contract or duties which have to be carried out as part of a contract or something which has to be agreed before a contract becomes valid 条款;条件: conditions of employment or conditions of service = terms of a contract of employment 雇用条款或服务条件; conditions of sale = agreed ways in which a sale takes place (such as discounts or credit terms)销售条件; on condition that = provided that 在…条件下;如果: They were granted the lease on condition that they paid the legal costs.在他们支付诉讼费用条件下,同意他们这项租赁. (b) general state 状况;状态: The union has complained of the bad working conditions in the factory.工会对工厂中的恶劣的工作状况表示不满. Item sold in good condition. 销售正品。What was the condition of the car when it was sold? 这辆小汽车被出售时,其状态如何? adverse trading conditions 不利的经营状况

◇ **conditional** a. provided that certain things take place 有条件的;视…而定的: to give a conditional acceptance = to accept, provided that certain things happen or certain terms apply 给予一个有条件的承兑; The offer is conditional on the board's acceptance. = provided the board accepts.这项提议以董事会接受为条件。He made a conditional offer. = He offered to buy, provided that certain terms applied.他发出一项有条件的要约。

**condominium** n. US system of ownership, where a person owns an apartment in abuilding, together with a share of the land, stairs, roof, etc. (美)公寓私有共有制(对一幢建筑物拥有一套公寓并享有土地、楼梯、屋顶等)

**conduct** v. to carry on 处理;指导: to conduct negotiations 进行谈判; The chairman conducted the negotiations very efficiently.董事长主持的谈判卓有成效。

**conference** n. (a) meeting of people to discuss problems 会议;讨论会: to be in conference = to be in a meeting 在开会中; conference phone = telephone so arranged that several people can speak into it from around a table 电话会议; conference room = room where small meetings can take place 会议室; press conference = meeting where newspaper and TV reporters are invited to hear news of a new product or a takeover bid, etc.新闻发布会;记者招待会; sales conference = meeting of sales managers, representatives, publicity staff, etc., to discuss future sales plans 销售会议 (b) meeting of an association or a society or a union(协会、联合会等召开的)会议: the annual conference of the Electricians' Union 电工协会年会; the conference of the Booksellers' Association 书商协会会议; The conference agenda or the agenda of the conference was drawn up by the secretary.会议的议事日程是由秘书草

拟的。Trades Union Conference (TUC) = association of British trade unions (英)工会联盟

**confidence** n. (a) feeling sure or being certain 自信；信心；信任：The sales teams do not have much confidence in their manager. 销售组对他们的经理缺乏信心。The board has total confidence in the managing director. 董事会对总经理完全信任。(b) in confidence = in secret 私下；秘密地：I will show you the report in confidence. 私下我将给你看该报告。

◇ **confidence trick** n. business deal where someone gains another person's confidence and then tricks him(信任)骗局；欺诈

◇ **confidence trickster** n. person who carries out a confidence trick on someone 骗子；玩骗局的人

◇ **confident** a. certain or sure 确信的；有自信心的：I am confident the turnover will increase rapidly. 我确信营业额将会迅速增加。Are you confident the sales team is capable of handling this product? 你对销售组经销这项产品有信心吗？

◇ **confidential** a. secret or not to be told or shown to other people 秘密的；机密的：He sent a confidential report to the chairman. 他向主席递交了一份机密报告。Please mark the letter "Private and Confidential". 请在函件上注明"私人和机密"字样。

◇ **confidentiality** n. being secret 秘密性；机密性：He broke the confidentiality of the discussions. = He told someone about the secret discussions. 他泄露了讨论的机密。

**confirm** v. to say that something is certain 证实；确认：to confirm a hotel reservation or a ticket or an agreement or a booking 确认旅馆订房订票或批准协议或证实预订；to confirm someone in a job = to say that someone is now permanently in the job 确认某人工作更永久性

◇ **confirmation** n. (a) being certain 确认；确定：confirmation of a booking = checking that a booking is certain 证实预订 (b) document which confirms something 批准书；确认书：He received confirmation from the bank that the deeds had been deposited. 他从银行接到了契约已被寄存的确认书。

**conflict** n. conflict of interest = situation where a person may profit personally from decisions which he takes in his official capacity 利益冲突

**confuse** v. to make it difficult for someone to understand something or to make something difficult 混淆；使混乱：The chairman was confused by all the journalists' questions. 主席被所有新闻工作者的提问弄胡涂了。To introduce the problem of VAT will only confuse the issue. 引进增值税的问题只能给问题造成混乱。

**conglomerate** n. group of subsidiary companies linked together and forming a group making very different types of products 企业集团；多种行业的联合大企业(经营不同类型产品的大公司)

**congratulate** v. to give someone your good wishes for having done something well 祝贺；道贺：The sales director congratulated the salesmen on doubling sales. 销售部主任祝贺销售人员将销售额翻了一翻。I want to congratulate you on your promotion. 我祝贺你晋升。

◇ **congratulations** pl. n. good wishes 祝贺；贺词：The staff sent him their congratulations on his promotion. 工作人员送去对他晋升的贺信。

**conman** n. informal = CONFIDENCE TRICKSTER 骗子
NOTE: plural is conmen

**connect** v. (a) to link or to join 连接；

联系：The company is connected to the governmentbecause the chairman's father is a minister. 该公司与政府有联系，因为董事长的父亲是一位部长。(b) The flight from New York connects with a flight to Athens. = The plane from New York arrives in time for passengers to catch the plane to Athens. 本次从纽约起飞的航班与飞往雅典的航班相接。

◇ **connecting flight** n. plane which a passenger will be on time to catch and which will take him to his final destination 中转航班飞机(旅客及时赶上一架班机到达目的地)：Check at the helicopter desk for connecting flights to the city centre. 在直升飞机工作台核对一下去市中心的中转航班。

◇ **connection** n. (a) link or something which joins 连接；联系：Is there a connection between his argument with the director and his sudden move to become warehouse manager? 他与主任的争论和他突然调任仓库管理员两者之间有什么联系吗? in connection with = referring to 涉及；关于：I want to speak to the managing director in connection with the sales forecasts. 我想与总经理谈谈关于销售额预测。(b) connections = people you know or customers or contacts 人事关系(顾客或有联系的客户)：He has useful connections in industry. 他在工业界有用得着的关系(户)。

**conservative** a. careful or not overestimating 保守的；谨慎的：a conservative estimate of sales 一项保守的销售估算；His forecast of expenditure is very conservative. 他所做的支出预测非常保守。at a conservative estimate = calculation which probably underestimates the final figure 按保守的估计：Their turnover has risen by at least 20% in the last year, and that is probably a conservative estimate. 去年，他们的营业额至少

上升20%，恐怕这可能是一个保守的估计。

◇ **conservatively** ad. not overestimating 保守地：The total sales are conservatively estimated at £2.3m. 总销售是2.3万英磅，这是个保守的估算。

**consider** v. to think seriously about something 考虑：to consider the terms of a contract = to examine and discuss if the terms are acceptable 考虑合同的条款

◇ **consideration** n. (a) serious thought 考虑：We are giving consideration to moving the head office to Scotland. 我们正考虑将总公司迁到苏格兰。(b) something valuable exchanged as part of a contract 对价(作为合同的一部分，用来交换有价值的东西)：for a small consideration = for a small fee or payment 为了一点微薄的对价
NOTE: no plural for (a)

**considerable** a. quite large 很大的；相当大的：We sell considerable quantities of our products to Africa. 我们的产品大量销往非洲。They lost a considerable amount of money on the commodity market. 他们在商品市场上损失了一大笔钱。

◇ **considerably** ad. quite a lot 相当大地；Sales are considerably higher than they were last year. 销售额比去年的要高得多。

**consign** v. to consign goods to someone = to send goods to someone for him to use or to sell for you(把货物交付给某人出售或使用)寄售

◇ **consignation** n. act of consigning 委托；寄售

◇ **consignee** n. person who receives goods from someone for his own use or to sell for the sender 受托人；承销人；收货人

◇ **consignment** n. (a) sending of goods to someone who will sell them for you 托付；寄售：consignment note = notesaying that goods have been sent 寄售通知书；goods on consignment = goods kept for another company to be sold on their behalf for a commission 寄售货物（b）group of goods sent for sale 寄售品；A consignment of goods has arrived. 一批寄售货物已经到达。We are expecting a consignment of cars from Japan. 我们正期待着来自日本的一批寄售小汽车。

◇ **consignor** n. person who consigns goods to someone 寄售人；发货人；委托人

**consist of** v. to be formed of 由 … 组成：The trade mission consists of the sales directors of ten major companies. 该贸易代表团由十家大公司的销售经理组成。The package tour consists of air travel, six nights in a luxury hotel, all meals and visits to places of interest 旅行社代办的一揽子旅游，包括空中旅行、在豪华大饭店住六夜、包餐和参观名胜。

**consolidate** v. （a）to put the accounts of several subsidiary companies into the accounts of the main group(将小公司或附属公司的帐户)合并；联合；（b）to group goods together for shipping 集中；聚集(装运)

◇ **consolidation** n. grouping together of goods for shipping 集中(装船)

◇ **consolidated** a. （a）consolidated accounts = accounts of subsidiary companies grouped together into theaccounts of the parent company 合并(子公司)帐户（b）consolidated shipment = goods from different companies grouped together into a singleshipment 集中装船

**consols** pl. n. GB government bonds which pay an interest but do not have a maturity date(英)政府债券(英国政府发行的一种债券,支付利息但无偿还日期)

**consortium** n. group of companies which work together 联营企业；(国际)财团：a consortium of Canadian companies or a Canadian consortium 一个加拿大联营公司；A consortium of French and British companies is planning to construct the new aircraft. 英法联营飞机公司正计划造新型飞机。

**constitution** n. written rules or regulations of a society or association or club or state 章程；宪法：Under the society's constitution, the chairman is elected for a two-year period. 协会的章程规定,当选的主席任期为两年。Payments to officers of the association are not allowed by the constitution. 依据章程,不允许付款给协会官员。

◇ **constitutional** a. according to a constitution 符合宪法的；宪法的：The reelection of the chairman is not constitutional. 主席连任是不符合宪法的。

**construct** v. to build 建造：The company has tendered for the contract to construct the new airport. 该公司已对承建新机场的合同投了标。

◇ **construction** n. building 建造：construction company = company which specializes in building 建筑公司；under construction = being built 正在施工：The airport is under construction. 该机场正在施工。

◇ **constructive** a. which helps in the making of something 建设性的：She made some constructive suggestions for improving management - worker relations. 她对改善劳资双方关系提出了一些有建设性的建议。We had a constructive proposal from a distribution company in Italy. 一家意大利的销售公司向我们提出了一项建设性建议。constructive dismissal = situation when a worker leaves his job voluntarily but because of pressure from the management 推定性解雇

◇ **constructor** n. person or company which constructs 建造者；营造商

**consult** v. to ask an expert for advice 请教；咨询：He consulted his accountant about his tax. 关于税款,他请教了他的会计。

◇ **consultancy** n. act of giving specialist advice 提供咨询；咨询公司：a consultancy firm 咨询公司：He offers a consultancy service. 他提供咨询服务。

◇ **consultant** n. specialist who gives advice 顾问：engineering consultant 工程顾问；management consultant 管理顾问；tax consultant 税收顾问

◇ **consulting** a. person who gives specialist advice 顾问的；咨询的：consulting engineer 咨询工程师

**consumable** a. consumable goods = goods which are bought by members of the public and not by companies 消费品

◇ **consumables** pl. n. = CONSUMABLE GOODS 消费品

◇ **consumer** n. person or company which buys and uses goods and services 用户；消费者：Gas consumers are protesting at the increase in prices. 煤气用户正竭力反对煤气涨价。The factory is a heavy consumer of water. 该厂为耗水大户。consumer council = group representing the interests of consumers 消费者协会；consumer credit = credit given by shops, banks and other financial institutions to consumers so that they can buy goods 消费者信贷；consumer durables = items such as washing machines or refrigerators or cookers which are bought and used by the public 耐用消费品(如家用电器)；consumer goods = goods bought by consumers or by members of the public 消费品；consumer panel = group of consumers who report on products they have used so that the manufacturers can improve them or

use what the panel says about them in advertising 消费者反馈研究小组 US consumer price index = index showing how prices of consumer goods have risen over aperiod of time, used as a way of measuring inflation and the cost of living (美)消费品价格指数；consumer protection = protecting consumers against unfair or illegal traders 消费者的保护；consumer research = research into why consumers buy goods and what goods theyreally want to buy 消费者研究；consumer resistance = lack of interest by consumers in buying a product 消费者反感；消费阻力：The latest price increases have produced considerable consumer resistance. 最近的价格上涨已经引起了相当大的消费阻力。consumer society = type of society where consumers are encouraged to buy goods 消费者社会；consumer spending = spending by consumers 消费者开销

**consumption** n. buying or using goods or services 消费(量)；消耗：a car with low petrol consumption 耗油量低的小汽车；The factory has a heavy consumption of coal. 该厂为耗煤大户。home consumption or domestic consumption = use of something in the home 国内消费
NOTE: no plural

**contact** 1. n. (a) person you know or person you can ask for help or advice 熟人：He has many contacts in the city. 在本市他有很多熟人？Who is your contact in the ministry? 部里谁是你的熟人？(b) act of getting in touch with someone 接触；联系：I have lost contact with them. = I do not communicate with them any longer. 我已经和他们失去了联系。He put me in contact with a good lawyer. = He told me how to get in touch with a good lawyer. 他让我与一个好律师取得联系。
NOTE: no plural for (b)
2. v. to get in touch with someone or to

communicate with someone 接触；联系：
He tried to contact his office by phone. 他
试图打电话与他的公司取得联系。
Can you contact the managing director at
his club? 你能和在俱乐部的总经理取
得联系吗？

**contain** v. to hold something inside 容
纳；包含：Each crate contains two computers and their peripherals. 每个板条箱
内装有两台计算机及其辅助设备。A
barrel contains 250 litres. 一桶盛 250
升。We have lost a file containing important documents. 我们丢失了一个装
有重要文件的文件夹。

◇ **container** n. (a) box or bottle or
can, etc. which can hold goods 容器（如
盒、瓶、桶等）：The gas is shipped in
strong metal containers. 这种气体用坚
固的金属容器装运。The container
burst during shipping. 该容器在运输期
间爆烈。(b) very large metal case of a
standard size for loading and transporting
goods on trucks, trains and ships 集 装 箱
container ship 集 装 箱 船；container
berth；集装箱船泊位；container port 集
装箱港口；container terminal 集装箱码
头；to ship goods in containers 用集装箱
运货；a container – load of spare parts
= a shipment of spare parts sent in a
container 用集装箱运的备件

◇ **containerization** n. putting into
containers；shipping in containers 集装
箱化；集装箱运输

◇ **containerize** v. to put goods into
containers；to ship goods in containers 用
集装箱发运；使集装箱化

**contango** n. payment of interest by a
stockbroker for carrying payment for
shares from one account day to the next
交易延期费；延期交割费：contango day
= day when the rate of contango payments is fixed 升水日；转期日；交易延
期费结算日

**content** n. the ideas inside a letter, etc.

内容：the content of the letter = the real meaning of the letter 信件内容

◇ **contents** pl. n. things contained or
what is inside something 所容之物：The
contents of the bottle poured out onto the
floor. 瓶中所装之物倾倒在地上。
The customs officials inspected the contents of the crate. 海关官员检查了板
条箱内的东西。the contents of the letter = the words written in the letter 信
中的词语

**contested takeover** n. takeover where
the board of the company do not recommend it to the shareholders and try to
fight it 有异义的兼并；角逐兼并（公司
的董事会不向其股东提议，而企图为之
奋斗）

**contingency** n. possible state of emergency when decisions will have to be tak-
en quickly 紧急情况；突发性：contin-
gency fund or contingency reserve =
money set aside in case it is needed urgently 应急费用或应急储备金；contin-
gency plans = plans which will be put
into action if something happens which no
one expects 应急（方案）措施；to add on
10% to provide for contingencies = to
provide for further expenditure which
may be incurred 追加 10% 的应急费供
突发事件之用；We have built 10% for
contingencies into our cost forecast. 我们
将 10% 的应急费用计入了成本预测。

◇ **contingent** a. (a) contingent expenses = expenses which will be incurred only if something happens 意外费
用；或有费用 (b) contingent policy =
policy which pays out only if something
happens (as if the person named in the
policy dies before the person due to
benefit) 意外保险单（当某种意外事情
发生，如在某人可得保险赔偿费之前死
去，而交付款项的保险单）

**continue** v. to go on doing something or
to do something which you were doing

earlier 恢复；继续：The chairman continuedspeaking in spite of the noise from the shareholders. 尽管股东们喧哗不止，董事长照讲不误。The meeting started at 10 a. m. and continued until six p. m.. 会议从上午十点一直开到下午六点。Negotiations will continue next Monday. 谈判将于下星期一继续进行。

◇ **continual** a. which happens again and again 不断的；频繁的：Production was slow because of continual breakdowns. 由于不断的发生故障，生产进展缓慢。

◇ **continually** ad. again and again 不断地；频繁地：The photocopier is continually breaking down. 这台复印机不停地出现故障。

◇ **continuation** n. act of continuing 继续；频繁

◇ **continuous** a. with no end or with no breaks 继续的；持续的；频繁的；continuous production line 流水作业生产线；连续生产线；continuous feed = device which feeds continuous stationery into a printer 电脑里连续填纸的装置；continuous stationery = paper made as one long sheet, used in the computer printers 很长不分开的打印纸(电脑用)

**contra** 1. n. contra account = account which offsets another account 抵销帐户；对销帐户；contra entry = entry made in the opposite side of an account to make an earlier entry worthless (i. e. a debit against a credit)对销分录；对销帐项；per contra or as per contra = words showing that a contra entry has been made 在另一方的；对应的 2. v. to contra an entry = to enter a similar amount in the opposite side of an account 对销分录；对销帐项

**contraband** n. contraband (goods) = goods brought into a country illegally, without paying customs duty 走私货；违禁品

**contract** 1. n. (a) legal agreement between two parties 合同；契约：to draw up a contract 草拟一项合同；to draft a contract 起草一项合同；to sign a contract 签署一项合同；The contract is binding on both parties. = Both parties signing the contract must do what is agreed. 双方均受合同的约束。under contract = bound by the terms of a contract 受合同约束的：The firm is under contract to deliver the goods by November. 公司必须履行合同于 11 月份交货。to void a contract = to make a contract invalid 使合同无效；contract of employment = contract between management and employee showing all conditions of work 雇用合同；招聘合同；service contract = contract between a company and a director showing all conditions of work 服务合同；exchange of contracts = point in the sale of a property when the buyer and seller both sign the contract of sale which then becomes binding 交换买卖合同

(b) contract law or law of contract = laws relating to agreements 合同法；by private contract = by private legal agreement 私人合同(协议)；contract note = note showing that shares have been bought or sold but not yet paid for 股票买卖合同通知 (c) agreement for supply of a service or goods 供应协议：contract for the supply of spare parts 供应备件的协议；to enter into acontract to supply spare parts 达成供应备件的协议；to sign a contract for £10,000worth of spare parts 签署一项价值 10,000 英磅的备件的协议；to put work out to contract = to decide that work should be done by another company on a contract, rather than employing members of staff to do it 包出去；让人承包；to award a contract to a company or to place a contract with a company = to decide that a company shall have the contract to do workfor you 将合同授于一个公司; to tender for a contract = to put forward an estimate of cost for work under contract 为获得合同投标; conditions of contract or contract conditions 合同的条件; breach of contract = breaking the terms of a contract 违反合同;违约; The company is in breach of contract. = The company has failed to do what was agreed in the contract. 公司不履行合同。contract work = work done according to a written agreement 承包工作 2. v. to agree to do some work by contract 订合同(包工): to contract to supply spare parts or to contract for the supply of spare parts 签订供应备件的合同; The supply of spare parts was contracted out to Smith Ltd. = Smith Ltd was given the contract for supplying spare parts. 备件的供应合同给史密斯有限公司。to contract out of an agreement = to withdraw from an agreement with written permission of the other party(经过对方书面同意)退出协议;收回协议;

◇ **contracting** a. contracting party = person or company which signs a contract 合同的当事人;缔约方

◇ **contractor** n. person or company which does work according to a written agreement 订约人;承包商: haulage contractor = company which transports goods by contract 运货承包商; government contractor = company which supplies the government with goods by contract(负责向政府供应的)承包商

◇ **contractual** a. according to a contract 根据合同的: contractual liability = legal responsibility for something as stated in a contract 合同规定的义务; to fulfill your contractual obligations = to do what you have agreed to do in a contract 履行你的合同义务; He is under no contractual obligation to buy. = He has signed no agreement to buy. 他没有购买(商品)的合同义务。

◇ **contractually** ad. according to a contract 根据合同地: The company is contractually bound to pay his expenses. 根据合同由公司支付他的费用。

**contrary** n. opposite 相反; 对立面: failing instructions to the contrary = unless different instructions are given 若无相反的指示; on the contrary = quite the opposite 相反地: The chairman not annoyed with his assistant – on the contrary, he promoted him. 董事长没被其助手所恼怒,相反还提升了他的职务。

**contribute** v. to give money or to add to money 缴款;捐款;捐助: to contribute 10% of the profits 捐10%的利润; He contributed to the pension fund for 10 years. 他向退休基金会缴款已达10年之久。

◇ **contribution** n. money paid to add to a sum 缴款;捐款: contribution of capital = money paid to a company as additional capital 缴入资本; employer's contribution = money paid by an employer towards a worker's pension(雇主给工人付的)养老金; National Insurance contributions = money paid each month by a worker and the company to the National Insurance 国民保险缴款; pension contributions = money paid by a company or worker into a pension fund 养老金缴款

◇ **contributor** n. contributor of capital = person who contributes capital 缴入资本者

◇ **contributory** a. (a) contributory pension plan or scheme = pension plan where the employee has to contribute a percentage of salary 分担退休金缴款计划 (b) which helps to cause 使起作用的: Falling exchange rates have been a contributory factor in or to the company's loss of profits. 汇率的持续下降一直是

公司利润损失的一个因素。

**con trick** n. informal = CONFI-
DENCE TRICK 骗局

**control** 1. n. (a) power or being able
to direct something 控制;管理: The
company is under the control of three
shareholders.该公司受控于三家股东。
The family lost control of its business. 该
家族控制不住其企业。to gain control
of a business = to buy more than 50%
of the shares so that you can direct the
business 获得对一个企业的控制能力;
to lose control of a business = to find
that you have less than 50% of the
shares in a company, and so are not
longer able to direct it 失去对一个企业
的控制能力(b) restricting or checking
something or making sure that something
is kept in check 控制;查验: under control = kept in check 处于控制之下;
Expenses are kept under tight control. 开
支受到严格控制。The company is try-
ing to bring its overheads back under
control.公司正努力使其经常性管理费
用再次得以控制。out of control = not
kept in check 失去控制;不受控制;
Costs have got out of control. 成本已经
失控。budgetary control = keeping
check on spending 预算控制; credit
control = checking that customers pay
on time and do not exceed their credit
limits 信贷控制; quality control =
making sure that the quality of a product
is good 质量检查; stock control = making sure that movements of stock are noted 存贷控制;库存品控制(c) exchange
controls = government restrictions on
changing the local currency into foreign
currency 外汇控制;外汇管制: The
government has imposed exchange
controls. 政府对外汇实行管制。They
say the government is going to lift exchange controls. 他们说政府打算取消
外汇管制。price controls = legal measures to prevent prices rising too fast 价

格控制;物价管制(d) control group =
small group which is used to check a
sample group 样品检查小组; control
systems = systems used to check that a
computer system is working correctly(计
算机)控制系统 2. v. (a) to control a
business = to direct a business 控制某
企业; The business is controlled by a
company based in Luxemburg.该企业由
一家总部设在卢森堡的公司控制。
The company is controlled by the majority shareholder.该公司被占多数的股东
的控制。(b) to make sure that something is kept in check or is not allowedto
develop 控制;抑制: The government is
fighting to control inflation or to control
the rise in the cost of living. 政府正在为
抑制通货膨胀或控制生活费用的上涨
而斗争。

NOTE: controlling - controlled

◇ **controlled** a. ruled or kept in check
抑制的;受到控制的: government -
controlled = ruled by a government 受
政府控制的; controlled economy = e-
conomy where the most business activity
is directed by orders from the government 受控制的经济

◇ **controller** n. (a) person who controls (especially the finances of a
company)控制人;监督人(特别是控制
公司财务的人); stock controller =
person who notes movements of stock 库
存品管理员(b) US chief accountant in
a company(美)公司的总会计师

◇ **controlling** a. to have a controlling
interest in a company = to own more
than 50% of the shares so that you can
direct how the company is run 在公司中
拥有控制权(益)

**convene** v. to ask people to come together 召集: to convene a meeting of
shareholders 召集股东开会。

**convenience** n. at your earliest convenience = as soon as you find it possible

方便的时候请尽早: convenience foods = food which is prepared by the shop before it is sold, so that it needs only heating to be made ready to eat 方便食品; ship sailing under a flag of convenience = flying the flag of a country which may have no ships of its own but allows ships of other countries to be registered in itsports 挂它国国旗航行的船只

◇ **convenient** a. suitable or handy 合适的;方便的: A bank draft is a convenient way of sending money abroad. 银行汇票是一种向国外汇款的方便方法。Is 9.30 a convenient time for the meeting? 9 点 30 分是开会(或会面)的合适时间吗?

**convenor** n. trade unionist who organizes union meetings 组织工会会议的工会会员

**conversion** n. change 改变;转换 (a) conversion of funds = using money which does not belong to you for a purpose for which it is not supposed to be used 挪用资金 (b) conversion price or conversion rate = rate at which a currency is changed into a foreign currency; price at which preference shares are converted into ordinary shares 兑换价或换算率

◇ **convert** v. to change money of one country for money of another 兑换(将一国币换或另一国货币): We converted our pounds into Swiss francs. 我们将英镑兑换成瑞士法郎。to convert funds to one's own use = to use someone else's money for yourself 挪用他人的钱

◇ **convertibility** n. ability to exchange one currency for another easily 可兑换性(能容易地将一种货币转换成另一种货币的能力)

◇ **convertible** a. convertible currency = currency which can be exchanged for another easily 可兑换货币;自由外汇: convertible loan stock = stock which can be exchanged for shares at a later date 可转换的借贷债券

**conveyance** n. legal document which transfers a property from the seller to the buyer 财产转让证书(将财产权从卖方转让给买方的法律文件)

◇ **conveyancer** n. person who draws up a conveyance 起草财产权转让证书的人

◇ **conveyancing** n. legally transferring a property from a seller to a buyer 将财产权由卖方转让与买方; do－it－yourself conveyancing = drawing up a legal conveyance without the help of a lawyer 自己起草财产权转让证书

**cooling off** n. cooling off period = during an industrial dispute, a period when negotiations have to be carried on and no action can be taken by either side; period when a person is allowed to think about something which he has agreed to buy on hire－purchase and possibly change his mind 争执双方的冷静期(对是否最终同意分期付款租购的思考的一段时间)或劳资争执双方冷静下来使谈判得以进行的冷却时间

**co－op** n. = CO－OPERATIVE 2

◇ **co－operate** v. to work together 合作: The governments are co－operating in the fight against piracy. 政府间进行合作与专利侵权行为进行计争。The two firms have co－operated on the computer project. 这两家公司在计算机项目上进行了合作。

◇ **co－operation** n. working together 合作: The project was completed ahead of schedule with the co－operation of the workforce. 在工人们的合作下项目提前完成。

◇ **co－operative** 1. a. willing to work together 顾意合作的: The workforce has not been co－operative over the management's productivity plan. 工人们没有在管理人员所制定的提高生产率

的计划上进行合作。co - operative society= society where the customers and workers are partners and share the profits 商业合作社 2. n. business run by a group of workers who are the owners and who share the profits 合作社(由工人经营,工人既是业主义又是共同分享利润者); agricultural co - operative 农业合作社; to set up a workers' co - operative 成立一个工人合作社

**co - opt** v. to co - opt someone onto a committee = to ask someone to join a committee without being elected 吸收(或指定)某人参加委员会

**co - owner** n. person who owns something with another person 共同所有者;与别人共同拥有某物的人: The two sisters are co - owners of the property. 这对姐妹是该财产的共同所有人。

◇ **co - ownership** n. arrangement where partners or workers have shares in a company 共同所有权;共有权(合伙人或工作人员在公司中拥有股份的一种协定)

**copartner** n. person who is a partner in a business with another person 合作者;合伙人

◇ **copartnership** n. arrangement where partners or workers have shares in the company 合作;合伙

**cope** v. to manage to do something 应付;对付: The new assistant manager coped very well when the manager was on holiday. 在经理度假期间,助理经理把工作应付得很好。The warehouse is trying to cope with the backlog of orders. 仓库人员正在设法应付订单的积压。

**copier** n. = COPYING MACHINE, PHOTOCOPIER 影印机;复印机

**coproperty** n. ownership of property by two or more people together 财产的共有权

◇ **coproprietor** n. person who owns a property with another person or several other people 与别人共同拥有财产的人

**copy** 1. n. (a) document which is made to look the same as another 复印件: carbon copy = copy made with carbon paper 复写本;副本; certified copy = document which is certified as being the same as another 经核证的副本; file copy = copy of a document which is filed in an office for reference 卷宗复印件 (b) document 文件: fair copy or final copy = document which is written or typed with no changes or mistakes 誊清本或清稿; hard copy = printout of a text which is on a computer or printed copy of something which is on microfilm (计算机)硬拷贝;复印件; rough copy = draft of a document which, it is expected, will have changes made to it 草稿; top copy = first or top sheet of a document which is typed with carbon copies 打字正本 (c) publicity copy = text of a proposed advertisement before it is printed 供宣传的文本: She writes copy for a travel firm. 她为一家旅游公司写了一份做广告的文字说明。Knocking copy = advertising material which criticizes competing products 贬低他人产品的广告 (d) a book or a newspaper 一本书;一份报纸; Have you kept yesterday's copy of "The Times"? 你有昨日的《时代》周刊吗? I read it in the office copy of "Fortune"; 我从办公室一份《幸福》杂志上读到的。Where is my copy of the telephone directory? 我的电话号码簿在哪里?

NOTE: no plural for (c)

2. verb. to make a second document which is like the first 复印: He copied the company report at night and took it home. 夜里他复印了一份公司报告并将它带回家。

◇ **copier or copying machine** n. machine which makes copies of documents 复印机

◇ **copyright** 1 . n. legal right (lasting forfifty years after the death of a writer) which a writer has to publish his own work and not to have it copied 版权(作者有出版他本人作品不让他人抄袭的合法权利, 作者死后可延长 50 年): copyright act = Act of Parliament making copyright legal, and controlling the copying of copyright material 版权法案; copyright law = laws concerning copyright 版权法 work which is out of copyright = work by a writer who has been dead for fifty years 已不再拥有版权的作品; work still in copyright = work by a living writer, or by a writer who has not been dead for fifty years 仍拥有版权的作品; infringement of copyright or copyright infringement = act of illegally copying a work which is in copyright 侵犯版权; copyright notice = note in a book showing who owns the copyright and the date of ownership 版权通知或版权记录

NOTE: no plural

2 . v. to confirm the copyright of a written work by inserting a copyright notice and publishing the work 获得版权(用刊登版权通知和出版作品的方法对某一书面作品版权进行确认) 3. a. covered by the laws of copyright 受版权保护的; 获得版权的: It is illegal to photocopy a copyright work. 复印受版权保护的作品是非法的。

◇ **copyrighted** a. in copyright 取得版权;版权所有

**copy typing** n. typing documents from handwritten originals, not from dictation 按手写本文件打字而不是口授打字

◇ **copy typist** n. person who types documents from handwritten originals, not from dictation 按文件的手写本而不是以口授进行打字的打字员

**copywriter** n. person who writes advertisements 广告文字撰稿人

**corner** 1 . n. ( a ) place where two streets or two walls join 街角或墙角: The Post Office is on the corner of the High Street and London Road. 邮局位于大马路和伦敦路的拐角处。corner shop = small general store in a town on a street corner 街头小店; (b) place where two sides join 两边相交处: The box has to have specially strong corners. 这个盒子的内角必须特别结实。The corner of the crate was damaged. 木条箱的箱角被损坏。(c) situation where one person or a group controls the supply of a certain commodity 垄断(由一个人或一个集团对某一商品供给进行控制的情况)

2 . v. to corner the market = to own most or all of the supply of a certain commodity and so control the price 垄断市场: The syndicate tried to corner the market in silver. 该企业集团试图垄断白银市场。

**corp** US = CORPORATION

**corporate** a. referring to a whole company 公司的: corporate image = idea which a company would like the public to have of it 公司形象; corporate plan = plan for the future work of a whole company 公司计划; corporate planning = planning the future work of a whole company 公司规划; corporate profits = profits of a corporation 公司利润

◇ **corporation** n. ( a ) large company 大公司: finance corporation = company which provides money for hire purchase 金融公司; corporation tax = tax on profits made by companies 公司税 (b) US company which is incorporated in the United States ( 在美国组建的) 公司: corporation income tax = tax on profits made by incorporated companies 公司所得税

**correct** 1 . a. accurate or right 准确的; 正确的: The published accounts do not give a correct picture of the company's financial position. 所发表的报导没能准确说明公司的财务状况。2. v. to remove mistakes from something 更正；纠正: The accounts department have corrected the invoice. 会计处已更正了发票上的错误。You will have to correct all these typing errors before you send the letter. 在发信前，你必须更正所有打字错误。

◇ **correction** n. making something correct 纠正; change which makes something correct 更正: He made some corrections to the text of the speech. 他对演讲稿作了一些修改。

**correspond** v. (a) to correspond with someone = to write letters to someone 与某人通信 (b) to correspond with something = to fit or to match something 与某事一致；相配

◇ **correspondence** n. letters which are exchanged 书信往来；互相写的信件: business correspondence = letters concerned with a business 商业信函; to be in correspondence with someone = to write letters to someone and receive letters back 与某人通信; correspondence clerk = clerk whose responsibility it is to answer correspondence 文书(专门复信) NOTE: no plural

◇ **correspondent** n. (a) person who writes letters 写信的人 (b) journalist who writes articles for a newspaper on specialist subjects 记者; a financial correspondent 写金融文章的记者; the "Times" business correspondent《时代》周刊商务记者; He is the Paris correspondent of the "Telegraph" 他是驻巴黎的《电讯》报记者。

**cost** 1. n. (a) amount of money which has to be paid for something 费用；花费: What is the cost of a first class ticket to New York? 去纽约的头等票多少钱一张? Computer costs are falling each year. 计算机的费用每年都在下减。We cannot afford the cost of two telephones. 我们付不起两部电话的费用。to cover costs = to produce enough money in sales to pay for the costs of production 捞回成本；弥补成本; The sales revenue barely covers the costs of advertising or the manufacturing costs. 销售收入仅能补偿广告费或生产费用。to sell at cost = to sell at a price which is the same as the cost of manufacture or the wholesale cost 按成本价出售; fixed costs = business costs which do not rise with the quantity of the product made 固定成本; labour costs = cost of hourly – paid workers employed to make a product 劳动力成本; manufacturing costs or production costs = costs of making a product 制造成本或生产成本; operating costs or running costs = cost of the day – to – day organization of a company 营业成本或日常费用; variable costs = production costs which increase with the quantity of the product made (such as wages, raw materials) 可变成本; cost accountant = accountant who gives managers information about their business costs 成本会计员(师); cost accounting = specially prepared accounts of manufacturing and sales costs 成本会计；成本核算; cost analysis = calculating in advance what a new product will cost 成本分析; cost centre = group or machine whose costs can be itemized and to which fixed costs can be allocated 成本项目; cost, insurance and freight = estimate of a price, which includes the cost of the goods, the insurance and the transport charges 成本加保险和运费; 到岸价; cost price = selling price which is the same as the price which the seller paid for the item (i.e. either the manufacturing cost or the wholesale price) 成本价格; cost of sales = all the costs of a product sold, including manufacturing costs and the staff costs of the production department 销售成本（b）costs ＝ expensesinvolved in a court case 诉讼费用；to pay costs ＝ to pay the expenses of a court case 支付诉讼费用；The judge awarded costs to the defendant. 法官裁决由被告支付诉讼费用。Costs of the case will be borne by the prosecution. 诉讼案的费用由原告来承担。2. v. （a）to have a price 值（多少钱）：How much does the machine cost? 这台机器的价钱是多少？This cloth costs ￡10 a metre. 这种布售价每米为10英磅。（b）to cost a product ＝ to calculate how much money will be needed to make a product, and so work out its selling price 计算产品的成本

◇ **cost – benefit** n. cost – benefit analysis ＝ examining the ratio between costs and benefits, especially in comparing different production processes 成本效益分析

◇ **cost – cutting** n. reducing costs 减少费用；降低费用：We have taken out the telex as a cost – cutting exercise. 作为降低费用的一种做法我们没打电传。

◇ **cost – effective** a. which gives value, especially when compared with something else 费用低廉的；本轻利厚的（特别是与其它事相比产生价值）：We find advertising in the Sunday newspapers very cost – effective. 我们发现星期日在报纸上做广告费用相当低廉。

◇ **cost – effectiveness** n. being cost – effective 成本效益：Can we calculate the cost – effectiveness of air freight against shipping by sea? 我们能计算出空运与海运比较的成本效益吗？

◇ **costing** n. calculation of the manufacturing costs, and so the selling price of a product 成本核算：The costings give us a retail price of ￡2.95. 经成本核算，我们将零售价定为2.95英磅。We cannot do the costing until we have details of all the production expenditure. 在未获得所有生产开支的细节前，我们不能进行成本核算。

◇ **costly** a. expensive or costing a lot of money 花钱多的；昂贵的

◇ **cost of living** n. money which has to be paid for food, heating, rent etc. 生活费用（为食品、取暖、房租…等所必须付出的钱）：to allow for the cost of living in the salaries 在工资中估及到生活费用；cost – of – living allowance ＝ addition to normal salary to cover increases in the cost ofliving 生活费津贴；cost – of – living bonus ＝ extra money paid to meet the increase in the cost of living 生活费补贴；cost – of – living increase ＝ increase in salary to allow it to keep up with the increased cost of living 因生活费上涨而增加的工资；cost – of – living index ＝ way of measuring the cost of living which is shown as a percentage increase on the figure for the previous year 生活费用指数

◇ **cost plus** n. system of charging, where the buyer pays the costs plus a percentage commission to the seller 成本加利润（费用）（指在实际成本之外另加一定的金额）：We are charging for the work on a cost plus basis. 我们根据成本加费用的方法为我们的工作收费。

◇ **cost – push inflation** n. inflation caused by increased wage demands which lead to higher prices and in turn lead to further wage demands 成本推动型通货膨胀（由于薪水提高，成本增加而造成物价上涨所引起的通货膨胀）

**council** n. official group chosen to run something or to advise on aproblem 委员会；顾问委员会：consumer council ＝ group representing the interests of consumers 消费者利益保护委员会；消费者权益委员会 town council ＝ representatives elected to run a town 市政会；镇议会

**counsel** n. lawyer acting for one of the

parties in a legal action (在诉讼中代表一方当事人的) 出庭律师: defence counsel 辨护律师; prosecution counsel 原告律师; GB Queen's Counsel = senior lawyer(英)高级律师

NOTE: no plural

**count** v. (a) to add figures together to make a total 计算: He counted up the sales for the six months to December. 他将一直到 12 月份的共 6 个月的销售额进行了计算。(b) to include 把…算入内: Did you count my trip to New York as part of my sales expenses? 你是否将我去纽约的旅行费用算在我销售开支之内?

◇ **counting house** n. department dealing with cash 会计室;(管现金的)帐房

◇ **count on** v. to expect something to happen 期待;指望: They are counting on getting a good response from the TV advertising. 他们指望电视广告会得到好的反响。Do not count on a bank loan to start your business. 别指望用银行贷款开业。

**counter** n. long flat surface in a shop for displaying and selling goods 柜台: over the counter = legally 公开的;合法的; goods sold over the counter = retail sales of goods in shops 商店公开零售的货物; Some drugs are sold over the counter, but others need to be recommended by a doctor. 有些药可由商店出售,但有些药则需要医生的推荐。over - the - counter sales = legal selling of shares which are not listed in the official Stock Exchange list 场外合法出售(未在官方证券交易所挂牌上市的股票), under the counter = illegally 私下出售; 黑市销售; under - the - counter sales = black market sales 黑市销售; bargain counter = counter where things are sold cheaply 处理商品柜台; 廉价商品柜台; check - in counter = place where plane passengers have to check in 机场检票

处; ticket counter = place where tickets are sold 售票处; trade counter = shop in a factory or warehouse where goods are sold to retailers (工厂或仓库里) 向零售商出售货物的商店; glove counter = section of a shop where gloves are sold 手套柜台; counter staff = sales staff who serve behind counters 柜台后的销售人员

**counter -** prefix against 前缀, 表示 "反", "逆"

◇ **counterbid** n. higher bid in reply to a previous bid 还价;还盘(作为对前一次出价的答复, 出更高的价): When I bid £ 20 he put in a counterbid of £ 25. 当我出价 20 英磅时, 他还价为 25 英磅。

◇ **counter - claim** 1. n. claim for damages made in reply to a previous claim 反要求;反索赔(作为对先前索赔要求的签复提出的损失赔偿要求): Jones claimed £ 25,000 in damages against Smith, and Smith entered a counter - claim of £ 50,000 for loss of office. 琼斯要求史密斯赔偿 25,000 英磅, 史密斯为失去职务提出 50,000 英磅的反索赔。2. v. to put in a counter - claim 提出反索赔: Jones claimed £ 25,000 in damages and Smith counter - claimed £ 50,000 for loss of office. 琼斯提出 25,000 英磅的赔偿费, 史密斯为失去职务提出 50,000 英磅的反要求。

◇ **counterfeit** 1. a. false or imitation (money) 假钞票 2. v. to make imitation money 伪造货币

◇ **counterfoil** n. slip of paper kept after writing a cheque or an invoice or a receipt, as a record of the deal which has taken place 存根;票根(作为对已发生交易的记录,写完支票或发票或收据后留下的字条)

◇ **countermand** v. to countermand an order = to say that an order must not be carried out 撤消命令或取消订单

◇ **counter – offer** n. higher offer made in reply to another offer 还盘；反要约(作为对另一发盘的答复所作之更高发盘或要约)? Smith Ltd made an offer of £1m for the property, and Blacks-replied with a counter – offer of £1.4m 史密斯有限公司对该财产的发盘(或要约)为100万英磅, 对此的答复, 布莱克公司的还盘(或反要约)为140万英磅。

◇ **counterpart** n. person who has a similar job in another company 在另一公司有类似职位的人：John is my counterpart in Smith's. = He has the same post as I have here. 约翰在史密斯公司的职位与我相对应(等)。

◇ **countersign** v. to sign a document which has already been signed by someoneelse 会签；连署(在已由他人签字的文件上签字)：All cheques have to be countersigned by the finance director. 所有支票必须再由财务主任签字。The sales director countersigns all my orders. 销售主任对我所有订单进行会签。

**country** n. (a) land which is separate and governs itself 国家：The contract covers distribution in the countries of the Common Market. 合同包括在共同市场国家的(商品)销售。Some African countries export oil. 某些非洲国家出口石油。the Organization of Petroleum Exporting Countries 石油出口国组织；The managing director is out of the country. = He is on a business trip abroad 总经理(或常务董事)在国外。(b) land which is not near a town 乡村：Distribution is difficult in country areas. 在乡村地区销售有困难。His territory is mainly the country, but he is based in the town. 他的经营地域主要是乡村, 但他的总部设在城里。

**couple** n. two things or people taken together 对；双；两个：We only have e-nough stock for a couple of weeks. 我们

仅存下两周的库存。A couple of the directors were ill, so the board meeting was cancelled. 有两个董事病了, 所以董事会会议被取消。The negotiations lasted a couple of hours. = The negotiations went on for about two hours. 谈判大约持续了两小时。

**coupon** n. (a) piece of paper used in place of money 取代货币的券或票证；gift coupon = coupon from a store which is given as a gift and which must be exchanged in that store 赠券 (b) piece of paper which replaces an order form 取代订单的票券；coupon ad = advertisement with a form attached, which is to be cut out and returned to the advertiser with your name and address if you want further information about the product advertised 附进一步索取产品信息表格的广告；reply coupon = form attached to a coupon ad, which must be filled in andreturned to the advertiser 产品信息索取表 (c) interest coupon = slip of paper attached to a government bond certificate whichcan be cashed to provide the annual interest 息票；cum coupon = with a coupon attached 附有息票；ex coupon = without the interest coupons 不带息票

**courier** n. (a) motorcyclist who takes messages from one place another in a town 信使 (b) person who goes with a party of tourists to guide them on a package tour 导游

**course** n. (a) in the course of = during or while something is happening 在…过程中；In the course of the discussion, the managing director explained the company's expansion plans. 在讨论时, 总经理解释了公司发展计划。Sales have risen sharply in the course of the last few months. 在过去几个月里, 销售额锐增。(b) series of lessons 课程：She has finished her secretarial course. 她修完了秘书课。The company has paid for her to attend a course for trainee sales managers. 公司为她参加销售经理班学习支付费用。(c) of course = naturally 当然; Of course the company is interested in profits. 公司自然对利润感兴越。Are you willing to go on a sales trip to Australia? – of course! 你愿意去澳大利亚搞推销吗？那当然!

**court** n. place where a judge listens to a case and decides legally which of the parties in the argument is right 法院: court case = legal action or trial 诉讼案件; to take someone to court = to tell someone to appear in court to settle an argument 让某人出庭; 起诉某人; A settlement was reached out of court or the two parties reached an out – of – court settlement. = The dispute was settled between the two parties privately without continuing the court case. 在法庭外达成和解或当事人在法庭外达成和解。

**covenant** 1. n. legal contract 契约: deed of covenant = officially signed agreement to pay someone a sum of money each year 立书保证(正式签订的每年向某人支付一笔款项的契据) 2. v. to agree to pay a sum of money each year by contract 立契约(以合同方式同意每年支付一笔款项); to covenant to pay £10 per annum 立契约同意每年支付10英磅

**cover** 1. n. (a) thing put over a machine, etc. to keep it clean 覆盖物: Put the cover over your micro when you leave the office. 你离开办公室时将微处理机罩上。Always keep a cover over the typewriter. 每次都得将打字机盖上。(b) insurance cover = protection guaranteed by an insurance policy 保险范围; Do you have cover against theft? 你投俞窃的保险了吗? to operate without adequate cover = without being protected by insurance 在没有适当投保的情况下营运; to ask for additional cover = to ask the insurance company to in-

crease the amount for which you are insured 要求获得追加保险; full cover = insurance against all risks 保全险; cover note = letter from an insurance company giving details of an insurance policy and confirming that the policy exists 暂保单; 承保通知书; 保险证明书

NOTE: the US English for this is binder (c) security to guarantee a loan 贷款抵押: Do you have sufficient cover for this loan? 你有足够的贷款抵押吗? (d) (in restaurant) cover charge = charge in addition to the charge for food(在饭店)额外收费 (e) dividend cover = ratio of profits to dividend 股利比率;利润股息比率; (f) to send something under separate cover = in a separate envelope 另函寄某物; to send a magazine under plain cover = in an ordinary envelope with no company name printed on it 用普通信封寄杂志 2. v. e (a) to put something over a machine, etc. to keep it clean 遮盖(机器等物): Don't forget to cover your micro before you go home. 在回家前别忘记将微处理机盖上。(b) to cover a risk = to be protected by insurance against a risk 风险投保; to be fully covered = to have insurance against all risks 保全险; The insurance covers fire, theft and loss of work. 对火灾、盗窃与失业投保。(c) to have enough money to pay 清偿: to ask for security against a loan which you are making 为贷款担保; The damage was covered by the insurance. = The insurance company paid for the damage. 损坏由保险公司清偿。to cover a position = to have enough money to be able to pay for a forward purchase 有足够的钱作期货购买 (d) to earn enough money to pay for costs, expenses etc. (挣足够的钱)支付: We do not make enough sales to cover the expense of running the shop. 我们的销售不足以支付商店的管理费用。Breakeven point is reached when sales cover all costs. 当销

售款能支付所有费用时，就是收支平衡。The dividend is covered four times. = Profits are four times the dividend paid out. 有四倍于股息的利润。

◇ **coverage** n. (a) press coverage or media coverage = reports about something in the newspapers or on TV, etc. 报纸或新闻报导：The company had good media coverage for the launch of its new model. 对该公司推出新型号有不少好的报导。(b) US protection guaranteed by insurance(美)保险范围(由保险公司保证); Do you have coverage against fire damage? 你投火灾险了吗？NOTE: no plural

◇ **covering letter or covering note** n. letter or note sent with documents to say why you are sending them 伴书；详函

**crane** n. machine for lifting heavy objects 起重机：The container slipped as the crane was lifting it onto the ship. 当起重机将集装箱往船上吊时，集装箱滑落了。They had to hire a crane to get the machine into the factory. 全们必须租吊车将机器吊进工厂。

**crash** 1. n. (a) accident to a car or plane or train(汽车、飞机或火车发生的)事故：The car was damaged in the crash. 小汽车在撞车事故中受损。The plane crash killed all the passengers or all the passengers were killed in the plane crash. 所有乘客在飞机失事中罹难。(b) financial collapse 倒闭；崩溃：financial crash 金融上的失败；He lost all his money in the crash of 1929. 在 1929 年的股市大萧条中他损失了所有的钱。2. v. (a) to hit something and be damaged 撞击受损：The plane crashed into the mountain. 飞机与山相撞。The lorry crashed into the post office. 卡车撞进了邮局。(b) to collapse financially 破产：The company crashed with debts of over £1 million. 该公司因负债 100 万英磅

而破产。

**crate** 1. n. large wooden box 大木条箱：a crate of oranges 一(大木条)箱的柑桔 2. v. to put goods into crates(将货物)装入木条箱

**create** v. to make something new 创造；创立：By acquiring small unprofitable companies he soon created a large manufacturing group. 用收购不盈利小公司的方法，他很快创立了一个大型工业制造集团。The government scheme aims at creating new jobs for young people. 政府新计划的目标是为年青人创造就业机会。

◇ **creation** n. making 创造：job creation scheme = government - backed scheme to make work for the unemployed 创造就业机会的计划(政府支持的)

**credere** see DEL CREDERE

**credit** 1. n. (a) time given to a customer before he has to pay 缓付款的期限；to give someone six months' credit 6 个月的缓付款的期限；to sell on good credit terms 以优惠的信贷条件出售(货物)；extended credit = credit on very long repayment terms 延期信贷；interest - free credit = arrangement to borrow money without paying interest on the loan 无息信贷；long credit = terms allowing the borrower a long time to pay 长期信贷；open credit = bank credit given to good customers without security 无担保信贷；short credit = terms allowing the customer only a short time to pay 短期信贷；credit account = account which a customer has with a shop which allows him to buy goods and pay for them later 赊欠帐户；to open a credit account 开立赊欠帐户；credit agency or US credit bureau = company which reports on the creditworthiness of customers to show whether they should be allowed credit 信用调查所或(美)征信

所；credit bank = bank which lends money信用银行；信贷银行；credit control = check that customers pay on time and do not owe more thantheir credit limit 信贷控制；credit facilities = arrangement with a bank or supplier to have credit so as tobuy goods 信贷手段；信用服务；credit freeze or credit squeeze = period when lending by banks is restricted by the government 信贷冻结或信贷紧缩；letter of credit = letter from a bank, allowing someone credit and promising to repay at a later date 信用证；信用状；irrevocable letter of credit = letter of credit which cannot be cancelled不可撤消的信用证；credit limit = fixed amount which is the most a customer can owe on credit 信贷限额；He has exceeded his credit limit. = He has borrowed more money than he is allowed. 他已超过信贷限额。to open a line of credit or a credit line = to make credit available to someone 开始发放信贷业务；credit rating = amount which a credit agency feels a customer should be allowed to borrow 信用定额；信用能力；信用地位；on credit = without paying immediately 赊帐；to live on credit 靠赊帐生活；We buy everything on sixty days credit. 我们买任何东西都是 60 天后付款。The company exists on credit from its suppliers. 该公司靠供应商的信贷生存。(NOTE: no plural) (b) money received by a person or company and recorded in the accounts(个人或公司所开帐户上的)贷方；to enter £100 to someone's credit 将 100 记入某人帐户的贷方；to pay in £100 to thecredit of Mr Smith 将 100 英磅记在史密斯先生的贷方；debit and credit = money which a company owes and which it receives 借贷；借方和贷方；credit balance = balance in an account showing that more money has been received than is owed by the company 贷方余额；The account has a credit balance of £1,000.该帐户的贷方余额为 1,000 英磅。credit column = right-hand column in accounts showing money received 贷方栏；credit entry = entry on the credit side of an account 贷方分录；credit note = note showing that money is owed to a customer 付款通知；贷项清单：The company sent the wrong order and so had to issue a credit note. 公司寄错了定单，因此必须签发一张付款通知。credit side = right-hand side of accounts showing money received 贷方；account in credit = account where the credits are higher than the debits 贷方余额的帐款；bank credit = loans or overdrafts from a bank to a customer 银行信贷；tax credits = part of a dividend on which the company has already paid tax, so that the shareholder is not taxed on it 赋税减免 2. v. to put money into someone's account；(将钱)入帐：to note money received in an account(将收到的钱)记入贷方：to credit an account with £100 or to credit £100 to an account 将 100 英磅帐户的记入贷方

◇ **credit card** n. plastic card which allows you to borrow money and to buy goods without paying for them immediately 信用卡(不立即为自己所购货物支付和允许你借钱的塑料卡片)

◇ **creditor** n. person who is owed money 债权人（别人欠他钱的人)：creditors' meeting = meeting of all persons to whom a bankrupt company owes money, to decide how to obtain the money owed 债权人会议

◇ **credit union** n. US group of people who pay regular subscriptions which are used to help members of the group who are ill or in financial difficulties(美)信用合作社或互助储金会(定期交纳认缴款,用来帮助生病和有财政困难的会员)

◇ **credit－worthy** a. able to buy

goods on credit 信用(贷)可靠性的

◇ **creditworthiness** n. ability of a customer to pay for goods bought on credit 客户信贷可靠性

**crew** n. group of people who work on a plane or ship, etc. 全体机务人员或船员; The ship carries a crew of 250. 该船有 250 个船员。

**crime** n. act which is against the law 犯罪; 罪行: Crimes in supermarkets have risen by 25％. 超级市场的犯罪率上升了 25％。

◇ **criminal** a. illegal 犯法的: Misappropriation of funds is a criminal act. 侵吞公款是犯法行为。criminal action = court case brought by the state against someone who ischarged with a crime(由政府提起的控告某人犯罪的)刑事诉讼

**crisis** n. serious economic situation where decisions have to be taken rapidly 危机(必须迅速决策的严峻的经济形势); international crisis 国际性危机; banking crisis 银行危机; financial crisis 财政危机; to take crisis measures = to take severe measures rapidly to stop a crisis developing 采取克服危机的举措
NOTE: plural is crises

**criticize** v. to say that something or someone is wrong or is working badly, etc. 批评: The MD criticized the sales manager for not improving the volume of sales. 总经理批评销售经理没能增加销售额。The design of the new catalogue has been criticized. 新目录本的设计受到批评。

**cross** v. (a) to go across 穿过: Concorde only takes three hours to cross the Atlantic. 协和式飞机横越大西洋只需 3 小时。To get to the bank, you turn left and cross the street at the post office. 你向左拐，在邮局处穿过马路就可到达银行。(b) to cross a cheque = to write two lines across a cheque to show that it has to be paid into a bank 给

支票划横线(表示必须向银行付款); crossed cheque = cheque which has to be paid into a bank 划线支票

◇ **cross holding** n. situation where two companies hold shares in each other 交叉持股(两个公司互相持有对方公司的股份)

◇ **cross off** v. to remove something from a list 划掉: He crossed my name off his list. 他将我的名字从名单上划掉。You can cross him off our mailing list. 你可从通信录上将他的名字删掉。

◇ **cross out** v. to put a line through something which has been written 划掉: She crossed out £ 250 and put in £ 500. 她划掉 250 英磅改为 500 英磅。

◇ **cross rate** n. exchange rate between two currencies expressed in a third currency 套汇汇率;交叉汇率(用第三国货币表示的两种货币之间的兑换率)

**crude** (oil) n. raw petroleum, taken from the ground 原油: The price for Arabian crude has slipped. 阿拉伯国家的原油价格已经下降。
NOTE: no plural

**cubic** a. measured in volume by multiplying length, depth and width 立方的: The crate holds six cubic metres. 该大木条箱的容积为 6 个立方米。cubic measure = volume measured in cubic feet or metres 立方单位制
NOTE: cubic is written in figures as$^3$; 6m$^3$ = six cubic metres; 10ft3 = ten cubic feet

**cum** prep. with 带有;附有: cum dividend = price of a share including the next dividend still to be paid 带股息; cum coupon = with a coupon attached 附息票的债券

**cumulative** adjective which is added automatically each year (每年自动) 累积的: cumulative interest = interest which is added to the capital each year 累计利息; cumulative preference share or US cumulative preferred stock = preference sharewhich will have the dividend paid at a later date even if the company is not able to pay a dividend in the current year 累积优先股

**currency** n. money in coins and notes which is used in a particular country 货币(在某一特定国家使用的硬币和纸币）: convertible currency = currency which can easily be exchanged for another 可兑换货币；foreign currency = currency of another country 外币；foreign currency account = bank account in the currency of another country (e.g. a dollar account) 外币帐户；foreign currency reserves = a country's reserves in currencies of other countries 外币储备；hard currency = currency of a country which has a strong economy and which can be changed into other currencies easily 硬通货币；to pay for imports in hard currency 以硬通货币来支付进口商品；to sell raw materials to earn hard currency 出售原材料赚取硬通货币；legal currency = money which is legally used in a country 法定货币；soft currency = currency of a country with a weak economy, which is cheap tobuy and difficult to exchange for other currencies 软货币；软通货；currency backing = gold or securities which maintain the international strength of a currency 用黄金或证券保持货币的国际实力；currency note = bank note 流通券；钞票：
NOTE: currency has no plural when it refers to the money of one country：He was arrested trying to take currency out of the country. 由于试图将货币带出国外,他被捕了。

**current** a. referring to the present time 现时代；当前的：current account = account in an bank from which the customer can withdraw money when he wants 活期存款帐户；to pay money into a current account 向活期帐户付款；current assets = assets used by a company in its ordinary work (such as materials, finished products, cash) 流动资产；current cost accounting = method of accounting which notes the cost of replacing assets at current prices, rather than valuing assets at their original cost 当期或现行成本会计；current liabilities = debts which a company has to pay within the next accounting period 流动负债；短期贷款；current price = today's price 时价；current rate of exchange = today's rate of exchange 现行汇率；current yield = dividend calculated as a percentage of the price paid per share 现行收益率；本期收益

◇ **currently** a. at the present time 当今；现在：We are currently negotiating with the bank for a loan. 我们正就贷款事宜与银行进行谈判。

**curriculum vitae** n. summary of a person's life story showing details of educationand work experience 简历；履历：Candidates should send a letter of application with a curriculum vitae to the personnel officer. 求职者应向人事官员寄一封附有履历的求职信。
NOTE: the plural is curriculums or curricula vitae. Note also that the US English is resume

**curve** n. line which bends round 曲线：The graph shows an upward curve. 图表显示的是向上曲线。sales curve = graph showing how sales increase or decrease 销售曲线

**cushion** n. (a) soft bag for sitting on 坐垫：She put a cushion on her chair as it was too hard. 因为椅子太硬她在上面放了一个坐垫。(b) money which allows you to make a loss 安全余量；缓冲 We have sums on deposit which are a useful cushion when cashflow is tight. 我们有存款,当现金吃紧时,这些钱是有用的缓冲。

**custom** n. (a) use of a shop by regular shoppers光顾; 惠顾: to lose someone's custom = to do something which makes a regular customer go to another shop 失去主顾的光顾; custom - built or custom - made = made specially for one customer(为顾客)定做的; 定制的: He drives a custom - built Rolls Royce. 他驾驶一辆定制的罗尔斯——罗伊斯小汽车。(b) the customs of the trade = general way of working in a trade 贸易惯例 NOTE: no plural for (a)

◇ **customer** n. person or company which buys goods 顾客: The shop was full of customers. 商店顾客盈门。Can you serve this customer first please? 你能先为这位顾客服务吗? He is a regular customer of ours. 他是我们的常客。customer appeal = what attracts customers to a product 顾客吸引; customer service department = department which deals with customers and their complaints and orders 顾客服务部

◇ **customize** v. to change something to fit the special needs of a customer 定制; 定做: We used customized computer terminals. 我们使用按顾客要求制作的计算机终端。

◇ **customs** pl. the government department which organizes the collection of taxes on imports; office of this department at a port or airport 海关(政府中组织征收进口货物税的部门, 由该部门在港口或机场设立的办事处): to go through the customs = to pass through the area of a port or airport where customs officials examine goods 通过海关的检查; to take something through the customs = to carry something illegal through the customs area without declaring it 在未报关情况下将东西带出海关区域; He was stopped by the customs. 他被海关拦住。Her car was searched by the customs. 海关搜查了她的汽车。

customs barrier = customs duty intended to prevent imports 关税壁垒; customs broker = person or company which takes goods through the customs for a shipping company 海关经纪人; customs clearance = document given by customs to a shipper to show that customs duty has been paid and the goods can be shipped 海关放行; 结关; to wait for customs clearance 等待结关 customs declaration = statement showing goods being imported on which duty will have to be paid 报关; to fill in a customs (declaration) form 填写报关表; customs duty = tax paid on goods brought into or taken out of a country 关税; The crates had to go through a customs examination. = The crates had to be examined by customs officials. 大木条箱必须办理验关手续. customs formalities = declaration of goods by the shipper and examination of them by the customs 海关手续; customs officers or customs officials = people working for the customs 海关官员; customs tariff = list of duties to be paid on imported goods 关税税则; customs union = agreement between several countries that goods can travel between them, without paying duty, while goods from other countries have to pay special duties 关税同盟

**cut** 1. n. (a) sudden lowering of a price or salary or numbers of jobs 降低; 削减 (价格或者工资或就业数目的突然下降): price cuts or cuts in prices; salary cuts or cuts in salaries 工资或薪金削减; job cuts = reductions in the number of jobs 就业削减; He took a cut in salary. = He accepted a lower salary. 他接受工资削减。(b) share in a payment 付款中的一份; He introduces new customers and gets a cut of the salesman's commission. 他介绍新客户, 分享推销人员的佣金。2. v. (a) to lower suddenly 突然减少: We are cutting prices on all our models. 我们正对所有型号的产品进行削价。to cut (back) production = to reduce the quantity of products made 削减:生产; The company has cut back its sales force. 公司裁减了销售人员的数目。We have taken out the telex in order to try to cut costs. 我们削减电传,尽量减少费用。(b) to stop or to reduce the number of something 停止或减少(某种东西的数目); to cut jobs = to reduce the number of jobs by making people redundant 减少就业人员; He cut his losses. = He stopped doing something which was creating a loss. 他不再亏本(他损失减少)

NOTE: cutting – cut – has cut

◇ **cutback** n. reduction 减少: cutbacks in government spending 政府开支的减少或削减

◇ **cut down (on)** v. to reduce suddenly the amount of something used 突然减少(所用东西的数量): The government is cutting down on welfare expenditure. 政府正在削减福利费开支。The office is trying to cut down on electricity consumption. 办公室正努力减少电的消耗。We have installed a word – processor to cut down on paperwork. 我们安装了一台文字处理机以减少文书工作量。

◇ **cut in** v. infml. to cut someone in on a deal = to give someone a share in the profits of a deal 让某人分享每笔交易的利润

◇ **cut – price** a. sold at a cheaper price than usual 削价的;减价的: cut – price goods 削价商品; cut – price petrol 削价汽油; cut – price store = store selling cut – price goods 出售削价商品的商店

◇ **cut – throat** a. cut – throat competition = sharp competition by cutting prices and offering highdiscounts 残酷无情的竞争

◇ **cutting** n. (a) cost cutting = reducing costs 成本削减;减少成本: We have made three secretaries redundant as part of our cost – cutting programme. 作为削减成本计划的一部分,我们解雇了三名秘书。price cutting = sudden lowering of prices 削价; price – cutting war = competition between companies to get a larger market share by cutting prices 削价战 NOTE: no plural (b) press cutting agency = company which cuts out references to a client from newspapersand magazines and sends them on to him 剪报服务公司; press cuttings = references to a client or person or product cut out of newspapers or magazines 剪报; We have a file of press cuttings on our rivals' products. 我们存有有关我们竞争者产品剪报档案。

NOTE: no plural for (a)

**cwt** = HUNDREDWEIGHT 英担;半公担

**CV** n. = CURRICULUM VITAE Please apply in writing, enclosing a current CV. 请以书面形式申请并附上现时履历一份。

**cycle** n. period of time when something leaves its original position and returns to it 周期(某种东西离开原来位置然后又返回的这段时间): economic cycle or trade cycle or business cycle = period during which trade expands, then slows down and then expands again 经济周期或贸易周期或商业周期

◇ **cyclical** a. which happens in cycles 周期性的: cyclical factors = way in which a trade cycle affects businesses 周期性因素

# Dd

**daily** a. done every day 每日的：daily consumption = amount used each day 日消费；daily production of cars = number of cars produced each day 汽车日产量；daily sales returns = reports of sales made each day 日销售收益表；a daily newspaper or a daily = newspaper which is produced every day 日报

**damage** 1. n. (a) harm done to thing 损害：fire damage = damage caused by a fire 火灾损失；storm damage = damage caused by a storm 风暴损失；to suffer damage = to be harmed 受损害；遭损；We are trying to assess the damage which the shipment suffered in transit. 我们正努力估计在运输途中货物的损坏情况。to cause damage = to harm something 引起损坏；The fire caused damage estimated at £ 100,000 火灾引起的损失估计为 100,000 英磅。damage survey = survey of damage done 损害调查；NOTE: no plural (b) damages = money claimed as compensation for harm done 损害赔偿金；to claim £ 1000 in damages；要求 10000 英镑的损害赔偿金；to be liable for damages 有支付损害赔偿金的责任；to pay £ 25,000 in damages 支付 25,000 英磅的损害赔偿金；to bring an action for damages against someone = to take someone to court and claim damages 对某人提出要求支付损失赔偿金诉讼 2. v. to harm 损坏：The storm damaged the cargo. 风暴损坏了货船。Stock which has been damaged by water. 被水损坏了的存货。

◇ **damaged** a. which has suffered damage or which has been harmed 受损的：goods damaged in transit 在运输途中受损的货物；fire-damaged goods = goods harmed in a fire 在火灾中损坏的货物

**damp down** v. to reduce 减少：to damp down demand for domestic con-sumption of oil 减少国内对石油的需求

**danger** n. possibility of being harmed or killed 危险：There is danger to the workforce in the old machinery. 老式机器对工人有危险。There is no danger of the sales force leaving. = It is not likely that the sales force will leave. 无销售人员离走的危险；in danger of = which may easily happen 有…的危险；The company is in danger of being taken over. 该公司有被接管的危险。She is in danger of being made redundant. 她有被解雇的危险。

◇ **danger money** n. extra money paid to workers in dangerous jobs 危险工作津贴：The workforce has stopped work and asked for danger money. 工人们已停止工作,要求获得危险工作津贴。

◇ **dangerous** a. which can be harmful 有危险的：dangerous job = job where the workers may be killed or hurt 危险工作

**data** n. information (letters or figures) available on computer 数据(计算机可提供的字母或数字)：data acquisition = getting information. 数据的获得；data bank or bank of data = store of information in a computer 数据库；data processing = selecting and examining data in a computer to produce special information 数据处理

NOTE: data is usually singular：The data is easily available. 数据垂手可得。

◇ **database** n. store of information in a large computer(大型计算机里的)数据库：We can extract the lists of potential customers from our database. 从数据库里我们可得到未来顾客的名单。

**date** 1. n. (a) number of day, month and year 日期：I have received your letter of yesterday's date. 我已收到你昨日的来信。date stamp = rubber stamp for marking the date on letters received 邮戳；date of receipt = date when something is received 收到日 (b) up to date = current or recent or modern 最新的: an up‐to‐date computer system 现代化的计算机系统; to bring something up to date = to add the latest information to something 使包含最新信息; to keep something up to date = to keep adding information to something so that it is always up to date 保持某物最新; We spend a lot of time keeping our mailing list up to date. 我们花了大量时间保持通信录最新。(c) to date = up to now 迄今为止;到现在为止: interest to date = interest up to the present time 迄今为止的利息 (d) out of date = old fashioned 过时的: Their computer system is years out of date. 他们的计算机落后许多年。They are still using out‐of‐date machinery. 他们仍在使用过了时的机器。(e) maturity date = date when a government stock will mature (政府公债)到期日: date of bill = date when a bill will mature 票据到期日; 2. v. to put a date on a document(在文件上)注明…日期: The cheque was dated March 24th. 发票的注明日期为 3 月 24 日。You forgot to date the cheque. 你忘记给支票填写日期。to date a cheque forward = to put a later date than the present one on a cheque 给支票的注明日期推后

◇ **dated** a. with a date written on it 注明日期的: Thank you for your letter dated June 15th. 谢谢你 6 月 15 日的来信。long‐dated bill = bill which is payable more than three months from now 长期汇票; short‐dated bill = bill which is payable within a few days 短期(即期)汇票

**day** n. (a) period of 24 hours 一天;一昼夜: There are thirty days in June. 六月份有 30 天。The first day of the month is a public holiday. 本月第一天为节假日。settlement day = day when accounts have to be settled 请算日;交割

日; three clear days = three whole working days 整整三天; to give ten clear days' notice 提前十整天通知; allow four clear days for the cheque to be paid into the bank 将支票支付给银行, 允许有四个整工作日的时间 (b) period of work from morning to night 工作日: She took two days off. = She did not come to work for two days. 她休了两天假。He works three days on, two days off. = He works for three days, then has two days' holiday. 他工作三天休息两天。to work an eight‐hour day = to spend eight hours at work each day 每天工作八小时; day shift = shift which works during the daylight hours such as from 8a. m. to 5.30 p. m. 日班; There are 150 men on the day shift. 150 名男工上日班。He works the day shift. 他上日班。day release = arrangement where a company allows a worker to go to college to study for one or two days each week 职工脱产学习按排; The junior sales manager is attending a day release course. 年青的销售经理在上脱产学习班。

◇ **daybook** n. book with an account of sales and purchases made each day. (记录每天买卖情况的)流水帐或日记帐。

◇ **day‐to‐day** a. ordinary or which goes on all the time 日常的;每天的: He organizes the day‐to‐day running of the company. 他负责公司的日常管理。Sales only just cover the day‐to‐day expenses. 销售仅能抵消日常开支。

◇ **day worker** n. person who works the day shift 上日班的工人

**DCF** = DISCOUNTED CASH FLOW 现金流量贴现

**dead** a. (a) not alive 死亡的: Six people were dead as a result of the accident. 由于该事故六人身亡。The founders of the company are all dead. 该公司的创建人均已故去。(b) not working 无活力

的：dead account = account which is no longer used 死帐；呆帐；The line went dead. = the telephone line suddenly stopped working. 电话线路中断。dead loss = total loss 全部损失；The car was written off as a dead loss. 汽车作为全损被注销。dead money = money which is not invested to make a profit(没有用来投资赚取利润的)闲置钱；dead season = time of year when there are few tourists about 旅游淡季

◇ **deadline** n. date by which something has to be done(做某事的)截止日期：to meet a deadline = to finish something in time 如期完成；We've missed our October 1st deadline. 我们错过了 10 月 1 日的最后期限。

◇ **deadlock** 1. n. point where two sides in a dispute cannot agree 僵局：The negotiations have reached a deadlock. 谈判陷入僵局。to break a deadlock = to find a way to start discussions again 打破僵局；2. v. to be unable to agree to continue discussing 陷入僵局：Talks have been deadlocked for ten days. = After ten days the talks have not produced any agreement. 谈判已僵持了十天。

◇ **deadweight** n. heavy goods like coal, iron or sand(按重量计算运费的货物)净重，笨重(货物)：deadweight cargo = heavy cargo which is charged by weight, not by volume 按净重计算运费的船货；deadweight capacity or deadweight tonnage = largest amount of cargo which a ship can carry safely 安全载重量；载重吨位

**deal** 1. n. (a) business agreement or affair or contract 商业协议；商业事务；商业合同：to arrange a deal or to set up a deal or to do a deal 安排或达成或做一笔交易；to sign a deal 签署一项商业合同；The sales director set up a deal with a Russian bank. 销售经理与一家俄罗斯银行达成一笔交易。The deal will be signed tomorrow. 协议明日签字。They did a deal with an American air line. 他们与美国航空公司做成一笔交易。to call off a deal = to stop an agreement 取消一项协议；When the chairman heard about the deal he called it off. 当董事长(或主席)听到此项协议时，即将其取消。cash deal = sale done for cash 现金交易；package deal = agreement where several different items are agreed at the same time 一揽子交易；They agreed a package deal, which involves the construction of the factory, training of staff and purchase of the product. 他们商定了一项一揽子协议，其中包括建工厂，培训人员和购买产品。(b) a great deal or a good deal of something = a large quantity of something 许多；大量：He has made a good deal of money on the stock market. 他在股票(或证券)市场上赚了一大笔钱。The company lost a great deal of time asking for expert advice. 公司在征求专家意见方面耗费了大量时间。2. v. (a) to deal with = to organize 处理；组织：Leave it to the filing clerk – he'll deal with 把它交给档案管理员，他会处理此事。to deal with an order = to supply an order 组织订货 (b) to trade or to buy and sell 做生意或做买卖：to deal with someone = to do business with someone 与某人做生意；to deal in leather or to deal in options = to buy and sell leather or options 买卖皮革或期权；He deals on the Stock Exchange. = His work involves buying and selling shares on the Stock Exchange for clients. 他在证券交易所做股票买卖生意。

◇ **dealer** n. person who buys and sells 商人：dealer in tobacco or tobacco dealer 烟草商；foreign exchange dealer = person who buys and sells foreign currencies 做外汇买卖的人；retail dealer = person who sells to the general public 零售

商; wholesale dealer = person who sells in bulk to retailers 批发商

◇ **dealing** n. (a) buying and selling on the Stock Exchange(指在证券交易所的股票或证券)交易. fair dealing = legal trade or legal buying and selling of shares 合法股票交易; foreign exchange dealing = buying and selling foreign currencies 外汇买卖; forward dealings = buying or selling commodities forward. 期货交易; insider dealing = illegal buying or selling of shares by staff of a company whohave secret information about the company's plans 内幕人交易;知情人交易; option dealing = buying and selling share options 期权交易; (b) buying and selling goods 商品买卖; to have dealings with someone = to do business with someone 与某人做买卖或做生意。

**dear** a. (a) expensive or costing a lot of money 昂贵的: Property is very dear in this area. 房地产在本地区很昂贵。dear money = money which has to be borrowed at a high interest rate 高利贷款 (b) way of starting a letter(信中抬头)尊敬的; 亲爱的: Dear Sir or Dear Madam = addressing a man or woman whom you do not know, or addressing a company 尊敬的先生或亲爱的女士; Dear Sirs = addressing a firm 亲爱的先生们;敬启者; Dear Mr Smith or Dear Mrs Smith or Dear Miss Smith = addressing a man or woman whom you know 尊敬的史密斯先生或亲爱的史密斯太太或亲爱的史密斯; Dear James or Dear Julia = addressing a friend or a person you do business with 尊敬的詹姆斯或亲爱的朱莉娅。

**death** n. act of dying 死亡: death benefit = insurance benefit paid to the family of someone who dies in an accident at work 死亡抚恤金; death in service = insurance benefit or pension paid when someone dies while employed by a company(由公司发放的)抚恤金或养老金;

US death duty or death tax = tax paid on the property left by a dead person (美)遗产税

**debenture** n. agreement to repay a debt with fixed interest using the company's assets as security 债券;借据(用公司资产作抵押, 按固定利息偿还债务的协议): The bank holds a debenture on the company. 银行持有该公司的债券。mortgage debenture = debenture where the lender can be repaid by selling the company's property 抵押债券;有抵押品的公司债券; debenture issue or issue of debentures = borrowing money against the security of the company's assets 债券的发行; debenture bond = certificate showing that a debenture has been issued 公司债券; debenture capital or debenture stock = capital borrowed by a company, using its fixed assets as security(以公司固定资产作抵押筹集的)债券资本或公司备用资本; debenture holder = person who holds a debenture for money lent 公司债券持有人; debenture register or register of debentures = list of debenture holders of a company 公司债券持有人名单。

**debit** 1. n. money which a company owes 借方(记入公司借方的款项): debits and credits = money which a company owes and money it receives 借方和贷方; debit balance = balance in an account, showing that the company owes more money than it has received 借方余额; debit column = left-hand column in accounts showing the money paid or owed to others 借方栏; debit entry = entry on the debit side of an account 借方分录; debit side = left-hand side of an account showing the money paid or owedto others 借方; debit note = note showing that a customer owes money 借方票据; We undercharged Mr Smith and had to send him a debit note for the extra amount. 我们少收了史密斯先生

的钱，必须寄他一份付余额的借据。directdebit = system where a customer allows a company to charge costs to his bank account automatically and where the amount charged can be increased or decreased with the agreement of the customer 直接借记；I pay my electricity bill by direct debit. 我以直接借记的方式支付电费。2. v. to debit an account = to charge an account with a cost 记入借方的帐户：His account was debited with the sum of £25. 将 25 英磅登入他的借方帐户。

◇ **debitable** a. which can be debited 可记入借方的

**debt** n. (a) money owed for goods or services 债务；欠款：The company stopped trading with debts of over £1 million. 由于欠一百多万英镑债务, 公司停止交易。to be in debt = to owe money 负债；欠债；He is in debt to the tune of £250. = He owes £250. 他负债总数达 250 英磅。to get into debt = to start to borrow more money than you can pay back 开始负债或欠债；The company is out of debt. = The company does not owe money any more. 公司已不欠债。to pay back a debt = to pay all the money owed 偿还债务；to pay off a debt = to finish paying money owed 还清债务；to service a debt = to pay interest on a debt 支付所欠债款的利息；The company is having problems in servicing its debts. 公司在偿还所欠债款利息方面遇到了问题。bad debt = money owed which will never be paid back 坏帐或呆帐；The company has written off £30,000 in bad debts. 公司注销了 30,000 英磅的呆帐。secured debts or unsecured debts = debts which are guaranteed or not guaranteed by assets 担保债务或非担保债务；debt collection = collecting money which is owed 收帐；debt collection agency = company which collects debts for a commission 债务托收代

理处；debt collector = person who collects debts 收帐的人；debts due = money owed which is due for repayment 到期债务 (b) funded debt = part of the British National Debt which pays interest, but where there is no date for repayment of the principal(英)长期债务（只付利息无本金偿还的确定日期）；the National Debt = money borrowed by a government 国债

◇ **debtor** n. person who owes money 债务人：debtor side = debit side of an account 借方；debtor nation = country whose foreign debts are larger than money owed to it by other countries 负债国

**deceit or deception** n. making a wrong statement to someone in order to trick him into paying money 欺骗某人使其：He obtained £10,000 by deception. 他用期骗手段获取 10,000 英磅。

**decentralize** v. to organize from various points, away from the centre 分散：The group has a policy of decentralized purchasing where each division is responsible for its own purchasing. 该集团实行分散购买政策, 按此政策每个部门负责自己的购买任务。

◇ **decentralization** n. organization from various points, away from the centre 分散：The decentralization of the buying departments. 购买部的分散化。

**decide** v. to make up your mind to do something 决定；决策；to decide on a course of action 就行动方向作出决定；to decide to appoint a newmanaging director 决定任命一名新总经理

◇ **deciding** a. deciding factor = most important factor which influences a decision 决定性因素

**decile** n. one of a series of nine figures below which one tenth or several tenths of the total fall 十分位数

**decimal** n. decimal system = system based on the number 10 十进制；correct to three places of decimals = correct to three figures after the decimal point ( e. g. 3.485)写到小数点后的第三位数, 如 3.485; decimal point = dot which indicates the division between the whole unit and its smaller parts (such as 4.75) 小数点

◇ **decimalization** n. changing to a decimal system 改成十进位制

◇ **decimalize** v. to change to a decimal system 改成十进位制

**decision** n. making up one's mind to do something 决定: to come to a decision or to reach a decision 决策; decision making = act of coming to a decision 作出决策;决策 the decision - making processes = ways in which decisions are reached 决策过程; decision maker = person who has to decide 决策人

**deck** n. flat floor in a ship 甲板;舱面: deck cargo = cargo carried on the open top deck of a ship 甲板货物; deck hand = ordinary sailor on a cargo ship 船面水手

**declaration** n. official statement 声明: declaration of bankruptcy = official statement that someone is bankrupt 宣布破产; declaration of income = statement declaring income to the tax office 收益申报; customs declaration = statement declaring goods brought into a country on which customs duty should be paid 报关单; VAT declaration = statement declaring VAT income to the VAT office 增值税申报单

◇ **declare** v. to make an official statement or to announce to the public 声明; 宣布; 申报: to declare someone bankrupt 宣布某人破产; to declare a dividend of 10% 宣布10%的股息或分红; to declare goods to the customs = to state that you are importing goods which are liable to duty 将物品向海关申报; The customs officials asked him if he had

anything to declare. 海关官员问他是否有东西要申报。to declare an interest = to state in public that you own shares in a company being investigated or that you are related to someone who can benefit from your contacts, etc. 公开宣布权益

◇ **declared** a. which has been made public or officially state 公开的;宣布了的: declared value = value of goods entered on a customs declaration 报关或申报价值

**decline** 1 n. gradual fall 跌落;逐步下降: the decline in the value of the franc 法朗价值的跌落; a decline in buying power 购买力的下降; The last year has seen a decline in real wages. 去年实际工资下降。2 v. to fall slowly 缓慢下降: Shares declined in a weak market. 在疲软的市场上股价下跌。Imports have declined over the last year. 去年进口下降。The economy declined during the last government. 上届政府当政期间经济下降。

**decontrol** v. to stop controls 解除管制;取消控制: to decontrol the price of petrol = to stop controlling the price of petrol so that it can be reached freely by the market 放开汽油价格; to decontrol wages = to allow wage increases to be given freely 解除对工资的控制
NOTE: decontrolling - decontrolled

**decrease** 1 n. fall or reduction 下降;减少: decrease in price 价格下降; decrease in value 价值下降; decrease in imports 进口下降; Exports have registered a decrease. 出口下降。Sales show a 10% decrease on last year 和去年相比, 销售有所下降。2 v. to fall or to become less 下降;减少: Imports are decreasing. 进口正在下降。The value of the pound has decreased by 5%. 英镑的价值已下降5%。

**deduct** v. to remove money from a total 扣除;减云: to deduct £3 from the price 从价格中扣除 3 英磅；to deduct a sumfor expenses 扣除开支金额；After deducting costs the gross margin is only 23%. 扣除成本毛利仅为 23%。Expenses are still to be deducted. 开支费用还得扣除。tax deducted at source = tax which is removed from a salary, interest payment ordividend payment on shares before the money is paid 从收入来源中扣除的赋税

◇ **deductible** a. which can be deducted 可减税的；可扣除的：tax – deductible = which can be deducted from an income before tax is paid 可课税减免的；These expenses are not tax – deductible. = Tax has to be paid on these expenses. 这些开支不能课税减免。

◇ **deduction** n. removing of money from a total or money removed from a total 扣除数：Net salary is salary after deduction of tax and social security. 净工资是指扣除课税和社会保险金后的工资。deductions from salary or salary deductions or deductions at source = money which a company removes from salaries to give to the government as tax, national insurance contributions, etc. (为交政府税与国民保险金公司所作的)工资扣除额；tax deductions = (i) money removed from a salary to pay tax 从工资中扣除的用来付税的钱 (ii) US business expenses which can be claimed against tax(美)企业开支的课税减免

**deed** n. legal document or written agreement 契约；证件：deed of assignment = document which legally transfers a property from a debtor to a creditor 移交凭证；财产转让凭证；deed of covenant = signed legal agreement to pay someone a sum of money every year 条约的契约（向某人每年支付钱款的法律文件）；deed of partnership = agreement which sets up a partnership 合伙契约；deed of transfer = document which transfers the ownership of shares 股票转让契约；title

deeds = document showing who owns a property 地契；所有权凭证；We have deposited the deeds of the house in the bank. 我们将房契存放在银行。

**defalcation** n. illegal use of money by someone who is not the owner but who has been trusted to look after it 盗用；侵吞公款(非法使用不属自己但由他保管的钱款)

**default** 1. n. failure to carry out the terms of a contract, especially failure to pay back a debt 违约；拖欠(特别是拖欠债务)：in default of payment = with no payment made 拖欠付款：The company is in default. = The company has failed to carry out the terms of the contract. 公司违约。by default = Because no one else will act 缺席；不出场；He was elected by default. = He was elected because all the other candidates withdrew. 由于其他侯选人未到场他被当选。

NOTE: no plural

2. v. to fail to carry out the terms of a contract, especially to fail to pay back a debt 违约(特别是拖欠付款)：to default on payments = not to make payments which are due under the terms of a contract 拖欠付款

◇ **defaulter** n. person who defaults 拖欠者；违约者

**defeat** 1. n. loss of a vote 失败；击败：The chairman offered to resign after the defeat of the proposal at the AGM. 在年度股东大会上建议未被采纳，董事长主动提出辞呈。2. v. to beat someone or something in a vote(在选举中)击败；受挫：The proposal was defeated by 10 votes to 23. 此项建议因 10 对 23 票受挫。He was heavily defeated in the ballot for union president. 在工会主席的选举中他惨遭失败。

**defect** n. something which is wrong or which stops a machine from working properly 缺点；毛病：a computer defect or a defect in the computer 计算机的毛病

◇ **defective** a. (a) faulty or not working properly 有缺点的；有缺陷的；有瑕庇的：The machine broke down because of a defective cooling system. 因冷却系统有毛病，机器出了故障。(b) not legally valid 法律上无效的：His title to the property is defective. 他的财产所有权在法律上是无效的。

**defence** or US **defense** n. (a) protecting someone or something against attack 保卫；防护：The merchant bank is organizing the company's defence against the takeover bid. 商业银行(或商人银行)正在组织公司防护自己以免遭兼并出价。(b) fighting a lawsuit on behalf of a defendant(诉讼中的)辨护：defence counsel = lawyer who represents the defendant in a lawsuit 辨护律师

◇ **defend** v. to fight to protect someone or something which is being attacked 防御；保护：The company is defending itself against the takeover bid. 公司正在保护自己以免遭兼并出价。He hired the best lawyers to defend him against the tax authorities. 他聘用了最好的律师以免遭受税务当局的侵害。to defend a lawsuit = to appear in court to state your case when accused of something 出庭辨护

◇ **defendant** n. person who is sued or who is accused of doing something to harm someone 被告

**defer** v. to put back to a later date or to postpone 推迟；延期：to defer payment 延期付款；The decision has been deferred until the next meeting. 被推迟到下次会议再作决定。NOTE: deferring - deferred

◇ **deferment** noun postponement or putting back to a later date deferment of payment 推迟；延期：deferment of a decision 决定或决策的推迟

◇ **deferred** a. put back to a later date 延期的：deferred creditor = person who is owed money by a bankrupt but who is paid only after all other creditors 迟偿债权人；deferred payment = payment for goods by instalments over a long period 延期付款 deferred stock = shares which receive a dividend after all other dividends have been paid 延期付息股票

**deficiency** n. lack 缺少：money lacking 缺钱；There is a £10 deficiency in the petty cash. 在小额现金中少了10英磅。to make up a deficiency = to put money into an account to balance it 在帐户上补上不足的金额

**deficit** n. amount by which spending is higher than income 赤字(开支超过了收入)：the accounts show a deficit. = The accounts show a loss. 帐户上有赤字。to make good a deficit = to put money into an account to balance it 弥补赤字；balance of payments deficit or trade deficit = situation when a country imports more than it exports 国际收支逆差或贸易逆差；deficit financing = planning by a government to borrow money to cover the shortf all between tax income and expenditure 赤字财政；赤字集资。

**deflate** v. to deflate the economy = to reduce activity in the economy by cutting the supply of money 紧缩通货

◇ **deflation** n. reduction in economic activity 通货紧缩；(减少经济活动)

◇ **deflationary** a. which can cause deflation 通货紧缩的：The government has introduced some deflationary measures in the budget. 在财政预算中政府提出了一些通货紧缩的措施。

**defray** v. to provide money to pay (costs) 支付：The company agreed to defray the costs of the exhibition. 公司同意支付展览会的开支。

**degearing** n. reduction in gearing or reducing a company's loan capital in relationto the value of its ordinary shares "去啮合"；（减少与普通股有关的借入资本）

NOTE: no plural

**delay** 1 n. time when someone or something is later than planned 耽搁；延误：There was a delay of thirty minutes before the AGM started or the AGM started after a thirty minute delay. 年度股东大会耽误了 30 分钟。We are sorry for the delay in supplying your order or in replying to your letter. 对提供订单货物或复信方面的耽搁，我们表示歉意。2 v. to be late 延期；耽搁：to make someone late 使某人迟到；He was delayed because his taxi had an accident. 因他的计程车出事故，他迟到了。The company has delayed payment of all invoices. 公司耽搁了对所有发票的支付。

**del credere** n. del credere agent = agent who receives a high commission because he guarantees payment by customers 保付货价代理人

**delegate** 1 n. person who represents others at a meeting 代表：The management refused to meet the trade union delegates. 管理部门拒绝会见工会代表。2 v. to pass authority or responsibility to someone else 授权；委托；委任：to delegate authority 授权；He cannot delegate . = He wants to control everything himself and refuses to give up any of his responsibilities to his subordinates. 他不能授权或委任他人。

◇ **delegation** n. (a) group of delegates 代表团：a Chinese trade delegation 一个中国贸易代表团；The management met a union delegation. 管理部门会见了一个工会代表团。(b) act of passing authority or responsibility to someone else 授权或委派代表

**delete** v. to cut out words in a document 删除：They want to delete all references

to credit terms from the contract. 他们想把所有涉及信贷的条件从合同中删除。The lawyers have deleted clause two. 律师已将条款 2 删掉。

**deliver** v. to transport goods to a customer 交付；递送：goods delivered free or free delivered goods = goods transported to the customer's address at a price which includes transport costs 免费送货；goods delivered on board = goods transported free to the ship or plane but not to the customer's warehouse 免费将货物运到船上或飞机上；delivered price = price which includes packing and transport 交货价；到货价（包括包装和运输费）

◇ **delivery** n. (a) delivery of goods = transport of goods to a customer's address 交货；parcels awaiting delivery 等待投递的包裹；free delivery or delivery free 免费发送货物；delivery date 交货日期；delivery within 28 days 在 28 天内交货；allow 28 days for delivery 允许交货期为 28 天；Delivery is not allowed for or is not included. 运输不在考虑之列或不包括在内。delivery note = list of goods being delivered, given to the customer with the goods 交货单；delivery order = instructions given by the customer to the person holding his goods, to tell him to deliver them 提货单；The store has a delivery service to all parts of the town. = The store will deliver goods to all parts of the town. 商店提供向该城镇所有地方送货的服务。delivery time = number of days before something will be delivered 交货期；发运货物时间；delivery van = goods van for delivering goods to retail customers 运货车；express delivery = very fast delivery 快运交货；recorded delivery = mail service where the letters are signed for by the person receiving them 有回执的邮递；We sent the documents (by) recorded delivery. 我们以有回执的邮递

方式将文件寄出。cash on delivery = paymentin cash when the goods are delivered 货到付款;交货付款;to take delivery of goods = to accept goods when they are delivered 提货;We took delivery of the stock into our warehouse on the 25th. 25 日我们将所提货物放进仓库。(b) goods being delivered 所发运的货物:We take in three deliveries a day. 每天我们收到三批货。There were four items missing in the last delivery. 在上次发来的那批货中少了四件。

(c) transfer of a bill of exchange 交割;汇票的转让

**demand** 1. n. (a) asking for payment 要求(付款):payable on demand = which must be paid when payment is asked for 见票付款;见票即付;demand bill = bill of exchange which must be paid when payment is asked for 即期汇票;即付票据;US demand deposit = money in a bank account which can be taken out when you want it by writing a cheque 美国即期或活期存款;final demand = last reminder from a supplier, after which he will sue for payment 最终要求(供应商的最后一次提醒)(b) need for goods at a certain price(要求按一定价格获得的货物)需求:There was an active demand for oil shares on the stock market. 在股市上石油股票十分畅销。to meet a demand or to fill a demand = to supply what is needed 满足需求;The factory had to increase production to meet the extra demand. 为满足额外需求,工厂不得不增加产量。The factory had to cut production when demand slackened. 当需求疲软时,工厂不得不减产。The office cleaning company cannot keep up with the demand for its services. 从事办公室打扫的公司跟不上对其服务的需求。There is not much demand for this item. = Not many people want to buy it. 对该商品的需求不大。This book is in great demand or there is a great demand for this book. = Many people want to buy it. 对这本书的需求很大。effective demand = actual demand for a product which can be paid for 有效需求;实际需求;demand price. = price at which a certain quantity of goods will be bought 需求价格;supply and demand = amount of a product which is available and the amount whichis wanted by customers 供求:law of supply and demand = general rule that the amount of a product which is availableis related to the needs of potential customers 供求规律;供求法则;2. v. to ask for something and expect to get it 要求;需要:She demanded a refund. 她要求退货款。The suppliers are demanding immediate payment of their outstanding invoices. 供应商要求对未支付的发票立即付款。

◇ **demand - led inflation** n. inflation caused by rising demand which cannot be met 需求引起通货膨胀

**demarcation dispute** n. argument between different trade unions over who shall do different parts of a job(工会之间的)分工争执:Production of the new car was held up by demarcation disputes. 新型汽车的生产因分工争执而耽搁。

**demise** n. (a) death 死亡:On his demise the estate passed to his daughter. 他死后,遗产由他的女儿继承。(b) granting of a property on a lease 租赁中的财产转让

NOTE: no plural for (a)

**demonetize** v. to stop a coin or note being used as money 停止使用(硬币和钞票)

◇ **demonetization** n. stopping a coin or note being used as money 废除或作废(硬币和钞票)

**demonstrate** v. to show how something works 展示;演示:He was demonstrating a new tractor when he was killed. 当

他被杀害时他正在演示一台新拖拉机时。The managers saw the new stock control system being demonstrated. 管理人员观看新存货控制系统的操作示范。

◇ **demonstration** n. showing how something works 示范；展示；We went to a demonstration of new telex equipment. 我们观看了新电传设备的操作示范。demonstration model = piece of equipment used in demonstrations and later sold off cheaply 展示的模型

◇ **demonstrator** n. person who demonstrates pieces of equipment 示范表演者

**demote** v. to give someone a less important job 降职；降级：He was demoted from manager to salesman. 他从经理降为销售员。She lost a lot of salary when she was demoted. 当她被降职时，她的薪水被减了许多。

◇ **demotion** n. giving someone a less important job 降职；降级：He was very angry at his demotion. 他因降职而十分愤怒。

**demurrage** n. money paid to a customer when a shipment is delayed at a portor by the customs 装卸误期费；滞期费

**denationalize** v. to put a nationalized industry back into private ownership 将国有变为私有；非国有化；The government has plans to denationalize the steel industry. 政府计划使钢铁工业转为私有。

◇ **denationalization** n. act of denationalizing 私有化；the denationalization of the aircraft industry 航空工业私有化

**denomination** n. unit of money (on a coin, banknote or stamp) 硬币，钞票或邮票上的货币单位：coins of all denominations 各种面额的硬币；small denomination notes 小额钞票；小额货币

**depart** v. (a) to leave 离开：The plane departs from Paris at 11.15. 飞机从巴黎起飞的时间为 11 点 15 分。(b) to depart from normal practice = to act in a different way from the normal practice 违反常规

◇ **department** n. (a) specialized section of a large company (一个大公司专业化的) 部门：complaints department 投诉部；申诉部；design department 设计部；dispatch department 发运部；export department 出口部 legal department 法律部；accounts department = section which deals with money paid or received 财会部；new issues department = section of a bank which deals with issues of new shares (新) 股票发行部；personnel department = section of a company dealing with the staff 人事部；head of department or department head or department manager = person in charge of a department 部门经理 (b) section of a large store selling one type of product (大商店出售某种产品的) 商品部：You will find beds in the furniture department. 你在家俱部可买到床。budget department = department in a large store which sells cheaper goods 廉价商品部 (c) section of the British government containing several ministries (英国政府中的) 部：the Department of Trade and Industry 贸易和工业部；the Department of Education and Science 教育和科学部

◇ **department store** n. large store with sections for different types of goods 百货商店；百货公司

◇ **departmental** a. referring to a department 部门的；departmental manager = manager of a department 部门经理

**departure** n. (a) going away 离开；出发：The plane's departure was delayed by two hours. 飞机延迟两小时起飞。departures = part of an airport terminal which deals with passengers who are leaving 航空终点站；起程旅客出口；

departure lounge = room in an airport where passengers wait to get on their planes 候机室 (b) new venture or a new type of business 新的商业冒险；新业务：Selling records will be a departure for the local bookshop. 销售唱片将是当地书店的一项新业务。

**depend** v. (a) to depend on = to need someone or something to exist 依赖；依靠：The company depends on efficient service from its suppliers. 该公司依赖供应商的有效服务。We depend on government grants to pay the salary bill. 我们靠政府拨款发工资。(b) to happen because of something 取决于：The success of the launch will depend on the publicity. 推出新产品的成功取决于宣传。depending on = which varies according to something 取决于；Depending on the advertising budget, the new product will be launched on radio or on TV. 在电台或是在电视上做新产品投放市场的广告宣传取决于广告预算。

**deposit** 1. n. (a) money placed in a bank for safe keeping or to earn interest 银行存款：certificate of deposit = certificate from a bank to show that money has been deposited 存款单；Bank deposits = all the money placed in banks 银行存款；Bank deposits are at an all-time high. 银行存款额达历史最高记录。fixed deposit = deposit which pays a fixed interest over a fixed period 定期存款；deposit account = bank account which pays interest but on which notice has to be given to withdraw money 存款帐户；deposit at 7 days' notice = money deposited which you can withdraw by giving seven days' notice 提前7天通知可提取的存款；deposit slip = piece of paper stamped by the cashier to prove that you have paid money into your account 存款单 (b) safe deposit = bank safe where you can leave jewellery or documents 银行的保管库；safe deposit box = small box which you can rent, in which you can keep jewellery or documents in a bank's safe 保险柜 (c) money given in advance so that the thing which you want to buy will not be sold to someone else 押金：to pay a deposit on a watch 付手表的押金；to leave £10 as deposit 留下10英磅的押金 2. v. (a) to put documents somewhere for safe keeping 存放：to deposit shares with a bank 将股票存放在银行；We have deposited the deeds of the house with the bank. 我们已将房契存放在这家银行。He deposited his will with his solicitor. 他将遗嘱寄存在他的律师处。(b) to put money into a bank account 储蓄：to deposit £100 in a current account 将100英磅存入活期存款帐户

◇ **depositary** n. US person or company with whom money or documents can be deposited (美) 保管人；受托人；保管处

◇ **depositor** n. person who deposits money in a bank 存款者

◇ **depository** n. (a) furniture depository = warehouse where you can store household furniture 家俱仓库 (b) person or company with whom money or documents can be deposited (货币或文件) 保管人；保管处

**depot** n. central warehouse for goods; centre for transport 主要仓库；运输中心：bus depot 汽车站；freight depot 货运站；goods depot；货栈；oil storage depot 石油储存站

**depreciate** v. (a) to reduce the value of assets in accounts 折旧 (减少帐上资产的价值)：We depreciate our company cars over three years. 我们将公司小汽车折旧三年。(b) to lose value 贬值：share which has depreciated by 10% over the year 在这一年中股票价值下减了10%；The pound has depreciated by 5% against the dollar. 英镑对美元的比

价下减了 5%。

◇ **depreciation** n. (a) reduction in value of an asset 折旧：depreciation rate = rate at which an asset is depreciated each year in the accounts 折旧率；accelerated depreciation = system of depreciation which reduces the value of assets at a high rate in the early years to encourage companies, as a result of tax advantages, to invest in new equipment 加速折旧；annual depreciation = reduction in the book value of an asset at a certain rate per year 年度折旧；straight line depreciation = depreciation calculated by dividing the cost of an asset by the number of years it is likely to be used. 直线法折旧(即年折旧额为资产使用年限除资产总成本计算的折旧方法)。
NOTE: no plural (b) loss of value 贬值：a share which has shown a depreciation of 10% over the year 一年里价值下降 10% 的股票；the depreciation of the pound against the dollar 英镑对美元的比价下降。

**depress** v. to reduce 减少：Reducing the money supply has the effect of depressing demand for consumer goods. 减少货币供应会产生降低对消费品需求的效果。

◇ **depressed** a. depressed area = part of a country suffering from depression 经济不景气地区；萧条地区：depressed market = market where there are more goods than customers 萧条的市场

◇ **depression** n. period of economic crisis with high unemployment and loss of trade 经济不景气；萧条：an economic depression 经济萧条：the Great Depression = the world economic crisis of 1929 –1933 大萧条

**dept** = DEPARTMENT 部门

**deputy** n. person who takes the place of another 代表；代理人：to act as deputy for someone or to act as someone's deputy 做某人的代表或代理人；deputy chairman 副主席；副董事长 deputy manager 副经理；deputy managing director 副总经理

◇ **deputize** v. to deputize for someone = to take the place of someone who is absent 充任代表或代理：He deputized for the chairman who had a cold. 因董事长感冒由他代任董事长之职。

**deregulation** n. US reducing government control over an industry(美)减少(对工业的)控制；解除控制：the deregulation of the airlines 解除对航空公司的控制

**describe** v. to say what someone or something is like 叙述；描绘；The leaflet describes the services the company can offer. 传单描述公司所能提供的服务。The managing director described the company's difficulties with cash flow. 总经理叙述了公司在现金流动方面所遇到的困难。

◇ **description** n. words which show what something is like 描绘；描述：false description of contents = wrongly stating the contents of a packet to trick customers into buying it 对包装的内容作欺诈性的说明；job description = official document from the management which says what a job involves 工作说明；职务说明；trade description = description of a product to attract customers 产品说明；商业说明；

**design** 1. n. planning or drawing of a product before it is built or manufactured (工业产品)设计：industrial design = design of products made by machines (such as cars and refrigerators)工业产品设计；product design = design of consumer products 消费品设计；design department = department in a large company which designs the company's products or its advertising(大公司的)产品广告设计部；design studio = independent firm which specializes in creating designs 设计公司 2. v. to plan or to draw something before it is built or manufactured 设计: He designed a new car factory. 他设计了一个新汽车工厂。 She designs garden furniture. 她设计花园家具。

◇ **designer** n. person who designs 设计者: She is the designer of the new computer 她是这台新计算机的设计师。

**designate** a. person who has been appointed to a job but who has not yet started work 已任命的(尚未就职): the chairman designate 已受任命而尚未就职的主席。

NOTE: always follows a noun

**desk** n. (a) writing table in an office, usually with drawers for stationery 办公桌: desk diary 办公桌上的工作日志; desk drawer 办公桌抽屉; desk light 台灯; a three - drawer desk = desk with three drawers 三屉办公桌; desk pad = pad of paper kept on a desk for writing notes 办公桌信笺 (b) cash desk or pay desk = place in a store where you pay for goods bought 收银处;商店的付款处: Please pay at the desk. 请在付款处付款 (c) section of a newspaper 编辑部: the city desk = the department which deals with business news 商业新闻编辑部

**despatch** = DISPATCH 发货

**destination** n. place to which something is sent or to which something is going 终点;目的地: The ship will take ten weeks to reach its destination. 该船需10周时间到达目的地。 final destination or ultimate destination = place reached at the end of a journey after stopping at several places en route 最终目的地

**detail** 1. n. small part of a description 细节;详情: The catalogue gives all the details of our product range. 该目录提供了我们产品范围的全部细节。 We are

worried by some of the details in the contract. 我们对合同中的一些细节不太放心。 in detail = giving many particulars 详细地; The catalogue lists all the products in detail 该目录详细地罗列了所有产品。 2. v. to list in detail 详细列出: The catalogue details the payment arrangements for overseas buyers. 该目录为海外购买者详细列出了付款方式。 The terms of the licence are detailed in the contract. 特许证的条款在合同中有详尽地叙述。

◇ **detailed** a. in detail 详细的: detailed account = account which lists every item 明细帐

**determine** v. to fix or to arrange or to decide 确定;决定: to determine prices or quantities 确定价格或数量; conditions still to be determined 仍待确定的条件

**Deutschmark** n. unit of money used in Germany 德国马克

NOTE: also called a mark; when used with a figure, usually written DM before the figure: DM250 ( say "two hundred and fifty Deutschmarks")

**devalue** v. to reduce the value of a currency against other currencies 使货币贬值: The pound has been devalued by 7%. 英镑贬值7%。 The government has devalued the pound by 7%. 政府使英镑贬值7%。

◇ **devaluation** n. reduction in value of a currency against other currencies 贬值: the devaluation of the franc 法郎贬值

**develop** v. (a) to plan and produce 开发;发展: to develop a new product 开发一种新产品 (b) to plan and build an area(计划与建设一个区域)开拓; to develop an industrial estate 建立工业开发区

◇ **developer** n. a property developer = person who plans and builds a group of new houses or new factories(房地产)

开发者

◇ **developing country or developing nation** n. country which is not fully industrialized 发展中国家

◇ **development** n. (a) planning the production of a new product(新产品的) 开发: research and development 研究与开发 (b) industrial development = planning and building of new industries in special areas 工业开发; development area or development zone = area which has been given special help from a government toencourage businesses and factories to be set up there 开发区

**device** n. small useful machine 器械: He invented a device for screwing tops on bottles. 他发明了一种拧瓶盖器。

**diagram** n. drawing which shows something as a plan or a map 图表;图解: diagram showing sales locations 销售分布图; He drew a diagram to show how the decision - making processes work. 他制作了一张决策程序图。The paper gives a diagram of the company's organizational structure. 该报提供一幅公司组织结构图。flow diagram = diagram showing the arrangement of work processes in a series 流水作业图

◇ **diagrammatic** a. in diagrammatic form = in the form of a diagram 图解的: The chart showed the sales pattern in diagrammatic form 该图从图解形式表示销售模式。

◇ **diagrammatically** a. using a diagram 用图解地方法: The chart shows the sales pattern diagrammatically. 该图用图解方法显示销售模式。

**dial** v. to call a telephone number on a telephone 拨（电话）号码: to dial a number; 打电话;拨电话号码; to dial the operator 拨总机号码; to dial direct = to contact a phone number without asking the operator to do it for you 直拨; You can dial New York direct from London. 你可从伦敦直拨纽约。

NOTE: GB English is dialling - dialled, but US spelling is dialing - dialed

◇ **dialling** n. act of calling a telephone number 拨电话号码: dialling code = special series of numbers which you use to make a call to another town or country 外埠电话号码; dialling tone = noise made by a telephone to show that it is ready for you to dial a number(电话)拨号音; international direct dialling = calling telephone numbers in other countries direct 国际直拨;

NOTE: no plural

**diary** n. book in which you can write notes or appointments for each day of the week 日记: desk diary 办公桌上的日程薄

**Dictaphone** n. trademark for a brand of dictating machine 一种口述记录机机牌号的商标

**dictate** v. to say something to someone who then writes down your words 口述; 使听写: to dictate a letter to a secretary. 向秘书口述一封信; He was dictating ordersinto his pocket dictating machine. 他向袖珍口述记录机口述他的指令或命令。dictating machine = machine which records what someone dictates, which a secretary can play back and type out the text. 记录机;口述记录机。

◇ **dictation** n. act of dictating 笔录; 听写: to take dictation = to write down what someone is saying 听写; The secretary was taking dictation from the managing director. 秘书正在笔录总经理的口述。dictation speed = number of words per minute which a secretary can write down in shorthand 听写速度

**differ** v. not to be the same as something else 不同;相异: The two products differ considerably - one has an electric motor, the other runs on oil. 这两种产品的区别相当大,一个有电动机,另一处则靠汽油运转。

◇ **difference** n. way in which two things are not the same 区别;差别: What is the difference between these two products? 这两种产品的区别是什么? differences in price or price differences 价格差异

◇ **different** a. not the same 不同的: Our product range is quite different in design from that of our rivals. 我们的产品系列设计与我们的竞争者的是大不一样的。We offer ten models each in six different colours. 我们提供十种型号,每种型号均有 6 种不同颜色。

◇ **differential** 1. a. which shows a difference 差别的: differential tariffs = different tariffs for different classes of goods 不同种类的商品的差别关税 2. n. price differential = difference in price between products in a range 价格差异: wage differentials = differences in salary between workers in similar types of jobs 工资差别; to erode wage differentials = to reduce differences in salary gradually 逐步减少工资差别

**difficult** a. not easy 困难的: The company found it difficult to sell into the Europeanmarket. 公司发现将产品打入欧洲市场有困难。The market for secondhand computers is very difficult at present. 目前旧计算机市场处于十分困难的境地。

◇ **difficulty** n. problem or thing which is not easy 困难;分歧: They had a lot of difficulty selling into the European market. 在向欧洲市场销售方面,他们碰到许多困难。We have had some difficulties with the customs over the export of computers. 在出口计算机问题上,我们与海关有一些分歧。

**digit** n. single number 单个数字: a seven - digit phone number 7 位数电话号码

◇ **digital** a. digital clock = clock which shows the time as a series of figures (such as12:05:23)数字显示钟: digital computer = computer which calculates on the basis of numbers 数字计算机

**dilution** n. dilution of equity or of shareholding = situation where the ordinary share capital of a company has been increased but without an increase in the assets, so that each share is worth less than before 股票的价值耗减
NOTE: no plural

**dime** n. US infml. ten cent coin 美国十美分的硬币

**diminish** v. to become smaller 缩小;变小: Our share of the market has diminished over the last few years. 过去几年我们产品市场份额已经缩小。law of diminishing returns = general rule that as more factors of production (land, labourand capital) are added to the existing factors, so the amount they produce is proportionally smaller 收益递减法则

**dip** 1. n. sudden small fall 突然略微下跌: Last year saw a dip in the company's performance. 去年公司经营利润小幅度下降。2. v. to fall in price 价格下跌: Shares dipped sharply in yesterday's trading. 在昨日的交易中股票价格锐减。
NOTE: dipping – dipped

**diplomat or diplomatist** n. person (such as an ambassador) who is the official representative of his country in another country 外交家;外交官

◇ **diplomatic** a. referring to diplomats 外交的: diplomatic immunity = being outside the control of the laws of the country you are living in because of being a diplomat 外交豁免; He claimed diplomatic immunity to avoid being arrested. 他提出外交豁免以避免被捕。to grant someone diplomatic status = to give someonethe rights of a diplomat 给予某人外交官地位

**direct** 1. v. to manage or to organize 管理；组织：He directs our South – East Asian operations. 他负责东南亚业务经营的管理。She was directing the development unit until last year. 到去年为止，她一直主持开发部的工作。2. a. straight or with no interference 直的；无干扰的：direct action = strike or go – slow, etc. 罢工；怠工；direct cost = production cost of a product 直接费；直接成本；direct debit = system where a customer allows a company to charge costs to his bank account automatically and where the amount charged can be increased or decreased with the agreement of the customer 直接借记；I pay my electricity bill by direct debit. 我用直接借记法支付电费。direct mail = selling a product by sending publicity material to possible buyers through the post 直接邮售；These calculators are only sold by direct mail. 这些计算器只以直接邮售方式出售。The company runs a successful direct – mail operation. 该公司经营直接邮售业务很成功。direct – mail advertising = advertising by sending leaflets to people through the post 直接邮售广告；direct selling = selling a product direct to the customer without goingthrough a shop 直接销售；direct taxation = tax, such as income tax, which is paid direct to the government 直接赋税；The government raises more money by direct taxation than by indirect. 政府用直接赋税比用间接赋税所筹资金多。3. a. straight or with no third party involved 直接地；不涉及第三者地：We pay income tax direct to the government. 我们直接向政府纳所得税。to dial direct = to contact a phone number yourself without asking the operator to do it for you（电话的）直拨；You can dial New York direct from London if you want. 你能从伦敦直接拨通纽约，如果你想这么做的话。

◇ **direction** n. (a) organizing or managing 组织；管理：He took over the direction of a multinational group. 他接管了一个跨国集团。(b) directions for use = instructions showing how to use something 使用说明

NOTE: no plural for (a)

◇ **directly** ad. (a) immediately 立即地：He left for the airport directly after receiving the telephone message. 在接完电话后他立即去机场。(b) straight or with no third party involved 直接地（无第三者介入）：We deal directly with the manufacturer, without using a wholesaler. 我们与制造商直接交易，不经过批发商。

◇ **director** n. (a) person appointed by the shareholders to help run a company 董事；经理：managing director = director who is in charge of the whole company 总经理；chairman and managing director = managing director who is also chairman of the board of directors 总经理兼董事长；board of directors = all the directors of a company 董事会；directors' report = annual report from the board of directors to the shareholders 董事会年度报告；associate director = director who attends board meetings but has not been elected by the shareholders 非正式董事；executive director = director who actually works full – time in the company 执行董事；non – executive director = director who attends board meetings only to give advice 非执行董事；outside director = director who is not employed by the company 外聘董事；(b) person who is in charge of a project, an official institute, etc. 主任；主持者；负责人：(某一官方机构的负责人等)；the director of the government research institute 政府研究所的主任；She was appointed director of the organization. 她被任命为该组织的负责人。

◇ **directorate** n. group of directors 董事会；理事会

◇ **directorship** n. post of director 董事职务：He was offered a directorship with Smith Ltd. 史密斯有限公司向他提供一个董事职务。

**directory** n. list of people or businesses with information about their addresses and telephone numbers 电话簿（记载人名、商号、电话号码和地址）：classified directory = list of businesses grouped under various headings, such as computer shops or newsagents 分类企业名录；commercial directory or trade directory = book which lists all the businesses and business people in a town 商业指南；street directory = list of people living in a street；map of a town which lists all the streets in alphabetical order in an index 路名指南；telephone directory = book which lists all people and businesses in alphabetical order with their phone numbers 电话号码本：to look up a number in the telephone directory 在电话号码本中查号；His number is in the London directory. 他的电话号码收在伦敦的电话本中。

**disallow** v. not to accept a claim for insurance 否决保险索赔：He claimed £2,000 for fire damage, but the claim was disallowed 他要求获得 2,000 英磅的火灾赔偿金，但此项索赔要求被否决。

**disaster** n. (a) very bad accident 灾难：Ten people died in the air disaster. 在空难中有十人丧生。(b) financial collapse 崩溃（指财政上）；The company is heading for disaster or is on a disaster course. = The company is going to collapse. 公司正走向破产。The advertising campaign was a disaster. = The

advertising campaign was very bad or did not have the required effect. 广告运动彻底失败。(c) accident in nature(自然)灾害：a storm disaster on the south coast 南部沿海的风暴灾害；flood disaster damage 火灾损失

◇ **disastrous** a. very bad 灾难性的：The company suffered a disastrous drop in sales 公司销售额大幅下降。

**disburse** v. to pay money 支出；付钱

◇ **disbursement** n. payment of money 付钱

**discharge** 1. n. (a) discharge in bankruptcy = being released from bankruptcy after paying one's debts 破产债务解除(令) (b) payment of debt 清偿债务：in full discharge of a debt = paying a debt completely 偿还全部债务；final discharge = final payment of what is left of a debt 最终一次偿还债务 (c) in discharge of his duties as director = carrying out his duties as director 履行董事职责 2. v. (a) to discharge a bankrupt = to release someone from bankruptcy because he has paid hisdebts 解除破产人(未偿还债务) (b) to discharge a debt or to discharge one's liabilities = to pay a debt or one's liabilities in full 解除债务 (c) to dismiss or to sack 解雇：to discharge an employee 解雇一名职员

**disciplinary** a. disciplinary procedure = way of warning a worker officially that he is breaking rules or that he is working badly 纪律的(惩戒)程序性

**disclaimer** n. legal refusal to accept responsibility 弃权声明；放弃要求

**disclose** v. to tell details 透露：The bank has no right to disclose details of my account to the tax office. 银行无权向税务局透露我的帐户细节。

◇ **disclosure** n. act of telling details 透露；披露细节：The disclosure of the takeover bid raised the price of the shares. 兼并出价详情的披露, 使股票价格上涨。

**discontinue** v. to stop stocking or selling or making (a product) 终止; 停止(购进或出售或生产某一产品); These carpets are a discontinued line. 这些地毯不再生产。

**discount** 1. n. (a) percentage by which a full price is reduced to a buyer by the seller(卖方给买方)折扣: to give a discount on bulk purchases 大宗(量)购买给折扣; to sell goods at a discount or at a discount price = to sell goods below the normal price 削价出售货物; basic discount = normal discount without extra percentages 基准折扣; We give 25% as a basic discount, but can add 5% for cash payment. 我们给 25% 的基准折扣, 用现金支付可加 5%。quantity discount = discount given to people who buy large quantities 数量折扣; 10% discount for quantity purchases = you pay 10% less if you buy a large quantity 给 10% 的数量折扣; 10% discount for cash or 10% cash discount = you pay 10% less if you pay in cash 10% 的现金折扣; trade discount = discount given to a customer in the same trade 行业折扣; (b) discount house = (i) financial company which specializes in discounting bills 贴现公司 (ii) shop which specializes in selling cheap goods bought at a high discount 廉价商店; discount rate = percentage taken when a bank buys bills 票据贴现率; discount store = shop which specializes in cheap goods bought at a high discount 折扣商店; 廉价商店 (c) shares which stand at a discount = shares which are lower in price than their face value 折扣股票; 低于面值的股票 2. v. to reduce prices to increase sales 打折扣: to discount bills of exchange = to buy bills of exchange for less than the value written on them in order to cash them later 汇票贴现; Shares are dis-

counting a rise in the dollar = Shares have risen in advance of a rise in the dollar price. 股票增值先于美元价值的上涨。discounted cash flow = calculating the forecast return on capital investment in current terms, with reductions for current interest rates 现金流量贴现; discounted value = difference between the face value of a share and its lower market price 贴现价值; 市场价与面值的差价

◇ **discountable** a. which can be discounted 可贴现的: These bills are not discountable. 这些汇票是不可贴现的。

◇ **discounter** n. person or company which discounts bills or sells goods at a discount. 贴现商(公司)廉价商店

**discover** v. to find something new 发现: We discovered that our agent was selling our rival's products at the same price as ours. 我们发现我们的代理人正在以相同的价格出售我们竞争者的产品。The auditors discovered some errors in the accounts. 审计人员发现帐户中有错误。

**discrepancy** n. situation where totals do not add up correctly in accounts 不一致; 差异: There is a discrepancy in the accounts. = There is an error. 帐上有差异。statistical discrepancy = amount by which sets of figures differ 统计差异

**discretion** n. being able to decide correctly what should be done 判断力; 决定能力: I leave it to your discretion. = I leave it for you to decide what to do. 我将它交与你决定。at the discretion of someone = if someone decides 由…自行决定; Membership is at the discretion of the committee. 会员(资格)由委员会决定。

NOTE: no plural

◇ **discretionary** a. which can be done if someone wants 自由决定的: the minister's discretionary powers = powers which the minister could use if he thoughthe should do so 部长的自由裁量权（酌处权）。

**discrimination** n. treating people in different ways because of class, religion, race, language, colour or sex 岐视：sexual discrimination or sex discrimination or discriminationon grounds of sex = treating men and women in different ways 性别岐视
NOTE: no plural

**discuss** v. to talk about a problem 讨论：They spent two hours discussing the details of the contract. 他们花了两小时讨论合同的细节。The committee discussed the question of import duties on cars. 委员会讨论小汽车的进口税问题。The board will discuss wage rises at its next meeting. 董事会将于下次会议讨论长工资事宜。We discussed delivery schedules with our suppliers. 我们与供应商讨论了交货日程安排事宜。

◇ **discussion** n. talking about a problem 讨论：After ten minutes' discussion the board agreed the salary increases. 讨论十分钟后，董事会同意给职工长工资。We spent the whole day in discussions with our suppliers. 我们花了一整天时间与我们的供应者商讨。

**disenfranchise** v. to take away someone's right to vote 剥夺某人的选举权：The company has tried to disenfranchise the ordinary shareholders. 公司试图剥夺普通股东的表决权。

**dishonour** v. to dishonour a bill = not to pay a bill 拒付汇票（或票据）：dishonoured cheque = cheque which the bank will not pay because there is not enough money in the account to pay it 不兑现的支票；空头支票

**disinflation** n. reducing inflation in the economy by increasing tax, reducing the level of money supply, etc. （用增加税收和减少货币供应方法）反通货膨胀；通货紧缩

**disinvest** v. to reduce investment by not replacing capital assets when they wear out 停止投资；投资减少

◇ **disinvestment** n. reduction in capital assets by not replacing them when they wear out 停止投资；投资减少
NOTE: no plural

**disk** n. round flat object, used to store information in computers(计算机上储存信息用的园形) 软盘：floppy disk = small disk for storing information through a computer 软磁盘；软塑料磁盘；hard disk = solid disk which will store a large amount of computerinformation in a sealed case 硬盘；disk drive = part of a computer which makes a disk spin round in order toread it or store information on it 软盘驱动器

◇ **diskette** n. very small floppy disk 小软磁盘

**dismiss** v. to dismiss an employee = to remove an employee from a job 解雇：He was dismissed for being late. 他因迟到而被解雇。

◇ **dismissal** n. removal of an employee from a job 解雇：constructive dismissal = situation where an employee leaves his job voluntarily, but because of pressure from the management 推定解雇；unfair dismissal = removing someone from a job for reasons which are not fair 不公正解雇；wrongful dismissal = removing someone from a job for reasons which are wrong 非法解雇；dismissal procedures = correct way of dismissing someone according to the contractof employment 解雇程序

**dispatch** 1. n. (a) sending of goods to a customer(向客户)发货：The strike held up dispatch for several weeks. 罢工已使货物的发运耽搁了几个星期。dispatch department = department which deals with the packing and sending of goods to customers 发运部；dispatch note = note saying that goods have been sent 发运单；dispatch rider = motorcyclist who delivers messages or parcels in a town 通讯员 (b) goods which have been sent 已发运货物：The weekly dispatch went off yesterday. 昨天已将每周应发运的货物运走。2. v. to send goods to customers 发货

◇ **dispatcher** n. person who sends goods to customers 发送者；调度员

**dispenser** n. machine which automatically provides something (an object or a drink or some food), often when money is put in 自动售货机：automatic dispenser 自动售货机 towel dispenser 自动纸巾机；cash dispenser = machine which gives out money when a special card is inserted and instructions given 自动提款机

**display** 1. n. showing of goods for sale 展销；The shop has several car models on display. 该商店正在展销几种型号的小汽车。an attractive display of kitchen equipment 吸引人的厨房设备展销；display advertisement = advertisement which is well designed to attract attention 具有吸引力的广告：display cabinet or display case = piece of furniture with a glass top or glass doors for showing goods for sale 陈列橱；display material = posters, photographs, etc., to be used to attract attention to goods which are for sale 产品广告资料；display pack or display box = special box for showing goods for sale 陈列柜；展销柜；The watches are prepacked in plastic display boxes. 手表事先装在塑料陈列盒子里。display stand or display unit = special stand for showing goods for sale 陈列台或展台；visual display unit or visual display terminal = screen attached to a computer which shows the information stored in the computer 直观显示终端 2. v. to show 展览；陈列：The company was displaying three new car models at the show. 在展览会上，公司陈列了三种型号的汽车。

**dispose** v. to dispose of = to get rid of or to sell cheaply 处理：to dispose of excess stock 处理多余库存；to dispose of one's business 将企业低价出售

◇ **disposable** a. (a) which can be used and then thrown away 一次性使用的；可随用随丢的；disposable cups 一次性使用的杯子 (b) disposable personal income = income left after tax and national insurance have been deducted 个人除税后的收入；个人收入中可任意支配的部分；可支配收入

◇ **disposal** n. sale 出售：disposal of securities or of property 证券或财产的出售；lease or business for disposal = lease or business for sale 租赁或企业的出售

**dispute** n. industrial disputes or labour disputes = arguments between management and workers (劳资)纠纷；(争议；争端；) to adjudicate or to mediate in a dispute = to try to settle a dispute between other parties 裁定或调停纠纷

**dissolve** v. to bring to an end 结束；终止；解散：to dissolve a partnership or a company 散伙或解散一个公司

◇ **dissolution** n. ending (of a partnership) 散伙；解散：

**distress merchandise** n. US goods sold cheaply to pay a company's debts (美)为偿还公司债务而廉价出售的商品

**distribute** v. (a) to share out dividends 分配或分享股息：Profits were distributed among the shareholders. 在股东中进行利润(红利)分配。(b) to send out goods from a manufacturer's warehouse to retailshops 分发(将货物从制造商的仓库发运到零售商店)：Smith Ltd distributes for several smaller companies. 史密斯有限公司为几家较小的公司发送货物。

◇ **distribution** n. (a) act of sending goodsfrom the manufacturer to the wholesaler and then to retailers 分发;发送(由制造商向批发商,再由批发商向零售商发运货物的行为): distribution costs 经销成本,销售成本; distribution manager 销售经理; channels of distribution or distribution channels = ways of sending goods from the manufacturer to the retailer 销售渠道; distribution network = series of points or small warehouses from which goods are sent all over a country 销售网 (b) distribution slip = paper attached to a document or a magazine showing all the people in an office who should read it 销售条
NOTE: no plural

◇ **distributor** n. company which sells goods for another company which makes them 销售公司(为生产厂家出售货物的公司); sole distributor = retailer who is the only one in an area who is allowed by the manufacturer to sell a certain product 独家销售; a network of distributors = a series of distributors spread all over a country 销售(商)网

◇ **distributorship** n. position of being a distributor for a company 销售商的地位

**district** n. section of a country or of a town(国家或城镇)地区;市区: district manager 地区经理; the commercial district or the business district = part of a town where offices and shops are located 商业区

**diversification** n. adding another quite different type of business to a firm's existing trade(商业经营的)多样化: product diversification or diversification into new products = adding new types of products to the range already made 产品多样化

◇ **diversify** v. (a) to add new types of business to existing ones 使多样化: to diversify into new products 搞产品的多样化 (b) to invest in different types of shares or savings so as to spread the risk of loss 多样化投资;分散投资(为减少风险)

**divest** v. to divest oneself of something = to get rid of something 摆脱;使舍弃: The company had divested itself of its US interests. 该公司摆脱了美国权益。

**divide** v. to cut into separate sections 分开;分割: The country is divided into six representative's areas. 这个国家划分为六个在下议院的议员区。The two companies agreed to divide the market between them. 这两家公司同意在他们之间划分市场。

**dividend** n. percentage of profits paid to shareholders 股息;红利: to raise or to increase the dividend = to pay out a higher dividend than in the previous year 提高股息; to maintain the dividend = to keep the same dividend as in the previous year 保持股息; to pass the dividend = to pay no dividend 不付股息; final dividend = dividend paid at the end of a year 年终分红; interim dividend = dividend paid at the end of a half-year 年中分红;临时分红; dividend cover = the ratio of profits to dividend 利润股息比例; The dividend is covered four times. = The profits are four times the dividend. 利润是股息的四倍。dividend warrant = cheque which makes payment of a dividend 股利息单;股息支票; dividend yield = dividend expressed as a percentage of the price of a share 股息收益率; cum dividend = share sold with the dividend still to be paid 带股息; ex dividend = share sold after the dividend has been paid 不带股息; The shares are quoted ex dividend. = The share price does not include the right to the dividend. 股票报价不带股息。

**division** n. (a) main section of a large

company(大公司)部门: marketing division营销部; production division 生产部; retail division 零售部; the paints division of ICI 帝国化学工业公司的油漆部; the hotel division of THF THF 公司的旅馆部; He is in charge of one of the major divisions of the company. 他是该公司一个主要部门的负责人。(b) company which is part of a large group 分公司: Smith's is now a division of the Brown group of companies. 史密斯公司现在是布朗公司集团中的一个分公司。

◇ **divisional** a. referring to a division 部门的: a divisional director 部门经理; the divisional headquarters 部门总部

**DIY** = DO‐IT‐YOURSELF 自己动手的

**DM or D‐mark** = DEUTSCHMARK, MARK 德国马克

**dock** 1. n. harbour or place where ships can load or unload(装卸货物的)码头: loading dock 装货码头; a dock worker 码头工人; the dock manager 码头管理人员; the docks = part of a town where the harbour is 港区; dock dues = money paid by a ship going into or out of a dock, used to keep the dock in good repair 码头费; 2. v. (a) to go into dock 靠码头: The ship docked at 17:00. 下午5点船靠码头。(b) to remove money from someone's wages 扣工资: We will have to dock his pay if he is late for work again. 如果上班他再迟到，我们将不得不扣他的工资。He had £20 docked from his pay for being late. 因迟到，他的工资被扣20英磅。

◇ **docker** n. person who works in a dock 码头工人

◇ **dockyard** n. place where ships are built 造船厂

**docket** n. list of contents of a package which is being sent(包裹上的)标签; 签条

**doctor** n. specialist who examines people when they are sick to see howthey can be made well 医生: The staff are all sent to see the company doctor once a year. 每年所有职员去该公司医生那里体检一次。doctor's certificate = document written by a doctor to say that a worker is ill and cannot work 医生证明; He has been off sick for ten days and still has not sent in a doctor's certificate. 他病了10天未上班，但一直未交医生证明。company doctor = (i) doctor who works for a company and looks after sickworkers 公司医生; (ii) specialist businessman who rescues businesses whichare in difficulties 经营专家

**document** n. paper with writing on it 文件: legal document 法律文件

◇ **documentary** a. in the form of documents 公文的; 文件的: documentary evidence 证明文件; 书面证据: documentary proof 书面证明; 书面证件; 书面证词

◇ **documentation** n. all documents referring to something 有关文件; 参考文件

Please send me the complete documentation concerning the sale NOTE: no plural. 请寄给我有关销售全部的文件。

**dogsbody** n. infml. person who does all types of work in an office for very low wages(办公室)勤杂工; 干杂活的人

**do‐it‐yourself** a. done by an ordinary person, not by a skilled worker 自制的; 自己动手的: do‐it‐yourself conveyancing = drawing up a legal conveyance by the person selling a property, without the help of a lawyer 自已起草的转让证书; do‐it‐yourself magazine = magazine with articles on work which the average person can do to repair or paint his house. 供自己动手者阅读的杂志。

**dole** n. money given by the government to unemployed people(政府发给)失业

救济金：He is receiving dole payments or he is on the dole. = He is receiving unemployment benefits. 他靠失业救济金生活。dole queues = lines of people waiting to collect the dole 领取失业救济金者的队

**dollar** n. (a) money used in the USA and other countries 元(美国和其他国家用的钱)：The US dollar rose 2%. 美元升值 2%。fifty Canadian dollars 50 加元；It costs sixAustralian dollars. 它值 6 澳元。five dollar bill = banknote for five dollars 5 元一张的钞票；(b) the currency used in the USA 美元；美金：dollar area = area of the world where the dollar is the main trading currency 美元区；dollar balances = a country's trade balances expressed in US dollars 用美元表示的贸易均衡状况；dollar crisis = fall in the exchange rate for the US dollar 美元危机；dollar gap or dollar shortage = situation where the supply of dollars is not enough to satisfy the demand for them from overseas buyers 美元短缺；dollar stocks = shares in US companies 美国公司股。NOTE: usually written $ before a figure：$ 250. The currencies used in different countries can be shown by the initial letter of the country：C $ (Canadian dollar) A $ (Australian dollar)，etc.

**domestic** a. referring to the home market or the market of the country where the business is situated 国内的(市场或企业所在地国家)：domestic sales 国内销售；domestic turnover 国内营业额；domestic consumption = consumption on the home market 国内消费；Domestic consumption of oil has fallen sharply. 国内石油消费税减。domestic market = market in the country where a company is based 国内市场；They produce goods for the domestic market. 他们为国内市场生产商品。domestic production = production of goods for domestic con-sumption 满足国内消费的生产

**domicile** 1. n. place where someone lives or where a company's office is registered 居住地；公司注册地 2. v. He is domiciled in Denmark. = He lives in Denmark officially. 他居住在丹麦。bills domiciled in France = bills of exchange which have to be paid in France 法国支付的汇票

**door** n. piece of wood or metal, etc. which closes the entrance to a building or room 门：The finance director knocked on the chairman's door and walked in. 主管财务的经理敲董事长的门并走了进去。The sales manager's name is on his door. 销售经理的名字贴在他门上。The store opened its doors on June 1st. = The store started in business on June 1st. 该商店于六月一日开业。

◇ **door - to - door** a. going from one house to the next, asking the occupiers to buy something or to vote for someone 挨门挨产(兜售商品或拉选票)；door - to - door canvassing 挨门挨户地游说；door - to - door salesman 挨门挨户的推销人员；door - to - door selling 挨门挨户的推销

**dot** n. small round spot 小圆点：The order form should be cut off along the line shown by the row of dots. 订货单应沿着虚线剪下。

◇ **dot - matrix printer** n. printer which makes letters by printing many small dots(一种能印出由许多网点组成字母的印刷机)点阵印刷机

◇ **dotted line** n. line made of a series of dots 点线；虚线：Please sign on the dotted line. 请在虚线上面签字。Do not write anything below the dotted line. 虚线下面不要写任何东西。

**double** 1. a. (a) twice as large or two times the size 加倍的；两倍的：Their turnover is double ours. 他们的营业额是我们的两倍。to be on double time =

to earn twice the usual wages for working on Sundays or other holidays 挣双工资；double - entry bookkeeping = system of bookkeeping where both credit and debit sides of an account are noted 复式簿记；double taxation = taxing the same income twice 双重课税；double taxation agreement = agreement between two countries that a person living in one country shall not be taxed in both countries on the income earned in the other country(指两国间)无双重课税的协议 (b) in double figures = with two figures or 10 to 99 两位数：Inflation is in double figures. 两位数的通货膨胀。We have had double - figure inflation for some years. 几年来我们都有两位数的通货膨胀。2 v. to become twice as big 是…的两倍；to make something twice as big 使增加一倍；We have doubled our profits this year or our profits have doubled this year. 今年我们的利润翻了一翻或增加了一倍。The company's borrowings have doubled. 公司的借款增加一倍。

◇ **double - book** v. to let the same hotel room or plane seat, etc., to more than one person at a time(将同一个旅馆房间、飞机座位…等)重复出租或出售：We had to change our flight as we were double - booked. 我们不得不改变航班，因为我们的座位是重复预定的。

◇ **double - booking** noun letting by a travel agent of the same hotel room or the same plane seat to more than one person at a time(同一旅馆房间、飞机座位等)重复预定

**Dow Jones Average** n. index of share prices on the New York Stock Exchange, based on a group of major companies(纽约证券交易所的)道琼斯平均指数：The Dow Jones Average rose ten points. 道琼斯平均指数上升了十个百分点。General optimism showed in the rise on the Dow Jones Average. 由于

道琼斯平均指数上升，人们普遍表现出乐观情绪。

**down** 1. ad. & prep in a lower position or to a lower position 在低处；向下：The inflation rate is gradually coming down. 通货膨胀率逐步下降。Shares are slightly down on the day. 白天股价有所下跌。The price of petrol has gone down. 汽油价格已经下跌。to pay money down = to make a deposit 付定金：He paid £50 down and the rest in monthly instalments. 他当场交付50英磅，其余则每月分期支付。2. v. to down tools = to stop working 放下工具(停止工作)

◇ **downgrade** v. to reduce the importance of someone or of a job 降级；降职：His job was downgraded in the company reorganization. 公司改组时他被降职。

◇ **down market** ad. & a. cheaper or appealing to a less wealthy section of the population(较便宜或面向较为不富裕的人)低挡品市场：The company has adopted a down - market image. 公司采用了低档品市场形象。The company has decided to go down market. = The company has decided to make products which appeal to a wider section of the public. 公司决定让自己的产品进入低档品市场。

◇ **down payment** n. part of a total payment made in advance 分期付款的定金；首次付款：He made a down payment of $100. 他付了100英磅定金。

◇ **downside** n. downside factor = possibility of making a loss (in an investment)(投资中)受损的因素：The sales force have been asked to give downside forecasts. = They have been asked for pessimistic forecasts. 让销售人员下调预测数字。

◇ **down time** n. time when a machine is not working because it is broken or being mended, etc.；time when a worker cannot work because machines have broken down, because components are not available, etc.(机器出故障、检修、缺少零配件所造成的)停工期；窝工时间

◇ **downtown** n. & ad. in the central business district of a town(城镇的)商业区：His office is in downtown New York. 他的办公室在纽约市的商业区。a downtown store 位于商业区的商店；They established a business downtown. 他们建立了一个商业区。

◇ **downturn** n. movement towards lower prices or sales or profits(价格或销售或利润的)下降趋势：a downturn in the market price 市场价格的下降趋势；The last quarter saw a downturn in the economy. 上个季度经济下降。

◇ **downward** ad. towards a lower position 向下的；下跌的

◇ **downwards** ad. towards a lower position 向下地：The company's profits have moved downwards over the last few years. 在过去几年中公司的利润日益减少。

**dozen** n. twelve 一打；12 个：to sell in sets of one dozen 以每一套一打出售；cheaper by the dozen = the product is cheaper if you buy twelve at a time 成打购买享受优惠

**draft** 1. n. (a) order for money to be paid by a bank 汇票：banker's draft 银行汇票；to make a draft on a bank = to ask a bank to pay money for you 向银行开汇票；sight draft = bill of exchange which is payable when it is presented 即期汇票；(b) first rough plan or document which has not been finished 草稿；草案：draft of a contract or draft contract 合同草稿：He drew up the draft agreement on the back of an envelope. 他在信封的背面草拟协议。The first draft of the contract was corrected by the managing director. 总经理对合同的第一稿进行了修改。The finance depart-

ment has passed the final draft of the accounts. 财务处通过了帐目的最后一稿。rough draft = plan of a document which may have changes made to it before it is complete 草稿 2. v. to make a first rough plan of a document 草拟；起草；to draft a letter 起草信函；to draft a contract 起草一份合同；The contract is still being drafted or is still in the drafting stage. 该合同仍处于草拟阶段。

◇ **drafter** n. person who makes a draft 起草人；拟搞人：the drafter of the agreement 协议的起草人

◇ **drafting** n. act of preparing the draft of a document 草拟：The drafting of the contract took six weeks. 合同的起草用了六周时间。

**drain** 1. n. (a) pipe for taking dirty water from a house 阴沟；排污水管 (b) gradual loss of money flowing away(指钱)花光；耗尽：The costs of the London office are a continual drain on our resources. 伦敦办事处的开支正在不断地耗尽我们的财力。2. v. to remove something gradually 花光；耗尽；The expansion plan has drained all our profits. 该发展计划已耗尽了我们全部的利润。The company's capital resources have drained away。公司的资本财力已被耗尽。

**draw** v. (a) to take money away 提款：to draw money out of an account 从帐户中提款；to draw a salary = to have a salary paid by the company 获得公司付给的薪金；The chairman does not draw a salary. 董事长不拿工资。(b) to write a cheque 开支票：He paid the invoice with a cheque drawn on an Egyptian bank. 他用一张一家埃及银行付款的支票来支付发票上的货款。

NOTE: drawing – drew – has drawn

◇ **drawback** n. (a) thing which is not convenient or likely to cause problems 不利条件；障碍：One of the main drawbacks of the scheme is that it will take six years to complete. 一个主要不利条件就是要花六年时间才能完成该项计划。(b) paying back customs duty when imported goods are then re - exported(进口货物,再出口时退还的进口税)退税

◇ **drawee** n. person or bank asked to make a payment by a drawer 受票人;付款人

◇ **drawer** n. person who writes a cheque or a bill asking a drawee to pay money to a payee(开支票或汇票要求受票人向收款人付钱的人)开票;出票人: The bank returned the cheque to drawer. = The bank would not pay the cheque because the person who wrote it did not have enough money in the account to pay it. 银行将支票退回给开票人。

◇ **drawing** n. drawing account = current account or account from which the customer may take money when he wants 提款帐户;往来帐户

◇ **draw up** v. to write a legal document 起草(一份法律文件): to draw up a contract or an agreement 起草一份合同或协议; to draw up a company's articles of association 起草公司章程

**drift** v. to move slowly 缓慢移动: Shares drifted lower in a dull market. 在呆滞的市场上,股票的价格缓慢下跌。Strikers are drifting back to work. 罢工者慢慢地开始复工。

**drive** 1. n. (a) energy or energetic way of working 干劲;积极性;能动性: economy drive = vigorous effort to save money or materials 节约运动; sales drive = vigorous effort to increase sales 促销运动; He has a lot of drive. = He is very energetic in business 他干劲十足。(b) part of a machine which makes other parts work(机器的)驱动装置; disk drive = part of a computer which makes the disk spin round in order to

store information on it 计算机的软盘驱动器 2. v. (a) to make a car or lorry, etc. go in a certain direction 驾驶;开车: He was driving to work when he heard the news on the car radio. 他正开车上班时,突然从汽车收音机中听到此消息。She drives a company car. 他驾驶一辆公司的小汽车。(b) He drives a hard bargain. = He is a difficult negotiator 他很善于讨价还价。

NOTE: driving - drove - has driven

**drop** 1. n. (a) fall 降低;下降: drop in sales 销售下跌; Sales show a drop of 10%. 销售额下降10%。a drop in prices 价格下跌 (b) drop shipment = delivery of a large order from the manufacturer direct to a customer's shop or warehouse without going through an agent or wholesaler(向顾客)直接装运(不经代理人或批发商直接向客户发运货物); 2. v. to fall 下跌;下降: Sales have dropped by 10% or have dropped 10%. 销售额下降10%。The pound dropped three points against the dollar. 英镑对美元的比价下跌了三个百分点。

NOTE: dropping - dropped

◇ **drop ship** v. to deliver a large order direct to a customer 直接发运

**drug** n. medicine 药;药物: a drug on the market = product which is difficult to sell because it has already been sold in large quantities and the market is satisfied 滞销商品

**dry** a. not wet 干的: dry goods = cloth, clothes and household goods 布类和家用商品; dry measure = way of calculating loose dry produce (such as corn)(度量衡)干量

**duck** see LAME DUCK

**dud** a. & n. infml. false or not good (coin or banknote)假硬币;假钞票;废钞票;伪钞: The £50 note was a dud. 这50英磅的钞票是伪钞。dud cheque = cheque which the bank refuses to pay because the personwriting it has not e-noughmoney in his account to pay it 作废的支票

**due** a. (a) owed 尚欠的：sum due from a debtor 债务人尚欠的款项；bond due for repayment 到期应偿还的债券；to fall due or to become due = to be ready for payment 到期；bill due on May 1st = bill which has to be paid on May 1st 5 月 1 日到期的汇票；balance due to us = amount owed to us which should be paid 应向我们支付的差额 (b) expected to arrive 应到达的；预期到达的：The plane is due to arrive at 10.30 or is due at 10.30. 飞机预定 10 点 30 分到达。(c) in due form = written in the correct legal form. 式地（按法律格式）；receipt in due form 正式的收条；contract drawn up in due form 正式拟定的合同；after due consideration of the problem = after thinking seriously about the problem 对这个问题经过认真的考虑后 (d) caused by 由于：Supplies have been delayed due to a strike at the manufacturers. 由于工厂罢工，供货被耽搁。The company pays the wages of staff who are absent due to illness. 公司给因病缺席的工人支付工资。

◇ **dues** pl n. (a) dock dues or port dues or harbour dues = payment which a ship makes to the harbour authorities for theright to use the harbour 码头费；港口费，(b) orders taken but not supplied until new stock arrives 未供订货；拖欠的订货

**dull** a. not exciting or not full of life 萧条的：dull market = market where little business is done 萧条的市场

◇ **dullness** n. being dull 萧条：the dullness of the market 市场的萧条

**duly** ad. (a) properly 合适地；恰当地：duly authorized representative 恰当地授权代表 (b) as was expected 按时地；如期地；We duly received his letter of 21st October. 我们按期收到他 10 月 21 日的来信。

**dummy** n. imitation product to test the reaction of potential customers to its design(用来试探未来购买者)仿制品：dummy pack = empty pack for display 样品包

**dump** v. to dump goods on a market = to get rid of large quantities of excess goods cheaply in an overseas market 倾销(在海外以低价倾销商品)：

◇ **dump bin** n. display container like a large box which is filled with goods for sale (出售货物用的)陈列集装箱

◇ **dumping** n. act of getting rid of excess goods cheaply in an overseas market 倾销(在海外市场低价倾销商品)：The government has passed anti－dumping legislation. 政府通过了反倾销法。dumping of goods on the European market 在欧洲市场倾销商品；panic dumping of sterling = rush to sell sterling at any price because of possible devaluation (因怕贬值)惊恐地低价抛售英磅
NOTE: no plural

**duplicate** 1. n. copy 副本：He sent me the duplicate of the contract. 他寄给我一份合同副本。duplicate receipt or duplicate of a receipt = copy of a receipt 收据的副本；in duplicate = with a copy receipt in duplicate = two copies of a receiptg 一式两份的收据；to print an invoice in duplicate 将发票印两份 2. v. (a) (of a bookkeeping entry) to duplicate with another = to repeat another entry or to be the same as another entry 与另一入帐重复 (b) to duplicate a letter = to make a copy of a letter 将信复印一份

◇ **duplicating** n. copying 复印；duplicating machine = machine which makes copies of documents 复印机；duplicating paper = special paper to be used in a duplicating machine 复印纸

◇ **duplication** n. copying of documents复印文件: duplication of work = work which is done twice without being necessary 重复劳动

◇ **duplicator** n. machine which makes copies of documents 复印

**durable** 1. a. durable goods = goods which will be used for a long time (such as washing machines or refrigerators)耐用品; durable effects = effects which will be felt for a long time 持久的影响; The strike will have durable effects on the economy. 罢工会对经济产生长远的影响。2. n. consumer durables = goods bought by the public which will be used for a long time(such as washing machines or refrigerators)耐用消费品

**Dutch** a. Dutch auction = auction where the auctioneer offers an item for sale at ahigh price and then gradually reduces the price until someonemakes a bid 喊价逐步减低的拍卖(逐步落价的荷兰式拍卖) to go Dutch = to share the bill in a restaurant 各人自己付帐

**dutiable items** a. dutiable goods or dutiable items = goods on which a customs duty has to be paid 征税的货物

◇ **duty** n. tax which has to be paid 应付的税: to take the duty off alcohol 酒精不付税; to put a duty on cigarettes 征香烟税 ad valorem duty = duty calculated on the sales value of the goods 从价税(按货物价格所征的税); customs duty or import duty = tax on goods imported into a country 海关税或进口税; excise duty = tax on goods (such as alcohol and petrol) which are produced in the country 国内货物税;消费税; goods which are liable to duty = goods on which customs or excise tax has to be paid 应付税的货物; duty - paid goods = goods where the duty has been paid 已付税货物; stamp duty = tax on legal documents (such as the conveyance of a propertyto a new owner)印花税; estate duty or US death duty = tax paid on the property left by a dead person 遗产税或美国继承税

◇ **duty - free** a. & ad. sold with no duty to be paid 免税: He bought a duty - free watch at the airport. or He bought the watch duty - free. 他在机场买了块免税手表。duty - free shop = shop at an airport or on a ship where goods can be bought without paying duty 免税商店。

# Ee

**e. & o. e.** = ERRORS AND OMISSIONS EXCEPTED 错误遗漏除外, 错漏不计。

**eager** a. wanting to do something 极想; 渴望: The management is eager to get into the Far Eastern markets. 管理部门极想把产品打入远东市场。Our salesmen are eager to see the new product range. 我们的销售人员急于想见到新产品系列。

**early** a。& adverh (a) before the usual time 早的 The mail left early. 邮件提前发出。early closing day = weekday when most shops in a town close in the afternoon(周日商店)提前关门; at your earliest convenience = as soon as possible请尽早(在你方便时) at an early date = very soon 很快 (b) at the beginning of a period of time 早期的: He took an early flight to Paris. 他乘早班飞机去巴黎。We hope for an early resumption of negotiations. = We hope negotiations will start again soon. 我们希望早日恢复谈判。

**earmark** v. to reserve for a special purpose 留作专用: to earmark funds for a project 为一个项目拨专款; The grant is earmarked for computer systems development. 此项拨款是专门用于计算机系统开发。

**earn** v. (a) to be paid money for working 赚;挣钱: to earn £ 50 a week 每周争 50 英磅; Our agent in Paris certainly does not earn his commission. 我们在巴黎的代理人当然不挣(拿)佣金。GB wife's earned income allowance = tax allowance to be set against money earned by the wife of the taxpayer(英)已婚妇女所得税补贴 (b) to produce interest or dividends 生利息;股息: What level of dividend do these shares earn? 这些股票能生多少股息? account which earns interest at 10% 能产生 10%利息的帐户

◇ **earning** n. earning capacity or earning power = amount of money someone should be able to earn 收益能力: He is such a fine dress designer that his earning power is very large. 他是一位精湛的女装设计师,因此收入很多。earning potential = amount of money a person should be able to earn 争钱潜力; amount of dividend a share should produce 挣股息的潜力

◇ **earnings** pl. n. (a) salary or wages, profits and dividends or interest received 薪水;工资;利润;股息;所获利息: compensation for loss of earnings = payment to someone who has stopped earning money or who is not able to earn money 无经济来源津贴; invisible earnings = foreign currency earned by a country in providing services (such as banking, tourism), not in selling goods 无形收益 (b) money which is earned in interest or dividend 股息;利息: earnings per share or earnings yield = money earned in dividends per share, shown as a percentage of the market price of one share 每股收益; gross earnings = earn-

ings before tax and other deductions 毛收益; price or earnings ratio (PorE ratio) = ratio between the market price of a share and the current dividend it produces(股票的)价格——收益率: These shares sell at a P or E ratio of 7. 这些股票按价格——收益率为 7 进行出售。retained earnings = profits which are not paid out to shareholders as dividend 保留盈余;保留收益

**earnest** n. money paid as a down payment 定金;保证金

**ease** v. to fall a little 略有下降: The share index eased slightly today. 今日股票指数稍有下降。

**easement** n. right which someone has to use land belonging to someone else (such as for a path to a garage)使用他人土地的权利;地役权

**easy** a. (a) not difficult 容易的;不难的: easy terms = terms which are not difficult to accept or price which is easy to pay 容易接受的条件; The shop is let on very easy terms. 以非常容易接受的条件出租此商店。The loan is repayable in easy payments. = with very small sums paid back regularly 贷款可以小金额分期偿还的。easy money = (i) money which can be earned with no difficulty 容易挣来的钱 (ii) money available on easy repayment terms 以低息借入的钱: easy money policy = government policy of expanding the economy by making moneymore easily available 金融缓和政策;宽松的货币政策 (b) easy market = market where few people are buying, so prices are low 价格低的市场: The Stock Exchange was easy yesterday. 昨日证券交易所交易平淡。Share prices are easier. = Prices have fallen slightly. 股票价格略有下跌。

◇ **easily** a. (a) without any difficulty 容易地: We passed through the customs easily. 我们很容易地通过了海关。(b) much or a lot (compared to something else)远远；无疑 He is easily our best salesman. 他无疑是我们最好的推销员。The firm is easily the biggest in the market. 该公司无疑是市场上的最大的一家。

**EC** = EUROPEAN COMMUNITY 欧共体

NOTE: EC is often used in the USA, while EEC is more common in GB English

**ECGD** = EXPORT CREDIT GUARANTEE DEPARTMENT 出口信贷保险部

**echelon** n. group of people of a certain grade in an organization(某一层或等级的)全体人员：the upper echelons of industry 工业部门有较高职位的阶层

**econometrics** pl. n. study of the statistics of economics, using computers 计量经济学(用计算机对经济学中的统计数字进行研究)

NOTE: takes a singular verb

**economic** a. (a) which provides enough money 合算的；有利可图的：The flat is let at an economic rent. 该单元房以有利可图的租金出租。It is hardly economic for the company to run its own warehouse. 该公司自己经营仓库是不合算的。(b) referring to the financial state of a country 经济的(指一国的经济情况)：economic planner 制定经济计划的人；economic planning 经济计划；the government's economic policy 政府的经济政策；the economic situation 经济形势；the country's economic system 国家经济制度；economic trends 经济趋势；economic crisis or economic depression = state where a country is in financial collapse 经济危机；经济萧条；The government has introduced import controls to solve the current economic crisis. 政府用控制进口方法解决当前的经济危机。economic cycle = period during which trade expands, then slows down, then expands again 经济周期；economic development = expansion of the commercial and financial situation 经济发展：The economic development of the region has totally changed since oil was discovered there. 自发现石油后，该地区的经济发展情况有了全新的变化。economic growth = increase in the national income 经济增长：The country enjoyed a period of economic growth in the 1960s. 60 年代该国经历了一段经济增长时期。economic indicators = statistics which show how the economy is going to perform in the short or long term 经济指标；economic sanctions = restrictions on trade with a country in order to make its government change policy 经济制裁：The western nations imposed economic sanctions on the country. 西方国家对该国实行经济制裁。the European Economic Community = the Common Market 欧洲经济共同体

◇ **economical** a. which saves money or materials or which is cheap 节省的；省钱的：economical car = car which does not use much petrol 节油小汽车；economical use of resources = using resources as carefully as possible 节约资源

◇ **economics** pl. n. (a) study of production, distribution, selling and use of goods and services 经济学(对生产、销售、货物与劳务使用和出售进行研究)：(b) study of financial structures to show how a product or service is costed and what returns it produces 经济核算(对金融结构的研究以表明产品或劳务的成本如何估计，以及它的效益是什么)；the economics of town planning；城市规划的经济核算；I do not understand the economics of the coal industry. 我不懂采煤业的经济核算。

NOTE: takes a singular verb

◇ **economist** n. person who specializes in the study of economics 经济学家：agricultural economist 农业经济学家

◇ **economize** v. to economize on petrol = to save petrol 节省汽油

◇ **economy** n. (a) being careful not to waste money or materials 节约；节省：an economy measure = an action to save money or materials 节约措施；to introduce economies or economy measures into the system = to start using methods to save money or materials 在该制度中引入节约举措；economies of scale = making a product more profitable by manufacturing it in larger quantities 规模经济；economy car = car which does not use much petrol 省油小汽车；economy class = cheapest class on a plane 经济舱位（乘飞机）；to travel economy class 乘坐经济舱位旅行；economy drive = campaign to save money or materials 节约运动；economy size = large size or large packet which is a bargain 经济包装；廉价包装 (b) financial state of a country or way in which a country makes and uses its money 经济状况：The country's economy is in ruins. 该国经济已崩溃。black economy = work which is paid for in cash or goods, but not declared to the tax authorities 非法经济活动（其报酬以现金或货物支付，不向税务局申报纳税）；capitalist economy = system where each person has the right to invest money, to work in business, to buy and sell with no restrictions from the state 资本主义经济；controlled economy = system where business activity is controlled by orders from the government 受控经济；free market economy = system where the government does not interfere in business activity in any way 自由市场经济；mixed economy = system which contains both nationalized industries and private enterprise 混合经济；planned economy = system where the government plans all business activity 计划经济

**ecu** or **ECU** n. = EUROPEAN CURRENCY UNIT 欧洲货币单位

**edge** 1 n. (a) side of a flat thing 边沿；边缘：He sat on the edge of the managing director's desk. 他坐在总经理办公桌边沿上。The printer has printed the figures right to the edge of the printout. 印刷机将数字正好打印在印刷输出片子的边缘。(b) advantage 优势；比…强：Having a local office gives us a competitive edge over Smith Ltd. 在当地设有办事处使我们胜史密斯有限公司一筹。to have the edge on a rival company = to be slightly more profitable or to have a slightly larger share of the market than a rival 稍胜竞争对手一筹；2. v. to move a little 徐徐移动：Prices on the stock market edged upwards today. 今日股市价格稍有上升。Sales figures edged downwards in January. 月份销售数字略有下降。

**editor** n. person in charge of a newspaper or a section of a newspaper (报纸)编辑：the editor of the "Times"《时代》周刊编辑；the City editor = business or finance editor of a British newspaper (英国报纸的)商业或金融版编辑

◇ **editorial** 1 a. referring to an editor 编辑的：editorial board = group of editors (on a newspaper, etc.) 编委会 2 n. main article in a newspaper, written by the editor 社论；评论

**EDP** = ELECTRONIC DATA PROCESSING 电子数据处理

**EEC** = EUROPEAN ECONOMIC COMMUNITY 欧洲经济共同体：EEC ministers met today in Brussels. 今日欧共体部长们在布鲁塞尔会晤。The USA is increasing its trade with the EEC. 美国与欧共体的贸易额正在增加。

**effect** 1 n. (a) result 结果；效果：The effect of the pay increase was to raise productivity levels. 增加工资的结果是

生产率水平的提高。terms of a contract which take effect or come into effect from January 1st = terms which start to operate on January 1st 1 月 1 日开始生效的合同条款；Prices are increased by 10% with effect from January 1st. = New prices will apply from January 1st. 价格上涨 10% 于 1 月 1 日生效。to remain in effect = to continue to be applied 仍有效（b）meaning 意思：clause to the effect that = clause which means that 条款大意是…；We have made provision to this effect. = We have put into the contract terms which will make this work. 我们已在合同中做了诸如此类意思的规定。（c）personal effects = personal belongings 动产；个人财物 2 v. to carry out 完成；履行；实现：to effect a payment = to make a payment 履行付款：to effect customs clearance = to clear something through customs 履行结关手续；to effect a settlement between two parties = to bring two parties together and make them agree to a settlement 在双方当事人之间实现和解

◇ **effective** a. （a）effective demand = actual demand for a product which can be paid for 实际需求；有效需求：effective yield = actual yield shown as a percentage 实际收益（b）effective date = date on which a rule or a contract starts to be applied 生效日：clause effective as from January 1st = clause which starts to be applied on January 1st 1 月 1 日开始生效的条款（c）which works or which produces results 有效的；产生效果的：Advertising in the Sunday papers is the most effective way of selling. 在星期日报纸上做广告是最有效的销售方法。see COST - EFFECTIVE

◇ **effectiveness** n. working or producing results 有效性：I doubt the effectiveness of television advertising. 我对电视广告的效果表示怀疑。see COST - EFFECTIVENESS

◇ **effectual** a. which produces a correct result 收效的；能奏效的

**efficiency** n. ability to work well or to produce the right result or the right work quickly 效率；功效：with a high degree of efficiency 有高效率；a business efficiency exhibition 商业效率展览；an efficiency expert 效率专家
NOTE: no plural

◇ **efficient** a. able to work well or to produce the right result quickly 有能力的；能胜任的：the efficient working of a system；制度的有效运转；He needs an efficient secretary to look after him. 他需要一个能力强的秘书来照顾他。efficient machine 效率高的机器

◇ **efficiently** adverb in an efficient way 高效地：She organized the sales conference very efficiently. 她高效地组织了这次销售会议。

**efflux** n. flowing out 流出：efflux of capital to North America 资本向北美的流动

**effort** n. using the mind or body to do something 努务；尽力：The salesmen made great efforts to increase sales. 销售人员尽力增加销售。Thanks to the efforts of the finance department, overheads have been reduced. 由于财务部门的努力管理费或间接费用减少。If we make one more effort, we should clear the backlog of orders. 如果再做一次努力，我们应能把积压的订单处理完。e. g. for example or such as 举例；例如：The contract is valid in some countries (e. g. France and Belgium) but not in others. 此合同在有些国家(如法国和比利时)有效的，但在其他国家则无效。

**EGM** = EXTRAORDINARY GENERAL MEETING 特别全会

**elastic** a. which can expand or contract easily because of small changes in price. 有弹性的(因价格的微小变化能容易扩大或缩小的)

◇ **elasticity** n. ability to change easily 弹性；弹力：elasticity of supply and demand = changes in supply and demand of an item depending on its market price 供给与需求的弹性
NOTE: no plural

**elect** v. to choose someone by a vote 选举：to elect the officers of an association 选举协会的办事员（高级职员）；She was elected president. 她当选为主席。

◇ **- elect** suffix person who has been elected but has not yet started the term of office 当选但尚未就任的人：She is the president - elect. 她是已当选但尚未就职的主席。
NOTE: the plural is presidents - elect

◇ **election** n. act of electing 选举：the election of officers of an association 协会官员的选举；the election of directors by the shareholders 股东选举董事；general election = choosing of representatives by all the voters in a country 大选

**electricity** n. current used to make light or heat or power 电；电流：The electricity was cut off this morning, so the computers could not work. 今晨断电，故计算机不能工作。Our electricity bill has increased considerably this quarter. 本季度我们的电费有相当大的增加。Electricity costs are an important factor in our overheads. 电费占经常性开支中很大一部分。

◇ **electric** a. worked by electricity 电动的：an electric typewriter 电动打字机

◇ **electrical** a. referring to electricity 电力的；电气科学的：The engineers are trying to repair an electrical fault. 工程师们正努力排除电力方面的故障。

**electronic** a. electronic data processing = selecting and examining data stored in a computer to produce information 电子数据处理；electronic engineer = engineer who specializes in electronic machines 电子工程师；electronic mail =

system of sending messages from one computer terminal to another, via telephone lines 电子邮件；electronic point of sale = system where sales are charged automatically to a customer's credit card and stock is controlled by the shop's computer 电子销售系统

◇ **electronics** pl. n. applying the scientific study of electrons to produce manufactured products, such as computers, calculators or telephones 电子学；电子：the electronics industry 电子工业；an electronics specialist or expert 电子专家；electronics engineer 电子工程师
NOTE: takes a singular verb

**element** noun basic part 成分；要素：the elements of a settlement 和解的要素

**elevator** n. US liftor machine which carries passengers or goods from one floor to another in a building（美）电梯：take the elevator to the 26th floor 乘电梯去 26 层

**eligible** a. person who can be chosen 适合被选的；有资格的：She is eligible for re - election. 她有资格再次当选。

◇ **eligibility** n. being eligible 有当选资格：The chairman questioned her eligibility to stand for re - election. 主席对她再次当选的资格表示怀疑。

**eliminate** v. to remove 排除；消除：to eliminate defects in the system. 排除系统中的缺陷；Using a computer should eliminate all possibility of error. 使用计算机应消除差错的一切可能性。

**embargo** 1 n. government order which stops a type of trade 禁止（贸易令）：to lay or put an embargo on trade with a country = to say that trade with a country must not take place 禁止与某国通商；The government has put an embargo on the export of computer equipment. 政府发出禁止计算机设备出口的命令。to lift an embargo = to allow trade to start again 解禁；解除禁令；The government has lifted the embargo on the exportof computers. 政府解除了对计算机设备出口的禁令。to be under an embargo = to be forbidden 受到禁止；在停止贸易中

NOTE: plural is embargoes

2 verb to stop trade or not to allow trade 停止贸易；不准贸易：The government has embargoed trade with the Eastern countries. 政府禁止与东方国家通商。

**embark** v. (a) to go on a ship 上船：The passengers embarked at Southampton. 旅客在南安普敦上船。(b) to embark on = to start 着手；开始从事：The company has embarked on an expansion programme. 公司已着手一项新的发展计划。

◇ **embarkation** n. going on to a ship or plane 上船；上飞机♠ port of embarkation = port at which you get on to a ship 乘船港；embarkation card = card given to passengers getting on to a plane or ship 登机卡；登船卡

**embezzle** v. to use money which is not yours, or which you are looking after for someone 盗用；挪用(公款…)贪污：He was sent to prison for six months for embezzling his clients' money. 他因盗用客户的钱款被监禁六个月。

◇ **embezzlement** n. act of embezzling 盗用；贪污：He was sent to prison for six months for embezzlement. 他因贪污被监禁六个月。

◇ **embezzler** n. person who embezzles 贪污者

**emergency** n. dangerous situation where decisions have to be taken quickly 紧急情况：The government declared a state of emergency. = The government decided that the situation was so dangerous that the police or army had to run the country. 政府宣布处于紧急状态。to take emergency measures = to take action rapidly to stop a crisis developing 采

取紧急措施：The company had to take emergency measures to stop losing money. 该公司必须采取应急措施中止亏损。emergency reserves = ready cash held in case it is needed suddenly 应急储备

**emoluments** pl. n. pay, salary or fees, or the earnings of directors who are not employees 薪俸；津贴等(指发给董事们而不是职员)

**employ** v. to give someone regular paid work 雇用；聘用：to employ twenty staff = to have twenty people working for you 雇用 20 名工作人员；to employ twenty new staff = to give work to twenty new people 雇用 20 名新工作人员

◇ **employed** 1 a. (a) in regular paid work 受雇的；就业的：He is not gainfully employed. = He has no regular paid work. 他没有一个拿固定薪金的工作。self - employed = working for yourself 为自己工作的；He worked in a bank for ten years but now is self - employed. 他在银行工作 10 年，现在他自己经营。(b) (money) used profitably 有利地使用(钱)：return against capital employed 使用资本的收益 2 pl. n. people who are working 受雇者：the employers and the employed 雇主与雇员；the self - employed = people who work for themselves 为自己工作的人；个体户

◇ **employee** n. worker or person employed by a company 工人；雇员：Employees of the firm are eligible to join a profit - sharing scheme. 该公司雇员有资格参予利润分红的计划。Relations between management and employees have improved. 劳资双方的关系已得到改善。The company has decided to take on new employees. 公司决定雇用新职员。

◇ **employer** n. person or company

which has regular workers and pays them 雇主: employers' organization or association = group of employers with similar interests 雇主组织或联合会; employer's contribution = money paid by an employer towards a worker's pension 雇主分担额(为工人退休金)

◇ **employment** n. regular paid work 受雇;雇用: full employment = situation where everyone in a country who can work has a job 全部就业; full - time employment = work for all of a working day 全日工作; to be in full - time employment 做全日工作; part - time employment = work for part of a working day 非全日工作; temporary employment = work which does not last for more than a few months 临时就业; to be without employment = to have no work 没有工作;失业; to find someone alternative employment = to find another job for someone 为某人找到另一个工作; conditions of employment = terms of a contract where someone is employed 聘用条件; contract of employment or employment contract = contract between management and an employee showing all the conditions of work 雇用合同或聘用合同; security of employment = feeling by a worker that he has the right to keep his job until he retires 就业保障; employment office or bureau or agency = office which finds jobs for people 职业介绍所
NOTE: no plural

**emporium** n. large shop 商场;大百货店
NOTE: plural is emporia

**empower** v. to give someone the power to do something 授权: She was empowered by the company to sign the contract. 她被公司授权签订此项合同。

**emptor** see CAVEAT

**empty** 1 a. with nothing inside 空的: The envelope is empty. 信封是空的。You can take that filing cabinet back to the storeroom as it is empty. 你可将此档案柜拿回仓库, 因为里面是空的。Start the computer file with an empty workspace. 将此计算机文件存于磁盘空余处。2 v. to take the contents out of something 倒出;腾空: She emptied the filing cabinet and put the files in boxes. 她将档案框腾空, 将档案放进盒子里。He emptied the petty cash box into his briefcase. 他将小现金盒中的现金倒入公文包中。

◇ **empties** plural noun empty bottles or cases 空瓶;空箱: returned empties = empty bottles which are taken back to a shop to get back a deposit paid on them 回收的空瓶子

**EMS** = EUROPEAN MONETARY SYSTEM 欧洲货币系统

**encash** v. to cash a cheque or to exchange a cheque for cash 支票兑现

◇ **encashable** a. which can be cashed 可兑现的

◇ **encashment** n. act of exchanging for cash 兑现

**enc or encl** = ENCLOSURE note put on a letter to show that a document is enclosed with it 附录;附寄物(随函)

**enclose** v. to put something inside an envelope with a letter 封入;(随函)附寄: to enclose an invoice with a letter 随函附上一张发票; I am enclosing a copy of the contract. 我随函附上一份合同。letter enclosing a cheque 附上一张支票的信函; Please find the cheque enclosed herewith. 兹随函附上一张支票。

◇ **enclosure** n. document enclosed with a letter 附件(随函): letter with enclosures 有附件的信函

**encourage** v. (a) to make it easier for something to happen 促进;怂恿: The general rise in wages encourages consumer spending. 工资的普遍提高促进

消费者的开支。Leaving your credit cardson your desk encourages people to steal or encourages stealing. 将信用卡留在你的办公桌上助长别人的偷窃。The company is trying to encourage sales by giving large discounts. 公司通过给予大幅折扣促进销售。(b) to help someone to do something by giving advice 鼓励: He encouraged me to apply for the job. 他鼓励我提出就业申请。

◇ **encouragement** n. giving advice to someone to help him to succeed 鼓励: The designers produced a very marketable product, thanks to the encouragement of the sales director. 由于销售经理的鼓励,设计人员设计出一种十分畅销的产品。

**end** 1 n. final point or last part 末尾;终点: at the end of the contract period 在合同期的末尾; at the end of six months = after six months have passed 六个月后; account end = the end of an accounting period 结算期的末尾; month end = the end of the month, when accounts have to be drawn up 月末结算; end product = manufactured product, made at the end of a production process 制成品;最终产品; After six months' trial production, the end product is still not acceptable. 经过六个月的试产后,最终产品仍不为人们接受。end user = person who actually uses a product 直接用户; The company is creating a computer with the end user in mind. 想到用户的需要公司正在创造一种新计算机。in the end = at last or after a lot of problems 最后;最终: In the end the company had to pull out of the US market. 最终公司不得不退出美国市场. In the end they signed the contract at the airport. 最后他们在机场签约。In the end the company had to call in the police. 最后公司不得不叫来警察。on end = for a long time or with no breaks 不停地;好久: The discussions contin-

ued for hours on end. 讨论无间断地持续了好几个小时。The workforce worked at top speed for weeks on end to finish the order on time. 工人们几周来一直连续地使劲干活为了按时完成订单任务。to come to an end = to finish 结束;完成: Our distribution agreement comes to an end next month. 我们的销售协议将于下月到期。2 v. to finish 结束 The distribution agreement ends in July. 该销售协议于七月终止。The chairman ended the discussion by getting up and walking out of the meeting. 董事长(主席)站起身来,退出会议,讨论也就结束了。

◇ **end in** v. to have as a result 以…结束;以…告终: The AGM ended in the shareholders fighting on the floor. 年度大会以股东们在地面上的搏斗而告终。

◇ **end up** v. to finish 结束;完成: We ended up with a bill for £10,000. 我们在最终结帐时付一万英镑。

**endorse** v. to endorse a bill or a cheque = to sign a bill or a cheque on the back to show that you accept it 背书(表示承兑汇票或支票)

◇ **endorsee** n. person whose name is written on a bill or a cheque as having the right to cash it 被背书人;受让人(其名字被写在汇票或支票上有权将其兑现的人)

◇ **endorsement** n. (a) act of endorsing; signature on a document which endorses it 背书;票据上签字 (b) note on an insurance policy which adds conditions to the policy 有条件的背书(给保险单附加条款的注释)

◇ **endorser** n. person who endorses a bill which is then paid to him 背书人(给向其付款的汇票背书的人)

**endowment** n. giving money to provide a regular income 捐款;资助: endowment insurance or endowment policy = insurance policy where a sum of money is paid to the insured person on a certain date, or to his heirs if he dies earlier 养老保险; endowment mortgage = mortgage backed by an endowment policy 以养老保险单作抵押的贷款

**energy** n. (a) force or strength 精力: He hasn't the energy to be a good salesman. 他没有精力成为一个好推销员。They wasted their energies on trying to sell cars in the German market. 他们试在德国市场出售小汽车，结果是白白浪费了精力。(b) power from electricity or petrol, etc. 能源, 能量: We try to save energy by switching off the lights when the rooms are empty. 我们用房间没人就关灯的方式来节约能源。If you reduce the room temperature to eighteen degrees, you will save energy. 如果将室内温度降至十八度, 你就能节省能源。NOTE: no plural for (b)

◇ **energetic** a. with a lot of energy 精力充沛的; 积极的: The salesmen have made energetic attempts to sell the product. 销售人员为出售产品作积极的尝试。

◇ **energy-saving** a. which saves energy 节省能源的: The company is introducing energy-saving measures. 该公司正在采取节能措施。

**enforce** v. to make sure something is done or is obeyed 厉行; 强制执行: to enforce the terms of a contract 强制执行合同条款

◇ **enforcement** n. making sure that something is obeyed 厉行; 强制执行: enforcement of the terms of a contract 合同条款的强制执行 NOTE: no plural

**engage** v. (a) to engage someone to do something = to make someone do something legally 使…保证; 使…从事: The contract engages us to a minimum annual purchase. 合同保证我们每年的最小购买量。(b) to employ 雇用: We have en-gaged the best commercial lawyer to represent us. 我们聘用了最好的商务律师作诉讼代理。The company has engaged twenty new salesmen. 公司雇用了二十名新推销员。(c) to be engaged in = to be busy with 忙于…: He is engaged in work on computers. 他正忙于计算机操作。The company is engaged in trade with Africa. 该公司与非洲做生意。

◇ **engaged** a. busy (telephone)(电话)占线: You cannot speak to the manager – his line is engaged. 你不能与经理通话, 电话占线。engaged tone = sound made by a telephone when the line dialled is busy(电话的)忙音: I tried to phone the complaints department but got only the engaged tone. 我试图给投诉部打电话, 但只听到忙音。

◇ **engagement** n. (a) agreement to do something 保证; 诺言: to break an engagement to do something = not to do what you have legally agreed 违背诺言: The company broke their engagement not to sell our rivals' products. 该公司违背了不出售我们竞争者产品的诺言。(b) engagements = arrangements to meet people 约会; 约见: I have no engagements for the rest of the day. 今天的其它时间我无约会。She noted the appointment in her engagements diary. 她在约见日记里记下这次会见。

**engine** n. machine which drives something 发动机: A car with a small engine is more economic than one with a large one. 带小发动机的小汽车比带大发动机的更经济。The lift engine has broken down again – we shall just have to walk up to the 4th floor. 电梯的引擎又坏了, 我们只好走到四楼。

◇ **engineer** n. person who looks after technical equipment 工程师: civil engineer = person who specializes in the construction of roads, bridges, railways, etc. 土木工程师; consulting engineer =

engineer who gives specialist advice 咨询工程师; product engineer = engineer in charge of the equipment for making a product 产品（设备）工程师; project engineer = engineer in charge of a project 项目工程师; programming engineer = engineer in charge of programming a computer system 程序工程师

◇ **engineering** n. science of technical equipment 工程学: civil engineering = construction of roads, bridges, railways, etc. 土木工程; the engineering department = section of a company dealing with equipment 工程部; an engineering consultant = an engineer who gives specialist advice 工程咨询人员
NOTE: no plural

**enquire** = INQUIRE ◇ **enquiry** = INQUIRY

**en route** a. on the way 在路上; 在途中: The tanker sank when she was en route to the Gulf. 在驶往海湾的途中油轮沉没。

**entail** 1 n. legal condition which passes ownership of a property only to certain persons 限定继承权（将财产只转移给某些人的法定条件）2 v. to involve 使必要; 需要: Itemizing the sales figures will entail about ten days' work. 逐条记载销售数字将需要大约 10 天时间。

**enter** v. (a) to go in 进入: They all stood up when the chairman entered the room. 当董事长主席步入房间时, 他们全体起立。The company has spent millions trying to enter the do - it - yourself market. 该公司花了几百万的钱, 试图打入"自己动手"市场。(b) to write 写; 登记: to enter a name on a list 在名单上写上名字; The clerk entered the interest in my bank book. 银行职员在我的存折上写上利息。to enter up an item in a ledger 将一笔帐登入分类帐册中; to enter a bid for something = to offer (usually in writing) to buy something 为

购买某物出价或递盘; to enter a caveat = to warn legally that you have an interest in a case, and that no steps can be taken without your permission 提出警告（从法律上提醒你在某案中享有的权益, 没有你的允许不能采取任何步骤）(c) to enter into = to begin to enter into relations with someone 开始与某人建立联系; to enter into negotiations with a foreign government 与某国政府进行谈判; to enter into a partnership with a legal friend 开始与一位合法的朋友合伙; to enter into an agreement or a contract 开始签订一项协议或合同

◇ **entering** n. act of writing items in a record 登记; 记下
NOTE: no plural

**enterprise** n. (a) system of carrying on a business 企业制度; 事业单位: free enterprise = system of business free from government interference 自由企业（不受政府干预）; private enterprise = businesses which are owned privately, not nationalized 私人企业; The project is completely funded by private enterprise. 此项工程的资金全部由私人企业提供。(b) business 企业: a small - scale enterprise = a small business 小型企业; a state enterprise = a state - controlled company 国营企业; Bosses of state enterprises are appointed by the government. 国营企业的老板由政府委派。
NOTE: no plural for (a)

**entertain** v. (a) to offer meals or hotel accommodation or theatre tickets, etc. to (business) visitors 招待; 款待 (b) to be ready to consider (a proposal) 准备考虑 1 一项建议) The management will not entertain any suggestions from the union representatives. 资方不会考虑工会代表的任何建议。

◇ **entertainment** n. offering meals, etc. to business visitors 招待; 款待: entertainment allowance = money which a manager is allowed by his company to spend on meals with visitors 招待补贴；entertainment expenses = money spent on giving meals to business visitors 招待费用

**entitle** v. to give the right to something 给予权利: He is entitled to a discount. = He has the right to be given a discount. 他有权获得折扣。

◇ **entitlement** n. right 权利: holiday entitlement = number of days' paid holiday which a worker has the right to take 休假权; She has not used up all her holiday entitlement. 她还未使用完她的休假权。pension entitlement = amount of pension which someone has the right to receive when he retires 养老金权利

**entrance** noun way in or going in 入口处；进口: The taxi will drop you at the main entrance. 计程车将把你送至主要入口处。Deliveries should be made to the London Road entrance. 货物应发运到论敦公路入口处。entrance (charge) = money which you have to pay to go in 门票费；Entrance is £1.50 for adults and £1 for children. 大人门票为1.50 英磅，儿童为1英磅。

**entrepot** n. entrepot port = town with a large international commercial port dealing in re – exports 转口港市

**entrepreneur** noun person who directs a company and takes commercial risks 企业家(管理公司并承担风险)

◇ **entrepreneurial** adjective taking commercial risks 冒商业风险的: an entrepreneurial decision 一个冒商业风险的决定

**entrust** v. to entrust someone with something or to entrust something to someone = to give someone the responsibility for looking after something 委托；托付: He was entrusted with the keys to the office safe. 办公室保险柜的钥匙交给他保管。

**entry** n. (a) written information put in an accounts ledger 入帐；分录: credit entry or debit entry = entry on the credit or debit side of an account 记入贷方或记入借方; single – entry bookkeeping = noting a deal with only one entry 单式薄记; double – entry bookkeeping = noting of both debit and credit sides of an account 复式薄记; to make an entry in a ledger = to write in details of a deal 在分类帐上详细入帐; contra entry = entry made in the opposite side of an account to make an earlier entry worthless (such as a debit entry against a credit) 对销分录; to contra an entry = to enter a similar amount on the opposite side of the account 对销分录；对销帐项 (b) act of going in; place where you can go in 进入；入口处: to pass a customs entry point 通过海关的入口处; entry of goods under bond 货物进入海关保税仓库；申报入关栈的货物; entry charge = money which you have to pay before you go in 入场费；门票费; entry visa = visa allowing someone to go into a country 入境签证; multiple entry visa = entry visa which allows someone to enter a country as often as he likes 多次入境签证

**envelope** n. flat paper cover for sending letters 信封: airmail envelope = very light envelope for airmail letters aperture envelope 航空信封; envelope with a hole in it so that the address on the letter inside can be seen 有标准径空的信封; window envelope = envelope with a hole covered with film so that the address on the letter inside can be seen 开窗信封; sealed or unsealed envelope = envelope where the flap has been stuck down to close it or envelope where the flap has been pushed into the back of the envelope 封口或不封口信封; to send the information in a sealed envelope 用封口信封

将信息寄出；a stamped addressed envelope= an envelope with your own address written on it and a stamp stuck on it to pay for return postage 贴有邮票具有本人地址的回邮信封；Please send a stamped addressed envelope for further details and our latest catalogue. 若需更多详情和我们最新目录请寄给我们一个帖有邮票并写好地址的回邮信封。

**epos or EPOS** = ELECTRONIC POINT OF SALE 电子销售点

**equal** 1 a. exactly the same 同样的；相等的：Male and female workers have equal pay. 男女工同酬。equal opportunities programme = programme to avoid discrimination in employment 就业机会均等

NOTE: the US equivalent is affirmative action 2 v. to be the same as 与…相等；等于：Production this month has equalled our best month ever. 本月产量与我们最好月份相同。

NOTE: equalling – equalled 使相等；but US: equaling – equaled

◇ **equalize** v. to make equal to equalize dividends 使股息(红利)相等

◇ **equalization** n. process of making equal

◇ **equally** ad. in the same way 同等地；同样地：Costs will be shared equally between the two parties. 成本由双方平摊。They were both equally responsible for the disastrous launch. 他们对这次损失掺重的产品上市要负同样的责任。

**equip** v. to provide with machinery 配备；装备：to equip a factory with new machinery 给工厂配备新机械：The office is fully equipped with word – processors. 办公室全部配备了文字处理机。

◇ **equipment** n. machinery and furniture required to make a factory or office work office equipment or business equipment 办公设备：office equipment supplier 办公设备供应商；office equipment catalogue. 办公设备目录本；capital equipment = equipment which a factory or office uses to work 资本设备；固定设备；主要设备；heavy equipment = large machines, such as for making cars or for printing 重型设备

NOTE: no plural

**equity** n. (a) right to receive dividends as part of the profit of a company in which you own shares 股息权(在某公司中拥有股份而获得作为公司利润一部分股息的权利)(b) shareholders' equity or equity capital = amount of a company's capital which is owned by shareholders 股本产权；产权资本；股本

◇ **equities** plural noun ordinary shares 普通股

**equivalence** n. being equivalent 相等；等值

◇ **equivalent** adjective to be equivalent to = to have the same value as or to be the same as 等价的；等量的：The total dividend paid is equivalent to one quarter of the pretax profits. 所付的全部股息等于纳税前利润的四分之一。

**ergonomics** pl. n. study of people at work and their working conditions 人类工程学；工效学(对在职的工作人员和他们工作条件进行研究)

NOTE: takes a singular verb

◇ **ergonomist** n. scientist who studies people at work and tries to improve their working conditions 人类工程学家

**erode** v. to wear away gradually 渐磨去；逐步减少：to erode wage differentials = to reduce gradually differences in salary between different grades 逐步减少工资差别

**error** n. mistake 差错；错误：He made an error in calculating the total. 算总数时他出了一个错。The secretary must have made a typing error. 秘书肯定有个打字错误。clerical error = mistake made in an office 文秘错误；笔误；computererror = mistake made by a computer 电脑错误；margin of error = number of mistakes which are accepted in a document or in a calculation 错误极限；errors and omissions excepted = words written on an invoice to show that the company has no responsibility for mistakes in the invoice 错误遗漏除外；有错当查；error rate = number of mistakes per thousand entries or per page 错误率；in error or by error = by mistake 弄错了；错误地：The letter was sent to the London office in error. 信被错误地发到伦敦办事处。

**escalate** v. to increase steadily 逐步上升；持续增加

◇ **escalation** n. escalation of prices = steady increase in prices 价格的逐步上涨；调价：escalation clause = ESCALATOR CLAUSE 合同的滑动条款

◇ **escalator clause** n. clause in a contract allowing for regular price increases because of increased costs 合同的滑动条款（因成本增加允许价格正常上涨的合同条款）

**escape** n. getting away from a difficult situation 逃脱；逃走：escape clause = clause in a contract which allows one of the parties to avoid carrying out the terms of the contract under certain conditions 免除条款；免责条款（允许合同当事人在某些情况下不执行合同条款）

**escrow** n. in escrow = held in safe keeping by a third party 由第三者妥为保管：document held in escrow = document given to a third party to keep and to pass on to someone when money has been paid 由第三者妥为保管的文件；US escrow account = account where money is held in escrow until a contract is signed or until goods are delivered, etc. （美）由第三者妥为保管帐户
NOTE: no plural

**espionage** n. industrial espionage = trying to find out the secrets of a competitor's work or products, usually by illegal means 工业间谍活动
NOTE: no plural

**essential** a. very important 必要的；必不可少的：It is essential that an agreement be reached before the end of the month. 月底前达成协议是很必要的。The factory is lacking essential spare parts. 工厂缺少必要的备用零件。

◇ **essentials** pl. n. goods or products which are very important 必需品

**establish** v. to set up or to make or to open 建立；设立；创力：The company has established a branch in Australia. 该公司在澳大利亚设立了一个分公司。The business was established in Scotland in 1823. 该企业于 1823 年在苏格兰创立。It is a young company – it has been established for only four years. 这是一个年轻的公司，开业仅四年。to establish oneself in business = to become successful in a new business 使某人在一个行业中立足

◇ **establishment** n. (a) commercial business 商社；企业：He runs an important printing establishment. 他经营一个重要的印刷企业。(b) establishment charges = cost of people and property in a company's accounts 企业费用；开办费（公司帐户中的人员和财产的费用）(c) number of people working in a company 机构；定员；编制：to be on the establishment = to be a full – time employee 在编制内；office with an establishment of fifteen = office with a budgeted staff of fifteen 编制为 15 人的办事处

**estate** n. (a) real estate = property (land or buildings) 房地产：estate agency = office which arranges for the sale of property 房地产代理处；estate agent = person in charge of an estate agency 房地

产经纪人；房地产中间商（b）industrial estateor trading estate = area of land near a town specially for factories and warehouses 工业用地或商业用地（c）property left by a dead person 遗产：estate duty = tax on property left by a dead person 遗产税

**estimate** 1 n. (a) calculation of probable cost or size or time of something 估计；评定(指估计成本或对规模或某事时间的计算)：rough estimate = very approximate calculation 粗略估计；at a conservative estimate = calculation which probably underestimates the final figure 保守的估计；Their turnover has risen by at least 20% in the last year, and that is a conservative estimate. 去年营业额至少增长 20%，这还是一个保守的估计。These figures are only an estimate. = These are not the final accurate figures. 这些数字仅仅是估算值。Can you give me an estimate of how much time was spent on the job? 这个工作要花多少时间, 你能估计一下吗？(b) calculation of how much something is likely to cost in the future, given to a client so as to get him to make an order 估算；估价(对未来某一时间可能的成本的估计, 以便让预客订购)；estimate of costs or of expenditure 成本或开支的估算；Before we can give the grant we must have an estimate of the total costs involved. 在拨款前我们必须对有关的总成本作个估算。to ask a builder for an estimate for building the warehouse 要求一个营造商对所建仓库的费用作一估价；to put in an estimate = to give someone a written calculation of the probable costs of carrying out a job 要求作出估算；Three firms put in estimates for the job. 三家公司要求对这项工作做出估算。2. v. (a) to calculate the probable cost or size or time of something 估计；评定：to estimate that it will cost £1m or to estimate costs at £1. 估计成

本将为一百万英镑；We estimate current sale at only 60% of last year. 我们估计目前的销售量仅占去年的 60%。(b) to estimate for a job = to state in writing the future costs of carrying out a piece of work so that a client can make an order 为做某事作出估算或估价：Three firms estimated for the fitting of the offices. 三家公司对办公室的装修作了估算。

◇ **estimated** a. calculated approximately 估计的：estimated sales；估计的销售额；estimated figure 估计数字

◇ **estimation** n. approximate calculation 估计

◇ **estimator** n. person whose job is to calculate estimates for carrying out work 估计者；预算者

**etc.** and so on 等等 The import duty is to be paid on luxury items including cars, watches, etc. 对诸如小汽车、手表…等奢侈品必须付进口税。

**Euro -** prefix referring to Europe or the European Community 指欧洲或欧洲共同体

◇ **Eurobond** n. bond issued by an international corporation or government outside its country of origin and sold to Europeans who pay in Eurodollars 欧洲债券(由国际性公司或政府在国外发行卖给欧洲人, 他们以欧洲美元支付的债券)：the Eurobond market 欧洲债券市场

◇ **Eurocheque** n. British cheque which can be cashed in a European bank 欧洲支票(可在欧洲银行兑现的英国支票)

◇ **Eurocurrency** n. European currencies used for trade within Europe but outside their countries of origin 欧洲货币(用来在自己国家以外的欧洲做贸易所使用的货币)：a Eurocurrency loan 欧洲货币贷款；the Eurocurrency market 欧洲货币市场

◇ **Eurodollar** n. US dollar in a Europeanbank, used for trade within Europe 欧洲美元(用来在欧洲做贸易,存在欧洲银行的美元): a Eurodollar loan 欧洲美元贷款; the Eurodollar market 欧洲美元市场

◇ **Euromarket** n. the European Economic Community seen as a potential market for sales 欧洲共同体市场;欧共体市场

◇ **Europe** n. group of countries to the West of Asia and the North of Africa 欧洲: Most of the countries of Western Europe are members of the Common Market. 大多数西欧国家是共同市场的成员国。Canadian exports to Europe have risen by 25%. 加拿大向欧洲的出口增加了 25%。

◇ **European** a. referring to Europe 欧洲的: the European Economic Community = the Common Market 欧洲经济共同体; the European Monetary System = system of controlled exchange rates between some member countries of the Common Market 欧洲货币体系(在同市场成员国之间控制汇率的系统)

**evade** v. to try to avoid something 逃避;避开: to evade tax = to try illegally to avoid paying tax 逃税

**evaluate** v. to calculate a value 评价;估计: to evaluate costs 估计成本

◇ **evaluation** noun calculation of value 估计;评价: job evaluation = examining different jobs within a company to see what skillsand qualifications are needed to carry them out 工作评价

**evasion** n. avoiding 逃避;避开: tax evasion = illegally trying not to pay tax 逃税

**evidence** n. written or spoken report at a trial documentary evidence = evidence in the form of documents 文件证据;书面或口头证据: The secretary gave evidence for or against her former

employer. = The secretary was a witness, and her report suggested that her former employer was not guilty or guilty. 秘书供给赞成或反对她过去老板(雇主)的证据。

NOTE: no plural

**ex-** pre. (a) out of or from 离开;交货: price ex warehouse price for a product which is to be collected from the manufacturer's or agent's warehouse and so does not include delivery 仓库交货价; price ex works or ex factory = price not including transport from the maker's factory 工厂交货价 (b) ex coupon = bond without the interest coupon 无息票债券: share quoted ex dividend = share price not including the right to receive the next dividend 不带股息报价的股票; The shares went ex dividend yesterday. 昨日股票价格是股息除外 (c) formerly 前;从前: Mr Smith, the ex-chairman of the company 前公司董事长史密斯先生 (d) ex-directory = telephone number which is not printed in the telephone book 未列入电话簿的: He has an ex-directory number. 他有一个未列入电话簿的号码。

**exact** a. very correct 准确的: The exact time is 10:27. 确切时间是 10 点 27 分。The salesgirl asked me if I had the exact sum, since the shop had no change. 女售货员问我所付的钱数是否正好,因为该商店没有零钱。

◇ **exactly** a. very correctly 准确地: The total cost was exactly £6,500. 总成本正好是 6500 英磅。

**examine** v. to look at someone or something very carefully to see if it can be accepted 检查: The customs officials asked to examine the inside of the car. 海关官员要求对小汽车的内部进行检查。The police are examining the papers from the managing director's safe. 警察正在检查

从总经理保险柜里取出的文件。

◇ **examination** n. （a） looking at something very carefully to see if it is acceptable 检查： customs examination = looking at goods or baggage by customs officials 海关检查 （b） test to see if someone has passed a course 考试；测验： He passed his accountancy examinations. 他通过会计学的考试。 She came first in the final examination for the course. 她在这门课的期末考试中获得第一名。 He failed his proficiency examination and so had to leave his job. 他没通过水平测试，因此不得不离职。

**example** n. something chosen to show 样品；范例： The motor show has many examples of energy - saving cars on display. 汽车展览会上展出了许多节能小汽车的样品。 for example = to show one thing out of many 例如；举例： The government wants to encourage exports, and, for example, it gives free credit to exporters. 政府鼓励出口，例如，向出口商提供自由信贷。

**exceed** v. to be more than 超过；多于…： discount not exceeding 15 % 不超过 15 % 的折扣； Last year costs exceeded 20 % of income for the first time. 去年开支第一次超过收入的 20 % 。 He has exceeded his credit limit. = He has borrowed more money than he is allowed. 他已超过他的信贷限额。

**excellent** a. very good 极好的；优秀的： The quality of the firm's products is excellent, but its sales force is not large enough. 该公司产品的质量极好，但销售队伍还不够大。

**except** preposition & conjunction not including 不包括；把…除外： VAT is levied on all goods and services except books, newspapers and children's clothes. 除书籍、报纸和童装外，对所有的货物与劳务都增收增值税。 Sales are rising in all markets except the Far East. 所有市场的销售都正在增加，但远东除外。

◇ **excepted** a. not including 不包括；除外： errors and omissions excepted = note on an invoice to show that the company has no responsibility for mistakes in the invoice 错误遗漏除外；有错当查

◇ **exceptional** a. not usual or different 特别的；异常的： exceptional items = items in a balance sheet which do not appear there each year 例外的项目

**excess** n. amount which is more than what is allowed 过多；过量： an excess of expenditure over revenue 超过收入的支出；超出额； excess baggage = extra payment at an airport for taking baggage which is heavier than the normal passenger's allowance 超重的行李； excess capacity = spare capacity which is not being used 剩余生产能力；过剩能力 excess fare = extra fare to be paid （such as for travelling first class with a second class ticket） 补票费； in excess of = above or more than 超过： quantities in excess of twenty - five kilos 数量超过 25 公斤； excess profits = profit which is more than what is thought to be normal 超额利润； excess profits tax = tax on excess profits 超额利润税

◇ **excessive** a. too large excessive costs 过份的；过度的

**exchange** 1 n. （a） giving of one thing for another 交换；互换： part exchange = giving an old product as part of the payment for a new one 部分抵价交易（以旧产品抵部分新产品的价格）； to take a car in part exchange 以部分抵价贸易方式买汽车； exchange of contracts = point in the sale of property when the buyer and the seller both sign the contract of sale which then becomes binding 买卖双方会签合同的交换 （b） foreign exchange = （i） exchanging the money of one country for that of another 外汇

(ii) money of another country 外国的货币：The company has more than £1m in foreign exchange. 该公司有价值一百多万英镑的外汇。foreign exchange broker = person who buys and sells foreign currency on behalf of other people 外汇经纪人；foreign exchange market = dealings in foreign currencies 外汇市场；He trades on the foreign exchange market. 他倒卖外汇。Foreign exchange markets were very active after the dollar devalued. 美元贬值后，外汇市场十分活跃。rate of exchange or exchange rate = price at which one currency is exchanged for another 汇率；兑换率；The current rate of exchange is 10.95 francs to the pound. 按目前的汇率，10.95法郎换1英镑。exchange control = control by a government of the way in which its currency may be exchanged for foreign currencies 外汇管制；The government had to impose exchange controls to stop the rush to buy dollars. 政府不得不实行外汇管制以停止对美元的抢购。exchange dealer = person who buys and sells foreign currency 外汇买卖人或外汇交易商；exchange dealings = buying and selling foreign currency 外汇交易；GB Exchange Equalization Account = account with the Bank of England used by the government when buying or selling foreign currency to influence the sterling exchange rate(英)外汇平衡帐户；exchange premium = extra cost above the normal rate for buying a foreign currency 汇兑贴水；外汇贴进；外汇升水 (c) bill of exchange = document which tells a bank to pay a person (usually used in foreign currency payments)汇票 (d) Stock Exchange = place where stocks and shares are bought and sold 证券交易所：The company's shares are traded on the New York Stock Exchange. 该公司的股票在纽约证券交易所进行买卖。He works on the Stock Exchange. 他在证券

交易的所工作。commodity exchange = place where commodities are bought and sold 商品交易所 NOTE：no plural for (b)

2 v. (a) to exchange one article for another = to give one thing in place of something else 交易；交换：He exchanged his motorcycle for a car. 他用摩托车换了辆汽车。If the trousers are too small you can take them back and exchange them for a larger pair. 如果裤子太小，你可拿回来换一条比较大的。Goods can be exchanged only on production of the sales slip. 只有凭产品销售单(小票)才能调换商品。(b) to exchange contracts = to sign a contract when buying a property (done by both buyer and seller at the same time)交换买卖双方会签合同 (c) to change money of one country for money of another 兑换货币：to exchange francs for pounds 将法郎况换成英镑

◇ **exchangeable** a. which can be exchanged 可交换的；可兑换的

◇ **exchanger** n. person who buys and sells foreign currency 外币交易商

**Exchequer** n. GB the Exchequer = government department dealing with public revenue (英)财政部：the Chancellor of the Exchequer = the chief British finance minister(英)财政大臣

**excise** 1. n. (a) excise duty = tax on certain goods produced in a country (such as alcohol)消费税(国内商品税)：to pay excise duty on wine 付酒税 (b) Customs and Excise or Excise Department = government department which deals with taxes on imports andon products such as alcohol produced in the country(英)税务局；关税与消费税局；Excise officer 税务官 2. v. to cut out 删去；切除：Please excise all references to the strike in the minutes. 请将会议记录中所有涉及罢工的部分删去。

◇ **exciseman** n. person who works in theExcise Department 税务员

**exclude** v. to keep out or not to include 把…排斥在外；不包括：The interest charges have been excluded from the document. 利息费用并未包括在单据内。Damage by fire is excluded from the policy. 火灾造成的损坏不包括在保险单中。

◇ **excluding** prep. not including 不包括；除外：All salesmen, excluding those living in London, can claim expenses for attending the sales conference. 除驻伦敦的人员外，全部销售人员都可要求获得参加销售会议的开支补贴。

◇ **exclusion** n. act of not including 不包括；除外：exclusion clause = clause in an insurance policy or warranty which says which items are not covered 除外责任条款(保险单中的)

◇ **exclusive** a. (a) exclusive agreement = agreement where a person is made sole agent for a product ina market 独家销售协议：exclusive right to market a product = right to be the only person to market the product 独家出售某产品的权利 (b) exclusive of = not including 不包括：All payments are exclusive of tax. 所有付款都不包括税款。The invoice is exclusive of VAT. 发票不包括增值税。

◇ **exclusivity** n. exclusive right to market a product 独家销售权

**excuse** 1. n. reason for doing something wrong 借口；托辞：His excuse for not coming to the meeting was that he had been told about it only the day before. 他没参加这次会议的借口是：在开会前一天已有人告诉过他有关会议的情况。The managing director refused to accept the sales manager's excuses for the poor sales. = He refused to believe that there was a good reason for the poor sales. 总经理不接受销售经理为销售状况不好所做的辨解。2 v. to forgive a small mistake 原谅(小错误)：She can be excused for not knowing the French for" photocopier". (我们)可原谅她不知道"影印机"法语名称。

**execute** v. to carry out (an order)履行(定单)

◇ **execution** n. carrying out of an order 履行；实行；执行：stay of execution = temporary stopping of a legal order 延期执行；The court granted the company a two - week stay of execution. 法院准许该公司延期两周交货。

NOTE: no plural

◇ **executive** 1. a. which puts decisions into action 执行的；实施的：executive committee = committee which runs a society or a club 执行委员会；executive director = director who actually works full - time in the company 执行董事；常务董事；executive powers = right to put decisions into actions 执行权；He was made managing director with full executive powers over the European operation. 他被任命为总经理，对在欧洲的业务经营具有完全的执行权。2. n. person in a business who takes decisions or manager or director 主管人员；经理；sales executive 销售管理人员；senior or junior executive 高级或初级管理人员；account executive = employee who is the link between his company and certain customers 客户执行人；客户经理；chief executive = executive director in charge of a company 常务董事长

**executor** n. person who sees that the terms of a will are carried out 遗嘱执行人：He was named executor of his brother's will. 他被提名当他兄弟的遗嘱执行人。

**exempt** 1. a. not covered by a law; not forced to obey a law 豁免；免除：exempt from tax or tax - exempt = not required to pay tax. 免税；As a non - profit -

making organization we are exempt from tax. 作为一个非赢利机构，我们不纳税。2 v. to free something from having tax paid on it or from having to pay tax 使免除: Non‑profit‑making organizations are exempted from tax. 非赢利组织不交营业税。Food is exempted from sales tax. 食品免征销售税。The government exempted trusts from tax. 政府免征信托(财产)税。

◇ **exemption** n. act of exempting something from a contract or from a tax 豁免；免除: exemption from tax or tax exemption = being free from having to pay tax 免税; As a non‑profit‑making organization you can claim tax exemption. 作为一个非赢利性机构，你们能提出免税要求。

**exercise** 1. n. use of something 行使；执行: exercise of an option = using an option or putting an option into action 行使选择权 2. v. to use 行使；执行: to exercise an option = to put an option into action 行使选择权; He exercised his option to acquire sole marketing rights for the product. 他使用选择权，获得该产品的独家销售权。The chairwoman exercised her veto to block the motion. 女董事长(主席)行使否决权，以阻止该提议的通过。

**ex gratia** a. an ex gratia payment = payment made as a gift, with no other obligations 惠给金；补偿款

**exhibit** 1. n. (a) thing which is shown 陈列品；展品: The buyers admired the exhibits on our stand. 购买者夸奖我们展台上的展品。(b) single section of an exhibition 展览会的一个分部: The British Trade Exhibit at the International Computer Fair 国际计算机展览会英国商品展示区 2. v. to exhibit at the Motor Show = to display new models of cars 在汽车展览会上展示

◇ **exhibition** n. showing goods so that buyers can look at them and decide what to buy 展览会: The government has sponsored an exhibition of good design. 政府主办了一个精心设计的展览会。We have a stand at the Ideal Home Exhibition. 我们在"理想住宅"展览会上有一个展台。the agricultural exhibition grounds 农业展览会场地; exhibition room or hall = place where goods are shown so that buyers can look at them and decide what to buy 展室或展厅; exhibition stand = separate section of an exhibition where a company exhibits its products or services 展台

◇ **exhibitor** n. person or company which shows products at an exhibition 展出者；展出厂商

**exist** v. to be 存在: I do not believe the document exists ‑ I think it has been burnt. 我不相信文件还存在一我认为它已被烧毁。

**exit** n. way out of a building 出口处: The customers all rushed towards the exits. 顾客都涌向出口处。fire exit = door which leads to a way out of a building if there is a fire 太平门

**ex officio** a. & ad. because of an office held 职权上的；按照职权地: The treasurer is ex officio a member or an ex officio member of the finance committee. 按职务规定，财务主任是财务委员会委员。

**expand** v. to increase or to get bigger or to make something bigger 增加；扩大；扩充: an expanding economy 发展的经济; The company is expanding fast. 公司正在迅速发展。We have had to expand our sales force. 我们不得不扩大销售队伍。

◇ **expansion** n. increase in size 扩大: the expansion of the domestic market 国内市场的扩大; The company had difficulty in financing its current expansion programme. 公司为现行发展计划提供

资金有困难。GB business expansion scheme = system where money invested in a new company for some yearsis free from tax 英国企业发展计划

**expect** v. to hope that something is going to happen 期待;盼望;预期: We are expecting him to arrive at 10:45. 我们预计他 10 点 45 分钟到达。 They are expecting a cheque from their agent next week. 他们正盼望下周收到代理人的一张支票。 The house was sold for more than the expected price. 房子出售的价格比预料的高。

◇ **expectancy** n. life expectancy = number of years a person is likely to live. 预期寿命;预期数

**expenditure** n. amounts of money spent 费用;开支;支出: below - the - line expenditure = exceptional payments which are separated from a company's normal accounts 线下项目开支; capital expenditure = money spent on fixed assets (such as property or machinery)资本支出;基本建设费用; the company's current expenditure programme = the company's spending according to the current plan 公司现行支出计划; heavy expenditure on equipment = spending large sums of money on equipment 大规模设备投资

NOTE: no plural

◇ **expense** n. (a) money spent 开支;花费: It is not worth the expense. 它不值得花钱。 The expense is too much for my bank balance. 开支太大,超出了我银行余额。 at great expense = having spent a lot of money 费用很多; He furnished the office regardless of expense. = without thinking how much it cost. 他为办公室配备家俱时不在乎花钱多少。 (b) expense account = money which a businessman is allowed by his company to spend on travelling and entertaining clients in connection with his business 营业费用帐户: I'll put this lunch on my expense account. 我将把这次午餐的开销记入我的营业费用帐户。 Expense account lunches form a large part of our current expenditure. 午餐费用成为我们现在开支帐户的一个主要部分。

NOTE: no plural

◇ **expenses** pl. n. money paid for doing something 费用: The salary offered is £10,000 plus expenses. 提供的薪水为 1 万英镑,外加额外的开支。 all expenses paid = with all costs paid by the company 支付所有费用(开支); The company sent him to San Francisco all expenses paid. 公司派他去旧金山,所有费用由公司支付。 to cut down on expenses = to try to reduce spending 减少开支; allowable expenses = business expenses which are allowed against tax 可列支的费用; business expenses = money spent on running a business, not on stock or assets 企业开支;营业费用; entertainment expenses = money spent on giving meals to business visitors 招待费用; fixed expenses = money which is spent regularly (such as rent, electricity, telephone)固定费用; incidental expenses = small amounts of money spent at various times, in addition tolarger amounts 零星支出;临时费;杂费; legal expenses = money spent on fees paid to lawyers 诉讼费;法律费; overhead expenses or general expenses or running expenses = money spent on the day - to - day cost of a business 间接费用;一般费用;管理费用;经常费用; travelling expenses = money spent on travelling and hotels for business purposes 差旅费

◇ **expensive** a. which costs a lot of money 昂贵的: First - class air travel is becoming more and more expensive. 坐飞机头等舱旅行变得越来越昂贵。

**experience** 1. n. having lived through various situations and therefore knowing how to make decisions 经验;经历: He is a man of considerable experience. 他是一个颇有经验的人。She has a lot of experience of dealing with German companies. 她有对付德国公司方面的丰富的经验。He gained most of his experience in the Far East. 他大多数的经验是在远东获得的。Some experience is required for this job. 这项工作需要一些经验。2. v. to live through a situation 经历: The company experienced a period of falling sales. 该公司经历了一段销售下降的时期。

◇ **experienced** a. person who has lived through many situations and has learnt from them 有经验的: He is the most experienced negotiator I know. 他是我知道的最富有经验的谈判者。We have appointed a very experienced woman as sales director. 我们委派了一名很有经验的妇女当销售经理。

**expert** n. person who knows a lot about something 专家: an expert in the field of electronics or an electronics expert 电子(学)专家; The company asked a financial expert for advice or asked for expert financial advice. 公司向金融专家征求意见。expert's report = report written by an expert 专家的报告

◇ **expertise** n. specialist knowledge 专业知识: We hired Mr Smith because of his financial expertise or because of his expertise in the African market. 我们雇用了史密斯先生, 因为他有金融专业知识, 或者因为他有非洲市场的专业知识。
NOTE: no plural

**expiration** n. coming to an end 终止; 满期: expiration of an insurance policy 保险单到期; to repay before the expiration of the stated period 在约定期到期前偿还; on expiration of the lease = when the lease comes to an end 在租赁期满时
NOTE: no plural

◇ **expire** v. to come to an end 期满; 终结; 终止: The lease expires in 1987. 租赁于 1987 年到期。His passport has expired. = His passport is no longer valid. 他的护照已到期。

◇ **expiry** n. coming to an end 期满; 终止: expiry of an insurance policy 保险单满期; expiry date = date when something will end 到期日; 截止日

**explain** v. to give reasons for something 说明; 解释: He explained to the customs officials that the two computers were presents from friends. 他向海关官员解释这两台计算机是朋友送的礼物。Can you explain why the sales in the first quarter are so high? 你能解释一下为什么第一季度销售额如此高吗? The sales director tried to explain the sudden drop in unit sales. 销售经理试图解释单位销售额突然下降的原因。

◇ **explanation** n. reason for something 解释; 说明: The VAT inspector asked for an explanation of the invoices. 增值税稽查员要求对发票进行说明。At the AGM, the chairman gave an explanation for the high level of interest payments. 在股东年度大会上, 董事长对高利息支付作了解释。

**exploit** v. to use something to make a profit 利用; 开发: The company is exploiting its contacts in the Ministry of Trade. 公司正在利用与贸易部的关系。We hope to exploit the oil resources in the China Sea. 我们希望开发中国海的石油资源。

**explore** v. to examine carefully 仔细检查; 研究: We are exploring the possibility of opening an office in London. 我们正在研究在伦敦开设办事处的可能性。

**export** 1. n. (a) exports = goods sent to a foreign country to be sold 出口: Exports to Africa have increased by 25%. 对非洲的出口增长了 25%。(b) action of sending goods to a foreign country to be sold 出口：the export trade or the exportmarket 出口贸易；出口市场；export department = section of a company which deals in sales to foreign countries 出口部；export duty = tax paid on goods sent out of a country for sale 出口税；export house = company which specializes in the export of goods made by other manufacturers 出口公司；export licence = government permit allowing something to be exported 出口许可证；The government has refused an export licence for computer parts. 政府拒绝发计算机零件的出口许可证。export manager = person in charge of an export department in a company 出口部经理；Export Credit Guarantee Department = British government department which insures exports sold on credit（英）出口信货担保部

NOTE: usually used in the plural, but the singular form isused before a noun

2. v. to send goods to foreign countries for sale 出口：50% of our production is exported. 我们生产量的50%供出口。The company imports raw materials and exports the finished products. 公司进口原料而出口成品。

◇ **exportation** n. act of sending goods to foreign countries for sale 出口；外销
NOTE: no plural

◇ **exporter** n. person or company or country which sells goods in foreign countries 出口商；出口公司；输出国：a major furniture exporter 一家主要家俱出口商；Canada is an important exporter of oil or an important oil exporter. 加拿大是重要的石油出口国。

◇ **exporting** a. which exports 出口的：oil exporting countries = countries which produce oil and sell it to other countries 石油输出国

**exposition** n. US = EXHIBITION

**exposure** n. amount of risk which a lender runs 风险程度；风险：He is trying to cover his exposure in the property market. 他正试图对房地产市场上的风险进行投保。
NOTE: no plural

**express** 1. a. (a) rapid or very fast 快的；快速的：express letter 快递信；express delivery 快速发运 (b) clearly shown in words 明确的：The contract has an express condition forbidding sale in Africa. 合同条件中明确规定，禁止在非洲出售。2. v. (a) to put into words or diagrams（用文字或图表）表示；表达：This chart shows home sales expressed as a percentage of total turnover. 该图显示的住宅销售额是以占总营业额的百分比来表示的。(b) to send very fast 快递：We expressed the order to the customer's warehouse. 我们把定货快递到客户的仓库。

◇ **expressly** adv. clearly in words 明确地；明白地：The contract expressly forbids sales to the United States. 合同明确规定不准向美国出售。

**ext** = EXTENSION

**extend** v. (a) to make available or to give 提供；给予：to extend credit to a customer 向一客户提供信贷 (b) to make longer 延长：to extend a contract for two years 将合同延长两年

◇ **extended credit** n. credit allowing the borrower a very long time to pay（允许借款人长期信贷）展期信用证：We sell to Australia on extended credit. 我们以展期信用证向澳大利亚销售产品。

◇ **extension** n. (a) allowing longer time 展期；延长：to get an extension of credit = to get more time to pay back 使信贷展期；将偿还期期延长；extension of a contract = continuing the contract for a further period 合同的延长 (b)（in an office）individual telephone linked to the main switchboard 电话分机：Can you get me extension 21. 你能给我接21

号分机吗? Extension 21 is engaged. 21号分机占线。The sales manager is on extension 53. 销售经理的分机号为53。

◇ **extensive** a. very large or covering a wide area 广泛的；辽阔的：an extensive network of sales outlets 广阔的销售批发店网络

**external** a. (a) outside a country 对外的；外国的：external account = account in a British bank of someone who is living in another country 外国人帐户；external trade = trade with foreign countries 对外贸易 (b) outside a company 外界的；外面的：external audit = audit carried out by an independent auditor 外来审计；外界审计

**extra** 1. a. which is added or which is more than usual 额外的；外加的；另收的：There is no extra charge for heating. 没有额外的取暖费用。to charge 10% extra for postage 外加10%的邮资费；He had £25 extra pay for working on Sunday. 因星期日工作,他外加25英磅的工资。Service is extra. 服务费另收。2. pl. n. extras = items which are not included in a price 外加；附加：Packing and postage are extras. 包装和邮费另收。

**extract** n. printed document which is part of a larger document 摘录；摘记：He sent me an extract of the accounts. 他寄给我一份帐户摘要。

**extraordinary** a. different from normal 不平常的；非常的：Extraordinary General Meeting = special meeting of shareholders or members of a club, etc., to discuss an important matter which cannot wait until the next AGM 特别大会；to call an Extraordinary General Meeting 召集特别大会；extraordinary items = items in accounts which do not appear each year 例外项目；非常项目；The auditors noted several extraordinary items in the accounts. 审计人员记下了帐户中

几个例外项目。

**extremely** adv. very much 极其；非常：It is extremely difficult to break into the US market. 打入美国市场极其困难。Their management team is extremely efficient. 他们的管理班子极有效率。

# Ff

**face value** n. value written on a coin or banknote or share 面值；面额(指硬币,钞票或股票)

**facility** n. (a) being able to do something easily 才能；技能；能力：We offer facilities for payment. 我们提供付款方便。(b) total amount of credit which a lender will allow a borrower 贷款限额：credit facilities = arrangement with a bank on supplier to have credit so as to buy goods 信贷股务；overdraft facility = arrangement with a bank to have an overdraft 透支贷款 (c) facilities = equipment or buildings which make it easy to do something 设施；设备；工具：storage facilities 存储设施；harbour facilities 港口设备；transport facilities 运输设备；There are no facilities for passengers. 没有供旅客使用的旅行工具。There are no facilities for unloading or There are no unloading facilities. 没有卸货的设备。(d) US single large building(美)单独一座大建筑物：We have opened our new warehouse facility. 我们已开放了一个大型仓库。

**facsimile** n. facsimile copy = exact copy of a document 复制本

**fact** n. something which is true and real 事实；真相：The chairman asked to see all the facts on the income tax claim. 董

事长要求看所有付所得税要求的实情。
The sales director can give you the facts and figuresabout the African operation. 销售经理能给你提供有关非洲经营状况的事实与数字。the fact of the matter is = what is true is that 事情的真相是；The fact of the matter is that the product does not fit the market. 事情的真相是，该产品不适合这个市场。in fact = really 事实上；The chairman blamed the finance director for the loss when in fact he was responsible for it himself. 董事长将事实上该由他本人负责的损失归咎于财务经理。

◇ **fact - finding** a. looking for information 实情调查的：a fact - finding mission = visit, usually by a group of people, to search for information about a problem 实情调查小组的使命；The minister went on a fact - finding tour of the region. 部长对该地区作了一次实情调查旅行。

**factor** 1. n. (a) thing which is important or which influences 要素；因素：The drop in sales is an important factor in the company's lower profits. 销售额下降是公司利润较低的一个重要因素。cost factor = problem of cost 费用因素；cyclical factors = way in which a trade cycle affects businesses 周期性因素；deciding factor = most important factor which influences a decision 决定性因素；load factor = number of seats in a bus or plane or train which are occupied by passengers who have paid the full fare 装载系数；负荷系数；factors of production = things needed to produce a product (land, labour and capital)生产要素 (b) by a factor of ten = ten times 十倍 (c) person or company which is responsible for collecting debts for companies, by buying debts at a discount on their face value 债务保收代理商 2. v. to buy debts from a company at a discount 贷款保收；从事客帐代理的业务

◇ **factoring** n. business of buying debts at a discount 贷款保收：factoring charges = cost of selling debts to a factor for a commission 贷款保收代理费用

**factory** n. building where products are manufactured 工厂：car factory 小汽车工厂；shoe factory 鞋厂；factory hand or factory worker = person who works in a factory 工厂工人；factory inspector or inspector of factories = government official who inspects factories to see if they are well run 工厂监察员；the factory inspectorate = all factory inspectors 工厂视察团；factory price or price ex factory = price not including transport from the maker's factory 出厂价；工厂交货价；factory unit = single building on an industrial estate 工业区中的单个建筑

**fail** v. (a) not to do something which you were trying to do 不做；失败：The company failed to notify the tax office of its change of address. 公司没将其地址变动通知税务部门。The prototype failed its first test. 生产原型的第一次试验失败。(b) to be unsuccessful commercially 失败；破产：The company failed . = The company went bankrupt. 公司破产。He lost all his money when the bank failed. 由于银行倒闭，他损失了所有的钱。

◇ **failing** 1. n. weakness 弱点：The chairman has one failing – he goes to sleep at board meetings. 董事长有一个弱点，他老在董事会会议上睡觉。2. prep. if something does not happen 如果没有…，若无…时：failing instructions to the contrary = unless someone gives opposite instructions 若无相反指示时；failing prompt payment = if the payment is not made on time 若不及时付款；failing that = if that does not work 若那不奏效；Try the company secretary, and failing that the chairman

先试试公司的秘书,若不行再找董长。

◇ **failure** n. ( a ) breaking down or stopping 垮台;失败;停止: the failure of the negotiations 谈判的失败 ( b ) failure to pay a bill = not having paid the bill 未支付汇票 ( c ) commercial failure = financial collapse or bankruptcy 商业上的失败;破产: He lost all his money in the bank failure. 银行的倒闭使他失去了所有的钱。

**fair** 1 . n. trade fair = large exhibition and meeting for advertising and selling acertain type of product 贸易展览会: to organize or to run a trade fair 组织或举办贸易展览会; The fair is open from 9a.m. to 5 p.m.. 展览会开放时间为上午九点到下午五点。The computer fair runs from April 1st to 6th. 计算机展览会从 4 月 1 日开到 4 月 6 日。There are two trade fairs running in London at the same time – the carpet manufacturers' and the computer dealers'. 在伦敦同时举办了两个交易会——一个是地毯厂家交易会,另一个是计算机交易商办的。2 . a . ( a ) honest or correct 诚实的;正确的: fair deal = arrangement where both parties are treated equally 公平交易; The workers feel they did not get a fair deal from the management. 工人们感到他们未能从资方(管理部门)获得公平待遇。fair dealing = legal buying and selling of shares 公平交易 ( 股票 ); fair price = good price for both buyer and seller 公平价格; fair trade = (i) international business system where countries agree not to charge import duties on certain items imported from their trading partners 国际互惠贸易 (ii) US = RESALE PRICE MAINTENANCE( 美 )维持转卖价格; fair trading or fair dealing = way of doing business which is reasonable and does not harm the consumer 互惠贸易;公平交易; GB Office of Fair Trading = government department which protects con-

sumers against unfair or illegal business (英)公正贸易局; fair wear and tear = acceptable damage caused by normal use 正常损耗; The insurance policy covers most damage, but not fair wear and tear to the machine. 保险单为大多数损失提供保险,但不包括机器正常损耗。( b ) fair copy = document which is written or typed with no changes or mistakes 誊清本

◇ **fairly** ad. quite 相当: The company is fairly close to financial collapse. 公司已很接近破产。She is a fairly fast keyboarder. 她是一个相当快的键盘排字员。

**faith** n. to have faith in something or someone = to believe that something or a person is good or will work well 相信;信心: The salesmen have great faith in the product. 销售人员对此产品信心十足。The sales teams do not have much faith in their manager. 销售组不太信任他们的经理。The board has faith in the managing director's judgement. 董事会相信董事长的判断。to buy something in good faith = to buy something thinking that is of good quality or that it has not been stolen or that it is not an imitation 购买自认信得过的东西

NOTE: no plural

◇ **faithfully** ad. yours faithfully = used as an ending to a formal business letter not addressed to a named person 你的忠实的(正式信函中礼仪结尾用语)

NOTE: not used in US English

**fake** 1 . n. imitation or copy made for criminal purposes 伪造品;赝品: The shipment came with fake documentation. 发运来的货物用的是伪造单据。2 . v. to make an imitation for criminal purposes 伪造: faked documents 伪造单据; He faked the results of the test. 他伪造了试验结果。

**fall** 1 . n. sudden drop or suddenly becoming smaller or loss of value 下降；跌落：a fall in the exchange rate 汇率下降；a fall in the price of gold 金价下跌；a fall on the Stock Exchange 证券交易所的股票价格下跌；Profits showed a 10％ fall.利润下减了 10％。2. v. (a) to drop suddenly to a lower price 下跌；下降：Shares fell on the market today. 今日股市下跌。Gold shares fell 10％ or fell 45 cents on the Stock Exchange. 金矿股票价下跌 10％或金矿股票在证券交易所下跌了 45 美分。The price of gold fell for the second day running. 黄金价格已连续两天下跌。The pound fell against other Europeancurrencies. 英镑对其它欧洲货币的比价下跌。(b) to happen or to take place 发生；正当；适逢：The public holiday falls on a Tuesday. 节假日正逢星期二。payments which fall due = payments which are now due to be made 到期的支付

NOTE: falling – fell – has fallen

◇ **fall away** v. to become less 减少：Hotel bookings have fallen away since the tourist season ended. 自旅游旺季结束后，旅馆预订减少。

◇ **fall back** v. to become lower or cheaper after rising in price 回落（价格上涨后下跌）：Shares fell back in light trading. 由于交易清谈，股票价格回落。

◇ **fall back on** v. to have to use money kept for emergencies 不得不动用：to fall back on cash reserves 不得不动用现金储备

◇ **fall behind** v. to be late in doing something 落后；拖欠：He fell behind with his mortgage repayments. 他拖欠了抵押付还款。

◇ **falling** a. which is growing smaller or dropping in price 衰弱的；下跌的：a falling market = market where prices are coming down 市场价格正在下跌；the falling pound = the pound which is losing its value against other currencies

正在不断贬值的英镑

◇ **fall off** v. to become lower or cheaper or less 降低；减少：Sales have fallen off since the tourist season ended. 自旅游旺季结束后销售额减少。

◇ **fall out** v. The bottom has fallen out of the market. = Sales have fallen below what previously seemed to be their lowest point. 销售额暴跌，比预想的最低点还要低。

◇ **fall through** v. not to happen or not to take place 中断；落空：The plan fell through at the last moment. 计划在最后一刻化为泡影。

**false** a. not true or not correct 不真实的；不正确的：to make a false entry in the balance sheet 在资产负债表中作了不真实的入帐；false pretences = doing or saying something to cheat someone 欺诈；He was sent to prison for obtaining money by false pretences. 他因用欺诈方法获得钱款而被送进监狱。false weight = weight on shop scales which is wrong and so cheats customers 假重量；分量不足；短斤缺两

◇ **falsify** v. to change something to make it wrong 篡改；伪造：to falsify the accounts 篡改帐目；伪造帐目帐目

◇ **falsification** n. action of making false entries in accounts 弄虚作假；伪造

**famous** a. very well known 著名的；有名的：The company owns a famous department store in the centre of London. 公司在伦敦中心拥有一个著名的百货大楼。

**fancy** a. (a) fancy goods = small attractive items 花哨的小工艺品 (b) fancy prices = high prices 高价：I don't want to pay the fancy prices they ask in London shops. 我不想支付伦敦商店所要的高价。

**fare** n. price to be paid for a ticket to travel 票价：Train fares have gone up by 5％. 火车票价上涨了 5％。The government is asking the airlines to keep air fares down. 政府要求航空公司减低机票价格。concessionary fare = reduced fare for certain types of passenger (such as employees of the transport company) 优惠的票价：full fare = ticket for a journey by an adult paying the full price 全票；成人票；half fare = half – price ticket for a child 半票；儿童票；single fare or US one – way fare = fare for a journey from one place to another 单程票；return fare or US round – trip fare = fare for a journey from one place to another and back again 往返票

**farm** 1. n. property in the country where crops are grown or where animals are raised for sale 农场；collective farm = state – owned farm which is run by the workers 集体农庄；fish farm = place where fish are grown for food 养鱼场；mixed farm = farm which has both animals and crops 混合农场 2. v. to own a farm 种植；养殖：He farms 150 acres. 他种 150 英亩地。

◇ **farming** n. job of working on a farm or of raising animals for sale or of growing crops for food 耕种；养殖；务农：chicken farming 养鸡；fish farming 养鱼；mixed farming 混合农场经营

◇ **farm out** v. to farm out work = to hand over work for another person or company to do it for you 将工作包给别人做：She farms out the office typing to various local bureaux. 她将办公室打字工作包给各个地方办事处。

**fast** a. & ad. quick or quickly 快的（地）；迅速的（地）：The train is the fastest way of getting to our supplier's factory. 乘火车是到我们供应商工厂的最快途径。Home computers sell fast in the pre – Christmas period. 圣诞节前家庭电脑很抢手。

◇ **fast – moving or fast – selling** a. fast – selling items = items which sell fast 卖得快的商品；畅销货：Dictionaries are not fast – moving stock. 字典不是畅销货。

**fault** n. (a) being to blame for something which is wrong 过错；过失：It is the stock controller's fault if the warehouse runs out of stock. 仓库货物供应不上是仓库管理人员的过失。The chairman said the lower sales figures were the fault of a badly motivated sales force. 董事长说销售额较低是销售人员积极性不高造成的。(b) wrong working 缺点；故障：The technicians are trying to correct a programming fault. 技术人员正努力排除程序故障。We think there is a basic fault in the product design. 我们认为在产品设计中有一个根本的缺陷。

◇ **faulty** a. which does not work properly 有缺陷的；有缺点的：faulty equipment 有缺陷的设备；They installed faulty computer programs. 他们装有缺陷的计算机程序。

**favour or** US **favor** 1 n. (a) as a favour = to help or to be kind to someone 爱护；好感：He asked the secretary for a loan as a favour. 他要求秘书帮他争取贷款。(b) in favour of = in agreement with or feeling that something is right 赞同；支持：Six members of the board are in favour of the proposal, and three are against it. 董事会有六个成员赞同此项建议，但有三个成员反对。2. v. to agree that something is right or to vote for something 赞同；拥护：The board members all favour Smith Ltd as partners in the project. 董事会一致赞同史密斯有限公司作此项目的合伙人。

◇ **favourable** a. which gives an advantage 有利的：favourable balance of trade = situation where a country's exports are more than the imports 贸易顺差；有利的贸易平衡；on favourable terms = on specially good terms 按有利的条件；

The shop is let on very favourable terms. 商店按很优惠的条件出租。

◇ **favourite** a. which is liked best 特别喜爱的；最喜欢的: This brand of chocolate is a favourite with the children's market. 这种牌子的巧克力是极受儿童市场喜爱的。

**fax or FAX** n. & v. informal = FACSIMILE COPY 传真(本): We will send a fax of the design plan. 我们将此设计计划发传真。I've faxed the documents to our New York office. 我们已将这些文件发传真给我们的纽约办事处。

**feasibility** n. ability to be done 可行性: to report on the feasibility of a project 报告项目的可行性; feasibility report = report saying if something can be done 可行性报告; to carry out a feasibility study on a project = to carry out an examination of costs and profits to see if the project should be started 对项目进行可行性研究

NOTE: no plural

**federal** a. referring to a system of government where a group of states are linked together in a federation, especially the central government of the United States 联邦制的(特别指美国的中央政府): Most federal offices are in Washington. 美国大多数联邦政府的办事部门设在华盛顿。

◇ **the Fed** n. US informal = FEDERAL RESERVE BOARD 美国联邦储备委员会(简称)

◇ **Federal Reserve Bank** n. US one of the twelve central banks in the USA which are owned by the state and directed by the Federal Reserve Board 美国联邦储备银行(美国 12 个中央银行之一，它属于州，但受美国联邦储备委员会的领导)

◇ **Federal Reserve Board** n. US government organization which runs the central banks in theUSA 联邦储备委员会(美国政府管理中央银行的组织)

◇ **federation** n. group of societies or companies or organizations which have a central organization which represents them and looks after their common interests 联盟；联邦；联合会: federation of trades unions 工会联合会; employers' federation 雇主联合会

**fee** n. (a) money paid for work carried out by a professional person(such as an accountant or a doctor or a lawyer)酬金；报酬: We charge a small fee for our services. 我们的服务收费很低。director's fees 经理的酬金; consultant's fee 顾问酬金 (b) money paid for something 费用: entrance fee or admission fee 入场费；门票费; registration fee 登记费；注册费

**feed** 1. n. device which puts paper into a printer or into a photocopier 进料器；影印机的进纸器: The paper feed has jammed. 进纸器塞住(被卡)了。continuous feed = device which feeds in continuous computer stationery into aprinter 连续进纸器; sheet feed = device which puts in one sheet at a time into a printer 单页进纸器

2 v. to put information into a computer (将信息输入计算机)输入 NOTE: feeding – fed

◇ **feedback** n. information, especially about people's reactions 反馈: Have you any feedback from the sales force about the customers' reaction to the new model? 你是否从销售人员那儿获得关于客户对新型号的反馈信息?

NOTE: no plural

**feint** n. very light lines on writing paper 淡格线；隐格线

**ferry** n. boat which takes passengers or goods across water 渡船: We are going to take the night ferry to Belgium. 我们打算夜里坐摆渡船去比利时。car ferry = ferry which carries cars 汽车渡轮;

passenger ferry = ferry which only carriespassengers 旅客渡轮

**fetch** v. (a) to go to bring something 拿来;取来: We have to fetch the goods from the docks. 我们必须从码头取货物。It is cheaper to buy at a cash and carry warehouse, provided you have a car to fetch the goods yourself. 如果你有汽车自己取货的话,在仓库现款取货买东西便宜。(b) to be sold for a certain price 售得;卖得: to fetch a high price 卖得好价;卖高价; It will not fetch more than £200. 它卖不到 200 英磅。These computers fetch very high prices on the black market. 这些计算机在黑市上卖好价钱。

**few** a. & n. (a) not many 很少;不多;少数: We sold so few of this item that we have discontinued the line. 这种商品我们只卖出很少几个,因此我们已停止这门生意。Few of the staff stay with us more than six months. 工作人员中没有几个和我们共处的时间达六个月以上的。(b) a few = some 一些: A few of our salesmen drive Rolls - Royces. 我们有一些销售人员贺驶罗尔斯-罗伊斯汽车。We get only a few orders in the period from Christmas to the New Year. 圣诞节到新年这段时间内我们只能收到为数不多的几张定单。

**fiat** n. fiat money = coins or notes which are not worth much as paper or metal, but are said by the government to have a value 不兑现货币;法定货币

**fictitious** a. false or which do not exist 假的;虚构的: fictitious assets = assets which do not really exist, but are entered as assets to balance the accounts 虚假资产;虚帐

**fiddle** 1. n. informal cheating 欺骗行为: It's all a fiddle. 这完全是一种欺骗行为。He's on the fiddle. = He is trying to cheat. 他试图搞欺骗。2. v. informal to cheat 伪造;欺骗: He tried to

fiddle his tax returns. 他试图伪造纳税申报单。The salesman was caught fiddling his expense account. 这个销售员因伪造费用帐户被捕。

**fide** see BONA FIDE

**fiduciary** a. & n. (person) acting as trustee for someone else 信托的;受托人

**field** n. (a) piece of ground on a farm 田野;田地: The cows are in the field. 牛在田间。(b) in the field = outside the office or among the customers 在现场;在实地: We have sixteen reps in the field. 我们有 16 个销售代表在销售现场。first in the field = first company to bring out a product or to start a service 率先生产;率先制造; Smith Ltd has a great advantage in being first in the field with a reliable electric car. 史密斯有限公司具有率先生产可靠电动汽车的巨大优势。field sales manager = manager in charge of a group of salesmen 实地销售经理; field work = examination of the situation among possible customers 现场工作;实地考察工作; He had to do a lot of field work to find the right market for the product. 为给产品找到合适的市场,他必须做许多实地考察工作。

**FIFO** = FIRST IN FIRST OUT 先进先出法

**fifty - fifty** a. & a. half 平分;均摊;各半: to go fifty - fifty = to share the costs equally 使…平分; He has a fifty - fifty chance of making a profit. = He has an equal chance of making a profit or a loss. 他有二分之一的赢利机会。

**figure** n. (a) number or cost written in numbers 数字;费用: The figure in the accounts for heating is very high. 帐户中的取暖费用很高。He put a very low figure on the value of the lease. = He calculated the value of the lease as very low. 他以低价出租。

(b) figures = written numbers 数值: sales figures = total sales 销售额; to work out the figures = to calculate 算出数值；His income runs into five figures or he has a five – figure income. = His income is more than £10, 000. 他的收入已超过五位数。in round figures = not totally accurate, but correct to the nearest 10 or 100 估计数；用整数表示；They have a workforce of 2, 500 in round figures. 他们大约有 2500 个工人。(c) figures = results for a company 公司的成效：the figures for last year or last year's figures 去年公司的成效或成果

**file** 1. n. (a) cardboard holder for documents, which can fit in the drawer of a filing cabinet 文件夹；卷宗；档案夹：Put these letters in the customer file. 将这些信件归入客户档案夹中。Look in the file marked "Scottish sales". 看一下标有"苏格兰销售"的卷宗。box file = cardboard box for holding documents 盒装档案 (b) documents kept for reference 档案 to place something on file = to keep a record of something 将…存档；to keep someone's name on file = to keep someone's name on a list for reference 将某人的名字(姓名)入档；file copy = copy of a document which is kept for reference in an office 档案副本；card – index file = information kept on filing cards 卡片索引 (c) section of data on a computer (such as payroll, address list, customer accounts)存储资料；计算机文件(如计算机中有关工资, 通讯录, 客户帐户)：How can we protect our computer files? 如何保护我们的计算机文件？2. v. (a) to file documents = to put documents in order so that they can be found easily 将文件档：The correspondence is filed under "complaints". 该信函已收入"投诉"卷宗。(b) to make an official request 提出；提交：to file a petition in bankruptcy = to ask officially to be made bankrupt or to ask officially for someone else to be made

bankrupt 提出破产申请 (c) to register something officially 登记；注册：to file an application for a patent 提出专利申请；to file a return to the tax office 向税务部门提出税款申报

◇ **filing** n. documents which have to be put in order 档案；归档：There is a lot of filing to do at the end of the week. 周末有很多旧档工作要做。The manager looked through the week's filing to see what letters had been sent. 经理仔细查看了一周的档案, 以便了解寄出什么样信件。filing basket or filing tray = container kept on a desk for documents which have to be filed 档案筐或档案公文格；filing cabinet = metal box with several drawers for keeping files 档案柜；filing card = card with information written on it, used to classify information into the correct order 档案分类卡片；filing clerk = clerk who files documents 档案管理员；filing system = way of putting documents in order for reference 档案制度

NOTE: no plural

**fill** 1. v. (a) to make something full 使充满；填满：We have filled our order book with orders for Africa. 我们的定货簿里已填满了非洲的定单。The production department has filled the warehouse with unsellable products 生产部门将卖不出的产品塞满了仓库。(b) to fill a gap = to provide a product or service which is needed, but which no one has provided before 填补：The new range of small cars fills a gap in the market. 新的小型汽车系列填补了市场空白。(c) to fill a post or a vacancy = to find someone to do a job 填补空缺；派人担任：Your application arrived too late – the post has already been filled. 你的申请表来得太晚, 这个职务已有人担任。

◇ **filler** n. something which fills a space 填塞物：stocking filler = small item which can be used to put into a Christmasstocking 袜子填塞物；圣诞袜(给儿童圣诞礼物塞入袜中)参看 see SHELF FILLER

◇ **fill in** v. to write in the blank spaces in a form 填入；填上：Fill in your name and address in block capitals. 用大写字母填上你的姓名与地址。

◇ **filling station** n. place where you can buy petrol 加油站：He stopped at the filling station to get some petrol before going on to the motorway. 在上高速公路前他将车子停在加油站加油。

◇ **fill out** v. to write the required information in the blank spaces in a form 填写；填好：To get customs clearance you must fill out three forms. 要获得结关证，你必须填写三张表格。

◇ **fill up** v. (a) to make something completely full 填满；装满：He filled up the car with petrol. 他将汽车加足了油。My appointments book is completely filled up. 我的约会登记簿写得满满的。(b) to finish writing on a form 填写；填上：He filled up the form and sent it to the bank. 他填完表格后就将它寄给银行。

**final** a. last or coming at the end of a period 最终的；最后的：to pay the final instalment 支付最后一次的分期付款；to make the final payment 最后一次付款；to put the final details on a document 将最后的细节写入文件；final date for payment = last date by which payment should be made 最终付款日；final demand = last reminder from a supplier, after which he will sue for payment 最后付款要求；final discharge = last payment of what is left of a debt 最后债务偿还；final dividend = dividend paid at the end of the year 年终分红(分股息)；final product = manufactured product, made at the end of a production process 最终产品；成品

◇ **finalize** v. to agree final details 最后定下；最后决定：We hope to finalize the agreement tomorrow. 我们希望明天将协议最终定下来。After six weeks of negotiations the loan was finalized yesterday. 经过六周谈判，贷款协定终于在昨天敲定。

◇ **finally** ad. in the end 最终；最后；终于：The contract was finally signed yesterday. 合同终于在昨日签订。After weeks of trials the company finally accepted the computer system. 经过数周试验后，公司终于接受该计算机系统。

**finance** 1. n. (a) money used by a company, provided by the shareholders or by loans 经费；资金(由股东提供或通过贷款筹措)：Where will they get the necessary finance for the project? 他们将从哪儿获得项目所需的资金? finance company or finance corporation or finance house = company which provides money for hire‐purchase 金融公司；finance market = place where large sums of money can be lent or borrowed 金融市场；high finance = lending, investing and borrowing of very large sums of money, organized by financiers 巨额融资 (b) money (of a club, local authority, etc.) 财务；财政(俱乐部或地方政府的钱)：She is the secretary of the local authority finance committee. 她是当地政府财政委员会的秘书。(c) finances = money or cash which is available 资金；财源：the bad state of the company's finances 公司资金状况不佳 2. v. to provide money to pay for something 为…提供资金：to finance an operation 为一项业务经营提供资金

◇ **Finance Act** n. GB annual act of parliament which gives the government the power to obtain money from taxes as proposed in the Budget 财政法案(英国议会制订的从国家预算的税收中获得的财源)

◇ **financial** a. concerning money 金融的；财政的：financial adviser = person or company which gives advice on financial matters for a fee 金融顾问；财务咨询机构；financial assistance = help in the form of money 财政援助；financial correspondent = journalist who writes articles on money matters for anewspaper 金融记者；financial position = state of a company's bank balance (assets and debts) 财务状况；金融形势；He must think of his financial position. 他必须考虑他的财政状况。financial resources = money which is available for investment 财政资源；资金；a company with strong financial resources 有充足资金的公司；financial risk = possibility of losing money 金融风险；There is no financial risk in selling to East European countries on credit. 向东欧赊销没有金融风险。financial statement = document which shows the financial situation of a company 财务报表；财务报告；The accounts department has prepared a financial statementfor the shareholders. 会计处已为股东准备好财务报表。Financial Times (Ordinary) index = index published by the "Financial Times", giving share prices on the London Stock Exchange based on a group of major companies "金融时报" 指数；financial year = the twelve months' period for a firm's accounts 会计年度；财政年度

◇ **financially** ad. regarding money 经费上；财政上：company which is financially sound = company which is profitable and has strong assets 资金充足的公司；财政实力雄厚的公司

◇ **financier** n. person who lends large amounts of money to companies 金融家 (向公司发放巨额贷款的人)

◇ **financing** n. providing money 提供资金；筹措资金：The financing of the project was done by two international banks. 为该项目提供资金的是两家国际银行。deficit financing = planning by a government to borrow money to cover the shortfall between expenditure and income from taxation 赤字财政

**find** v. (a) to get something which was not there before 寻得；找到：to find backing for a project 为一个项目寻求支持 (b) to make a legal decision in court 裁决：The tribunal found that both parties were at fault. 法庭裁决双方都有责任。The judge found for the defendant. = The judge decided that the defendant was right. 法官作出有利于被告的裁决。

NOTE: finding - found

◇ **findings** pl. n. the findings of a commission of enquiry = the recommendations of the commission 调查结果

◇ **find time** v. to make enough time to do something 找到时间：We must find time to visit the new staff sports club. 我们必须找时间访问新的职工俱乐部。The chairman never finds enough time to play golf. 董事长从未找到足够的时间打高尔夫球。

**fine** 1. n. money paid because of something wrong which has been done 罚款；罚金；He was asked to pay a $25,000 fine. 要求他付 2.5 万美元的罚款。We had to pay a $10 parking fine. 我们不得不付 10 美元的停车罚款。2. v. to punish someone by making him pay money 处以罚款；处以罚金：to fine someone £2,500 for obtaining money by false pretences 因某人骗取钱财要他付 2500 英磅罚款 3. ad. very thin or very small 细小地；略微地：We are cutting our margins very fine. = We are reducing our margins to the smallest possible. 我们正将利润削减到最低点。

**finish** 1. n. (a) final appearance 最后一道工序；抛光；涂饰：The product has an attractive finish. 这产品有着很吸引人的涂饰。(b) end of a day's trading on the Stock Exchange 证券交易所交易日最后时刻: Oil shares rallied at the finish. 在证券交易所交易日的最后时刻石油股票价回稳。2. v. (a) to do something or to make something completely 完成;结束: The order was finished in time. 订单及时完成。She finished the test before all the other candidates. 她先于其他所有投考者结束考试。(b) to come to an end 结束;终止: The contract is due to finish next month. 合同于下月终止。

◇ **finished** a. finished goods = manufactured goods which are ready to be sold 成品

**fink** n. US informal worker hired to replace a striking worker(美)工人罢工时之替工;工贼

**fire** 1. n. thing which burns 火;火灾: The shipment was damaged in the fire on board the cargo boat. 发运的货物被货船上的一场火灾所损坏。Half the stock was destroyed in the warehouse fire. 一半的存货被仓库火灾所毁灭。to catch fire = to start to burn 着火; The papers in the waste paper basket caught fire. 废纸篓里的文件着火。fire damage = damage caused by fire 火损; He claimed £250 for fire damage. 他要求获得 250 英磅的火灾损失赔偿金。fire - damaged goods = goods which have been damaged in a fire 火灾损坏的货物; fire door = special door to prevent fire going from one part of a building to another 防火安全门; fire escape = door or stairs which allow staff to get out of a building which is on fire 太平梯;安全出口; fire hazard or fire risk = situation or goods which could start a fire 火险; That warehouse full of paper is a fire hazard. 那个堆满纸的仓库是一个引起火灾的隐患。fire insurance = insurance against damage by fire 火灾保险 2. v.

to fire someone = to dismiss someone from a job 解雇;开除: The new managing director fired half the sales force. 新上任的总经理解雇了一半的销售人员。to hire and fire = to employ new staff and dismiss existing staff very frequently 频繁聘用和解雇

◇ **fireproof** a. which cannot be damaged by fire 防火的: We packed the papers in a fireproof safe. 我们将文件装在防火的保险箱内。It is impossible to make the office completely fireproof. 不可能使办公室完全防火。

**firm** 1. n. business or partnership 企业;公司: He is a partner in a law firm. 他是一位律师事务所的合伙人。a manufacturing firm 一家从事工业制造的公司; an important publishing firm 一个重要的出版公司 2. a. (a) which cannot be changed 坚定的;不能改变的; to make a firm offer for something 为…递实盘; to place a firm offer for two aircraft 为两架飞机递实盘; They are quoting a firm price of £1.32 per unit. 他们正在为每单位报价,定为 1.32 英磅(不能减价)。(b) not dropping in price, and possibly going to rise 坚挺的;有可能回升的: Sterling was firmer on the foreign exchange markets. 外汇市场上的英镑价格较坚挺。Shares remained firm. 股票价格仍然坚挺。3. v. to remain at a price and seem likely to go up 稳定;坚挺: The shares firmed at £1.50. 股价坚挺,每股为 1.50 英磅。

◇ **firmness** n. being steady at a price or being likely to rise 稳定;坚挺: the firmness of the pound 英镑的坚挺

◇ **firm up** v. to finalize or to agree final details 使确定: We expect to firm up the deal at the next trade fair. 我们希望下一次贸易展览会上将这项交易确定下来。

**first** n. person or thing which is there at the beginning or earlier than others 第

一: Our company was one of the first to sell into the Europeanmarket. 我们公司是第一批向欧洲市场销售的公司之一。
first quarter = three months' period from January to the end of March 第一季度; first half or first half – year = six months' period from January to the end of June 上半年; 前半年; first in first out 先进先出 (i) redundancy policy, where the people who have been working longest are the first to be made redundant 精简政策 (工龄长的人首先被解雇) (ii) accounting policy where stock is valued at the price of the oldest purchases. 会计政策 (存货先进先出计价法)

◇ **first – class** a. & n. (a) top quality or most expensive 第一流的; 上等的; 最贵的: He is a first – class accountant. 他是个第一流的会计人员。(b) most expensive and comfortable type of travel or type of hotel 头等的 (旅行或旅馆): to travel first – class. 坐头等座旅行; First – class travel provides the bestservice. 坐头等座旅行能获得最好的服务。a first – class ticket 头等座的票; to stay in first – class hotels 住在第一流旅馆; first – class mail = GB most expensive mail service, designed to be faster; US mail service for letters and postcards (英) 最贵的快递邮件; 第一类邮件; (美) 平信 (信件和明信片的邮政服务); A first – class letter should get to Scotland in a day. 用快邮件寄的信当天可到苏格兰。

◇ **first – line** a. first – line management = the managers who have immediate contact with the workers 第一线的管理人员

**fiscal** a. referring to tax or to government revenues 财政的; 国库的: the government's fiscal policies 政府的财政政策; fiscal measures = tax changes made by a government to improve the working of the economy 财政措施; fiscal year = twelve – month period on which taxes are calculated (in the UK, April 6th to April 5th) 财政年度

**fit** v. to be the right size for something 适合于: The paper doesn't fit the typewriter. 这种纸不适合这个打字机。
NOTE: fitting – fitted

◇ **fit in** v. to make something go into a space 放进去: Will the computer fit into that little room? 计算机能放进这个小房间吗? The chairman tries to fit in a game of golf every afternoon. 董事长试图每天下午安排一场高尔夫球赛。My appointments diary is full, but I shall try to fit you in tomorrow afternoon. 我的约会登记本已安排得满满的, 但我将努力把你安排在明天下午。

◇ **fit out** v. to provide equipment or furniture for a business 装备; 配备: They fitted out the factory with computers. 他们给工厂配备了计算机。The shop was fitted out at a cost of £10,000. 为该商店提供必要设备花了一万英镑。fitting out of a shop = putting shelves or counters in for a new shop 为商店提供必要设备 (货贺, 柜台…)

◇ **fittings** pl. n. items in a property which are sold with it but are not permanently fixed (such as carpets or shelves) 可移动的装置: fixtures and fittings = objects in a property which are sold with the property, both those which cannot be removed and those which can 房产中不能够移动的装置和可移动的装置

**fix** v. (a) to arrange or to agree 安排; 使确定; 固定: to fix a budget 使预算确定下来; to fix a meeting for 3 p.m. 安排下午3时召开会议; The date has still to be fixed. 日期还未确定。The price of gold was fixed at $300. 黄金价格定为300美元。The mortgage rate has been fixed at 11%. 抵押借款率已定为11%。(b) to mend 修理: The technicians are coming to fix the telephone switchboard.

技术人员将来修理电话总机。Can you fixthe photocopier? 你能修理这台影印机吗?

◇ **fixed** a. permanent or which cannot be removed 固定的: fixed assets = property or machinery which a company owns and uses 固定资产; fixed capital = capital in the form of buildings and machinery 固定资本; fixed costs = costs paid to produce a product which do not increase with the amount of product made (such as rent)固定成本; fixed deposit = deposit which pays a stated interest over a set period 定期存款; fixed expenses = money which is spent regularly ( such as rent, electricity, telephone)固定费用; fixed income = income which does not change (as from an annuity)固定收入; fixed - interest investments = investments producing an interest which does not change 固定利息投资; fixed - price agreement = agreement where a company provides a service or a product at a price which stays the same for the whole period of the agreement 固定价格协议; fixed scale of charges = rate of charging which cannot be altered 固定收费率

◇ **fixer** n. informal person who has a reputation for arranging business deals (often illegally)代人安排生意而闻名的人;中介人(常为非法)

◇ **fixing** n. (a) arranging 安排: fixing of charges 费用安排; fixing of a mortgage rate 确定抵押贷款利率 (b) price fixing = illegal agreement between companies to charge the same price 限价;定价(非法):for competing products 对竞争产品要同样的价格 (c) the London gold fixing = system where the world price for gold is set each day in London 伦敦黄金定价制度
NOTE: no plural

◇ **fixtures** pl. n. items in a property which are permanently attached to it (such as sinks and lavatories)固定的装置物(如洗涤槽…): fixtures and fittings = objects in a property which are sold with the property, both those which cannot be removed and those which can (房产中)不可移动的装置和可移动的装置

◇ **fix up with** v. to arrange 安排;准备: My secretary fixed me up with a car at the airport. 我的秘书为我在机场准备一辆小车。Can you fix me up with a room for tomorrow night? 明晚你能为我安排一个房间吗?

**flag** 1. n. (a) piece of cloth with a design on it which shows which country it belongs to 国旗: a ship flying a British flag 挂英国国旗的船; ship sailing under a flag of convenience = ship flying the flag of a country which may have no ships of its own, but allows ships of other countries to be registered in its ports 挂方便船旗航行的船(指在外国登记的船只,而挂该国国旗) (b) mark which is attached to information in a computer so that the information can be found easily(计算机上)信息的标志 2. v. to insert marks on information in a computer so that the information can be found easily(计算机上)插入信息的标志
NOTE: flagging - flagged

**flat** 1. a. (a) falling because of low demand 萧条的;不景气的: The market was flat today. 今日市场疲软。(b) fixed or not changing 固定的;一律的;统一的: flat rate = charge which always stays the same 统一收费率; We pay a flat rate for electricity each quarter.我们每季度所付电费是一样的。He is paid a flat rate of £2 per thousand.给他的费用是固定的,每千个付2英磅。2. n. set of rooms for one family in a building with other sets of similar rooms 一套房间(单元楼房): He has a flat in the centre of town. 在市中

心他有一套单元房。She is buying a flat close to her office. 她正购买一套离她办公室近的单元房。company flat = flat owned by a company and used by members of staff from time to time 公司的单元房

NOTE: US English is apartment

◇ **flat out** ad. working hard or at full speed 竭尽全力；用全速：The factory worked flat out to complete the order on time. 工厂竭尽全力以及便时完成定单。

**flea market** n. market, usually in the open air, for selling cheap secondhand goods 跳骚市场(通常在露天出售便宜的旧货)

**fleet** n. group of cars belonging to a company and used by its staff 车队(属于公司的，能被职员使用)：a company's fleet of representatives' cars 公司代表用车辆；公司推销员用车辆；a fleet car = car which is one of a fleet of cars 车队中一辆车；fleet discount = specially cheap price for purchase or rental of a company's cars 购买或租用公司车队车辆时的折扣；fleet rental = renting all a company's cars at a special price 租用公司车的租价

**flexible** a. which can be altered or changed 弹性的；灵活的：flexible budget 弹性预算；flexible prices 灵活的价格；有伸缩预算；flexible pricing policy 灵活的定价政策；flexible working hours = system where workers can start or stop work at different hours of the morning or evening provided that they work a certain number of hours per day or week 弹性工作制

◇ **flexibility** n. being easily changed 弹性；灵活性：There is no flexibility in the company's pricing policy. 公司的定价政策毫无灵活性。

NOTE: no plural

◇ **flexitime** n. system where workers can start or stop work at different hours of the morning or evening, provided that they work a certain number of hours per day or week 弹性作小时制(只要干完每天或每周规定工作小时，就可自行决定上下班)：We work flexitime. 我们实行弹性工作小时制。The company introduced flexitime working two years ago. 两年前公司采用了弹性工作小时制。

NOTE: no plural

**flier or flyer** n. (a) high flier = (i) person who is very successful or who is likely to rise to a very important position 有成就的人；有野心的人 (ii) share whose market price is rising rapidly 价格迅速上涨的股票 (b) small advertising leaflet designed to encourage customers to ask for more information about the product for sale 小广告传单(鼓励顾客询问有关出售产品信息)

**flight** n. (a) journey by an aircraft, leaving at a regular time 航班；班机：Flight AC 267 is leaving from Gate 46. AC267. 班机从46号门起飞。He missed his flight. 他误了航班。I always take the afternoon flight to Rome. 我总是乘坐下午的班机去罗马。If you hurry you will catch the six o'clock flight to Paris 如果你抓紧的话，你可赶上六点钟去巴黎的航班。(b) rapid movement of money out of a country because of a lack of confidence in the country's economic future 资金外流(由于对某国的经济缺管信心，将大量货币迅速转移到国外)：the flight of capital from Europe into the USA 资本从欧洲迅速外流到美国。the flight from the franc into the dollar 法郎逃逸转换成美元 (c) series of steps 等级：top – flight = in the most important position or very efficient 身居要职的；最高层次的；效力十分高的；Top – flight managers can earn very high salaries. 身居要职的经理能拿很高的薪水。

**flip chart** n. way of showing information to a group of people by writing on large sheets of paper which can then be turned over to show the next sheet 活动挂图；配套挂图

**float 1.** n. (a) cash taken from a central supply and used for running expenses 备用零钱（供日常开支用）: The sales reps have a float of £100 each. 销售代表每人有 100 英磅备用零钱。cash float = cash put into the cash box at the beginning of the day to allow business to start 备用现金; We start the day with a £20 float in the cash desk. 一天的营业开始前我们在收银处准备了 20 英磅的备用现金。(b) starting a new company by selling shares in it on the Stock Exchange 筹资创办（在证券交易所出售股票开办公司）: The float of the new company was a complete failure. 筹资创办这个新公司彻底地失败了。2. v. (a) to float a company = to start a new company by selling shares in it on the Stock Exchange 筹资开办公司: to float a loan = to raise a loan on the financial market by asking banks and companies to subscribe to it 筹集贷款 (b) to let a currency find its own exchange rate on the international markets and not be fixed 汇率浮动: The government has let sterling float. 政府让英镑汇率浮动。The government has decided to float the pound. 政府决定使英镑的汇率浮动。

◇ **floating 1.** n. (a) floating of a company = starting a new company by selling shares in it on the Stock Exchange 筹资创办公司 (b) the floating of the pound = letting the pound find its own exchange rate on the international market 将英镑汇率浮动
NOTE: no plural
**2.** a. which is not fixed 浮动的；不固定的: floating exchange rates 浮动汇率; the floating pound 浮动汇率的英镑

**flood 1.** n. large quantity 大量: We re-ceived a flood of orders. 我们收到大量定单。Floods of tourists filled the hotels. 旅馆内住满了旅游者。2. v. to fill with a large quantity of something 将…装满: The market was flooded with cheap imitations. 大量廉价的假冒伪劣商品充斥市场。The sales department is flooded with orders or with complaints. 销售部收到大量订单或大量投诉。

**floor** n. (a) part of the room which you walk on 地面；地板: floor space = area of floor in an office or warehouse 面积; We have 3,500 square metres of floor space to let. 我们有 3500 平方米面积供出租。the factory floor = main works of a factory 工厂的场地; on the shop floor = in the works or in the factory or among the ordinary workers 在车间;在工厂;在普通工人中间; The feeling on the shop floor is that the manager does not know his job. 工厂车间的工人感到,这位经理对自己的工作不熟悉。(b) all rooms on one level in a building 楼层: The shoe department is on the first floor(英)鞋部在二楼。Her office is on the 26th floor.(英)她的办公室在 27 楼。US floor manager = person in charge of the sales staff in a department store(美)百货公司主管营业员的经理
NOTE: the numbering of floors is different in GB and the USA. The floor at street level is the ground floor in GB, but the first floor in the USA. Each floor in the USA is one number higher than the same floor in GB.

◇ **floorwalker** n. employee of a department store who advises the customers, and supervises the shop assistants in a department 百货公司巡视员（为顾客咨询）

**flop 1.** n. failure or not being a success 失败: The new model was a flop. 新型号是个失败。2. v. to fail or not to be a success 失败;不成功: The flotation of the new company flopped badly. 筹资创

办的这家新公司一败涂地。

NOTE: flopping – flopped

◇ **floppy** 1. a. floppy disk = small disk for storing information in a computer 软磁盘 2. n. small disk for storing computer information 软磁盘: The data is on 5 inch floppies 数据存放在 5 英寸的软磁盘上。

**flotation** n. the flotation of a new company = starting a new company by selling shares in it(用出售股票)筹资创办一个新公司

**flotsam** n. flotsam and jetsam = rubbish floating in the water after a ship has been wrecked and rubbish washed on to the land 废物(船舶失事后垃圾漂在水面冲到岸上)

NOTE: no plural

**flourish** v. to be prosperous or to do well in business 兴隆;繁荣: The company is flourishing. 公司生意兴隆。Trade with Nigeria flourished. 与尼日利亚的贸易十分红火。

◇ **flourishing** a. profitable 成功的;蒸蒸日上的: flourishing trade = trade which is expanding profitably 欣欣向荣的贸易; He runs a flourishing shoe business. 他所经营的鞋业生意兴隆。

**flow** 1. n. (a) movement the flow of capital into a country 资本向某一国流动; the flow of investments in to Japan 投资流入日本 (b) cash flow = cash which comes into a company from sales and goes out in purchases or overhead expenditure 现金流动; discounted cash flow. = Calculation of forecast sales of a product in current terms with reductions for current interest rates 现金流量贴现; The company is suffering from cash flow problems = Cash income is not coming in fast enough to pay for the expenditure going out. 公司正受到现金流量的困挠。(c) flow chart or flow diagram = chart which shows the arrangement of

work processes in a series 工作流程图 2. v. to move smoothly 顺利进行: Production is now flowing normally after the strike. 罢工后,生产正恢复正常。

**fluctuate** v. to move up and down 波动: Prices fluctuate between £1.10 and £1.25. 价格在 1.10 英磅和 1.25 英磅之间波动。The pound fluctuated all day on the foreign exchange markets. 一天来,英磅在外汇市场上一直上下波动。

◇ **fluctuating** a. moving up and down 波动: fluctuating dollar prices 波动的美元价格

◇ **fluctuation** n. up and down movement the fluctuations of the franc 法郎的波动: the fluctuations of the exchange rate 外汇兑换率的波动

**fly** v. to move through the air in an aircraft 飞行: The chairman is flying to Germany on business. 董事长将飞往德国出差。The overseas sales manager flies about 100,000 miles a year visiting the agents. 负责海外销售的经理每年坐飞机的行程达 10 万英里,去各地访问代理人。

◇ **fly – by – night** a. company which is not reliable or which might disappear to avoid paying debts 无信用的;不可靠的: I want a reputable builder, not one of these fly by night outfits. 我要一个声誉好的营造商,而不是一个不可靠的单位。

**FOB or f.o.b.** = FREE ON BOARD 船上交货价;离岸价

**fold** v. (a) to bend a flat thing, so that part of it is on top of the rest 折叠: She folded the letter so that the address was clearly visible 她将信折叠起来,以便使地址清晰可见。(b) informal to fold (up) = to stop trading 歇业;关闭: The business folded up last December. 商行于去年 12 月停业。The company folded with debts of over £1m. 该公司由于拖欠 100 万英磅债务已倒闭。

◇ **- fold** suffix times 倍: four - fold = four times 四倍

◇ **folder** n. cardboard envelope for carrying papers 纸夹;文书夹: Put all the documents in a folder for the chairman. 帮董事长将所有文件放在文件夹中。

**folio** 1. n. page with a number, especially two facing pages in an account book which have the same number 帐簿中左右相对的两页有相同的号码,但只算作一页 2. v. to put a number on a page 编上页码

**follow** v. to come behind or to come afterwards 继…之后;跟随: The samples will follow by surface mail. 样品将用平邮随后寄出。We will pay £10,000 down, with the balance to follow in six months' time. 我们将先付 1 万英磅定金,其余则在六个月内付清。

◇ **follow up** v. to examine something further 进一步观察: I'll follow up your idea of putting our address list on to the computer. 我将进一步考虑你将地址表输入计算机的想法。to follow up an initiative = to take action once someone else has decided to do something 贯彻某人的决定

◇ **follow - up letter** n. letter sent to someone who has not acted on the instructions in a previous letter, or to discuss in more detail points which were raised earlier 后续信件;补充信件

**food** n. things which are eaten 食物;食品: He is very fond of Indian food. 他很喜欢印度食品。The food in the staff restaurant is excellent. 职工食堂的食品好极了。

◇ **foodstuffs** pl. n. essential foodstuffs = very important food, such as bread or rice 基本食品(如面包或米饭)

**foolscap** n. large size of writing paper 大页纸: The letter was on six sheets of foolscap. 信是写在六张大页纸上。a foolscap envelope = large envelope

which takes foolscap paper 用大页纸做的信封
NOTE: no plural

**foot** 1. n. (a) part of the body at the end of the leg 脚: on foot = walking 步行; The reps make most of their central London calls on foot. 推销代表步行访问了伦敦中心区大多数地方。The rush hour traffic is so bad that it is quicker to go to the office on foot. 在上下班高峰时间,交通十分拥挤,走着去办公室要更快一些。(b) bottom part 底部: He signed his name at the foot of the invoice. 他在发票底部签了他的名字。(c) measurement of length ( = 30cm)英尺(30 厘米): The table is six feet long. 这张桌子长六英尺。My office is ten feet by twelve. 我的办公室是 10 × 12 英尺。
NOTE: the plural is feet for (a) and (c); there is no plural for (b). In measurements, foot is usually written ft or after figures: 10ft; 10'
2. v. (a) to foot the bill = to pay the bill 付帐: The director footed the bill for the department's Christmas party. 经理为该部门圣诞宴会付帐。(b) US to foot up an account = to add up a column of numbers(美)累加一栏数字;总计

**forbid** v. to tell someone not to do something or to say that something must not be done 不允许;禁止;不准: The contract forbids resale of the goods to the USA. 合同不允许将货物返销美国。The staff are forbidden to use the front entrance. 工作人员不准使用前面的入口处。
NOTE: forbidding - forbade - forbidden

**force** 1. n. (a) strength 力量: to be in force = to be operating or working 生效;起作用; The rules have been in force since 1946. 这些法规自 1946 年起生效。to come into force = to start to operate or work 开始生效;开始实施; The

new regulations will come into force on January1st. 新规章将于 1 月 1 日生效。 (b) group of people 一群人: labour force or workforce = all the workers in a company or in an area 所有工人;劳动力; The management has made an increased offer to the labourforce. 厂方给工人们开了一个更高的价钱。 We are opening a new factory in the Far East because of the cheap local labour force. 我们正在远东开办一个新工厂,因为当地可提供廉价劳动力。 sales force = group of salesmen 销售队伍 (c) force majeure = something which happens which is out of the control of the parties who have signed a contract (such as strike, war, storm)不可抗力(如罢工,战争,风暴)
NOTE: no plural for (a) and (c)
2. v. to make someone do something 强迫;迫使: Competition has forced the company to lower its prices. 竞争迫使公司减价。
◇ **forced** a. forced sale = sale which takes place because a court orders it or because itis the only way to avoid a financial crisis 强制出售;被迫出售
◇ **force down** v. to make something become lower 迫使 … 下降: to force prices down = to make prices come down 迫使价格下跌; Competition has forced prices down. 竞争迫使价格下跌。
◇ **force up** v. to make something become higher 迫使…上升: to force prices up = to make prices go up 迫使价格上升; The war forced up the price of oil. 战争迫使油价上升。
**forecast** 1. n. description or calculation of what will probably happen in the future 预测;预报: The chairman did not believe the sales director's forecast of higher turnover. 董事长不相信销售经理所做的营业额偏高的预测。 We based our calcu lations on the forecast

turnover. 我们是以预测的营业额为根据进行计算的。 cash flow forecast = forecast of when cash will be received or paid out 现金流动预测; population forecast = calculation of how many people will be living in a country orin a town at some point in the future 人口预测; sales forecast = calculation of future sales 销售预测 2. v. to calculate or to say what will probably happen in the future 预测: He is forecasting sales of £2m. 他预测销售额将为 200 万英磅。 Economists have forecast a fall in the exchange rate. 经济学家预测,汇率要下降。
NOTE: forecasting – forecast
◇ **forecasting** n. calculating what will probably happen in the future 预测: manpower forecasting = calculating how many workers will be needed in the future, and how many will actually be available 劳动力预测
NOTE: no plural
**foreclose** v. to sell a property because the owner cannot repay money which he has borrowed (using the property as security)取消赎回权: to foreclose on a mortgaged property 取消抵押财产的赎回权
◇ **foreclosure** n. act of foreclosing 取消赎回权
**foreign** a. not belonging to one's own country 外国的: Foreign cars have flooded our market. 外国车允斥着我们的市场。 We are increasing our trade with foreign countries. 我们将增加对外贸易。 foreign currency = money of another country 外国货币; foreign goods = goods manufactured in other countries 外国商品; foreign investments = money invested in other countries 外国的投资; foreign money order = money order in a foreign currency which is payable to someone living in a foreign country 外币

汇款单; foreign trade = trade with othercountries 对外贸易

◇ **foreign exchange** n. exchanging the money of one country for that of another 外汇: foreign exchange broker or dealer = person who deals on the foreign exchange market 外汇交易商; foreign exchange dealing = buying and selling foreign currencies 外汇买卖或交易; the foreign exchange markets = market where people buy and sell foreign currencies 外汇市场; foreign exchange reserves = foreign money held by a government to support its own currency and pay its debts 外汇储备; foreign exchange transfer = sending of money from one country to another 外汇转移

◇ **foreigner** n. person from another country 外国人

**foreman or forewoman** n. skilled worker in charge of several other workers 工头(男或女)

NOTE: plural is foremen or forewomen

**forex or Forex** = FOREIGN EXCHANGE 外汇

**forfeit** 1. n. taking something away as a punishment 没收: forfeit clause = clause in a contract which says that goods or deposit will betaken away if the contract is not obeyed 没收(解约)条款(合同中); The goods were declared forfeit. = The court said that the goods had to be taken away from their owner. 货物宣布没收。2. v. to have something taken away as a punishment 将…没收: to forfeit a patent = to lose a patent because payments have not been made 没收专利权; to forfeit a deposit = to lose a deposit which was left for an item because you have decided not to buy that item 没收押金

◇ **forfeiture** n. act of forfeiting a property 没收

NOTE: no plural

**forge** v. to copy money or a signature illegally or to make a documentwhich looks like a real one 伪造(货币,签字,文件): He tried to enter the country with forged documents. 他试图以伪造的证件进入这个国家。

◇ **forgery** n. (a) making an illegal copy 伪造(文件): He was sent to prison for forgery. 他因伪造罪入狱。

NOTE: no plural (b) illegal copy 伪造物(文件): The signature was proved to be a forgery. 这个签名证明是伪造的。

**forget** v. not to remember 忘记: She forgot to put a stamp on the envelope. 她忘了在信封上贴邮票。Don't forget we're having lunch together tomorrow. 别忘了我们明天一起用午餐。

NOTE: forgetting - forgot - forgotten

**fork - lift truck** n. type of small tractor with two metal arms in front, used for lifting and moving pallets 铲车; 叉车; 叉式升降机

**form** 1. n. (a) form of words = words correctly laid out for a legal document 行文格式: receipt in due form = correctly written receipt 正式收据 (b) official printed paper with blank spaces which have to befilled in with information 单; 表格: You have to fill in form A20. 你必须填表格 A20。customs declaration form 海关申报单; a pad of order forms 一叠定货单; 定货簿; application form = form which has to be filled in to apply for something 申请表; claim form = form which has to be filled in when making an insurance claim 保险索赔表

2. v. to start or to organize 成立; 组织: The brothers have formed a new company. 几个弟兄成立一家新公司。

◇ **formation or forming** n. act of organizing 组织; 成立: the formation of a new company 组建新公司

NOTE: no plural

**forma** see 参看 PRO FORMA

**formal** a. clearly and legally written 正式的: to make a formal application 正式提出申请; to send a formal order 寄送一份正式订单

◇ **formality** n. something which has to be done to obey the law 例行手续; 正式手续: customs formalities = declaration of goods by the shipper and examination of them by the customs 海关手续

◇ **formally** a. in a formal way 正式地: We have formally applied for planning permission for the new shopping precinct. 我们已就允许规划商业区事宜提出正式申请。

**former** a. before or at an earlier time. 前任的; 早先的: The former chairman has taken a job with the rival company. 前任董事长已在一家竞争对手的公司里找到工作。

◇ **formerly** ad. at an earlier time 从前; 以前: He is currently managing director of Smith Ltd, but formerly he worked for Jones. 现在他是史密斯有限公司的总经理，但过去他为琼斯公司工作。

**fortnight** n. two weeks 两周: I saw him a fortnight ago. 我于两周前见过他。 We will be on holiday during the last fortnight of July. 我们将在七月的最后两周度假。

**fortune** n. large amount of money 财产; 财富: He made a fortune from investing in oil shares. 他从石油股票投资中发了大财。 She left her fortune to her three children. 她将财产留给她的三个孩子。

**forward** 1. a. in advance or to be paid at a later date 预定的; 远期的: forward buying or buying forward = buying shares or currency or commodities at today's price for delivery at a later date 预购; forward contract = agreement to buy foreign currency or shares or commodities for delivery at a later date at a certain price 远期合同; 期货合同; forward market = market for purchasing foreign currency or oil or commodities for delivery at a later date 期货市场; forward (exchange) rate = rate for purchase of foreign currency at a fixed price for delivery at a later date 期货汇率; 远期外汇汇率; What are the forward rates for the pound? 英镑的期货汇率是多少? forward sales = sales for delivery at a later date 期货销售 2. ad. (a) to date a cheque forward = to put a later date than the present one on a cheque 倒填日期: carriage forward or freight forward = deal where the customer pays for transporting the goods 运费交货时付; 运费到付; charges forward = charges which will be paid by the customer 费用后付(由客户以后支付) (b) to buy forward ( = to buy foreign currency before you need it, in order to becertain of the exchange rate 预购(外币): to sell forward = to sell foreign currency for delivery at a later date 提前出售(外币); 期货出售 (c) balance brought forward or carried forward = balance which is entered in an account at the end of a period and is then taken to be the starting point of the next period 上期结转; 余额承前 3. v. to forward something to someone = to send something to someone 转交; 转运: to forward a consignment to Nigeria 将一批货转到尼日利亚; Please forward or to be forwarded = words written on an envelope, asking the person receiving it to send it on to the person whose name is written on it 请转交

◇ **(freight) forwarder** n. person or company which arranges shipping and customs documents for several shipments from different companies, putting them together to form one large shipment 转运商; 运输报关代理人（为不同公司的货

物安排运输和备好海关文件)

◇ **forwarding** n. (a) arranging shipping and customs documents 代运；转运：air forwarding = arranging for goods to be shipped by air 航空代运；forwarding agent = FORWARDER 转运商；运输报关代理；forwarding instructions or instructions for forwarding = instructions showing how the goods are to be shipped and delivered 转运说明书 (b) forwarding address = address to which a person's mail can be sent on 信件转寄地址

NOTE: no plural

**foul** a. foul bill of lading = bill of lading which says that the goods were in bad condition when received by the shipper 不洁提单；不完全提单

**founder** n. person who starts a company 创始人：founder's shares = special shares issued to the person who starts a company 发起人股票

**fourth** a. coming after third 第四的：fourth quarter = period of three months from October to the end of the year 第四季度

**Fr** = FRANC 法郎

**fraction** n. very small amount 小部份；微量：Only a fraction of the new share issue was subscribed. 新发行的股票中仅有很小一部分被认购。

◇ **fractional** a. very small 微不足道的；很小的：fractional certificate = certificate for part of a share 零星股票的凭证

**fragile** a. which can be easily broken 易坏的；易碎的：There is an extra premium for insuring fragile goods in shipment. 对发运货物中的易碎品要多收保险费。

**franc** n. money used in France, Belgium, Switzerland and many other countries 法郎(在法国、比利时、瑞士以及许多其它国家所用货币)：French

francs or Belgian francs or Swiss francs 法国法郎；比利时法郎；瑞士法郎；It costs twenty – five Swiss francs. 这值 25 瑞士法郎。franc account = bank account in francs 法郎帐户

NOTE: in English usually written Fr before the figure：Fr2, 500 ( say："two thousand, five hundred francs")。Currencies of different countries can be shown by the initial letters of the countries: FFr (French francs)；SwFr (Swiss francs)；BFr (Belgian francs)

**franchise** 1. n. licence to trade using a brand name and paying a royalty forit 特许经销权(要获得该权必须支付特许使用费)：He has bought a printing franchise or a hot dog franchise. 他已买到印刷特许经营权或热狗的特许经营权。2. v. to sell licences for people to trade using a brand name and paying a royalty 赋与特许权：His sandwich bar was so successful that he decided to franchise it. 他的三明治柜台生意十分兴隆，因此他决定获得三明治的经营特许权。

◇ **franchisee** n. person who runs a franchise 特许证持有人

◇ **franchiser** n. person who licenses a franchise 授予特许权者

◇ **franchising** n. act of selling a licence to trade as a franchise 出售特许权：He runs his sandwich chain as a franchising operation 他以特许专营权企业的身份对三明治连锁店进行管理。

NOTE: no plural

◇ **franchisor** n. = FRANCHISER

**franco** ad. free 免费地

**frank** v. to stamp the date and postage on a letter 盖邮戳：franking machine = machine which marks the date and postage on letters so that the sender does not need to use stamps 盖"邮资已付"邮戳的机器

**fraud** n. making money by making people believe something which is not true

欺诈；欺骗：He got possession of the property by fraud. 他用欺诈方式占有了这项房地产。He was accused of frauds relating to foreign currency. 指控他犯有外币诈骗罪。to obtain money by fraud = to obtain money by saying or doing something to cheat someone 用欺诈的方式获得钱；fraud squad = special police department which investigates frauds 调查欺诈警察队

◇ **fraudulent** a. not honest or aiming to cheat people 不诚实的；欺诈性的：a fraudulent transaction 一笔欺骗性的交易

◇ **fraudulently** ad. not honestly 不诚实地；欺骗地：goods imported fraudulently 用欺骗方式进口的货物

**free** 1. a. & ad. (a) not costing any money 免费：to be given a free ticket to the exhibition 给一张免费参观展览会的票：The price Catalogue sent free on request. 一经要求可免费寄送目录本。carriage free = the customer does not pay for the shipping 运费免付；free gift = present given by a shop to a customer who buys a certain amount of goods 赠品；There is a free gift worth £25 to any customer buying a washing machine. 任何一个购买洗衣机的顾客都可得到价值 25 英磅的赠品。free sample = sample given free to advertise a product 免费的样品（做广告用）；free trial = testing of a machine with no payment involved 免费试机；to send a piece of equipment for two weeks' free trial 发送一种供两周免费试用的设备；free of charge = with no payment to be made 免费；free on board = (i) price including all the seller's costs until the goods are on the ship for transportation 船上交货价 (ii) US price includes all the seller's costs until the goods are delivered to a certain place(美)指在某地交货价；free on rail = price including all the seller's costs until the goods are delivered

to the railway for shipment 铁路交货价 (b) with no restrictions 自由的；自由地：free collective bargaining = negotiations over wage increases and working conditions between the management and the trade unions 自由集体谈判；free competition = being free to compete without government interference 自由竞争；free currency = currency which is allowed by the government to be bought and sold without restriction 自由通货；free enterprise = system of business with no interference from the government 自由企业制；free market economy = system where the government does not interfere in business activity in any way 自由市场经济制；free port or free trade zone = port or area where there are no customs duties 自由港或自由贸易区；free of tax or tax-free = with no tax having to be paid 免税；He was given a tax-free sum of £25,000 when he was made redundant. 在他被解雇时，他得到不必纳税的 25000 英磅。interest free of tax or tax-free interest 利息免税；interest-free credit or loan = credit or loan where no interest is paid by the borrower 无息信贷或贷款；free of duty or duty-free = with no duty to be paid 免征关税；免税；to import wine free of duty or duty-free 进口酒免税；free trade = system where goods can go from one country to another without any restrictions 自由贸易制；The government adopted a free trade policy. 政府实行自由贸易政策。free trade area = group of countries practising free trade 自由贸易区；free trader = person who is in favour of free trade 主张自由贸易的人 (c) not busy or not occupied 不忙；未被占用的：Are there any free tables in the restaurant? 饭店里有空桌子吗？I shall be free in a few minutes. 几分钟后我有空。The chairman always keeps Friday afternoon free for a game of bridge. 董事长总是将星期五下午留出来打桥牌。2. v. to make something available or easy 使…容易；使可获得：The government's decision has freed millions of pounds for investment. 政府的这项决策使成百万英磅用于投资。

◇ **freehold** n. freehold property = property which the owner holds for ever and on which no rent is paid 终身持有不付租金的房地产

◇ **freeholder** n. person who owns a freehold property 不动产的终身所有者

◇ **freelance** 1. a. & n. independent worker who works for several different companies but is not employed by any of them 自由职业者(为几家公司工作，但未被它们中任何一家雇用)：We have about twenty freelances working for us or about twenty people working for us on a freelance basis. 大约有 20 名自由职业者为我们工作。She is a freelance journalist. 她是一个不受雇的自由记者。2. ad. selling one's work to various firms, but not being employed by any of them 独立地；自由地：He works freelance as a designer. 他是一个不受雇于任何人的设计师。3. v. (a) to do work for several firms but not be employed by any of them 无契约自由工作：She freelances for the local newspapers. 她作为自由职业者为地方报社工作。(b) to send work out to be done by a freelancer 向自由职业者提供工作：We freelance work out to several specialists. 我们向几位自由工作专家提供工作。

◇ **freelancer** n. freelance worker 不受雇于任何雇主的工人

◇ **freely** ad. with no restrictions 自由地：Money should circulate freely within the Common Market. 货币应在共同市场内自由流通。

◇ **freephone** n. GB system where one can telephone to reply to an advertisement or to place an order or to ask for in-formation and the seller paysfor the call (英)免费电话服务制度(对广告答覆和订货以及要求卖方提供商品信息电话用由卖方支付)

◇ **freepost** n. GB system where one can write to an advertiser or to place anorder or to ask for information to be sent, and the seller pays the postage 免费邮寄制度(向广告人写信或向卖方订货和询问信息的信件，其邮资全部由卖方承担)

**freeze** 1. n. credit freeze = period when lending by banks is restricted by the government 信贷冻结；wages and prices freeze or a freeze on wages and prices = period when wages and prices are not allowed to be increased 工资和价格冻结 2 v. to keep money or costs, etc., at their present level and notallow them to rise 冻结(将货币或成本等保持在现在水平，不允许它们增加)：We have frozen expenditure at last year's level. 我们已将开支保持在去年的水平。to freeze wages and prices 冻结工资和价格；to freeze credits 冻结信贷；to freeze company dividends 冻结公司的股息

NOTE: freezing – froze – has frozen

◇ **freeze out** v. to freeze out competition = to trade successfully and cheaply and so prevent competitors from operating 把竞争排斥在外。

**freight** 1. n. (a) cost of transporting goods by air, sea or land 运费：At an auction, the buyer pays the freight. 拍卖时,买方支付运费。Freight charges or freight rates = money charged for transporting goods 运费；Freight charges have gone up sharply this year. 今年运费猛涨。freight costs = money paid to transport goods 运费；freight forward = deal where the customer pays for transporting the goods 运费由提货人照付 (b) air freight = shipping of goods in an aircraft 空运：to send a shipment by air freight空运货物；air freight charges or rates = money charged for sending goods by air 航空运费；空运之费（c）goods which are transported（运送的）货物：to take on freight = to load goods onto a ship, train or truck 装货（将货物装上船；火车或卡车）；US freight car = railway wagon for carrying goods（美）货车；freight depot = central point where goods are collected before being shipped 货物积存处；freight elevator = strong lift for carrying goods 运送货物的电梯；升降机；freight plane = aircraft which carries goods, not passengers 运货（飞）机；freight train = train used for carrying goods 货（运列）车 2. v. to freight goods = to send goods 发运货物：We freight goods to all parts of the USA. 我们向美国各地方运送货物。

◇ **freightage** n. cost of transporting goods 运费

◇ **freighter** n. （a）aircraft or ship which carries goods 货物运载工具（如飞机, 船舶…）（b）person or company which organizes the transport of goods 运输或运输公司

◇ **freightliner** n. train which carries goods in containers 集装箱列车：The shipment has to be delivered to the freightliner depot. 要运输的货物必须运到集装箱列车站。

**frequent** a. which comes or goes or takes place often 时常的；频繁的：There is a frequent ferry service to France. 有经常去法国的摆渡服务。We send frequent telexes to New York. 我们频频向纽约发电传。How frequent are the planes to Birmingham? 每隔多长时间有去伯明翰的飞机?

◇ **frequently** ad. often 时常地；频繁地：The photocopier is frequently out of use. 这台影印机经常不用。We telex our NewYork office very frequently - at least four times a day. 我们十分频繁地向纽约办事处打电传，至少一天 4 次。

**friendly society** n. group of people who pay regular subscriptions which are used to help members of the group when they are ill or in financial difficulties 互济会；互助会(用大家定期交纳的会员费对生病或碰到经济财政困难的会员进行帮助的组织)

**fringe benefits** pl. n. extra items given by a company to workers in addition to a salary（such as company cars, private health insurance)附加福利（除工资外，公司给职工提供的额外好处, 如用公司的车、私人健康保险）

**front** n.（a）part of something which faces away from the back 前面；前部：The front of the office building is on the High Street. 办公楼面向一条大马路或一条主要街道。The front page of the company report has a photograph of the managing director. 公司报告的扉页有总经理的照片。Our ad appeared on the front page of the newspaper. 我们的广告登在报纸的第一版。（b）in front of = before or on the front side of something 在…前面：They put up a"for sale" sign in front of the factory. 他们在工厂前面立了一块"待售"的牌子。The chairman's name is in front of all the others on the staff list. 在职员名单上, 董事长的名字排在第一个。（c）business or person used to hide an illegal trade 掩护人或企业(指非法贸易)：His restaurant is a front for a drugs organization. 他的餐馆是一个吸毒组织的掩护处。（d）money up front = payment in advance 预付：They are asking for £10,000 up front before they will consider the deal. 在考虑这笔交易前，他们要求先预付 1000 英磅。He had to put money up front before he could clinch the deal. 他必须先预付一笔钱, 才能达成这笔交易。

◇ **front - line** a. front - line management = managers who have immediate contactwith the workers 第一线管理人员

◇ **front man** n. person who seems honest but is hiding an illegal trade 为他人非法活动做掩护的人

**frozen** a. not allowed to be changed or used 冻结的：frozen account = bank account where the money cannot be changed or used because of a court order 冻结帐户；frozen assets = a company's assets which by law cannot be sold because someone has a claim against them 冻结资产；frozen credits = credit in an account which cannot be moved 冻结贷款；呆欠；His assets have been frozen by the court. = The court does not allow him to sell his assets. 他的资产被法院冻结。see also FREEZE

**ft** = FOOT

**fuel** 1. n. material (like oil, coal, gas) used to give power 燃料：The annual fuel bill for the plant has doubled over the last years. 工厂年燃料费用在过去几年翻了一翻。He has bought a car with low fuel consumption. 他买到一辆省燃料的小车。2. v. to add to 增加；引起：Market worries were fuelled by news of an increase in electricity charges. 电费增加的消息更增添了对市场担忧。The rise in the share price was fuelled by rumours of a takeover bid. 股票价格上涨是由合并递价的传闻所引起的。

**fulfil or** US **fulfill** v. to complete something in a satisfactory way 圆满完成；履行：The clause regarding payments has not been fulfilled. 付款条款没能履行。to fulfil an order = to supply the items which have been ordered 履行订单；We are so understaffed that we cannot fulfil any more orders before Christmas. 我们人手太少，在圣诞前不能完成更多的订单。

◇ **fulfilment** n. carrying something out in a satisfactory way 完成：order fulfilment = supplying items which have been ordered 完成订单；履行定单

**full** a. (a) with as much inside it as possible 充满的；挤满的：The train was full of commuters. 火车里充满了通勤者(坐火车上下班的人)。Is the container full yet? 集装箱装满了吗？We sent a lorry full of spare parts to our warehouse. 我们向仓库发了一辆满载零件的卡车。When the disk is full, don't forget to make a backup copy. 当软盘存满信息后,别忘搞一个备用拷贝。(b) complete or including everything 全部的：We are working at full capacity. = we are doing as much work as possible. 我们竭尽全力地工作。full costs = all the costs of manufacturing a product, including bothfixed and variable costs 全部成本；full cover = insurance cover against all risks 完全承保；in full discharge of a debt = paying a debt completely 完全清偿债务；full employment = situation where all the people who can work have jobs 充分就业；full fare = ticket for a journey by an adult at full price 全票；大人票；full price = price with no discount 全价(没有折扣的)；He bought a full‑price ticket. 他买了一张全票。(c) in full = completely 全部地：Give your full name and address or your name and address in full. 提供你的全名和地址! He accepted all our conditions in full. 他全部接受了我们的条件。full refund or refund paid in full 全部退款；He got a full refund when he complained about the service. 当他对服务提出抗议时,他获得全部退款。full payment or payment in full = paying all money owed 全部付还

◇ **full‑scale** a. complete or very thorough 完全的；彻底的：The MD ordered a full‑scale review of credit terms. 总经理命令对信贷的条件进行彻底的审核。

◇ **full‑time** a. & ad. working all the

normal working time (i. e. about eight hoursa day, five days a week) 全日的；全日地：She is in full‒time work or She works full‒time or She is in full‒time employment；她是一个全职雇员。他是全职雇员中一员。

◇ **full‒timer** n. person who works full‒time 全职工作人员

◇ **fully** ad. completely 完全地；完整地；圆满地：fully‒paid shares = shares where the full face value has been paid 已全部缴款的股票；fully paid‒up capital = all money paid for the issued capital shares 全部缴清股本

**function** 1. n. duty or job 职责；职务；职能：management function or function of management = the duties of being a manager 管理的职能 2. v. to work 运转；起作用：The advertising campaign is functioning smoothly. 广告运动开展顺利。The new management structure does not seem to be functioning very well. 新管理机构似乎运转得不好。

**fund** 1. n. money set aside for a special purpose 专款；基金：contingency fund = money set aside in case it is needed urgently 应急基金；pension fund = money which provides pensions for retired members of staff 抚恤基金；退休基金；the International Monetary Fund = (part of the United Nations) a type of bank which helps member states in financial difficulties, gives financial advice to members and encourages world trade 国际货币基金组织 2. pl. n. (a) money which is available for spending 资金：The company has no funds to pay for the research programme. 公司没有钱来支付研究计划的费用。The company called for extra funds. = The company asked for more money. 公司需要额外的资金。to run out of funds = to come to the end of the money available 用完资金；public funds 公共基金；公款；The

cost was paid for out of public funds. 用公款支付费用。conversion of funds = using money which does not belong to you for a purpose forwhich it is not supposed to be used 侵吞他人的资金；挪用他人的资金；to convert funds to another purpose = to use money for a wrong purpose 挪用或侵吞资金；to convert funds to one's own use = to use someone else's money for yourself 侵吞他人款项或资金 (b) GB the Funds = government stocks and securities(英)政府的债券与证券 3. v. to provide money for a purpose 提供资金：to fund a company = to provide money for a company to operate 为一个公司提供资金；The company does not have enough resources to fund its expansion programme. 公司没有足够的财力资源为扩展计划提供资金。

◇ **funded** a. backed by long‒term loans 长期贷款资助的：long‒term funded capital 用长期贷款筹措资本；GB funded debt = part of the National Debt which pays interest, but where there is no date for repayment of the principal(英)国债的一部分,付利息而本金的偿还不定。

◇ **funding** n. (a) providing money for spending 提供资金：The bank is providing the funding for the new product launch. 银行为新产品投放市场提供资金。(b) changing a short‒term debt into a long‒term loan 将短期债款转变为长期贷款：The capital expenditure programme requires long‒term funding. 资本支出计划需将短期借款转变或长期贷款。

NOTE: no plural

**furnish** v. (a) to supply or to provide 提供 (b) to put furniture into an office or room 为…配备家俱：He furnished his office with secondhand chairs and desks；他为办公室配备了旧的桌椅。The company spent £10,000 on furnishing the chairman's office. 公司为给董事长办公室配备家俱花了 10,000 英磅。furnished accommodation = flat or house, etc. which is let with furniture) in it 带家俱的住处（出租）

**furniture** n. chairs, tables, beds, etc. 家俱：office furniture = chairs, desks, filing cabinets used in an office 办公室家俱；He deals in secondhand office furniture. 他从事办公室旧家俱的交易。an office furniture store 办公家俱商店；furniture depository = warehouse where you can store the furniture from a house 家俱仓库

**further** 1. a. (a) at a larger distance away 更远的：The office is further down the High Street. 办公室在大马路的再往南那头。The flight from Paris terminates in New York – for further destinations you must change to internal flights. 从巴黎开出的航班停在纽约，还想远行你必须换乘国内航班。(b) additional or extra 进一步的；另外的：Further orders will be dealt with by our London office. 额外订单由我们伦敦办事处处理。Nothing can be done while we are awaiting further instructions. 在我们等待进一步指示期间，我们什么也干不了。to ask for further details or particulars；要求获得更多详情或细节；He had borrowed £100,000 and then tried to borrow a further £25,000. 他已借了 100,000 英磅，然后还试图再借 25,000 英磅。The company is asking for further credit. 公司要求更多的信贷。He asked for a further six weeks to pay. 他要求再给六周的时间来付款。(c) further to = referring to something in addition 再；参照：further to our letter of the 21st = in addition to what we said in our letter 参照我们 21 日信件；further to your letter of the 21st = here is information which you asked for in your letter 参照一下你 21 日的信件

further to our telephone conversation =

here is some information which we discussed 参照我们的电话交谈 2. v. to help or to promote 帮助；促进：He was accused of using his membership of the council to further his own interests. 有人指控他用委员会委员身份谋私利益。

**future** 1. a. referring to time to come or to something which has not yet happened 未来的：future delivery = delivery at a later date 远期交货；期货交割 2. n. time which has not yet happened 将来；未来；以后：try to be more careful in future 努力在将来变得更加谨慎；In future all reports must be sent to Australia by air. 以后所有报告必须寄往澳大利亚。◇ **futures** pl. n. trading in shares or commodities for delivery at a later date 期货交易（股票，商品）：Gold rose 5% on the commodity futures market yesterday. 昨日商品期货市场上的金价上涨了 5%。

# Gg

**g** = GRAM

**gain** 1 n. (a) increase or becoming larger gain in experience = getting more experience 经验的增长；gain in profitability = becoming more profitable 利润的增加 (b) increase in profit or price or value (价格，价值，利润的) 上涨：Oil shares showed gains on the Stock Exchange. 石油股票在证券交易所的价格呈上涨趋势。Property shares put on gains of 10% – 15%. 房地产股票价上涨了 10% 到 15%。capital gains = money made by selling a fixed asset 资本收益；资本利得；capital gains tax = tax paid on capital gains 资本收益税；资本

利得税; short – term gains = increase inprice made over a short period 价格短期上涨 2 v. (a) to get or to obtain 获得; 取得: He gained some useful experience working in a bank. 在银行工作期间, 他取得了一些有用的经验。to gain control of a business = to buy more than 50% of the shares so that you can direct the business 获得企业的控制权 (b) to rise in value 增值: The dollar gained six points on the foreign exchange markets. 美元在外汇市场上增值了六个百分点。

◇ **gainful** a. gainful employment = employment which pays money 有报酬的工作

◇ **gainfully** adverb gainfully employed = working and earning money 有酬劳地受雇

**gallon** n. measure of liquids ( = 4. 5 litres)加仑( = 4. 5 升): The car does twenty – five miles per gallon or the car does twenty – five miles to the gallon. = The car uses one gallon of petrol in travelling twenty – five miles. 这辆汽车每加仑汽油跑 25 英里。
NOTE: usually written gal after figures: 25gal

**galloping inflation** n. very rapid inflation which is almost impossible to reduce 恶性通货膨胀; 难以控制的通货膨胀

**gap** n. empty space 空缺; 空白: gap in the market = opportunity to make a product which is needed but which no one has sold before 市场空白; to look for or to find a gap in the market; 寻找市场空白或空缺; This computer has filled a real gap in the market. 这种计算机实在是填补了市场的一个空白。dollar gap = situation where the supply of dollars is not enough to satisfy the demand for them from overseas buyers 美元短缺; trade gap = difference in value between a country's imports and exports 贸易逆差; 入超

**gate** n. (a) door leading into a field 大门 (b) door leading to an aircraft at an airport(飞机场通向飞机的)门: Flight AZ270 is now boarding at Gate 23. 乘坐 AZ270 的旅客请于 23 号门登机。(c) number of people attending a sports match(体育比赛的)观众人数: There was a gate of 50, 000 at the football final. 观看这场足球决赛的观众达 5 万人。

**gather** v. (a) to collect together or to put together 搜集; 收集: He gathered his papers together before the meeting started. 在开会前, 他将所有文件收集在一起。She has been gathering information on import controls from various sources. 她从各个渠道搜集有关进口控制的情报。(b) to understand or to find out 认为: I gather he has left the office. 我想他已离开办公室。Did you gather who will be at the meeting? 在你看来, 谁将参加这次会议?

**GATT** = GENERAL AGREEMENT ON TARIFFS AND TRADE 关贸总协定

**gazump** v. He was gazumped. = His agreement to buy the house was cancelled because someone offered more money. 由于别人提高房价, 他的购房协议被取消。

◇ **gazumping** n. offering more money for a house than another buyer has done, so as to be sure of buying it 比另一买主出更高的价钱买房; 抬价买房

**GDP** = GROSS DOMESTIC PRODUCT 国内生产总值

**gear** v. (a) to link to or to connect with 与 … 相联系: Bank interest rates are geared to American interest rates. 银行利率与美国利率相联系。Salary geared to the cost of living. = Salary which rises as the cost of living increases. 工资与生活费用挂钩。(b) a company which is highly geared or a highly – geared company = company which has a high proportion of its funds from fixed - interest borrowings 负债经营的公司；债台高筑的公司

◇ **gear up** v. to get ready 准备好；to gear up for a sales drive = to make all the plans and get ready for a sales drive 准备好开展一场推销运动；The company is gearing itself up for expansion into the African market. 公司正准备打入非洲市场。

◇ **gearing** n. (a) ratio between a company's capital borrowed at fixed interest and the value of its ordinary shares 举债经营或借入资本与股东的比例结合(以固定利率借入资本与普通股价之间的比) (b) borrowing money at fixed interest which is then used to produce more money than the interest paid 负债或举债经营(按固定利息借钱，用来赚比所付利息更多的钱)
NOTE: no plural

**general** a. (a) ordinary or not special 一般的：general expenses = all kinds of minor expenses or money spent on the day - to - day costs of running a business 总务费用；日常性管理费用；general manager = manager in charge of the administration of a company 总经理；general office = main administrative office of a company 总务处 (b) dealing with everything or with everybody 总的；综合性的：general audit = examining all the books and accounts of a company 全面审计；一般审计；general average = sharing of the cost of lost goods between all parties to an insurance 共同海损；general election = election of a government by all the voters in a country 大选；普选；general meeting = meeting of all the shareholders of a company 股东大会；general strike = strike of all the workers in a country 总罢工；Annual General Meeting = meeting of all the shareholders, when the company's fi-

nancial situation is discussed with the directors 年度股东大会；Extraordinary General Meeting = special meeting of shareholders to discuss an important matter 特别股东大会 (c) the General Agreement on Tariffs and Trade = international organization which aims to try to reduce restrictions in trade between countries 贸易关税总协定 (d) general trading = dealing in all types of goods 综合贸易：general store = small country shop which sells a large range of goods 杂货店

◇ **generally** a. normally or usually 一般地；通常地：The office is generally closed between Christmas and the New Year. 办事处在圣诞节与新年之间一般不办公。We generally give a 25% discount for bulk purchases. 我们一般给大批量购买者打25%的折扣。

**generous** a. (person) who is glad to give money (人)慷慨的；大方的：The staff contributed a generous sum for the retirement present for the manager. 职工们慷慨解囊，给经理购买退休礼品。

**gentleman** n. (a) "gentlemen" = way of starting to talk to a group of men "先生们"(向一群男性讲话时间，表示礼貌)："Good morning, gentlemen; 先生，早晨好! If everyone is here, the meeting can start"；如果每人已到此，会议可开始。"Well, gentlemen, we have all read the report from our Australian office" "先生们! 我们都已阅读过来自澳大利亚办事处的报告。" "Ladies and gentlemen" = way of starting to talk to a group of women and men "女士们! 先生们!" (b) man 男士：gentleman's agreement or US gentlemen's agreement = verbal agreement between two parties who respect each other 君子协定；They have a gentleman's agreement not to trade in each other's area. 他们之间有一个不在互相区域内进行贸易的君子协定。

**genuine** a. true or real 真的: This old table is genuine. 这张旧桌子是真货。a genuine leather purse 真皮钱包; the genuine article = real article, not an imitation 真货; genuine purchaser = someone who is really interested in buying 真买主

◇ **genuineness** n. being real or not being an imitation 真正; 非伪造

**get** v. (a) to receive 收到: We got a letter from the solicitor this morning. 今晨我们收到一封律师的来信。When do you expect to get more stock? 你们何时有望进得更多的货? He gets £250 a week for doing nothing. 他什么也不干, 每周白拿 250 英镑。She got £5,000 for her car. 她的车卖了 5000 英镑。(b) to arrive at a place 到达某地: The shipment got to Canada six weeks late. 所运货物晚了 6 个星期才到达加拿大。She finally got to the office at 10:30. 她最终于 10 时 30 分到达办公室。
NOTE: getting – got – has got or US gotten

◇ **get across** v. to make someone understand something 使人了解或接受: The manager tried to get across to the workforce why some people were being made redundant. 经理努力让工人们理解为什么要将一些人解雇。

◇ **get along** v. to manage 对付; 设法做到: We are getting along quite well with only half the staff. 我们只用一半的工作人员, 工作仍进展得不错。

◇ **get back** v. to receive something which you had before 取回; 收回: I got my money back after I had complained to the manager. 我向经理申诉后, 拿回了我们钱。He got his initial investment back in two months. 两个月后, 他就收回了自己的最初投资。

◇ **get on** v. (a) to work or to manage 干, 处理: How is the new secretary getting on? 新秘书工作干得如何? (b) to succeed 成功: My son is getting on well – he has just been promoted. 我儿子干得很成功, 刚刚晋升。

◇ **get on with** v. (a) to be friendly or to work well with someone 相处得很好: She does not get on with her new boss. 她与新老板相处地不好。(b) to go on doing work 继续工作: The staff got on with the work and finished the order on time. 职工们继续工作并及时地完成了订单。

◇ **get out** v. (a) to produce something (on time) 生产; 公布: The accounts department got out the draft accounts in time for the meeting. 财会部门为会议及时地公布帐目草稿。(b) to sell an investment 出售(投资); 退出: He didn't like the annual report, so he got out before the company collapsed. 他不满意这个上年度报告, 因此在公司例闭前抽出了自己的投资。

◇ **get out of** v. to stop trading in (a product or an area) 停止; 放弃: The company is getting out of computers. 公司已停止做计算机生意。We got out of the South American market. 我们退出南美市场。

◇ **get round** v. to avoid 避开: We tried to get round the embargo by shipping from Canada. 我们试图从加拿大发运以避开禁运。

◇ **get through** v. (a) to speak to someone on the phone 与某人通电话: I tried to get through to the complaints department. 我尽力与投诉部门通(电)话。(b) to be successful 成功: He got through his exams, so he is now a qualified engineer. 他通过了考试现在已是一名合格的工程师。(c) to try to make someone understand 使人理解: I could not get through to her that I had to be at the airport by 2:15. 我无法让她理解, 我必须在 2 时 15 分赶到机场。

**gift** n. thing given to someone 礼物; 礼

品：gift coupon or gift token or gift voucher = card, bought in a store, which is given as a present and which must be exchanged in that store for goods 赠券；We gave her a gift token for her birthday. 我们送给她一张生日礼券。

**gift shop** = shop selling small items which are given as presents 礼品商店；gift inter vivos = present given to another living person 生前的赠物；free gift = present given by a shop to a customer who buys a certain amount of goods. 免费赠送品

◇ **gift - wrap** v. to wrap a present in attractive paper 礼品包装：Do you want this book gift - wrapped? 你要给这本书进行礼品包装吗？

◇ **gift - wrapping** n. (a) service in a store for wrapping presents for customers 礼品包装业务 (b) attractive paper for wrapping presents 包装礼品的包装纸

**gilts** plural noun GB government securities 英国金边证券；优等证券（信用很高的英国证券）

◇ **gilt - edged** a. investment which is very safe 投资可靠的：gilt - edged stock or securities = government securities 金边债券；政府证券

**gimmick** n. clever idea or trick 骗人的花招：a publicity gimmick 一种宣传花招；The PR men thought up this new advertising gimmick. 公关人员想出了这种新的广告花招。

**giro** n. the giro system = banking system in which money can be transferred from one account to another without writing a cheque 直接转帐制；GB National Giro = banking system, run by the Post Office, which allows account holders to move money from one account to another free of cost 邮政汇款；a giro cheque 直接转帐支票；giro account 直接转帐帐户；giro account number 直接转帐帐户号码；She put £25 into her giro account. 她在直接转帐帐户上存了 25 英镑。to pay by bank giro transfer 通过银行直接转帐划拨支付

◇ **Girobank** n. bank in a giro system 直接转帐银行；a National Girobank account 一个国家直接转帐银行帐户

**give** v. (a) to pass something to someone as a present 馈赠；给：The office gave him a clock when he retired. 他退休时，办事处送给他一个钟。(b) to pass something to someone 交给：She gave the documents to the accountant. 他将文件交给了会计。Can you give me some information about the new computer system? 你能给我提供一些新计算机系统的信息吗？Do not give any details to the police. 不要向警察提供任何细节。(c) to organize 组织；举行：The company gave a party on a boat to publicize its new discount system. 公司在船上举行了一次聚会，为其新的折扣制度做宣传。

NOTE: giving - gave - has given

◇ **give away** v. to give something as a free present 赠送：We are giving away a pocket calculator with each £10 of purchases. 每次购买 10 英镑的商品，我们赠送一个袖珍计算器。

◇ **giveaway** 1 a. to sell at giveaway prices = to sell at very cheap prices 大廉价 2 n. thing which is given as a free gift when another item is bought 赠品

**glue** 1 n. material which sticks items together 胶水：She put some glue on the back of the poster to fix it to the wall. 她用胶水涂在招贴画的背面，将它贴在墙上。The glue on the envelope does not stick very well. 信封上的胶水粘性不好。2. v. to stick things together with glue(用胶水)粘：He glued the label to the box. 他将标签粘在盒子上。

**glut** 1 n. a glut of produce = too much produce, which is then difficult to sell 过剩的产品：a coffee glut or a glut of coffee 过多的咖啡；glut of money = situation where there is too much money available to borrowers 过多的货币 2. v. to fill the market with something which is then difficult to sell(使某种商品)充斥市场：The market is glutted with cheap cameras. 廉价的照相机充斥市场 NOTE: glutting – glutted

**gm** = GRAM

**gnome** n. informal. the gnomes of Zurich = important Swiss international bankers(非正式)瑞士的大银行家们

**GNP** = GROSS NATIONAL PRODUCT 国民生产总值

**go** v. (a) to move from one place to another 去；走到：The cheque went to your bank yesterday. 支票昨日到了你们银行。The plane goes to Frankfurt, then to Rome. 此飞机先飞到法兰克福，然后去罗马。He is going to our L agos office. 他正去我们拉各斯的办公室。(b) to be placed 放在；置于：The date goes at the top of the letter. 日期写在信封的顶部。NOTE: going – went – has gone

◇ **go – ahead** 1 n. to give something the go – ahead = to approve something OR to say that something can be done 批准：His project got a government go – ahead. 他的项目已获政府批准。The board refused to give the go – ahead to the expansion plan. 董事会拒绝批准此项发展计划。2 a. energetic or keen to do well 有朝气的；进取心的：He is a very go – ahead type. 他属于有进取心类型的人。She works for a go – ahead clothing company. 她任职于一家兴旺发达的服装公司。

◇ **go back on** v. not to do what has been promised 食言；违背：Two months later they went back on the agreement. 两个月后，他们违背了协议。

◇ **going** a. (a) active or busy 活跃的；忙碌的：to sell a business as a going con-

cern = to sell a business as an actively trading company 将企业当作经营发达的公司出售；It is a going concern. = The company is working . (and making a profit). 这是一家生意兴隆的公司。(b) the going price = the usual or current price or the price which is being charged now 现价；时价；What is the going price for secondhand 1975 Volkswagens? 1975 年的"大众牌"二手货汽车的时价为多少? the going rate = the usual or current rate of payment 现行收费；We pay the going rate for typists. 我们按现行收费标准给打字员付款。The going rate for offices is £ 10 per square metre. 办公室的现行收费标准为每平米 10 英镑。

◇ **going to** v. to be going to do something = to be just about to start doing something 开始从事；打算做：The firm is going to open an office in New York next year. 公司即将在纽约开设办事处。When are you going to answer my letter? 你何时会回我的信?

◇ **go into** v. (a) to go into business = to start in business 从商：He went into business as a car dealer. 他作为一个汽车商步入商界。She went into businessin partnership with her son. 她与儿子合伙，开始从商。(b) to examine carefully 仔细检查：The bank wants to go into the details of the inter – company loans 银行想他细检查一下公司间贷款细节。

◇ **go on** v. (a) to continue 继续：The staff went on working in spite of the fire. 尽管发生火灾，职工们还继续工作。The chairman went on speaking for two hours. 董事长连续讲了二个小时。(b) to work with 以…为依据：The figures for 1982 are all he has to go on. 他必须以 1982 的所有数值作为依据。We have to go on the assumption that sales will not double next year. 我们只能有这样的假定，即明年的销售量不会增

加一倍。

NOTE: you go on doing something

◇ **go out** v. to go out of business = to stop trading 停止贸易: The firm went out of business last week. 该公司上周停止贸易。

**goal** n. aim or something which you try to do 目标: Our goal is to break even within twelve months. 我们的目标是在12个月内达到收支相抵。The company achieved all its goals. 公司达到了它所有的规定目标。

**godown** n. warehouse (in the Far East) 仓库; 贷栈(在远东)

**gofer** n. US person who does all types of work in an office for low wages(美)勤杂工

**gold** n. (a) very valuable yellow metal 黄金: to buy gold. 购买黄金; to deal in gold 经营黄金交易; gold coins 金币; gold bullion = bars of gold 金条 (b) the country's gold reserves = the country's store of gold kept to pay international debts 该国的黄金储备; the gold standard = linking of the value of a currency to the value of a quantity of gold 金本位; The pound came off the gold standard. = The pound stopped being linked to the value of gold. 英镑停止使用金本位。(c) gold point = amount by which a currency which is linked to gold can vary in price 黄金输入点 (d) gold shares or golds = shares in gold mines 金矿股票

NOTE: no plural, except for (d)

◇ **golden handshake or** US **golden parachute** n. large, usually tax - free, sum of money given to a director who retires from a company before the end of his service contract 大笔退休金(给提前退休的董事或经理): When the company was taken over, the sales director received a golden handshake of £25,000. 当接收该公司时, 销售经理们得到

25000 英磅退休金。

◇ **goldmine** n. mine which produces gold 金矿: That shop is a little goldmine. = That shop is a very profitable business. 那个商店财源滚滚。

**good** a. (a) not bad 好的: a good buy = excellent item which has been bought cheaply 低价购进上等品; to buy something in good faith = to buy something thinking it is of good quality or that it has not been stolen or that it is not an imitation 买信誉好的东西 (b) a good deal of = a large quantity of 大量: We wasted a good deal of time discussing the arrangements for the AGM. 在讨论年度股东大会安排方面我们浪费了大量的时间。The company had to pay a good deal for the building site. 公司为买建筑用地要付大量的钱。a good many = very many 许多; A good many staff members have joined the union. 许多职员加入工会。

◇ **goods** pl. n. (a) goods and chattels = moveable personal possessions 私人动产; 个人动产 (b) items which can be moved and are for sale 商品: goods in bond = imported goods held by the customs until duty is paid 保税货物; capital goods = machinery, buildings and raw materials which are used to make other goods 资本货物; consumer goods or consumable goods = goods bought by the general public and not by businesses 消费品; dry goods = cloth and clothes 布和衣服; finished goods = manufactured goods which are ready to be sold 成品; household goods = items which are used in the home 家用商品; luxury goods = expensive items which are not basic necessities 奢侈品; manufactured goods = items which are made by machine 工业制品 (c) goods depot = central warehouse where goods can be stored until they are moved 货物集散处; 货物集散中心仓库; goods train = train for carrying freight 货车

◇ **goodwill** n. good reputation of a business 商业信誉;企业声誉: He paid £10,000 for the goodwill of the shop and £4,000 for the stock. 他为该商店的声誉付了 10000 英磅,为其存货付 4000 英磅。
NOTE: no plural

**go – slow** n. slowing down of production by workers as a protest against the management 怠工: A series of go – slows reduced production. 连续的怠工使生产降低。

**govern** v. to rule a country 统治: The country is governed by a group of military leaders. 国家由一伙军界领导人统治。

◇ **government** n. (a) organization which administers a country 政府: central government = main organization dealing with the affairs of the whole country 中央政府; local government = organizations dealing with the affairs of a small area of the country 地方政府; provincial government or state government = organization dealing with the affairs of a province or of a state 省政府或州政府 (b) coming from the government or referring to the government 来自政府;涉及政府的: government employees 政府雇员; local government staff 地方政府官员; government intervention or intervention by the government 政府干预; a government ban on the import of arms 政府对武器进口的禁令; a government investigation into organized crime 政府对有组织犯罪的调查; Government officials prevented him leaving the country. 政府官员阻止他离开这个国家。Government policy is outlined in the booklet. 这本小册子概述了政府的政策。Government regulations state that import duty has to be paid on luxury items. 政府条例规定奢侈品必须

交纳进口税。He invested all his savings in government securities. 他把自己的全部储蓄都投资于政府债券了。government support = financial help given by the government 政府资助; The computer industry relies on government support. 计算机业依赖于政府资助。government annuity = money paid each year by the government 政府年金; government contractor = company which supplies goods or services to the government on contract 政府承包人(商)

◇ **governmental** a. referring to a government 涉及及政府的

◇ **government – backed** a. backed by the government 政府扶持的

◇ **government – controlled** a. under the direct control of the government 政府控制的: Ad cannot be placed in the government – controlled newspapers. 广告不能刊登在政府控制的报纸上。

◇ **government – regulated** a. regulated by the government 政府管理的

◇ **government – sponsored** a. encouraged by the government and backed by government money 政府赞助的: He is working in a government – sponsored scheme to help small businesses. 他正致力于一个政府赞助的扶持小企业的方案。

**grace** n. favour shown by granting a delay 宽限;缓期 to give a creditor a period of grace or two weeks' grace 给债权人一个宽限期或两个星期的宽限
NOTE: no plural

**grade** 1. n. level or rank 品位或等级: top grade of civil servant 最高级公务人员; to reach the top grade in the civil service 晋升到最高级公务人员; high – grade = of very good quality 优质; high – grade petrol 优质汽油; a high – grade trade delegation = a delegation made up of important people 高级贸易代表团; low – grade = not very important or not of very good quality 低级或低质量；a low – grade official from the Ministry of Commerce 商业部一位低级职员；The car runs well on low – grade petrol. 这个汽车使用低质汽油运行良好。top – grade = most important or of the best quality 最高级或质量最佳；top – grade petrol 优质汽油 2. v. (a) to sort something into different levels of quality(按质量)分级；分等：to grade coal 给煤分级 (b) to make something rise in steps according to quantity(按质量制定)级差：graded advertising rates = rates which become cheaper as you take more advertising space 分级付广告费；graded tax = tax which rises according to income 等级税收 (c) graded hotel = good quality hotel 高级旅馆；星级旅馆

**gradual** a. slow or step by step 慢慢的；逐渐的：1984 saw a gradual return to profits. 1984 年呈现出逐步恢复赢利的局面。His CV describes his gradual rise to the position of company chairman. 他的履历说明了他是一步一步地晋升到公司董事长的职位。

◇ **gradually** ad. slowly or step by step 慢慢地；逐步地：The company has gradually become more profitable. 公司已逐步变得有更多赢利。She gradually learnt the details of the import – export business. 她逐步弄懂了进出口业务的细节。

**graduate** n. person who has a degree from a university or polytechnic(大学或理工学院)毕业生：graduate entry = entry of graduates into employment with a company 毕业生在公司就业；the graduate entry into the civil service 毕业生在政府文职机构就业；graduate training scheme = training scheme for graduates 毕业生训练计划；graduate trainee = person in a graduate training scheme 接受毕业培训生

◇ **graduated** a. rising in steps according to quantity(按数量)累进的：graduated income tax 累进所得税；graduated pension scheme = pension scheme which is calculated on the salary of each person in the scheme 累进退休金方案；graduated taxation = tax system where the percentage of tax paid rises as the income rises 累进税收

**gram** or **gramme** n. measure of weight (one thousandth of a kilo)重量单位"克" NOTE: usually written g or gm with figures: 25g

**grand** 1 a. important 重要的：grand plan = major plan 重要的计划；He explained his grand plan for redeveloping the factory site. 他解释了重新拓展厂址的重要的规划。grand total = final total made by adding several subtotals 总量 2 n. informal one thousand pounds or dollars 一千英磅或一千美元；They offered him fifty grand for the information. 他们支付给他 50000 美元 (或英镑)的情报费。 NOTE: no plural

**grant** 1 n. money given by the government to help pay for something 政府拨款：The laboratory has a government grant to cover the cost of the development programme. 实验室得到一笔政府拨款用于扩建方案所需开支。The government has allocated grants towards the costs of the scheme. 政府已拨款用于此方案所需开支。grant – aided scheme = scheme which is funded by a government grant 政府拨款资助的方案 2 v. to agree to give someone something 给与：to grant someone a loan or a subsidy 给与某人一笔贷款或补助金；The local authority granted the company an interest – free loan to start up the new factory. 地方政府给与公司一笔无息贷款以建立新的工厂。

**graph** n. diagram which shows statistics as a drawing 统计图表：to set out the results in a graph 把结果体现在统计图表 上；to draw a graph showing the rising profitability 画统计图表显示不断增长的利润；The sales graph shows a steady rise. 销售额曲线图显示出稳步上升的趋势。graph paper = special paper with many little squares, used for drawing graphs 座标纸

**gratia** see EX GRATIA

**gratis** ad. free or not costing anything 免费：We got into the exhibition gratis. 我们免费进入展览会。

**gratuity** n. money given to someone who has helped you 赏金：The staff are instructed not to accept gratuities. 指示职工们不接受赏金。

**great** a. large 大：a great deal of = very much 大量；He made a great deal of money on the Stock Exchange. 在证券交易所他赚到很多钱。There is a great deal of work to be done before the company can be made really profitable. 在公司能真正盈利之前尚有大量工作要做。

**greenback** n. US inmal dollar bill(美) 美钞

◇ **green card** n. (a) special British insurance certificate to prove that a car is insured for travel abroad(英)绿色保险卡 (b) work permit for a person going to live in the USA(美)绿卡

◇ **greenmail** n. making a profit by buying a large number of shares in a company, threatening to take the company over, and then selling the shares back to the company at a higher price 绿票讹诈(购进某公司大量股票，形成吞并之势，然后以更高价将股票回卖给该公司从中牟利)

NOTE: no plural

◇ **Green Paper** n. report from the British government on proposals for a new law to be discussed in Parliament 绿色文件；绿皮书(英政府关于一项需在议会讨论的新法令提议的报告)

◇ **green pound** n. value of the British pound as used in calculating agricultural prices and subsidies in the EEC 绿色英镑(用于欧共体计算农业价格与补贴)

**grid** n. system of numbered squares 座标方格体系：grid structure = structure based on a grid 座标方格体系结构

**grievance** n. complaint made by a trade union or a worker to the management 抱怨；申诉：grievance procedure 申诉程序

**gross** 1 n. twelve dozen（144）罗（12打）：He ordered four gross of pens. 他订购了四罗钢笔。

NOTE: no plural 2. a. (a) total or with no deductions 总量：gross earnings = total earnings before tax and other deductions 总收益(扣税前)；gross income or gross salary = salary before tax is deducted 工资总收入；gross margin = percentage difference between sales income and the cost of sales 毛利；gross profit = profit calculated as sales income less the cost of sales 毛利润；gross receipts = total amount of money received before expenses are deducted 收入总额；总收入；gross yield = profit from investments before the deduction of tax 毛收益率；税前投资收益 (b) gross domestic product = annual value of goods sold and services paid for inside a country 国内生产总值；gross national product = annual value of goods and services in a country including income from other countries 国民生产总值 (c) gross tonnage = total amount of space in a ship 总吨数；gross weight = weight of both the container and its contents 毛重 3. ad. with no deductions 不扣除地；总共地：His salary is paid gross. 工资全部发给他。4 v. to make a gross profit 获…毛利润；总共赚得：The group grossed £25m in 1985. 1985 年这个集团共赚得毛利 2500 万英磅。

**ground** n. (a) soil or earth 土壤；地面：

The factory was burnt to the ground. = The factory was completely destroyed in a fire. 工厂焚为平地。ground hostess = woman who looks after passengers at the airport before they board the plane 地勤小姐; ground landlord = person or company which owns the freehold of a property which is then leased and sub-leased 房地产主或房地产公司; ground lease = first lease on a freehold building 不动产的出租; ground rent = rent paid by a lessee to the ground landlord 地租 (b) grounds = basic reasons 理由: Does he have good grounds for complaint? 他的抱怨有充分理由吗? There are no grounds on which we can be sued. 没有理由对我们起诉。What are the grounds for the demand for a pay rise? 要求增加工资的理由是什么?

◇ **ground floor** n. floor (in a shop or office) which is level with the ground (英)底层;(美)第一层: The men's department is on the ground floor. 男子用品部在第一层。He has a ground - floor office. 他有一个在一楼的办公室。

NOTE: in the USA this is the first floor

**group** 1. n. (a) several things or people together 组;群: A group of the staff has sent a memo to the chairman complaining about noise in the office. 一群职工给董事长送去了一份备忘录,抱怨办公室内有噪音。(b) several companies linked together in the same organization 集团: the group chairman or the chairman of the group 集团董事长; group turnover or turnover for the group 集团营业额; the BPCC group BPCC 集团; group results = results of a group of companies taken together 集团的成果;公司的成果 2. v. to group together = to put several items together 聚集: Sales from six different agencies are grouped together under the heading "European sales". 六个不同机构的销售额汇总在"欧洲销售额"这个标题下。

**grow** v. to become larger 发展: The company has grown from a small repair shop to a multinational electronics business. 公司已从一个小维修店发展成为一垮国电子企业. Turnover is growing at a rate of 15% per annum. 营业额正以年 15% 的速度递增。The computer industry grew fast in the 1980s. 20 世纪 80 年代计算机工业迅速发展。

NOTE: growing – grew – has grown

◇ **growth** n. increase in size 发展;增长: The company is aiming for growth. = ··· is aiming to expand rapidly. 公司正打算扩建。economic growth = rate at which a country's national income grows 经济增长; a growth area or a growth market = an area where sales are increasing rapidly 迅速发展地区或市场; a growth industry = industry which is expanding rapidly 迅速发展中的工业; growth rate = speed at which something grows 增长速度;增长率; growth share or growth stock = share which people think is likely to rise in value 增值股票或增值债券

NOTE: no plural

**guarantee** 1. n. (a) legal document which promises that a machine will work properly or that an item is of good quality 担保;保证: certificate of guarantee or guarantee certificate 保证书; The guarantee lasts for two years. 担保期为 2 年。It is sold with a twelve - month guarantee. 销售的商品有 12 个月担保期。The car is still under guarantee. = is still covered by the maker's guarantee. 这辆汽车仍处于担保期内。(b) promise that someone will pay another person's debts 担保: to go guarantee for someone = to act as security for someone's debts 为某人之债务作担保 (c) thing given as a security 担保物: to leave share certificates as a guarantee 把股票留下作为担保物 2. v. to give a promise that something will happen 担保；保证：to guarantee a debt = to promise that you will pay a debt made by someone else 给一笔债款做担保：to guarantee an associate company = to promise that an associate company will pay its debts 给一个联营公司做担保；to guarantee a bill of exchange = to promise that the bill will be paid 给汇票做担保；The product is guaranteed for twelve months. = The manufacturer says that the product will work well for twelve months, and will mend it free of charge if it breaks down. 此产品有 12 个月的担保期。guaranteed wage = wage which a company promises will not fall below a certain figure 保证工资(工资的最低限度)

◇ **guarantor** n. oun person who promises to pay someone's debts 担保人：He stood guarantor for his brother. 他为他兄弟做担保人。

**guess** 1. n. calculation made without any real information 估算；猜测：The forecast of sales is only a guess. 销售额的预测只是一种估算。He made a guess at the pretax profits. = He tried to calculate roughly what the pretax profits would be. 他对税前利润作了估计。It is anyone's guess. = No one really knows what is the right answer. 这仅仅是大家的猜测而已。2. v. to guess (at) something = to try to calculate something without any information 估算；猜测：They could only guess at the total loss. 他们对于全部损失只能作大概估算。The sales director tried to guess the turnover of the Far East division. 销售经理试图对远东分公司的营业额做出估算。

◇ **guesstimate** n. imal rough calculation 粗略估算

**guideline** n. unofficial suggestion from the government as to how something should be done 指导方针：The government has issued guidelines on increases in incomes and prices. 政府对于工资和物价增长已发布了指导方针。The increase in retail price breaks or goes against the government guidelines. 零售价格的增长违背政府的指导方针。

**guild** n. association of merchants or of shopkeepers 同业公会：trade guild 商贸同业公会；the guild of master bakers 面包师同业公会

**guillotine** n. machine for cutting paper 切纸机

**guilty** a. (person) who has done something wrong 有罪的：He was found guilty of libel. 发现他犯诽谤罪. The company was guilty of not reporting the sales to the auditors. 公司没有向审计员汇报销售额是有罪的。

**gum** n. glue 胶；胶水：He stuck the label to the box with gum. 他用胶水把商标贴在盒子上。

◇ **gummed** a. with glue on it 带胶的：gummed label = label with dry glue on it, which has to be made wet to make it stick 带胶的标签

# Hh

**ha** = HECTARE 公顷

**haggle** v. to discuss prices and terms and try to reduce them 讨价还价；争论不休：to haggle about or over the details of a contract 对合同的细节争论不休；After two days' haggling the contract was signed. 经过两天的讨价还价合同才签定。

**half** 1 n. one of two parts into which something is divided 一半；二分之一：

The first half of the agreement is acceptable. 协议 的 前半部分 是 可接受的。the first half or the second half of the year = the periods from January 1st to June 30th or from June 30th to December 31st 前半年 或 后半年；We share the profits half and half. = We share the profits equally. 我们平分利润。NOTE: plural is halves 2 a. divided into two parts 一半的；二分之一的；Half a per cent or a half per cent = 0.5% 百分之零点五；His commission on the deal is twelve and a half per cent = 12.5%. 在这笔交易中他的佣金是 12.5%。half a dozen or a half - dozen = six 半打；六；to sell goods off at half price = at 50% of the price for which they were sold before 按原价的二分之一将商品售出；a half - price sale = sale of all goods at half the price 半价销售。

◇ **half - dollar** n. US fifty cents 五十美分；半美元

◇ **half - year** n. six months of an accounting period 财会年度的半年：first half - year or second half - year = first six months or second six months of a company's accounting year(公司财会年度的) 前半年 或 后半年；to announce the results for the half - year to June 30th or the first half - year's results = results for the period January 1st to June 30th 宣布(财会年度)前半年的成果；We look forward to improvements in the second half - year. 我们期望(财会年度)后半年能有所改进。

◇ **half - yearly** 1 a. happening every six months or referring to a period of six months 每半年的：half - yearly accounts 半年帐目；half - yearly payment 每半年支付的款额；half - yearly statement 每半年一次的报表；a half - yearly meeting 每半年一次的会议 2. ad. every six months 每半年地：we pay the account half - yearly. 我们每半年支付一次帐款。

**hallmark** 1 n. mark put on gold or silver items to show that the metal is of the correct quality(金银器皿上表示成色或纯度的)检验印记 2 v. to put a hallmark on a piece of gold or silver 在(金品或银品)上盖检验印记：a hallmarked spoon 有成色印记的调羹

**hammer** 1 n. auctioneer's hammer = wooden hammer used by an auctioneer to hit his desk, showing that an item has been sold 拍卖商的木锤：to go under the hammer = to be sold by auction 被拍卖；All the stock went under the hammer = All the stock was sold by auction. 所有的存货都被拍卖。2 v. to hit hard 猛击；to hammer the competition = to attack and defeat the competition 全力投入竞争并取胜；to hammer prices = to reduce prices sharply 大幅度降价。

◇ **hammered** a. ( on the Stock Exchange) He was hammered. = He was removed from the Stock Exchange because he could not pay his debts. 击锤宣布他不再是证券交易所的会员。

◇ **hammering** n. (a) beating 击败：The company took a hammering in Europe. = The company had large losses in Europe or lost parts of its European markets. 在欧洲市场上这个公司遭受了巨大损失。We gave them a hammering. = We beat them commercially. 我们挤跨了他们的生意。(b) (on the Stock Exchange) removal of a member because he cannot pay his debts(交易所)击锤宣布(某人无力偿债不再成为其成员)

◇ **hammer out** v. to hammer out an agreement = to agree something after long and difficult negotiations 努力达成协议：The contract was finally hammered out. 经过艰苦谈判合同终于签订。

**hand** n. (a) part of the body at the end

of each arm 手: to shake hands = to hold someone's hand when meeting to show you are pleased to meet him or to show that an agreement has been reached 握手: the two negotiating teams shook hands and sat down at the conference table. 谈判双方握手并坐在会议桌旁。 to shake hands on a deal = to shake hands to show that a deal has been agreed 握手成交。(b) by hand = using the hands, not a machine 手工; 用手: These shoes are made by hand. 这些鞋是手工制作的 to send a letter by hand = to ask someone to carry and deliver a letter personally, not sending it through the post 由某人亲手转交信件。(c) in hand = kept in reserve 手头(拥有): balance in hand or cash in hand = cash held to pay small debts and running costs 手头余额; 手头现金: We have £10,000 in hand. 我们手头有一万英磅。 work in hand = work which is in progress but not finished 在制作中; 在进行中。(d) goods left on hand = unsold goods left with the retailer or manufacturer 未售出商品: They were left with half the stock on their hands. 他们还有一半的存货未脱手。(e) to hand = here or present 近在手边; I have the invoice to hand. = I have the invoice in front of me 我这里有那张发票。(f) show of hands = vote where people show how they vote by raising their hands 举手表决: The motion was carried on a show of hands. 提议由举手表决而通过。(g) to change hands = to be sold to a new owner 转卖: The shop changed hands for £100,000. 商店以十万英磅转卖他人。(h) note of hand = document where someone promises to pay money at a stated time without conditions(无条件付款的承诺文件)本票; 期票; 付款单: In witness whereof, I set my hand. = I sign as a witness. 我作为见证人签了字。(i) worker 人手: to take on ten more hands 再补充十个人手; deck hand = ordinary sailor on a ship 水手; factory hand = worker in a factory 工厂工人。

◇ **handbill** n. sheet of printed paper handed out to members of the public as an advertisement 传单。

◇ **handbook** n. book which gives instructions on how something is to be used 说明书; 手册: The handbook does not say how you open the photocopier. 说明书没说明怎样打开影印机。Look in the handbook to see if it tells you how to clean the typewriter. 查一下说明书看看是否讲到如何清洗打字机。service handbook = book which shows how to service a machine 维修手册

◇ **hand in** v. to deliver (a letter) by hand 递交: He handed in his notice or he handed in his resignation. = He resigned. 他递交了他的辞职书。

◇ **hand luggage** n. small cases which passengers can carry themselves (and so can take with them into a plane) 手提行李箱。

◇ **handmade** a. made by hand, not by machine 手工制做的; He writes all his letters on handmade paper. 他写信全是用手工制信纸。

◇ **hand - operated** a. worked by hand, not automatically 手工操作的: a hand - operated machine 手工操作的机器。

◇ **handout** n. (a) publicity handout = information sheet which is given to members of the public 宣传传单。(b) free gift 施舍物; 救济品: The company exists on handouts from the government. 公司靠着政府的施舍而生存。

◇ **hand over** v. to pass something to someone 移交; She handed over the documents to the lawyer. 她把文件移交给律师。he handed over to his deputy. = He passed his responsibilities to his deputy. 他把职责移交给他的副手。

◇ **handover** n. passing of responsibilities to someone else 职责移交：The handover from the old chairman to the new went very smoothly. 原任董事长向新任董事长的职责移交工作进行得很顺利。When the ownership of a company changes, the handover period is always difficult. 公司的所有权转变时，职责移交期总是困难的。

◇ **handshake** n. golden handshake = large, usually tax - free, sum of money given to a director who retires from a company before the end of his service contract 大笔退休金；The retiring director received a golden handshake of £25,000. 退职董事接到一笔 2,5000 英磅的高额退职金。

◇ **handwriting** n. writing done by hand 手写：Send a letter of application in your own handwriting = written by you with a pen, and not typed 请寄一份手写申请书。
NOTE: no plural

◇ **handwritten** a. written by hand, not typed It is more professional to send in a typed rather than a handwritten letter of application. 寄一份打印的申请书比手写的申请书更为正式。

**handle** v. (a) to deal with something or to organize something 处理；组织；The accounts department handles all the cash. 会计部门管理所有的现金。We can handle orders for up to 15,000 units. 我们能够处理多达 15000 件的订单。They handle all our overseas orders. 他们负责处理我们所有的海外订单。(b) to sell or to trade in (a sort of product)经营某项产品：We do not handle foreign cars. 我们不经营外国汽车。They will not handle goods produced by other firms. 他们不经营其他公司生产的商品。

◇ **handling** n. moving something by hand or dealing with something 手工搬运或经营管理：handling charges = money to be paid for packing and invoicing or for dealing with something in general or for moving goods from one place to another 手续费、管理费；搬运费：The bank adds on a 5% handling charge for changing travellers' cheques. 银行加收5%作为换购旅行支票的总现费。materials handling = moving materials from one part of a factory to another in an efficient way 原材料搬运；货物搬运

**handy** a. useful or convenient 有用的；方便的：They are sold in handy - sized packs. 它们以方便的包装规格售出。This small case is handy for use when travelling. 这个小箱子旅游时使用很方便。

**hang** v. to attach something to a hook, nail, etc. 挂：Hang your coat on the hook behind the door. 把你的外衣挂在门后的钩子上。He hung his umbrella over the back of his chair. 他把雨伞挂在他的椅子背上。
NOTE: hanging - hung

◇ **hang on** v. to wait (while phoning) 不挂断电话：If you hang on a moment, the chairman will be off the other line soon. 你别挂，稍等，董事长将很快挂断另一条线的电话。

◇ **hang up** v. to stop a telephone conversation by putting the telephone back on its hook 挂断电话；When I asked him about the invoice, he hung up. 当我问他有关发票之事，他挂断了电话。

**happen** v. to take place by chance 偶然发生：The contract happened to arrive when the managing director was away on holiday. 当总经理外出度假时，那份合同恰巧到了。He happened to be in the shop when the customer placed the order. 当那位顾客订货时他正好在商店里。What has happened to = What went wrong with or What is the matter with or Where is. 出什么问题了：What hashappened to that order for Japan? 日本的那份订货单出什么问题了？

**happy** a. very pleased 高兴的：We will be happy to supply you at 25% discount. 我们乐意给你打 25% 的折扣。The MD was not at all happy when the sales figures came in. 销售额数字送来时总经理一点都不高兴。

**harbour** n. port or place where ships come to load or unload 港口／码头：harbour dues = payment which a ship makes to the harbour authorities for the right to use the harbour 港务税；harbour installations or harbour facilities = buildings or equipment in a harbour 港口设备

**hard** 1 a. (a) strong or not weak 强硬的：to take a hard line in trade union negotiations = to refuse to accept any proposal from the other side 在工会谈判中采取强硬路线 (b) difficult 困难的：These typewriters are hard to sell. 这些打字机销售困难。It is hard to get good people to work on low salaries. 以低工资雇佣能干的人是困难的。(c) solid hard cash = money in notes and coins which is ready at hand 现金；硬币；He paid out £100 in hard cash for the chair. 他花了 100 英磅现金买了把椅子。hard copy = printout of a text which is on a computer or printed copy of a document which is on microfilm 硬拷贝；He made the presentation with diagrams and ten pages of hard copy hard disk = computer disk which has a sealed case and can store large quantities of information（计算机信息存储）硬盘。(d) hard bargain = bargain with difficult terms 条件苛刻的交易；to drive a hard bargain = to be a difficult negotiator 拼命讨价还价；迫使对方接受苛刻条件 to strike a hard bargain = to agree a deal where the terms are favourable to you 以有利于自己的条件成交；after weeks of hard bar-

gaining = after weeks of difficult discussions 经过几个星期的讨价还价。(e) hard currency = currency of a country which has a strong economy and which can be changed into other currencies easily 硬通货；exports which can earn hard currency for the Soviet Union 能为苏联挣回硬通货的出口商品；These goods must be paid for in hard currency. 这些商品需用硬通货支付。a hard currency deal 一笔用硬通货支付的交易。2 ad. with a lot of effort 努力地；The sales team sold the new product range hard into the supermarkets. 销售组努力将新产品系列打入超级市场。If all the workforce works hard, the order should be completed on time. 如果所有的工人都努力工作，定货应能按时完成。

◇ **harden** v. Prices are hardening. = are settling at a higher price 价格上涨。

◇ **hardness** n. hardness of the market = being strong or not being likely to fall 市场坚挺

◇ **hard sell** n. to give a product the hard sell = to make great efforts to persuade people to buy it（对产品的）硬行推销：He tried to give me the hard sell. = He put a lot of effort into trying to make me buy. 他竭尽全力地说服我购买商品

◇ **hard selling** n. act of selling by using great efforts A lot of hard selling went into that deal 经过竭力推销才达成那笔交易。

◇ **hardware** n. (a) computer hardware = machines used in data processing, including the computers and printers, but not the programs 计算机硬件；hardware maintenance contract 计算机硬件维修合同 (b) military hardware = guns or rockets or tanks, etc. 军事武器。(c) solid goods for use in the house (such as frying pans or hammers) 家用五金制品；a hardware shop 五金店。

NOTE: no plural

**harm** 1 n. damage done 危害: The recession has done a lot of harm to export sales. 经济衰退对于出口贸易造成了很严重的危害。
NOTE: no plural 2 v. to damage 危害: The tad pullicity has harmed the company's reputation. 少量的的广告宣传危害了公司声誉。

**hatchet man** n. recently appointed manager, whose job is to make staff redundant and reduce expenditure. (负责精简职工并减少开支的经理)替上司做恶人的人;走狗

**haul** n. distance travelled with a load of cargo 拖运距离: It is a long haul from Birmingham to Athens. 从伯明翰到雅典是一漫长的拖运距离. short – haul flight = flight over a short distance (up to 1000 km)短距离飞行; long – haul flight = long – distance flight, especially between continents 长短离飞行

◇ **haulage** n. (a) road haulage = moving of goods by road 公路运输: road haulage depot = centre for goods which are being moved by road, and the lorries which carry them 公路运输仓库; haulage contractor = company which arranges for goods to be moved by road or rail under contract 公路铁路承运公司; haulage costs or haulage rates = cost or rates of transporting goods by road 公路运输费; haulage firm or company = company which transports goods by road. 公路运输公司 (b) cost of transporting goods by road 公路运输费用; Haulage is increasing by 5% per annum. 公路运输费以每年5%速度增长。
NOTE: no plural

◇ **haulier** n. road haulier = company which transports goods by road 公路承运公司

**haven** n. safe place 避难所;安全地方: tax haven = country where taxes are low which encourages companies to set up their main offices there 低税国

**hawk** v. to sell goods from door to door or in the street 叫卖;兜售: to hawk something round = to take a product or an idea or a project to various companies to see if one will accept it 四处兜售(某产品、点子计或划); He hawked his idea for a plastic car body round all the major car constructors. 他向各个主要的汽车制造商那里兜售他的塑料车身的想法。

◇ **hawker** n. person who sells goods from door to door or in the street 走街串户的小贩

**hazard** n. fire hazard = situation or goods which could start a fire 起火的危险物;火灾隐患: That warehouse full of wood and paper is a fire hazard. 那座堆满木头和纸张的库房是个火灾隐患。

**head** 1 n. (a) most important person 首脑;首长; head of department or department head = person in charge of a department 部门主任或负责人。(b) most important or main 首要或主要: head clerk 领班店员; head porter 领班搬运工; head salesman 领班销售员; head waiter 领班服务员; head buyer = most important buyer in a department store 大主顾; head office = main office, where the board of directors works and meets 总公司;总店;总行 (c) top part or first part 顶部或第一部分; Write the name of the company at the head of the list. 将公司的名称写在目录的上端。(d) person 人: Rqepresentatives cost on average £25,000 per head per annum. 代表们每年人均花费25,000英磅。(e) heads of agreement = draft agreement with not all the details complete 协议要点草案。2 v. (a) to be the manager or to be the most important person 领导; to head a department 领导或管理一个部门; He is heading a buying mission to China. 他正率领一采购代表团前往中国。(b) to be first 居于首位: The two largest oil companieshead the list of stock market results. 两个最大的石油公司在让券交易数目一览表中居于首位。

◇ **headed** a. headed paper = notepaper with the name of the company and its address printed on it 有抬头的便笺纸; 眉笺。

◇ **head for** v. to go towards 走向: The company is heading for disaster. = The company is going to collapse. 这个公司正走向于崩溃。

◇ **headhunt** v. to look for managers and offer them jobs in other companies 物色人才: He was headhunted = he was approached by a headhunter and offered a new job. 他受到荐举人才的人推荐。

◇ **headhunter** n. person or company which looks for top managers and offers them jobs in other companies 荐举人才的人或公司。

◇ **heading** n. (a) words at the top of a piece of text 标题: Items are listed under several headings. 在几个标题下面列出的商品。Look at the figure under the heading "Costs 85 - 86". 检查标题为 "85年到86年费用"下面的数字。(b) letter heading or heading on notepaper = name and address of a company printed at the top of a piece of notepaper 信头

◇ **headlease** n. lease from a freehold owner to a lessee 不动产拥有者租给承租人。

◇ **headquarters** plural n. main office, where the board of directors meets and works 总部: The company's headquarters are in New York. 公司总部设在纽约。divisional headquarters = main office of a division of a company 分公司总部; to reduce headquarters staff = to have fewer people working in the main office 精简总部工作人员。

◇ **head up** v. to be in charge of 负责: He has been appointed to head up our European organization. 任命他负责我们欧洲组织工作。

**health** n. (a) being fit and well, not ill 健康: GB Health and Safety at Work Act = Act of Parliament which rules how the health of workers should be protected by the companies they work for 英国劳动健康安全法: health insurance = insurance which pays the cost of treatment for illness, especially when travelling abroad 健康保险; a private health scheme = insurance which will pay for the cost of treatment in a private hospital, not a state one 私人健康保险计划 (b) to give a company a clean bill of health = to report that a company is trading profitably 向公司汇报赢利
NOTE: no plural

◇ **healthy** a. a healthy balance sheet = balance sheet which shows a good profit 高盈利的资产负债表: The company made some very healthy profits or a very healthy profit. = made a large profit 公司取得了高额利润。

**hear** v. (a) to sense a sound with the ears 听: You can hear the printer in the next office. 你能听到隔壁办公室那位印刷工人说话。The traffic makes so much noise that I cannot hear my phone ringing. 街道上的车辆噪音太杂我听不到电话铃响。(b) to have a letter or a phone call from someone 收到(信件); 听(电话): We have not heard from them for some time. 我们有一段时间没收到他们的信了。We hope to hear from the lawyers within a few days. 我们希望这几天能接到律师的来信。
NOTE: hearing - heard

**heavy** a. (a) large or in large quantities 大量的; 多的: a programme of heavy investment overseas 大量海外投资的计划; He had heavy losses on the Stock Exchange. 在证券市场的交易中他损失

惨重。The company is a heavy user of steelor a heavy consumer of electricity; 这个公司使用钢材或电的大户。The gove rnment imposed a heavy tax on luxury goods. 政府对奢侈品征收重税。heavy costs or heavy expenditure = spending large sums of money 大量花销;大量开支;(b) which weighs a lot 沉重的: The Post Office refused to handle the package because it was too heavy. 邮局拒绝邮寄这个包裹,因为它太重。heavy industry = industry which makes large products (such as steel bars, ships or railway lines) 重工业; heavy machinery = large machines 重型机械

◇ **heavily** ad. He is heavily in debt = he has many debts. 他负债累累。They are heavily into property. = They have large investments in property. 他们大量投资于房地产。The company has had to borrow heavily to repay its debts = the company has had to borrow large sums of money. 公司不得不大量借款以偿还债务。

**hectare** n. measurement of area of land ( = 2.47 acres)( = 2.47acres)公顷( = 2.47公亩)

NOTE: usually written ha after figures: 16ha

**hectic** a. wild or very active 激烈的;活跃的: a hectic day on the Stock Exchange 证券交易所中活跃的一天;After last week's hectic trading, this week has been very calm. 经过上个星期的繁忙交易,这个星期市况变得非常静。

**hedge** 1 n. protection 保护; a hedge against inflation = investment which should increase in value more than the increase in the rate of inflation 为避免通货膨胀而采取保值措施而购; He bought gold as a hedge against exchange losses. 他购买了黄金以避免汇兑损失。2 v. to hedge one's bets = to make investments in several areas so as to be protected against loss in one of them 多方投资以弥补单方损失; to hedge against inflation = to buy investments which will rise in value faster than the increase in the rate of inflation 为避免通货膨胀损失而套购升值的证券

◇ **hedging** n. buying investments at a fixed price for delivery later, so as to protect oneself against possible loss 对冲买卖;套头保值交易;海琴

**height** n. (a) measurement of how tall or high something is 高度: What is the height of the desk from the floor? 这个桌子离地面的高度是多少? He measured the height of the room from floor to ceiling. 他测量了房间从地面到天花板的高度。(b) highest point 最高点: It is difficult to find hotel rooms at the height of the tourist season. 在旅游季节的高峰期很难找到旅馆房间。

NOTE: no plural

**heir** n. person who will receive property when someone dies 继承人: His heirs split the estate between them 他的继承人分了财产。

**helicopter** n. aircraft with a large propeller on top which allows it to lift straight off the ground 直升飞机: He took the helicopter from the airport to the centre of town. 他乘直升飞机从机场飞至镇中心。It is only a short helicopter flight from the centre of town to the factory site. 从镇中心到工厂工地坐直升飞机只需一会儿时间。

**help** 1 n. thing which makes it easy to do something 帮助: She finds the word - processor a great help in writing letters. 她发现文字处理机在写作中帮助极大。The company was set up with financial help from the government. 这个公司在政府的财政资助下建立起来。Her assistant is not much help in the office - he cannot type or drive. 她的助手在办公室中帮助不大,他既不会打字

也不会开车。

NOTE: no plural

2 v. to make it easy for something to be done 帮助: He helped the salesman carry his case of samples. 他帮助推销员搬运样品箱。The computer helps in the rapid processing of orders or helps us to process orders rapidly. 计算机有助于订单的快速处理。The government helps exporting companies with easy credit. 政府以宽松的信贷帮助出口公司。

NOTE: you help someone or something to do something

**hereafter** ad. from this time on 此后

◇ **hereby** ad. in this way or by this letter 特此或在此信中: We hereby revoke the agreement of January 1st 1982 我们在此撤消 1982 年 1 月 1 日的协议。

◇ **herewith** ad. together with this letter 随函: Please find the cheque enclosed herewith. 请查收随函附上的支票

**hereditament** n. property, including land and buildings 不动产

**hesitate** v. not to be sure what to do next 犹豫; the company is hesitating about starting up a new computer factory. 公司对建立新的计算机厂犹豫不决。She hesitated for some time before accepting the job. 她犹豫一段时间才接受了这项工作。

**hidden** a. which cannot be seen 隐藏的; hidden asset = asset which is valued much less in the company's accounts than its true market value 帐外资产;隐匿资产; hidden reserves = illegal reserves which are not declared in the company's balance sheet 隐蔽公积金;隐蔽准备金; hidden defect in the program = defect which was not noticed when the program was tested 方案中不易察觉的缺陷

**high** 1 a. (a) tall 高的: The shelves are 30 cm high; 架子有 30 公分高。The door is not high enough to let us get the machines into the building. 门不够高我们不能将机器搬进这座楼房。They are planning a 30 - storey high office block. 他们计划建设一座 30 层高的办公大楼。(b) large or not low 大的;高的: High overhead costs increase the unit price. 高额的间接费用开销增加了单价。High prices put customers off. 因价格高顾客不登门了。They are budgeting for a high level of expenditure. 他们正在为一笔高额支出做预算。investments which bring in a high rate of return 带来高收益的投资; High interest rates are killing small businesses. 高利率正在扼杀小企业。high finance = lending, investing and borrowing of very large sums of money organized by financiers 巨额融资; high flier = person who is very successful or who is likely to get a very important job; share whose market price is rising rapidly 事业高度成功者;价格飞涨的股票; high sales = large amount of revenue produced by sales 高额销售收入; high taxation = taxation which imposes large taxes on incomes or profits 高税 highest tax bracket = the group which pays the most tax 最高税级; high volume (of sales) = large number of items sold 高销售额 (c) highest bidder = person who offers the most money at an auction. (拍卖中)出价最高者; The property was sold to the highest bidder. 房地产卖给了出价最高者。a decision taken at the highest level = decision taken by the most important person or group 最高层次决策 2 ad. prices are running high = prices are above their usual level 价格上涨。3 n. point where prices or sales are very large 最高点: Share prices have dropped by 10% since the high of January 2nd; 股价已从 1 月 2 日的最高点跌了 10%。the highs and lows on the Stock Exchange 证券交易所中股价的最高点和最低点; sales volume has reached an all - time high. = has reached the highest point it has ever been at 销售量已经达到历史最高点。

◇ **high - grade** a. of very good quality 优质的; high - grade petrol 优质汽油; a high - grade trade delegation = a delegation made up of very important people 高级贸易代表团

◇ **high - income** a. which gives a large income 高收入的; high - income shares; 高收益股票 a high - income portfolio 高收益有价证券

◇ **high - level** a. (a) very important 高级的; a high - level meeting or delegation = meeting or delegation of the most important people ( such as ministers, managing directors)高级会议或高级代表团; a high - level decision = decision taken by the most important person or group 高层次决策 (b) high - level computer language = programming language which uses normal words and figures 计算机高级语言

◇ **highly** ad. very 高度地; highly - geared company = company which has a high proportion of its funds from fixed - interest borrowings 高度负债经营的公司; highly - paid = earning a large salary 高报酬; highly - placed = occupying an important post 地位高的: The delegation met a highly - placed official in the Trade Ministry. 代表团会见了商贸部的一名高级官员。highly - priced = with a large price 高价的; She is highly thought of by the managing director = The managing director thinks she is very competent. 董事长对她评价很高。

◇ **high pressure** n. strong force by other people to do something 高压:压力大 working under high pressure = working with a manager telling you what to do and to do it quickly or with customers asking for supplies urgently 在高压下工作; high - pressure salesman = salesman who forces the customer to buy something he does not really need 倾力向顾客推销的销售人员; high - pressure sales techniques or high - pressure selling = forcing a customer to buy something he does not really want 倾力推销术。

◇ **high - quality** a. of very good quality 优质的; high - quality goods 优质商品; high - quality steel 优质钢

◇ **High Street** n. main shopping street in a British town (英) 主要街道; the High Street shops 主要街道上的商店; a High Street bookshop 主要街道上的书店 the High Street banks = main British banks which accept deposits from individual customers 主要街上的大银行

**hike** 1 n. US increase 增长: pay hike = increase in salary 工资增长 2 v. US to increase 增长: The union hiked its demand to $3 an hour. 工会要求每小时工资增长到3美元。

**hire** 1 n. (a) paying money to rent a car or boat or piece of equipment for a time 租用; Car hire 汽车出租; truck hire 卡车出租; car hire firm or equipment hire firm = company which owns cars or equipment and lends them to customers for a payment 汽车出租公司或设备出租公司; hire car = car which has been rented 租出的汽车; He was driving a hire car when the accident happened. 当事故发生时他正驾驶着一辆租来的汽车。(b) "for hire" = sign on a taxi showing it is empty"待租"的标记 (c) US for hire contract = freelance contract (美) 临时工合同; 自由职业合同: to work for hire = to work freelance 做雇工 2 v. (a) to hire staff = to engage new staff to work for you 雇用新职员; to hire and fire = to employ new staff and dismiss existing staff frequently 雇用和解雇; We have hired the best lawyers to represent us. 我们已聘用了最好的律师做我们的诉讼代理。 They hired a small company to paint the offices. 他们雇用了一个小公司来油漆办公室。(b) to hire a car or a crane = to pay money to use a car or a crane for a time 租用汽车或起重机; He hired a truck to move his furniture. 他租用了一辆卡车搬运他的家具。(c) to hire out cars or equipment = to lend cars or equipment to customers who pay for their use 出租汽车或出租设备

◇ **hired** a. a hired car = car which has been rented 已租出汽车

◇ **hire purchase** n. system of buying something by paying a sum regularly each month 租购(分期付款购买法): to buy a refrigerator on hire purchase 用租购方式购置电冰箱; to sign a hire – purchase agreement = to sign a contract to pay for something by instalments 签署一个租购协议; hire – purchase company = company which provides money for hire purchase 从事租购业务的公司

◇ **hiring** n. employing 雇用: Hiring of new personnel has been stopped. 已停止雇用新人员

**historic or historical** a. which goes back over a period of time 历史的: historic(al) cost = actual cost of something which was made some time ago 原始成本;历史成本; historical figures = figures which were current in the past 历史上的数字;过去通用的数字

**hit** v. (a) to knock against something 碰撞: he hit his head against the table. 他头撞在桌子 We have hit our export targets. = We have reached our targets. 我们已经达到了我们的出口指标。(b) to hurt or to damage 打击;毁坏; The company was badly hit by the falling exchange rate. 因兑换率的不断下跌公司遭到严重打击。 Our sales of summer clothes have been hit by the bad

weather. 天气不好影响了我们的夏季服装销售 The new legislation has hit the small companies hardest. 新法律对小型企业的打击最为惨重。
NOTE: hitting – hit

**hive off** v. to split off part of a large company to form a smaller subsidiary 分散经营: The new managing director hived off the retail sections of the company. 新任总经理使公司的零售部门的业务分散经营。

**hoard** v. to buy and store food in case of need or to keep cash insteadof investing it 囤积

◇ **hoarder** n. person who buys and stores food in case of need 囤户;贮藏者

◇ **hoarding** n. (a) hoarding of supplies = buying large quantities of money or food to keep in case of need 囤积生活必需品 (b) advertisement hoarding = large board for posters 大型广告牌
NOTE: no plural for (a)

**hold** v. (a) to own or to keep 拥有;持有: he holds 10% of the company's shares. 他持有 10% 的公司股票。 You should hold these shares – they look likely to rise. = You should keep these shares and not sell them. 你应该留住这些股票,看来它们要升值了。(b) to contain 容纳: The carton holds twenty packets. 纸板盒里装有 20 个包。 Each box holds 250 sheets of paper. 每个盒子里装有 250 张纸。 A bag can hold twenty kilos of sugar. 每个袋子能装 20 公斤糖。(c) to make something happen 举行: to hold a meeting or a discussion 举行会议或讨论; The computer show will be held in London next month;计算机展览会将于下个月在伦敦举行。 Board meetings are held in the boardroom. 董事会会议在会议室举行。 The AGM will be held on March 24th. 年度股东大会将于 3 月 24 日举行。 The receiver will hold an auction of the company's assets.

该破产管理人将要举行一个公司财产拍卖。The accountants held a review of the company's accounting practices. 会计们对公司的会计实务进行审查（d）（on telephone）hold the line please = please wait（打电话）请稍等；The chairman is on the other line - will you hold? 董事长正在接另一个电话, 请稍等好吗?

NOTE: holding - held

◇ **hold back** v. to wait or not to go forward 等候；克制：Investors are holding back until after the Budget. = Investors are waiting until they hear the details of the Budget before they decide whether to buy or sell. 投资者们等候着, 直至预算方案出台。He held back from signing the lease until he had checked the details = he delayed signing the lease until he had checked the details. 他检查了所有细节后才在租借契约上签字。Payment will be held back until the contract has been signed = Payment will not be made until the contract has been signed. 要到合同签定后才付款。

◇ **hold down** v. (a) to keep at a low level 压制；压低；压抑：We are cutting margins to hold our prices down. 我们正削减利润以压低物价。(b) to hold down a job = to manage to do a difficult job 保住一份工作

◇ **holder** n. (a) person who owns or keeps something 拥有人；持有人；holders of government bonds or bondholders 政府债券持有人；holder of stock or of shares in a company 公司股票持有人；holder of an insurance policy or policy holder 保险单持有人；credit card holder = person who has a credit card 信用卡持有人；debenture holder = person who holds a debenture for money lent 公司债券持有人 (b) thing which keeps something or which protects something 支持物；保护物；card holder or message

holder = frame which protects a card or a message 卡片夹子或文件夹子；credit card holder = plastic wallet for keeping credit cards 信用卡夹子

◇ **holding** n. (a) group of shares owned 所持的股份：He has sold all his holdings in the Far East. 他卖掉了在远东所持的全部股份。The company has holdings in German manufacturing companies. 这个公司拥有德国制造公司的股份。(b) cross holdings = situation where two companies own shares in each other in order to stop each from being taken over 相互持有股票（两公司互持对方股票, 以防被对方吞并）；the two companies have protected themselves from takeover by a system of cross holdings. 这两个公司通过相互持有对方股票以防自己被对方吞并。

◇ **holding company** n. company which exists only to own shares in subsidiary companies 控股公司

◇ **hold on** v. to wait or not to change 等待；继续：The company's shareholders should hold on and wait for a better offer. = They should keep their shares and not sell them. 公司股东仍应留住股票并等待更有利的报价。

◇ **hold out for** v. to wait and ask for 坚持要求：You should hold out for a 10% pay rise. = Do not agree to a pay rise of less than 10%. 你应坚持要求增加10%的工资。

◇ **hold over** v. to postpone or to put back to a later date 推迟；延期：Discussion of item 4 was held over until the next meeting. 第四条的讨论延期至下次会议。

◇ **hold to** v. not to allow something to change 坚持；遵循：We will try to hold him to the contract. = We will try to stop him going against the contract. 我们将努力地使他遵循合同。The government hopes to hold wage increases to

5%. = The government hopes that wageincreases will not be more than 5%. 政府希望工资增长率为5%。

◇ **hold up** v. (a) to stay at a high level 持续(高水平); Share prices have held up well; 股价一直不跌。Sales held up during the tourist season. 旅游旺季销售额持续看好。(b) to delay 耽搁; The shipment has been held up at the customs. 装运的货物耽搁在海关。Payment will be held up until the contract has been signed. 直到合同签订后才付款。The strike will hold up dispatch for some weeks. 罢工将使发货耽搁几个星期。

◇ **hold－up** n. delay 耽搁: The strike caused hold－ups in the dispatch of goods. 罢工耽搁了货物发送。

**holiday** n. (a) bank holiday = weekday which is a public holiday when the banks are closed New Year's Day is a bank holiday 银行假日; public holiday = day when all workers rest and enjoy themselves instead of working 公共节假日; statutory holiday = holiday which is fixed by law 法定节假日; The office is closed for the Christmas holiday. 圣诞节办事处不办公。(b) period when a worker does not work, but rests, goes away and enjoys himself 假期: to take a holiday or to go on holiday 度假; When is the manager taking his holidays? 经理什么时候去度假? My secretary is off on holiday tomorrow; 我的秘书明天休假。He is away on holiday for two weeks. 他通常外出休假两个星期。The job carries five weeks' holiday. = One of the conditions of the job is that you have five weeks' holiday/这项工作有五个星期休假。the summer holidays = holidays taken by the workers in the summer when the weather is good and children are not at school 暑假; holiday entitlement = number of days' paid holiday which a worker has the right to take 法

定节假日天数; holiday pay = salary which is still paid during the holiday 假日工资 (c) tax holiday = period when a new business is exempted from paying tax 免税期

**home** n. (a) Place where a person lives 家; please send the letter to my home address, not my office. 请把信寄到我家中别寄到办公室。(b) home country = country where a company is based home sales or sales in the home market = sales in the country where a company is based 本国(公司总部所在国) home－produced products = products manufactured in the country where the company is based本国的销售额 (c) house 住宅: new home sales = sales of new houses 新住宅销售; home loan = loan by a bank or a building society to a person buying a house 买房贷款

◇ **homegrown** a. which has been developed in a local area or in a country where the company is based 本地区或本国(发展起来)的; a homegrown computer industry 国内计算机工业; India's homegrown car industry 印度国内汽车工业

◇ **homemade** a. made in a home 家庭自制的: homemade jam 家庭自制果酱。

◇ **homeowner** n. person who owns a private house 私房房主: homeowner's insurance policy = insurance policy covering a house and its contents and the personal liability of the people living in it 私房房主的房屋保险单

◇ **homeward** a. going towards the home country 回国的;归国的: homeward freight 发往本国的运费; homeward journey 归国旅途

◇ **homewards** a. towards the home country 向家乡;本国: cargo homewards 运往本国的货物

**hon** = HONORARY hon sec = honorary secretary 名誉秘书长

**honest** a. respected or saying what is right受尊敬的；诚实的；to play the honest broker = to act for the parties in a negotiation to try to make them agree to a solution 充当诚实的中间人

◇ **honestly** a. saying what is right or not cheating 坦诚地

**honorarium** n. money paid to a professional person, such as an accountant or a lawyer, when he does not ask for a fee 酬金,谢礼。

NOTE: plural is honoraria

◇ **honorary** a. person who is not paid a salary 名誉的；honorary secretary 名誉秘书；义务秘书；honorary president 名誉总裁；honorary member = member who does not have to pay a subscription 名誉会员

**honour** v. to pay something because it is owed and is correct 承兑(承认并如期付款)；to honour a bill 承兑票据；to honour a signature = to pay something because the signature is correct 承认签字并付款

**hope** v. to expect or to want something to happen 希望：We hope to be able to dispatch the order next week. 我们希望下个星期能发出订货。He is hoping to break into the US market. 他希望能打入美国市场。They had hoped the TV commercials would help sales. 他们希望电视广告能有助于销售。

**horizontal** a. flat or going from side to side, not up and down 水平的；横向的；horizontal integration = joining similar companies or taking over a company in the same line of business 横向联合；horizontal communication = communication between workers at the same level 横向联系

**horse trading** n. hard bargaining which ends with someone giving something in return for a concession from the other side 双方讨价还价后互相让步的交易

**hostess** n. woman who looks after passengers or clients 女服务员；女老板：air hostess = woman who looks after passengers in a plane 空中小姐；ground hostess = woman who looks after passengers before they get into the plane 地勤小姐

**hot** a. (a) very warm 火热：The staff complain that the office is too hot in the summer and too cold in the winter. 职员们抱怨办公室里夏天太热而冬天太冷。The drinks machine sells coffee, tea and hot soup. 饮料机出售咖啡、茶和热汤。Switch off the machine if it gets too hot. 机器太烫就关机。(b) not safe or very bad 危险的；很糟糕；to make things hot for someone = to make it difficult for someone to work or to trade 使某人不好办某事；Customs officials are making things hot for the drug smugglers. 海关人员使得毒品走私犯的活动陷于困境。hot money = money which is moved from country to country to get the best interest rates 游资；He is in the hot seat. = His job involves making many difficult decisions. 他处在困难局面之中。

**hotel** n. building where you can rent a room for a night, or eat in a restaurant 旅馆；饭店 hotel bill 旅馆帐单；hotel expenses 旅馆开支；住宿费；hotel manager 旅馆经理；hotel staff 饭店员工；hotel accommodation = rooms available in hotels 旅馆客房：All hotel accommodation has been booked up for the exhibition. 所有的旅馆客房都由展览会预定了。hotel chain or chain of hotels = group of hotels owned by the same company 联锁旅馆；the hotel trade = business of running hotels 旅馆经营业

◇ **hotelier** n. person who owns or manages a hotel 旅馆老板或经营人

**hour** n. (a) period of time lasting sixty minutes 小时；to work a thirty - five hour week = to work seven hours a day each weekday 一星期工作 35 小时 We work an eight – hour day. = We work for eight hours a day, e.g. from 8.30 to 5.30 with one hour for lunch. 我们每日工作 8 小时。(b) sixty minutes of work 工时: He earns £ 4 an hour. 他每工时挣 4 英磅。We pay £ 6 an hour. 我们每小时支付 6 英磅 to pay by the hour = to pay people a fixed amount of money for each hour worked 按工时付酬 (c) banking hours = time when a bank is open for its customers 银行营业时间: You cannot get money out of a bank outside banking hours. 非银行营业时间你不能从银行取钱。office hours = time when an office is open 办公时间: Do not telephone during office hours. 办公时间不要打电话。outside hours or out of hours = when the office is not open 非办公时间: He worked on the accounts out of hours. 他下班后继续算帐。The shares rose in after – hours trading. = In trading after the Stock Exchange had closed. 在证券交易所关门后的交易中股票价格上涨。

◇ **hourly** a. per hour 每小时地; hourly – paid workers = workers paid at a fixed rate for each hour worked 钟点工 hourly rate = amount of money paid for an hour worked 小时工资额

**house** n. (a) building in which someone lives 房屋;住宅: house property = private houses, not shops, offices or factories 私人房产; house agent = estate agent who deals in buying or selling houses 房地产经纪人 (b) company 公司; a French business house 一家法国商业公司; the largest London finance house 伦敦最大的金融公司; He works for a broking house or a publishing house. 他为一家经纪业公司或一家出版公司工作。clearing house = central office where clearing banks exchange cheques 票据交换所; discount house = financial company which specializes in discounting bills 票据贴现公司; export house = company which specializes in the export of goods manufactured by other companies 出口公司;出口行; house journal or house magazine or US house organ = magazine produced for the workers or shareholders in a company to give them news about the company 内部发行的刊物; house telephone = internal telephone for calling from one office to another 内部电话 (c) the House = the London Stock Exchange 伦敦证券交易所

◇ **household** n. people living in a house 家人;家庭: household expenses = money spent on running a private house 家庭开支; household goods = goods which are used in a house 家庭日用品

◇ **householder** n. person who owns a private house 房主;户主

◇ **house starts or US housing starts** pl. n. number of new private houses or flats of which the construction has begun during a year 一年中开始新建的房数

◇ **house – to – house** ad. going from one house to the next, asking people to buy something or to vote for someone 挨户的 ( 推销或拉选票 ) house – to – house canvassing 挨户兜售; house – to – house salesman 挨户的推销员; house – to – house selling 挨户推销

**HP** = HIRE PURCHASE 租购

**hundredweight** n. weight of 112 pounds (about fifty kilos) 英担(等于 112 磅或约 50 公斤)
NOTE: usually written cwt after figures: 20cwt

**hurry** 1 n. doing things fast 赶快;勿忙: There is no hurry for the figures, we do not need them until next week. 这些数字不急用,我们下星期才需要它们。in a hurry = very fast 急忙;勿促

地：The sales manager wants the report ina hurry. 销售经理急需这个报告。2 verb to do something or to make something or to go very fast 急忙、匆忙：催促 The production team tried to hurry the order through the factory. 生产组试图通过工厂催促订货。The chairman does not want to be hurried into making a decision. 董事长不想让人推他做出决定。The directors hurried into the meeting. 董事们匆忙走进会场。

◇ **hurry up** v. to make something go faster 赶快；催促：Can you hurry up that order – the customer wants it immediately? 因顾客急需, 你能催促一下那个订货吗?

**hurt** v. to harm or to damage 伤害损害：The bad publicity did not hurt our sales. 不利宣传并没有损害我们的销售。Sales of summer clothes were hurt by the bad weather. 夏季服装的销售, 因不良的天气而受到影响。The company has not been hurt by the recession. 公司没因经济衰退而遭受损失。
NOTE: hurting – hurt

**hype** 1 n. excessive claims made in advertising 大肆宣传：all the hype surrounding the launch of the new soap 围绕着新型肥皂投放市场的大肆宣传 2 v. to make excessive claims in advertising 大做广告宣传

**hyper –** prefix meaning very large 很大
◇ **hyperinflation** n. inflation which is so rapid that it is almost impossible to reduce 恶性(极度)通货膨胀。
NOTE: no plural

◇ **hypermarket** n. very large supermarket, usually on the outside of a large town 特大超级市场

# Ii

**idea** n. thing which you think of 主意：One of the salesman had the idea of changing the product colour. 一个推销员有一个改变产品颜色的主意。The chairman thinks it would be a good idea to ask all directors to itemize their expenses. 董事长认为详细列明开支是个好主意。

**ideal** a. perfect or very good for something 理想的：This is the ideal site for a new hypermarket. 这是建立新的大超级市场理想场所。

◇ **Ideal Home Exhibition** n. annual exhibition in London showing new houses, new kitchens, etc. (每年在伦敦举办的新房屋, 新厨房等展示会)理想住宅展览会

**idle** a. (a) not working 闲置的；不做事的：2,000 employees were made idle by the recession. 由于经济衰退, 两千名雇员闲着没事做。(b) idle machinery or machines lying idle = machinery not being used 闲置的机器 (c) idle capital = capital not being used productively 闲置资本 money lying idle or idle money = money which is not being used to produce interest or which is not invested in business 闲置资金

**i.e.** that is 即：The largest companies, i.e. Smith's and Brown's, had a very good first quarter. 最大的公司, 即史密斯和布朗公司第一季度首战大捷。The import restrictions apply to expensive items, i.e. items costing more than $2,500. 进口限制适用于昂贵物品, 即价格高于 2,500 美元的物品。

**illegal** a. not legal or against the law 非法的
◇ **illegality** n. being illegal 非法(性)

◇ **illegally** ad. against the law 非法地；He was accused of illegally importing arms into the country. 他被指控非法进口武器。

**illicit** a. not legal or not permitted 违法的；违禁的；illicit sale of alcohol 酒类私卖；trade in illicit alcohol 酒类的非法交易；酒类私售交易

**ILO** = INTERNATIONAL LABOUR ORGANIZATION 国际劳工组织

**image** n. general idea which the public has of a product or a company 形象：They are spending a lot of advertising money to improve the company's image；他们花了大量广告费以改善公司的形象。the company has adopted a down-market image. 公司采纳了建立低档商品市场的形象。brand image = picture which people have in their minds of a product associated with the brand name 商标形象；corporate image = idea which a company would like the public to have of it 公司形象；to promote a corporate image = to publicize a company so that its reputation is improved 改善公司形象

**IMF** = INTERNATIONAL MONETARY FUND 国际货币基金组织

**imitate** v. to do what someone else does 模仿；效法：They imitate all our sales gimmicks. 他们模仿我们所有的销售招花招。

◇ **imitation** n. thing which copies another 仿造品；仿制品：beware of imitations = be careful not to buy low quality goods which are made to look like other more expensive items 谨防假冒

**immediate** a. happening at once 立刻的：He wrote an immediate letter of complaint. 他随即写了一封投诉信。Your order will receive immediate attention. 你的订货将得到立即的关注。

◇ **immediately** ad. at once 立刻：He immediately placed an order for 2,000 boxes. 他立刻预订了 2000 箱。As soon as he heard the news he immediately telexed his office. 听到消息后，他马上给办公室打电传。Can you phone immediately when you get the information? 得到情报后你能立刻打电话吗？

**immovable** a. which cannot be moved 不动的；immovable property = houses and other buildings on land 不动产。

**immunity** n. protection against arrest 豁免权：diplomatic immunity = being outside a country's laws because of being a diplomat 外交豁免权；He was granted immunity from prosecution = he was told he would not be prosecuted. 他被给予诉讼豁免权。

NOTE: no plural

**impact** n. shock or strong effect 强烈影响：the impact of new technology on the cotton trade；新技术对棉花贸易的强烈影响；The new design has made little impact on the buying public. 新设计对于购买公众没有什么影响 。NOTE: no plural

**imperfect** a. not perfect 不完善的：sale of imperfect items 残次商品销售；to check a batch for imperfect products 检查一批产品中的残次品

◇ **imperfection** n. part of an item which is not perfect 残次品；to check a batch for imperfections 检一批货物中的残次品。

**impersonal** a. without any personal touch or as if done by machines 不受个人情感影响的；an impersonal style of management 不受个人情感影响的管理风格

**implement** 1 n. tool or instrument used to do some work 工具；器具 2. v. to put into action 实施；实现；to implement an agreement 使协议生效；实施协议。

◇ **implementation** n. putting into action 实行；实施：the implementation of new rules 实施新规定。

NOTE: no plural

**import** 1 n. ( a ) Imports = goods brought into a country from abroad for sale 进口货; Imports from Poland have risen to $1m a year. 来自波兰的进口货已增加到每年 100 万美元。 invisible imports = services ( such as banking, tourism ) which are paid for in foreign currency 无形进口; visible imports = real goods which are imported 有形的进口 ( b ) import ban = forbidding imports 禁止进口: The government has imposed an import ban on arms. 政府下令禁止进口武器。 import duty = tax on goods imported into a country 进口税; import levy = tax on imports, especially in the EEC a tax on imports of farm produce from outside the EEC(欧共体外进口农产品)的进口征税; import licence or import permit = government licence or permit which allows goods to be imported 进口许可证; import quota = fixed quantity of a particular type of goods which the government allows to be imported 进口配额; The government has imposed an import quota on cars. 政府对汽车实行了进口配额。 import surcharge = extra duty charged on imported goods, to try to prevent them from being imported and to encourage local manufacture 进口附加税( 对进口商品加征的关税, 目的在限制进口和鼓励地方工业 )

NOTE: usually used in the plural, but the singular form is used before a noun

2 v. to bring goods from abroad into a country for sale 进口: The company imports television sets from Japan. 公司从日本进口电视机。 This car was imported from France. 这辆汽车是从法国进口的。 The union organized a boycott of imported cars. 协会组织对进口汽车的联合抵制。

◇ **importation** n. act of importing 进口: The importation of arms is forbidden. 武器进口是禁止的。

NOTE: no plural

◇ **importer** n. person or company which imports goods 进口商; a cigar importer 雪茄烟进口商; The company is a big importer of foreign cars. 这个公司是一家大的外国汽车进口公司。

◇ **import - export** a. dealing with both bringing foreign goods into a country and sending locally made goods abroad 进出口的: import - export trade 进出口贸易; He is in import - export. 他从事进出口贸易。

◇ **importing** 1 a. which imports 进口的: oil - importing countries 石油进口国; an importing company 进口公司 2 n. act of bringing foreign goods into a country for sale 进口: The importing of arms into the country is illegal. 武器进口是非法的。

NOTE: no plural

**importance** n. having a value or mattering a lot 重要; The bank attaches great importance to the deal. 银行重视这笔交易。 NOTE: no plural

◇ **important** a. which matters a lot 重要的: He left a pile of important papers in the taxi. 他把一叠重要的文件忘在出租汽车里。 She has an important meeting at 10.30. 10 时 30 分他有个重要会议。 He was promoted to a more important job. 他被提升到一个更重要的职位。

**impose** v. to put a tax or a duty on goods 征税: to impose a tax on bicycles 对自行车征税; The government imposed a special duty on oil. 政府对石油征收特殊税。 The customs have imposed a 10% tax increase on luxury items. 海关对奢侈品增税 10%。 ( b ) to put aban on goods 禁止: They tried to impose a ban on smoking. 他们试图禁止吸烟。 The unions have asked the government to impose trade barriers on foreign cars. 工

会要求政府对外国汽车实行贸易壁垒。

◇ **imposition** n. putting a tax on goods or services 征税

NOTE: no plural

**impossible** a. which cannot be done 不可能的: Getting skilled staff is becoming impossible. 获得有技术的职员正变得不可能。Government regulations make it impossible for us to export. 政府条例的使我们不可能出口。

**impound** v. to take something away and keep it until a tax is paid 扣押: The customs impounded the whole cargo. 海关扣押了全部货物。

◇ **impounding** n. act of taking something and keeping it until a tax is paid 扣押

NOTE: no plural

**imprest** n. the imprest system = system of controlling petty cash, where cash is paid out against a written receipt and the receipt is used to get more cash to bring the float to the original level 定额备用金制度;定额资金预付制。

**improve** v. to make something better or to become better 增进;改善: We are trying to improve our image with a series of TV commercials. 我们正以一系列电视广告来改善我们的形象。They hope to improve the company's cash flow position. 他们希望改善公司的现金流动状况。We hope the cash flow position will improve or we will have difficulty in paying our bills. 我们希望现金流动状况将得到改善,否则我们会难于支付帐单。Export trade has improved sharply during the first quarter. = Export trade has increased. 第一季度的出口贸易迅速增长。

◇ **improved** a. better 改善的: The union rejected the management's improved offer. 工会拒绝接受资方改进后的提议。

◇ **improvement** n. (a) getting better 增进;改善: There is no improvement in the cash flow situation. 现金流动状况没有得到改善。Sales are showing a sharp improvement over last year. 去年销售情况大有改善。(b) thing which is better 好转: improvement on an offer = making a better offer 发盘的改善

◇ **improve on** v. to do better than 改进: He refused to improve on his previous offer. = He refused to make a better offer. 他拒绝改进其前的发盘。

**impulse** n. sudden decision 冲动;即兴: impulse buying = buying things which you have just seen, not because you had planned to buy them 即兴购买; The store puts racks of chocolates by the checkout to attract the impulse buyer. 商店在验货收款台旁放了几架子巧克力以吸引即兴购买者。impulse purchase = thing bought as soon as it is seen 即兴购置的货物; to do something on impulse = to do something because you have just thought of it, not because it was planned 凭一时冲动做某事。

**in** = INCH 英寸。

**inactive** a. not active or not busy 不活跃的;不繁忙的: inactive market = stock market with few buyers or sellers 交易不活跃的股票市场。

**Inc** US = INCORPORATED(美)组成公司的

**incentive** n. thing which encourages staff to work better 奖励: staff incentives = pay and better conditions offered to workers to make them work better 职工奖励; incentive bonus or incentive payment = extra pay offered to a worker to make him work better 奖金; incentive scheme = plan to encourage better work by paying higher commission or bonuses 奖励计划; Incentive schemes are boosting production. 奖励计划正使产量提高。

**inch** n. measurement of length ( = 2.

54cm)英寸。

NOTE: usually written in or ” after figures: 2in or 2”

**incidental** 1 a. which is not important, but connected with something else 不重要的；附带的: incidental expenses = small amounts of money spent at various times in addition to larger amounts 杂费 2. n. incidentals = incidental expenses 杂费。

**include** v. to count something along with other things 包括；包含: The charge includes VAT. 索价中包括增值税。The total comes to £1,000 including freight. 总价为1,000英磅，其中包括运费。The total is £140 not including insurance and freight. 总价为140英磅，不包括保险和运费。The account covers services up to and including the month of June. 这个帐目包括劳务费，结止到并包括六月份在内。

◇ **inclusive** a. which counts something in with other things 在内的；包含的: inclusive of tax 包括税收; not inclusive of VAT 不包括增值税; inclusive sum or inclusive charge = charge which includes all costs 全部费用; The conference runs from the 12th to the 16th inclusive. = It starts on the morning of the 12th and ends on the evening of the 16th. 会议从12日早开始到16日晚结束。

**income** n. (a) money which a person receives as salary or dividends 收入: annual income = money received during a calendar year 年收入; disposable income = income left after tax and national insurance have been deducted 可支配的收入; earned income = money received as a salary or wages 劳动所得；劳动收入; earned income allowance = tax allowance to be set against money earned by the wife or children of the main taxpayer 劳动所得的税收补贴; fixed income = income which does not change from year to year 固定收入; gross income = income before tax has been deducted 总收入；毛收入; net income = income left after tax has been deducted 净收入; private income = income from dividends or interest or rent which is not part of a salary(来自红利、利息租金)工资外的私人收入; personal income = income received by an individual person 个人所得; retained income = profits which are not paid out to shareholders as dividends 保留盈余；留存收益; unearned income = money received from interest or dividends 非劳动所得; lower or upper income bracket = groups of people who earn low or high salaries considered for tax purposes 低或高收入阶层; He comes into the higher income bracket. = He is in a group of people earning high incomes and therefore paying more tax. 他属于高收入阶层。(b) the government's incomes policy = the government's ideas on how incomes should be controlled 政府控制的收入政策 (c) income tax = tax on a person's income 所得税; income tax form = form to be completed which declares all income to the tax office 所得税申报表; declaration of income or income tax return = statement declaring income to the tax office 所得税申报 (d) money which an organization receives as gifts or from investments 赠款；投资收益; The hospital has a large income from gifts. 医院从馈赠礼品中获得一大笔收入。(e) US income statement = accounts for a company which show expenditure and sales balanced to give a final profit or loss (美)损益表

**incoming** a. (a) incoming call = phone call coming into the office from someone outside 打进来的电话; incoming mail = mail which comes into an office 寄来的邮件 (b) which have recently been elected or appointed 新当选的；新任命

的：the incoming board of directors = the new board which is about to start working 新当选的董事会；the incoming chairman or president 新的董事长或总裁

**incompetent** a. who cannot work well 无能的；不能胜任的：The sales manager is quite incompetent. 销售经理很不称职。The company has an incompetent sales director. 公司有个不称职的销售董事。

**inconvertible** a. (currency) which cannot be easily converted into other currencies 不能兑换的。

**incorporate** v. (a) to bring something in to form part of a main group 合并：Income from the 1984 acquisition is incorporated into the accounts. 1984 年收购的收入已并入帐中。(b) to form a registered company 组建一个注册公司. a company incorporated in the USA 一个在美国组建的公司；an incorporated company 一个股份有限公司；J. Doe Incorporated 杰、多伊股份有限公司

◇ **incorporation** n. act of incorporating a company 合并；组建公司

**incorrect** a. wrong or not correct 错误的；不正确的：The minutes of the meeting were incorrect and had to be changed. 会议记录有错误，必须加以改正。

◇ **incorrectly** a. wrongly or not correctly 错误地；The package was incorrectly addressed. 包裹上的地址错了。

**increase** 1 n. (a) growth or becoming larger 增加；增多：increase in tax or tax increase 增加税收；increase in price or price increase 涨价；Profits showed a 10% increase or an increase of 10% on last year. 与去年相比利润有 10% 的增长。increase in the cost of living = rise in the annual cost of living 生活费的增长 (b) higher salary (工资) 增长 increase in pay or pay increase 报酬增加；

increase in salary or salary increase 工资增长；The government hopes to hold salary increases to 3%. 政府希望工资增长率控制在 3%。He had two increases last year = His salary went up twice. 去年他两次加工资。cost – of – living increase = increase in salary to allow it to keep up with higher cost of living 生活费用增长；merit increase = increase in pay given to a worker whose work is good 功绩酬劳增加 (c) on the increase = growing larger or becoming more frequent 增加中；正在增加：Stealing in shops is on the increase. 商店中的偷盗正在增加。2 v. (a) to grow bigger or higher 增大；增长：Profits have increased faster than the increase in the rate of inflation. 利润增长高于通货膨胀率增长。Exports to Africa have increased by more than 25%. 对非洲出口增长了 25% 以上。The price of oil has increased twice in the past week. 上星期石油两次提价。to increase in price = to cost more 提价；to increase in size or in value = to become larger or more valuable 增大或增值 (b) The company increased his salary to £20,000. = The company gave him a rise in salary to £20,000. 公司将他的工资加到 20,000 英磅。

◇ **increasing** a. which is growing bigger 正在增长的：increasing profits 不断增长的利润；The company has an increasing share of the market. 这个公司拥有的市场份额不断增大。

◇ **increasingly** a. more and more 渐增地；日益地：The company has to depend increasingly on the export market. 公司只得越来越依赖于出口市场。

**increment** n regular automatic increase in salary 常规增额；常规增值：annual increment 年度增长 salary which rises in annual increments of £500 = each year the salary is increased by £500 年工资增长额为 500 英磅

◇ **incremental** a. which rises automatically in stages 增长的；incremental cost = cost of making a single extra unit above the number already planned 边际成本；增支成本；incremental increase = increase in salary according to an a-greed annual increment 每年有规律的提薪；incremental scale = salary scale with regular annual salary increases 常规增薪比例或幅度

**incur** v. to make yourself liable to 招致：to incur the risk of a penalty = to make it possible that you risk paying a penalty 招致罚款的危险；to incur debts or costs = to do something which means that you owe money or that you will have to pay costs 招致负债或支付费用；The company has incurred heavy costs to implement the expansion programme. = The company has had to pay large sums of money. 公司为实施这项扩建计划已支付巨额费用。

NOTE: incurring – incurred

**indebted** a. owing money to someone 负债的；to be indebted to a property company 负债于房地产公司。

◇ **indebtedness** n. state of indebtedness = being in debt or owing money 负债境况。

**indemnification** n. payment for damage 赔偿

◇ **indemnify** v. to pay for damage to indemnify someone for a loss 赔偿某人的损失；

◇ **indemnity** n. guarantee of payment after a loss 赔偿金：He had to pay an indemnity of £100. 他必须支付100英磅赔偿金。letter of indemnity = letter promising payment as compensation for a loss 赔偿金担保书

**indent** 1 n. (a) order placed by an importer for goods from overseas 国外定货单：He put in an indent for a new stock of soap. 他向国外发了订货单以订购一种新上市的肥皂。(b) line of typing which starts several spaces from the left – hand margin 缩排（打字时第一行的开端要从左边空白边起空出几个格）2 v. (a) to indent for something = to put in an order for something 订购；向国外定货：The department has indented for a new computer. 这个部门已向国外订购一台新的电子计算机。(b) to start a line of typing several spaces from the left – hand margin 缩排；Indent the first line three spaces. 第一行缩进三个字母的间隔。

**indenture** 1 n. indentures or articles of indenture = contract by which an apprentice works for a master for some years to learn a trade(师徒之间的)合同或契约 2 v. to contract with an apprentice who will work for some years to learn a trade 签订学徒合同：He was indentured to a builder. 他与一个建筑公司签订了学徒合同。

**independent** a. free or not controlled by anyone 独立的：independent company = company which is not controlled by another company 独立公司；independent trader or independent shop = shop which is owned by an individual proprietor, not by a chain 独立商店；the independents = shops or companies which are owned by private individuals 个体商店或公司

**index** n. (a) list of items classified into groups or put in alphabetical order(按类型分组的或按字母顺序排列的)索引：index card = small card used for filing 索引卡片；card index = series of cards with information written on them, kept in a special order so that the information car be found easily 卡片式索引；index letter or number = letter or number of an item in an index 索引的字母或数字 (b) regular statistical report which shows rises and falls in prices, etc. 指数（一种能反映价格等变化趋势的常规统

计数字）: growth index = index showing how something has grown 增长指数; cost – of – living index = way of measuring the cost of living, shown as a percentage increase on the figure for the previous year 生活费用指数; retail price index or US consumer price index = index showing how prices of consumer goods have risen over a period of time, used as a way of measuring inflation and the cost of living 零售价格指数或美国的日用品价格指数; wholesale price index = index showing rises and falls of prices of manufactured goods as they leave the factory 批发价指数 the Financial Times Index = index which shows percentage rises or falls in shares prices on the London Stock Exchange based on a small group of major companies《金融时报》股票价格指数(反映建立在少数大公司基础上的伦敦股票交易所的股价变化情况) index number = number which shows the percentage rise of something over a period of time 指数(数字)
NOTE: plural is indexes or indices

◇ **indexation** n. linking of something to an index 指数化: indexation of wage increases = linking of wage increases to the percentage rise in the cost of living 工资增长指数化。
NOTE: no plural

◇ **index – linked** a. which rises automatically by the percentage increase in the cost of living 指数相联的: index – linked pensions 指数相联的退休金; His pension is index – linked. 他的退休金是与生活费用指数相联的。index – linked government bonds 与生活费用指数相联的政府债券保值的政府债券。

**indicate** v. to show 表明: the latest figures indicate a fall in the inflation rate 最新数字表明通货膨胀率下降。Our sales for 1985 indicate a move from the home market to exports. 我们 1985 年的销售额表明了产品从国内市场转向出口贸易的。

◇ **indicator** n. thing which indicates 指标; government economic indicators = statistics which show how the country's economy is going to perform in the short or long term 政府经济指标。

**indirect** a. not direct 间接的: indirect expenses or costs = costs which are not directly attached to the making of a product ( such as cleaning, rent, administration) 间接费用或成本; indirect labour costs = costs of paying workers who are not directly involved in making a product ( such as secretaries, cleaners) 间接人工成本; indirect taxation = taxes ( such as sales tax) which are not paid direct to the government 间接税收; The government raises more money by indirect taxation than by direct. 政府从间接税收中比从直接税收中筹措到更多资金。

**individual** 1 n. one single person 个人; 个体; savings plan made to suit the requirements of the private individual 为满足私人个体的要求而设立的储蓄业务 2 a. single or belonging to one person 个人的: a pension plan designed to meet each person's individual requirements 为满足每个人的要求而设立的退休金制度。Wc sell individual portions of ice cream. 我们出售单份冰淇淋。US Individual Retirement Account = private pension plan, where persons can make contributions separate from a company pension plan 美国个人退休金帐户

**inducement** n. thing which helps to persuade someone to do something 引诱物: They offered him a company car as an inducement to stay. 他们为引诱他留下给他提供了一辆公司汽车。

**induction** n. starting a new person in a new job 就职: induction courses or induction training = courses to train people starting new jobs 就职培训。

NOTE: no plural

**industry** n. (a) all factories or companies or processes involved in the manufacturing of products 工业: All sectors of industry have shown rises in output. 工业中各个部门产量都有增加。basic industry = most important industry of a country (such as coal, steel, agriculture) 基础工业; a boom industry or a growth industry = industry which is expanding rapidly 迅速发展的工业; heavy industry = industry which deals in heavy raw materials (such as coal) or makes large products (such as ships or engines) 重工业; light industry = industry making small products (such as clothes, books, calculators) 轻工业; primary industry = industry dealing with basic raw materials (such as coal, wood, farm produce) 基本工业; 初级工业; 第一产业; secondary industry = industry which uses basic raw materials to produce manufactured goods 第二产业; service industry or tertiary industry = industry which does not produce raw materials or manufacture products but offers a service (such as banking, retailing, accountancy) 服务业; 第三产业 (b) group of companies making the same type of product 行业; the aircraft industry 飞机制造业; the building industry 建筑业; the car industry 汽车制造业; the food processing industry 食品加工业; the mining industry 采矿业; the petroleum industry 石油工业。

◇ **industrial** 1 a. referring to manufacturing work 工业的: industrial accident = accident which takes place at work 工伤事故; to take industrial action = to go on strike or go - slow 罢工; 怠工; industrial capacity = amount of work which can be done in a factory or several factories 工业生产能力; industrial centre = large town with many industries 工业中心; GB industrial court or industrial tribunal = court which can decide in industrial disputes if both parties agree to ask it to judge between them (英) 工业法庭; 处理劳资纠纷法院; industrial design = design of products made by machines (such as cars, refrigerators) 工业设计; industrial disputes = arguments between management and workers 劳资纠纷; industrial espionage = trying to find out the secrets of a competitor's work or products, usually by illegal means 工业间谍活动; industrial estate or industrial park = area of land near a town specially for factories and warehouses 工业区; industrial expansion = growth of industries in a country or a region 工业发展; industrial injuries = injuries which happen to workers at work 工伤; industrial processes = processes involved in manufacturing products in factories 工业加工; 工业过程; industrial relations = relations between management and workers 劳资关系; good industrial relations = situation where management and workers understand each others' problems and work together for the good of the company 良好的劳资关系; industrial training = training of new workers to work in an industry 行业培训; land zoned for light industrial use = land where planning permission has been given to build small factories for light industry 划作轻工业建厂的土地 2 n. industrials = shares in manufacturing companies 工业股票

◇ **industrialist** n. owner or director of a factory 工业家。

◇ **industrialization** n. changing of an economy from being based on agriculture to industry 工业化:
NOTE: no plural

◇ **industrialize** v. to set up industries in a country which had none before 工业化; industrialized societies = countries which have many industries 工业化国家

**inefficiency** n. lack of efficiency 低效率：The report criticized the inefficiency of the sales staff. 这个报告批评了销售人员的低工作效率。

◇ **inefficient** adjective not efficient or not doing a job well 低效率的；an inefficient sales director 低效率的销售主任。

**inertia** n. being lazy 懒惰：inertia selling = method of selling items by sending them when they have not been ordered and assuming that if the items are not returned, the person who has received them is willing to buy them 惰性推销。
NOTE: no plural

**inexpensive** a. cheap or not expensive 便宜的；花费不多的

◇ **inexpensively** adv. without spending much money 便宜地；花费不多地

**inferior** a. not as good as others 劣质的：inferior products or products of inferior quality 劣质产品

**inflate** v. (a) to inflate prices = to increase prices without any reason 哄抬物价；Tourists don't want to pay inflated London prices. 旅游者们不愿意支付哄抬起来的伦敦价格。(b) to inflate the economy = to make the economy more active by increasing the money supply 扩大货币供给以活跃经济。

◇ **inflated** a. (a) inflated prices = prices which are increased without any reason 供抬起来的物价 (b) inflated currency = currency which is too high in relation to other currencies 膨胀的通货。

◇ **inflation** n. situation where prices rise to keep up with increased production costs 通货膨胀（由于生产成本的增加而引起的物价上涨）：We have 15% inflation or inflation is running at 15%. = Prices are 15% higher than at the same time last year. 目前我们的通货膨胀率为15%。to take measures to reduce inflation 采取措施降低通货膨胀；High interest rates tend to increase inflation. 高利率趋于增加通货膨胀. rate of inflation or inflation rate = percentage increase in prices over a twelve - month period 年通货膨胀率；galloping inflation or runaway inflation = very rapid inflation which it is almost impossible to reduce 失去控制的恶性通货膨胀；spiralling inflation = inflation where price rises make workers ask for higher wages which then increase prices again 螺旋式通货膨胀。
NOTE: no plural

◇ **inflationary** adjective which tends to increase inflation 通货膨胀的；inflationary trends in the economy 经济中的通货膨胀趋势；The economy is in an inflationary spiral. = in a situation where price rises encourage higher wage demands which in turn make prices rise 经济处于螺旋式通货膨胀中。anti - inflationary measures = measures to reduce inflation 抑制通货膨胀举措

**inflow** n. flowing in 流入；inflow of capital into the country = capital which is coming into a country in order to be invested 资金向国内流入

**influence** 1 n. effect which is had on someone or something 影响：The price of oil has a marked influence on the price of manufactured goods. 石油价格对于工业品价格有明显的影响。We are suffering from the influence of a high exchange rate. 我们因高兑换率的影响正蒙受着损失。2 v. to have an effect on someone or something 影响：The board was influenced in its decision by the memo from the managers. 董事会在作决议时受到经理们的备忘录的影响。The price of oil has influenced the price of manufactured goods；石油价格已影响着工业制品的价格。High inflation is influencing our profitability. 高通货膨胀正影响着我们的利润。
NOTE: you influence someone to do something

**influx** n. rushing in 涌进：an influx of

foreign currency into the country 外币涌入; an influx of cheap labour into the cities 廉价劳动力涌入城市。
NOTE: plural is influxes

**inform** v. to tell someone officially 通知: I regret to inform you that your tender was not acceptable. 我很遗憾地通知您,您的投标未被接受。We are pleased to inform you that your offer has been accepted. 我们高兴地通知您,您的发盘被接受了。We have been informed by the Department of Trade that new tariffs are coming into force. 贸易部通知我们新的关税将开始生效。

◇ **information** n. (a) details which explain something 资料;消息;情报;信息: Please send me information on or about holidays in the USA. 请寄给我有关美国节假日方面的资料。Have you any information on or about deposit accounts? 你有关于储蓄帐户方面的资料吗? I enclose this leaflet for your information. 兹随函附上份这传单供您参考。to disclose a piece of information 披露一条消息;to answer a request for information 回答信息请求; For further information, please write to Department 27. 要知进一步消息请写信给部门第 27 号。disclosure of confidential information = telling someone information which should be secret 泄露机密情报; flight information = information about flight times 飞行航班信息; tourist information = information for tourists 旅游信息; (b) information technology = working with computer data 信息处理技术; information retrieval = storing and then finding data in a computer 信息检索 (c) information bureau or information office = office which gives information to tourists or visitors 情报局或信息办公室; information officer = person whose job is to give information about a company or an organization or a government department to the public; person whose job is to give information to other departments in the same organization 信息员(传递、公布信息、情报的人员)
NOTE: no plural; for one item say a piece of information

**infrastructure** n. (a) basic structure 基本结构: the company's infrastructure = how the company is organized 公司中的组织结构 (b) basic services 基础设施 a country's infrastructure = the road and rail systems, education and legal systems, etc. 国家的基础设施。

**infringe** v. to break a law or a right 犯法;侵权: to infringe a copyright = to copy a copyright text illegally 侵犯版权; to infringe a patent = to make a product which works in the same way as a patented product and not pay a royalty to the patent holder 侵犯专利权

◇ **infringement** n. breaking a law or a right 犯法;侵权: infringement of copyright or copyright infringement = act of illegally copying a work which is in copyright 侵犯版权; infringement of patent or patent infringement 侵犯专利权。

**ingot** n. bar of gold or silver 金绽或银绽。

**inherit** v. to get something from a person who has died 继承: When her father died she inherited the shop. 父亲死后她继承了商店。He inherited £10,000 from his grandfather. 他从祖父那里继承了 10,000 英磅。

◇ **inheritance** n. property which is received from a dead person 继承物。
NOTE: no plural

**in－house** ad. & a. working inside a company's building(公司)内部的(地): the in－house staff 内部工作人员; we do all our data processing in－house 我们在公司内部完成所有的数据处理。in－house training = training given to staff at their place of work 岗位培训;内部培训。

**initial** 1 a. first or starting 最初的;开始的: initial capital = capital which is used to start a business 创办资本; He started the business with an initial expenditure or initial investment of £500. 他以 500 英磅的创办资本开始创业。initial sales = first sales of a new product 最初销售; The initial response to the TV advertising has been very good. 对电视广告的最初反映是很好的。2 n. initials = first letters of the words in a name 姓名起首的大写字母; What do the initials IMF stand for? IMF 的起首大写字母代表什么? The chairman wrote his initials by each alteration in the contract he was signing. 董事长在他正签署的合同的每一更改之处的旁边写上他的姓名起首字母。3 v. to write your initials on a document to show you have read it and approved 签上姓名起首字母以示读过并同意; to initial an amendment to a contract 在合同的更改处签上姓名起首字母; Please initial the agreement at the place marked with an X. 请在协议书上标有 X 的地方签上姓名起首字母。

**initiate** v. to start 开始; to initiate discussions 开始讨论。

◇ **initiative** n. decision to start something 率先;主动: to take the initiative = to decide to do something 采取主动; to follow up an initiative = to take action once someone else has decided to do something 跟随率先行动

**inject** v. to inject capital into a business = to put money into a business 向企业投入资本。

◇ **injection** n. a capital injection of £100,000 or an injection of £100,000 capital = putting £100,000 into an existing business 十万英磅的资本投入。

**injunction** n. court order telling someone not to do something 禁令: He got an injunction preventing the company from selling his car. 他接到禁止公司出售他的汽车的命令。The company applied for an injunction to stop their rival from marketing a similar product. 公司申请用指令去禁止他们的对手销售一种类似产品。

**injure** v. to hurt (someone)伤害: Two workers were injured in the fire. 两个工人在火灾中受伤。

◇ **injured party** n. party in a court case which has been harmed by another party 被害者;受害的一方。

◇ **injury** n. hurt caused to a person 伤害; injury benefit = money paid to a worker who has been hurt at work 工伤补助; industrial injuries = injuries caused to workers at work 工伤

**inking pad** n. small pad with ink on it, used for putting ink on a rubber stamp 印台

**inland** a. (a) inside a country 国内的: inland postage = postage for a letter to another part of the country 国内邮政; inland freight charges = charges for carrying goods from one part of the country to another 国内运费 (b) GB the Inland Revenue = government department dealing with tax (英)国内税务局; He received a letter from the Inland Revenue. 他收到了国内税务局的一封信。

**innovate** v. to bring in new ideas or new methods 革新

◇ **innovation** n. new idea or new method or new product 革新

◇ **innovative** a. (person or thing) which is new and makes changes 革新的

◇ **innovator** n. person who brings in new ideas and methods 革新者

**input** 1 n. input of information or computer input = data fed into a computer 信息输入;计算计输入: input lead = lead for connecting the electric current to the machine 输入线; input tax = VAT paid on goods or services which a company buys 投入税 2 v. to input information = to put data into a computer 输入信息。

NOTE: inputting – inputted

**inquire** v. to ask questions about something 询问: He inquired if anything was wrong. 他询问是否出什么问题了。She inquired about the mortgage rate. 她询问抵押率之事。"Inquire within" = ask for more details inside the office or shop (办公室或商店中)询问欲知详情请进内。

◇ **inquire into** v. to investigate or to try to find out about something 调查: We are inquiring into the background of the new supplier. 我们正在调查新供应商的背景。

◇ **inquiry** n. official question 询问: I refer to your inquiry of May 25th 我参照您 5 月 25 日的询问信。All inquiries should be addressed to this department. 所有的询问信都应寄到这个部门。

**insert** 1 n. thing which is put inside something 插入物: an insert in a magazine mailing or a magazine insert = advertising sheet put into a magazine when it is mailed 杂志加页广告 2 v. to put something in 插入: to insert a clause into a contract 合同中加了一项条款; to insert a publicity piece into a magazine mailing 在邮寄的杂志中插入一张广告。

**inside** 1 a. & ad. in, especially in a company's office or building 内部或在里面的(地): We do all our design work inside. 我们在室内进行所有的设计工作。inside worker = worker who works in the office or factory (not in the open air, not a salesman) 室内工作人员; 2 preposition in 在……内: There was nothing inside the container; 容器内什么也没有。We have a contact inside our rival's production department who gives us very useful information. 我们与竞争对手的生产部门内部有联系,他们给我们提供有用的信息。

◇ **insider** n. person who works in an organization and therefore knows its secrets 内部知情者: insider dealings or insider trading = illegal buying or selling of shares by staff of a company who have secret information about the company's plans 内幕交易;知情人交易。

**insolvent** a. not able to pay debts 无偿还能力的;破产的: He was declared insolvent. = He was officially stated to be insolvent. 他被宣布破产。

◇ **insolvency** n. not being able to pay debts 无力偿付;破产 He was in a state of insolvency = He could not pay his debts. 他处于无力偿付境地。

NOTE: no plural

**inspect** v. to examine in detail 检验: to inspect a machine or an installation 检验机器或设备; to inspect the accounts 检验帐目; to inspect products for defects = to look at products in detail to see if they have any defects 检验产品的瑕疵

◇ **inspection** n. close examination of something 检验: to make an inspection or to carry out an inspection of a machine or an installation 对机器或设备进行检验; inspection of a product for defects 检验产品的瑕疵; to carry out a tour of inspection = to visit various places or offices or factories to inspect them 进行巡回检查; to issue an inspection order = to order an official inspection 发布视察令; inspection stamp = stamp placed on something to show it has been inspected 检验盖章

◇ **inspector** n. official who inspects 检查员: inspector of factories or factory inspector = government official who inspects factories to see if they are safely run 工厂检查员; inspector of taxes or tax inspector = official of the Inland

Revenue who examines tax returns and decides how much tax people should pay 税务检查员; inspector of weights and measures = government official who inspects weighing machines and goods sold in shops to see if the quantities and weights are correct 度量衡检查员。

◇ **inspectorate** n. all inspectors 检查团; the factory inspectorate = all inspectors of factories 工厂检查团

**inst** = INSTANT 本月的: your letter of the 6th inst = your letter of the 6th of this month 你本月 6 日的信

**instability** n. being unstable or moving up and down 不稳定: period of instability in the money markets = period when currencies fluctuate rapidly 货币市场不稳定时期。

NOTE: no plural

**install** v. to put (a machine) into an office or into a factory 安装; to install new machinery 安装新机器; to install a new data processing system 安装新数据处理系统。

◇ **installation** n. (a) machines, equipment and buildings 装备; 设备; 设施; harbour installations; 码头设施; The fire seriously damaged the oil installations. 火灾严重地破坏了石油装备。(b) putting new machines into an office or a factory 安装: to supervise the installation of new equipment 监督新设备安装。

◇ **instalment or US installment** n. part of a payment which is paid regularly until the total amount is paid 分期付款: The first instalment is payable on signature of the agreement. 在协议上签字时支付第一次分期付款。The final instalment is now due = the last of a series of payments should be paid now. 最后一次分期付款现已到期。to pay £ 25 down and monthly instalments of £ 20 = to pay a first payment of £ 25 and the rest

in payments of £ 20 each month 先付 25 英磅定金,其余的每月分期支付 20 英磅; to miss an instalment = not to pay an instalment at the right time 未按时支付分期付款。

◇ **installment plan** n. US system of buying something by paying a sum regularly each month 美国分期付款购物法; to buy a car on the installment plan 用分期付款方法购买汽车。

NOTE: GB English is hire purchase

**instance** n. particular example or case 实例证: In this instance we will overlook the delay. 在这种情况下我们可宽容这种拖延。

**instant** a. (a) this month 本月; our letter of the 6th instant = our letter of the 6th of this current month 我们本月 6 日的信 (b) immediately available 立即的: instant credit 立即可获信贷

**institute** 1 n. official organization 机构; research institute = organization set up to do research 研究所 2 v. to start 开始; 着手: to institute proceedings against someone 对某人提起诉讼。

◇ **institution** n. organization or society set up for a particular purpose 机构; 协会; financial institution = bank or investment trust or insurance company whose work involves lending or investing large sums of money(银行、投资信托公司、保险公司等)金融机构

◇ **institutional** a. referring to a financial institution 金融机构的: institutional buying or selling = buying or selling shares by financial institutions 金融机构的股票买卖; institutional investors = financial institutions who invest money in securities 金融机构投资者

**instruct** v. (a) to give an order to someone 指示; to instruct someone to do something = to tell someone officially to do something 指示某人做某事; He instructed the credit controller to take action. 他指示信贷管理员采取行动。(b) to instruct a solicitor = to give orders to a solicitor to start legal proceedings on your behalf 指示律师提起诉讼。

◇ **instruction** n. order which tells what should be done or how something is to be used 指令；指示：He gave instructions to his stockbroker to sell the shares immediately. 他指示他的股票经纪人立即卖掉股票。

to await instructions = to wait for someone to tell you what to do 等候指令；to issue instructions = to tell everyone what to do 发出指示；in accordance with or according to instructions = as the instructions show 按照指令；failing instructions to the contrary = unless someone tells you to do the opposite 当无相反的指示；forwarding instructions or shipping instructions = details of how goods are to be shipped and delivered 货物装运指示(需知)

◇ **instructor** n. person who shows how something is to be done 指导者

**instrument** n. (a) tool or piece of equipment 工具；仪器：The technician brought instruments to measure the output of electricity. 技术员带来仪器测量电的输出功率。(b) legal document 法律文件；票据；negotiable instrument = document (such as a bill of exchange or a cheque) which can be exchanged for cash 可转让票据；可流通票据(汇票、支票等可兑现票据)

**insure** v. to have a contract with a company where, if regular small payments are made, the company will pay compensation for loss, damage, injury or death 保险；投保(同保险公司签定合同，并定期向公司交纳少量保险金，保险公司将赔偿付款人损失、损坏或伤亡等)：to insure a house against fire 给房屋保火险；to insure someone's life 给某人保人寿险：He was insured for £100,000. 他

被投保的全额为 100,000 英磅。to insure baggage against loss 保行李觅失险；to insure against bad weather 投保天气险；to insure against loss of earnings 保收入损失险；the life insured = the person whose life is covered by a life assurance 保人寿险；the sum insured = the largest amount of money that an insurer will pay under an insurance 投保金额；保险额

◇ **insurable** a. which can be insured 可保险的

◇ **insurance** n. (a) agreement that in return for regular small payments, a company will pay compensation for loss, damage, injury or death 保险合同：to take out an insurance against fire = to pay a premium, so that if a fire happens, compensation will be paid 投保火险；to take out an insurance on the house = to pay a premium, so that if the house is damaged compensation will be paid 办理房屋保险；The damage is covered by the insurance . = The insurance company will pay for the damage. 损坏由保险公司赔偿。Repairs will be paid for by the insurance. 修理费用将由保险公司支付。to pay the insurance on a car = to pay premiums to insure a car 交付汽车保险费 (b) accident insurance = insurance which will pay if an accident takes place 事故保险；car insurance or motor insurance = insuring a car, the driver and passengers in case of accident 汽车保险或机动车辆保险；comprehensive insurance = insurance which covers against all risks which are likely to happen 综合保险；endowment insurance = situation where a sum of money is paid to the insured person on a certain date or to his heir if he dies before that date 养老保险；fire insurance = insurance against damage by fire 火险；house insurance = insuring a house and its contents against damage 住宅保险；life insurance = situation which pays a sum of money when someone dies 人寿保险; medical insurance = insurance which pays the cost of medical treatment, especially when travelling abroad 医疗保险; term insurance = life insurance which covers a person's life for a fixed period of time 定期人寿保险; third – party insurance = insurance which pays compensation if someone who is not the insured person incurs loss or injury 第三者责任保险; whole – life insurance = insurance where the insured person pays premiums for all his life and the insurance company pays a sum when he dies 终身人寿保险。 (c) insurance agent or insurance broker = person who arranges insurance for clients 保险经纪人; insurance claim = asking an insurance company to pay for damage 保险索赔; insurance company = company whose business is to receive payments and pay compensation for loss or damage 保险公司; insurance contract = agreement by an insurance company to insure 保险合同; insurance cover = protection guaranteed by an insurance policy 保险范围; insurance policy = document which shows the conditions of an insurance 保险单; insurance premium = payment made by the insured person to the insurer 保险费; (d) GB National Insurance = state insurance, organized by the government, which pays for medical care, hospitals, unemployment benefits, etc. 英国国民保险; National Insurance contributions = money paid by a worker and the company each month to the National Insurance 国民保险付款

◇ **insurer** n. company which insures 保险公司, 保险商

NOTE: no plural for (b), (c) and (d). Note also that for lifeinsurance, GB English prefers to use assurance, assure, assurer

**intangible** a. which cannot be touched 无形的: intangible assets = assets which have a value, but which cannot be seen ( such as goodwill, patent or a trademark) 无形资产。

**integrate** v. to link things together to form one whole group 联合; 一体化

◇ **integration** n. bringing several businesses together under a central control 联合; 一体化; horizontal integration = joining similar companies or taking over a company in the same line of business as yourself 横向联合; vertical integration = joining business together which deal with different stages in the production or sale of a product 纵向联合

**intend** v. to plan or to expect to do something 打算: The company intends to open an office in New York next year. 公司打算明年在纽约设一个办事处。 We intend to offer jobs to 250 unemployed young people. 我们打算为250名无业青年提供就业。

**intensive** a. intensive farming = farming small areas of expensive land, using machines and fertilizers to obtain high crops 集约农业; capital – intensive industry = industry which needs a large amount of capital investment in plant to make it work 资本密集的工业; labour – intensive industry – industry which needs large numbers of workers or where labour costs are high in relation to turnover 劳动密集的工业

**intent** n. what is planned 意向: letter of intent = letter which states what a company intends to do if something happens 意向书

**inter –** prefix between 之间: inter – bank loan = loan from one bank to another 银行间贷款; 银行间内业拆借; The inter – city rail services are good. = Train services between cities are good. 城市间铁路交通是发达的。 inter – company dealings = dealings between two companies in the same group 同业间的交易；inter – company comparisons = comparing the results of one company with those of another in the same product area 同业间互相比较。

**interest** 1 n. (a) special attention 兴趣：The MD takes no interest in the staff club；总经理对职工俱乐部不感兴趣。The buyers showed a lot of interest in our new product range. 顾客对我们的新产品系列很感兴趣。(b) payment made by a borrower for the use of money, calculated as a percentage of the capital borrowed 利息(按借款的百分率计算, 所付的金额)；simple interest = interest calculated on the capital only, and not added to it 单利；compound interest = interest which is added to the capital and then earns interest itself 复利；accrual of interest = automatic addition of interest to capital 自动计息；应付利息；accrued interest = interest which is accumulating and is due for payment at a later date 应计利息；back interest = interest which has not yet been paid 欠付利息；fixed interest = interest which is paid at a set rate 固定利息；high or low interest = interest at a high or low percentage 高利息或低利息；interest charges = cost of paying interest 利息费用；interest rate or rate of interest = percentage charge for borrowing money 利率；interest – free credit or loan = credit or loan where no interest is paid by the borrower 无息信贷或无息贷款；The company gives its staff interest – free loans. 公司给予其职工无息贷款。(c) money paid as income on investments or loans. 投资利息或贷款利息；The bank pays 10% interest on deposits. 银行支付10%的存款利息。to receive interest at 5%；得到5%的利息；The loan pays 5% interest. 贷款要支付5%利息。deposit which yields or gives or produces or bears 5% interest 利息为5%的存款；account which earns interest at 10% or which earns 10% interest 获利10%的帐户；interest – bearing deposits = deposits which produce interest 有息存款 (d) money invested in a company or financial share in a company 权益；股树权；beneficial interest = situation where someone is allowed to occupy or receive rent from a house without owning it 受惠权益；He has a controlling interest in the company. = He owns more than 50% of the shares and so can direct how the company is run. 他拥有对公司的控制权。life interest = situation where someone benefits from a property as long as he is alive 终身权益；majority interest or minority interest = situation where someone owns a majority or a minority of shares in a company 多数股权(股份)或少数股权益(股份)：He has a majority interest in a supermarket chain. 他在连锁超级市场中拥有多数股权益。to acquire a substantial interest in the company = to buy a large number of shares in a company 购买某公司的大量股权；to declare an interest = to state in public that you own shares in a company 公开宣布拥有某公司股份

NOTE: no plural for (a), (b) and (c) 2 v. to attract someone's attention 使发生兴趣；使注意：He tried to interest several companies in his new invention. 他试图使几个公司关注他的新发明。interested in = paying attention to 对某事感兴趣：The managing director is interested only in increasing profitability. 总经理只对增加利润感兴趣。

interested party = person or company with a financial interest in a company 有利害关系之一方

◇ **interesting** a. which attracts attention 令人感兴趣的；有趣的：They made us a very interesting offer for the factory. 他们对该工厂的发价使我们十分感兴趣。。

**interface** 1 n. link between two different computer systems or pieces of hardware 接口；界面 2 v. to meet and act with 联系；联接：The office micros interface with the mainframe computer at head office. 办公室的微型计算机与总部的主机是联系在一起的。

**interfere** v. to get involved or to try to change something which is not your concern 干预；干涉

◇ **interference** n. the act of interfering 干预；干涉：The sales department complained of continual interference from the accounts department. 销售部分抱怨来自会计部门的不断干预。

**interim** n. interim dividend = dividend paid at the end of a half – year 期中股利；interim payment = payment of part of a dividend 期中支付；interim report = report given at the end of a half – year 年中报告；in the interim = meanwhile or for the time being 其间；暂时

**intermediary** n. person who is the link between parties who do not agree or who are negotiating 中间人；调解人：He refused to act as an intermediary between the two directors. 他拒绝充当两个董事之间的调解人。

**internal** a. (a) inside a company 内部的：We decided to make an internal appointment. = We decided to appoint an existing member of staff to the post, and not bring someone in from outside the company. 我们决定指定内部人员担任这一职位。internal audit = audit carried out by a department within the company 内部审计；internal audit department or internal auditor = department or member of staff who audits the accounts of the company he works for 内部审计部门或内部审计员；internal telephone = telephone which is linked to other phones in an office 内部电话 (b) inside a country 国内的：an internal flight = flight to a town inside the same country 国内航班；US Internal Revenue Service = government department which deals with tax(美)国内税务局；internal trade = trade between various parts of a country 国内贸易。

◇ **internally** adv. inside a company 内部地：The job was advertised internally. 这项招工只在内部作了广告。

**international** a. working between countries 国际的：international call = telephone call to another country 国际电话；international dialling code = number used to make a telephone call to another country 国际电话拨码；International Labour Organization = section of the United Nations, an organization which tries to improve working conditions and workers' pay in member countries 国际劳工组织；international law = laws governing relations between countries 国际法；the International Monetary Fund = (part of the United Nations) a type of bank which helps member states in financial difficulties, gives financial advice to members and encourages world trade 国际货币基金组织；international trade = trade between different countries 国际贸易

**interpret** v. to translate what someone has said into another language 翻译：My assistant knows Greek, so he will interpret for us. 我的助手懂希腊语，因此他会为我们做翻译。

◇ **interpreter** n. person who translates what someone has said into another language 口译者；译员：My secretary will act as interpreter. 我的秘书将充当翻译。

**intervene** v. to try to make a change in a system 介入；干预：to intervene in a dispute = to try to settle a dispute. 试图调停争端

◇ **intervention** n. acting to make a

change in a system 干预：the government's intervention in the foreign exchange markets 政府对外汇市场的干预；the central bank's intervention in the banking crisis 中央银行在金融危机中的干预；the government's intervention in the labour dispute 在劳资争端中政府的调停；intervention price = price at which the EEC will buy farm produce which farmers cannot sell, in order to store it 干预价格。

**interview** 1 n. (a) talking to a person who is applying for a job(对求职者的)面试：We called six people for interview. 我们给六个人打了电话，通知他们前去面试。I have an interview next week or I am going for an interview next week. 下星期我要前去面试。(b) asking a person questions as part of an opinion poll(民意测验中的个别)采访 2 v. to talk to a person applying for a job to see if he is suitable 面试：We interviewed ten candidates, but did not find anyone suitable. 我们面试了十位候选人，但未发现适合的人选。

◇ **interviewee** n. person who is being interviewed 参加面试者；被接见者；被采访者。

◇ **interviewer** n. person who is conducting the interview 接见者；会见者；面试者；

**inter vivos** phr. gift inter vivos = gift given to another living person(在存者之间的)捐赠

**intestate** a. to die intestate = to die without having made a will 死后未留下遗嘱。

**intransit** ad. goods in transit = goods being transported 运输中的商品

**intray n. basket on a desk for letters or memos which have been received and are waiting to be dealt with** 公文筐；文件筐；公文格

**introduce** v. to make someone get to know a new person or thing 介绍；to introduce a client = to bring in a new client and make him known to someone 介绍一个新客户；to introduce a new product on the market = to produce a new product and launch it on the market 在市场上推出一个新产品

◇ **introduction** n. (a) letter making someone get to know another person 介绍信：I'll give you an introduction to the MD - He is an old friend of mine. 我给你一封递交给总经理的介绍信，他是我的一个老朋友。(b) bringing into use 采用：the introduction of new technology = putting new machines (usually computers) into a business or industry 采用新技术；引进新技术

◇ **introductory** a. introductory offer = special price offered on a new product to attract customers 优待发价(为打开销路)

**invalid** a. not valid or not legal 无效的；非法的：permit that is invalid 无效的许可证；claim which has been declared invalid 宣布无效的索赔或要求权

◇ **invalidate** v. to make something invalid 使无效：Because the company has been taken over, the contract has been invalidated. 因为公司被兼并了，合同已无效。

◇ **invalidation** n. making invalid 无效。

◇ **invalidity** n. being invalid 无效力：the invalidity of the contract 合同的无效力

**invent** v. to make something which has never been made before 发明：She invented a new type of computer terminal. 她发明了一种新型计算机终端。Who invented shorthand? 谁发明了速记？The chief accountant has invented a new system of customer filing. 主任会计发明了一新的顾客存档体系。

◇ **invention** n. thing which has been

invented 发明: He tried to sell his latest invention to a US car manufacturer. 他试图把他的最新发明出售给美国汽车制造商。

◇ **inventor** n. person who invents something 发明者: He is the inventor of the all－plastic car. 他是全塑料汽车的发明者。

**inventory** 1 n. (a) stock or goods in a warehouse or shop 存货: to carry a high inventory 备有充足的库存; to aim to reduce inventory 旨在减少库存; inventory control = system of checking that there is not too much stock in a warehouse, but just enough to meet requirements 库存管理 (b) list of the contents of a house for sale, of an office for rent, etc. 财产目录: to draw up an inventory of fixtures 出固定资产的目录; to agree the inventory = to agree that the inventory is correct 承认财产目录。 2 v. to make a list of stock or contents 编制存货清单或财产目录。

**invest** v. (a) to put money into shares, bonds, a building society, hoping that it will produce interest and increase in value 投资: He invested all his money in an engineering business. 将所有的钱投资于一个建造业。 She was advised to invest in real estate or in government bonds. 别人劝她投资于房地产或政府债券。 to invest abroad = to put money into shares or bonds in overseas countries 对外投资 (b) to spend money on something which you believe will be useful 花钱购买(认为是有用之物): to invest money in new machinery 花钱买机械; to invest capital in a new factory 把资本投资于建新工厂

◇ **investment** n. (a) placing of money so that it will increase in value and produce interest 投资: They called for more government investment in new industries; 他们要求政府将更多的资金

投资于新兴工业。 investment in real estate 房地产投资; to make investments in oil companies 投资于石油公司; return on investment = interest or dividends shown as a percentage of the money invested 投资利润率 (b) shares, bonds, deposits bought with invested money(股票、债券等金融)投资: long－term investment or short－term investment = shares, etc., which are likely to increase in value over a long or short period 长期投资或短期投资; safe investment = shares, etc. which are not likely to fall in value 安全投资; blue－chip investments = risk－free shares of good companies 无风险股票投资; He is trying to protect his investments. = He is trying to make sure that the money he has invested is not lost. 他正试图保护他的投资。 (c) investment adviser = person who advises people on what investments to make 投资顾问; investment company or investment trust = company whose shares can be bought on the Stock Exchange, and whose business is to make money by buying and selling stocks and shares 投资公司或投资信托; investment grant = government grant to a company to help it to invest in new machinery 投资拨款; investment income = income ( such as interest and dividends) from investments 投资收益; 投资收入

◇ **investor** n. person who invests money 投资者: the small investor or the private investor = person with a small sum of money to invest 小规模投资者或私人投资者; the institutional investor = organization (like a pension fund or insurance company) with large sums of money to invest 公共机构投资者

**investigate** v. to examine something which may be wrong 调查

◇ **investigation** n. examination to find out what is wrong 调查: to conduct an investigation into irregularities in share dealings 对股票交易的不规律性进行调查

◇ **investigator** n. person who investigates 调查者: government investigator 政府调查人

**invisible** 1 a. invisible assets = assets which have a value but which cannot be seen (such as goodwill or patents) 无形资产: invisible earnings = foreign currency earned by a country by providing services, not selling goods 无形收益; invisible imports or exports = services which are paid for in foreign currency or earn foreign currency without actually selling a product (such as banking or tourism) 无形进出口 2 pl. n. invisibles = invisible imports and exports 无形进出口;无形贸易。

**invite** v. to ask someone to do something or to ask for something 邀请: to invite someone to an interview 邀请某人来面谈或面试;to invite someone to join the board 邀请某人加入董事会; to invite shareholders to subscribe a new issue 邀请股东们认购新发行的股票; to invite tenders for a contract 招标订立合同

◇ **invitation** n. asking someone to do something 邀请: to issue an invitation to someone to join the board 邀请某人加入董事会; invitation to tender for a contract 招标订立合同; invitation to subscribe a new issue 认购新发行股票的邀请

**invoice** 1 n. (a) note asking for payment for goods or services supplied 发(货)票; Your invoice dated November 10th. 你的发票注明日期是 11 月 10 日。They sent in their invoice six weeks late. 晚六个星期他们送来了发票。to make out an invoice for £250 开一张 250 英磅发票; to settle or to pay an invoice 结清或支付一张发票 The total is payable within thirty days of invoice. =

The total sum has to be paid within thirty days of the date on the invoice. 全部款项要在开发票后三十天内付清 VAT invoice = invoice which includes VAT 包括增值税的发票 (b) invoice clerk = office worker who deals with invoices 开发票的人: invoice price = price as given on an invoice (including discount and VAT)发票票面价格; total invoice value = total amount on an invoice, including transport, VAT, etc. 发票总价值 2 v. to send an invoice to someone 寄发票: to invoice a customer 给顾客寄发票; We invoiced you on November 10th. = We sent you the invoice on November 10th 我们于 11 月 10 日给你寄了发票。

◇ **invoicing** n. sending of an invoice 开发票: our invoicing is done by the computer 我们这里开发票是用计算机。invoicing department = department in a company which deals with preparing and sending invoices 发票管理部门; invoicing in triplicate = preparing three copies of invoices 开一式三份的发票; VAT invoicing = sending of an invoice including VAT 开包括增值税的发票
NOTE: no plural

**inward** a. towards the home country;向内的;进口的: inward bill = bill of lading for goods arriving in a country 进口提单; inward mission = visit to your home country by a group of foreign businessmen 外国代表团的访问。

**IOU** n. = I OWE YOU signed document promising that you will pay back money borrowed 借据: to pay a pile of IOUs 支付许多借据

**IRA** US = INDIVIDUAL RETIREMENT ACCOUNT(美)个人退休帐户。

**irrecoverable** a. which cannot be recovered 不能恢复的;不能回收的 irrecoverable debt = debt which will never be paid 不能回收的欠款或债务

**irredeemable** a. which cannot be redeemed 不能偿还的: irredeemable bond = bond which has no date of maturity and which therefore provides interest but can never be redeemed at full value 本金不能偿还债券

**irregular** a. not correct or not done in the correct way 不正规的;非正式的: irregular documentation 不正规的单据; This procedure is highly irregular. 这个程序是很不正规的。

◇ **irregularity** n. (a) not being regular or not being on time 不正规;不准时: the irregularity of the postal deliveries 邮递的不准时 (b) irregularities = things which are not done in the correct way and which are possibly illegal 违章;违规之事: to investigate irregularities in the share dealings 调查股票交易中的非法行为。

**irrevocable** a. which cannot be changed 不可改变的;不可撤消的: irrevocable acceptance = acceptance which cannot be withdrawn 不可撤消的承兑; irrevocable letter of credit = letter of credit which cannot be cancelled or changed 不可撤消信用证

**IRS** US = INTERNAL REVENUE SERVICE(美)国内税务局;国内收入署。

**issue** 1 n. giving out new shares 发行;新股票: bonus issue or scrip issue = new shares given free to shareholders 发行红股; issue of debentures or debenture issue = borrowing money by giving lenders debentures 发行公司债券; issue of new shares or share issue = selling new shares in a company to the public 新股票发行; rights issue = giving shareholders the right to buy more shares at a lower price 股权发行; new issues department = section of a bank which deals with issues of new shares in companies 新股票发行部门; issue price = price of shares when they are offered for sale for the first time 股票发行价格 2 v. to put out or to give out 开立;发行;发布: to issue a letter of credit 开信用证; to issue shares in a new company 发行新公司的股票; to issue a writ against someone 发出针对某人的书面命令; The government issued a report on London's traffic. 政府发布了伦敦交通的报告。

◇ **issued** a. issued capital = amount of capital which is given out as shares to shareholders 已发行股本; issued price = price of shares in a new company when they are offered for sale for the first time 发行新公司股票价格

◇ **issuing** n. which organizes an issue of shares 发行; issuing bank or issuing house = bank which organizes the selling of shares in a new company. 发行(股票)银行

**IT** = INFORMATION TECHNOLOGY 信息技术

**item** n. (a) thing for sale 商品: cash items = goods sold for cash 收取现金的商品; We are holding orders for out of stock items. = for goods which are not in stock 我们持有一些要现货的订单。Please find enclosed an order for the following items from your catalogue. 兹随函附上一份订单,订购你方目录中的下列商品。(b) piece of information 一条;一则; items on a balance sheet 资金平衡表中的项目: extraordinary items = items in accounts which do not appear each year and need to be noted 帐目中的特别项目; item of expenditure = goods or services which have been paid for and appear in the accounts 帐目中的支出项目 (c) point on a list 条款: We will now take item four on the agenda. = We will now discuss the fourth point on the agenda. 我们将讨论议事日程上的第4项。

◇ **itemize** v. to make a detailed list of

things. 详细列明；Itemizing the sales figures will take about two days 详细列明销售额数字要花费大约两天时间。
itemized account = detailed record of money paid or owed 明细帐目；itemized invoice = invoice which lists each item separately 逐项列明的发票

**itinerary** n. list of places to be visited on one journey 旅行路线；旅行计划：a salesman's it inerary 推销员的旅行路线

# Jj

**jam** 1 n. (a) sweet food made with fruit and sugar 果酱 (b) blocking 阻塞：traffic jam = situation where there is so much traffic on the road that it moves only very slowly 交通阻塞 2 v. to stop working or to be blocked 出故障；挤满：The paper feed has jammed；进纸处卡住了。The switchboard was jammed with calls. 电话总机占线。
NOTE: jamming - jammed

**jetsam** n. flotsam and jetsam = rubbish floating in the water after a ship has been wrecked and rubbish washed on to the land(船只遇难后漂浮在水面的或冲刷到岸边的)废弃物
NOTE: no plural

**jettison** v. to throw cargo from a ship into the sea to make the ship lighter(将船货抛入海中以减轻船体重量)抛弃

**jingle** n. advertising jingle or publicity jingle = short and easily remembered tune to advertise a product on television, etc. (电视等宣传广告中简短而熟悉的音乐旋律)广告音乐

**job** n. (a) piece of work 一件工作 to do a job of work = to be given a job of work to do 做一项工作：to do odd jobs = to do various pieces of work 打零工：He does odd jobs for us around the house. 他在我们家中做杂活。odd - job - man = person who does various pieces of work 做零工的人；to be paid by the job = to be paid for each piece of work done 按工付酬 (b) order being worked on(履行下达)任务：We are working on six jobs at the moment 目前我们正忙于六项下达任务；The shipyard has a big job starting in August. 从八月开始造船厂要有一项大任务。(c) regular paid work. 工作；职位：He is looking for a job in the computer industry. 他正在计算机行业中寻找工作。He lost his job when the factory closed. 工厂倒闭,他失业了。She got a job in a factory. 她在一家工厂找到了工作。to apply for a job in an office 申请一份办公室工作；office job or white - collar job = job in an office 办公室工作；to give up one's job = to resign from one's work 辞去工作；to look for a job = to try to find work 寻找工作；to retire from one's job = to leave work and take a pension 退休；to be out of a job = to have no work 失业 (d) job analysis = detailed examination and report on the duties of a job 工作分析；job application or application for a job = asking for a job in writing 工作申请书；You have to fill in a job application form. 你得先填写工作申请表。job centre = government office which lists jobs which are vacant 求职中心；job classification = describing jobs listed under various classes 工作分类；job creation scheme = government - backed plan to make work for the unemployed 就业计划；job description = official document from the management which says what a job involves 工作说明；job evaluation = examining different jobs within an organization to see what skills and qualifications are needed to carry themout 工作评价; job satisfaction = a worker's feeling that he is happy in his place of work and pleased with the work he does 工作的满意感; job security = feeling which a worker has that he has a right to keep his job, or that his job will never end 工作安全感; job specification = very detailed description of what is involved in a job 工作详情况明; job title = name given to a person in a certain job 工作职称; Her job title is "Chief Buyer." 她的工作头街是"主任采购员"。on - the - job training = training given to workers at their place of work 在职岗位培训; off - the - job training = training given to workers away from their place of work (i.e. at a college)脱产培训 (e) job lot = group of miscellaneous items sold together 零星物整批交易; He sold the household furniture as a job lot. 他将家中家具成批卖掉。(f) difficulty 费力的事; 难做的事: They will have a job to borrow the money they need for the expansion programme. 他们将费很大的劲去筹借扩建计划所需的用款。We had a job to find a qualified secretary. 我们难以找到合格的秘书。

◇ **jobber** n. (a) (stock) jobber = person who buys and sells shares from other traders on the Stock Exchange 股票经纪人 (b) US wholesaler(美)批发商

◇ **jobbing** n. (a) (stock) jobbing = buying and selling shares from other traders on the Stock Exchange 股票买卖 (b) doing small pieces of work 做零工的: jobbing gardener or jobbing printer = person who does odd jobs in the garden or who does smallprinting jobs 做零工的园丁或做零件的印刷工

◇ **jobless** n. the jobless = people with no jobs or the unemployed 无业者; 失业者

**join** v. (a) to put things together 连接:

The offices were joined together by making a door in the wall. 在墙上凿了门, 办公室连接在一起了。If the paper is too short to take all the accounts, you can join an extra piece on the bottom. 如果这张纸太短而不能写下所有帐目, 你可以在底下接上一张纸。(b) to join a firm = to start work with a company 加入一个公司: He joined on January 1st = He started work on the January 1st. 他于 1 月 1 日开始工作。(c) to join an association or a group = to become a member of an association or a group 加入某协会或团体: All the staff have joined the company pension plan; 所有的职工都已加入公司的养老金计划。He was asked to join the board; 邀请他加入委员会。Smith Ltd has applied to join the trade association 史密斯有限公司已经申请加入贸易协会。

**joint** a. (a) combined or with two or more organizations linked together 联合的;共同的: joint commission of inquiry or joint committee = commission or committee with representatives of various organizations on it 职工调查委员会或联合委员会; joint discussions = discussions between management and workers before something is done 共同讨论; joint management = management done by two or more people 共同管理; joint venture = very large business project where two or more companies join together 合资经营 (b) joint account = bank account for two people 联合帐户; joint - stock bank = bank which is a public company quoted on the Stock Exchange 合股银行; joint - stock company = public company whose shares are owned by very many people 股份公司( (c) one of two or more people who work together or who are linked 共同的;联合的; joint beneficiary 共同受益人; joint managing director 联合总经理; joint owner 共同拥有者; joint signatory 联合

签署人；joint ownership = owning of a propertyby several owners 共同所有权

◇ **jointly** ad. together with one or more other people 联合地；共同地：to own a property jointly 共同拥有一份财产；to manage a company jointly 联合管理一家公司；They are jointly liable for damages. 他们共同负责支付损坏赔偿金。

**journal** n. (a) book with the account of sales and purchases made each day 日记帐 (b) magazine 期刊；house journal = magazine produced for the workers in a company to give them news about the company 内部期刊；trade journal = magazine produced for people or companies in a certain trade 贸易期刊。

◇ **journalist** n. person who writes for a newspaper 记者

**journey** n. long trip, especially a trip done by a salesman 旅行：He planned his journey to visit all his accounts in two days. 他计划在两天内走访他的全部客户。journey order = order given by the shopkeeper to a salesman when he calls 旅行订购(店主向来访的推销员定货)

**judge** 1 n. person who decides in a legal case 法官：The judge sent him to prison for embezzlement. 因为贪污，法官使他入狱。2 v. to decide 判断；认为：He judged it was time to call an end to the discussions. 他认为该结束讨论了。

◇ **judgement or judgment** n. legal decision or official decision 判决；裁决：to pronounce judgement or to give one's judgement on something = to give an official or legal decision about something 宣布裁决或判决；judgment debtor = debtor who has been ordered by a court to pay a debt 判定债务人

NOTE: the spelling judgment is used by lawyers

**judicial** a. referring to the law 司法的：judicial processes = the ways in which

the law works 司法程序

**jumble sale** n. sale of odd secondhand items organized by a club or organization to raise money 旧货慈善义卖

**jump** 1 n. sudden rise 猛增：jump in prices 物价暴涨；jump in unemployment figures 失业人数猛增 2 v. (a) to go up suddenly 猛增：Oil prices have jumped since the war started. 战争开始后，石油价格暴涨。Share values jumped on the Stock Exchange. 证券交易所的股价猛增。(b) to go away suddenly 突然私自离开：to jump bail = not to appear in court after having been released on bail 保释后即刻离去；to jump the gun = to start to do something too early or before you should 过早地开始某事；抢跑；to jump the queue = to go in front of someone who has been waiting longer 不按次序排队；加塞；They jumped the queue and got their export licence before we did. 他们加塞儿比我们先得到了出口许可证。to jump ship = to leave a ship where you work as a sailor and not to go back(水手)私自离航船

◇ **jumpy** a. nervous or excited 神经紧张的；兴奋的：The market is jumpy = The stock market is nervous and share prices are likely to fluctuate. 证券市场上股价急剧波动的。

**junior** 1 a. younger or lower in rank 年幼的；下级的：junior clerk = clerk, usually young, who has lower status than a senior clerk 低级职员；junior executive or junior manager = young manager in a company 年轻的经理；junior partner = person who has been made a partner more recently than others 最新合伙人；John Smith, Junior = the younger John Smith (i.e. the son of John Smith, Senior)小史密期 2 n. (a) barrister who is not a Queen's counsel(不是皇家律师) 小律师 (b) office junior = young man or woman who does all types of work in an office 办公室勤杂人员

**junk** n. rubbish or useless items 废物：
You should throw away all that junk. 你
应扔掉所有那些废物。junk bonds =
bonds raised as debentures on the security of a company which is the subject of a
takeover bid 不值钱的债券；垃圾债券；
junk mail = advertising material sent
through the post 邮寄的广告；三等邮件
NOTE：no plural

**jurisdiction** n. within the jurisdiction
of the court = in the legal power of a
court 在法庭的管辖权范围之内

# Kk

**K** abbrev. one thousand 一千；"salary：
￡15K + " = salary more than ￡15,
000 per annum 工资：每年超过 15000
英镑

**keen** a. (a) eager or active 迫切的；活
跃的：keen competition = strong competition 激烈竞争；We are facing some
keen competition from European
manufacturers. 我们正面临来自欧洲制
造商的激烈竞争。keen demand wide
demand 迫切需求；There is a keen demand for home computers. 目前，对国产
计算机的需求很旺。(b) keen prices =
prices which are kept low so as to be
competitive 有竞争性的价格：Our
prices are the keenest on the market. 我
们的价格在市上是最有竞争性的。

**keep** v. (a) to go on doing something 保
持；继续：They kept working, even
when the boss told them to stop. 甚至当
老板让他们停工时，他们还继续干。
The other secretaries complain that she
keeps singing when she is typing. 其他的

秘书们抱怨她在打字时不断地唱歌。
(b) to do what is necessary 履行；遵守：
to keep an appointment = to be there
when you said you would be 遵守约见；
赴约；to keep the books of a company or
to keep a company's books = to note
the accounts of a company accurately 记
载公司帐册（c) to hold items for sale or
for information 保存：We always keep
this item in stock. = We always have
this item in our warehouse or shop. 我们
库房中总存有这种货物。to keep
someone's name on file = to have
someone's name on a list for reference 将
某人名字存档（d) to hold things at a
certain level 保持：We must keep our
mailing list up to date. 我们必须保持我
们邮寄通信名单是最新的。to keep
spending to a minimum 保持最低开支。
The price of oil has kept the pound at a
high level. 石油价格使英镑保持高价。
The government is encouraging firms to
keep prices low. 政府正鼓励公司保持
低价格。
NOTE：keeping – kept

◇ **keep back** v. to hold on to something which you could give to someone
不透露；隐瞒；to keep back information
or to keep something back from someone
不透露情报或对某人隐瞒某事；to
keep ￡10 back from someone's salary
从某人的工资中扣留 10 英磅。

◇ **keeping** n. safe keeping = being
looked after carefully 妥善保管：We put
the documents into the bank for safe
keeping. 我们把文件存入银行为了妥
善保管。
NOTE：no plural

◇ **keep on** v. to continue to do something 继续：The factory kept on working
in spite of the fire. 尽管遭火灾，工厂继
续开工。We keep on receiving orders for
this item although it was discontinued
two years ago. 虽然两年前这种商品就
已停产，但我们现在还仍然收到其订

单。

◇ **keep up** v. to hold at a certain high level 使居高不下；We must keep up the turnover in spite of the recession. 尽管经济衰退我们必须保持高营业额。She kept up a rate of sixty words per minute for several hours. 她保持了几个小时内每分钟 60 个词的高速度。

**key** n. (a) piece of metal used to open a lock 钥匙：We have lost the keys to the computer room. 我们丢失了计算机房的钥匙。key money = premium paid when taking over the keys of a flat or office which you are renting 钥匙押金 (b) part of a computer or typewriter which you press with your fingers 按键：there are sixty - four keys on the keyboard 键盘上有 64 个按键。control key = key on a computer which works part of a program 控制键；shift key = key which makes a typewriter or computer move to capital letters 大小字型变换按键 (c) important 重要：key factor 重要因素；key industry 重要工业；key personnel 重要人物；key post 重要岗位；key staff 重要人员。

◇ **keyboard** 1 n. part of a typewriter or computer with keys which are pressed to make a letter or figure 键盘；qwerty keyboard = English language keyboard, where the first letters are Q - W - E - R - T - Y 以字母 Q - W - E - R - T - Y 为首的英语键盘；The computer has a normal qwerty keyboard. 这个计算机有个普通的 qwerty 键盘。2 v. to press the keys on a keyboard to type something 用键盘打字：He is keyboarding our address list. 他正操作键盘打出我们的通讯录。

◇ **keyboarder** n. person who types information into a computer 键盘操作人员

◇ **keyboarding** n. act of typing on a keyboard 键盘操作：Keyboarding costs have risen sharply. 键盘操作费用陡涨。NOTE: no plural

◇ **keypad** n. small keyboard 小型键盘：numeric keypad = part of a computer keyboard which is a programmable set of numbered keys 数字键

**kg** = KILOGRAM 公斤

**kickback** n. illegal commission paid to someone（especially a government official）who helps a business deal 非法回扣或酬金

**killing** n. informal huge profit 巨额利润：He made a killing on the stock market. 他在证券市场中发了大财。

**kilo or kilogram** n. measure of weight（= one thousand grams）公斤

◇ **kilobyte** n. unit of storage in a computer（= 1,024 bytes）千字节（计算机存储单位）

◇ **kilometre or US kilometer** n. measure of length（= one thousand metres）公里：The car does fifteen kilometres to the litre. = The car uses a litre of petrol to travel fifteen kilometres. 这辆车 1 公升油能行驶 15 公里。

**kind** n. sort or type 种类：The printer produces two kinds of printout. 这台打印机能打印输出两种结果。Our drinks machine has three kinds of soups. 我们的饮料机能制成三种汤汁。payment in kind = payment made by giving goods or food, but not money 以实物支付。

**kiosk** n. small wooden shelter, for selling goods out of doors 售货亭：a newspaper kiosk 卖报亭；telephone kiosk = shelter with a public telephone in it 电话亭。

**kite** n. (a) to fly a kite = to put forward a proposal to try to interest people 试探（舆论）：kite flier = person who tries to impress by putting forward a proposal（舆论）试探者；kite - flying = trying to impress by putting forward grand plans（舆论）试探 (b) GB kite

mark = mark on goods to show they
meetofficial standards(英)规格说明的
标志。

**kitty** n. money which has been collected
by a group of people to be used later
(such as for an office party)(某团体为
做某事)所集之资金;共同的储金。

**km** = KILOMETRE 公里。

**knock** v. (a) to hit something 撞击;
敲: He knocked on the door and went
in. 他敲门并走进去。She knocked her
head on the filing cabinet. 她把头撞在了
档案柜上。(b) to knock the competition
= to hit competing firms hard by vigorous selling 沉重地打击竞争对手;
knocking copy = advertising material
which criticizes competing products. 批
评竞争对方产品的宣传材料 。

◇ **knock down** v. to knock something
down to a bidder = to sell something at
an auction (拍卖中)击锤成交: The
stock was knocked down to him for
£10,000. 存货以 10,000 英磅拍卖给
他。

◇ **knockdown** n. knockdown prices
= very low prices 很低价格: He sold
me the car at a knockdown price. 他以很
低价格把汽车卖给了我。

◇ **knock off** v. (a) to stop work 停工
(b) to reduce a price by an amount 削
价: He knocked £10 off the price for
cash. 为收取现金他削价 10 英磅。

◇ **knock - on effect** n. effect which
an action will have on other situations 连
锁影响: The strike by customs officers
has had a knock - on effect on car production by slowing down exports of cars.
海关人员的罢工使汽车出口速度减慢,
对于汽车生产产生了连带影响。

**know** v. (a) to learn or to have information about something 知道: I do not
know how a computer works. 我不知道
计算机是怎样工作的。Does he know
how long it takes to get to the airport?

他知道到机场要用多长时间吗? The
managing director's secretary does not
know where he is. 总经理的秘书不知道
他在哪里。(b) to have met someone 认
识; Do you know Mr Jones, our new
sales director? 你认识我们的新销售董
事琼斯先生吗? He knows the African
market very well. 他很熟悉美国市场。
NOTE: knowing - known

◇ **know - how** n. knowledge about
how something works or how something
is made 专门技术;决窍: electronic
know - how 电子技术; to acquire computer know - how 获得计算机技术;决
窍
NOTE: no plural

◇ **knowledge** n. what is known 知道;
知识: He had no knowledge of the
contract. = He did not know that the
contract existed. 他不知道这项合同。
NOTE: no plural

# Ll

l = LITRE(英)公升

**label** 1 n. (a) piece of paper or card attached to something to show its price or
an address or instructions for use 标记;
标签: gummed label = label which you
wet to make it stick on the item 自带胶
性的标签; self - sticking label = sticky
label, ready to stick on an item 自带粘
胶的标签; tie - on label = label with a
piece of string attached so that it can be
tied on to an item 带有细绳子的标签
(b) address label = label with an address on it 地址标签; price label = label
showing a price 价格标签; quality label
= label which states the quality of some-

thing 说明物品质量的标签 (c) own labelgoods = goods specially produced for a store with the store's name on them 为(某店特制的商品)贴有自用标签的商品 2 v. to attach a label to something 给……贴标签: incorrectly labelled parcel = parcel with the wrong information on the label 错贴标签的包裹

NOTE: labelling – labelled but US labeling – labeled

◇ **labelling** n. putting a label on something 贴标签: labelling department = section of a factory where labels are attached to the product 贴标签的部门

NOTE: no plural

**laboratory** n. place where scientific research is carried out 实验室; The product was developed in the company's laboratories. 这个产品是在公司实验室中所制成的。All products are tested in our own laboratories. 所有产品都是在我们自己的实验室检验。

**labour** or US labor n. (a) heavy work (繁重的)劳动: manual labour = work done by hand 体力劳动; to charge for materials and labour = to charge for both the materials used in a job and also the hours of work involved 索取材料费和劳动费; labour costs or labour charges = cost of the workers employed to make a product ( not including materials or overheads)劳动成本或劳动费用; indirect labour costs = cost of wages of workers who are not directly involved in making the product (such as secretaries, cleaners) 间接劳动成本; Labour is charged at £5 an hour. = Each hour of work costs £5. 每小时的劳动费用是5英磅。(b) workers or the workforce 工人;劳动力: casual labour = workers who are hired for a short period 短工; cheap labour = workers who do not earn much money 廉价劳力; local labour = workers recruited near a factory, not brought in from somewhere else 本地工

人; organized labour = workers who are members of trade unions 加入工会的工人; skilled labour = workers who have special knowledge or qualifications 技术工人; labour force = all workers 劳动力; The management has made an increased offer to the labour force. 资方已提高了对工人的报价。We are setting up a factory in the Far East because of the cheap labour force available. 我们正在远东建立工厂,因为那里提供廉价劳动力。labour market = number of workers who are available for work 劳动力市场; 25,000 young people have left school and have come on to the labour market. = 25,000 people have left school and become available for work. 25,000 名年轻人已离校并进入劳动力市场。labour shortage or shortage of labour = situation where there are not enough workers to fill jobs 劳动力短缺; labour – intensive industry = industry which needs large numbers of workers or where labour costs are high in relation to turnover 劳动密集的工业。(c) labour disputes = arguments between management and workers 劳资争端; labour laws or labour legislation = laws relating to the employment of workers 劳动法; labour relations = relations between management and workers 劳资关系; US labor union = organization which represents workers who are its members in discussions about wages and conditions of work with management(美国)工会 (d) International Labour Organization = section of the United Nations which tries to improve working conditions and workers' pay in member countries 国际劳工组织

NOTE: no plural

◇ **labourer** n. person who does heavy work(体力)劳动者: agricultural labourer = person who does heavy work on a farm 农业劳动者; casual labourer =

worker who can be hired for a short peri-od临时工; manual labourer = person who does heavy work with his hands 体力劳动者。

◇ **labour – saving** a. which saves you doing hard work 节约劳动的: a labour – saving device 节省劳力的设备。

**lack** 1 n. not having enough 短缺: lack of data or lack of information = not having enough information 数据或情报短缺; The decision has been put back for lack of up – to – date information. 因为缺少最新情报,决策被推迟执行。lack of funds = not enough money 资金短缺; The project was cancelled because of lack of funds. 因资金短缺该项目被取消。NOTE: no plural 2 v. not to have enough of something 短缺; The company lacks capital. 公司缺乏资金。The sales staff lack motivation. = The sales staff are not motivated enough. 销售人员缺乏动力或积极性。

**ladder** n. series of steps made of wood or metal which can be moved about, and which you can climb 梯子: You will need a ladder to look into the machine. 你需要上梯子去查看机器。promotion ladder = series of steps by which people can be promoted 晋升阶梯; By being appointed sales manager, he moved several steps up the promotion ladder. 他被任命为销售经理,在晋升阶梯上一下连跳了几级。

**laden** a. loaded 满载的: fully – laden ship = ship with a full cargo 满载货物的船只; ship laden in bulk = ship which has a loose cargo ( such as corn ) which is not packed in containers 满载散装货物的船只

**lading** n. loading or putting goods on a ship 装货: bill of lading = list of goods being shipped, which the transporter gives to the person sending the goods to show that they have been loaded 提货单 NOTE: no plural

**laissez – faire economy** n. economy where the government does not interfere because it believes it is right to let the e-conomy run itself 自由放任经济不干预经济(政府对经济活动采取不干预,任其自由发展的方针)。

**lame** a. walking badly because of a bad leg 跛腿的;瘸的

◇ **lame duck** n. company which is in financial difficulties 陷于财政困境的企业; The government has refused to help lame duck companies. 政府拒绝援助陷入财政困境的企业。

**land** 1 n. area of earth 土地: land agent = person who runs a farm or a large area of land for someone 地产管理人; GB land register = register of land, showing who owns it and what buildings are on it (英)土地登记; land registration = system of registering land and its owners 地籍登记体制; land registry = government office where land is registered 地籍登记处(部门) land taxes = taxes on the amount of land someone owns 地税;田赋 2 v. (a) to put goods or passengers on to land after a voyage by sea or by air 着陆;卸货: to land goods at a port 港口卸货; to land passengers at an airport 将旅客降落在机场; landed costs = costs of goods which have been delivered to a port, unloaded and passed through customs 卸岸成本 (b) to come down to earth after a flight 着陆; The plane landed ten minutes late. 飞机推迟十分钟着陆。

◇ **landing** n. landing card = card given to passengers who have passed customs and can land from a ship or an aircraft 登陆卡; landing charges = payment for putting goods on land and the customs duties 卸货费用; landing order = permit which allows goods to be unloaded into a bonded warehouse without payingcustoms duty 卸货通知；(海关)起货令。

◇ **landlady** n. woman who owns a property which she lets 出租房地产的女主人；女房东

◇ **landlord** n. person or company which owns a property which is let 出租房地产拥有者；地主；男房东：ground landlord = person or company which owns the freehold of a property which is then let and sublet 建筑物地产主；Our ground landlord is an insurance company. 我们的建筑物地产主是一家保险公司。

◇ **landowner** n. person who owns large areas of land 地主；土地所有者

**language** n. words spoken or written by people in a certain country 语言：The managing director conducted the negotiations in three languages. 总经理用三种语言进行谈判。programming language = system of signs, letters and words used to instruct a computer 机算机程序设计语言；What language does the program run on? 这个程序使用什么(计算机设计)语言？

**lapse** 1 n. a lapse of time = a period of time which has passed 过去的一段时间 2 v. to stop being valid or to stop being active 失效；失去活力：The guarantee has lapsed. 保证书已失效了。to let an offer lapse = to allow time to pass so that an offer is no longer valid 使出价过时失效

**large** a. very big or important 很大的；很重要的：Our company is one of the largest suppliers of computers to the government. 我们公司是政府最大的计算机供应商之一。He is our largest customer. 他是我们最大的客户。Why has she got an office which is larger than mine? 为什么她得到的办公室比我的大？

◇ **largely** ad. mainly or mostly 主要地；大部分：our sales are largely in the home market. 我们的销售大部分是在国内市场。They have largely pulled out of the American market. 他们已几乎全部从美国市场中撤出。

◇ **large－scale** a. working in a large way, with large numbers of people or large amounts of money involved 大规模的：large－scale investment in new technology 对新技术大规模投资；large－scale redundancies in the construction industry 建筑工业中大量裁员或解雇

**last** 1 a. & ad. (a) coming at the end of a series 最终；Out of a queue of twenty people, I was served last. 我是排队的20人中最后被接待的人。This is our last board meeting before we move to our new offices；这是我们搬进新办公室前的最后一次董事会会议。We finished the last items in the order just two days before the promised delivery date. 正好在许诺交货期的前两天我们完成了订货单上最后所列商品。last quarter = period of three months to the end of the financial year (财政年度的) 第四季度 (b) most recent or most recently 最近：Where is the last batch of orders? 最近的那批订单在哪里？The last ten orders were only for small quantities 最近的10张订单都是小批量订货。last week or last month or last year = the week or month or year before this one 上星期、上月或去年；Last week's sales were the best we have ever had. 上星期的销售是我们有史以来最好的。The sales managers have been asked to report on last month's drop in unit sales. 要求销售经理对上月的单位销售量的下降作出报告。Last year's accounts have to be ready by the AGM. 去年的帐目必须在年度股东大会之前准备好。(c) the week or month or year before last = the week or month or year before the one before this 前个星期、前个月或前年；

Last year's figures were bad, but they were an improvement on those of the year before last. 去年的收益不好,但比起前年来有改善。2 v. to go on or to continue 继续: The boom started in the 1970s and lasted until the early 1980s. 繁荣期始于 20 世纪 70 年代,并一直持续到 80 年代早期。The discussions over redundancies lasted all day. 对裁员问题的讨论持续了一整天。

◇ **last in first out** n. (a) redundancy policy, where the people who have been most recently appointed are the first to be made redundant 后进者先出(企业精简人员时,最晚到企业就职的人最先受到裁减的裁员政策) (b) accounting method where stock is valued at the price of the latest purchases 后进先出计价法(库存按最近购买价格作价的方法)

**late** 1 a. (a) after the time stated or agreed 迟: We apologize for the late arrival of the plane from Amsterdam. 我们很抱歉,来自阿姆斯特丹的飞机晚点了。There is a penalty for late delivery. = If delivery is later than the agreed date, the supplier has to pay a fine. 延期交货要罚款。(b) at the end of a period of time 末期的: latest date for signature of the contract = the last acceptable date for signing the contract 合同签定的最后日期 (c) latest = most recent 最新的: He always drives the latest model of car. 他总是驾驶最新式的汽车。Here are the latest sales figures 这里是最新销售数字。2 ad. after the time stated or agreed 误时: The shipment was landed late; 卸货误期了。The plane was two hours late 飞机晚点两个小时。

◇ **late - night** a. happening late at night 深夜的; He had a late - night meeting at the airport. 他在飞机场参加了一个深夜召开的会议。Their late - night negotiations ended in an agreement which was signed at 3 a.m. 他们深夜举行的谈判以凌晨 3 时签定的协议而宣

告结束。

**launch** 1 v. to put a new product on the market (usually spending money on advertising it) 投放市场: They launched their new car model at the motor show. 在汽车博览会上,他们推出了新型汽车。The company is spending thousands of pounds to launch a new brand of soap. 他们花费几千英磅推出一种新型肥皂。2 n. act of putting a new product on the market 新产品的投放市场;推出新产品: The launch of the new model has been put back three months. 新型产品投放市场推迟了三个月。The company is geared up for the launch of the new brand of soap。公司已准备好将新型肥皂投放市场。The management has decided on a September launch date. 管理部门决定将新产品上市日期定在九月份的某一天。

◇ **launching** n. act of putting a new product on the market 投放市场: launching costs = costs of publicity for a new product 投放市场费用; launching date = date when a new product is officially shown to the public for the first time 新产品首次投放市场日期; launching party = party held to advertise the launching of a new product 产品投放市场而进行的聚会
NOTE: no plural

**launder** v; to pass illegal profits or money which has not been taxed, etc. into the normal banking system 非法转移(将非法利润或逃税资金等划入正常的银行系统): to launder money through an offshore bank 通过境外银行将非法资金划放银行系统或通过境外银行"洗钱"。

**law** n. (a) laws = rules by which a country is governed and the activities of people and organizations controlled 法律;法条: labour laws = laws concerning the employment of workers 劳动法;

(b) law = all the laws of a country taken together 法; civil law = laws relating to arguments between individuals and the rights of individuals 民法; commercial law = laws regarding business 商法; 商事法; company law = laws which refer to the way companies work 公司法; contract law or the law of contract = laws relating to private agreements 合同法; copyright law = laws concerning the protection of copyright 版权法; criminal law = laws relating to crime 刑法; international law = laws referring to the way countries deal with each other 国际法; maritime law or the law of the sea = laws referring to ships, ports, etc. 海商法; law courts = place where a judge listens to cases and decides who is right legally 法院; to take someone to law = to tell someone to appear in court to settle an argument 对某人进行起拆; inside the law or within the law = obeying the laws of a country 合法; against or outside the law = not according to the laws of a country 违法; The company is operating outside the law. 这个公司正违法经营。 to break the law = to do something which is not allowed by law 犯法; He is breaking the law by selling goods on Sunday. 他于星期日销售商品是违法的。 You will be breaking the law if you try to take that computer out of the country without an export licence. 假若你在没有出口许可证的情况下试图把那台计算机带到国外, 你会犯法的。 (c) general rule 规律; law of supply and demand = general rule that the amount of a product which is available is related to the needs of the possible customers 商品供求规律; law of diminishing returns = general rule that as more factors of production (land, labour and capital) are added to the existing factors, so the amount they produce is proportionately smaller 报酬递减规律 (当生产力达到

一定水平后, 生产要素投入的增加不能导致产品产量的同比例增长的规律)

NOTE: no plural for (b)

◇ **lawful** a. acting within the law 合法的: lawful practice = action which is permitted by the law 合法行为; lawful trade = trade which is allowed by law 合法贸易

◇ **lawfully** ad. acting within the law 合法地

◇ **lawsuit** n. case brought to a court 诉讼案件; to bring a lawsuit against someone = to tell someone to appear in court to settle an argument 对某人提起诉讼; to defend a lawsuit = to appear in court to state your case 出庭辩护

◇ **lawyer** n. person who has studied law and can act for people on legal business 律师: commercial lawyer or company lawyer = person who specializes in company law or who advises companies on legal problems 商事法律师或公司律师; international lawyer = person who specializes in international law 国际法律师; maritime lawyer = person who specializes in laws concerning ships 海事法律师

**lay** v. to put 放置; to lay an embargo on trade with a country = to forbid trade with a country 规定与一个国家禁止贸易往来。

NOTE: laying – laid

◇ **lay off** v. (a) to lay off workers = to dismiss workers for a time (until more work is available) 临时解雇工人: The factory laid off half its workers because of lack of orders. 因为缺少订货, 工厂临时解雇了一半工人。 (b) to lay off risks = to protect oneself against risk in one investment by making other investments 分散风险 (投资者通过多方投资以分散因单方投资所承受的风险)

◇ **lay – off** n. action of dismissing a worker for a time 临时解雇; The recession has caused hundreds of lay-offs in thecar industry. 经济衰退已经造成汽车行业中几百人临时解雇。

◇ **lay out** v. to spend money 花钱：We had to lay out half our cash budget on equipping the new factory. 我们得花去现金预算的一半用于新工厂的装备。

◇ **layout** n. arrangement of the inside of a building 布局：They have altered the layout of the offices. 他们改变了办公室内的布局。

◇ **lay up** v. to stop using a ship because there is no work 闲置（船只）；Half the shipping fleet is laid up by the recession. 由于经济衰退，船队中一半的船只被闲置。

**lazy** a. (person) who does not want to work 懒惰的：She is too lazy to do any overtime. 她太懒从不加班。He is so lazy he does not even send in his expense claims on time. 他很懒，甚至从不及时提交费用要求。

**lb** = pound 磅

**L/C** = LETTER OF CREDIT 信用证

**lead** v. (a) to be the first or to be in front 领先：The company leads the market in cheap computers. 在经销廉价计算机方面，这个公司在市场上处于领先地位。(b) to be the main person in a group 率领：She will lead the trade mission to Nigeria. 她将率领贸易代表团赴尼日利亚。The tour of American factories will be led by the minister. 部长将率团巡视美国各工厂。

NOTE: leading - led

◇ **leader** n. (a) person who manages or directs others 领导人：the leader of the construction workers' union or the construction workers' leader 建筑工人工会的领导人；She is the leader of the trade mission to Nigeria. 她是赴尼日利亚访问的贸易代表团团长。The minister was the leader of the party of industrialists on a tour of American factories.

部长是参观美国工厂工业家团体的团长。(b) product which sells best 最畅销产品：a market leader = product which sells most in a market or company which has the largest share of a market 市场上销路最好产品或占最大市场份额的公司；loss-leader = article which is sold very cheaply to attract customers (为吸引顾客而廉价售销商品)。(c) important share or share which is often bought or sold on the Stock Exchange 重要的股票(常指在证券交易所进行买卖的股票)

◇ **leading** a. most important 最重要的；主要的：Leading industrialists feel the end of the recession is near. 主要的工业家们认为经济衰退即将结束。Leading shares rose on the Stock Exchange. 证券交易所的主要股票涨价。leading shareholders in the company forced a change in management policy. 公司的主要股东迫使管理部门改变方针。They are the leading company in the field. 他们是这个领域中最重要的公司。

◇ **lead time** n. time between deciding to place an order and receiving the product 订货至交货时间：The lead time on this item is more than six weeks. 这种货物的订货至交货间隔期为六个多星期。

◇ **lead (up) to** v. to be the cause of 导致；为…做准备：The discussions led to a big argument between the management and the union. 这场讨论导致了一场资方与工会之间的大辩论。We received a series of approaches leading up to the takeover bid. 我们收到了为合并递价做准备的一系列方法。

**leaflet** n. sheet of paper giving information, used to advertise something 传单：to mail leaflets or to hand out leaflets describing services 邮寄或散发有关服务说明的传单；They made a leaflet mailing to 20,000 addresses. 他向

二万处寄这种宣传传单。

**leak** v. to pass on a secret 泄露: Information on the contract was leaked to the press. 有关合同的消息泄露给新闻界。They discovered the managing director was leaking information to a rival company. 他们发现总经理正向竞争的公司泄露信息。

◇ **leakage** n. amount of goods lost in storage (by going bad or by being stolen or by escaping from the container)漏损；漏耗；(储存中因变质偷盗或散露)

**leap – frogging** a. leap – frogging pay demands = pay demands where each section of workers asks for higher pay to do better than another section, which then asks for further increases in turn 竞相提高工资要求(工人们在工作中互相攀比, 以求取得高于其它部门工人的报酬)

**lease** 1 n. (a) written contract for letting or renting of a building or a piece of land or a piece of equipment for a period against payment of a fee 租约(出租人向承租人出租建筑物、土地或设备并收取租金作为报酬的书面合同)；long lease or short lease = lease which runs for fifty years or more or for up to two or three years 长期租赁办公楼；to take an office building on a long lease 长期租约或短期租约；We have a short lease on our current premises. 我们目前用的房屋是以短期租约租下的。to rent office space on a twenty – year lease 以 20 年租约租下的办公场地；full repairing lease = lease where the tenant has to pay for all repairs to the property)租户支付全部修理费用的租约；headlease = lease from the freeholder to a tenant 由世袭地产保有人向租户进行的租赁；sublease or underlease = lease from a tenant to another tenant. 从一个承租人到另一个承租人的租约；The lease expires or runs out in 1989. = The lease

comes to an end in 1989. 这个租约于 1989 年到期。on expiration of the lease = When the lease comes to an end. 当租约终止时 (b) to hold an oil lease in the North Sea = to have a lease on a section of the North Sea to explore for oil 持有在北海地区勘探石油的租约 2 v. (a) to let or rent offices or land or machinery for a period 出租或办公室或土地机械: to lease offices to small firms 把办公室租给了小公司；to lease equipment 出租设备 (b) to use an office or land or machinery for a time and pay a fee 租用办公室或土地或机械 to lease an office from an insurance company 租用保险公司的办公室；All our company cars are leased. 我们公司所有的汽车都是租来的。

◇ **lease back** v. to sell a property or machinery to a company and then take it back on a lease 回租(把财产或机械等出售给某公司,然后再将出售物租回)；They sold the office building to raise cash, and then leased it back for twenty – five years. 他们将办公楼售出以筹资,然后将其回租 25 年。

◇ **lease – back** n. arrangement where property is sold and then taken back on a lease 回租: They sold the office building and then took it back under a lease – back arrangement. 他们出售了办公楼,然后以回租方式将其租回。

◇ **leasehold** n. & a. holding property on a lease 租借物；租赁的: leasehold property 租借房地产；The company has some valuable leaseholds. 这个公司有些有价值的租借物。to buy a property leasehold 购买租赁的房地产

◇ **leaseholder** n. person who holds a property on a lease 租借人；承租人

◇ **leasing** n. which leases or working under a lease 租借；租赁业务: The company has branched out into car leasing. 这个公司开拓出汽车租赁业务。an e-

quipment – leasing company 设备租赁公司; to run a copier under a leasing arrangement 以租借协议方式经营复印机
NOTE: no plural see also LESSEE

**leave** 1 n. permission to be away from work 假期: six weeks' annual leave = six weeks' holiday each year 每年六个星期假期; leave of absence = being allowed to be away from work 获准的假; maternity leave = permission given to a woman to be away from work to have a baby 产假; sick leave = period when a worker is away from work because of illness 病假; to go on leave or to be on leave = to be away from work 度假; She is away on sick leave or on maternity leave. 她在休病假或休产假。
NOTE: no plural
2 v. (a) to go away from 离开; He left his office early to go to the meeting. 他提前离开办公室去开会了。The next plane leaves at 10.20. 下一班飞机于 10 时 20 分起飞。(b) to resign 辞职; He left his job and bought a farm. 他辞去工作买了一个农场。
NOTE: leaving – left

◇ **leave out** v. not to include 遗漏;略去: She left out the date on the letter. 她漏掉了写信日期。The contract leaves out all details of marketing arrangements. 这个合同略去了销售安排的所有细节。

**ledger** n. book in which accounts are written 帐目: bought ledger or purchase ledger = book in which expenditure is noted 购进货分类帐; bought ledger clerk or sales ledger clerk = office worker who deals with the bought ledger or the sales ledger 购货分类帐记帐员或销售分类帐记帐员; nominal ledger = book which records a company's income and expenditure in general 记载收入和支出的总帐; payroll ledger = list of staff and their salaries 工资帐; sales ledger = book in which sales are noted 销售分类帐

**left** a. on the side of the body which usually has the weaker hand or not right 左边的: The numbers run down the left side of the page. 数字排列在该页的左边。Put the debits in the left column. 把借方记入左栏内。see also LEAVE

◇ **left – hand** a. belonging to the left side 左边的;左手边的: The debits are in the left – hand column in the accounts. 借方记在帐户的左边栏里。He keeps the personnel files in the left – hand drawer of his desk. 他把个人档案存放在书桌的左边抽屉里。

◇ **left luggage office** n. room where suitcases can be left while passengers are waiting for a plane or train 行李寄存处。

**legacy** n. property given by someone to someone else at his death 遗产

**legal** a. (a) according to the law or allowed by the law 合法: The company's action was completely legal. 公司的行为完全合法。(b) referring to the law 法律的; to take legal action = to sue someone or to take someone to court 起诉; to take legal advice = to ask a lawyer to advise about a legal problem 进行法律咨询; legal adviser = person who advises clients about the law 法律顾问;律师; GB legal aid = government scheme where someone who has little money can have his legal expenses paid for him(英) 法律援助; legal claim = statement that someone owns something legally 在法律权利要求; He has no legal claim to the property. 他对此项财产不拥有合法要求权。legal costs or legal charges or legal expenses = money spent on fees to lawyers 诉讼费用; legal currency = money which is legally used in a country 法定货币; legal department or legal section = section of a company dealing with legal matters 公司处理法律事务的部门; legal expert = person who knows a lot about the law 法律专家; legal holiday = day when banks and other businesses are closed 公休日; 法定节假日; legal tender = coins or notes which can be legally used to pay a debt (small denominations cannot be used to pay large debts) 合法货币。

◇ **legality** n. being allowed by law 合法性; There is doubt about the legality of the company's action in dismissing him. 对于公司解雇他的行为的合法性存在着怀疑。

◇ **legalize** v. to make something legal 合法化

◇ **legalization** n. making something legal 合法化

◇ **legally** adv. according to the law 依法地; 从法律方面: The contract is legally binding. = According to the law, the contract has to be obeyed. 这个合同在法律上有拘束力。The directors are legally responsible = the law says that the directors are responsible. 这个董事是负有法律责任的。

**legatee** n. person who receives property from someone who has died 财产继承人。

**legislation** n. laws 法律; 立法: labour legislation = laws concerning the employment of workers 劳动立法。

NOTE: no plural

**lend** v. to allow someone to use something for a period 借出; 借给: to lend something to someone or to lend someone something 将某物借给某人或借给某人某物; He lent the company money or he lent money to the company. 他借给公司钱或他把钱借给了公司。to lend money against security 以保证金或抵押而借钱 (给别人); The bank lent him £50,000 to start his business. 银行借给他 60,000 英磅去开业。

NOTE: lending - lent

◇ **lender** n. person who lends money

贷款人; 出借者: lender of the last resort = central bank which lends money to commercial banks 最后借贷银行 (中央银行)

◇ **lending** n. act of letting someone use money for a time 借出; 放款: lending limit = limit on the amount of money a bank can lend 贷款限额

NOTE: no plural

**length** n. (a) measurement of how long something is 长度: The boardroom table is twelve feet in length. 董事会办公室中桌子的长度是 12 英尺。Inches and centimetres are measurements of length. 英寸和厘米是长度计量单位。(b) to go to great lengths to get something = to do anything (even commit a crime) to get something 不遗余力地去做某事: They went to considerable lengths to keep the turnover secret. 他们竭力将营业额保密。

**less** 1 a. smaller than or of a smaller size or of a smaller value 小于; 比较小的; 比较少的: We do not grant credit for sums of less than £100. 我们不给予金额少于 100 英磅的信贷。He sold it for less than he had paid for it. 他以低于进价的价格将它卖掉。2 prep. minus or with a sum removed 扣除; purchase price less 15% discount 购买价减去 15% 折扣; interest less service charges 利息减去服务费用。

**lessee** n. person who has a lease or who pays money for a property he leases 承租人。

◇ **lessor** n. person who grants a lease on a property 出租人。

**let** 1 v. to lend a house or an office or a farm to someone for a payment 出租 (房屋、地产等以获取租金): to let an office = to allow someone to use an office for a time in return for payment of rent 租出办公室; offices to let = offices which are available to be leased by companies 待

出租的办公室。

NOTE: letting – let

2 n. period of the lease of a property 租借期: They took the office on a short let. 他们短期租借了办公室。

◇ **let – out clause** n. clause which allows someone to avoid doing something in a contract 放宽条款(允许某方不执行合同中某些规定的条款): He added a let – out clause to the effect that the payments would be revised if the exchange rate fell by more than 5%. 他补充了一个放宽条款,大意是如果兑换率降低5%以上,付款额应做修改。

**letter** n. (a) piece of writing sent from one person or company to another to give information 信件: business letter = letter which deals with business matters 商务信件; circular letter = letter sent to many people 通知;通函; covering letter = letter sent with documents to say why they are being sent 详函;伴书; follow – up letter = letter sent to someone after a previous letter or after a visit 后续信件; private letter = letter which deals with personal matters 私人信件; standard letter = letter which is sent without change to various correspondents 标准信函 (b) letter of acknowledgement = letter which says that something has been received 收悉通知书; letters of administration = letter given by a court to allow someone to deal with the estate of someone who has died 财产管理委任书: letter of allotment or allotment letter = letter which tells someone how many shares in a new company he has been allotted 派股通知书; letter of application = letter in which someone applies for a job 工作申请书; letter of appointment = letter in which someone is appointed to a job 委任书; letter of comfort = letter supporting someone who is trying to get a loan 安慰函(表明对某人的贷款承担义务的信); letter of complaint = letter in which someone complains 投诉信; letter of credit = letter from a bank allowing someone credit and promising to repay at a later date 信用证; letter of indemnity = letter promising payment of compensation for a loss 赔偿保证书 letter of intent = letter which states what a company intends to do if something happens 意向书; letters patent = official document which gives someone the exclusive right to make and sell something which he has invented 专利证书 letter of reference = letter in which an employer recommends someone for a new job 推荐信 (c) air letter = special thin blue paper which when folded can be sent by air without an envelope 航空邮笺; airmail letter = letter sent by air 航空信; express letter = letter sent very fast 快信; registered letter = letter which is noted by the post office before it is sent, so that compensation can be claimed if it is lost 挂号信 (d) to acknowledge receipt by letter = to write a letter to say that something has been received 写信证实收悉 (e) written or printed sign (such as A, B, C, etc.)字母; Write your name and address in block letters or in capital letters. 用印刷体或大写字母写下你的名字和地址。

◇ **letterhead** n. name and address of a company printed at the top of a piece of notepaper 信头(印刷在信纸上方的公司名称、地址)

**letting** n. letting agency = agency which deals in property to let 出租代理机构; furnished lettings = furnished property to let 带有家具的房地产出租。

**level** 1 n. position where high is large and low is small 水平: low level of productivity or low productivity levels 低生产水平; to raise the level of employee benefits 提高雇员福利水平; to lower the level of borrowings 降低借贷水平; high level of investment = large amount of money invested 高水平投资；a deci-sontaken at the highest level = decision taken by the most important person or group 最高级决策；low‑level = not very important 低水平；a low‑level delegation 低级代表团；high‑level = very important 高级别；a high‑level meeting or decision 高级会议或决策；decisions taken at managerial level = de-cisions taken by managers 经理级的决策；manning levels or staffing levels = number of people required in each de-partment of a company to do the work efficiently 职工配备水准(为有效工作，企业的各部门职工所需的人数 2 v. to level off or to level out = to stop rising or falling 使稳停在一个水平上；Profits have levelled off over the last few years; 过去的几年中利润额没有什么变化。Prices are levelling out. 物价平稳。NOTE: levelling‑levelled but US lev-eling‑leveled

**leverage** n. (a) influence which you can use to achieve an aim 影响力：He has no leverage over the chairman. 他对于董事长没有什么影响力。(b) relation be-tween a company's capital borrowed at a fixed interest and the value of its ordi-nary shares 杠杆作用(企业中以固定利息借贷资金与企业自有普通股资金的关系) (c) borrowing money at fixed in-terest which is then used to produce more money than the interest paid 举债经营；杠杆效果(企业利用固定利息借贷资金增加企业利润高于所付利息)
NOTE: no plural

◇ **leveraged buyout** n. buying all the shares in a company by borrowing money against the security of the shares to be bought 负债买下一个公司的所有股票

**levy** 1 n. money which is demanded and collected by the government 政府税收：capital levy = tax on the value of a person's property and possessions 个人资产税；import levy = tax on imports,

especially in the EEC a tax on imports of farm produce from outside the EEC 进口税(特别是欧共体对来自其外部的进口农产品的税收)；levies on luxury items = taxes on luxury items 奢侈品税；training levy = tax to be paid by compa-nies to fund the government's training schemes 培训税(公司上交的资助政府培训计划) 2 v. to demand payment of a tax or an extra payment and to collect it 征税；征集；The government has decid-ed to levy a tax on imported cars. 政府决定对进口汽车征税。to levy a duty on the import of luxury items 对奢侈品进口征税；to levy members for a new club house = to ask members of the club to pay for the new building 向俱乐部成员收取俱乐部新房屋费。

**liability** n. (a) being legally responsible for damage or loss, etc. 责任；义务：to accept liability for something = to agree that you are responsible for something 承担某事的责任；to refuse liability for something = to refuse to agree that you are responsible for something 拒绝为某事承担责任；contractual liability = le-gal responsibility for something as stated in a contract 契约责任；合同义务；employers' liability insurance = insur-ance to cover accidents which may hap-pen at work, and for which the company may be responsible 雇主责任保险；lim-ited liability = situation where someone's liability for debt is limited by law 有限责任(债务的偿还责任是受法律限制的)；limited liability company = compa-ny where a shareholder is responsible for repaying the company's debts only to the face value of the shares he owns 有限责任公司(公司股东偿付公司债务时只限于其拥有的公司股票票面额) (b) lia-bilities = debts of a business(企业)债务；负债：The balance sheet shows the company's assets and liabilities. 资产负债表表明了企业的资产和负债。cur-

rent liabilities = debts which a company shouldpay within the next accounting period 短期债务; long - term liabilities = debts which are not due to be paid for some time 长期债务; He was not able to meet his liabilities . = He could not pay his debts. 他无力偿还债务. to discharge one's liabilities in full = to pay everything which you owe 清偿全部债务
NOTE: no plural for (a)

◇ **liable** a. (a) liable for = legally responsible for 负有责任的; The customer is liable for breakages. 顾客对于破损是有责任的。The chairman was personally liable for the company's debts. 董事长对于公司的负债是负有个人责任。(b) liable to = which is officially due to be paid 应支付的; goods which are liable to stamp duty 应支付印花税的商品。

**libel** 1 n. untrue written statement which damages someone's character 文字诽谤; action for libel or libel action = case in a law court where someone says that another person has written a libel 对文字诽谤提起诉讼 2 v. to libel someone = to damage someone's character in writing 用文字对某人进行诽谤
NOTE: libelling - libelled but US libeling - libeled. Compare SLANDER

**licence** or US license n. (a) official document which allows someone to do something 执照;许可证: driving licence = document which allows someone to drive a car or a truck, etc. 驾驶证; Applicants should hold a valid driving licence. 申请者应持有有效的驾驶证. import licence or export licence allow goods to be exported or imported 进口许可证或出口许可证; liquor licence = government document allowing someone to sell alcohol 售酒许可证; off licence = licence to sell alcohol to be drunk away from the place where it is bought; shop which sells alcohol for drinking at home 出售外

饮酒的许可证; (b) goods manufactured under licence = goods made with the permission of the owner of the copyright or patent 经过版权或专利所有者允许而制做的特许产品

◇ **license** 1 n. US = LICENCE(美) 许可证;执照 2 v. to give someone official permission to do something 许可: licensed to sell beers, wines and spirits 被批准销售啤酒、果酒和烈性酒; to license a company to manufacture spare parts 批准一个公司生产零部件; She is licensed to run an employment agency. 批准她开一个职业介绍所。

◇ **licensee** n. person who has a licence, especially a licence to sell alcohol or to manufacture something 执照持有者(特别是售酒或制做某物的许可)

◇ **licensing** n. which refers to licences 特许;特许权: a licensing agreement 特许权协议; licensing laws 许可证法; GB licensing hours = hours of the day when alcohol can be sold(英)特许售酒时间。

**lien** n. legal right to hold someone's goods and keep them until a debt has been paid. 留置权(留置债务人财产直至偿清债务的权力)

**lieu** n. in lieu of = instead of 代替: She was given two months' salary in lieu of notice . = She was given the salary and asked to leave immediately. 没有给她离职通知而是给了她两个月的工资让她当即离职。

**life** n. (a) time when a person is alive 一生: for life = for as long as someone is alive 终身; His pension gives him a comfortable income for life. 他的养老金使他终身享有丰厚的收入。life annuity or annuity for life = annual payments made to someone as long as he is alive 终身年金; life assurance or life insurance = insurance which pays a sum of money when someone dies or at a certain date if he is still alive 人寿保险; the life assured or the life insured = the person whose life has been covered by the life assurance 作了人寿保险的人; life expectancy = number of years a person is likely to live 平均寿命; life interest = interest in a property which stops when a person dies 终身财产所有权 (b) period of time something exists 有效期; the life of a loan 贷款期限; during the life of the agreement 协议有效期间; shelf life of a product = length of time during which a product can stay in the shop and still be good to use 产品储存期

◇ **lifeboat** n. boat used to rescue passengers from sinking ships 救生船; lifeboat operation = rescue of a company (especially of a bank) which is in difficulties 挽救工作后进先出对陷入困境的公司,特别是银行的挽救

**LIFO = LAST IN FIRST OUT** 后进先出

**lift** 1 n. machine which takes people or goods from one floor to another in a building 电梯; He took the lift to the 27th floor. 他乘电梯到第 27 层楼。The staff could not get into their office when the lift broke down, 电梯出毛病时职工们不能进入他们的办公室。2 v. to take away or to remove 解除; The government has lifted the ban on imports from Japan. 政府解除了从日本进口的禁令。to lift trade barriers 解除贸易壁垒; The minister has lifted the embargo on the export of computers to East European countries. 部长已解除了计算机出口东欧国家的禁运令。

**light** a. not heavy 轻的; Shares fell back in light trading. = Shares lost value on a day when there was little business done on the Stock Exchange. 证券市场交易冷落股价回落。light industry = industry which makes small products (such as clothes, books, calculators) 轻工业。

**limit** 1 n. point at which something ends or point where you can go no further 限制; to set limits to imports or to impose import limits = to allow only a certain amount of imports 实行进口限制; age limit = top age at which you are allowed to do a job 年龄限制; There is an age limit of thirty – five on the post of buyer. 采购员职务的年龄限制在 35 岁。credit limit = largest amount of money which a customer can borrow 信贷限额; He has exceeded his credit limit . = He has borrowed more money than he is allowed. 他已经超过了信贷限额。lending limit = restriction on the amount of money a bank can lend 银行贷款限额; time limit = maximum time which can be taken to do something 时间限制; They set a time limit for acceptance of the offer. 他们对接受报价做了时间限制。weight limit. = maximum weight 重量限制 2 v. to stop something from going beyond a certain point 限制; The banks have limited their credit. = The banks have allowed their customers only a certain amount of credit. 银行已限制了他们的信贷额。Each agent is limited to twenty – five units = Each agent is allowed only twenty – five units to sell. 每个代理商限于出售 25 件套。

◇ **limitation** n. (a) act of allowing only a certain quantity of something 限制; limitation of liability = making someone liable for only a part of the damage or loss 责任限制(对于损失只承担部分责任); time limitation = amount of time available 时间限制; The contract imposes limitations on the number of cars which can be imported. 合同强行限制汽车的进口数量。(b) statute of limitations = law which allows only a certain amount of time (a few years) for someone to claim damages or property 限制法规;时效法(对某人要求赔偿损失或财产,法律只允许一定时间)

◇ **limited** a. restricted or not open 有限制的; limited market = market which can take only a certain quantity of goods 有限市场; limited liability company = company where a shareholder is responsible for the company's debts only to the face value of his shares 有限责任公司; private limited company = company with a small number of shareholders, whose shares are not traded on the Stock Exchange 股票不公开上市的私营有限公司 Smith and Sons, Ltd 史密斯和桑斯有限公司; Public Limited Company = company whose shares can be bought on the Stock Exchange 股票公开上市有限公司(其股票在证券市场公开交易); Smith and Sons, plc 史密斯和桑斯股票公开上市有限公司。

◇ **limiting** a. which limits 限制的; a limiting clause in a contract 合同中的限制条款; The short holiday season is a limiting factor on the hotel trade. 短暂的休假季节是旅馆业的限制因素。

**line** n. (a) long mark 线条; paper with thin blue lines 带有兰色细线条的纸张; I prefer notepaper without any lines. 我喜欢没有任何直线条的信纸。He drew a thick line across the bottom of the column to show which figure was the total. 他在这栏的底部横划一条粗线表明总数所在。(b) shipping line or airline = large shipping or aircraft company which carries passengers or cargo 航运公司;航空公司; Profits of major airlines have been affected by the rise in fuel prices. 主要的航空公司的利润受到燃料涨价的影响。(c) line of business or line of work = type of business or work 职业;行业; What is his line? 他干哪一行? 或他经营什么? line of product or product line = series of different products which form a group, all made by the same company 产品种类; We do not stock that line. 我们没有那种产品的存货。Computers are not one of our best-selling lines. 计算机不是我们销路最佳产品。They produce an interesting line in garden tools 他们生产一种有趣的园艺(花园)工具。(d) row of letters or figures on a page 文字或数字的行; bottom line = last line in accounts, showing the net profit 底行; The boss is interested only in the bottom line. 老板只对底行感兴趣。to open a line of credit or a credit line = to make credit available to someone 开出信贷限额 (e) assembly line or production line = production system where the product (such as a car) moves slowly through a factory with new sections added to it as it goes along. 工厂中的生产;流水线; He works on the production line or he is a production line worker in the car factory. 他在汽车制造厂生产流水线上工作。(f) line chart or line graph = chart or graph using lines to indicate values 线形图表或线状图; line printer = machine which prints information from a computer one line at a time 行式打印机 (g) line of command or line management or line organization = organization of a business where each manager is responsible for doing what his superior tells him to do(企业中)逐级领导(对上一级领导)负责制;垂直负责制 (h) telephone line = wire along which telephone messages travel 电话线; The line is bad. = It is difficult to hear clearly what someone is saying. 电话线路很差劲。a crossed line = when two telephone conversations get mixed 电话串线; The line is engaged. = The person is already speaking on the phone 电话占线。The chairman is on the other line. = The chairman is speaking on his second telephone. 董事长正在用另一部电话通话。outside line = line from an internal office telephone system to the main telephone exchange 电话外线。

◇ **lined** a. with lines 带线的; He

prefers lined paper for writing notes. 他喜欢用带线的纸做笔记。

◇ **liner** n. large passenger ship 大客轮

**link** v. to join or to attach to something else 连接；联系；to link pensions to inflation 把退休金与通货膨胀相联系；His salary is linked to the cost of living. 他的工资是与生活费用相联系的。to link bonus payments to productivity 奖金额与劳动生产率挂钩。

**liquid** a. liquid assets = cash, or bills which can easily be changed into cash 流动资产或变现资产(现金和应收帐款等容易转变为现金的资产)；to go liquid = to convert as many assets as possible into cash 把资产变现金

◇ **liquidate** v. to liquidate a company = to close a company and sell its assets 清算公司资产；to liquidate a debt = to pay a debt in full 偿清债务；to liquidate stock = to sell stock to raise cash 出售库存筹集资金

◇ **liquidation** n. (a) liquidation of a debt = payment of a debt 偿清债务 (b) closing of a company and selling of its assets 清算(关闭公司并出售其财产)；The company went into liquidation. = The company was closed and its assets sold. 公司被清算。compulsory liquidation = liquidation which is ordered by a court 强制性清算；voluntary liquidation = situation where a company itself decides it must close 企业自愿停业清算。

◇ **liquidator** n. person named to supervise the closing of a company which is in liquidation 清算人(由法院指定的监督清算破产企业的人)

◇ **liquidity** n. having cash or assets which can be changed into cash 流动性(指企业拥有现金和变现资产来偿付其债务的能力)；liquidity crisis = not having enough liquid assets 变现资产危机；头寸危机

**lira** n. money used in Italy 里拉(意大利货币)；The book cost 2,700 lira or L2,700 这本书值 2,700 里拉。

NOTE: lira is usually written L before figures: L2,700

**list** 1 n. (a) several items written one after the other 清单；list of products or product list 产品清单 stock list 存货清单；to add an item to a list 在清单上加上一项；to cross an item off a list 在清单上划去一项；address list or mailing list = list of names and addresses of people and companies 通讯录；black list = list of goods or companies or countries which are banned for trade 黑名单(禁止从事交易的商品、公司和国家的清单)；picking list = list of items in an order, but listed according to where they can be found in the warehouse 货物清单；(按照货物在库房中存放位置编制) (b) catalogue 目录：list price = price as given in a catalogue 价格目录 price list = sheet giving prices of goods for sale 商品价格表；价目表；2 v. (a) to write a series of items one after the other 列出清单；to list products by category 按产品类别列出清单；to list representatives by area 按地区列出推销员的名单；to list products in a catalogue 把产品列在目录中；The catalogue lists twenty - three models of washing machines. 目录中列出了 23 种样式的洗衣机。(b) listed company = company whose shares can be bought or sold on the Stock Exchange (股票)挂牌上市的公司；listed securities = shares which can be bought or sold on the Stock Exchange or shares which appear on the official Stock Exchange list 上市证券；挂牌证券

◇ **listing** n. (a) Stock Exchange listing = being on the official list of shares which can be bought or sold on the Stock Exchange 证券交易所上市股票挂牌；The company is planning to obtain a Stock Exchange listing. 公司想在证券交易所挂牌上市。(b) computer listing

= printout of a list of items taken from the data stored in a computer 计算机打印清单; listing paper = Paper made as a long sheet, used in computer printers 计算机的打印机用的长条纸张

**literature** n. written information about something 印刷品;(情报信息方面) please send me literature about your new product range. 请寄给我有关你们新产品种类的印刷品。

NOTE: no plural

**litigation** n. the bringing of a lawsuit against someone 诉讼

NOTE: no plural

**litre or** US **liter** n. measure of liquids 升(容量单位); The car does fifteen kilometres to the litre or fifteen kilometres per litre. = The car uses one litre of petrol to travel fifteen kilometres. 这辆汽车每升汽油可行驶 15 公里。

NOTE: usually written L after figures: 251

**lively** a. lively market = active stock market, with many shares being bought or sold 交易频繁证券市场。

**living** n. 生活 cost of living = money which a person has to pay for rent, food, heating, etc. 生活费用; cost - of - living index = way of measuring the cost of living which is shown as a percentage increase on the figure for the previous year 生活费用指数(生活费用比前一年增长的百分比); He does not earn a living wage. = He does not earn enough to pay for essentials. (food, heat, rent)他的收入不足以支付基本生活费用。standard of living or living standards = quality of personal home life (amount of food, clothes bought, size of the family car, etc.)生活水准; Living standards fell as unemployment rose. 失业上升时,生活水平下降了。

NOTE: no plural **Lloyd's** n. central London insurance market 劳合社(伦敦中心保险市场); Lloyd's Register = classified list showing details of all the ships in the world(英)劳合船级社年鉴(世界上所有船只详情分类清单); ship which is A1 at Lloyd's = ship in very good condition 劳合社 A1 级船(最高效能的船)

**load** 1 n. (a) goods which are transported 运载的货物: load of a lorry or of a container = goods carried by a lorry or container 卡车或集装箱装载的货物; lorry - load or container - load = amount of goods carried on a lorry or container 卡车或集装箱的货物载运量; A container - load of spare parts is missing. 一集装箱运载的零部件丢失了。They delivered six lorry - loads of coal. 他们发运了六卡车的煤。commercial load = amount of goods or number of passengers which a bus or train or plane has to carry to make a profit 商业装载量 maximum load = largest weight of goods which a lorry or plane can carry 最大载运量; load - carrying capacity = amount of goods which a lorry is capable of carrying 装载能力; load factor = number of seats in a bus or train or plane which are occupied by passengers who have paid the full fare 负载量;装载系数 (b) workload = amount of work which a person has to do 工作量定额: He has difficulty in coping with his heavy workload. 他难于应付他的繁重的工作量定额。2 v. (a) to load a lorry or a ship = to put goods into a lorry or a ship for transporting 给卡车或船装货; to load cargo onto a ship 向船上装货; a truck loaded with boxes 装载着箱子的卡车; a ship loaded with iron 装载着铁的船; fully loaded ship = ship which is full of cargo 满载货物的船 (b) (of ship) to take on cargo 承载货物; The ship is loading a cargo of wood 该船正在承载木材。(c) to put a program into a computer 向计算机输入程序; Load the word - processing program before you start keyboarding. 开始键盘操作前,先

输入文字处理程序。

◇ **loading** n. loading bay = section of road in a warehouse where lorries can drive in to be loaded 装卸场道; loading dock = part of a harbour where ships can load or unload 船只装卸货物的码头; loading ramp = raised platform which makes it easier to load goods onto a lorry 装货起用的可升降平台。

NOTE: no plural

◇ **load line** n. line painted on the side of a ship to show where the water should reach for maximum safety if the ship is fully loaded 吃水线(这是船只吃水的最大安全限度)

**loan** 1 n. money which has been lent 贷款; loan capital = part of a company's capital which is a loan to be repaid at a later date(企业的)借入资本; loan stock = money lent to a company at a fixed rate of interest 贷款债券; convertible loan stock = money which can be exchanged for shares at a later date 可换成股票的贷款债券; bank loan = money lent by a bank 银行贷款; bridging loan = short - term loan to help someone buy a new house when he has not yet sold his old one 过渡贷款; government loan = money lent by the government 政府贷款; home loan = loan by a bank or building society to help someone buy a house 住房贷款; short - term loan or long - term loan = loans which have to be repaid within a few weeks or some years 短期贷款或长期贷款; soft loan = loan (from a company to an employee or from one government to another) with no interest payable 无利息贷款; unsecured loan = loan made with no security 无担保贷款 2 v. to lend 借出

**lobby** 1 n. group of people who try to influence members of parliament, members of town councils, etc. 游说团(对国会议员、城镇委员会成员等施加影响;; the energy - saving lobby = people who try to persuade members of parliament to pass laws to save energy 节能议案的游说团 2 v. to try to influence members of parliament, members of town councils, etc. 游说; The group lobbied the chairmen of all the committees. 该团体对所有的委员会主席进行游说。

**local** 1. a. referring to a particular area, especially one near where a factory or an office is based 本地的(特别是某工厂或办公室所在地附近地区); local authority = elected section of government which runs a small area of the country 地方当局; local call = telephone call to a number in the same area as the person making the call 本地电话; local government = elected administrative bodies which run areas of the country 地方政府; local labour = workers who are recruited near a factory, and are not brought there from a distance 本地劳动力 2 n. US branch of a trade union(美)分工会

◇ **locally** ad. in the area near where an office or factory is based 本地: We recruit all our staff locally. 我们的所有职工都是在本地招聘的。

**locate** v. to be located = to be in a certain place 位于某地; The warehouse is located near to the motorway. 仓库位于高速公路附近。

◇ **location** n. place where something is 地点; The company has moved to a new location = the company has moved to a new office or a different town. 公司已移至新地点。

**lock** 1 n. device for closing a door or box so that it can be opened only with a key 锁; The lock is broken on the petty cash box. 零用现金箱的锁坏了。I have forgotten the combination of the lock on my briefcase. 我忘记我的手提箱上号码锁的号码了。2 v. to close a door with a key, so that it cannot be opened 锁门；The manager forgot to lock the door of the computer room. 经理忘记锁计算机房的门了。The petty cash box was not locked. 零用现金箱没上锁。

◇ **lock out** v. to lock out workers = to shut the factory door so that workers cannot get in and so force them not to work until the conditions imposed by the management are met 闭厂（不准工人进入工作地点，直至纠纷依雇主条件解决为止）

◇ **lockout** n. industrial dispute where the management will not let the workers into the factory until they have agreed to the management's conditions 闭厂；不准进工厂；（在劳资纠纷中，厂方不让工人进入工厂直至工人同意厂方提出的条件）

◇ **lock up** v. to lock up a shop or an office = to close and lock the door at the end of the day's work 关门上锁（将商店或办公室）；to lock up capital = to have capital invested in such a way that it cannot be used for other investments 使资本搁置或使资金呆滞（投资项目局限性大，以至限制了资金向更有利的项目转移）

◇ **locking up** n. the locking up of money in stock = investing money in stock so that it cannot be used for other, possibly more profitable, investments 资金搁置在证券上（投资于证券，以至限制了资金向其他更有利的投资项目转移）。

◇ **lock - up** a. lock - up shop = shop which has no living accommodation and which the proprietor locks at night when it is closed 打烊；上锁的商店（店内无住宿设施，店主于晚间关门上锁）

**lodge** v. to lodge a complaint against someone = to make an official complaint about someone 投诉某人；to lodge money with someone = to deposit money with someone 把钱存于某人处；to lodge securities as collateral = to put securities into a bank to be used as collateral for a loan 把证券存入银行作为贷款抵押

**log** v. to write down all that happens 记录；to log phone calls = to note all details of phone calls made 详细记录电话内容。
NOTE: logging - logged

**logo** n. symbol or design or group of letters used by a company as a mark on its products and in advertising 标识语（产品及广告上使用的，作为某公司标志的符号、图案或一组字母）

**long** 1 a. for a large period of time 长时间的；long credit = credit terms which allow the borrower a long time to pay 长期信贷；in the long term = over a long period of time 从长远的观点看来 to take the long view = to plan for a long period before current investment becomes profitable 从长远的观点看问题；作长远打算 2 n. longs = government stocks which mature in over fifteen years' time 15年以上到期的政府债券。

◇ **long - dated** a. long - dated bills = bills which are payable in more than three months' time 远期票据（支付期为3个月以上）

◇ **long - distance** a. a long - distance call = telephone call to a number which is not near 长途电话；long - distance flight = flight to a destination which is a long way away 长距离飞行

◇ **longhand** n. handwriting where the words are written out in full and not typed or in shorthand 普通手写字体；Applications should be written in longhand and sent to the personnel officer. 申请书应手书并送交给人事官员。

◇ **long - haul** a. over a long distance 长距离的；long - haul flight = long - distance flight especially between continents 长距离飞行

◇ **long – range** a. for a long period of time in the future 长时期的; long – range economic forecast = forecast which covers a period of several years 长期经济预测

◇ **long – standing** a. which has been arranged for a long time 长期存在的; long – standing agreement 长期协议; long – standing customer or customer of long standing = person who has been a customer for many years 老主顾(长期顾客)

◇ **long – term** a. on a long – term basis = for a long period of time 长时期; long – term debts = debts which will be repaid many years later 长期债务; long – term forecast = forecast for a period of over three years(三年以上的)长期预测; long – term loan = loan to be repaid many years later 长期贷款; long – term objectives = aims which will take years to achieve 长期目标

**loophole** n. to find a loophole in the law = to find a means of legally avoiding the law(寻找法律)漏洞; to find a tax loophole = to find a means of legally not paying tax 寻找可逃税漏洞。

**loose** a. not packed together 松散的; loose change = money in coins 零钱; to sell loose sugar or to sell sugar loose = to sell sugar in separately weighed quantities, not in packets 出售散装食糖。

◇ **loose – leaf book** n. book with loose pages which can be taken out and fixed back in again on rings 活页书。

**lorry** n. large motor vehicle for carrying goods 大卡车: He drives a five – ton lorry. 他驾驶一辆五吨运货车。heavy lorry = very large lorry which carries heavy loads 重型大卡车; lorry driver = person who drives a lorry 卡车司机
NOTE: US English is truck

**lose** v. (a) not to have something any more 遗失;失去; to lose an order = not to get an order which you were hoping to get 失去一张订单; During the strike, the company lost six orders to American competitors. 罢工期间, 公司有 6 张订单落入到美国对手那里。to lose control of a company = to find that you have less than 50% of the shares and so are no longer able to direct the company(因拥有的股票不到 50%)失去对公司的控制; to lose customers = to have fewer customers 失去顾客; Their service is so slow that they have been losing customers. 他们的服务如此缓慢使其顾客越来越少。She lost her job when the factory closed. = She was made redundant. 工厂关闭, 她失去了工作。(b) to have less money 亏损; He lost £25,000 in his father's computer company. 他在父亲的计算机公司亏损了 25,000 英磅。The pound has lost value = the pound is worth less 英磅贬值。(c) to drop to a lower price 贬值; The dollar lost two cents against the yen. 与日元相比美元贬值两美分。Gold shares lost 5% on the market yesterday. 在昨天的股市上, 金矿股票贬值(下跌了)5%。
NOTE: losing – lost

◇ **lose out** v. to suffer as a result of something 损失; The company has lost out in the rush to make cheap computers. 在制做廉价计算机热潮中公司遭受了损失。

**loss** n. (a) loss of customers = not keeping customers because of bad service or high prices, etc. 失去顾客(因劣质服务或高价格等原因) loss of an order = not getting an order which was expected. 失去一份订单。The company suffered a loss of market penetration = the company found it had a smaller share of the market 公司遭到市场渗透的打击。compensation for loss of earnings =

payment to someone who has stopped earningmoney or who is not able to earn money 对失去收入的人的补助; compensation for loss of office = payment to a director who is asked to leave a company before his contract ends 职务丢失补偿(对合同未满而被要求离职的董事的补偿) (b) having less money than before or not making a profit 亏损; 不赢利; The company suffered a loss. = The company did not make a profit. 公司遭受亏损。to report a loss = not to show a profit in the accounts at the end of the year 年终帐面上亏损; The company reported a loss of £1m on the first year's trading. 在帐面上, 公司第一年的贸易有100万英磅的亏损。capital loss = loss made by selling assets 资本损失; The car was written off as a dead loss or a total loss = the car was so badly damaged that the insurers said it had no value. 这辆车已完全报损。paper loss = loss made when an asset has fallen in value but has not been sold 帐面亏损(未售出的固定资产因贬值造成的损失); trading loss = situation where the company's receipts are less than its expenditure 营业亏损; at a loss = making a loss or not making any profit 亏损; 不赢利; The company is trading at a loss. 公司正亏损经营。He sold the shop at a loss. 他亏本卖了商店。to cut one's losses = to stop doing something which was losing money 停止亏损经营 (c) being worth less or having a lower value 贬值; 跌价; Shares showed losses of up to 5% on the Stock Exchange. 股票在证券市场下跌5%。 (d) loss in weight = goods which weigh less than when they were packed 重量损耗(商品重量比其包装时减轻); loss in transport = amount of weight which is lost while goods are being transported 商品运输中的重量损耗

◇ **loss – leader** n. article which is sold at a loss to attract customers 为吸引顾客亏本售出的货物: We use these cheap films as a loss – leader. 我们用这些廉价胶卷作为吸引顾客而亏本售出商品。

**lot** n. (a) large quantity 大量: a lot of people or lots of people are out of work 大量人员失业。(b) group of items sold together at an auction(在拍卖中)多样东西一起出售的物件; to bid for lot 23 批号为第23号商品出价; At the end of the auction half the lots were unsold. 拍卖结束时一半的拍卖物未售出。(c) group of shares which are sold 售出一批股票; to sell a lot of shares 出售许多股票; to sell shares in small lots 小批出售股票 (d) US piece of land, especially one to be used for redevelopment(美)一块地(尤指重新开发用地)。

**lottery** n. game where numbered tickets are sold and prizes given for some of the numbers 彩票; 抽彩给奖(出售印有数字的彩票, 其中某些彩票上的数字可以中奖)

**lounge** n. comfortable room 休息室; departure lounge = room in an airport where passengers wait to board their planes 机场候机室; transit lounge = room in an airport where passengers wait for connecting flights 机场中转休息室

**low** 1. a. small or not high 小; 低; Low overhead costs keep the unit cost low. 经常性开支低使得单位产品成本低。We try to keep our wages bill low. 我们尽量使工资开支低一些。The company offered him a mortgage at a low rate of interest. 公司提供给他一笔低利率抵押贷款。The pound is at a very low rate of exchange against the dollar. 英磅对美元的汇率很低。Our aim is to buy at the lowest price possible. 我们想以尽可能低的价格购买。Shares are at their lowest for two years. 股价处于两年来的最低点。low sales = small amount of money produced by sales 收入低微的销售;

low volume of sales = small number of itemssold 低销售额; The tender will go to the lowest bidder. = The contract will be awarded to the person who offers the best terms. 出最低价的人中标。2 n. point where prices or sales are very small 低点(价格或销售额); Sales have reached a new low. 销量又进入低点。the highs and lows on the stock market 证券市场上的最高和最低点; Shares have hit an all – time low. = shares have reached their lowest price ever. 股价跌落到历史的最低点。

◇ **lower** 1. a. smaller or less high 较小的;较低的: a lower rate of interest;较低的利息率; Sales were lower in December than in November. 12 月的销售最比 11 月的低。2 v. to make smaller or less expensive 降低; to lower prices to secure a larger market share 降低价格以占领更大市场份额; to lower the interest rate 降低利率。

◇ **lowering** n. making smaller or less expensive 降低;减少: lowering of prices 降低价格; We hope to achieve low prices with no lowering of quality. 我们希望在不降低质量的前提下降低价格。NOTE: no plural

◇ **low – grade** a. not very important or not of very good quality 低级的;低质量的: a low – grade official from the Ministry of Commerce:商业部低级官员; The car runs best on low – grade petrol. 这辆汽车使用低质汽油运行良好。

◇ **low – level** a. (a) not very important 低级的: A low – level delegation visited the ministry. 一个低级代表团到部里访问。a low – level meeting decided to put off making a decision. 一个低级会议决定推迟做决定。

(b) low – level computer language = programming language similar to machine code 计算机低级语言。

◇ **low – pressure** a. low – pressure sales = sales where the salesman does not force someone to buy, but only encourages him to do so 低压力销售(推销员不迫使顾客购买而是鼓励顾客购买)。

◇ **low – quality** a. not of good quality 低质量的:They tried to sell us some low – quality steel. 他们试图卖给我们一些低质钢材。

**Loyalty** n. brand loyalty = feeling of a customer who always buys the same brand of product(产品的商标)信任感; feeling of a customer who always buys the same brand of customer loyalty = feeling of customers who always shop at the same shop 顾客(对某商店)的信任感

**Ltd** = LIMITED

**luggage** n. suitcases or bags for carrying clothes when travelling 手提箱;手提包: hand luggage or cabin luggage = small cases which passengers can take with them into the cabin of a plane or ship 可随身携带的手提行李; free luggage allowance = amount of luggage which a passenger can take with him free of charge 可免费随身携带的手提物限量 NOTE: no plural; to show one suitcase, etc., say a piece of luggage

**lull** n. quiet period 平静时期; After last week's hectic trading this week's lull was welcome. 经过上星期的狂热的交易,这个星期的平静受到欢迎。

**lump** n. lump sum = money paid in one single amount, not in several small sums 一次总付的金额; When he retired he was given a lump – sum bonus. 退休时他得到一笔一次性支付的奖金。She sold her house and invested the money as a lump sum. 她卖了房子并把全部得款作为一次性投资。

**lunch** n. meal eaten in the middle of the day 午餐; The hours of work are from

9.30 to 5.30 with an hour off for lunch; 工作时间是从 9:30 到 5:30，其中除去一个小时的午餐时间。The chairman is out at lunch. 总裁出去用午餐了。business lunch = meeting between businessmen where they have lunch together to discuss business deals 业务性午餐。

◇ **lunch hour or lunchtime** n. time when people have lunch 午餐时间: The office is closed during the lunch hour or at lunchtimes. 午餐时间办公室关门。

◇ **luncheon voucher** n. 雇主免费给雇员的午餐代金券

**luxury** n. expensive thing which is not necessary but which is good to have 奢侈物品; luxury items or luxury goods 奢侈品或奢侈商品; a black market in luxury articles 奢侈品黑市(场)

# Mm

**m** = METRE, MILE, MILLION 米; 英里; 百万

**M1** British measure of money supply, including all coins and notes plus personal money in current accounts. 英国货币供应量 M1(包括流通中的货币和活期存款)(狭议)

◇ **M2** British measure of money supply, including coins and notes and personal money in current and deposit accounts. 英国货币供应量 M2(包括流通中的货币、个人活期存款和个人定期存款)

◇ **M3** British measure of money supply, including coins and notes, personal money in current and deposit accounts, government deposits and deposits in currencies other than sterling. 英国货币供应量 M3(包括流通中的货币、个人活期存款、个人定期存款、政府存款和英磅外其他通币的存款)(广义); £ M3 = British measure of sterling money supply, including coins and notes, personal money in current and deposit accounts and government deposits. 英国英磅供应量 £ M3(包括流通中货币、个人活期存款、个人定期存款和政府存款)
NOTE: say "sterling M3"

**machine** n. (a) device which works with power from a motor 机器; 机械: adding machine = machine which adds numbers 加数器; copying machine or duplicating machine = machine which makes copies of documents 复印机; dictating machine = machine which records what someone dictates, which a typist can then play back and type out 口述记录器; automatic vending machine = machine which provides food or drink when money is put in it 自动售货机; machine shop = place where working machines are placed 机械车间; machine tools = tools worked by motors, used to work on wood or metal 机床 (b) machine - made or machine - produced = manufactured by a machine, not by people 机制的 (c) machine code or machine language = instructions and information shown as a series of figures (0 and 1) which can be read by a computer 电子计算机密码或电子计算机语言; machine - readable codes = sets of signs or letters (such as bar codes, post codes) which a computer can read 计算机可读的代码

◇ **machinery** n. (a) machines 机械: idle machinery or machinery lying idle = machines not being used 闲置机械; machinery guards = pieces of metal to prevent workers from getting hurt by the moving parts of a machine 机械保护罩 (b) organization or system 机构; 体制:

the government machinery 政府机构；the machinery of local government 地方政府机构；administrative machinery 管理机构；the machinery for awarding government contracts 签奖政府合同的机构

NOTE: no plural

◇ **machinist** n. person who works a machine 机械师

**macro -** prefix very large, covering a wide area 很大；复盖面广泛；宏观的：macro - economics = study of the economics of a whole area or whole industry or whole group of the population or whole country, in order to help in economic planning 宏观经济学

**Madam** n. formal way of addressing a woman, especially one whom you do not know 女士(特别是称呼陌生的妇女)：Dear Madam = beginning of a letter to a woman whom you do not know 亲爱的女士；Madam Chairman = way of addressing a woman who is in the chair at the meeting 女主席(对会议女主席的称谓)

**made** a. produced or manufactured 生产的；制造的：made in Japan or Japanese made 日本制造；see also MAKE

**magazine** n. paper, usually with pictures, which comes out regularly, every month or every week 杂志：computer magazine = magazine with articles on computers and programs 计算机杂志；do - it - yourself magazine = magazine with articles on work which the average person can do to repair or paint the house《自己动手》杂志；house magazine = magazine produced for the workers in a company to give them news of the company's affairs 公司内部杂志；trade magazine = magazine produced for people or companies in certain trades 行业杂志；travel magazine = magazine with articles on holidays and travel 旅游杂志；

women's magazine = magazine aimed at the women's market 妇女杂志；magazine insert = advertising sheet put into a magazine when it is mailed or sold 杂志加页广告；to insert a leaflet in a specialist magazine = to put an advertising leaflet into a magazine before it is mailed or sold 将广告单插入要邮寄的专业杂志中；magazine mailing = sending of copies of a magazine by post to subscribers 杂志邮寄

**magnate** n. important businessman 工商业巨头：a shipping magnate 船业巨头

**magnetic tape or** infml. **mag tape** n. plastic tape for recording information on a large computer 大型计算机使用的磁带

**mail** 1 n. (a) system of sending letters and parcels from one place to another 邮寄：to put a letter in the mail 寄信(将信邮寄)；The cheque was lost in the mail. 支票在邮寄中丢失。The invoice was put in the mail yesterday. 发票昨天寄出去了。Mail to some of the islands in the Pacific can take six weeks. 寄往太平洋的某些岛屿邮件要花六个星期。by mail = using the postal services, not sending something by hand or by messenger 邮寄；to send a package by surface mail = to send a package by land or sea, not by air 通过陆地或水上邮寄包裹；by sea mail = sent by post abroad, using a ship 海上邮寄；to receive a sample by air mail = by post using a plane 收到了航空邮寄的样品；We sent the order by first - class mail. = by the most expensive mail service, designed to be faster 我们把订单用第一等邮件寄出去了。electronic mail = system of sending messages from one computer to another, using the telephone lines 电子邮件(用电话线路电脑传送信息)(b) letters sent or received 信件；Has the mail arrived yet? 信来了吗？to open the mail 打开信；拆信；Your cheque arrived inyesterday's mail. 你的支票是昨天寄到。My secretary opens my mail as soon as it arrives. 我的秘书一接到我的信就把它打开了。The receipt was in this morning's mail. 收据在今天早晨寄到的。incoming mail = mail which arrives 送进来的邮件；outgoing mail = mail which is sent out 送出去的邮件；mail room = room in an office where incoming letters are sorted and sent to each department, and where outgoing mail is collected for sending 邮件收发室 (c) direct mail = selling a product by sending publicity material to possible buyers through the post 直接邮寄：The company runs a successful direct - mail operation.这个公司成功地开展了直接邮寄业务。These calculators are sold only by direct mail. 这些计数器通过直接邮寄进行销售。direct - mail advertising = advertising by sending leaflets to people by post 直接邮寄产品广告；mail shot = leaflets sent by mail to possible customers 邮寄给可能的买主的广告单 NOTE: no plural

2 v. to send something by post 邮寄；to mail a letter 寄信：We mailed our order last Wednesday. 上星期三我们寄出了订单。

◇ **mail box** n. one of several boxes where incoming mail is put in a large building；box for putting letters, etc. which you want to post 信箱

◇ **mailing** n. sending something in the post 邮寄：the mailing of publicity material 邮寄宣传材料；direct mailing = sending of publicity material by post to possible buyers 直接邮寄（产品宣传材料）；mailing list = list of names and addresses of people who might be interested in a product or list of names and addresses of members of a society 通讯录（某产品预期购买者的通讯录或某社会团体成员）；His name is on our mailing list.

他的名字在我们的通讯录中。to build up a mailing list 建立通讯录；to buy a mailing list = to pay a society, etc. money to buy the list of members so that you can use it to mail publicity material （向某团体）购买（其成员）通讯录（以便向他们邮寄产品宣传材料）；mailing piece = leaflet suitable for sending by direct mail 适合直接邮寄的传单；mailing shot = leaflets sent by mail to possible customers 邮寄给可能买主的广告单

◇ **mail - order** n. system of buying and selling from a catalogue, placing orders and sending goods by mail 邮购；mail - order business or mail - order firm or mail - order house = company which sells a product by mail 邮购公司或邮购商店；mail - order catalogue = catalogue from which a customer can order items to be sent by mail 邮购商品目录

**main** a. most important 主要的：main office 总部；main building 主建筑；one of our main customers 我们的一个主要顾客；US Main Street = most important street in a town, where the shops and banks are(美)（城镇中商店和银行所在的）大街；大马路

◇ **mainframe** n. large computer(大型计算机的)中央处理机：The office micro interfaces with the mainframe in the head office.办公室的微机与总部的中央处理机相互联结。

◇ **mainly** adv. mostly or usually 主要地：Their sales are mainly in the home market. 他们的销售主要是在国内市场. We are interested mainly in buying children's gift items. 我们主要对购买儿童礼品感兴趣。

**maintain** v. (a) to keep something going or working 保持：to maintain good relations with one's customers 与其顾客保持良好关系；to maintain contact with an overseas market 与海外市场保持联系 (b) to keep something working at the same level 维持某一水平: The company has maintained the same volume of business in spite of the recession. 尽管经济衰退,公司还是维持了原来的业务量。to maintain an interest rate at 5% 维持5%的利率; to maintain a dividend = to pay the same dividend as the previous year 维持以往的股息水平

◇ **maintenance** n. (a) keeping things going or working 保持: maintenance of contacts 保持联系; maintenance of supplies 保持供应 (b) keeping a machine in good working order 维修: maintenance contract = contract by which a company keeps a piece of equipment in good working order 设备维修合同; We offer a full maintenance service. 我们提供全面的设备维修服务。

**majeure** see FORCE MAJEURE

**major** a. important 主要的; major shareholder = shareholder with a large number of shares 主要股东;大股东

◇ **majority** n. larger group than all others 多数: majority of the shareholders = more than 50% of the shareholders 多数股东; The board accepted the proposal by a majority of three to two. = Three members of the board voted to accept and two voted against. 董事会以三比二多数接受这项建议。majority vote or majority decision = decision made after a vote according to the wishes of the largest group 多数人的投票或多数人的决定; majority shareholding or majority interest = group of more than half of all the shares in a company(某公司的)多数股份或多数股权; a majority shareholder = person who owns more than half the shares in a company 拥有多数股份的人或股东

**make** 1 n. type of product manufactured 牌子;式样: Japanese makes of cars 日本牌子的汽车; a standard make of equipment 标准式样的设备; What make

is the new computer system or what is the make of the new computer system? 新计算机系统是什么型号的? 2 v. (a) to produce or to manufacture 生产;制造: to make a car or to make a computer 生产汽车或计算机; The workmen spent ten weeks making the table. 工人花了十周时间做这张桌子。The factory makes three hundred cars a day. 工厂一天生产300辆汽车。(b) to sign or to agree 签署或达成: to make a deal or to make an agreement 达成交易或达成协议; to make a bid for something = to offer to buy something 出价;投标; to make a payment = to pay 支付; to make a deposit = to pay money as a deposit 付定金 (c) to earn or to increase in value 挣钱;增值: He makes £50,000 a year or £25 an hour. 他一年挣50,000英磅或一个小时挣25英磅。The shares made $2.92 in today's trading. 在今天的交易中股票增值2.92美元. (d) to make a profit or to make a loss = to have more money or less money after a deal 赢利或亏损; to make a killing = to make a very large profit 获得巨额利润 NOTE: making – made

◇ **make good** v. (a) to repair or to compensate 修复;补偿: The company will make good the damage. 公司将补偿损坏。to make good a loss 补偿损失 (b) to be a success 成功: A local boy made good. = local person who becomes successful 一个本地男孩获得了成功。

◇ **make out** v. to write 写: to make out an invoice 开发票; The bill is made out to Smith & Co. 帐单是开给史密斯公司的。to make out a cheque to someone = to write someone's name on a cheque 给某人开支票。

◇ **make over** v. to transfer property legally(合法地)转让财产; to make over the house to one's children 将房屋转让给孩子们

◇ **make up** v. (a) to compensate for

something 补偿：to make up a loss or to makeup the difference = to pay extra so that the loss or difference is covered 弥补损失或补齐差额（b）to make up accounts = to complete the accounts 结清帐目

◇ **make up for** v. to compensate for something 补偿；to make up for a short payment or to make up for a late payment 补齐付款差额或补偿延期支付。

◇ **maker** n. person who makes something 制做者：a major car maker 大汽车制造商；a furniture maker 家具制造商；decision maker = person who decides or who takes decisions 决策人

◇ **making** n. production of an item 制做：Ten tons of concrete were used in the making of the wall. 砌墙用了 10 吨混凝土。decision making = act of coming to a decision 决策

**maladministration** n. incompetent administration 管理不善

**mall** n. US shopping mall = enclosed covered area for shopping, with shops, restaurants, banks and other facilities（美）购物中心（包括商店、饭店、银行和其他设施）

**man** 1 n. person or ordinary worker 人；一般工人：All the men went back to work yesterday. 所有的工人昨天都复工。2 v. to provide the workforce for something 提供劳动力；配备人员：to man a shift 为倒班配备人员；to man an exhibition 为办展览会配备人员：The exhibition stand was manned by three salesgirls. 展台配备了三个女售货员。see also MANNED, MANNING

**manage** v. (a) to direct or to be in charge of 指挥；负责：to manage a department 负责某部门；to manage a branch office 负责某分部（公司）(b) to manage property = to look after rented property for the owner（代替房地产主）照管房子 (c) to manage to = to be able

to do something 能应付：Did you manage to see the head buyer? 你设法见到了那位重要买主吗？She managed to write six orders and take three phone calls all in two minutes. 她设法 在两分钟内写完六张订单并接三个电话。

◇ **manageable** a. which can be dealt with easily 可解决的：difficulties which are still manageable 仍属可以解决的困难；The problems are too large to be manageable. 问题大得无法解决。

◇ **management** n. (a) directing or running a business 管理：to study management 研究经营管理；good management or efficient management 好的或有效的经营管理；bad management or inefficient management 不佳的或低效的经营管理；a management graduate or a graduate in management 管理专业的本科毕业生；line management = organization of a business where each manager is responsible for doing what his superior tells him to do 垂直管理；portfolio management = buying and selling shares by a person or by a specialist on behalf of a client 有价证券管理；product management = directing the making and selling of a product as an independent item 产品管理；management accountant = accountant who prepares specialized information for managers so that they can make decisions 管理会计员；management accounts = financial information (on sales, costs, credit, profitability) prepared for a manager（为经理准备的）企业财务情况的报告；management committee = committee which manages a club, a pension fund, etc. 管理委员会；management consultant = person who gives advice on how to manage a business 管理顾问；management course = training course for managers 管理课程；management by objectives = way of managing a business by planning work for the managers and testing to see if it is

completed correctly and on time 目标管理制度(为各级经理确立明确工作目标以作为衡量标准来检验其工作完成情况的管理制度); management team = a group of managers working together 管理人员队伍; management techniques = ways of managing a business 管理技术; management training = training managers by making them study problems and work out ways of solving them 企业管理培训; management trainee = young person being trained to be a manager 参加企业管理培训的学员 (b) group of managers or directors 管理部门: The management has decided to give an overall pay increase. 管理部门决定给全体职工长工资。top management = the main directors of a company 最高管理部门(层); middle management = the department managers of a company who carry out the policy set by the directors and organize the work of a group of workers 中层管理部门, (包括公司的各部门经理,其职责是执行董事会制定的政策并组织工人们生产)
NOTE; no plural for (a)

◇ **manager** n. (a) head of a department in a company 经理: a department manager 部门经理; personnel manager 人事经理; production manager 生产经理; sales manager 销售经理; accounts manager = head of the accounts department 会计部门经理; area manager = manager who is responsible for the company's work (usually sales) in an area 地区(销售)经理; general manager = manager in charge of the administration in a large company 总经理 (b) person in charge of a branch or shop 分公司经理;商店经理: Mr Smith is the manager of our local Lloyds Bank. 史密斯先生是我们当地劳埃德银行的经理。The manager of our Lagos branch is in London for a series of meetings. 我们拉各斯分公司经理正在伦敦参加一系列会议。

bank manager = person in charge of a branch of a bank 银行分行经理或行长; branch manager = person in charge of a branch of a company 分公司经理

◇ **manageress** n. woman who runs a shop, or a department 女经理(商店或百货公司)

◇ **managerial** a. referring to managers 管理上的: managerial staff 管理人员; to be appointed to a managerial position = to be appointed a manager 任经理的职务; decisions taken at managerial level = decisions taken by managers 经理做出的决定

◇ **managership** n. job of being a manager 经理职务: After six years, he was offered the managership of a branch in Scotland. 六年后任命他为英格兰分支机构的经理。

◇ **managing** a. managing director = director who is in charge of a whole company 总经理: chairman and managing director = managing director who is also chairman of the board of directors 兼任总经理董事长

**mandate** n. bank mandate = written order allowing someone to sign cheques on behalf of a company(委托某人代表公司在支票上签字的)委托书

**mandatory** a. mandatory meeting = meeting which all members have to attend 全体人员都须参加的会议;指令性会议

**man - hour** n. work done by one man in one hour 工时(一人一小时之工作): One million man - hours were lost through industrial action. 在工人罢工期间损失了 100 万工时。

**manifest** n. list of goods in a shipment 运货清单: passenger manifest = list of passengers on a ship or plane 旅客名单(航船或飞机上的)

**manilla** n. thick brown paper 马尼拉纸(褐色厚纸): a manilla envelope 马尼拉

纸信封
NOTE: no plural

**manipulate** v. to manipulate the accounts = to make false accounts so that the company seems profitable 做假帐: to manipulate the market = to work to influence share prices in your favour 操纵股市

◇ **manipulation** n. stock market manipulation = trying to influence the price of shares 操纵股市

◇ **manipulator** n. stock market manipulator = person who tries to influence the price of shares in his own favour 股市操纵者(试图控制股价以从中渔利的人)

**manned** a. with someone working on it 由人操纵的: The switchboard is manned twenty - four hours a day. 电话总机是一天 24 小时由人操纵的。The stand was manned by our sales staff. 摊位配备了我们的销售人员。

◇ **manning** n. people who are needed to do a work process 人员配置: manning levels = number of people required in each department of a company to do the work efficiently 人员配备水平(公司每一部门所需人员配置量); manning agreement or agreement on manning = agreement between the company and the workers about how many workers are needed for a certain job(劳资之间对某项具体工作的)人员配置协议
NOTE: no plural

**manpower** n. number of workers 人力;劳动力数量: manpower forecasting = forecasting how many workers will be needed, and how many will be available 劳力预测; manpower planning = planning to obtain the right number of workers in each job 劳动力规划; manpower requirements = number of workers needed 所需劳动力数量; manpower shortage or shortage of manpower =

lack of workers 劳动力短缺;人力不足
NOTE: no plural

**manual** 1 a. done by hand or done using the hands 手工的: manual labour or manual work = heavy work done by hand 体力劳动; manual labourer = person who does heavy work with his hands 体力劳动者; manual worker = person who works with his hands 手工劳动者,体力劳动者 2 n. book of instructions 手册: operating manual = book showing how to operate a machine 操作手册: service manual = book showing how to service a machine 维修手册

◇ **manually** adv. done by hand, not by a machine 手工地: Invoices have had to be made manually because the computer has broken down. 因为计算机坏了,只好手工开发票了。

**manufacture** 1 v. to make a product for sale, using machines 制造: manufactured goods 机制品; The company manufactures spare parts for cars. 这个公司制做汽车零部件。 2 n. making a product for sale, using machines 制造: products of foreign manufacture = products made in foreign countries 外国制造的产品
NOTE: no plural

◇ **manufacturer** n. person or company which produces machine - made products 制造商(者);制造公司: foreign manufacturers 外国制造商(公司); cotton manufacturer 棉花生产商; sports car manufacturer 运动车制造商; manufacturer's recommended price = price at which the manufacturer suggests the product should be sold on the retail market, though often reduced by the retailer 制造厂商推出的产品零售价(零售商常将此价格降低); All typewriters - 20% off the manufacturer's recommended price. 所有的打字机——均比厂家零售价低 20%。

◇ **manufacturing** n. producing machine-made products for sale 制造,生产: manufacturing overheads 制造费用; manufacturing processes 加工;制造工序; manufacturing capacity = amount of a product which a factory is capable of making 生产能力; manufacturing costs = costs of making a product 产品制造成本; manufacturing industries = industries which take raw materials and make them into finished products 加工制造业;制造业

NOTE: no plural

**margin** n. (a) difference between the money received when selling a product and the money paid for it 价差;利润: gross margin = percentage difference between the unit manufacturing cost and the received price 毛利; net margin = percentage difference between received price and all costs, including overheads 净利润; We are cutting our margins very fine. = We are reducing our margins to the smallest possible to be competitive. 我们将利润削减至尽可能的低。Our margins have been squeezed. = Profits have been reduced because our margins have to be smaller to stay competitive. 我们的利润减少了。(b) extra space or time allowed 余地(空间或时间上); margin of error = number of mistakes which are accepted in a document or in a calculation 差错限度; safety margin = time or space allowed for something to be safe 安全极限; margin of safety = sales which are above the breakeven point 保险幅度;安全边际(高于保本点销售额)

◇ **marginal** a. (a) marginal cost = cost of making a single extra unit above the number already planned 边际成本(高于计划数量的每增一单位产品所需成本): marginal pricing = making the selling price the same as the marginal cost 边际定价(按边际成本制定销售价); marginal rate of tax = percentage of tax which a taxpayer pays at the top rate 边际税率(纳税人所纳最高税率); marginal revenue = income from selling a single extra unit above the number already sold 边际收入(每增加——单位产品出售所得收入)(b) not very profitable or hardly worth the money paid 获利很少的;无利可图的: marginal return on investment 投资收益低微; marginal land = land which is almost not worth farming 边际土地(产品销售收入仅敷生产成本的地土地); marginal purchase = thing which a buyer feels is only just worth buying 边际购买(勉强购买划得来的东西)

**marine** 1 a. referring to the sea 海洋的: marine insurance = insurance of ships and their cargoes 海运保险; marine underwriter = person who insures ships and their cargoes 海运保险商 2 n. the merchant marine = all the commercial ships of a country 商船

◇ **maritime** adjective referring to the sea 海洋的; maritime law = laws referring to ships, ports, etc. 海事法;海商法(有关船只、港口等的法律); maritime lawyer = lawyer who specializes in legal matters concerning ships and cargoes 海商法律师; maritime trade = transporting commercial goods by sea 海上贸易

**mark** 1 n. (a) sign put on an item to show something 标志;标记: assay mark = hallmark or mark put on gold or silver items to show that the metal is of the correct quality(金银器上质量检验)烙印或标记; GB kite mark = mark on goods to show that they meet official standards(英)商品合格的标记 (b) money used in Germany 马克(德国货币单位): The price is twenty - five marks. 价钱是 25 马克。The mark rose against the dollar. 马克对美元的比价上升了。

NOTE: usually written DM after a figure:25DM. Also called Deutschmark, D‑Mark 2 v. to put a sign on something 做标记: to mark a product "For export only" 在产品上印上"只供出口"; article marked at £1.50 标价为 1.50 英磅的商品; to mark the price on something 在某物上标价

◇ **mark down** v. to make lower 降低: to mark down a price = to lower the price of something 降价; This range has been marked down to $24.99. 这种商品已降价到 24.99 美元。We have marked all prices down by 30% for the sale. 这次降价销售中我们将所有商品降价 30%。

◇ **mark‑down** n. (a) reduction of the price of something to less than its usual price 降价 (b) percentage amount by which a price has been lowered 降价率: We have used a 30% mark‑down to fix the sale price 我们用 30% 的降价率来定销售价。

◇ **marker pen** n. felt pen which makes a wide coloured mark 粗头彩色笔

◇ **mark up** v. to increase 增加: to mark prices up = to increase prices 提价; These prices have been marked up by 10%. 这些物价已提价了 10%。

◇ **mark‑up** n. (a) increase in price 提价: We put into effect a 10% mark‑up of all prices in June. 我们于六月份实行 10% 的全面提价。(b) amount added to the cost price to give the selling price 加价: We work to a 3.5 times mark‑up or to a 350% mark‑up. = We take the unit cost and multiply by 3.5 to give the selling price. 我们按单位成本 3.5 倍或 350% 标价。

**market** 1 n. (a) place (often in the open air) where farm produce is sold(出售农产品的)集市(通常是露天): fish market 鱼市; flower market 花市; open‑air market 露天市场; Here are this week's market prices for sheep. 这是本星期的羊市价格。flea market = market for secondhand goods 跳蚤市场; market day = day when a market is regularly held 集市日; Tuesday is market day, so the streets are closed to traffic. 星期二是集市日,因此大街上禁止车辆通行。market dues = rent for a stall in a market 租金(租用市场货摊)(b) the Common Market = the European Economic Community 欧洲共同市场(即欧洲经济共同体); the Common Market agricultural policy or the Common Market ministers 欧洲经济共同体农业政策或欧洲经济共同体部长(c) place where a product might be sold or group of people who might buy a product 市场: home or domestic market = market in the country where the selling company is based 国内市场: Sales in the home market rose by 22%. 国内市场的销售量提高了 22%。(d) possible sales of a certain type of product or demand for a certain type of product 销路;需求: The market for home computers has fallen sharply. 国产计算机市场需求已大幅度下降。We have 20% of the British car market. 我们占有 20% 的英国汽车(需求)市场。There is no market for electric typewriters. 电子打字机没有销路。a growth market = market where sales are likely to rise rapidly 发展迅速的市场;销售行情看好; the labour market. = number of workers available for work 劳动力市场; 25,000 graduates have come on to the labour market. = They have become available for work because they have left college. 25,000 名毕业生已进入劳动力市场。the property market = sales of houses 房地产市场 (e) the black market = buying and selling goods in a way which is not allowed by law 黑市: There is a flourishing black market in spare parts for cars. 汽车零部件黑市兴隆。to pay black market prices

= to pay high prices to get items which arenot easily available 付黑市价购买 (f) a buyer's market = market where goods are sold cheaply because there is little demand 买方市场(商品供大于求而有利于买方的市场); a seller's market = market where the seller can ask high prices because there is a large demand for the product 卖方市场(商品供不应求而利于卖方的市场) (g) closed market = market where a supplier deals with only one agent or distributor and does not supply any others direct 闭锁市场(卖方只对一家机构或经销商售其商品) free market economy = system where the government does not interfere in business activity in any way 自由市场经济; open market = market where anyone can buy and sell 公开市场(任何人都可以在此从事贸易) (h) capital market = place where companies can look for investment capital 资本市场; the foreign exchange markets = places where currencies are bought or sold 外汇市场; forward markets = places where foreign currency or commodities can be bought or sold for delivery at a later date 期货市场(买卖的外币或商品是在未来的规定日期交割的市场); money market or finance market = place where large sums of money are lent or borrowed 金融市场; (i) commodity market = place where commodities are bought or sold 商品市场; stock market = place where shares are bought and sold 股票市场; The market in oil shares was very active. or There was a brisk market in oil shares. 石油股票交易活跃。 to buy shares in the open market = to buy shares on the Stock Exchange, not privately 在公开市场(证券交易所)购买股票; over - the - counter market = secondary market in shares which are not listed on the main Stock Exchange 场外交易市场(这里经营非挂牌股票的二级市场) (j) market analysis = detailed examination and report on a market 市场分析; market capitalization = value of a company calculated by multiplying the price of its shares on the Stock Exchange by the number of shares issued 市场资本总额(以公司在证券交易所发行的股票价格乘以其发行数量所得公司的价值); market economist = person who specializes in the study of financial structures and the return on investments in the stock market 市场经济学家; market forces = influences on the sales of a product 市场力量; market forecast = forecast of prices on the stock market 市场预测; market leader = company with the largest market share 占有最大市场份额的公司;市场领导; We are the market leader in home computers. 我们公司拥有最大的国产计算机市场。 market opportunities = possibility of finding new sales in a market 市场机会; market penetration or market share = percentage of a total market which the sales of a company cover 市场渗入或市场份额(某公司销售额占该市场总销售额的百分比); We hope our new product range will increase our market share. 我们希望我们的新产品系列将增加我们的市场份额。 market price = price at which a product can be sold 市场销售价格; market rate = normal price in the market 市场正常价格; We pay the market rate for secretaries. or We pay secretaries the market rate. 我们以市场正常价格支付秘书工资。 market research = examining the possible sales of a product before it is put on the market 市场研究; market trends = gradual changes taking place in a market 市场趋势;市场展望; market value = value of a product or of a company if sold today 市场价值 (k) up market or down market = more expensive or less expensive 高档品市场或低档品市场; to go up market or to go down market = to make products which appeal to a wealthy section of the market or to a wider, less wealthy, section of the market 转向高档品或低档品市场 (1) to be in the market for secondhand cars = to look for secondhand cars to buy 寻购旧汽车; to come on to the market = to start to be sold 开始投放市场; This soap has just come on to the market. 这种肥皂刚刚投放市场。to put something on the market = to start to offer something for sale 向市场投放某种产品; They put their house on the market. 他们把房屋投放市场出售。I hear the company has been put on the market. 我听说公司产品已上市。The company has priced itself out of the market. = The company has raised its prices so high that its products do not sell. 这家公司抬价过高而断了自己的销路。2 v. to sell (products) 出售(产品): This product is being marketed in all European countries 这种产品正在欧洲所有国家出售。

◇ **marketable** a. which can be sold easily 适销的; 有销路的

◇ **marketing** n. techniques used in selling a product (such as packaging, advertising, etc.) 产品推销; 销售术; marketing agreement = contract by which one company will market another company's products 销售协议; marketing department = department in a company which specializes in using marketing techniques to sell a product 销售部; marketing manager = person in charge of a marketing department 销售经理; marketing policy or marketing plans = ideas of how the company's products are going to be marketed 产品售销政策或销售计划; to plan the marketing of a new product 计划新产品的推销 NOTE: no plural

◇ **market - maker** n. person who buys and sells shares for clients on the Stock Exchange 股票经纪人

◇ **marketplace** n. (a) open space in the middle of a town where a market is held 露天集市 (b) place where goods are sold 市场: Our salesmen find life difficult in the marketplace. 我们的推销员发现在市场上日子不好过。What is the reaction to the new car in the marketplace? or What is the marketplace reaction to the new car? 对于新汽车市场上有什么反应?

**mart** n. market or place where things are sold 商业中心; 市场: car mart 汽车市场; auction mart = auction rooms 拍卖市场

**mass** n. (a) large group of people 群众: mass marketing = marketing which aims at reaching large numbers of people 大规模的销售; mass media = means of communication which reach large numbers of people (such as radio, television, newspapers) 大众传播媒介(如收音机, 电视和报纸等); mass unemployment = unemployment of large numbers of workers 大量人员失业 (b) large number 大量: We have a mass of letters or masses of letters to write. 我们有大量的信要写。They received a mass of orders or masses of orders after the TV commercials. 做电视广告后他们收到大量订单。

◇ **mass - produce** v. to manufacture in large quantities 大规模生产: to mass - produce cars 大规模生产汽车

◇ **mass production** n. manufacturing large quantities of products 大量生产; 大规模生产

**master** n. main or original 主要部分; 原物: master copy of a file = main copy of a computer file, kept for security purposes 计算机安全存档中的原本

**material** n. (a) substance which can be used to make a finished product 材料; 原料: building materials = bricks, cement, etc., used in building 建筑材料; raw materials = substances which have not been manufactured (such as wool, wood, sand) 原材料; synthetic materials = substances made as products of a chemical process 人工合成材料; materials control = system to check that a company has enough materials in stock to do its work 材料管理; 材料的控制; materials handling = moving materials from one part of a factory to another in an efficient way 材料(在厂内的)管理 (b) display material = posters, photographs, etc., which can be used to attract attention to goods which are for sale 展示商品资料(广告画,照片)

**maternity** n. becoming a mother 母性: maternity benefit = money paid by the National Insurance to a mother when she has her child 产妇津贴; maternity leave = permission for a woman to be away from work to have a baby 产假

**matter** 1 n. (a) problem 问题; 事情: It is a matter of concern to the members of the committee. = The members of the committee are worried about it. 这是个令委员会成员们感到关注的问题。(b) printed matter = printed books, newspapers, publicity sheets, etc. 印刷材料; 印刷品: publicity matter = sheets or posters or leaflets used for publicity 宣传品 (c) question or problem to be discussed 问题: the most important matter on the agenda 议事日程中最重要的问题; We shall consider first the matter of last month's fall in prices. 我们首先要考虑上个月跌价的问题。NOTE: no plural for (b) 2 v. to be important 具有重要性: Does it matter if one month's sales are down? 如果某个月的销售额下降了,这关系大吗?

**mature** 1 a. mature economy = fully developed economy 成熟经济; 充分发展的经济 2 v. bills which mature in three weeks' time = bills which will be due

for payment in three weeks 三个星期后到期的汇票

◇ **maturity** n. date of maturity or maturity date = date when a government stock or an assurance policy or a debenture will become due for payment 到期日 (政府债券、保险单、公司债券等证券的): amount payable on maturity 到期承保人的应付款项 = amount received by the insured person when the policy becomes mature 到期承保人的应付款项

**maximization** n. making as large as possible 最大限度: profit maximization or maximization of profit 最大限度增加利润

◇ **maximize** v. to make as large as possible 把……增加(或扩大)到最大限度: to maximize profits 最大限度利润

**maximum** 1 n. largest possible number or price or quantity 最大限度: up to a maximum of £10 = no more than £10 最多不超过 10 英磅的; to increase exports to the maximum = as much as possible 最大限度增加出口; It is the maximum the insurance company will pay. 这是保险公司所能付给的最大金额。NOTE: plural is maxima 2 a. largest possible 最大限度的: maximum income tax rate or maximum rate of tax 最大限度的所得税率; maximum load 最大限度负载; maximum production levels 最高限度生产水平; maximum price 最高价格; to increase production to the maximum level = as much as possible 增加生产至最高水平

**MD** = MANAGING DIRECTOR 总经理. The MD is in his office. 总经理在他的办公室里。 She was appointed MD of a property company. 她被认命为某房地产公司的总经理。

**mean** 1 a. average 平均的: mean annual increase 平均年增长; mean price = average price of a share in a day's trad-

ing(某股票交易的)日平均价格 2 n.
averageor number calculated by adding
several figures together and dividing by
the number of figures added 平均;平均
数: Unit sales are over the mean for the
first quarter or above the first quarter
mean. 单位产品销售额超过了第一季
度的平均数。

◇ **means** pl. n. (a) way of doing
something 方法: Air freight is the
fastest means of getting stock to South
America. 空运是把货物运送到南美的
最快方法。Do we have any means of
copying all these documents quickly? 我
们有什么办法把所有这些文件很快复
印出来呢? (b) money or resources 资
金;资源: The company has the means
to launch the new product. 公司有资金
向市场投放新产品。Such a level of investment is beyond the means of a small
private company. 这样的投资水平超
过了小型私人企业的资力。means test
= inquiry into how much money someone earns to see if he is eligible for state
benefits 收入调查;家庭资金来源调查
(对申请国家生活补贴的人所进行的家
庭收入情况调查). He has private
means. = He has income from dividends
or interest or rent which is not part of his
salary. 他有工资外收入(如租金股息或
利息)。

**measure** he has income from dividends
or interest or rent which is not part of his
salary 计贴;

**measure** 1. n. (a) way of calculating
size or quantity 计量;衡量: cubic measure = volume in cubic feet or metres,
calculated by multiplying height, width
and length 体积; dry measure = way of
calculating the quantity of loose dry
goods (such as corn) 干货量; square
measure = area in square feet or metres,
calculated by multiplying width and
length 面积;计算; inspector of weights
and measures = government inspector

who inspects weighing machines and
goods sold in shops to see if the quantities
and weights are correct 度量衡检查员;
as a measure of the company's performance = as a way of judging if the
company's results are good or bad 公司
工作业绩的衡量法 (b) made to mea-
sure = made specially to fit 依尺寸定
做: He has his clothes made to measure.
他的衣服是依尺寸定做的。(c) tape
measure = long tape with centimetres or
inches marked on it, used to measure
how long something is 卷尺 (d) type of
action 措施; to take measures to prevent
something happening = to act to stop
something happening 采取措施防止某
事发生; to take crisis or emergency
measures = to act rapidly to stop a crisis
developing 采取紧急措施; an economy
measure = an action to save money 节约
措施; fiscal measures = tax changes
made by the government to improve the
working of the economy 财政措施; as a
precautionary measure = to prevent
something taking place 作为预防措施;
safety measures = actions to make sure
that something is safe 安全措施 2. v.
(a) to find out the size or quantity of
something; to be of a certain size or
quantity 量度(大小,多少); to measure
the size of a package; (测)量色裹的尺
寸; a package which measures 10cm by
25cm or a package measuring 10cm by
25cm 尺寸为 10cm×25cm 的包裹 (b)
to measure the government's performance = to judge how well the government is doing 衡量政府的业绩

◇ **measurement** n. (a) measurements
= size (in inches, centimetres, etc.) 尺
码: to write down the measurements of a
package 记下包裹的尺寸 (b) way of
judging something 衡量方法; performance measurement or measurement of
performance 工作业绩衡量; measure-
ment of profitability = way of calculat-

ing how profitable something is 利润率的(能力的)衡量

◇ **measuring tape** n. long tape with centimetres or inches marked on it, used to measure how long something is 卷尺

**mechanic** n. person who works with engines or machines 机械师；car mechanic 汽车机械师

◇ **mechanical** a. worked by a machine 机械的；a mechanical pump 机械泵

◇ **mechanism** n. way in which something works 途径；机制：a mechanism to slow down inflation；减慢通货膨胀的途径；the company's discount mechanism 公司的折扣机制

◇ **mechanize** v. to use machines in place of workers 使机械化：The country is aiming to mechanize its farming industry. 国家目标是使农业机械化。

◇ **mechanization** n. using machines in place of workers 机械化；farm mechanization or the mechanization of farms 农业机械化

**media** n. the media or the mass media = means of communicating information to the public (such as television, radio, newspapers)大众传播媒介；新闻媒介：The product attracted a lot of interest in the media or a lot of media interest. 产品引起了大众传播媒介的很大兴趣。media analysis or media research = examining different types of media (such as the readers of newspapers, television viewers) to see which is best for promoting a certain type of product 新闻媒介分析或调查(对各种可用来做某种商品广告的传播媒介进行效果分析)；media coverage = reports about something in the media 大众传播媒介的报导；We got good media coverage for the launch of the new model. 传播媒介对我们的新型产品投放市场作了有利的报导。

NOTE: media is followed by a singular or plural verb

**median** n. point in the middle of a list of numbers 中位数

**mediate** v. to try to make the two sides in an argument come to to an agreement 调停；调解：to mediate between the manager and his staff；在经理和他的职员之间进行调解；The government offered to mediate in the dispute. 政府主动提出为争端进行调解

◇ **mediation** n. attempt by a third party to make the two sides in an argument agree 调解；调停；The employers refused an offer of government mediation. 雇主拒绝政府提供的调解。The dispute was ended through the mediation of union officials. 通过工会官员的调解解决了争端。

◇ **mediator** n. official mediator = government official who tries to make the two sides in an industrial dispute agree 政府调解员(为劳资争端双方进行调解的)

**medical** n. referring to the study or treatment of illness 医疗的：medical certificate = certificate from a doctor to show that a worker has been ill 医疗证明；medical inspection = examining a place of work to see if the conditions will not make the workers ill 医疗视察(检查工作环境是否符合人体健康要求)；medical insurance = insurance which pays the cost of medical treatment especially when travelling abroad 医疗保险；medical officer of health = person responsible for the health services in a town 负责医疗服务的官员；He resigned for medical reasons. = He resigned because he was too ill to work. 他因健康原因辞职了。

**medium** 1. a. middle or average 中间的；平均的：The company is of medium size 这个公司具有中等规模。2. n. (a) way of doing something or means of doing something 方法；媒介：advertising medium = type of advertisement (such as a TV commercial)广告宣传媒介；

The product was advertised through the medium of the trade press. 产品通过商业新闻界做的广告。(b) mediums = government stocks which mature in five to fifteen years' time 债券（政府发行的5年到15年偿还）NOTE: plural for (a) is media

◇ **medium – sized** a. a medium – sized engineering company = company which is neither very large nor very small 一个中等规模的工程公司

◇ **medium – term** a. referring to a point between short term and long terms 中期的; medium – term forecast = forecast for two or three years 中期预测（两年或三年的）

**meet** v. (a) to come together with someone 会见: to meet a negotiating committee 会见某谈判委员会; to meet an agent at his hotel 在他的旅馆会见某代理人; The two sides met in the lawyer's office. 双方在律师办公室会面。(b) to be satisfactory for 满足: to meet a customer's requirements 满足顾客的需求; to meet the demand for a new product = to fill the demand for a product 满足对新产品的需求; We will try to meet your price. = We will try to offer a price which is acceptable to you. 我们会尽量满足您的出价。They failed to meet the deadline. = They were not able to complete in time. 他们未能按期完成。(c) to pay for 支付: to meet someone's expenses 支付某人的开销; The company will meet your expenses. 公司将支付你的开销。He was unable to meet his mortgage repayments. 他无力支付他所抵押款的偿还。NOTE: meeting – met

◇ **meet with** verb (a) US to come together with someone(美)与某人会见; I hope to meet with him in New York. = I hope to meet him in New York. 我希望在纽约与他会面。(b) His request met with a refusal. = His request was refused. 他的要求遭到拒绝。

◇ **meeting** n. (a) coming together of a group of people 会面; 会议: management meeting 管理人员会议; staff meeting 职工会议; board meeting = meeting of the directors of a company 公司董事会会议; general meeting or meeting of shareholders or shareholders' meeting = meeting of all the shareholders of a company or meeting of all the members of a society 全体股东大会; Annual General Meeting = meeting of all the shareholders when a company's financial situation is discussed with the directors 年度股东大会; Extraordinary General Meeting = special meeting of shareholders to discuss an important matter(讨论重大问题的)股东特别大会议 (b) to hold a meeting = to organize a meeting of a group of people 召开会议; 举行会议; The meeting will be held in the committee room. 会议将在委员会办公室召开。to open a meeting = to start a meeting 开始会议; to conduct a meeting = to be in the chair for a meeting 主持会议; to close a meeting = to end a meeting 结束会议; to address a meeting = to speak to a meeting 在会上讲话; to put a resolution to a meeting = to ask a meeting to vote on a proposal 会议就某提议进行表决

**megabyte** n. storage unit in computers, equal to 1,048,576 bytes 兆位(计算机中的存储单位, 相当于1,048,576字节)

**member** n. (a) person who belongs to a group or a society 成员; members of a committee or committee members 委员会成员 They were elected members of the board. 他们被选为董事会成员。ordinary member = person who pays a subscription to belong to a group 一般成员; honorary member = special person who does not have to pay a subscription 名誉成员 (b) organization which belongs to a society 成员（组织）: the membercountries of the EEC 欧洲经济共同体的成员国; the members of the United Nations 联合国成员国; the member companies of a trade association 贸易协会的会员公司

◇ **membership** n. (a) belonging to a group 社员或会员地位（资格）; membership qualifications 成员资格; conditions of membership 获得成员资格的应具备条件; membership card 会员卡; to pay your membership or your membership fees 交纳你的会员费; Is Austria going to apply for membership of the Common Market? 奥地利打算申请加入共同市场吗?(b) all the members of a group 全体成员: The membership was asked to vote for the new president. 要求全体成员投票选举新总裁。the club's membership secretary = committee member who deals with the ordinary members of a society 俱乐部会员秘书; The club has a membership of five hundred. = The club has five hundred members. 俱乐部有 500 个成员。

**memo** n. short message sent from one person to another in the same organization 便函（公司或机构内部彼此之间行文）; to write a memo to the finance director 给财务主任写便函; to send a memo to all the sales representatives 给所有销售代表寄去一份便函; according to your memo about debtors 按照你的有关债务人的便函; I sent the managing director a memo about your complaint. 我给总经理送去了有关你的投诉的便函。

◇ **memo pad** n. pad of paper for writing short notes 便函簿

◇ **memorandum** n. short message 便笺; memorandum (and articles) of association = legal document setting up a limited company and giving details of its aims, directors, and registered office 公司组织章程

**memory** n. facility for storing of data in a computer 存储器（计算机中存储信息用的）

**mention** v. to talk about something for a short time 提及: The chairman mentioned the work of the retiring managing director. 董事长提到了即将退休的总经理的工作。Can you mention to the secretary that the date of the next meeting has been changed? 你能跟秘书提一提下次会议已改期之事吗?

**mercantile** a. commercial 商业的; mercantile country = country which earns income from trade（商业发达的）贸易国家; mercantile law = laws relating to business 商法; mercantile marine = all the commercial ships of a country 商船（队）

**merchandise** 1 n. goods which are for sale or which have been sold 商品: The merchandise is shipped through two ports. 商品通过两个港口装运。NOTE: no plural 2 v. to sell goods by a wide variety of means, including display, advertising, sending samples, etc. 推销商品（例如商品展示、广告宣传、寄送样品等）; to merchandise a product 推销一种产品。

◇ **merchandiser** n. person or company which organizes the display and promotion of goods 商人; 从事商业的公司（组织展览促销）

◇ **merchandising** n. organizing the display and promotion of goods for sale 推销（组织产品展览及促销产品的活动）; merchandising of a product 推销一种产品; merchandising department 产品促销部门;

**merchant** n. (a) businessman who buys and sells goods (especially imported goods) in bulk for retail sale 商人（特别是进口商）: coal merchant 煤炭商: tobacco merchant 烟草商; wine merchant 酒类商 (b) merchant bank = bank which lends money to companies and deals in international finance 商人(业)银行(向公司提供贷款并从事国际金融业务的银行); merchant banker = person who has a high position in a merchant bank 商人(业)银行的银行家或高级职员; merchant navy or merchant marine = all the commercial ships of a country 商船; merchant ship or merchant vessel = commercial ship or ship which carries a cargo 商船或货船

◇ **merchantman** n. commercial ship 商船

**merge** v. to join together 合并: The two companies have merged. 这两个公司已合并了。The firm merged with its main competitor. 该公司和它的主要竞争对手合并了。

◇ **merger** n. joining together of two or more companies 吸收;合并;吞并(两个或更多公司间的合并): As a result of the merger, the company is the largest in the field. 合并的结果是这家公司成为其领域中最大一家公司。

**merit** n. being good or efficient 优点;功绩; merit award or merit bonus = extra money given to a worker because he has worked well(对工作效绩突出的人给予额外的)奖赏或奖金; merit increase = increase in pay given to someone because his work is good 功绩加薪; merit rating = judging how well a worker does his work, so that he can be paid according to merit 人事考核,工资评定

**message** n. piece of news which is sent to someone 消息; to send a message 发出消息;送讯; I will leave a message with his secretary. 我会给他的秘书留言。Can you give the director a message from his wife? 你能把他的妻子的信带给董事吗? He says he never received the message. 他说他从未接到这个消息。

**messenger** n. person who brings a message 信使;通信员: He sent the package by special messenger or by motorcycle messenger. 他用特殊的信使或用摩托信使发送包裹。office messenger = person who carries messages from one person to another in a large office 大办公处内传递消息的人; messenger boy = young man who carries messages 传递消息的年轻人;信童

**Messrs** n. plural form of Mr; used only in names of firms 先生(Mr 的复数形式,只用于商号名称): Messrs White and Smith 华特与史密斯公司

**method** n. way of doing something 方法: a new method of making something or of doing something 制造某物或做某事的新方法; What is the best method of payment? 什么是最好的支付方式? His organizing methods are out of date. 他的组织方法过时了。Their manufacturing methods or production methods are among the most modern in the country. 他们的生产方式是国内最先进的。time and method study = examining the way in which something is done to see if a cheaper or quicker way can be found 时间和方法研究(通过对工作方法的研究寻求更高效简捷的工作方法)

**metre** or **US meter** n. measure of length (= 3.4 feet) 米(长度衡量单位等于3.4英尺) NOTE: usually written m after figures: The case is 2m wide by 3m long. 这箱子2米宽3米长。

◇ **metric** a. using the metre as a basic measurement 公制的(以米作为度量单位); metric ton or metric tonne = 1000 kilograms 公吨(相当于1000公斤); the metric system = system of measuring, using metres, litres and grams 公制;十进位制(以公尺、公升、克等作为度量单位的度量体系)

**mg** = MILLIGRAM 毫克(千分之一克)

**mi** = MILE 英里

**micro** n. microcomputer 微型计算机；微机：We put the sales statistics on to the office micro. 我们把销售统计数字输入办公室的微型电子计算机中。Our office micro interfaces with the mainframe computer in London. 我们办公室的微机与伦敦总机相联接。

◇ **micro-** prefix very small 很小 micro - economics = study of the economics of persons or single companies 微观经济学

◇ **microcomputer** n. small computer for general use in the home or office(一般家用或办公用的)小型计算机；微机

◇ **microfiche** n. index sheet, made of several microfilm photographs 微缩胶片(用缩微胶片制成的、有摄制内容的胶片) We hold our records on microfiche. 我们把记录保存在缩微胶片上。

◇ **microfilm** 1 n. roll of film on which a document is photographed in very small scale 缩微胶卷(印刷物等摄制成的极微小的胶片)；We hold our records on microfilm. 我们把记录保存在缩微胶卷上 2 v. to make a very small scale photograph 摄制成缩微胶片；把…拍摄在缩微胶卷上；Send the 1980 correspondence to be microfilmed or for microfilming. 把 1980 年的信函送去摄制成缩微胶卷。

◇ **microprocessor** n. small computer processing unit 微处理机

**mid-** prefix middle 中间；from mid - 1982 = from the middle of 1982 1982 年年中；The factory is closed until mid - July. 工厂关闭直至七月中旬。

◇ **mid - month** a. taking place in the middle of the month 月中：mid - month accounts 月中帐户

◇ **mid - week** a. which happens in the middle of a week 一星期中间的：the mid - week lull in sales 一周中间销售呆滞

**middle** a. in the centre or between two points 中心的；中间的；middle management = department managers in a company, who carry out the policy set by the directors and organize the work of a group of workers 公司中层管理人员(其职能是执行董事们制定的政策并组织工人生产)

◇ **middle - income** a. people in the middle - income bracket = people with average incomes, not very high or very low 中等收入阶层的人

◇ **middleman** n. businessman who buys from the manufacturer and sells to the public 中间商；We sell direct from the factory to the customer and cut out the middleman 我们从工厂向顾客直接销售，绕过了中间商。
NOTE: plural is middlemen

◇ **middle - sized** a. neither small nor large 中等规模的；a middle - sized company 中等规模的公司

**mile** n. measure of length ( = 1.625 kilometres) 英里(长度单位，相当于 1.625 公里)：The car does twenty - five miles to the gallon or twenty - five miles per gallon. = The car uses one gallon of petrol to travel twenty - five miles. 这辆汽车每加仑油能行驶 25 英里。
NOTE: miles per gallon is usually written mpg after figures: The car does 25mpg.

◇ **mileage** n. distance travelled in miles 里程(按英里计算的行驶距离)；mileage allowance = money allowed as expenses to someone who uses his own car for business travel 里程补助；the salesman's average annual mileage = the number of miles which a salesman drives in a year 推销员的年驾驶里程数
NOTE: no plural

**mill** n. building where a certain type of material is processed or made 工厂：After lunch the visitors were shown round the mill. 午饭后带领来访者参观工厂。 Cotton mill = factory where raw cotton is processed 绵纺厂; paper mill = factory where wood is made into paper 造纸厂;

**milligram** n. one thousandth of a gram 毫克(千分之一克)

NOTE: usually written mg after figures

◇ **millilitre** n. one thousandth of a litre 毫升(千分之一升)

NOTE: usually written ml after figures

◇ **millimetre** n. one thousandth of a metre 毫米

NOTE: usually written mm after figures

**million** num. 1,000,000 一百万; The company lost £10 million in the African market. 公司在非洲市场损失了 1000 万英磅。 Our turnover has risen to $13.4 million 我们的营业额已增加到 1340 万美元。( $13.4m)

NOTE: can be written m figures: $5m (say "five million dollars")

◇ **millionaire** n. person who has more than one million pounds 百万富翁; dollar millionaire = person who has more than one million dollars 美元百万富翁; paper millionaire = person who owns shares which, if sold, would be worth one million pounds or dollars 拥有价值为百万英磅或百万美元股东

**min** = MINUTE, MINIMUM 分钟、最低限度

**mine** 1 n. hole in the ground for digging out coal, gold, iron etc. 矿井: The mines have been closed by a strike. 由于罢工矿井关闭了。 2 v. to dig and bring out coal, gold, etc. 采矿: The company is mining coal in the south of the country. 该公司正在国家的南部开采煤矿。 mining concession = right to use a piece of land for mining 矿山开采特许权

**mini-** prefix very small 很小

◇ **minibudget** n. interim statement

about financial plans from a finance minister 小预算; 临时性的预算(财政部长对于财政计划的报告)

◇ **minicomputer** n. computer which is larger than a micro but smaller than a mainframe 微型计算机

◇ **minicontainer** n. small container 小容器; 小集装箱

◇ **minimarket** n. very small self-service store 小型的自选商场

**minimal** a. the smallest possible 最小的: There was a minimal quantity of imperfections in the batch. 这批产品的残次品极少。 The head office exercises minimal control over the branch offices. 总部对分部实行最低程度的控制。

◇ **minimize** v. to make something seem to be very small and not very important 轻视, 不看重; 对…低估: Do not minimize the risks involved. 不要低估所涉的风险。 He tends to minimize the difficulty of the project. 他常常低估该项目的困难。

◇ **minimum** 1 n. smallest possible quantity or price or number 最低限度: to keep expenses to a minimum 使费用开支维持在最低水平; to reduce the risk of a loss to a minimum 把损失的风险减少至最低限度

NOTE: plural is minima or minimums 2 a. smallest possible 最低限度的: minimum dividend = smallest dividend which is legal and accepted by the shareholders 最低限度股息; minimum payment = smallest payment necessary 最低偿付额(支付) minimum quantity = smallest quantity which is acceptable 最低数量; minimum wage = lowest hourly wage which a company can legally pay its workers 最低时工资

**minister** n. member of a government who is in charge of a ministry 部长: a government minister 政府部长; the Minister of Trade or the Trade Minister

贸易部部长; the Minister of Foreign Affairsor the Foreign Minister 外交部部长

NOTE: in the USA, they are called secretary: the Secretary for Commerce 商业部部长

◇ **ministry** n. department in the government 政府部门; He works in the Ministry of Finance or the Finance Ministry. 他在财政部工作。He is in charge of the Ministry of Information or of the Information Ministry. 他负责政府情报部。a ministry official or an official from the ministry 政府部门官员

NOTE: in GB and the USA, important ministries are called departments: the Department of Trade and Industry 贸易与工业部; the Commerce Department 商业部

**minor** a. less important 较次要的: minor expenditure 次要开支; minor shareholders 次要股东; a loss of minor importance = not a very serious loss 不严重的损失

◇ **minority** n. number or quantity which is less than half of the total 少数: A minority of board members opposed the chairman. 董事会成员中的少数人反对董事长。minority shareholding or minority interest = group of shares which are less than one half of the shares in a company 持有少数股权或少数股份; minority shareholder = person who owns a group of shares but less than half of the shares in a company 次要股东(拥有的股票少于公司全部股票半数的股东); in the minority = being fewer than half 处于少数; Good salesmen are in the minority in our sales team. 在我们的推销队伍中好的推销员占少数。

**mint** 1 n. factory where coins are made 制币厂 2 v. to make coins 制硬币

**minus** 1 prep. less or without 较少; 没有: Net salary is gross salary minus tax and National Insurance deductions. 净工资是工资总额减去税收和扣除国民保险。Gross profit is sales minus production costs. 毛利润是销售额减去生产成本。2 a. The accounts show a minus figure. = show that more has been spent than has been received 帐目中出现负数。minus factor = unfavourable factor 不利因素; To have lost sales in the best quarter of the year is a minus factor for the sales team. 对于销售人员来讲,在一年中最有利的季节失去产品销售是个不利因素。

**minute** 1 n. (a) one sixtieth part of an hour 分钟: I can see you for ten minutes only. 我只能接见你十分钟。If you do not mind waiting, Mr Smith will be free in about twenty minutes' time. 如果您能等一下,史密斯先生20分钟后就有空了。(b) the minutes of the meeting = notes of what happened at a meeting, written by the secretary 会议记录: to take the minutes = to write notes of what happened at a meeting. 做会议记录; The chairman signed the minutes of the last meeting. = He signed them to show that they are a correct record of what was said and what decisions were taken. 主席在上次的会议记录上签了名。This will not appear in the minutes of the meeting. = This is unofficial and will not be noted as having been said. 这将不记入会议记录中。2 v. to put something into the minutes of a meeting 记入会议记录; The chairman's remarks about the auditors were minuted. 董事长对审计员的评论记入了会议记录。I do not want that to be minuted or I want that not to be minuted. = Do not put that remark into the minutes of the meeting. 我不希望那一点被记入会议记录。

◇ **minutebook** n. book in which the minutes of a meeting are kept 会议记录本

**misappropriate** v. to use illegally moneywhich is not yours, but with which you have been trusted 非法侵占(挪用)经管资金

◇ **misappropriation** n. illegal use of money by someone who is not the owner but who has been trusted to look after it 非法侵占(挪用)经管资金

**misc** = MISCELLANEOUS 混杂的

**miscalculate** v. to calculate wrongly 错算；误算：The salesman miscalculated the discount, so we hardly broke even on the deal. 推销员算错了折扣，因此在这项交易中我们几乎不能收支抵销。

◇ **miscalculation** n. mistake in calculating 计算差错

**miscellaneous** a. various or mixed or not all of the same sort 多种类的；混杂的：miscellaneous items 杂项；杂物 a box of miscellaneous pieces of equipment 一箱各种各样的设备；miscellaneous expenditure 杂项支出

**miscount** 1 n. mistake in counting 计算差错 2 v. to count wrongly 错算：The shopkeeper miscounted, so we got twenty-five bars of chocolate instead of two dozen 店主算错了数，我们得到了 25 块巧克力而不是 24 块。

**misdirect** v. to give wrong directions 指错方向

**mismanage** v. to manage badly 管理不善。

◇ **mismanagement** n. bad management 管理不善；The company failed because of the chairman's mismanagement. 因为董事长的管理不善公司倒闭了。

NOTE: no plural

**misrepresent** v. to report facts wrongly 误报；误述；错误说明；

◇ **misrepresentation** n. wrongly reporting facts 误报；误述 fraudulent misrepresentation = giving someone wrong information in order to cheat him 欺骗性的陈述

**Miss** n. title given to a woman who is not married 小姐：Miss Smith is our sales manager. 史密斯小姐是我们的销售经理。

**miss** v. (a) not to hit 未击中；The company has missed its profit forecast again. 公司又未达到其利润预测。The sales team has missed its sales targets. 销售人员未达到其销售目标。(b) not to meet 错过：I arrived late, so missed most of the discussion。我迟到了，错过了大部分讨论。He missed the chairman by ten minutes. = He left ten minutes before the chairman arrived. 他早走 10 分钟而未能见到董事长。

**mission** n. group of people going on a journey for a special purpose 特使团；代表团：trade mission = visit by a group of businessmen to discuss trade 贸易代表团；He led a trade mission to China. 他率贸易代表团来中国。inward mission = visit to your home country by a group of foreign businessmen 来访商团；outward mission = visit by a group of businessmen to a foreign country 出访商团；a fact-finding mission = visit to an area to search for information about a problem 实情调查团

**mistake** n. wrong action or wrong decision 错误；弄错：to make a mistake = to do something wrong 出差错；The shop made a mistake and sent the wrong items. 商店出了差错而送错了货。There was a mistake in the address. 地址中有一处错误(地址有误). She made a mistake in addressing the letter. 她写信时写错了地址。by mistake = in error or wrongly 弄错，误为；They sent the wrong items by mistake. 他送错了货。She put my letter into an envelope for the chairman by mistake. 她把给我的信误装入寄给董事长的信封里。

**misunderstanding** n. lack of agreement or mistake 误解: There was a mis-understandingover my tickets. 对我的票发生了误解。

**misuse** n. wrong use 错用: misuse of funds or of assets 资金或财产的错误使用

**mix** 1 n. things put together 混合: product mix = range of different products which a company has for sale 产品组合; sales mix = sales and profitability of a wide range of different products 销售组合 2 v. to put different things together 混合: I like to mix business with pleasure – why don't we discuss the deal over lunch? 我喜欢把业务和娱乐合二为一——我们为什么不能边用午餐边谈生意呢?

◇ **mixed** a. (a) of different sorts or of different types together 混合的: mixed economy = system which contains both nationalized industries and private enterprise 混合经济; mixed farm = farm which has both animals and crops(既有畜牧业又有农业的)混合型农场;多种经营农场 (b) neither good nor bad 混合的(既不好也不坏)

**ml** = MILLILITRE 毫升

**mm** = MILLIMETRE 毫米

**mobile** a. which can move about 可移动的: mobile shop = van fitted out like a small shop which travels round selling groceries or vegetables 流动售货车;流动商店; mobile workforce = workers who move from place to place to get work 流动劳动力

◇ **mobility** n. being able to move from one place to another 流动性: mobility of labour = situation when workers agree to move from one place to another to get work 劳动力的流动性
NOTE: no plural

◇ **mobilize** v. to bring together, especially to fight 动员;调动: to mobilize capital = to collect capital to support

something 调集资本; to mobilize resources to defend a takeover bid = to get the support of shareholders, etc., to stop a company being taken over 动员公司力量以防公司被合并

**mock – up** n. model of a new product for testing or to show to possible buyers 用来做实验或用来向顾客展示的新产品模型。

**mode** n. way of doing something 方式: mode of payment = way in which payment is made (such as cash or cheque) 付款方式

**model** 1 n. (a) small copy of something to show what it will look like when finished 模型: He showed us a model of the new office building. 他给我们看了个新办公楼的模型。(b) style or type of product 产品样式或类型: This is the latest model. 这是最新产品样式。The model on display is last year's. 展示的产品是去年的样式。He drives a 1985 model Ford. 他驾驶着一辆 1985 年样式的福特车。demonstration model = piece of equipment used in demonstrations and then sold cheaply 展品 (c) person whose job is to wear new clothes to show them to possible buyers 服装模特 (d) economic model = computerized plan of a country's economic system, used for forecasting economic trends 经济型模式 2 a. which is a perfect example to be copied 标准的: a model agreement 标准合同 3 v. to wear new clothes to show them to possible buyers 模特儿展示服装
NOTE: modelling – modelled but US modeling – modeled

**modem** n. device which links a computer to the telephone line, allowing data to be sent from one computer to another(电脑联网装置)调制解调器

**moderate** 1 a. not too large 适度的: The trade union made a moderate claim.

工会提出适度要求。The government proposeda moderate increase in the tax rate. 政府建议税收率适度增长。2 v. to make less strong or less large 缓和；减轻：The union was forced to moderate its claim. 工会被迫缓和了其提出的要求。

**modern** a. referring to the recent past or the present time 现代的：It is a fairly modern invention – it was patented only in the 1960s. 这是个相当现代的发明——它是在 20 世纪 60 年代才得到发明的专利。

◇ **modernize** v. to make modern 使现代化：He modernized the whole product range. 他使所有产品系列现代化了。

◇ **modernization** n. making modern 现代化：the modernization of the workshop 工厂车间的现代化

**modest** a. small 小的：Oil shares showed modest gains over the week's trading. 石油股票价在上星期的交易中略有上升。

**modify** v. to change or to make something fit a different use 改变；修正；改装：The management modified its proposals. 管理部人员修改了其提议。This is the new modified agreement. 这是新修改的协议。The car will have to be modified to pass the government tests. 这部汽车必须改装以通过政府检验。The refrigerator was considerably modified before it went into production. 这冰箱在投产前做了相当大的改装。

◇ **modification** n. change 改变；改装：to make or to carry out modifications to the plan 对计划进行修改；The new model has had several important modifications. 新模型有几处重大改动。We asked for modifications to the contract. 我们要求对合同做修改。

**modular** a. made of various sections 组件的

**momentum** n. movement forwards 推进力；动力；势头：to gain or to lose mo-

mentum = to move faster or more slowly 势头在增强或在减弱；The strike is gaining momentum. = More workers are joining the strike. 罢工愈演愈烈或罢工势头正在加大。
NOTE: no plural

**monetary** a. referring to money or currency 货币的；the government's monetary policy = the government's policy relating to finance (bank interest rates, taxes, government expenditure and borrowing) 政府的货币政策（如银行利息、税收、政府支出和借贷等政策）；monetary standard = fixing of a fixed exchange rate for a currency 货币本位制（确定某种货币的固定的兑换率）；the international monetary system = methods of controlling and exchanging currencies between countries 国际货币制度（国家间货币控制和兑换的制度）；the European Monetary System = system of controlled exchange rates between some member countries of the Common Market 欧洲经济共同体货币制度（一些共同体成员国之间有关控制兑换率的制度）；The International Monetary Fund = (part of the United Nations) a type of bank which helps member states in financial difficulties, gives financial advice to members and encourages world trade 国际货币基金(组织)(旨在帮助其成员国解决财政困难、给予财政建议并鼓励其国际贸易的银行)；monetary unit = standard currency in a country (the pound, the dollar, the franc, etc.) 货币单位

◇ **monetarism** n. idea that inflation can be controlled by regulating the amount of money available in the economy 货币主义(认为通过控制货币发行量可以控制通货膨胀的经济主张)
NOTE: no plural

◇ **monetarist** 1 n. person who believes in monetarism and acts accordingly 货币主义者 2 a. according to monetarism 货

币主义的；monetarist theories 货币主义理论

**money** n. (a) coins and notes used for buying and selling 金钱；货币：to earn money = to have a salary 挣钱；to earn good money = to have a large salary 挣很多钱；to lose money = to make a loss or not to make a profit 亏损或不赢利；The company has been losing money for months. = The company has been working at a loss. 几个月来公司一直在亏损。to get your money back = to earn enough to cover your original investment 把最初的投资赚回来；to make money = to make a profit 赢利；to put money into the bank = to deposit money into a bank account 把钱存入银行；to put money into a business = to invest money in a business 将钱投入于企业；He put all his redundancy money into a shop. 他把所有剩余资金都投入了一家商店。to put money down = to pay cash, especially as a deposit 支付现金（特指支付定金）；He put £25 down and paid the rest in instalments. 他付了 25 英磅的定金,其余的分期付款。cheap money = money which can be borrowed at a low rate of interest 低利率借款；danger money = extra salary paid to workers in dangerous jobs 危险工作的津贴；dear money = money which has to be borrowed at a high rate of interest 高利率借款；easy money = money which can be earned with no difficulty 容易挣的钱；钱来得容易；Selling insurance is easy money. 出售保险容易赚钱。hot money = money which is moved from country to country to get the best returns 游资（在国家之间转移以取得高利率的资金）；paper money = money in notes, not coins 纸币 ready money = cash or money which is immediately available 现金；立即得到的款项；money lying idle = money not being used to produce interest 闲置资金；They are worth a lot of

money. = They are valuable. 它们值许多钱。(b) money supply = amount of money which exists in a country 货币供应：money markets = markets for buying and selling short - term loans 货币市场；The international money markets are nervous. 国际货币市场摇摆不定。money rates = rates of interest for borrowers or lenders 借贷款利率 (c) money order = document which can be bought for sending money through the post 汇票；汇款单：foreign money order or international money order or overseas money order = money order in a foreign currency which is payable to someone living in a foreign country 国际汇款单；对外汇款单；

NOTE: no plural for (a), (b) and (c) (d) monies = sums of money 货币总额；monies owing to the company 对某公司的欠款总额；to collect monies due 收回全部到期款项

◇ **moneylender** n. person who lends money at interest 放款人

◇ **money - making** a. which makes money 能赚钱的：a money - making plan 一个能赚钱的计划

◇ **money - spinner** n. item which sells very well or which is very profitable 销路好或赢利高的商品；能赚钱的商品

**monitor** 1 n. screen (like a TV screen) on a computer 计算机荧光屏；监视器 2 v. to check or to examine how something is working 检查；监视：He is monitoring the progress of sales. 他正监视着销售进展。How do you monitor the performance of the sales reps? 你是怎样检查销售代表们的工作情况的？

**monopoly** n. situation where one person or company controls all the market in the supply of a product 垄断：to have the monopoly of alcohol sales or to have the alcohol monopoly 垄断酒类销售；to be in a monopoly situation；处于垄断状况；

The company has the absolute monopoly of imports of French wine. 这公司对法国酒进口拥有绝对垄断权。The factory has the absolute monopoly of jobs in the town. 镇子里这家工厂在提供就业机会方面拥有绝对垄断权。public monopoly or state monopoly = situation where the state is the only suppliers of a product or service ( such as the Post Office, the coal industry, etc.) 国家垄断；GB the Monopolies Commission = organization which examines takeovers and mergers to make sure that a monopoly is not being created(英)垄断委员会(对于企业间的接管和合并进行监查以保证不产生垄断的组织)

NOTE: trust is used more often in US English

◇ **monopolize** v. to create a monopoly or to get control of all the supply of a product 垄断；独占

◇ **monopolization** n. making a monopoly 垄断；独占

**month** n. one of twelve periods which make a year 月：The company pays him £100 a month. 公司每月付给他100英磅。He earns £2,000 a month. 他一个月挣2,000英磅。bills are due at the end of the current month 本月底应付的帐单或汇票；calendar month = whole month as on a calendar 历月；paid by the month = paid once each month 按月付款；to give a customer two months' credit = to allow a customer to pay not immediately, but after two months 允许给顾客两个月的信贷

◇ **month end** n. the end of a calendar month, when accounts have to be drawn up 月末(此时要结算帐目；) month - end accounts 月末帐目

◇ **monthly** 1 a. happening every month or which is received every month 每月的：monthly statement 月报表；monthly payments 每月支付；He is pay-ing for his car by monthly instalments. 他按月分期付款的方式支付他的购(汽)车款。My monthly salary cheque is late. 我的月工资支票来迟了。monthly ticket = ticket for travel which is good for one month 月票 2 adv. every month 每月 to pay monthly 每月支付：The account is credited monthly. 每月给帐户记入贷方。

**moonlight** v. infml. to do a second job for cash (often in the evening) as well as a regular job 从事第二职业；兼职

◇ **moonlighter** n. person who moonlights 兼干第二职业的人

◇ **moonlighting** n. doing a second job 从事第二职业：He makes thousands a year from moonlighting. 他每年可从兼职工作中挣几千元钱。

**mooring** n. place where boats can be tied up in a harbour 码头停船处；系船处

**moratorium** n. temporary stop to repayments of money owed 延期偿付权；延缓偿付期：The banks called for a moratorium on payments. 银行要求延缓款项偿付期。

NOTE: plural is moratoria

**mortality tables** pl. n. chart, used by insurers, which shows how long a person of a certain age can be expected to live on average 死亡统计表(保险公司用来表示某一年令的人平均寿命的表格)

**mortgage** 1 n. agreement where someone lends money to another person so that he can buy a property, the property being the security; money lent in this way 抵押贷款：to take out a mortgage on a house 以一幢房屋作抵押；to buy a house with a £20,000 mortgage 以20,000英磅的抵押贷款购买一座房子；mortgage payments = money paid each month as interest on a mortgage, plus repayment of a small part of the capital borrowed 抵押款偿付：endowment mortgage = mortgage backed by an endowmentpolicy 以养老保险单做为抵押的贷款；first mortgage = main mortgage on a property 第一抵押权；second mortgage = further mortgage on a property which is already mortgaged 第二抵押权(抵押的财产上作再次抵押)；to foreclose on a mortgaged property = to sell a property because the owner cannot repay money which he has borrowed, using the property as security 取消抵押房地产的赎回权；to pay off a mortgage = to pay back the principal and all the interest on a loan to buy a property 偿清抵押贷款本金和利息；mortgage bond = certificate showing that a mortgage exists and that property is security for it 抵押债券；mortgage debenture = debenture where the lender can be repaid by selling the company's property 公司抵押债券；mortgage famine = situation where there is not enough money available to offer mortgages to house buyers 抵押贷款紧缺；mortgage queue = list of people waiting for mortgages 申请抵押贷款人名单 2. v. to accept a loan with a property as security 抵押：The house is mortgaged 这房屋作为贷款抵押了。He mortgaged his house to set up in business. 他抵押了房屋取得贷款去开办企业。

◇ **mortgagee** n. person or company which lends money for someone to buy a property 承受抵押者,受押人

◇ **mortgager or mortgagor** n. person who borrows money to buy a property 抵押者

**most** 1. n. very large amount or quantity 大多数；大量：Most of the staff are graduates. 大多数职工是大学毕业生。Most of our customers live near the factory. 大多数顾客住在工厂附近。Most of the orders come in the early part of the year.大多数订货单于年初达到。2. a. Very large number of most orders are dealt with the same day.大多数订单是当天处理的。Most salesmen have had a course of on‐the‐job training. 大多数推销员参加了岗位培训课程。

◇ **most favoured nation** n. country which has the best trade terms 最惠国(享有最优惠贸易条件的国家) most‐favoured‐nation clause = agreement between two countries that each will offer the best possible terms in commercial contracts 最惠国条款

◇ **mostly** ad. mainly or generally 多数；通常：The staff are mostly girls of twenty to thirty years of age. 多数职员是 20 至 30 岁的女孩子。He works mostly in the London office. 他通常在伦敦办事处工作。

**motion** n. (a) moving about 动作：time and motion study = study in an office or factory of the time taken to do certain jobs and the movements workers have to make to do them 工时和动作研究 (b) proposal which will be put to a meeting to vote on 动议；提议：to propose or to move a motion 提出一项动议；The meeting voted on the motion. 会议就动议进行表决。to speak against or for a motion 发言反对或赞同某项提议；The motion was carried or was defeated by 220 votes to 196. 提议以 220 票对 196 票被通过或被否决。to table a motion = to put forward a proposal for discussion by putting details of it on the table at a meeting 提出动议(在会议上将其细节摆在桌面上进行讨论)
NOTE: no plural

**motivated** a. highly motivated sales staff. = sales staff who are very eager to sell 干劲十足的销售人员

◇ **motivation** n. encouragement or being eager to sell 激发积极性；干劲；The sales staff lack motivation . = The sales staff are not motivated enough. 销售人员缺乏销售积极性。

NOTE: no plural

**motor** n. car motor insurance = insuring a car, the driver and the passengers in case of accident 汽车保险

**mountain** n. pile or large heap 成堆; 大量: I have mountains of typing to do. 我有大量的打字工作要干。 There is a mountain of invoices on the sales manager's desk. 销售经理的桌上堆着大量的发票。 butter mountain = large amount of unsold butter kept in storage 库存大量黄油。

**mounting** a. increasing 增长的: He resigned in the face of mounting pressure from the shareholders. 面临来自股东们日益增长的压力，他辞职了。 The company is faced with mounting debts. 公司债台高筑。

◇ **mount up** v. to increase rapidly 迅速增长: Costs are mounting up. 成本正迅速增长。

**move** v. (a) to go from one place to another 移动: The company is moving from London Road to the centre of town. 公司正从伦敦路搬往城镇中心。 We have decided to move our factory to a site near the airport. 我们已决定把工厂搬到机场附近。 (b) to be sold or to sell 出售: The stock is starting to move. 存货开始被售出。 The salesmen will have to work hard if they want to move all that stock by the end of the month. 如果推销员们在月底售出所有存货，就得努力工作。 (c) to propose formally that a motion be accepted by a meeting 动议: He moved that the accounts be agreed. 他提议通过报告。 I move that the meeting should adjourn for ten minutes. 我提议会议应休息 10 分钟。

◇ **moveable** 1 a. which can be moved 可移动的: moveable property 动产 2 pl. n. moveables = moveable property 动产

◇ **movement** n. (a) changing position or going up or down 移动; 活动: movements in the money markets 金融市场动向; cyclical movements of trade 商业贸易的循环运动; movements of capital = changes of investments from one country to another 资本流动; 资金动向; stock movements = passing of stock into or out of the warehouse 货物的进出库情况; All stock movements are logged by the computer. 所有的货物进出库情况都是由计算机记录的。 (b) group of people working towards the same aim 运动: the labour movement 劳工运动; the free trade movement 自由贸易运动

◇ **mover** n. person who proposes a motion 提议人

**mpg** = MILES PER GALLON 汽车每加仑汽油可行里程

**Mr** n. title given to a man 先生: Mr Smith is the Managing Director. 史密斯先生是总经理。

**MRP** = MANUFACTURER'S RECOMMENDED PRICE 厂商推荐价

**Mrs** n. title given to a married woman 夫人: The chair was taken by Mrs Smith. 史密斯夫人当会议主席。

**Ms** n. title given to a woman where it is not known if she is married, or where she does not wish to indicate if she is married or not 女士(对于不知婚否或本人不原说明婚否的妇女的称谓); Ms Smith is the personnel officer. 史密斯女士是人事部门高级职员。

**multi‑** prefix referring to many things 多的

◇ **multilateral** a. between several parties 多边的; 多方的: a multilateral agreement 多边协议; multilateral trade = trade between several countries 多边贸易

◇ **multimillion** a. referring to several million pounds or dollars 几百万英磅或美元的: They signed a multimillion pound deal. 他们签了一项几百万英磅的交易。

◇ **multimillionaire** n. person who owns several million pounds or dollars 拥有几百万英磅或美元的富翁

◇ **multinational** n. company which has branches or subsidiary companies in several countries 跨国公司 The company has been bought by one of the big multinationals. 这个公司被一家大跨国公司买下。

**multiple** 1 a. many 多的: multiple entry visa = visa which allows a visitor to enter a country many times 可多次入境的签证; multiple store = one store in a chain of stores 连锁商店;分店; multiple ownership = situation where something is owned by several parties jointly 多方共同拥有 2 n. company with stores in several different towns 在几个城镇中都有商号的公司

**multiply** v. (a) to calculate the sum of various numbers repeated a certain number of times 乘;使相乘: to multiply twelve by three 12 乘以 3; Square measurements are calculated by multiplying length by width. 面积是通过长乘以宽来计算的。(b) to grow or to increase 增长: Profits multiplied in the boom years. 兴旺之年利润增长。

◇ **multiplication** n. act of multiplying 乘法运算: multiplication sign = sign used to show that a number is being multiplied by another 乘号
NOTE: no plural

**municipal** a. referring to a town 市政的: municipal taxes 市政税收; municipal offices 市政办公室

**Murphy's law** n. law, based on wide experience, which says that in commercial life if something can go wrong it will go wrong 墨菲定律(根据经验,在商业方面如果某事可能出差错,终将出差错。)

**mutual** a. belonging to two or more people 共有的: mutual (insurance) company = company which belongs to insurance policy holders 互助保险公司; US mutual funds = organizations which take money from small investors and invest it in stocks and shares for them, the investment being in the form of shares in the fund(美)互助基金(以股份形式筹资并投资于证券市场为股东谋利的组织)

# Nn

**nail** n. small piece of metal, used to attach things together 铁钉: to pay on the nail = to pay promptly or to pay rapidly 立即付款

**naira** n. money used in Nigeria 奈拉(尼日利亚货币单位
NOTE: no plural; naira is usually written N before figures: N2,000 say "two thousand naira"

**name** n. word used to call a thing or a person 名称;人名; I cannot remember the name of the managing director of Smith's Ltd. 我记不住史密斯有限公司董事长的名字。His first name is John, but I am not sure of his other names. 他名叫约翰,但我不清楚他的第二个名字和姓。brand name = name of a particular make of product 商标名称; corporate name = name of a large corporation 大公司名称; under the name of = using a particular name 以…命名; trading under the name of "Best Foods" = using the name "Best Foods" as a commercial name, but not the name of the company 以"美食"的名字做生意

◇ **named** a. person named in the policy = person whose name is given on an insurance policy as the person insured 在保单中所指名的人

**nation** n. country and the people living in it 国家；most favoured nation = country which has the best trade terms 最惠国；most - favoured - nation clause = agreement between two countries that each will give the other the best possible trade terms in commercial contracts 最惠国条款；the United Nations = organization linking almost all countries in the world 联合国

◇ **national** a. referring to a particular country 国家的：national advertising = advertising in every part of a country, not just in the capital 全国性的广告宣传；We took national advertising to promote our new 24 - hour delivery service. 我们做全国性的广告来宣传我们的 24 小时递送服务。national campaign = sales or publicity campaign in every part of a country 全国性销售活动；全国性宣传活动；the National Debt = money borrowed by a government 国债；GB National Health Service = scheme for free medical and hospital service for everyone, paid for by the National Insurance(英)国民保健制度；national income = value of income from the sales of goods and services in a country 国民收入；GB National Insurance = state insurance which pays for medical care, hospitals, unemployment benefits, etc. (英)国民保险制度 National Insurance contributions = money paid into the National Insurance scheme by the employer and the worker 国民保险缴款；national newspapers or the national press = newspapers which sell in all parts of a country 全国性报刊；gross national product = annual value of goods and services in a country including income from other countries 国民生产总值(国家全

年生产的产品和劳务总值, 包括来自其他国家收入)；GB National Savings = savings scheme for small investors run by the Post Office(including a savings bank, savings certificates and premium bonds)(英)国民储蓄制(邮政为小额投资者开办储蓄银行、办理存单和有奖公债)

◇ **nationality** n. He is of British nationality = He is a British citizen. 他是英国国籍。

◇ **nationalize** v. to put a privately - owned industry under state ownership and control 国有化：The government are planning to nationalize the banking system. 政府正打算将银行系统国有化。

◇ **nationalized** a. nationalized industry = industry which was privately owned, but is now owned by the state 国有化了的工业

◇ **nationalization** n. taking over of private industry by the state 国有化

◇ **nationwide** a. all over a country 全国范围的：The union called for a nationwide strike. 工会号召全国范围的罢工。We offer a nationwide delivery service. 我们提供全国范围的送货服务。The new car is being launched with a nationwide sales campaign. 新型汽车用开展全国范围的销售活动投放市场。

**nature** n. kind or type 类型；种类；What is the nature of the contents of the parcel? 这个包裹里装的是哪种类型东西？The nature of his business is not known. 不知道他的公司是属哪种类型的。

◇ **natural** a. (a) found in the earth 自然的；天然的；自然界中的：natural gas 天然气；natural resources = raw materials (such as coal, gas, iron) which are found in the earth 自然资源 (b) not made by people 天然的：natural fibres 天然纤维 (c) normal 正常的；It was natural for the shopkeeper to feel annoyed when the hypermarket was set up closeto his shop. 当特大超级市场挨着这家商店建立起来时,店主感到苦脑是正常的。natural wastage = losing workers because they resign or retire, not through redundancy or dismissals 正常的减员; The company is hoping to avoid redundancies and reduce its staff by natural wastage. 公司不希望裁减职工而希望通过正常的减员来减少其职工。

**navy** n. merchant navy = all the commercial ships of a country 商业船队

**NB** = NOTE 纸币、票据

**necessary** a. which has to be done or which is needed 必需的;需要的: It is necessary to fill in the form correctly if you are not to have difficulty at the customs. 如果你不想在海关遇到麻烦,就必须正确地填写表格。Is it really necessary for the chairman to have six personal assistants? 董事长真有必要要六个人事助理吗? You must have all the necessary documentation before you apply for a subsidy. 你须持有全部必要的文件才能申请补助。

◇ **necessity** n. thing which is absolutely important, without which nothing can be done 必需品: Being unemployed makes it difficult to afford even the basic necessities. 失业使人连基本生活必需品都买不起了。

**negative** a. meaning "no" 否定的: The answer was in the negative = the answer was "no" 回答是否定的。negative cash flow = situation where a company is spending more money than it receives 负现金流(量)

**neglected** a. not well looked after 被忽略的; neglected shares = shares which are not bought or sold often 被忽视的股票; Bank shares have been a neglected sector of the market this week. 这个星期银行股票是证券市场上被忽视的股票。neglected business = company

which has not been actively run by its owners and could therefore do better 管理被忽视的企业

**negligence** n. lack of proper care or not doing a duty 疏忽;失职: criminal negligence = not doing a duty with the result that harm is done to the interests of people 刑法上的过失

NOTE: no plural

◇ **negligible** a. very small or not worth bothering about 无足轻重的;可以忽略的; not negligible = quite large 不容忽略的

**negotiable** a. not negotiable = which cannot be exchanged for cash 不能兑换成现金的; "not negotiable" = words written on a cheque to show that it can be paid only to a certain person(写在支票上)"不可转让"的字样; negotiable cheque = cheque made payable to bearer (i. e. to anyone who holds it)可转让支票; negotiable instrument = document (such as a bill of exchange, or cheque) which can beexchanged for cash 可转让票据;流通票据(汇票或支票)

◇ **negotiate** v. to negotiate with someone = to discuss a problem formally with someone, so as to reach anagreement 谈判;协商: The management refused to negotiate with the union. 管理部门(资方)拒绝与工会谈判。to negotiate terms and conditions or to negotiate a contract = to discuss and agree terms of a contract 商谈各项条款和条件或商定一项合同; He negotiated a £250,000 loan with the bank = He came to an agreement with the bank for a loan of £250,000.他与银行达成一项250,000英磅的货款协议。negotiating committee = group of representatives of management or unions whonegotiate a wage settlement 谈判委员会

◇ **negotiation** n. discussion of terms and conditions to reach an agreement 谈

判；contract under negotiation = contractwhich is being discussed 谈判中的合同；a matter for negotiation = something which must be discussed before a decision isreached 需经协商的事；to enter into negotiations or to start negotiations = to start discussing a problem 开始谈判；to resume negotiations = to start discussing a problem again, after talks have stoppedfor a time 重新恢复谈判；to break off negotiations = to refuse to go on discussing a problem 中断谈判；to conduct negotiations = to negotiate 进行谈判；Negotiations broke down after six hours = Discussions stopped because no agreement was possible. 六个小时后，谈判失败。pay negotiations or wage negotiations = discussions between management and workers about pay 工资谈判

◇ **negotiator** n. (a) person who discusses with the aim of reaching an agreement 谈判者；协商者：an experienced union negotiator = member of a union who has a lot of experience of discussingterms of employment with management 有经验的工会谈判代表。(b) GB person who works in an estate agency (英)房地产代理机构的工作人员

**net** 1. a. (a) price or weight or pay, etc. after all deductions have been made 净价；净重；净支付；net assets or net worth = value of all the property of a company after taking away what the company owes 净资产或资产净值 net cash flow = difference between money coming in and money going out of afirm 净现金流量；net earnings or net income = total earnings of a business after tax and other deductions 企业净收益或净收入 net income or net salary = person's income which is left after taking away tax and otherdeductions 工资净得；净工资 net loss = actual loss, after deducting overheads 净损失；net margin = net

profit shown as a percentage of sales 净利润率：net price = price which cannot be reduced by a discount 净价；net profit = result where income from sales is more than all expenditure 净利润；net receipts = receipts after deducting commission or tax or discounts, etc.纯收入；net sales = sales less damaged or returned items 净销售额；net weight = weight of goods after deducting the weight of packagingmaterial and container 净重；net yield = profit from investments after deduction of tax 净收益 (b) terms strictly net = payment has to be the full price, with no discount allowed 不打折扣的全价支付

NOTE: the spelling nett is sometimes used on containers

2 v. to make a true profit 净得，赢利：to net a profit of ￡10,000 获得净利润 10,000 英磅。

NOTE: netting - netted

**network** 1 n. system which links different points together 网络：a network of distributors or a distribution network = series of points or warehouses from which goods are sent allover a country 销售网络；computer network = computer system where several micros are linked so that theyall draw on the same database 计算机网络；television network = system of linked television stations covering the wholecountry 电视网；2. v. to link together in a network 联网；to network a television programme = to send out the same television programme through several TVstations 电视台联网(播出相同电视节目)；networked system = computer system where several micros are linked together sothat they all draw on the same database 计算机联网体系

**new** a. recent or not old 最近的；新的：under new management = with a new owner 在新的管理部门领导之下；new issue = issues of new shares 发行新股

票；new issues department = section of abank which deals with issues of new shares 新股票发行部门；new technology = electronic instruments which have recently been invented 新工艺, 新技术

◇ **news** n. information about things which have happened 新闻: business news 商业新闻；financial news 财政金融新闻；Financial markets were shocked by the news of the devaluation. 金融市场被货币贬值的新闻所震惊。news agency = office which distributes news to newspapers and televisioncompanies 通讯社；news release = sheet giving information about a new event which is sent tonewspapers and TV and radio stations so that they can use it 新闻稿；The company sent out a news release about the new managing director. 公司发了一份有关新任总经理的新闻稿件.

◇ **newsagent** n. person who runs a shop selling newspapers and magazines 报刊经销商

◇ **newsletter** n. company newsletter = printed sheet or small newspaper giving news about a company 公司的新闻简报

**niche** n. special place in a market, occupied by one company(公司在市场所占)特殊地位

**nickel** n. US five cent coin(美)五分硬币

**night** n. period of time from evening to morning 夜晚；夜间: night safe = safe in the outside wall of a bank where money and documents can be deposited at night using a special door(银行)夜间保险箱；night shift = shift which works at night 夜班；There are thirty men on the night shift. 夜班有 30 个人。He works nights or he works the night shift. 他上夜班。

**nil** n. zero or nothing 零；无；to make a nil return;没获得收益；The advertising budget has been cut to nil. 广告预算被削减为零。

**No = NUMBER** 数字

**no - claims bonus** n. reduction of premiums on an insurance policy because no claims have been made 无索赔奖金(因无保险索赔而减少应缴保险费)

**nominal** a. (a) very small (payment) 金额极小的: We make a nominal charge for our services. 我们收取少量的(手续费)服务费。They are paying a nominal rent. 他们付一小笔租金。(b) nominal capital = the total of the face value of all the shares in a company 票面股本或名义资本(某公司股票的票面总额)；nominal ledger = general accounts book showing income and expenditure 会计总帐；nominal value = face value or value written on a share or a coin or a banknote 面值

**nominate** v. to suggest someone or to name someone for a job 提名；指派: to nominate someone to a post = to appoint someone to a post without an election 提名某人到某工作岗位；to nominate someone as proxy = to name someone as your proxy 指派某人为代理人

◇ **nomination** n. act of nominating 提名；委任

◇ **nominee** n. person who is nominated, especially someone who is appointed to deal with financial matters on your behalf 被任命者, 被提名者；被推荐者(特别是被指定代表他人处理财金事物的人)；nominee account = account held on behalf of someone 代理帐户

**non -** prefix not 不

◇ **non - acceptance** n. situation where the person who is to pay a bill of exchange does not accept it 拒绝承兑

◇ **non - contributory** a. non - contributory pension scheme = pension scheme where the employee does not make any contributions and the company payseverything 不缴纳退休金制度（不用职工付钱的，而由业主单方支付退休基金的办法）; The company pension scheme is non - contributory. 这个公司的退休基金计划是不缴纳费用。

◇ **non - delivery** n. situation where something is not delivered 无送货，未交付

◇ **non - durables** pl. n. goods which are used up soon after they have been bought(such as food, newspapers) 非耐用品(食品、报纸等买后很快就消费掉的)

◇ **non - executive** a. non - executive director = director who attends board meetings and gives advice, but does not work full - time for the company 非常务董事，非执行董事

◇ **non - feisance** n. not doing something which should be done by law 不履行义务，失职

◇ **non - negotiable** a. non - negotiable instrument = document (such as a crossed cheque) which cannot be exchanged for cash 不能兑现的票据；不可转让票据

◇ **non - payment** n. non - payment of a debt = not paying a debt due 没支付到期债务

◇ **non profit - making organization or US non - profit corporation** n. organization (such as a club) which is not allowed by law tomake a profit(俱乐部等法定的)非赢利组织: Non - profit - making organizations are exempted from tax. 非赢利组织是免税的。

◇ **non - recurring** a. non - recurring items = special items in a set of accounts which appear only once 帐目中的特殊或临时项目

◇ **non - refundable** a. which will not be refunded 不可偿还的: non - refundable deposit 不能偿还的定金或押金

◇ **non - resident** n. person who is not considered a resident of a country for tax purposes 非某国家居民（从纳税的角度) He has a non - resident bank account. 他有一个非本国居民银行帐户。

◇ **non - returnable** a. which cannot be returned 不退还的: non - returnable packing = packing which is to be thrown away when it has been used and not returned to the sender(一次性使用的货物)不能退回的包装

◇ **non - stop** a. & ad. without stopping 不中断的: They worked non - stop to finish the audit on time. 他们不停地工作以按期完成审计工作。

◇ **non - taxable** a. which is not subject to tax 免税的: non - taxable income 免税收益

◇ **non - union** a. company using non - union labour = company employing workers who do not belong to trade unions 雇佣非工会成员的公司

◇ **non - voting** a. non - voting shares = shares which do not allow the shareholder to vote at meetings 无表决权的股票

**norm** n. the usual quantity or the usual rate 正常标准；平均数: The output from this factory is well above the norm for the industry or well above the industry norm. 这个厂的产量远远高于同行业的正常标率。

◇ **normal** a. usual or which happens regularly 正常的；正规的: Normal deliveries are made on Tuesdays and Fridays. 正常的发货日期是星期二和星期五。 Now that the strike is over we hope to resume normal service as soon as possible. 既然罢工已结束，我们希望尽早恢复正常的服务。 under normal conditions = if things work in the usual way 在正常情况下: Under normal conditions a package takes two days to get to

Copenhagen. 在正常情况下, 包裹用两天时间到达哥本哈根。

**notary public** n. lawyer who has the authority to witness documents and spoken statements, making them official 公证人 (通常由律师担任)
NOTE: plural is notaries public

**note** 1. n. (a) short document or short piece of information 简短文件; 短讯: advice note = written notice to a customer giving details of goods ordered and shipped but not yet delivered 通知书 (告诉顾客货已装船但还未运出的); contract note = note showing that shares have been bought or sold but not yet paid for 买卖股票通知 cover note = letter from an insurance company giving details of an insurance policy and confirming that the policy exists 暂保单; 保险证明书; covering note = letter sent with documents to explain why you are sending them 附信; 伴书; credit note = note showing that money is owed to a customer 贷记报单; 贷方票据; 欠条; debit note = note showing that a customer owes money 借记报单; 借方票据; 借条; We undercharged Mr Smith and had to send him a debit note for the extra amount. 我们少收了史密斯先生的钱, 只得给他寄去一张借条索要欠款。delivery note = list of goods being delivered, given to the customer with the goods 交货单 dispatch note = note saying that goods have been sent 发货单; note of hand or promissory note = document stating that someone promises to pay an amount of money on a certain date 期票或本票 (b) short letter or short piece of information 便条; 短信: to send someone a note; 给某人送一个便条; I left a note on his desk. 我在他桌上留了张便条。She left a note for the managing director with his secretary. 她给董事长留了个便条, 并将其交给了他的秘书。(c) bank note or currency note =

piece of printed paper money 纸币; 钞票: a £5 note 一张 5 英磅纸币; He pulled out a pile of used notes. 他掏出一叠旧纸币。2. v. to write down details of something and remember them 详细记下; 笔录; We note that the goods were delivered in bad condition. 我们将货物运送中的损坏情况记录下来。Your order has been noted and will be dispatched as soon as we have stock. 你的订货已做记载, 一经有货我们将马上发送。Your complaint has been noted. 你的投诉已做了记载。

◇ **notebook** n. book for writing notes in 笔记本

◇ **notepad** n. pad of paper for writing short notes 便笺簿

◇ **notepaper** n. good quality paper for letters 信笺

**notice** n. (a) piece of written information 通告; 通知: The company secretary pinned up a notice about the pension scheme. 公司秘书贴出一张退休金方案通告。copyright notice = note in a book showing who owns the copyright and the date of ownership 版权通告; 版权记录 (b) official warning that a contract is going to end or that terms are going to be changed 正式通知 (合同将到期条款将会改变): until further notice = until different instructions are given. 在另行通知以前; You must pay £200 on the 30th of each month until further notice. 在另行通知前你必须在每月 30 日支付 200 英磅。(c) written announcement that a worker is leaving his job on a certain date 离职通知书; period of notice = time stated in the contract of employment which the worker or company has to allow between resigning or being fired and the worker actually leaving his job 辞职或离职预选通知期; We require three months' notice; 我们要求提前三个月的通知。He gave six months' notice. 他

提前六个月通知。We gave him three months' wages in lieu of notice. 我们给了他三个月的工资而来向他发离职通知。She gave in or handed in her notice. = She resigned 她递交了她的离职通知期报告。He is working out his notice = he is working during the time between resigning and actually leaving the company. 他在离职通知和实际离开公司期间仍在工作。(d) time allowed before something takes place 提前通知期；at short notice = with very little warning 在短时间内；The bank manager will not see anyone at short notice. 提前短时间预约，银行经理不会接见任何人。You must give seven days' notice of withdrawal. = You must ask to take money out of the account seven days before you want it. 你要取款，必须提前七天通知银行。(e) legal document (such as telling a tenant to leave property which he is occupying) 通告；通令；to give a tenant notice to quit 让房客迁出通告；to serve notice on someone = to give someone a legal notice 给某人警告 NOTE: no plural for (b), (c), (d) and (e)

◇ **noticeboard** n. board fixed to a wall where notices can be put up 布告栏：Did you see the new list of prices on the noticeboard? 你看到布告栏上新的价目表了吗？

**notify** v. to notify someone of something = to tell someone something formally 通知；通告：They were notified of the arrival of the shipment. 通知他们船货到达日。

◇ **notification** n. informing someone 通知

**notional** a. probable but not known exactly or not quantifiable 概念上的；名义上的；理论上的；notional income = invisible benefit which is not money or goods and services 理论上的收入（非资金、商品、劳务等无形利益）；notional rent = sum put into accounts as rent where the company owns the building it is occupying and so does not pay an actual rent 名义上的房租（对于公司自己拥有的房屋，只需把房租划入帐目中而不必实际支付的房租）

**nought** n. number 0 零之数目字(0)：A million pounds can be written as "£ 1m" or as one and six noughts. 一百万英磅可以写作"1m"或"1后面加六个零(即1,000,000)"。 NOTE: nought is commoner in GB English; in US English, zero is more usual

**null** a. with no meaning or which cannot legally be enforced 无意义的；法律上无效的：Contract was declared null and void = The contract was said to be not valid. 合同被宣告无效。to render a decision null = to make a decision useless or to cancel a decision 使得某决定无效（废弃某定议）

◇ **nullification** n. act of making something invalid 废弃

◇ **nullify** v. to make something invalid or to cancel something 使无效；取消某事

**number** 1. n. (a) quantity of things or people 数量：The number of persons on the payroll has increased over the last year. 去年工资单上的雇员人数增加了。The number of days lost through strikes has fallen. 因罢工而失去的工作日减少了。the number of shares sold 售出的股票数量；a number of = some 一些：A number of the staff will be retiring this year. 一些职工今年将退休。(b) written figure 数码：account number 帐号；batch number 批号；cheque number 支票号码；invoice number 发票号码；order number 订货单号码；page number 页数；serial number 顺序排列的数字；序号；phone number or telephone number 电话号码; box number = reference numberused when asking for mail to be sent to a post office or when asking for replies to an advertisement to be sent to the newspaper's offices 邮政信箱号码; Please reply to Box No. 209. 回信请寄 209 号信箱。index number = (i) number of something in an index 索引中的条码 (ii) number showing the percentage rise of something over a period 指数 NOTE: often written No. with figures 2. v. to put a figure on a document 编号: to number an order 给订货单编号; I refer to your invoice numbered 1234. 我查阅你们编号为 1234 的发票。numbered account = bank account (usually in Switzerland) which is referred toonly by a number, the name of the person holding it being kept secret 编号帐户(按帐户编号查找帐户,其帐户持有人的名字是保密的)

◇ **numeric or numerical** a. referring to numbers 数字的: in numerical order = in the order of figures (such as 1 before 2, 33 before 34)按数字顺序; File these invoices in numerical order 按编号顺序把这些发票入档。numeric data = data in the form of figures 数字资料; numeric keypad = part of a computer keyboard which is a programmable set ofnumbered keys 数字键(计算机键盘上的)

# Oo

**O & M** = ORGANIZATION AND METHODS 组织与方法

**OAP** = OLD AGE PENSIONER 领取养老金者;领取退休金者;领取抚恤金者

**oath** n. legal promise stating that something is true 誓言;誓约: He was under oath. = He had promised in court to say what was true. 他宣过誓(在法庭)。

**object** v. to refuse to do something or to say that you do not accept something 拒绝;反对;拒绝接受: to object to a clause in a contract 反对(或拒绝接受)合同中某一项条款
NOTE: you object to something

◇ **objection** n. to raise an objection to something = to object to something(对某事)提出异议;反对: The union delegates raised an objection to the wording of the agreement. 工会代表们对这项协议的措辞提出异议。

**objective** 1. n. something which you try to do 目标;目的: The company has achieved its objectives. 公司已达到了其目标。We set the salesforces certain objectives. 我们对销售人员规定明确的目标。long-term objective or short-term objective = aim which you hope to achieve within a few years or a few months 长期目标;近期目标; management by objectives = way of managing a business by planning work for the managers to do and testing if it is completed correctly and on time 目标管理(制度) 2. a. considered from a general point of view not from that of the person involved 客观的: You must be objective in assessing the performance of the staff. 你必须客观地评价职员们的工作表现。to carry out an objective survey of the market 对市场进行客观调查

**obligate** v. to be obligated to do something = to have a legal duty to do something 有责任;的有义务的(去做某事)

◇ **obligation** n. (a) duty to do something 责任;义务: to be under an obligation to do something = to feel it is your duty to do something 有义务做某事:

There is no obligation to buy. 没有购买的义务。to be under no obligation to do something 无义务做某事; He is under no contractual obligation to buy. = He has signed no contract which forces him to buy. 他没有合同上的购买义务。to fulfill one's contractual obligations = to do what is stated in a contract 履行合同义务; two weeks' free trial without obligation = the customer can try the item at home for two weeks withouthaving to buy it at the end of the test 免费试用两星期 (b) debt 债务: to meet one's obligations = to pay one's debts 偿还债务

◇ **obligatory** a. necessary according to the law or rules(在法律上)必须的; 义务的: Each person has to pass an obligatory medical examination. 每个人都必须通过体检。

◇ **oblige** v. to oblige someone to do something = to make someone feel he must do something 使(某人)有义务(做某事): He felt obliged to cancel the contract. 他认为有必要取消合同。

**obsolescence** n. act of going out of date, and therefore becoming less useful and valuable 即将过时; 逐渐无用; 即将无价值: built - in obsolescence or planned obsolescence = situation where the manufacturer designs his products to become out of date so that the customers can be pressed to replace them with new models 内在(指商品)陈旧性; 计划好的过时(制造商设计产品时, 有意使其很快成为过时货, 因而用户不得不购买新产品取而代之)
NOTE: no plural

◇ **obsolescent** a. becoming out of date 逐渐被废弃的: 即将过时的

◇ **obsolete** a. no longer used 已不用的; 已废弃的: When the office was equipped with word - processors the typewriters became obsolete. 办公室配备了文字处理机, 那么打字机就用不着了。

**obtain** v. to get 得到; 获得: to obtain supplies from abroad 获得外援; We find these items very difficult to obtain. 我们发现这些商品非常难以买到。to obtain an injunction against a company 得到针对某公司的禁令; He obtained control by buying the founder's shareholding. 他因买下创始人的股份而得到控股权。

◇ **obtainable** a. which can be got 可获得的; 能取得的: Prices fall when raw materials are easily obtainable. 当原材料容易买到时, 价格就会降低。Our products are obtainable in all computer shops. 我们的产品在所有的计算机商店有售。

**occasional** a. which happens from time to time 偶尔的; 时有发生的

**occupancy** n. act of occupying a property (such as a house, an office, aroom in a hotel)占有(房屋、办公室或旅馆中的套房等): with immediate occupancy = empty and available to be occupied immediately 即期占有(指随时可以立即使用与占用); occupancy rate = average number of rooms occupied in a hotel over a period oftime shown as a percentage of the total number of rooms 客房率: During the winter months the occupancy rate was down to 50%. 冬季的几个月里, 客房率降到5%。
NOTE: no plural

◇ **occupant** n. person or company which occupies a property(财产)占有者; 占有人

◇ **occupation** n. (a) occupation of a building = act of occupying a building 居住 (b) job or work 工作; 职业 What is her occupation? 她从事什么工作? His main occupation is house building. 他主要从事房屋建筑业。(c) occupations = types of work 各种工作; 工种: people in professional occupations 从事各种专业工作的人们

◇ **occupational** a. referring to a job 职业的: occupational accident = accident which takes place at work 工伤; occupational disease = disease which affects people in certain jobs 职业病; occupational hazards = dangers which apply to certain jobs 职业危险; Heart attacks are one of the occupational hazards of directors. 心脏病是董事们的职业危害病之一。occupational pension scheme = pension scheme where the worker gets a pension from the company he has worked for 职业养老金(退休金、抚恤金)计划

◇ **occupier** n. person who lives in a property 居住者: beneficial occupier = person who occupies a property but does not own it fully 有使用权的人(指占用但并非全部拥有房产的人); owner-occupier = person who owns the property in which he lives 住用自己房屋的人

◇ **occupy** v. (a) to live or work in a property (such as a house, an office, a hotel room) 居住; 工作(在房子、办公室、旅馆客房): All the rooms in the hotel are occupied. 饭店的全部客房都已住满。The company occupies three floors of an office block. 这家公司占用了办公大楼的三层楼房。(b) to occupy a post = to be employed in a job 充任; 受雇.

**odd** a. (a) odd numbers = numbers (like 17 or 33) which cannot be divided by two 奇数: Odd-numbered buildings or buildings with odd numbers are on the south side of the street. 单号楼房在马路的南侧。(b) a hundred odd = approximately one hundred 100 多; keep the odd change = keep the small change which is left over 集攒零钱 (c) one of a group 单个的; 零散的: an odd shoe = one shoe of a pair 单只鞋; We have a few odd boxes left. = We have a few boxes left out of the total shipment. 我们还剩下几只零散的箱子。odd lot =

group of miscellaneous items for sale at an auction 零星交易量(拍卖时出售的多种混杂在一起的项目); to do odd jobs = to do various pieces of work 打杂; 做零工 (d) odd sizes = strange sizes which are not usual 特殊规格、尺寸或号码

◇ **odd-job-man** n. person who does various pieces of work 打零工者; 干杂役者

◇ **oddments** pl. n. items left over 剩余物; 残余物; pieces of large items sold separately 大型零卖物品

**off** 1. ad. (a) not working or not in operation 不工作的; 不运转的: The agreement is off. 协议不发生作用了。They called the strike off. 他们取消了罢工。(b) taken away from a price 降价; 低于: These carpets are sold at £25 off the marked price. 这些地毯以低于标价25英镑售出。We give 5% off for quick settlement. 为了迅速结帐, 我们降价5%。2. prep. (a) away from a price 削价; 降低: to take £25 off the price 降价25英磅; We give 10% off our normal prices. 我们的降价幅度为正常(标准)价格的10%。(b) away from work 离岗; 休假: to take time off work 休假; We give the staff four days off at Christmas. 在圣诞节时我们给全体职工放四天假。It is the secretary's day off tomorrow. 明天该秘书休假。

**offer** 1. n. (a) statement that you are willing to pay a certain amount of money to buy something 出价; 发价; to make an offer for a company 出价购买一家公司: He made an offer of £10 a share. 他的发价是10英磅一股。We made a written offer for the house. 我们做出书面发价购买这座房子。£1,000 is the best offer I can make. 1,000英磅是我所能出的最好发价。to accept an offer of £1,000 for the car 接受这辆汽车1000英磅的报价; The house is under offer. = Someone has made an offer to buythe house and the offer has been accepted provisionally. 这幢房子已有人发价购买。We are open to offers. = We are ready to discuss the price which we are asking. 我们的发价是未定的。cash offer = being ready to pay in cash 现钞出价; or near offer = or an offer of a price which is slightly less than the price asked 近似发价(略低于索价的出价): The car is for sale at £2,000 or near offer. 这辆车售价为 2000 英磅或略低于售价(也可考虑)。(NOTE: often shortened to o.n.o.) (b) statement that you are willing to sell something 出售; 发盘; 要约: offer for sale = situation where a company advertises new shares for sale 标价出售(新股票); offer price = price at which new shares are put on sale 出售价(指新股票上市出售的价格) (c) He received six offers of jobs or six job offers. = Six companies told him he could have a job with them. 有六家公司向他提供工作机会。(d) bargain offer = sale of a particular type of goods at a cheap price 优惠发价; 廉价出售: This week's bargain offer – 30% off all carpet prices. 本周所有地毯价格优惠降价 30%。introductory offer = special price offered on a new product to attract customers 开售价; 引导价; 优待发价(为吸引客户的购买新产品所报的特别价格); special offer = goods put on sale at a specially low price 特别(优惠)报价: We have a range of men's shirts on special offer. 我们有男士系列衬衫, 价格特别优惠。2. v. (a) to offer someone a job = to tell someone that he can have a job in your company 提供就业机会; 主动(给某人)提供工作: He was offered a directorship with Smith Ltd. 史密斯有限公司请他出任董事。(b) to say that you are willing to pay a certain amount of moneyfor something 出价; 报价: to offer someone £100,000 for his house 出价 100,000 英磅购买某人的房子; He offered £10 a share 他出价 10 英磅一股。(c) to say that you are willing to sell something 愿意出售: We offered the house for sale. 我们标价出售此房。

**office** n. (a) set of rooms where a company works or where business is done 办公室; 营业处; 事务所: branch office = less important office, usually in a different town or country from the main office 分公司; 分处; 分行; 分所; head office or main office = office building where the board of directors works and meets 总公司; 总部; 总行; GB registered office = office address of a company which is officially registeredwith the Companies' Registrar(英)注册(法定)办公所在地 (b) office block or a block of offices = building which contains only offices 办公大楼; office boy = young man who works in an office, usually taking messagesfrom one department to another 办公室的工友; 办公室的勤杂员; office equipment = furniture and machines needed to make an office work 办公设备; office hours = time when an office is open 办公时间; 营业时间; open during normal office hours 正常营业时间开门; Do not telephone during office hours. 上班时间别打电话。The manager can be reached at home out of office hours. 工作时间外, 可打电话到经理家中。office junior = young man or woman who does all types of work in an office 年轻勤杂工; office space or office accommodation = space available for offices or occupied by offices 办公所占面积; We are looking for extra office space 我们正在寻找额外办公场地。office staff = people who work in offices 办公室职员; office supplies = stationery and furniture used in an office 办公用品及家具; an office supplies firm = company which sells office supplies 办公用品用具公司; for office use only = something which must only be used in an office 办公专用; office worker = person who works in an office 办公室工作人员 (c) room where someone works and does business 办公室;营业所;事务所: come into my office 走进我的办公室; The manager's office is on the third floor. 经理的办公室在四楼。(d) booking office = office where you can book seats at a theatre or tickets for the railway 订票处 (剧院或车站); box office = office at a theatre where tickets can be bought(剧院)售票处; employment office = office which finds jobs for people 职业介绍所; general office = main administrative office in a company(公司)总部;总务处; information office = office which gives information to tourists or visitors 咨询处;问询处; inquiry office = office where someone can answer questions from members of thepublic 问询处; ticket office = office where tickets can be bought 售票处 (e) GB government department(英)政府部门;部; the Foreign Office = ministry dealing with foreign affairs(英)外交部; the Home Office = ministry dealing with the internal affairs of the country 内政部;内务部; Office of Fair Trading = government department which protects consumers against unfair or illegal business 保护消费者权益局 (f) post or position 位置;地位: He holds or performs the office of treasurer. 他担任会计职务。high office = important position or job 重要职位;重要工作: compensation for loss of office = payment to a director who is asked to leave a company before his contract ends 提前离职津贴(合同期满前就被要求离职的董事所应得到的补偿金)

**officer** n. (a) person who has an official position 官员: customs officer = person working for the customs 海关官员; fire safety officer = person responsible for fire safety in a building 防火安全(官)员; information officer = person who gives information about a company or about agovernment department to the public 信息员;新闻发布人; personnel officer = person who deals with the staff, especially interviewing newworkers 主管人事的负责人;负责人事的官员; training officer = person who deals with the training of staff 训练官;教练;教官: the company officers or the officers of a company = the main executives or directors of a company 公司高级职员(指董事或经理)(b) official ( usually unpaid) of a club or society, etc. 社团或俱乐部等团体中的领导人(通常不计报酬); the election of officers of an association 协会领导人的选举

**official** 1. a. (a) from a government department or organization 官方的;政府的: on official business 因公务;正值公务: He left official documents in his car. 他将政府公文忘在了汽车里。She received an official letter of explanation. 她收到了一封解释性的公函。speaking in an official capacity = speaking officially 以官方身份讲;正式地讲; to go through official channels = to deal with officials, especially when making a request 通过官方渠道;与官方打交道; the official exchange rate = exchange rate which is imposed by the government 官方汇率: The official exchange rate is ten to the dollar, but you can get twice that on the black market. 美元的官方汇率是 10 比 1,但在黑市上你可获得双倍。(b) done or approved by a director or by a person in authority 有权威的: This must be an official order - it is written on the company's notepaper. 这肯定是正式命令——因为公司记事本上已记录在案。The strike was made official. = The local strike was approved by the main trade union office. 这次罢工是正式批准的。(c) the official receiver

= government official who is appointed toclose down a company which is in liquidation 官方破产事务官(指负责处理停业及破产事务的官员): 2. n. person working in a government department 政府官员: Airport officials inspected the shipment. 机场官员检查了这批货物。 Government officials stopped the import licence. 政府官员停止这张进口许可证的使用。 customs official = person working for the customs 海关官员; high official = important person in a government department 高级官员; minor official = person in a low position in a government department 职位低的官员; Some minor official tried to stop my request for building permission. 某位职位低的官员试图阻止我申请建筑许可(证)。 top official = very important person in a government department 最高级官员(指政府部门); union officials = paid organizers in a trade union 工会组织者;工会领导人(指工会中领取薪金报酬的组织者)

◇ **officialese** n. language used in government documents which can be difficultto understand 官话;公文用语;公文体

◇ **officially** ad. in an official way 官方地;正式地;权威地: Officially he knows nothing about the problem, but unofficially he has given us a lot of advice about it 从官方讲,他对该问题一无所知,但对此他非官方地给我们提出许多忠告。

**officio** see EX OFFICIO 依官职的:依职权地

**off - licence** n. GB (a) licence to sell alcohol for drinking away from the place where you buy it(英)准许出售店外饮酒的执照(指只许买酒带到店外饮用)(b) shop which sells alcohol for drinking at home 出售在家饮用酒的酒店

**offload** v. to pass something which is not wanted to someone else 转手;脱手

(将不要的东西): to off load excess stock = to try to sell excess stock 抛售(倾销)过剩库存; to offload costs onto a subsidiary company = to try to get a subsidiary company to pay some charges so as to reduce tax 由附属公司(子公司)支付部分费用

NOTE: you offload something from a thing or person onto another thing or person

**off - peak** a. not during the most busy time 非高峰期的;淡季的; during the off - peak period = at the time when business is less busy 非高峰期;在淡季: off - peak tariff or rate = lower charges used when the service is not busy 非高峰期优惠价,非高峰期收费

**off - season** 1. a. off - season tariff or rate = cheap fares which are charged in a season when there is less business 淡季优惠价 2. n. less busy season for travel (usually during the winter) 旅游淡季(一般指冬季); to travel in the off - season 淡季旅游; Air fares are cheaper in the off - season. 淡季旅游机票较便宜。

**offset** v. to balance one thing against another so that they cancel eachother out 抵消;冲销;补偿: to offset losses against tax 税抵消损失; Foreign exchange losses more than offset profits in the domestic market. 外汇损失大大地抵销了国内利润。

NOTE: offsetting - offset

**off - shore** a. & ad. (a) on an island or in the sea near to land 近海的;离岸的;境外的: off - shore oil field 近海油田: off - shore oil platform 海上石油平台;近海石油平台 (b) on an island which is a tax haven 避税岛上的; off - shore fund = fund which is based in the Bahamas, etc. 国外资金;境外基金

**off - the - job** a. off - the - job training = training given to workers away from their place of work (suchas at a college or school)脱产培训

**oil** n. natural liquid found in the ground, used to burn to give power 石油：oil – exporting countries = countries which produce oil and sell it to others 石油输出国；oil field = area of land or sea under which oil is found 油田；油矿：the North Sea oil fields 北海油田；oil – importing countries = countries which import oil 石油进口国；oil – producing countries = countries which produce oil 产油国；oil platform or oil rig = large construction with equipment for making holes in the ground to find oil 油井平台；石油井架；oil well = hole in the ground from which oil is pumped 油井

**old** a. having existed for a long time 长久的；年老的：The company is 125 years old next year. 该公司到明年就有125年的历史了。We have decided to get rid of our old computer system and install a new one. 我们决定换掉老式计算机系统而安装一套新的。

◇ **old age** n. period when a person is old 老年：old age pension = state pension given to a man who is 65 or a woman who is 60 养老年金；old age pensioner = person who receives the old age pension 养老金领取者

◇ **old – established** a. (company or brand) which has been in existence for a long time 老字号的(公司或商标)；(公司)成立已久的

◇ **old – fashioned** a. out of date or not modern 过时的；老式的：He still uses an old – fashioned typewriter. 他还用着老式打字机。

**ombudsman** n. official who investigates complaints by the public against government departments 巡视官；调查官(专门调查公众对政府各部门之投诉的官员)
NOTE: plural is ombudsmen

**omit** v. (a) to leave something out or not to put something in 省略；遗漏：The secretary omitted the date when typing the contract. 秘书在打印合同时漏掉了日期。(b) not to do something 疏忽；忽略：He omitted to tell the managing director that he had lost the documents. 他忘记告诉总经理，他丢失了那些文件。
NOTE: omitting – omitted

◇ **omission** n. thing which has been omitted 省略；删除；遗漏：errors and omissions excepted = words written on an invoice to show that the company has no responsibility for mistakes in the invoice 差错遗漏除外；有错当查(发票上常用的短语，指公司对发票上的误差和遗漏概不负责)

**omnibus** n. omnibus agreement = agreement which covers many different items 统括协议；多项协议(协定或契约)

**on** prep. (a) being a member of a group 成员之一；委员之一；为…之一员：to sit on a committee 担任委员；She is on the boards of two companies. 她是两家公司董事会的成员。We have 250 people on the payroll. 在工资册上我们有250人。She is on our full – time staff. 她是一名全日制(在职)工作人员。(b) in a certain way on a commercial basis 以商业标准；以商业基本原理：to buy something on approval 进行包退包换购买的；on the average 平均地；按平均数计算；to buy a car on hire – purchase 以租购方式购买汽车；to get a mortgage on easy terms 以宽松的条件获得抵押贷款 (c) at a time 在…之时；当…之时：on weekdays 在平时每天；The shop is closed on Wednesday afternoons. 这家商店星期三下午停业。on May 24th 在5月24日那天 (d) doing something 正在做某事：The director is on holiday. 这位董事正在度假。She is in the States on business. 她正在美国出差。The switchboard operator is on duty from 6 to 9. 电话总机接线员6点到9点值班。

**oncosts** pl. n. fixed costs or money paid

in producing a product which does not rise with the quantity of the product made 固定成本(指不随产量变化的成本)

**on line or online** ad. linked directly to a mainframe computer(直接与主机)相联地;直接地; The sales office is on line to the warehouse. 营业部与仓库的计算机联网。We get our data on line from the stock control department. 我们直接从存货控制部(或库存管理部)得到数据。

**on – the – job** a. on – the – job training = training given to workers at their place of work 在职训练;就地培训

**one – man** a. one – man business or firm or company or operation = business run by one person alone with no staff or partners 个体经营;独资经营;个体户

◇ **one – off** a. done or made only once 一次性的: one – off item 一次性商品; one – off deal 一次性处理;一次性经营; 一次性买卖与交易

◇ **one – sided** a. which favours one side and not the other in a negotiation 单方面的;偏袒一方的;片面的: one – sided agreement 片面协议;单方同意

◇ **one – way** a. one – way ticket = ticket for a journey from one place to another 单程票; US one – way fare = fare for a journey from one place to another (美)单程费用;单程车费; one – way trade = situation where one country sells to another, but does not buy anything in return 单方贸易;单向贸易

◇ **one – way street** n. street where the traffic is allowed to go only in one direction 单行道: The shop is in a one – way street, which makes it very difficult for parking. 这家商店位于单行道边,很难停放汽车。

**onerous** a. heavy or needing a lot of effort or money 繁重的;艰巨的;有偿的: The repayment terms are particularly onerous. = The loan is particularly difficult to pay back 付还条件特别艰巨。

**o.n.o.** = OR NEAR OFFER 接近售价

**OPEC** = ORGANIZATION OF PETROLEUM EXPORTING COUNTRIES 石油输出国组织

**open** 1. a. (a) at work or not closed 开着的;营业的: The store is open on Sunday mornings. 这家商店星期日上午营业。Our offices are open from 9 to 6. 我们的办事处从早上9点开到下午6点。They are open for business every day of the week. 他们这周每天都开门营业。(b) ready to accept something 随时准备接受的;开放的: The job is open to all applicants. = Anyone can apply for the job. 这个工作向所有申请者开放。We will keep the job open for you until you have passed your driving test. = We will not give the job to anyone else, and will wait until you have passed your test. 我们将为你保留这个工作直到你通过驾驶考试。open to offers = ready to accept a reasonable offer 随时准备接受出价: The company is open to offers for the empty factory. = The company is ready to discuss an offer which is lower than the suggested price. 公司随时准备接受对这家空闲工厂的发价。(c) open account = unsecured credit or amount owed with no security 赊欠帐户;未清帐户;往来帐户: open cheque = cheque which is not crossed and can be cashed anywhere 普通支票(指未划线的并可在任何银行兑付的支票); open credit = bank credit given to good customers without security up to a certain maximum sum 无担保信用贷款;无担保信贷; open market = market where anyone can buy or sell 公开市场;自由市场 to buy shares on the open market = to buy shares on the Stock Exchange, not privately(在在证券交易所)公开购买股票; open ticket = ticket which can be used on any date 无定期票(哪天都可使

用的票）2. v. (a) to start a new businessworking 开业: She has opened a shop in the High Street. 她在大马路上开了一家商店。We have opened an office in London. 我们在伦敦开了一家事务所。(b) to start work or to be at work 开张; 开始营业: The office opens at 9 a.m.. 办事处上午 9 点开门营业。We open for business on Sundays. 星期日我们营业。(c) to begin 开始: to open negotiations = to begin negotiating 开始谈判; 开始协商: He opened the discussions with a description of the product. 开始讨论时他对该产品进行了描述。The chairman opened the meeting at 10.30. 主席于 10 时 30 分宣布开会。(d) to start or to allow something to start 开立; 允许开始: to open a bank account 立银行帐户; to open a line of credit 开立信用贷款额度; 开立融通额度; to open a loan 开始放款 (e) The shares opened lower. = Share prices were lower at the beginning of the day's trading. 股票开盘价格较低。

◇ **open – ended or US open – end** a. with no fixed limit or with some items not specified 无限定的; 开放的; open – ended agreement 无限制协约

◇ **opening** 1. n. (a) act of starting a new business 开业; 开放: the opening of a new branch 新建分店的开业; the opening of a new market or of a new distribution network 新市场的开张或新销售网开张 (b) opening hours = hours when a shop or business is open 营业时间; (c) job openings = jobs which are empty and need filling 工作空缺; We have openings for office staff. 我们还缺办公室职员。a market opening = possibility of starting to do business in a new market 市场空缺 2. a. at the beginning or first 开始的; 起初的: opening balance = balance at the beginning of an accounting period 期初余额(结余)(指期初开始时的帐户余额); opening bid =

first bid at an auction 首次出价(在拍卖射); opening entry = first entry in an account 开始分录(帐册上的头笔记录); opening price = price at the start of the day's trading 开盘价格; opening stock = stock at the beginning of the accounting period 期初存货(指会计期初始的存货)

◇ **open – plan** a. open – plan office = large room divided into smaller working spaces with no fixed divisions between them 敞开式办公室(一个大房间分割成许多办公场地)

◇ **open up** v. to open up new markets = to work to start business in markets where such business hasnot been done before 开发新市场

**operate** v. (a) to work 工作; 运转; 实行; 生效; The new terms of service will operate from January 1st. 新的服务条款将于 1 月 1 日实行。The rules operate on inland postal services. 这些规定用于国内邮政。(b) to operate a machine = to make a machine work 开动一台机器; 操作一台机器; He is learning to operate the new telephone switchboard. 他正在学习操作这部新的电话总机。

◇ **operating** n. general running of a business or of a machine 营业; 经营; 操作; operating budget = forecast of income and expenditure over a period of time 营业预算; 业务收支预算; 经营预算(指定期收支预算); operating costs or operating expenses = costs of the day – to – day organization of a company 经营成本; 营业费用; 日常费用; operating manual = book which shows how to work a machine 使用说明书; 操作手册; operating profit or operating loss = profit or loss made by a company in its usual business 营业利润或营业亏损; operating system = the main program which operates a computer 操作系统(计算机)

NOTE: no plural

◇ **operation** n. (a) business organization and work 企业机构；企业业务活动：the company's operations in West Africa 公司在西非的业务活动；He heads up the operations in Northern Europe. 他是公司驻北欧机构的主管（他负责领导北欧的业务活动）。operations review = examining the way in which a company or department works to see how it can be made more efficient and profitable 企业业务审核(指对企业或部门的经营方式进行检查审核以确保其效率更高,利润更大)；a franchising operation = selling licences to trade as a franchise 出售专卖权的业务活动 (b) Stock Exchange operation = buying or selling of shares on the Stock Exchange 证券交易业务 (c) in operation = working or being used 在实行中；在生效中；在实施中：The system will be in operation by June. 这项制度将于六月份实行。The new system came into operation on June 1st. 这项新制度将于6月1日开始生效。

◇ **operational** a. (a) referring to how something works 操作上的；经营上的；业务上的；营业的：operational budget = forecast of expenditure on running a business 经营预算；营业预算；operational costs = costs of running a business 经营成本；营业成本；operational planning = planning how a business is to be run 经营规划；营业计划；operational research = study of a company's way of working to see if it can be made more efficient and profitable 运筹学(对企业经营方式进行研究以确保其经济效益的一门学科) (b) The system became operational on June 1st. = The system began working on June 1st. 这项制度6月1日起生效(实施)。

◇ **operative** 1. a. to become operative = to start working 开始实施；开始生效；The new system has been operative since June 1st. 自6月1日以来一直实施该项新制度。2 n. person who operates a machine which makes a product 工人；技工

◇ **operator** n. (a) person who works a machine 操作工；操作人员：a keyboard operator 键盘操作员；a telex operator 电传员；(b) person who works a telephone switchboard 电话接线员；接线生；switchboard operator 电话接线员 to call the operator or to dial the operator 打电话或拨电话给接线员；to place a call through or via the operator 通过总机接通电话 (c) (on the Stock Exchange) person who buys and sells shares hoping to make a quick profit(股票证券交易所的)经纪人；经营者 (d) tour operator = person or company which organizes package tours 旅游经纪人或旅游公司

**opinion** n. (a) public opinion = what people think about something 公众舆论；opinion poll or opinion research = asking a sample group of people what their opinion is, so as to guess the opinion of the whole population 民意调查；民意测验；Opinion polls showed that the public preferred butter to margarine. 民意调查表明:公众更喜欢黄油而不是人造奶油。Before starting the new service, the company carried out nationwide opinion polls. 推出新的服务方式前,公司进行了全国范围的民意调查。(b) piece of expert advice 判断；意见：The lawyers gave their opinion. 律师们提出他们的意见。to ask an adviser for his opinion on a case 请顾问对一案例做出判断(表发意见)

**opportunity** n. situation where you can do something successfully 机遇；机会；时机；良机：investment opportunities or sales opportunities = possibilities for making investments or sales which will be profitable 投资机会；销售机会；a market opportunity = possibility of going into a market for the first time 市场

机会(指有可能首先打入市场的机会);
employment opportunities or job opportunities = new jobs being available 就业机会;工作机会; The increase in export orders has created hundreds of job opportunities. 出口订单的增加提供了数以百计的就业机会。

**oppose** v. to try to stop something happening; to vote against something 阻止;反对: A minority of board members opposed the motion. 少数董事们反对这项动议。 We are all opposed to the takeover. 我们全部反对这种兼并。

**opposite** n. opposite number = person who has a similar job in another company (在别的公司)居相同职务的人;职务相等的人: John is my opposite number in Smith's. = John has the same job in Smith's as I have here. 约翰在史密斯公司和我在此做同样的工作。

**optimal** a. best 最好的;最理想的;最适宜的

◇ **optimism** n. being sure that everything will work out well 乐观;乐观主义: He has considerable optimism about sales possibilities in the Far East. 他对在远东的销售机会相当乐观。 market optimism = feeling that the stock market will rise 市场乐观主义(指股票市场将有好的趋势)
NOTE: no plural

◇ **optimistic** a. feeling sure that everything will work out well 乐观的;乐观主义的: He takes an optimistic view of the exchange rate. = He expects the exchange rate will go in his favour. 他对汇率(汇价)持乐观态度。

◇ **optimum** a. best 最适宜的;最佳条件的: The market offers optimum conditions for sales. 市场为销售提供了最佳条件。

**option** n. (a) option to purchase or to sell = giving someone the possibility to buy or sell something within a period of time 选购权,购买选择权; first option = allowing someone to be the first to have the possibility of deciding something 首选权;优选权(指允许某人享有第一选择决定权); to grant someone a six-month option on a product = to allow someone six months to decide if he wants to be the agent or if he wants to manufacture the product 允许某人对一项产品(的代理权或生产权)享有六个月的选择决定权; to take up an option or to exercise an option = to accept the option which has been offered and to put it into action. 行使选择权;实施选择权; He exercised his option or he took up his option to acquire sole marketing rights to the product. 他行使了获得这项产品的独家销售的选择权。 I want to leave my options open. = I want to be able to decide what to do when the time is right. 我要保留选择权。 to take the soft option = to decide to do something which involves the least risk, effort or problems 采取软选择(或安全选择)(指在风险最小,最省力,问题最少时做出选择决定) (b) (Stock Exchange) call option = option to buy shares at a certain price(股票交易术语)买入选择权;购买权(指在股票交易中,以某种价格买入股票的选择权力); put option = option to sell shares at a certain price 售出选择权(指在股票市场中,以某种价格出售股票的选择权力); share option = right to buy or sell shares at a certain price at a time in the future 任选股权(指以某一价格在未来某一时间内买卖股票的权力); stock option = right to buy shares at a cheap price given by a company to its employees 购股选择权(公司或企业给予雇员优惠选购本公司股票的权力); option contract = right to buy or sell shares at a fixed price 股票选择权合同或契约; option dealing or option trading = buying and selling share options 选择权交易

◇ **optional** a. which can be added if the customer wants 选择的；附加的：The insurance cover is optional. 保险范围可以随意选择。optional extras = items (such as a radio) which can be added (to a car) if wanted 额外附加商品

**order** 1. n. (a) arrangement of records (filing cards, invoices, etc.) (档案、发票等的) 顺序；次序：alphabetical order = arrangement by the letters of the alphabet (A, B, C, etc.) 按字母排列之顺序 (如 A, B, C 等)：chronological order = arrangement by the order of the dates 按照年代顺序排列；The reports are filed in chronological order. 报告是按年代日期顺序归挡的。numerical order = arrangement by numbers 按照号码 (数字) 排列顺序；Put these invoices in numerical order. 把这些发票按其号码顺序放好。(b) working arrangement 工作状况；运转状况；正常状况；machine in full working order = machine which is ready and able to work properly 运转良好的机器；The telephone is out of order. = The telephone is not working 电话坏了。Is all the documentation in order? = Are all the documents valid and correct? 是否所有这些文件有效和正确？(c) pay to Mr Smith or order = pay money to Mr Smith or as he orders 付钱给史密斯先生或其指定人；pay to the order of Mr Smith = pay money directly into Mr Smith's account 把汇票直接划到史密斯先生的帐户上。(d) official request for goods to be supplied 正式定货；定购：to give someone an order or to place an order with someone for twenty filing cabinets 向某人订购 20 个文件柜 (或公文柜)；to fill or to fulfil an order = to supply items which have been ordered 交付订货；完成订单 We are so understaffed we cannot fulfil any more orders before Christmas. 我们因为缺少人手，所以圣诞节前无法交付更多的订

货。to supply an order for twenty filing cabinets 交付 20 个文件柜的订货；purchase order = official paper which places an order for something 购货订单；订购单；order fulfilment = supplying items which have been ordered 订单交货；订货交付；Terms: cash with order = The goods will be supplied only if payment in cash is made at the same time as the order is placed. 专用术语：订货付现。items available to order only = items which will be manufactured only if someone orders them 必须预先订购的商品才可供货；on order = ordered but not delivered 已定购 (而尚未交货的)：This item is out of stock, but is on order. 这项产品全部售空 (已无存货)，但已经订购了。unfulfilled orders or back orders or outstanding orders = orders received in the past and not yet supplied 拖欠订单；拖欠订货；order book = record of orders 订货记录；订货薄：The company has a full order book . = It has enough orders to work at full capacity. 该公司的货物被订购一空 (公司订货薄已满)。telephone orders = orders received over the telephone 电话订货；Since we mailed the catalogue we have had a large number of telephone orders. 我们寄出产品目录后，收到了大量的电话订货。a pad of order forms = a pad of blank forms for orders to be written on (可一页页扯下使用的) 一本空白的订货本 (薄) (e) item which has been ordered 订货：The order is to be delivered to our warehouse. 这批订货将送到我们的库房。order picking = collecting various items in a warehouse to make up an order to be sent to a customer 订货提取 (f) instruction 指示；说明：delivery order = instructions given by the customer to the person holding his goods, telling him to deliver them 提货单；出货单；交货单 (g) document which allows money to be paid to someone 汇款单；汇票：He sent us an order on the Chartered Bank. 他寄给我们一张由特许银行付款的汇款单。banker's order or standing order = order written by a customer asking a bank to make a regular payment 银行本票;银行指令; He pays his subscription by banker's order. 他用银行本票支付购股金。money order = document which can be bought for sending money through the post 邮政汇票 2. v. (a) to ask for goods to be supplied 订货;订购: to order twenty filing cabinets to be delivered to the warehouse 订购 20 个向仓库交货的公文柜; They ordered a new Rolls Royce for the managing director. 他们为总经理订购了一部新罗尔斯－罗伊斯高级轿车。(b) to put in a certain way 整理;安排: The address list is ordered by country. 这本通讯录是按国家顺序整理的。That filing cabinet contains invoices ordered by date. 那个文件柜中的发票是按日期顺序整理好的。

**ordinary** a. normal or not special 正常的;普通的: ordinary member = person who pays a subscription to belong to a group 普通会员; ordinary shares = normal shares in a company, which have no special bonuses orrestrictions 普通股(公司中没有特殊红利和限制的股份); ordinary shareholder = person who owns ordinary shares in a company 普通股东;普通股票持有者

**organization** n. (a) way of arranging something so that it works efficiently 组织: The chairman handles the organization of the AGM.董事长负责年度股东大会组织。The organization of the group is too centralized to be efficient.团体组织过于集中,以致影响效率。the organization of the head office into departments 将总公司组织成各个部门; organization and methods = examining how an office works, and suggesting how it can bemade more efficient 组织与方法审查; organization chart = list of people working in various departments, showing how a company or office is organized 组织系统图; line organization = organization of a business where each manager is responsible for doing what his superior tells him to do 垂直组织,垂直负责制(企业内部每一位经理只对他自己的直接上司所授的命令负责的制度及管理方汉)(b) group or institution which is arranged for efficient work 组织;机构(为提高工作效率而设置: the Organization of Petroleum Exporting Countries = group of major countries who are producers and exporters ofoil 石油输出国组织; a government organization = official body, run by the government 政府机构; a travel organization = body representing companies in the travel business 旅行社;旅游机构; an employers' organization = group of employers with similar interests 雇主协会;雇主联合会

NOTE: no plural for (a)

◇ **organize** v. to arrange something so that it works efficiently 组织: The company is organized into six profit centres . 公司被组成六个利润中心。The group is organized by areas of sales. 这个集团是按销售区域组织的。organized labour = workers who are members of trade unions 加入工会的工人

◇ **organizational** a. referring to the way in which something is organized 有组织的;组织上的: The paper gives a diagram of the company's organizational structure. 文件中有一个(给出了)这家公司组织结构图。

◇ **organizer** n. person who arranges things efficiently 组织者;建立者

◇ **organizing committee** n. group of people who arrange something 组织委员会: He is a member of the organizing committee for the conference. 他是大会组织委员会的成员之一。

**oriented or orientated** a. working in a certain direction 定向的；定位的；以…为导向的：profit – oriented company = company which does everything to make a profit 纯追求利润的公司；export – oriented company = company which produces goods mainly for export 产品主要供出口的公司

**origin** n. where something comes from 起源；开端产地：spare parts of European origin 欧洲生产的机器零件；certificate of origin = document showing where goods were made 商品产地证明书；原产地证书：country of origin = country where a product is manufactured 出产地；原产地；产品原产国

◇ **original** 1. a. which was used or made first 最早的；原始的：They sent a copy of the original invoice. 他们邮来一份原始支票的复印件。He kept the original receipt for reference. 他保留正本（原始的）收据以便参考。2. n. first copy made 原文；原件；正本；正文：Send the original and file two copies。寄送原本并将两本复印件存档。

◇ **originally** ad. first or at the beginning 最初地；原始地；超初地

**ounce** n. measure of weight ( = 28 grams) 盎司（度量单位：一盎司 = 28 克）
NOTE: usually written oz after figures

**out** ad. (a) on strike 罢工：The workers have been out on strike for four weeks. 工人们已经罢工四个星期了。As soon as the management made the offer, the staff came out. 管理部门一表态，职工们便罢工了。The shop stewards called the workforce out. 工厂的工人代表号召工人罢工。(b) to be out = to be wrong in calculating something 计算失误；The balance is £10 out. 余额有10英磅的计算失误。We are £20, 000 out in our calculations. = We have £20,000 too much or too little. 我们计算中有 20,000 英磅的计算错误。

◇ **outbid** v. to offer a better price than someone else 出高价；出价高于(他人)：We offered £100, 000 for the warehouse, but another company outbid us. 我们出价 1000,000 英磅购买这个库房，但另一家公司出价高于我们。
NOTE: outbidding – outbid

◇ **outfit** n. small, sometimes badly run, company 小公司(指规模小而又经营不善的公司)：They called in a public relations outfit. 他们召请了一个公共关系公司。He works for some finance outfit. 他在为某个金融公司工作。

◇ **outflow** n. outflow of capital from a country = capital which is sent out of a country for investment abroad 资金外流；国家资产外流

◇ **outgoing** a. (a) outgoing mail = mail which is being sent out 外寄邮件；外发邮件 (b) the outgoing chairman or the outgoing president = chairman or president who is about to retire 即将离职退休的董事长或总裁

◇ **outgoings** pl. n. money which is paid out 支出；开销

◇ **out – house** a. working outside a company's buildings 室外工作的；户外工作的：the out – house staff 室外工作人员；We do all our data processing out – house. 我们在室外做全部数据处理。

◇ **outlay** n. money spent or expenditure 支出；费用；开支：capital outlay = money spent on fixed assets ( such as property, machinery, furniture) 基建投资；资本支出；for a modest outlay = for a small sum 小笔花费；少量支出

◇ **outlet** n. place where something can be sold 市场；销路；商行；商店：retail outlets = shops which sell to the general public 零售商店

◇ **outline** 1. n. general description, without giving many details 概要；大纲：They drew up the outline of a plan or an outline plan. 他们拟定了计划概要。 outlineplanning permission = general permission to build a property on a piece of land, but not final because there are no details 草案许可；概要计划许可 2. v. to make a general description 梗概；概括：The chairman outlined the company's plans for the coming year. 董事长概述了公司明年的计划。

◇ **outlook** n. view of what is going to happen in the future 展望；前景；看法：The economic outlook is not good. 经济前景不乐观。The stock market outlook isworrying. 股票市场前景令人担忧。

◇ **out of court** ad. & a. A settlement was reached out of court. = A dispute was settled between two parties privately without continuing a court case. 庭外达成和解（私了）：They are hoping to reach an out‐of‐court settlement. 他们希望达成庭外和解。

◇ **out of date** a. & ad. old‐fashioned or no longer modern 过时的；陈旧的；不流行的：Their computer system is years out of date. 他们的电脑系统已过时多年。They are still using out‐of‐date equipment. 他们仍在使用陈旧的设备。

◇ **out of pocket** a. & ad. having paid out money personally 赔钱；自己掏腰包支付：The deal has left me out of pocket. 这笔交易由我自己付款。out‐of‐pocket expenses = amount of money to pay a worker back for his own money which he has spent on company business 付现费用；付实费用

◇ **out of stock** a. & ad. with no stock left 无存货；已售完：Those records are temporarily out of stock. 那些唱片暂时无货。Several out‐of‐stock items have been on order for weeks. 几个星期以来一直有人订购几种脱销的产品。

◇ **out of work** a. & ad. with no job 失业的；无业的：The recession has put millions out of work. 这次经济衰退造成数百万人的失业。The company was set up by three out‐of‐work engineers. 该公司是由三位失业的工程师创建的。

◇ **output** 1. n. (a) amount which a company or a person or a machine produces 产量；生产额：Output has increased by 10%. 产量增加了 10%。25% of our output is exported. 我们产量的25%是供出口。output per hour = amount produced in one hour 单位时间产量（按小时计算的产量）；output bonus = extra payment for increased production 超产奖；output tax = VAT charged by a company on goods or services sold 对出售的商品和劳务所征增值税 (b) information which is produced by a computer(计算机的输出)信息；数据

NOTE: no plural

2. v. to produce (by a computer)(由计算机）输出：The printer will output colour graphs. 这台打印机将输出彩色图表。That is the information outputted from the computer. 那是从计算机输出的信息。

NOTE: outputting‐outputted

◇ **outright** ad. & a. completely 彻底地；全部地：to purchase something outright or to make an outright purchase = to buy something completely, including all rights in it 一次性全部买下（包括其中所有权利）

◇ **outsell** v. to sell more than someone 销售多于…；比…更多地销售：The company is easily outselling its competitors. 公司的销售额轻而易举地超过竞争对手。

NOTE: outselling‐outsold

◇ **outside** a. & ad. not in a company's office or building 在外面的；在室外的：to send work to be done outside = to send work to be done in other offices 把工作让别的单位干；outside office hours = when the office is not open 非营业时间; outside dealer = person who is not a member of the Stock Exchange but is allowed to trade 场外交易人(非证券交易所成员,但被允许进行证券交易者); outside director = director who is not employed by the company 外界董事;外部董事(非受雇于企业的董事); outside line = line from an internal office telephone system to the main telephone exchange 电话外线; You dial 9 to get an outside line. 要外线请拨 9。outside worker = worker who does not work in a company's offices 未在公司办公室工作工人

◇ **outsize** n. size which is larger than usual 特大型;超常规号码: an outsize order = a very large order 超常规订货;特大量订货

◇ **outstanding** a. not yet paid or completed 未偿付的;未解决的: outstanding debts = debts which are waiting to be paid 未偿还债务; outstanding orders = orders received but not yet supplied 未交订货; What is the amount outstanding? = how much money is still owed? 还欠多少? matters outstanding from the previous meeting = questions which were not settled at the previous meeting 上次会议遗留下未解决的问题

◇ **out tray** n. basket on a desk for letters or memos which have been dealt with and are ready to be dispatched 文件筐

◇ **outturn** n. amount produced by a country or company 产量;产出

◇ **outvote** v. to defeat in a vote 得票多于(对方);投票压倒(对方): The chairman was outvoted. = The majority voted against the chairman. 该主席在选举中得票少于他人(即主席在选举中失利).

◇ **outward** a. going away from the home country 远离家乡的;向外的;海外的: The ship is outward bound. 这艘船是开往国外的。On the outward voyage the ship will call in at the West Indies. 在海外航行中,这艘轮船将在西印度群岛停靠。outward cargo or outward freight = goods which are being exported 出口货物;外销货; outward mission = visit by a group of businessmen to a foreign country 商务出访

◇ **outwork** n. work which a company pays someone to do at home 可在家进行的工作;外勤工作

◇ **outworker** n. person who works at home for a company 在家工作的雇员;外勤人员

**over** 1. prep. (a) more than 多于: The carpet costs over £100. 这条地毯价值100多英磅。packages not over 200 grams 不超过 200 克的包(装); The increase in turnover was over 25%. 营业额增长超过了 25%。(b) compared with 比较: increase in output over last year 较之去年的增产额; increase in debtors over the last quarter's figure 债务人较之去年第四季度有所增加 (c) during 在…期间: Over the last half of the year profits doubled. 在去年下半年利润增加了一倍。2. ad. held over to the next meeting = postponed or put back to the next meeting 推迟到下次会议; to carry over a balance = to take a balance from the end of one page or period to the beginning of the next(将帐目或余额)结转下页;结转余款 3. pl. n. overs = extra items above the agreed total 额外商品; The price includes 10% overs to compensate for damage. 价格包括 10% 的额外赔偿费。

◇ **over −** prefix more than 多于;高于;超过 shop which caters to the over − 60s = shop which has goods which appeal to people who are more than sixty years old 迎合(吸引)60 岁以上老年人的商店

◇ **overall** a. covering or including everything全面的；总体的；包括一切的：Although some divisions traded profitably, the company = The company reported an overall fall in profits. = The company reported a general fall in profits 根据帐目，尽管有些部门的生意盈利，但公司的总利润下降了。overall plan = plan which covers everything 全盘计划；全面规划

◇ **overbook** v. to book more people than there are seats or rooms available 超额预订（客房或座位）：The hotel or the flight was overbooked. 这家旅馆（或这次航班）已超额预订。

◇ **overbooking** n. booking of more people than there are seats or rooms available. 超额预订

◇ **overbought** a. having bought too much 过多购买；买空；多头：The market is overbought. = Prices on the stock market are too high, because there have been too many buyers. 股票市场买主太多价格过高。

◇ **overcapacity** n. unused capacity for producing something 生产力过剩

◇ **overcapitalized** a. with more capital in a company than it needs 投资过多的；资本额过多

◇ **overcharge** 1. n. charge which is higher than it should be 过高的收费：to pay back an overcharge 付还多开的帐款；2. v. to ask too much money 要价过多；要价过高：They overcharged us for meals. 他们过多地索要我们的伙食费。We asked for a refund because we had been overcharged. 因为他们索费过高，所以我们要求退款。

◇ **overdraft** n. amount of money which a person withdraws from his account and which is more than he has in the account 透支；(借款人从自己的帐户上提取超过其存款的款项)：The bank has allowed me an overdraft of

£5,000. 银行允许我透支 5,000 英磅。overdraft facilities. = arrangement with a bank to have an overdraft 透支额；透支款项；We have exceeded our overdraft facilities. = We have taken out more than the overdraft allowed by the bank. 我们超过了透支额度。

◇ **overdraw** v. to take out more money from a bank account than there is init 透支；超支：Your account is overdrawn or you are overdrawn = You have paid out more money from your account than you have in it. 你透支了。NOTE: overdrawing - overdrew - overdrawn

◇ **overdue** a. which has not been paid on time 过期未付的；过期的：Interest payments are three weeks overdue. = interest payments which should have been made three weeks ago 付息已过期三周了。

◇ **overestimate** v. to think something is larger or worse than it really is 过高估计：He overestimated the amount of time needed to fit out the factory. 他过多地估计了装备这家工厂的时间。

◇ **overextend** v. the company overextended itself. = The company borrowed more money than its assets would allow. 这家公司负债超出了它的资产允许范围。

◇ **overhead** 1. a. overhead costs or expenses = money spent on the day - to - day cost of a business 企业日常管理费的；经常性开支的；间接费用的：overhead budget = plan of probable overhead costs 普通费用预算；间接费用预算 2. n. overheads or US overhead = costs of the day - to - day running of a business 企业日常管理费用；间接费用；企业一般管理费：The sales revenue covers the manufacturing costs but not the overheads. 销售收入与生产成本持平，但却不抵企业一般管理费。

◇ **overlook** v. (a) to look out over 眺望；俯瞰：The Managing Director's office overlooks the factory. 总经理的办公室俯视着那家工厂。(b) not to pay attention to 忽略；未注意：In this instance we will overlook the delay. 在这种情况下，我们不介意延缓。

◇ **overmanning** n. having more workers than are needed to do a company's work 人浮于事；人员配备过多：to aim to reduce overmanning 意于裁减多余的人员

◇ **overpaid** a. paid too much 多付的；过多偿付的：Our staff are overpaid and underworked. 我们的职员挣得多，干得少。

◇ **overpayment** n. paying too much 多付钱；过多偿付的

◇ **overproduce** v. to produce too much 多付钱；过多偿付

◇ **overproduction** n. manufacturing too much of a product 生产过剩；过量生产

◇ **overrated** a. valued more highly than it should be 估价过高的；过高估计的：The effect of the dollar on European business cannot be overrated. 美元对欧洲商业的影响不能高估。Their "first - class service" is very overrated. "第一流服务水平"被过高估计了。

◇ **overrider or overriding commission** n. special extra commission which is above all other commissions 特别额外佣金（超过一般佣金水平）

◇ **overrun** v. to go beyond a limit 超过限度：The company overran the time limit set to complete the factory. 这家企业超过了本工厂限定完工的时间期限。NOTE: overrunning – overran – overrun

◇ **overseas** 1. a. across the sea or to foreign countries 海外的；国外的：an o-verseas call = phone call to another country 国外电话；the overseas division = section of a company dealing with trade with other countries 海外分部(分公司，分社，分店等)；overseas markets = markets in foreign countries 国外市场；海外市场；overseas trade = trade with foreign countries 对外贸易；海外贸易 2. n. foreign countries 外国；国外：The profits from overseas are far higher than those of the home division. 国外贸易利润大大高于国内分公司的利润。

◇ **overseer** n. person who supervises other workers 管理人；工头；监工

◇ **oversell** v. to sell more than you can produce 售出过多；卖空：He is oversold = He has agreed to sell more product than he can produce. 他是在卖空。（他的产品出售超过了产量。）The market is oversold. = Stock market prices are too low, because there have been too many sellers. 股票市场价格太低因抛售过多。NOTE: overselling – oversold

◇ **overspend** v. to spend too much 超支：to overspend one's budget = to spend more money than is allowed in the budget 支出超过预算；预算超支 NOTE: overspending – overspent

◇ **overspending** n. spending more than is allowed 超支；过度花费：The board decided to limit the overspending by the production departments. 该董事会决定限制生产部门的过度花费。

◇ **overstaffed** a. with more workers than are needed to do the work of the company 人员配备过多的；人浮于事的

◇ **overstock** 1. v. to have more stock than is needed 库存过剩；存货过多：to be overstocked with spare parts = to have too many spare parts in stock 零件库存过剩 2. pl. n. US overstocks = more stock than is needed to supply orders(美)备货过多；库存过剩：We will have to sell off the overstocks to make room in the warehouse. 为了腾出库房

场地,我们必须廉价出售存货。

◇ **oversubscribe** v. The share offer was oversubscribed six times. = People applied for six times as many new shares as were available. 股票认购已逾额六倍了(超额六倍)。

◇ **over‐the‐counter** a. over‐the‐counter sales = legal selling of shares which are not listed in the official Stock Exchange list(不通过证券交易所的)场外交易: This share is available on the over‐the‐counter market. 这种股票可以在场外交易市场买到。

◇ **overtime** 1. n. hours worked more than the normal working time 超时;加班时间: to work six hours' overtime 加班 6 小时; The overtime rate is one and a half times normal pay. 加班费是正常报酬的一倍半。 overtime ban = order by a trade union which forbids overtime work by itsmembers. 加班禁令;禁止加班(通告); overtime pay = pay for extra time worked 加班费
NOTE: no plural
2. ad. to work overtime = to work longer hours than in the contract of employment 加班工作:超时工作

◇ **overvalue** v. to give a higher value than is right 过高估计;定价过高: These shares are overvalued at £1.25. = The shares are worth less than the £1.25 for which they are selling. 这些股票价格定 1.25 英磅过高了。 The pound is overvalued against the dollar. = The exchange rate gives too many dollars to the pound, given the strength of the two countries' economies. 英磅对美元的比价过高。

◇ **overweight** a. The package is sixty grams overweight. = The package weighs sixty grams too much. 这个包裹超重 60 克。

◇ **overworked** a. having too much work to do 工作过度的;干活过多的:

Our staff complain of being underpaid and overworked 我们的职员抱怨挣得少,干活多。

**owe** v. to have to pay money 欠款;欠债;应付钱: He owes the bank £250,000. 他欠银行 250,000 英磅。 He owes the company for the stock he purchased. = He has not paid for the stock. 他欠着公司买股票的钱。

◇ **owing** a. (a) which is owed 欠着的;未付的;应付的: money owing to the directors 应付给董事们的钱; How much is still owing to the company by its debtors? 债务人还欠公司多少钱? (b) owing to = because of 因为;由于: The plane was late owing to fog. 由于有雾飞机晚点了。 I am sorry that owing to pressure of work, we cannot supply your order on time. 我很抱歉,因工作过于繁重,我们无法按时交货。

**own** v. to have or to possess 有;拥有;具有;占有: He owns 50% of the shares. 他拥有 50% 的股票。 a wholly‐owned subsidiary = a subsidiary which belongs completely to the parent company 完全由母公司拥有的附属公司; a state‐owned industry = industry which is nationalized 国营工业

◇ **own brand goods** n. products specially packed for a store with the store's name on them 标有自己店名的货物(产品)

◇ **owner** n. person who owns something 拥有者;所有人;物主;业主: sole owner = person who owns something by himself 唯一业主; owner‐occupier = person who owns and lives in a house(住自己的房子的)房主; goods sent at owner's risk = situation where the owner has to insure the goods while they are being transported 由业主(即货物发运人)承担风险的货物

◇ **ownership** n. act of owning something 所有(权);所有制: common or collective ownership = situation where a business is owned by the workers who work in it 集体所有制;共同所有权; joint ownership = situation where two people own the same property 共有制;共同所有权; public ownership or state ownership = situation where an industry is nationalized 公有制;国家所有制;公有产权; private ownership = situation where a company is owned by private shareholders 私有制;私人所有权; The ownership of the company has passed to the banks. = The banks have become owners of the company. 该企业所有权已转给银行。

NOTE: no plural

◇ **own label goods** n. goods specially produced for a store with store's name on them 标有本店店名的货物或商品。

**oz** = OUNCE(S) 盎斯

# Pp

**PA** = PERSONAL ASSISTANT 私人助理

**p.a.** = PER ANNUM 每年

**pack** 1. n. pack of items = items put together in a container for selling 包产品;包装产品; pack of cigarettes 一包香烟; pack of biscuits 一包饼干; pack of envelopes 一叠信封; items sold in packs of 200 = sold in boxes containing 200 items 产品以 200 个一包为单位出售; blister pack or bubble pack = type of packing where the item for sale is covered with astiff plastic cover sealed to a card backing 泡沫薄膜包装; display pack = specially attractive box for showing goods for sale 样品陈列包装;样本

包装; dummy pack = empty pack for display in a shop 陈列空包装; six‐pack = box containing six items ( often bottles)6 个一盒(一包) 2. v. to put things into a container for selling or sending 包装;装箱;打包; to pack goods into cartons 把货物打包装箱;把装物用纸板盒包装; The biscuits are packed in plastic wrappers. 这些饼干用塑料纸包装。The computer is packed in expanded polystyrene before being shipped. 这台计算机运送前用弹性聚苯乙烯包装。

◇ **package** 1. n. (a) goods packed and wrapped for sending by mail 包裹: The Post Office does not accept bulky packages. 邮局拒收体积大的邮包。The goods are to be sent in airtight packages. 这批货物应密封包装运送。(b) group of different items joined together in one deal 整体;整批;一揽子: pay package or salary package or US compensation package ‐ salary and other benefits offered with a job 一揽子工资;全部金酬; The job carries an attractive salary package. 这份工作具有诱人的丰厚工资与各种福利。 package deal = agreement where several different items are agreed at the same time 一揽子交易;整批交易; We are offering a package deal which includes the whole office computer system, staff training and hardware maintenance. 我们提供整套服务,其中包括提供办公计算机系统,人员培训和硬件维修。 package holiday or package tour = holiday or tour where the hotel, travel and meals are all included in the price 由旅行社代办的旅行; The travel company is arranging a package trip to the international computer exhibition. 旅游公司正在组织参加国际计算机展览的代办旅行。2. v. (a) to package goods = to wrap and pack goods in an attractive way 装饰包装货物 (b) to package holidays = to sell a holiday package including travel hotels and food 承办假日旅游

◇ **packaging** n. ( a ) the action of puttingthings into packages 打包;包装;装箱 ( b ) material used to protect goods which are being packed 包装材料;airtight packaging 密封包装;packaging material 包装材料 ( c ) attractive material used to wrap goods for display 有吸引力的供陈列用的包装材料
NOTE: no plural

◇ **packager** n. person who creates a book for a publisher 包装者;装订工

◇ **packer** n. person who packs goods 包装工;打包工

◇ **packet** n. small box of goods for selling 小包;小盒;小箱: packet of cigarettes 一小盒烟; packet of biscuits 一包饼干; packet of filing cards 小捆文件卡(档案卡); item sold in packets of 20 = sold in boxes containing 20 items each 20 个一盒出售的物品; postal packet = small container of goods sent by post 小件邮包

◇ **packing** n. ( a ) action of putting goods into boxes and wrapping them for shipping 包装;捆装: What is the cost of the packing? 包装费多少? Packing is included in the price. 价格中包括包装费。 packing case = large wooden box for carrying easily broken items 大的包装箱(木头); packing charges = money charged for putting goods into boxes 包装费;打包费; packing list or packing slip = list of goods which have been packed, sent with the goods to show they have been checked 包装货物详单;装箱单 ( b ) material used to protect goods 包装材料: packed in airtight packing 用密封材料包装的; non – returnable packing = packing which is to be thrown away when it has been used and not returned to the sender 一次性包装材料(不能退还)
NOTE: no plural

**pad** n. ( a ) pile of sheets of paper attached together on one side 便笺簿;拍纸簿 desk pad = pad of paper kept on a desk for writing notes 便笺簿;记事簿; memo pad or note pad = pad of paper for writing memos or notes 记事本;笔记本; phone pad = pad of paper kept by a telephone for noting messages 电话记录簿 ( b ) soft material like a cushion 软垫;垫子: The machine is protected by rubber pads. 这台机器用橡胶软垫保护着。 inking pad = cushion with ink in it, used to put ink on a rubber stamp 印台;印泥;印墨

**paid** a. with money given 支薪金的;付钱的 ( a ) paid holidays = holidays where the worker's wages are still paid even though he is not working 带薪假日 ( b ) paid assistant = assistant who receives a salary 领取薪金的助手 ( c ) which has been settled 已付清的: carriage paid 运费付讫;运费预付; tax paid 完税; paid bills = bills which have been settled 已付帐单; The invoice is marked "Paid". 发票上有"付讫"字样。 ( d ) paid – up capital = all money paid for the issued capital shares 已缴清资本;实收资本; paid – up shares = shares which have been completely paid for by the shareholder 实付股票;已缴清股票

**pallet** n. flat wooden base on which goods can be stacked for easyhandling by a fork – lift truck 货盘;托盘;夹板(供叉车装卸搬运货物用)

◇ **palletize** v. to put goods on pallets 货盘化;用货盘搬运: palletized cartons 托盘纸板箱

**pamphlet** n. small booklet of advertising material or of information 小册子

**panel** n. ( a ) flat surface standing upright 板;盘: display panel = flat area for displaying goods in a shop window 展销板; advertisement panel = specially designed large advertising space in a newspaper 广告版面 ( b ) panel of experts = group of people who give advice on a problem 专家小组; consumer panel = group of consumers who report on goods they have used so that the manufacturer can improve the goods, or use the consumers' reports in his advertising 用户小组;消费者小组

**panic** a. frightened 恐慌的;惊慌的; panic buying = rush to buy something at any price because stocks may run out or because the price may rise 抢购; panic buying of sugar or of dollars 抢购白糖或美元; panic selling of sterling = rush to sell sterling at any price because of possible devaluation 抛售英磅

**paper** n. (a) thin material for writing on or for wrapping 纸: brown paper = thick paper for wrapping parcels 牛皮纸; carbon paper = sheet of paper with a black stuff on one side used in a typewriter to make a copy 复写纸; He put the carbon paper in the wrong way round. 她把复写纸放反了。 duplicating paper = special paper to be used in a duplicating machine 复印纸; graph paper = paper with small squares printed on it, used for drawinggraphs 座标纸; headed paper = notepaper with the name and address of the company printed onit 有抬头的信纸;有抬头的便笺纸; lined paper = paper with thin lines printed on it 横线纸;条纹纸; typing paper = thin paper for use in a typewriter 打字纸; wrapping paper = paper for wrapping 包装纸 (NOTE: no plural) (b) paper bag = bag made of paper 纸袋; paper feed = device which puts paper into a printer or photocopier 进纸器 (c) papers = documents 文件;公文: He sent me the relevant papers on the case. 他给我送来了与这个案例有关的文件。 He has lost the customs papers. 他丢失了海关文件。 The office is asking for the VAT papers. 办公室需要增值税的文件。 (d) on paper = in theory 理论

上: On paper the system is ideal, but we have to see it working before we will sign the contract. 从理论上讲, 这个系统是理想的, 但在签合同之前, 我们必须看看它的运行情况。 paper loss = loss made when an asset has fallen in value but has not beensold 帐面亏损; paper profit = profit made when an asset has increased in value but has notbeen sold 帐面盈余;虚盈; paper millionaire = person who owns shares which, if he sold them, would make him a millionaire 股票值百万富翁 (e) documents which can represent money (bills of exchange, promissory notes, etc.) 商业票据;单据;证券(汇票和本票等); bankable paper = document which a bank will accept as security for a loan 可向银行贴现的票据; negotiable paper = document which can be transferred from one owner to another for money 可转让的票据;可流通的票据 (f) paper money or paper currency = banknotes 钞票;纸币 (g) newspaper 报纸; trade paper = newspaper aimed at people working in a certain industry 商业报;贸易报; free paper or giveaway paper = newspaper which is given away free, and which relies for its income on its advertising 免费报纸

◇ **paperclip** n. piece of bent wire, used to hold pieces of paper together 纸夹;环形针

◇ **paperwork** n. office work, especially writing memos and filling in forms 文书工作;卷案工作: Exporting to Russia involves a large amount of paperwork. 对俄罗斯出口还需做大量的文书工作。

NOTE: no plural

**par** a. equal or at the same price 等价; 票面价值: par value = face value or the value printed on a share certificate 票面价值;面值; shares at par = shares whose market price is the same as their face value 等价股票(面值与市价相

同）；平价股票；shares above par or belowpar = shares with a market price higher or lower than their par value 溢价股票或折价股票

**parachute** n. US golden parachute = large, usually tax – free, sum of money given to an executive who retires from a company before the end of his service contract(美国公司高级职员在合同期未满离任时所付的)高额的大笔免税款项

**paragraph** n. group of several lines of writing which makes a separate section 段落：the first paragraph of your letter or paragraph one of yourletter 你信件的第一段；Please refer to the paragraph in the contract on"hipping instructions". 清查阅合同中有关装船指令那段。

**parameter** n. fixed limit 参数；系数：The budget parameters are fixed by the finance director. 预算参数由财务主任定的。Spending by each department has to fall within certain parameters. 每个部门的开支必须属于确定的系数之内。

**parastatal** n. (in Africa) large state – controlled organization(非洲)大型国家机构；大的国控组织

**parcel** 1. n. (a) goods wrapped up in paper or plastic, etc., to be sent by post 包裹；邮包：to do up goods into parcels 把货物打包；将货物捆扎成包；to tie up a parcel = to fasten a parcel with string 把包裹捆扎紧；

parcel delivery service = private company which delivers parcels within a certain area 包裹投递服务，小件运送服务；parcels office = office where parcels can be handed in for sending by mail 包裹邮寄处；parcel post = mail service for sending parcels 包裹邮递；小件邮递；to send a box by parcel post 将盒子当包裹寄(由小件邮递寄送一个小盒子)；parcel rates = charges for sending parcels by post 包裹邮费；包裹寄费 (b) parcel of shares = group of shares (such as 50 or 100) which are sold as a group 一批股票；一宗股票；The shares are on offer in parcels of 50. 股票以每五十张为一宗出售。2. v. to wrap and tie to make a parcel 包装捆扎或打包：to parcel up a consignment of books 把一批邮寄的书打包

NOTE: parcelling – parcelled but US parceling – parceled

**parent** n. parents = father and mother 父母；双亲：parent company = company which owns more than 50% of the shares of anothercompany 母公司；控股公司

**pari passu** phr. equally 同等地；对等地：The new shares will rank pari passu with the existing ones. 新上市股票将与正在市场流通的股票同等。

**parity** n. being equal 同等；平等；等价：The female staff want parity with the men. = They want to have the same rates of pay and perks as the men. 女职工要求与男职工同工同酬。The pound fell to parity with the dollar. = the pound fell to a point where one pound equalled one dollar. 英磅下跌到与美元等价。

NOTE: no plural

**park** 1. n. open space with grass and trees 公园；公共游憩场：business park = group of small factories or warehouses, especially near a town 商业区；car park = place where you can leave your car 停车场；He left his car in the hotel car park. 他把车停放在旅馆的停车场。If the car park is full, you can park in the street for thirty minutes. 如果停车场已满，你可以把车停放在街道上 30 分钟。industrial park = area of land near a town specially set aside for factories and warehouses 工业区；science park = area near a town or university set aside for technological industries

科技园区 2. v. to leave your car in a placewhile you are not using it 停放车辆：The rep parked his car outside the shop. 这个推销员把车停放在商店外面。You cannot park here during the rush hour. 交通高峰时你不能把车停在这儿。Parking is difficult in the centre of the city. 在市中心停车很难。

**Parkinson's law** n. law, based on wide experience, that in business as in government the amount of work increases to fill the time available for it 帕金森定律——基于丰富广博的经验，商界与政界一样，用增加工作量，最大限度地利用一切可行的时间。

**part** n. (a) piece or section 部分；局部：Part of the shipment was damaged. 部分发运货物受到损坏。Part of the workforce is on overtime. 部分工人正在加班干活。Part of the expenses will be refunded. = Some of the expenses, but not all. 部分开支是可偿还的 (b) in part = not completely 部分地：to contribute in part to the costs or to pay the costs in part 支付部分成本 (c) spare part = small piece of machinery to replace a part of a machine whichis broken 零件；部件；机器备用件：The photocopier will not work — we need to replace a part or a part needs replacing. 影印机坏了，需要换个零件。(d) part - owner = person who owns something jointly with one or more other persons 合伙人；共有物主：He is part - owner of the restaurant. 他是这个饭店的合伙人。part - ownership = situation where two or more persons own the same property 合伙制，共有制 (e) part exchange = giving an old product as part of the payment for a new one 折旧换新：They refused to take my old car as part exchange for the new one. 他们拒绝接受我的旧车来折旧换新。part payment = paying of part of a whole payment 部分偿还；部分支付：I gave him ￡250 as

part payment for the car. 我给他 250 英镑作为这辆汽车的部分付款。part delivery or part order or part shipment = delivering or shipping only some of the items in an order 部分发运

◇ **part - time** a. & ad. not working for the whole working day 非全日制的；兼任的：She works part - time. 她不是全天上班。He is trying to find part - time work when the children are in school. 当孩子们上学时，他想找个兼职工作。a part - time worker 零工；非全日工；We are looking for part - time staff to work our computers. 我们正在寻找操作计算机的兼职人员。part - time work or part - time employment = work for part of a working day 非全日性工作；零活

◇ **part - timer** n. person who works part - time 零工；非全日工；兼职者

**partial** a. not complete 部分的；不完全的：partial loss = situation where only part of the insured property has been damaged or lost 部分亏损；部分损失；He got partial compensation for the damage to his house. = He was compensated for part of the damage. 他得到了房屋损失的部分赔偿。

**participation** n. taking part 参加；参与：worker participation = situation where the workers take part in making management decisions 工人参与
NOTE: no plural

◇ **participative** a. where both sides take part 双方参与的，共享的；分担的：We do not treat management - worker relations as a participative process. 我们不能视劳资关系为双方参与过程。

**particular** 1. a. special or different from others 特殊的；特别的；独特的：The photocopier only works with a particular type of paper. 影印机只能使用专用纸。particular average = situation where part of a shipment is lost or damaged and the insurance costs are borne by the owner of the lost goods and not shared among all the owners of the shipment 单独海损(海损的一种形式, 指航运中部分货运损失及保险费用只由损失货物货主承担, 而不在发运货物及其它所有人中分摊) 2. n. (a) particulars = details 详细说明; 细则; 详尽: sheet which gives particulars of the items for sale 所售物品详细说明的一页; The inspector asked for particulars of the missing car. 检查官询问了失踪汽车的详细情况。 to give full particulars of something = to list all the known details about something 列举出事情的全部细节 (b) in particular = specially or as a special point 特别地; 尤其是: Fragile goods, in particular glasses, need special packing. 易碎物品, 尤其是玻璃, 需要特殊包装。

**partly** ad. not completely 部分地; 不完全地: partly – paid capital = capital which represents partly – paid shares 部分支付资本; partly – paid up shares = shares where the shareholders have not paid the full facevalue 部分支付的股票; partly – secured creditors = creditors whose debts are not fully covered by the value ofthe security 部分担保的债权人

**partner** n. person who works in a business and has an equal share in it with other partners 合股人; 合伙人; 合作者: He became a partner in a firm of solicitors. 他成为一家律师事务所的合伙人。 active partner or working partner = partner who works in a partnership 参与经营的合伙人; 执行业务股东; junior partner or senior partner = person who has a small or large part of the shares in apartnership 小股东或大股东; sleeping partner = partner who has a share in a business but does not work in it. 不参与经营的合伙人; 不任职的股东

◇ **partnership** n. (a) unregistered business where two or more people share the risks and profits equally. 合伙; 合作企业; to go into partnership with someone 加入某人合作企业; to join with someone to form a partnership 与某人一起建立合作企业; to offer someone a partnership or to take someone into partnership with you = to have a working business and bring someone in to share it with you 与某人合伙 (合作); to dissolve a partnership = to bring a partnership to an end 解散合作关系; 散伙 (b) limited partnership = registered business where the liability of the partners is limited to the amount of capital they have each provided to the business and where the partners may not take part in the running of the business 有限合伙公司; 两合公司(责任限于对企业所投资本, 但合伙人不一定参与企业的管理)

**party** n. (a) company or person involved in a legal dispute or legal agreement 当事人; 一方; 参与者: One of the parties to the suit has died. 诉讼的一方已死亡。 The company is not a party to the agreement. 该公司不是本协议的当事人。 (b) third party = any third person, in addition to the two main people involved in a contract 第三方; 第三者: third party insurance or third party policy = insurance to cover damage to any person who is not one of the people named in the insurance contract (that is, not the insured person nor the insurance company) 第三者责任保险 (c) working party = group of experts who study a problem 工作组; 专家工作组: The government has set up a working party to study the problems of industrial waste. 政府指派了一个专家小组研究工业废物问题。 Professor Smith is the chairman of the working party on computers in society. 史密斯教授是上层社会计算机专家委员会主席。

**pass** 1. n. permit to allow someone to

go into a building 通行证；入场证：You need a pass to enter the ministry offices. 你需有一个通行证才能进入部长办公室。All members of staff must show a pass. 所有人员必须出示出入证。2. v. (a) to pass a dividend = to pay no dividend in a certain year 到期未付股利；不发放股利 (b) to approve 同意；批准；通过：The finance director has to pass an invoice before it is sent out. 支票开出前必须经财务主任批准。The loan has been passed by the board. 贷款事宜已经董事会批准。to pass a resolution = to vote to agree to a resolution 通过决议：The meeting passed a proposal that salaries should be frozen. 大会通过了冻结薪金的提议。(c) to be successful(成功地)通过：He passed his typing test. 他通过了打字测试。She has passed all her exams and now is a qualified accountant. 她通过了所有的考试，现在是一位合格的会计师。

◇ **passbook** n. book given by a bank or building society which shows money which you deposit or withdraw from your savings account or building society account 银行存折；住宅互助社团的帐户

◇ **pass off** v. to pass something off as something else = to pretend that it is another thing in order to cheat a customer 骗卖；出售假冒产品：He tried to pass off the wine as French, when in fact it came from outside the Common Market. 他企图将这种酒假冒或法国酒，而事宜上此酒来自共同市场以外的地方。

**passage** n. voyage by ship 航行

**passenger** n. person who travels in a plane, bus, taxi, plane, etc., but is not the driver or member of the crew 乘客；旅客；passenger terminal = air terminal for people going on planes, not for cargo 乘客侯机处；passenger train = train

which carries passengers but not freight 客车

**passport** n. official document proving that you are a citizen of a country, which you have to show when you travel from one country to another 护照：We had to show our passports at the customs post. 在海关关卡我们必须出示护照。His passport is out of date. 他的护照过期了。The passport officer stamped my passport. 这位海关官员在我的护照上盖了章。

**patent** 1. n. (a) official document showing that a person has the exclusive right to make and sell an invention 专利权；专利：to take out a patent for a new type of light bulb 得到了一种新型灯泡的专利权；to apply for a patent for a new invention 申请一项新发明专利；letters patent = official term for a patent 专利证；特许证；patent applied for or patent pending = words on a product showing that the inventor has applied for a patent for it 已申请专利；to forfeit a patent = to lose a patent because payments have not been made 失去专利(因无钱支付)；to infringe a patent = to make and sell a product which works in the same way as a patented product and not pay a royalty for it 侵犯专利；infringement of patent or patent infringement = act of illegally making or selling a product which is patented 专利侵权；侵犯专利权 (b) patent agent = person who advises on patents and applies for patents on behalf of clients 专利代理人；to file a patent application = to apply for a patent 提交专利申请；patent medicine = medicine which is registered as a patent 专利药品；patent office = government office which grants patents and supervises them 专利局；patent rights = rights which an inventor holds under a patent 专利权 2. v. to patent an invention = to register an invention with the patent office to prevent other people fromcopying it 取得一项发明专利权

◇ **patented** a. which is protected by a patent 有专利权的

**paternity** n. paternity leave = permission for a man to be away from work when his wife is having a baby 父亲假（指当妻子生育时, 丈夫可告假）

**pattern** n. (a) pattern book = book showing examples of design 图样书；样书 (b) general way in which something usually happens 模式；模型；类型：pattern of prices or price pattern 价格种类；pattern of sales or sales pattern 销售方式；pattern of trade or trading pattern = general way in which trade is carried on 贸易格局；贸易方式：The company's trading pattern shows high export sales in the first quarter and high home sales in the third quarter. 公司贸易格局表明，第一季度外销额高而第三季度内销额高。

**pawn** 1. n. to put something in pawn = to leave a valuable object with someone in exchange for a loan which has to be repaid if you want to take back the object 把…抵押出去；典当某物；to take something out of pawn = to repay the loan and so get back the object 赎回典当品；pawn ticket = receipt given by the pawnbroker for the object left in pawn 当票；典当凭据

NOTE: no plural

2. v. to pawn a watch = to leave a watch with a pawnbroker who gives a loan against it 把手表当掉；把手表做抵押

◇ **pawnbroker** n. person who lends money against the security of valuable objects 典当商；开当铺者

◇ **pawnshop** n. pawnbroker's shop 当铺；典当行

**pay** 1. n. (a) salary or wage or money given to someone for regular work 报酬；付款；工资：back pay = salary which has not been paid 欠薪；拖欠工资；basic pay = normal salary without extra payments 基本工资；基本薪金；take – home pay = pay left after tax and insurance have been deducted 实得工资；holidays with pay = holiday which a worker can take by contract and for which he is paid 有薪假期；unemployment pay = dole or money given by the government to someone who is unemployed 失业救济津贴 (b) pay cheque = monthly cheque which pays a salary to a worker 付薪支票；pay day = day on which wages are paid to workers ( usually Friday for workers paid once a week, and during the last week of the month for workers who are paid once a month)发薪日；pay negotiations or pay talks = discussions between management and workers about pay increases 加薪谈判；pay packet = envelope containing the pay slip and the cash pay 工资袋(其中装有工资单和现金)；pay rise = increase in pay 长工资；加薪；pay slip = piece of paper showing the full amount of a worker's pay, and the money deducted as tax, pension and insurance contributions 工资单 (c) pay desk = place in a store where you pay for goods bought 付款台；pay phone = telephone which works if you put coins into it 投币电话 2. v. (a) to give money to buy an item or a service 付款购物：to pay £1,000 for a car 花 1,000 英磅购买汽车；How much did you pay to have the office cleaned? 你花了多少钱请人把办公室打扫干净的? to pay in advance = to give money before you receive the item bought or before the service has been completed 预先付款；预付；We had to pay in advance to have the new telephone system installed. 装新电话系统我们必须预先付款。to pay in instalments = to give money for an item by giving small amounts regularly 分期

付款；We are paying for the computer bypaying instalments of £50 a month. 我们以每月 50 英磅分期付款支付这台计算机。to pay cash = to pay the complete sum in cash 现金支付；付现："pay cash" = words written on a crossed cheque to show that it can be paid in cash if necessary "付现"（划线支票上标明 "付现"二字，表明必要时，可用现金支付）；to pay by cheque = to pay by giving a cheque, not by using cash or credit card 支票付款；to pay by credit card = to pay, using a credit card and not a cheque or cash 信用卡支付（b）to give money 支付；付钱；to pay on demand = to pay money when it is asked for, not after a period of credit 索要即付；Please pay the sum of £10 . = Please give £10 in cash or by cheque. 请付 10 英磅。to pay a dividend = to give shareholders a part of the profits of a company 支付股息；These shares pay a dividend of 1.5p. 这些股票的股息为 1.5 便士。to pay interest = to give money as interest on money borrowed or invested 支付利息；付息；Building societies pay an interest of 10% . 住宅互助社团付息 10%。pay as you earn or US pay - as - you - go = tax system, where income tax is deducted from the salary before it is paid to the worker 预扣所得税（一种税收制度——支薪前从薪金中扣除所得税）（c）to give a worker money for work done 付薪；付给报酬：The workforce has not been paid for three weeks. 工人们已有三个星期未拿工钱了。We pay good wages for skilled workers. 我们给技术娴熟的工人付高薪。How much do they pay you per hour? 他们每小时付你多少钱? to be paid by the hour = to get money for each hour worked 计时付款；计时领取的报酬；to be paid at piece - work rates = to get money for each piece of work finished 计件付款，计件取酬（d）to give money which is owed

or which has to be paid 偿还；还帐：to pay a bill 支付帐单；to pay an invoice 支付发票上的款项；to pay duty on imports 进口产品的纳税；to pay tax 缴税（e）to pay a cheque into an account = to deposit money in the form of a cheque 支票转入帐户

NOTE: paying - paid

◇ **payable** a. which is due to be paid 到期应付的：payable in advance = which has to be paid before the goods are delivered 预先付款；payable on delivery = which has to be paid when the goods are delivered 货到即付；payable on demand = which must be paid when payment is asked for 索款即付；payable at sixty days = which has to be paid by sixty days after the date of invoice 60 天内付款；cheque made payable to bearer = cheque which will be paid to the person who has it, not to any particular name written on it 不记名支票；shares payable on application = shares which must be paid for when you apply to buy them 申请即付股票；accounts payable = money owed by a company 应付帐款；bills payable = bills which a debtor will have to pay 应付票据；Electricity charges are payable by the tenant. = The tenant (and not the landlord) must pay for the electricity. 电费由房客支付。

◇ **pay back** v. to give money back to someone 付还，偿付：to pay back a loan 偿还贷款；I lent him £50 and he promised to pay me back in a month. 我借给他 50 英磅，他答应一个月之内还给我。He has never paid me back for the money he borrowed. 他从我这儿借的钱从未还过。

◇ **payback** n. paying back money which has been borrowed 偿还；付还：payback clause = clause in a contract which states the terms for repaying a loan 偿还条款；payback period = period of time over which a loan is to be repaid or an investment is to pay for itself 偿还期(贷款偿还期或投资回收期) NOTE: no plural

◇ **paycheck** n. salary cheque given to an employee(付给雇员的)薪金支票

◇ **pay down** v. to pay money down = to make a deposit 付押金;付保证金: He paid £50 down and the rest in monthly instalments. 他先付 50 英磅定金,其余的按月分期付款

◇ **PAYE** = PAY AS YOU EARN 预扣所得税

◇ **payee** n. person who receives money from someone or person whose name ison a cheque 受款人;收款人

◇ **payer** n. person who gives money to someone 付款人; slow payer = person or company which does not pay debts on time 拖欠债务者(或公司); He is well known as a slow payer. 他是出名的债务拖欠者。

◇ **paying** 1. a. which makes a profit 赢利的;合算的; It is a paying business. 这是个赢利企业。 It is not a paying proposition. = It is not a business which is going to make a profit. 这是一个蚀本企业。 2. n. giving money 支付; paying of a debt 还债; paying – in book = book of forms for paying money into a bank account or building society 缴款簿;付款簿; paying – in slip = form which is filled in when money is being deposited in a bank account or building society 存款单 NOTE: no plural

◇ **payload** n. cargo or passengers carried by a ship or train or plane for which payment is made 酬载(收取运载费用的载货或载客量的船或火车或飞机)

◇ **payment** n. (a) giving money 支付;缴纳;付款; payment in cash or cash payment 付现;现金支付; payment by cheque 支票付款; payment of interest or interest payment 付息; payment on ac-count = paying part of the money owed 部分付欠款;赊帐付款; full payment or payment in full = paying all money owed 付清; payment on invoice = paying money as soon as an invoice is received 凭发票付款; payment in kind = paying by giving goods or food, but not money 实物支付; payment by results = money given which increases with the amount of work done or goods produced 凭最后结果付款;按成就付款;按劳付酬 (b) money paid 已付款项;付出款项: back payment = paying money which is owed 付欠款; deferred payments = money paid later than the agreed date 延期付款;延付货款; The company agreed to payments for three months. 公司同意延期三个月后付款。 down payment = part of a total payment made in advance 分期付款的定金,第一期付款; repayable in easy payments = repayable with small sums regularly 定期小额(偿还)付款; incentive payments = extra pay offered to a worker to make him work better 奖励金,奖励费; balance of payments = the international financial position of a country including visible and invisible trade 国际收支差额

◇ **pay off** v. (a) to finish paying money which is owed 清偿(债务): to pay off a mortgage 清偿抵押; to pay off a loan 清还贷款 (b) to pay all the money owed to someone and terminate his employment 付清工资并将其解雇: When the company was taken over the factory was closed and all the workers were paid off. 当公司被接管后,工厂关门了,付清所有工人的工资之后,工人被解雇了。

◇ **payoff** n. money paid to finish paying something which is owed 清偿费

◇ **pay out** v. to give money 支出;花费; The company pays out thousands of pounds in legal fees. 公司花了数千英磅的诉讼费。 We have paid out half our profits in dividends. 我们将一半的利润作为股息付出。

◇ **payout** n. money paid to help a company in difficulty or subsidy 补助金;补贴: The company only exists on payouts from the government. 这个公司仅靠政府救济补贴生存。

◇ **payroll** n. list of people employed and paid by a company or money paid by a company in salaries 工资表;发放工资额; The company has 250 on the payroll. 这个公司的工资表上有250人. payroll ledger = list of staff and their salaries 职员薪金表; payroll tax = tax on the people employed by a company 工薪金税;就业税

◇ **pay up** v. to give money which is owed 付清;缴清(股款);全部付清: The company only paid up when we sent them a letter from our solicitor. 当我们的律师把信寄给那家公司时,他们仅能付清所欠债务。He finally paid up six months late. 他终于还清了全部债务,但晚了6个月。

**P/E** abbreviation = PRICE/EARNINGS 价格/收益 P/E ratio = ratio between the market price of a share and the current dividend it produces 价格/收益比率(股票市场价格与每股股息之间的比率); The shares sell at a P/E ratio of 7. 这些股票以价格/收益比率为7出售。

**peak** 1. n. highest point 顶点;最高峰: peak period = time of the day when most commuters are travelling or when most electricity is being used, etc. (乘车或用电)高峰期; time of peak demand = time when something is being used most 需求高峰期; peak output = highest output 最高产量; peak year = best year or year when the largest quantity of products was produced or when sales were highest 最高产年景;最高记录年景; The shares reached their peak in January. 股票价于一月份达到最高峰。The share index has fallen 10% since the peak in January. 自一月份高峰期后,股票指数下降10%。2. v. to reach the highest point 达到顶点;达到高峰: Productivity peaked in January. 一月份生产率达到最高点。Shares have peaked and are beginning to slip back. 股价已达到最高点,现在正开始下滑。

**pecuniary** a. referring to money 金钱的: He gained no pecuniary advantage. = He made no profit. 他没赚到钱。(他没得到金钱上的好处)。

**peddle** v. to sell goods from door to door or in the street 挨户兜售;沿街叫卖

**peg** v. to hold something at a certain point 钉住;稳住: to peg prices = to fix prices to stop them rising 固定价格; to peg wage increases to the cost - of - living index = to limit increases in wages to the increases in the cost - of - living index 将工资增长钉住于生活费用指数增长

NOTE: pegging - pegged

**pen** n. thing for writing with, using ink 钢笔: felt pen = pen with a point made of hard cloth 毛毡笔; light pen = type of pen which when passed over a bar code can read it and send information back to a computer 计算机用笔; marker pen = pen which makes a wide coloured mark 粗头彩色笔

**penalty** n. punishment (such as a fine) which is imposed if something is not done 惩罚;罚金: penalty clause = clause which lists the penalties which will be imposed if the contract is not obeyed 罚款条款; The contract contains a penalty clause which fines the company 1% for every week the completion date is late. 合同包括罚款条款:延期完工按每星期处罚公司1%罚款。

◇ **penalize** v. to punish or to fine 惩

罚;罚款: to penalize a supplier for late deliveries;因推迟交货而对供货人罚款; They were penalized for bad service. 他们因劣质服务而受到罚款。

**pence** see PENNY

**pending** 1 a. waiting 等待的;待解决的: pending tray = basket on a desk for papers which cannot be dealt with immediately 文件筐,文件篮; patent pending = situation where an invention is put on the market before a patent is granted 待审查专利;专利未定 2. ad. pending advice from our lawyers = while waiting for advice from our lawyers 有待于向律师咨询

**penetrate** v. to penetrate a market = to get into a market and capture a share of it 打进市场;渗透市场

◇ **penetration** n. market penetration = percentage of a total market which the sales of a company cover 市场渗透(公司销售占整个市场的百分比)
NOTE: no plural

**penny** n. (a) GB small coin, of which one hundred make a pound 便士(1 英磅 =100 便士)
(NOTE: usually written p after a figure: 26p; the plural is pence) (b) US informal small coin, one cent

◇ **penny share or US penny stock** n. very cheap share, costing about 10p or less than $1 低价股票(价值约＋便士或少于一美元)

**pension** 1. n. (a) money paid regularly to someone who no longer works 养老金;退休金;抚恤金: retirement pension or old age pension = state pension given to a man who is over 65 or and woman who is over 60 退休金,养老金; government pension or state pension = pension paid by the state 政府抚恤金或养老金; occupational pension = pension which is paid by the company by which a worker has been employed 职业抚恤金或养老

金; portable pension = pension entitlement which can be moved from one company to another without loss (as a worker changes jobs)可转抚恤金或养老金;退休金; pension contributions = money paid by a company or worker into a pension fund 退休金缴纳或分担 (b) pension plan or pension scheme = plan worked out by an insurance company which arranges for a worker to pay part of his salary over many years and receive a regular payment when he retires 抚养金制;抚养金计划; company pension scheme = pension which is organized by a company for its staff 公司抚恤金制,公司养老金制(计划); He decided to join the company's pension scheme. 他决定参加公司养老金制。 contributory pension scheme. = scheme where the worker has to pay a proportion of his salary 分担退休金缴款计划; graduated pension scheme = pension scheme where the benefit is calculated as a percentage of the salary of each person in the scheme 分级养老金制; non - contributory pension scheme = scheme where the employer pays in all the money on behalf of the worker 不分担退休金缴款的养老制(计划)(由雇主支付全部退休金的养老金制); personal pension plan = pension plan which applies to one worker only, usually a self - employed person, not to a group 私人养老金制; portable pension plan = pension plan which a worker can carry from one company to another as he changes jobs 可转(随工作变动的)养老金制 (c) pension entitlement = amount of pension which someone has the right to receive when he retires 退休金权益; pension fund = money which provides pensions for retired members of staff 退休基金 2 v. to pension someone off = to ask someone to retire and take a pension 发给某人退休金并令其退休

◇ **pensionable** a. able to receive a pension可领取养老金的; pensionable age = age after which someone can take a pension 可领取养老金的年龄

◇ **pensioner** n. person who receives a pension 领取抚恤金(养老金,退休金)者: old age pensioner = person who receives the retirement pension 领取退休金者

**peppercorn rent** n. very small or nominal rent 名义租金;象征性租金: to pay a peppercorn rent 支付名义租金; to lease a property for or at a peppercorn rent 以名义租金或象征性租金出租房地产

**per** prep. (a) as per = according to 根据: as per invoice = as stated in the invoice 根据发票,凭发票; as per sample = as shown in the sample 按样品;与样品相符; as per previous order = according to the details given in our previous order 根据上次订单 (b) at a rate of 每: per hour or per day or per week or per year = for each hour or day or week or year 每小时,每天,每星期或每年; The rate is £5 per hour. 每小时收费5英磅。He makes about £250 per month. 他每日挣250英磅左右。We pay £10 per hour. = We pay £10 for each hour worked. 我们工作每小时付10英磅。The car was travelling at twenty - five miles per hour. = at a speed which covered 25 miles in one hour 这辆汽车每小时跑25英里。the earnings per share = dividend received by each share 每股收益; the average sales per representative = the average sales achieved by one representative 每个销售员的平均销售额; per head = for each person 每人; Allow £15 per head for expenses. 允许每人开支为15英磅。Representatives cost on average £25,000 per head per annum. 销售代表每年每人平均花费25000英磅。(c) out of(比率)…分之… The rate

of imperfect items is about twenty - five per thousand. 次品率约为 25‰。The birth rate has fallen to twelve per hundred. 出生率下降到12%。

◇ **per annum** ad. in a year 一年中: What is their turnover per annum? 他们每年的营业额是多少?

◇ **per capita** a. & ad. for each person 人均;每人;按人头: average income per capita or per capita income = average income of one person 人均国民收入; per capita expenditure = total money spent divided by the number of people involved 人均开支

◇ **per cent** a. & ad. out of each hundred or for each hundred 每百(%),百分之: 10 per cent = ten in every hundred 10%;百分之十: What is the increase per cent? 增长了百分之几? Fifty per cent of nothing is still nothing. 零的50%还是零。

◇ **percentage** n. amount shown as part of one hundred 百分比;百分率: percentage discount = discount calculated at an amount per hundred 赔现率,折扣率,折现率(以百分比计算); percentage increase = increase calculated on the basis of a rate for one hundred 按百分比增加; percentage point = one per cent 一个百分点,百分之一(1%)

◇ **percentile** n. one of a series of ninety - nine figures below which a certain percentage of the total falls 百分位数;按百等分排列的数值(99以下的百分数,按百等分顺序依次下降)

**perfect** 1. a. completely correct or with no mistakes 完美无缺的;准确无误的: We check each batch to make sure it is perfect. 我们检查了每一批货以确保准确无误。She did a perfect typing test. 她打字考试没出一点错误。2. v. to make something which is completely correct 使绝对正确;使完美无缺: He perfected the process for making high grade steel. 为炼出优质钢他完善地改进了生产流程。

◇ **perfectly** ad. with no mistakes or correctly 无误地；正确地：She typed the letter perfectly. 她打信准确无误。

**perform** v. to do well or badly 执行；进行；履行：How did the shares perform? = Did the shares go up or down? 股票行情如何？The company or the shares performed badly. = The company's share price fell. 公司经营或股票行情很差。

◇ **performance** n. way in which someone or something acts 表现；行为；经营：the poor performance of the shares on the stock market = the fall in the share price on the stock market 证券市场上股票经营惨淡；Last year saw a dip in the company's performance. 去年公司的业绩滑坡了。as a measure of the company's performance = as a way of judging if the company's results are good or bad 作为评估公司业绩的办法；performance of personnel against objectives = how personnel have worked, measured against the objectives set 以目标衡量个人业绩；performance review = yearly interview between a manager and each worker to discuss how the worker has worked during the year(年度)业绩审查；earnings performance = way in which shares earn dividends(股票)收益成绩；job performance = doing a job well or badly 工作业绩

**period** n. (a) length of time 期间；时期：for a period of time or for a period of months or for a six - year period 一段时间；几个月的时间；六年期间；sales over a period of three months 三个月的销售额；sales over the holiday period 假期销售额；to deposit money for a fixed period 定期存款；(b) accounting period = period of time at the end of which the firm's accounts are made up 会计期

◇ **periodic or periodical** 1. a. from time to time 周期的；间歇的：a periodic review of the company's performance 公司经营的定期检查 2. n. periodical = magazine which comes out regularly 期刊或杂志

**peripherals** pl. n. items of hardware (such as terminals, printers, monitors, etc.) which are attached to a main computer system 与主计算机系统相连接的硬件零件

**perishable** 1. a. which can go bad or become rotten easily 易坏的；易腐败的：perishable goods or items or cargo 易腐商品 2. pl. n. perishables = goods which can go bad easily 易腐商品，易腐货物

**perjury** n. telling lies when you have made an oath in court to say what is true (在法庭上作)伪证；伪誓；伪证罪：He was sent to prison for perjury. 他因作伪证而进监狱。She appeared in court on a perjury charge. 她因被指控作了伪证而出庭受审。

◇ **perjure** v. to perjure yourself = to tell lies when you have made an oath to say what is true 作伪证，假发誓

**perks** pl. n. extra items given by a company to workers in addition to their salaries (such as company cars, private health insurance)工资外福利；额外福利(任职带来的福利如使用公司汽车，投健康保险等)

**permanent** a. which will last for a very long time or for ever 持久的；永久的：He has found a permanent job. 他找到了一个持久固定的工作。She is in permanent employment. 她有固定工作。the permanent staff and part - timers 固定职员和临时工

◇ **permanency** n. being permanent 持久，永久；
NOTE: no plural

◇ **permanently** ad. for ever 持久地；

永久地

**permission** n. being allowed to do something 许可；允许：written permission = document which allows someone to do something 书面准许；文件许可；verbal permission = telling someone that he is allowed to do something 口头许可；to give someone permission to do something = to allow someone to do something 准许某人做某事；He asked the manager's permission to take a day off. 他请求经理批准他一天假。

**permit** 1. n. official document which allows someone to do something 执照；许可证：building permit = official document which allows someone to build on a piece of land 建筑许可证；export permit or import permit = official document which allows goods to be exported or imported 出口许可证或进口许可证；work permit = official document which allows someone who is not a citizen to work in a country 工作许可证，受雇许可证。2. v. to allow someone to do something 准许某人做某事：This document permits you to export twenty-five computer systems. 这个证件准许你出口 25 套计算机系统。The ticket permits three people to go into the exhibition. 这张票允许 3 人参观展览。

**per pro** = PER PROCURATIONEM with the authority of 经授权代理：The secretary signed per pro the manager. 秘书被授权代表经理签字。

**perquisites** pl. n. = PERKS 额外福利

**person** n. (a) someone or man or woman 人：insurance policy which covers a named person 记名保险单；the persons named in the contract = people whose names are given in the contract 合同中提名者；The document should be witnessed by a third person. = Someone who is not named in the document should

witness it. 此文件必须有第三者见证。(b) in person = someone himself or herself 亲自；本人：This important package is to be delivered to the chairman in person. = The package has to be given to the chairman himself (and not to his secretary, assistant, etc.). 这个重要的包裹必须亲自交给主席本人。He came to see me in person. = he himself came to see me. 他本人亲自来看我

◇ **person-to-person call** n. telephone call where you ask the operator to connect you with a named person 直通私人电话 (经电话接线员接通直接与指名受话人通话的电话)

◇ **personal** a. (a) referring to one person 个人的，私人的：personal allowances = part of a person's income which is not taxed 个人免税津贴；personal assets = moveable assets which belong to a person 私人动产；personal call = telephone call where you ask the operator to connect you with a particular person 私人电话 (经电话接线员接通与指名受话人直接通话的电话)；personal computer = small computer which can be used at home 家用计算机；personal effects or personal property = things which belong to someone 私人财产；个人财产；personal income = income received by an individual person before tax is paid 个人所得 (指纳税前个人的全部所得)；Apart from the family shares, he has a personal shareholding in the company. = He has shares which he owns himself. 除了家庭共同持有的股票之外，他个人还持有公司的股票。The car is for his personal use. = The car is for him to use himself. 这辆小轿车专供他个人使用。(b) private 私人的，私有的：I want to see the director on a personal matter. 我想就私人问题见一下董事。personal assistant = secretary who also helps the boss in various ways 私人助手

◇ **personalized** a. with the name or initialsof a person printed on it；(印有个人姓名的或姓名的首字母的)使成为私人的：personalized cheques 印有个人姓名的支票，私人支票；personalized briefcase 有个人姓名的公事包(公文包)

◇ **personally** ad. in person 亲自地；亲身地：He personally opened the envelope. 他亲自打开信。She wrote to me personally. 她亲自给我写信。

**personnel** n. people who work in a certain place or for a certain company 全体人员；职员：the personnel of the warehouse or the warehouse personnel 货栈职员；仓库全体人员；the personnel department = section of the company which deals with the staff 人事处；personnel management = organizing and training of staff so that they work well and profitably 人事管理；personnel manager = head of the personnel department 人事部经理

**persuade** v. to talk to someone and get him to do what you want 说服；使相信：After ten hours of discussion, they persuaded the MD to resign. 经过 10 小时的讨论，他们说服总经理辞职。We could not persuade the French company to sign the contract. 我们无法说服法国公司签署这份合

**peseta** n. money used in Spain 比塞塔(西班牙货币单位)
NOTE: usually written ptas after a figure: 2,000 ptas

**peso** n. money used in Mexico and many other countries 比索(用于墨西哥和其它许多国家)

**pessimism** n. expecting that everything will turn out badly 悲观主义；悲观：market pessimism or pessimism on the market. = Feeling that the stock market prices will fall 市场悲观主义(总以为股票将下跌)；There is considerable pessimism about job opportunities. 人们对就业机会相当悲观
NOTE: no plural

◇ **pessimistic** a. feeling sure that things will work out badly 悲观的；悲观主义的：He takes a pessimistic view of the exchange rate. = He expects the exchange rate to fall. 他对汇率抱悲观的看法。

**peter out** v. to come to an end gradually 逐渐消失；逐渐枯竭

**Peter principle** n. law, based on wide experience, that people are promoted until they occupy positions for which they are incompetent 彼得法则——基于广泛丰富的经验，人们只有胜任和职称后，才应晋升。

**petition** 1. n. official request 申请；请求；请愿书：to file a petition in bankruptcy = to ask officially to be made bankrupt or to ask officially for someone else to be made bankrupt 提出破产的申请 2. v. to make an official request 申请；请求：He petitioned the government for a special pension. 他向政府申请特别养老金(抚恤金)

**petrodollar** n. dollar earned by a country from exporting oil, then invested outside that country 石油美元(石油输出国所获得的美元盈余,然后用于国外投资)

**petrol** n. liquid, made from petroleum, used to drive a car engine 汽油：The car is very economic on petrol. 这车非常省油。We are looking for a car with a low petrol consumption. 我们正在寻找一辆耗油少的汽车
NOTE: no plural

◇ **petroleum** n. raw natural oil, found in the ground 石油：crude petroleum = raw petroleum which has not been processed 原油；petroleum exporting countries = countries which produce petroleum and sell it to others 石油输出

国；petroleum industry = industry whichuses petroleum to make other products（petrol, soap, etc.）石油工业；petroleum products = products（such as petrol, soap, paint）which are made fromcrude petroleum 原石油产品；petroleum revenues = income from selling oil 石油收益（卖石油所得）

**petty** a. not important 微小的；小额的：petty cash = small amount of money kept in an office to pay small debts 零用现金；备用小额金；petty cash book = book in which petty cash payments are noted 零用现金薄；petty cash box = locked metal box in an office where the petty cash is kept 零用现金箱；petty expenses = small sums of money spent 杂费；小额费用

**phase** n. period or part of something which takes place 阶段；时期：the first phase of the expansion programme 第一期扩建计划

◇ **phase in** v. to bring something in gradually 逐步采用；分阶段引入：The new invoicing system will be phased in over the next two months. 新发票制度将于今后两个月中逐步实行。

◇ **phase out** v. to remove something gradually 逐渐陶汰，逐渐撤退：Smith Ltd will be phased out as a supplier of spare parts. 作为零件供货商的，史密斯有限公司将被逐渐陶汰。

**phone** 1 n. telephone or machine used for speaking to someone over a long distance 电话：We had a new phone system installed last week. 上星期我们安装了新电话系统。house phone or internal phone = telephone for calling from one office to another 内线电话；by phone = using the telephone 打电话；to place an order by phone 打电话订货；to be on the phone = to be speaking to someone on the telephone 正在通话，正在打电话；She has been on the phone all morning. 她整个早上都在打电话. He spoke to the manager on the phone. 他在电话里跟经理谈过话。phone book = book which lists names of people and companies with their addresses and phone numbers 电话薄；Look up his address in the phone book. 在电话薄里查他的地址。phone call = speaking to someone on the phone(给某人)打电话；to make a phone call = to speak to someone on the telephone 接电话；to answer the phone or to take a phone call = to reply to a call on the phone 接电话：phone number = set of figures for a particular telephone 电话号码；He keeps a list of phone numbers in a little black book. 他把很多的电话号码记在一个小黑本子里。The phone number is on the company notepaper. 电话号码在公司的便条纸上。Can you give me your phone number? 能把你的电话号码给我吗？

2. v. to phone someone = to call someone by telephone 打电话。Don't phone me, I'll phone you. 别给我打电话，我会给你打。His secretary phoned to say he would be late. 他的秘书来电话说他可能会迟到。He phoned the order through to the warehouse. 他直接给仓库打电话订货。to phone for something = to make a phone call to ask for something；He phoned for a taxi. 他打电话要一辆出租车. to phone about something = to make a phone call to speak about something 打电话谈论某事；He phoned about the January invoice. 他打电话谈到一月份的发票问题。

◇ **phone back** v. to reply by phone 回电话：The chairman is in a meeting, can you phone back in about half an hour? 董事长正在开会，你半小时后再来电话好吗？Mr Smith called while you were out and asked if you would phone him back. 你不在时，史密斯先生来过电话，问你可否给他回个电话。

**photocopier** n. machine which makes a copy of a document by photographing andprinting it 复印机：

◇ **photocopy** 1. n. copy of a document made by photographing and printing it 影印本；复印本：Make six photocopies of the contract. 将此合同影印 6 份本。2. v. to make a copy of a document by photographing and printing it 影印；照相复制：She photocopied the contract. 她影印了这份合同

◇ **photocopying** n. making photocopies 影印：Photocopying costs are rising each year. 影印费逐年见涨。photocopying bureau = office which photocopies documents for companies which do not possess their own photocopiers 影印（室、社、所、处等）；There is a mass of photocopying to be done. = There are many documents waiting to be photocopied. 有许多文件都需要影印。NOTE: no plural

◇ **photostat** 1. n. trademark for a type of photocopy 一种影印机的商标 2. v. to make a photostat of a document 用直接影印机拍摄，直接影印复制

**pick** 1. n. thing chosen 选择物：Take your pick. = Choose what you want. 选择你想要的。the pick of the group = the best item in the group 这组商品之精华 2 v. to choose 选择；挑选：The board picked the finance director to succeed the retiring MD. 委员会选择财务主任接替即将退休的总经理。The Association has picked Paris for its next meeting. 协会选择巴黎为下次会址。

◇ **picking** n. order picking = collecting various items in a warehouse to make up an order to be sent to a customer 存货提取：picking list = list of items in an order, listed according to where they can be found in the warehouse 仓库存货提取单

◇ **pick out** v. to choose (something or someone) out of a lot 选出；挑出：He was picked out for promotion by the chairman. 他被董事长选中晋升。

◇ **pick up** v. to get better or to improve 改进；改善：Business or trade is picking up. 经营正在改善。

◇ **pickup** n. pickup (truck) = type of small van for transporting goods 小型轻便货车；小吨位货运汽车：pickup and delivery service = service which takes goods from the warehouse and delivers them to the customer 接送货物服务（将货物从仓库运送给客户的服务）

**picket** 1. n. striking worker who stands at the gate of a factory to try to persuade other workers not to go to work 纠察员（罢工时，在工厂门口劝说他人参加罢工的工人）：flying pickets = pickets who travel round the country to try to stop workers going to work 巡回纠察队；picket line = line of pickets at the gate of a factory 纠察线；警戒线；to man a picket line or to be on the picket line 守卫（坚守）在警卫线；to cross a picket line = to go into a factory to work, even though pickets are tryingto prevent workers from going in 越过纠察线；穿过警戒线 2. v. to picket a factory = to put pickets at the gate of a factory to try to prevent other workers from going to work 派纠察员在工厂门口阻止工人上工

◇ **picketing** n. act of standing at the gates of a factory to prevent workersgoing to work 纠察；警戒（以阻止工人上工）：lawful picketing = picketing which is allowed by law 合法纠察；合法警戒；mass picketing = picketing by large numbers of pickets who try to frighten workers who want to work 群众纠察；大批纠察；peaceful picketing = picketing which does not involve fighting 和平纠察；非武力纠察；secondary picketing = picketing of another factory, not directly connected with the strike, to prevent it supplying the striking factory or receiving supplies from it 二级纠察；二级警戒(另一个非罢工工厂的警戒,防止它去支持和援助正在罢工的工厂)

NOTE: no plural

**piece** n. small part of something 部份；件；个: to sell something by the piece 计件出售；零售；零卖; The price is 25p the piece. 价格是每个 25 便士。mailing piece = leaflet suitable for sending by direct mail 邮寄清单

◇ **piece rate** n. rate of pay for a product produced or for a piece of work done and not paid for at an hourly rate 按件付款；计件工资; to earn piece rates 挣计件工资

◇ **piecework** n. work for which workers are paid for the products produced or the piece of work done and not at an hourly rate 计件工作(以产品件数付钱的工作)

NOTE: no plural

**pie chart** n. diagram where information is shown as a circle cut up into sections of different sizes 圆形分析图；圆形分格统计图表(指用一个圆形分割成大小不同的部分来表示信息的图)

**pigeonhole** 1. n. one of a series of small spaces for filing documents or for putting letters for delivery to separate offices(鸽笼式)分类架；文件格; 2. v. to file a plan or document as the best way of forgetting about it 束之高阁: The whole expansion plan was pigeonholed. 整个扩建计划被搁置起来了。

**pile** 1. n. lot of things put one on top of the other 堆；一大堆: The Managing Director's desk is covered with piles of paper. 总经理的桌子上堆满了文件。She put the letter on the pile of letters waiting to be signed. 她把这封信放在一堆待签字的信上。2. v. to put things on top of one another 堆积；堆起: He piled the papers on his desk. 他把文件堆在桌上。

◇ **pile up** v. to put or get into a pile 堆积；积累起来: The invoices were piled up on the table. 桌上堆满了票据。Complaints are piling up about the after - sales service. 人们对售后服务抱怨日益增多。

**pilferage or pilfering** n. stealing small amounts of money or small items from an office or shop 小偷行为；小偷小摸

NOTE: no plural

**pilot** n. (a) person who flies a plane or guides a ship into port 飞行员；领港员；领航员 (b) used as a test, which if successful will then be expanded into a full operation 小规模试验: The company set up a pilot project to see if the proposed manufacturing system was efficient. 公司提出一个小规模试验方案以观设想的生产体系是否有效。The pilot factory has been built to test the new production processes. 为试验新的生产流程,这个小型试验厂已建成。He is directing a pilot scheme for training unemployed young people. 为了培训无业青年,他正在指导一个小规模试验生产计划。

**pin** 1. n. sharp piece of metal for attaching papers together, etc. 别针；大头针; drawing pin – pin with a flat head for attaching a sheet of paper to something hard 图钉; She used drawing pins to pin the poster to the door. 她用图钉把广告钉在门上。2. v. to attach with a pin 钉住(用钉): She pinned the papers together. 她用别针把文件在一起。Pin your cheque to the application form. 用别针将你的支票和申请表别在一起。

◇ **pin up** v. to attach something with pins to a wall 把…钉在(墙上): They pinned the posters up at the back of the exhibition stand. 他们将广告钉在展台背面。

**pint** n. measure of liquids ( = 0.568 of

a litre)品脱(＝0.568公升)

**pioneer** 1. n. first to do a type of work 先驱；先锋：pioneer project or pioneer development ＝ project or development which is new and has never been tried before 首创项目；开拓计划；开拓发展 2. v. to be the first to do something 当选锋；当先驱；开拓：The company pioneered developments in the field of electronics. 公司在电子领域进行了开拓性开发。

**pirate** 1 n. person who copies a patented invention or a copyright work and sells it 非法翻印者；侵犯版权(专利权)者；剽窃者：a pirate copy of a book 非法翻印本；(海)盗版本 2. v. to copy a copyright work 非法翻印；偷印：a pirated book or a pirated design 非法翻印的书；剽窃的设计方案；The designs for the new dress collection were pirated in the Far East. 新式服装的系列设计在远东被非法翻印(剽窃)。

◇ **piracy** n. copying of patented inventions or copyright works 侵犯版权；非法翻印；剽窃

NOTE: no plural

**pit** n. coal mine 煤矿；矿井

**pitch** n. sales pitch ＝ talk by a salesman to persuade someone to buy 竭力推销商品的宣传

**pix** pl. n. infml pictures (used in advertising or design)(非日式)照片；影片(用于广告和设计)

**place** 1. n. (a) where something is or where something happens 地点；场所；位置：to take place ＝ to happen 发生；The meeting will take place in our offices. 会议将在我们办公室召开。meeting place ＝ room or area where people can meet 会场；会址；place of work ＝ office or factory, etc. where people work 工作场所 (b) position (in a competition) 名次；位置：Three companies are fighting for first place in the homecomputer market. 三家公司正在争夺国内计算机市场的领先地位。(c) job 职位：He was offered a place with an insurance company. 保险公司向他提供一个职位。She turned down three places before accepting the one we offered 在接受我们提供的工作前,她拒绝了三处别的工作。(d) position in a text(文中的)一段落；页：She marked her place in the text with a red pen. 她用红笔在文中标出了她所读到的地方。I have lost my place and cannot remember where I have reached in my filing. 我读到哪里,找不到了,也想不起旧档归到什么地方。2. v. (a) to put 放；安置：to place money in an account ＝ to deposit money 存款；to place a block of shares ＝ to find a buyer for a block of shares 出售大宗股票；to place a contract ＝ to decide that a certain company shall have the contract to do work 认定合同；确定合同；to place something on file ＝ to file something 存档；归档 (b) to place an order ＝ to order something 订购；订货：He placed an order for 250 cartons of paper. 他订购了250个纸板箱。(c) to place staff ＝ to find jobs for staff 安排工作：How are you placed for work? ＝ Have you enough work to do? 怎么给你安排工作的?

◇ **placement** n. finding work for someone 安置工作；工作介绍

◇ **placing** n. the placing of a line of shares ＝ finding a buyer for a large number of shares in a new company or a company which is going public 大量配售新公司的股票

NOTE: no plural

**plain** a. (a) easy to understand 明白的；易理解的；清楚的：We made it plain to the union that 5% was the management's final offer. 我们使工会明白,资方最终提出为5%。The manager is a very plain - spoken man. ＝ The manager says exactly what he thinks. 经

理是位直言不讳的人。(b) simple 简单的;简洁的;平淡的: The design of the package is in plain blue and white squares. 包装设计是纯兰白方格相间。We want the cheaper models to have a plain design. 我们想要价格便宜的型号有一个简洁的设计。

◇ **plain cover** n. to send something under plain cover = to send something in an ordinary envelope with no company name printed on it 用普通信封寄出

**plaintiff** n. person who starts a legal action against someone 原告

**plan** 1. n. (a) organized way of doing something 计划;方案;规划: contingency plan = plan which will be put into action if something happens which no one expects to happen 应急方案,临时方案; the government's economic plans = government's proposals for running the country's economy 政府经济计划; a Five - Year Plan = proposals for running a country's economy over a five - year period 一个五年计划 (b) way of saving or investing money(存储或投资) 方案: investment plan 投资方案; pension plan 养老金计划; savings plan 储蓄计划 (c) drawing which shows how something is arranged or how something will be built 平面图;设计图;规划图: The designers showed us the first plans for the new offices. 设计人员给我们看了这座新的办公楼的第一稿平面图。floor plan = drawing of a floor in a building, showing where different departments are 楼层平面图; street plan or town plan = map of a town showing streets and buildings 街道平面图;城区设计图 2. v. to organize carefully how something should be done 计划;部署;规划: to plan for an increase in bank interest charges = to change a way of doing things because you think there will be an increase in bank interest charges 为银行提高利息而作出相应的部署; to plan

investments = to propose how investments should be made 计划投资
NOTE: planning – planned

◇ **planned** a. planned economy = system where the government plans all business activity 计划经济

◇ **planner** n. (a) person who plans 设计者;计划者;策划者: the government's economic planners = people who plan the future economy of the country for the government 政府经济规划者 (b) desk planner or wall planner = book or chart which shows days or weeks or months so that the work of an office can be shown by diagrams 台式图表;挂式图表

◇ **planning** n. (a) organizing how something should be done, especially how a company should be run to make increased profits 规划;计划;策划: long - term planning or short - term planning 长期规划或短期规划; economic planning = planning the future financial state of the country for the government 经济规划; corporate planning = planning the future financial state of a group of companies 公司规划; manpower planning = planning to get the right number of workers in each job 劳动力规划 (b) GB planning permission = official document allowing a person or company to plan new buildings on empty land(英)政府建筑许可证; to be refused planning permission 未得到建筑许可证; We are waiting for planning permission before we can start building. 我们正等待建筑许可证才能开工。The land is to be sold with planning permission. 这块地与建筑许可证一并出售。the planning department = section of a local government office which deals with requests for planning permission 建筑规划部;基建许可证发放部门
NOTE: no plural

**plane** n. aircraft or machine which flies

in the air, carrying passengers or cargo 飞机: I plan to take the 5 o'clock plane to New York. 我准备乘 5 点钟的飞机去纽约。He could not get a seat on Tuesday's plane, so he had to wait until Wednesday. 他买不到星期二的飞机票，只好等到星期三。There are ten planes a day from London to Paris. 每天有十次从伦敦飞往巴黎的飞机。

**plant** n. (a) machinery 机器;机械: plant-hire firm = company which lends large machines (such as cranes and tractors) to building companies 建筑机器出租行; 建筑机械租赁公司 (NOTE: no plural) (b) large factory 工厂: They are planning to build a car plant near the river. 他们计划在河边建一个汽车厂。to set up a new plant 建一个新工厂; They closed down six plants in the north of the country. 他们关闭了国内北部的六个工厂。He was appointed plant manager. 他被任命为厂长。

**platform** n. high pavement in a station, so that passengers can get on or off trains 站台;月台: The train for Birmingham leaves from Platform 12. 开往伯明翰的列车从 12 号站台开出。The ticket office is on Platform 2. 售票处在 2 号站台。

**PLC or plc** = PUBLIC LIMITED COMPANY 大众有限公司(公开上市有限公司)

**plead** v. to speak on behalf of a client in court 辩护

**pledge** 1. n. object given to a pawnbroker as security for money borrowed 抵押品;典当物: to redeem a pledge = to pay back a loan and interest and so get back the security 赎回抵押品; unredeemed pledge = pledge which the borrower has not claimed back by paying back his loan 未赎回的典当品 2. v. to pledge share certificates = to deposit share certificates with the lender as secu-

rity for money borrowed 以股票作抵押

**plenary** n. plenary meeting or plenary session = meeting at a conference when all the delegates meet together 全体会议;全会

**plough back** v. to plough back profits into the company = to invest the profits in the business (and not pay them out as dividends to the shareholders) by using them to buy new equipment or create new products(将利润)再投资以扩展业务

**plug** 1. n. (a) device at the end of a wire for connecting a machine to the electricity supply 插头;插销: The printer is supplied with a plug. 打印机的供给带插销。(b) to give a plug to a new product = to publicize a new product 宣传新产品 2. v. (a) to plug in = to attach a machine to the electricity supply 插上插头(以接通电源): He computer was not plugged in. 计算机没通电源。(b) to publicize or to advertise 宣传;作广告: They ran six commercials plugging holidays in Spain. 他们 6 次主办广告大肆宣传在西班牙的度假。(c) to block or to stop 阻塞;停止: The company is trying to plug the drain on cash reserves. 公司正在设法阻止现金储备外流

NOTE: plugging - plugged

**plummet or plunge** v. to fall sharply 暴跌;大降; 骤然跌落: Share prices plummeted or plunged on the news of the devaluation. 一有贬值的消息,股票价格就暴跌了。

**plus** 1. prep. (a) added to; 加;加上: His salary plus commission comes to more than £25,000. 他的薪金加佣金超过 25,000 英磅。Production costs plus overheads are higher than revenue. 生产成本加上间接费用高出营业收入。(b) more than 多于;超出: Houses valued at £100,000 plus. = Houses valued at over £ 100,000. 房屋价值超出了10,000 英磅。2. a. favourable or good and profitable 有利的;有增益的: A plus factor for the company is that the market is much larger than they had originally thought. 对公司一个有利的因素是市场比他们原先想象的要大得多。the plus side of the account = the credit side of the account 帐户的贷方; on the plus side = this is a favourable point 从有利的一面 (一点) 看; On the plus side, we must take into account the new productline. 从有利的一面看, 我们必须考虑新的生产线。3. n. a good or favourable point 盈余; 增益: To have achieved £ 1m in new sales in less than six months is certainly a plus for the sales team. 对销售组来说, 在不到六个月里新产品销售额为 100 万英磅的确是个增益(盈余)。

**p. m.** ad. in the afternoon or in the evening or after 12 o'clock midday 下午;午后: The train leaves at 6.50 p. m.. 火车下午 6 时 50 分开。If you phone New York after 6p. m. the calls are at a cheaper rate. 若下午六时后给纽约挂电话, 收费较便宜。

**PO** = POST OFFICE 邮电局

**pocket** n. pocket calculator or pocket diary = calculator or diary which can be carried in the pocket 袖珍计算器;袖珍日记本; to be £ 25 in pocket = to have made a profit of £ 25 赚了 25 英磅; to be £ 25 out of pocket = to have lost £ 25 赔了 25 英磅; out – of – pocket expenses = amount of money to pay back a worker for his own money which he has spent on company business 垫付的业务费

**point** 1. n. (a) place or position 地点;位置: point of sale = place where a product is sold (such as a shop)销售点; point of sale material = display material (such as posters, dump bins) to adver-

tise a product where it is being sold 展销点; breakeven point = position at which sales cover costs but do not show a profit 损益两平点;收支平衡点; customs entry point = place at a border between two countries where goods are declared to customs 进口报关处; starting point = place where something starts 起点 (b) decimal point = dot which indicates the division between a whole unit and its smaller parts (such as 4.25)小数点 (如 4.25) percentage point = 1 per cent 百分点;百分之一; half a percentage point = 0.5 per cent 百分之零点五; The dollar gained two points = The dollar increased in value against another currency by two hundredths of a cent. 美元增值了两个百分点。The exchange fell ten points. = The stock market index fell by ten units. 股票市场指数下跌十个点。2. v. to point out = to show 指出: The report points out the mistakes made by the company over the last year. 报告指出了公司在去年所犯的错误。He pointed out that the results were better than in previous years. 他指出结果比前几年都好。

**policy** n. (a) decisions on the general way of doing something 政策: government policy on wages or government wages policy 国家工资政策; the government's prices policy or incomes policy 国家价格或收入政策; the country's economic policy 国家经济政策; a company's trading policy 公司贸易政策; The government made a policy statement or made a statement of policy. = The government declared in public what its plans were. 政府做了政策说明。budgetary policy = policy of expected income and expenditure 预算政策 (b) company policy = the company's agreed plan of action or the company's way of doing things 公司的方针;公司的政策: What is the company policy on credit? 什么是公司的信贷方针? It is againstcompany policy to give more than thirty days' credit. 超过 30 天信用赊帐是违反公司政策的。Our policy is to submit all contracts to the legal department. 我们的方针是所有合同都必须呈交法律处。(c) insurance policy = document which shows the conditions of an insurance contract 保险单; an accident policy = an insurance contract against accidents 事故保险单; all - risks policy = insurance policy which covers risks of any kind, with no exclusions 全损保险单; a comprehensive or an all - in policy = an insurance which covers all risks 综合保险单; contingent policy = policy which pays out only if something happens (as if the person named in the policy dies before the person due to benefit)或有保险单(指当偶发事发生时才有的保险费, 如投保人死于他应受益之前); endowment policy = policy where a sum of money is paid to the insured person on a certain date, or to his estate if he dies earlier 养老保险单(指投保人到期日可领到一笔金额;若在到期日前死亡, 则按其资产领取一笔金额); policy holder = person who is insured by an insurance company 保险客户;投保人; to take out a policy = to sign the contract for an insurance and start paying the premiums 投保;申请保险; She took out a life insurance policy or a house insurance policy. 她投了人寿保险或房屋保险。The insurance company made out a policy or drew up a policy. = The company wrote the details of the contract on the policy. 这家保险公司开出了一张保险单。

**polite** a. behaving in a pleasant way 有礼貌的;客气的: We stipulate that our salesgirls must be polite to customers. 我们规定售货小姐们必须礼貌待客。We had a polite letter from the MD. 我们收到总经理的一封彬彬有礼的来信。

◇ **politely** ad. in a pleasant way 有礼貌地;客气地: She politely answered the customers' questions. 她很有礼貌地回答了顾客提出的问题。

**political** a. referring to a certain idea of how a country should be run 政治上的: political levy = part of the subscription of a member of a trade union which the union pays to support a political party 政治征税;政治征收; political party = group of people who believe a country should be run in a certain way 政党;政治党派

**poll** 1. n. opinion poll = asking a sample group of people, taken at random, what they feel about something, so as to guess the opinion of the whole population 民意测验: Opinion polls showed the public preferred butter to margarine. 民意测验表明公众喜欢黄油, 而不喜欢人造奶油。Before starting the service the company carried out a nationwide opinion poll. 公司在开始这项服务前, 先进行了全国性的民意测验。2. v. to poll a sample of the population = to ask a sample group of people what they feel about something 进行民意测验: to poll the members of the club on an issue = to ask the members for their opinion on an issue 就此问题征求俱乐部成员们的意见

◇ **pollster** n. expert in understanding what polls mean 民意测验专家

**polystyrene** n. expanded polystyrene = light solid plastic used for packing 弹力聚苯乙烯: The computer is delivered packed in expanded polystyrene. 计算机是用弹力聚苯乙烯塑料包装运送的。NOTE: no plural

**pool** 1. n. (a) typing pool = group of typists, working together in a company, offering a secretarial service to several departments 联合打字组 (b) unused supply 集中备用物资: a pool of unemployed labour or of expertise 备用就业劳

动力或专家意见之汇合 2. v. to pool resources = to put all resources together so as to be more powerful or profitable 集中各种资源

**poor** a. (a) without much money 穷的；贫穷的：The company tries to help the poorest members of staff with soft loans. 公司试图用长期低息贷款帮助那些经济窘困的职员。It is one of the poorest countries in the world. 该国是世界上最贫穷的国家之一。(b) not very good 不良的；低劣的；poor quality 质量低劣；poor service 劣质服务；poor turnround time of orders or poor order turnround time 周转时间紧的订货

◇ **poorly** ad. badly 拙劣地；不足地：The offices are poorly laid out. 办公室布置得很差。The plan was poorly presented. 计划写得很差。poorly – paid staff = staff with low wages 低薪职工

**popular** a. liked by many people 大众喜爱的；流行的；受欢迎的：This is our most popular model. 这是我们最流行的款式。The South Coast is the most popular area for holidays. 南部海岸是最受欢迎的度假区。popular prices = prices which are low and therefore liked 廉价；大众化的价格

**population** n. number of people who live in a country or in a town 人口；全体居民：Paris has a population of over one million. 巴黎有 100 多万人口。the working population 劳动人口；population statistic 人口统计；population trends 人口趋势；floating population = people who move from place to place 流动人口

**port** n. (a) harbour or place where ships come to load or unload 港；港市：the port of Rotterdam 鹿特丹港；inland port = port on a river or canal 内陆港口；to call at a port = to stop at a port to load or unload cargo 停靠港口；在港口停泊；port authority = organization which runs a port 港务局；port of call = port at which a ship often stops 停靠港；暂停港；port charges or port dues = payment which a ship makes to the port authority for the right to use the port 港口费用；入港费；港税；港口使用费；port of embarkation = port at which you get on a ship 启航港；port installations = buildings and equipment of a port 港口设施；commercial port = port which has only goods traffic 商务港；fishing port = port which is used mainly by fishing boats 渔港；free port = port where there are no customs duties to be paid 自由港；免税港 (b) part of a computer where a lead can be attached(计算机)端口

**portable** 1. a. which can be carried 便于携带的；手提的；轻便的：a portable computer or a portable typewriter 便携式计算机；手提打字机；portable pension = pension rights which a worker can take with him from one company to another as he changes jobs 可转的年金 2. n. a portable = a computer or typewriter which can be carried 便携式计算机或手提式打字机

**portfolio** n. a portfolio of shares = all the shares owned by someone 股份有价证券；portfolio management = buying and selling shares to make profits for a person 有价证券经营(管理)

**portion** n. small quantity, especially enough food for one person 份；一份：We serve ice cream in individual portions. 我们按份(供一人食用)供应冰琪淋(我们端上供每个人吃的冰琪淋。)

**p.o.s.** = POINT OF SALE 销售点

**position** n. (a) situation or state of affairs 状况；情况：What is the cash position? = What is the state of the company's current account? 现金状况如何？bargaining position = statement of position by one group during negotiations 谈判地位；谈判立场；to cover a position = to have enough money to pay for a forward purchase 轧平(有足够的钱支付期货的进货)(b) job or paid work in a company 职位；工作：to apply for a position as manager 申请经理职位；We have several positions vacant. 我们还有几个工作空缺。All the vacant positions have been filled. 所有空缺的职位全部满员。She retired from her position in the accounts department. 她从财务处的职位上退休的。He is in a key position. = He has an important job. 他身居要职。

**positive** a. meaning "yes" 确定的；肯定的：The board gave a positive reply. 董事会给予肯定答复。positive cash flow = situation where more money is coming in than is being spent 正向现金流

**possess** v. to own 拥有；占有：The company possesses property in the centre of the town. 这家公司在市中心拥有房地产。He lost all he possessed in the collapse of his company. 他在公司破产中丧失了他所拥有的一切。

◇ **possession** n. (a) owning something 持有；所有：The documents are in his possession. =′ He is holding the documents. 他持有这些文件。vacant possession = being able to occupy a property immediately after buying it because it is empty 空屋出卖(广告用语)；The property is to be sold with vacant possession。这房地产计划与空屋一起出售。(NOTE: no plural) (b) possessions = property or things owned 财产；所有物：They lost all their possessions in the fire. 他们在火灾中失去了他所拥有的一切。

**possible** a. which might happen 可能的：The 25th and 26th are possible dates for our next meeting. 我们下次的会议可能在 25 日和 26 日召开。It is possible that production will be held up by in-dustrial action. 生产可能因工业行动(罢工，怠工)而停顿。There are two possible candidates for the job. = Two candidates are good enough to be appointed. 这个工作有两位侯选人可被录用。

◇ **possibility** n. being likely to happen 可能；可能性：There is a possibility that the plane will be early. 飞机有可能提前起飞/到达。There is no possibility of the chairman retiring before next Christmas. 董事长不可能在明年圣诞节前退休。

**post** 1. n. (a) system of sending letters and parcels from one place to another 邮政；邮递：to send an invoice by post 邮寄发票；He put the letter in the post. 他将信投入邮箱。The cheque was lost in the post. 支票在邮寄过程中丢了。to send a reply by return of post = to reply to a letter immediately 由原送信人带回复信；由下一班回程邮递带回的回信；letter post or parcel post = service for sending letters or parcels 信件邮递；包裹邮寄；post room = room in an office where the post is sorted and sent to each department or collected from each de-partment for sending 邮件房；收发室 (b) letters sent or received 邮件：Has the post arrived yet? 邮件到了吗? My secretary opens the post as soon as it arrives. 邮件一到，我的秘书就立即将它打开。The receipt was in this morning's post. 收据是今天早晨寄来的。The letter did not arrive by first post this morning. 这封信不是今晨随第一批邮件抵达的 (c) job or paid work in a company 职位；工作：to apply for a post as cashier 申请出纳员职位；We have three posts vacant. 我们有三个工作空缺。All our posts have been filled. 职位全满了。We advertised three posts in the "Times" 我们在"泰晤士报"上登了广告招聘三人

NOTE：no plural for (a) or (b)

2. v. (a) to send something by post 邮
寄,邮送: to post a letter or to post a
parcel 寄信或寄包裹 (b) to post an entry = to transfer an entry to an account
过帐; to post up a ledger = to keep a
ledger up to date 过入分类帐(分户帐)
(c) to post up a notice = to put a notice
on a wall or on a noticeboard 张帖布告
(d) to post an increase = to let people
know that an increase has taken place 公
布(宣告)……增加

**post −** prefix later 在……之后;在后

**postage** n. payment for sending a letter
or parcel by post 邮费; 邮资: What is
the postage to Nigeria? 寄往尼日利亚
邮费是多少? postage paid = words
printed on an envelope to show that the
sender has paid the postage even though
there is no stamp on it 邮费付讫;邮资
已付; postage stamp = small piece of
paper attached to a letter or parcel to
show that you have paid for it to be sent
through the post 邮票
NOTE: no plural

**postal** a. referring to the post 邮局的;
邮政的: postal charges or postal rates =
money to be paid for sending letters or
parcels by post 邮费; 邮资; Postal
charges are going up by 10% in
September. 九月份邮资将上涨 10%。
postal order = document bought at a
post office, as a method of paying small
amounts of money by post 邮政汇票

**postcard** n. piece of cardboard for sending a message by post (often with a picture on one side) 明信片

**postcode** n. letters and numbers used to
indicate a town or street in an address on
an envelope 邮政编码;邮政号码
NOTE: US English is zip code

**postdate** v. to put a later date on a document 把日期填迟;填迟…日期: He
sent us a postdated cheque. 他寄给我们
一张填迟日期的支票。His cheque was

postdated to June. 他的支票日期填迟到
六月份。

**poster** n. large notice or advertisement
to be stuck up on a wall 大型广告(画);
海报

**poste restante** n. system where letters
can be addressed to someone at a post
office, where they can be collected 邮件
代存处: Send any messages to "Poste
Restante, Athens". 将一切电文发往雅
典邮件代存处。

**post free** ad. without having to pay any
postage 邮资免费;邮资付讫(地): The
game is obtainable post free from the
manufacturer. 买这种游戏用具由制造
商免费邮寄。

**postmark** 1. n. mark stamped by the
Post Office on a letter, covering thep-
ostage stamp, to show that the Post Office has accepted it 邮戳: letter with a
London postmark 盖有伦敦邮戳的信
2. v. to stamp a letter with a postmark
盖邮戳: The letter was postmarked
New York. 这封信盖着纽约的邮戳。

**post office** n. (a) building where the
postal services are based shop where you
can buy stamps, send parcels, etc. 邮电
所;邮政局: main post office 邮电总局;
sub − post office = small post office,
usually part of a general store 邮政处;邮
电分局 (b) the Post Office = national
organization which deals with sending
letters and parcels 邮电部; Post Office
officials or officials of the Post Office 邮
政官员; Post Office van 邮车; Post Office box number = reference number
given for delivering mail to a post office,
so as not to give the actual address of the
person who willreceive it 邮政信箱号码

**postpaid** a. with the postage already
paid 邮资已付的: The price is £5.95
postpaid. 价格(含邮资)为 5.95 英镑。

**postpone** v. to arrange for something to
take place later than planned 推迟;延

迟;延误: He postponed the meeting to tomorrow. 他将会议推迟到明天。They asked if theycould postpone payment until the cash situation was better. 他们请求可否等到现金情况好转时才付款。

◇ **postponement** n. arranging for something to take place later than planned 延期;推迟: I had to change my appointments because of the postponement of the board meeting. 因为董事会推迟召开,我只好变更约会时间。

**potential** 1. a. possible 可能的;潜在的: potential customers = people who could be customers 潜在的顾客; potential market = market which could be exploited 潜在市场; The product has potential sales of 100,000 units. = The product will possibly sell 100,000 units 这项产品有可能售出 10 万件。He is a potential managing director. = He is the sort of man who could become managing director. 他有潜力成为总经理。2 n. possibility of becoming something 潜力;潜能;潜势: share with a growth potential or with a potential for growth = share which is likely to increase in value 潜在长势股票;潜在升值股票; product with considerable sales potential = product which is likely to have very large sales 具有相当大销售潜力的产品; to analyze the market potential = to examine the market to see how large it possibly is 分析市场潜力; earning potential = amount of money which someone should be able to earn or amountof dividend which a share is capable of earning 收益潜在能力

**pound** n. (a) measure of weight ( = 0.45 kilos)磅(重量单位,1 磅 = 0.45 公斤): to sell oranges by the pound 按磅出售桔子; a pound of oranges 一磅桔子; Oranges cost 50p a pound. 桔子价格每磅为 50 硬士。NOTE: usually written lb after a figure: 25lb (b) money used in the UK and many other countries

英磅; pound sterling = official term for the British currency 英磅(英国货币的官方用语); a pound coin 一英磅的硬币; a five pound note 一张五英镑的纸币; It costs six pounds. 它值 6 英磅。the pound/dollar exchange rate 英磅对美元的汇率(汇价)
NOTE: usually written £ before a figure: £ 25

◇ **poundage** n. (i) rate charged per pound in weight 按每磅重量所收费用 (ii) tax charged perpound in value 按每英磅所征收的税款
NOTE: no plural

**power** n. (a) strength or ability 能力;力量: purchasing power = quantity of goods which can be bought by a group of people or with a sum of money 购买力; the purchasing power of the school market 学校市场购买力; The purchasing power of the pound has fallen over the last five years. 英磅的购买力在过去的五年里下降了。the power of a consumer group = ability of a group to influence the government or manufacturers 消费团体影响力; bargaining power = strength of one person or group when discussing prices or wages 讨价还价能力; earning power = amount of money someone should be able to earn 赚钱能力;收益能力; He is such a fine designer that his earning power is very large. 他是位出色的设计家,收入很高。borrowing power = amount of money which a company can borrow 借款能力;借款限额 (b) force or legal right executive power = right to act as director or to put decisions into action 行政权力; power of attorney = legal document which gives someone the right to act on someone's behalf in legal matters 委托书;授权书;代理权; the full power of the law = the full force of the law when applied 法律全部权力: We will apply the full power of the law to get possession of our property again.

我们将运用法律全部权力重新获得我们的财产。

**p. p.** v. = PER PROCURATIONEM 经由代理；由 … 代表签署：to p. p. a letter = to sign a letter on behalf of someone 由某人代签信件：The secretary p. p. 'd the letter while the manager was at lunch. 当经理吃午饭时，由秘书代签信件。

**PR** = PUBLIC RELATIONS 公共关系：A PR firm is handling all our publicity. 一家公共关系公司正在处理我们全部的广告宣传。He is working in PR. 他在公共关系公司做事。The PR people gave away 100,000 balloons. 公共关系公司的人们赠送了 10 万个气球。

**practice** n. (a) way of doing things 实践；做法：His practice was to arrive at work at 7:30 and start counting the cash. 他习惯早上 7 点 30 分上班，开始清点现金。business practices or industrial practices or trade practices = ways of managing or working in business, industry or trade 商业惯例；工业实践；贸易惯例；restrictive practices = ways of working which make people less free (such as stopping, by trade unions, of workers from doing certain jobs or not allowing customers a free choice of product)限制作业法；sharp practice = way of doing business which is not honest, but is not illegal 不择手段的做法(但不违法) code of practice = rules drawn up by an association which the members must follow when doing business 业务规则(商界) (b) in practice = when actually done 实施；实行：The marketing plan seems very interesting, but what will it cost in practice? 这个销售计划很令人感兴趣，但实施起来要花费多少呢？

**pre** - prefix before 在 … 之前；预先：a pre - stocktaking sale 存货盘点前销售；

盘存预售；There will be a pre - AGM board meeting. or There will be a board meeting pre the AGM. 年度股东大会召开前将开一次董事会议。The pre - Christmas period is always very busy. 圣诞节前这一段时间总是很繁忙的。

**precautionary** a. as a precautionary measure = in case something takes place 预防措施；应急措施

◇ **precautions** pl. n. care taken to avoid something unpleasant 预防；警惕；谨慎：to take precautions to prevent thefts in the office 提高警惕以防办公室失窃；The company did not take proper fire precautions. 公司未采取适当的防火措施。safety precautions = actions to try to make sure that something is safe 安全预防措施

**precinct** n. (a) pedestrian precinct or shopping precinct = part of a town which is closed to traffic so that people canwalk about and shop 行人专用区或购物区(城市步行区域，人们可四处走动与购物) (b) US administrative district in a town(美)行政区

**predecessor** n. person who had a job or position before someone else 前任；前辈：He took over from his predecessor last May. 去年五月份，他接替了前任。She is using the same office as her predecessor. 她用的是她前任的办公室。

**predict** v. to say that something will certainly happen 预言；预示；预告

**pre** - **empt** v. to get an advantage by doing something quickly before anyoneelse 抢先取得；预先占有；先买；先占：They staged a management buyout to pre - empt a takeover bid. 他们筹划买下资方的全部产权以便抢先得到兼并出价的好处。

◇ **pre** - **emptive** a. which has an advantage by acting early 优先的；先发制人的：pre - emptive strike against a takeover bid = rapid action taken to preventa takeover bid 对兼并出价来取先发制人的打击; a pre – emptive right = (i) right of a government or of a local authority to buy aproperty before anyone else 优先购买权(政府或地方当局先于他人购买资产的权利) (ii) US right of a shareholder to be first to buy a new stock issue(美)(股东的)优先购股权 (第一个购买新上市的股票的权利)

**prefer** v. to like something better than another thing 更喜欢; 偏爱: We prefer the small corner shop to the large supermarket. 与大型超级市场相比, 我们更喜欢那家拐角小商店. Most customers prefer to choose clothes themselves, rather than take the advice of the sales assistant. 大多数顾客更愿意自己选择衣服, 而不太爱采纳售货员的意见。

◇ **preference** n. thing which is preferred 偏爱, 优先: the customers' preference for small corner shops 顾客对拐角的那些小商店的偏爱; preference shares = shares (often with no voting rights) which receive their dividend before all other shares and which are repaid first (at face value) if the company is liquidated 优先股; preference shareholders = owners of preference shares 优先股股东; cumulative preference share = preference share where the dividend will be paid at a later date even if the company cannot pay a dividend in the current year 累积优先股(如当年利润不足发放利息时, 可累积至下一年度发放的优先股)

◇ **preferential** a. showing that something is preferred more than another 优先的; 优惠的: preferential creditor = creditor who must be paid first if a company is in liquidation 优先债权人; preferential duty or preferential tariff = special low rate of tax 优惠关税; preferential terms or preferential treatment = terms or way of dealing which is better

than usual 优惠条件; Subsidiary companies get preferential treatment when it comes to subcontracting work. 分公司承接转包(二包)工作时会得到优惠待遇。

◇ **preferred** a. preferred creditor = creditor who must be paid first if a company is in liquidation 优先债权人; preferred shares or US preferred stock = shares which receive their dividend before all other shares, and which are repaid first (at face value) if the company is in liquidation 优先股; US cumulative preferred stock = preference share where the dividend will be paid at a later date even if the company cannot pay a dividend in the current year(美)累积优先股

**pre – financing** n. financing in advance 先期货款

**prejudice** 1. n. harm done to someone 损害; 侵害: without prejudice = without harming any interests (words written on a letter to indicate that the writer is not legally bound to do what he offers to do in the letter)无损合法权益; to act to the prejudice of a claim = to do something which may harm a claim 作出有损于索赔权益之事 2. v. to harm to prejudice someone's claim 有损某人的合法权利要求

**preliminary** a. early or happening before anything else 初步的; 在前的: preliminary discussion or a preliminary meeting = discussion or meeting which takes place before the main discussion or meeting starts 初步讨论或预备会议

**premises** pl. n. building and the land it stands on 房屋及其周围土地: business premises or commercial premises = building used for commercial use 营业大楼; office premises or shop premises = building which houses an office or shop 办公楼; 商业大厦; lock – up premises = shop which is locked up at night when the owner goes home 上锁商店（夜间）licensedpremises = shop or restaurant or public house which is licensed to sell alcohol 特许售酒的商店，（饭店或酒店）；on the premises = in the building 室内，楼里；There is a doctor on the premises at all times. 楼里随时有医生值班。

**premium** n. (a) premium offer = free gift offered to attract more customers 随赠礼品；(b) insurance premium = annual payment made by the insured person or a company to an insurance company 保险费；additional premium = payment made to cover extra items in an existing insurance 追加保险费；You pay either an annual premium of £360 or twelve monthly premiums of £32. 你可一次性付360英磅的年度保险费，也可按月付，交12个月的，每月付32英磅。(c) amount to be paid to a landlord or a tenant for the right to take over a lease 顶费金；预付租金：flat to let with a premium of £10,000 公寓以10,000英磅为预付租金出租；Annual rent：£8,500, premium：£25,000 年租金为8,500英磅，顶费为25,000英磅 £25,000 (d) extra charge 额外价格；额外收费：exchange premium = extra cost above the normal rate for buying foreign currency 贴进；外汇升水；The dollar is at a premium. 美元高丁市价。shares sold at a premium = shares whose price is higher than their face value；new shares whose market price is higher than their issue price 溢价出售的股票 (e) GB premium bonds = government bonds；part of the national savings scheme, which pay no interest, but give the owner the chance to win a weekly or monthly prize （英）（有月奖但无利息的）有奖债券 (f) premium quality = top quality 优质；最高质量

**prepack or prepackage** v. to pack something before putting it on sale 预先包装：The fruit are prepacked or prepackaged in plastic trays. 水果用塑料盘预先包装。Thewatches are prepacked in attractive display boxes. 手表是用诱人的装饰盒预先包装好的

**prepaid** a. paid in advance 预付的；付讫的：carriage prepaid = note showing that the transport costs have been paid in advance "运费付讫"字样；prepaid reply card = stamped addressed card which is sent to someone so that he can reply without paying the postage（邮资）已预付的回言卡

◇ **prepay** v. to pay in advance 预付
NOTE: prepaying – prepaid

◇ **prepayment** n. payment in advance 预付金：to ask for prepayment of a fee = to ask for the fee to be paid before the work is done 要求预付酬金

**present** 1. n. thing which is given 礼物；赠品：These calculators make good presents. 这些计算器是很好的礼物。The office gave her a present when she got married. 她结婚时，公司送给她一件礼品。2. a. (a) happening now 现在的；目前的：The shares are too expensive at their present price. 这些股票现价太贵。What is the present address of the company? 现在公司的地址是什么？(b) being there when something happens 出席；在场：Only six directors were present at the board meeting. 只有六位董事出席了这次董事会。3. v. (a) to give someone something 给予，赠送：He was presented with a watch on completing twenty five years' service with the company. 他因25年效力于公司而赠送他一块手表。(b) to bring or send and show a document 出示；呈送；递上：to present a bill for acceptance = to send a bill for payment by the person who has accepted it 提请承兑（出示票据要求付款）；to present a bill for payment = to send a bill to be paid 提请付款；凭单付款

◇ **presentation** n. (a) showing a document 提示；递交：cheque payable on presentation = cheque which will be paid when it is presented 提示即兑支票；free admission on presentation of the card = you do not pay to go in if you show this card 免费入场券；示卡免费入场 (b) demonstration or exhibition of a proposed plan 介绍；展示：The manufacturer made a presentation of his new product lineto possible customers. 制造商向潜在客户们展示了新生产线。The distribution company made a presentation of the services they could offer. 这家销售公司介绍了他们能够提供的服务项目。We have asked two PR firms to make presentations of proposed publicity campaigns. 我们请了两家公共关系公司来介绍拟定的广告宣传活动。

◇ **present value** n. (a) the value something has now 现值：In 1974 the pound was worth five times its present value. 英磅在 1974 年是现值的五倍。(b) sum of money which if invested now at a given rate of interest would produce a certain amount in the future 本金现值（一笔金额按现有利率投资将来肯定盈利）

**preside** v. to be chairman 负责；主持：to preside over a meeting 主持会议；The meeting was held in the committee room, Mr Smith presiding. 会议在委员会房间召开，由史密斯先生主持。

◇ **president** n. head of a company or a club 董事长；总裁；总经理；会长：He was elected president of the sports club. 他被选为体育俱乐部的会长。A. B. Smith has been appointed president of the company. 史密斯被任命为公司总裁。
NOTE: in GB, president is sometimes a title given to a non - executive former chairman of a company; in the USA, the president is the main executive director of a company

**press** n. newspapers and magazines 报刊；杂志等刊物：the local press = newspapers which are sold in a small area of the country 地方报刊；the national press = newspapers which sell in all parts of the country 全国性发行的报纸；The new car has been advertised in the national press. 这种新型汽车已在全国性报纸上登了广告。We plan to give the product a lot of press publicity. 我们计划在刊物上对这项产品做大量的广告宣传。There was no mention of the new product in the press. 新闻界没有提到这项新产品。press conference = meeting where reporters from newspapers are invited to hear news of a new product or of a court case or of a takeover bid, etc. 记者招待会；新闻发布会；press coverage = reports about something in the press 新闻报导；采访报告；We were very disappointed by the press coverage of the new car. 我们对这种新型汽车的新闻报导大失所望。press cutting = piece cut out of a newspaper or magazine, which refers to an item which you find interesting 剪报；We have kept a file of press cuttings about the new car. 我们已将这种新型汽车的剪报归档。press release = sheet giving news about something which is sent to newspapersand TV and radio stations so that they can use the information 新闻稿；通讯稿；The company sent out a press release about the launch of the new car.公司发出了即将投放这种新型汽车的新闻稿。
NOTE: no plural

◇ **pressing** a. urgent 紧急的；迫切的：pressing engagements = meetings which have to be attended 紧急会议；pressing bills = bills which have to be paid 即付票据；必付票据

**pressure** n. something which forces you to do something 压力；强制；紧迫：He was under considerable financial pressure. = He was forced to act because he owed money. 他的财政压力很大(他经济上十分困窘)。to put pressure on someone to do something = to try to force someone to do something 施加压力迫使某人做某事；The group tried to put pressure on the government to act. 这个团体向政府施加压力迫使其采取行动。The banks put pressure on the company to reduce its borrowings. 银行界向这家公司施加压力,迫使其减少借款。working under high pressure = working with customers asking for supplies urgently or with a manager telling you to work faster 逼不得已工作；high - pressure salesman = salesman who forces a customer to buy something he does not really need 强行推销员(强行推销产品的销售人)；pressure group = group of people who try to influence the government or the local town council, etc. 压力集团(试图以高压手段去影响政府或地方议会的团体)

**prestige** n. importance because of high quality or high value, etc. 信誉；威望；威信：prestige advertising = advertising in high quality magazines to increase a company's reputation 商誉广告(在高质量杂志上作广告以提高公司的声望)；prestige product = expensive luxury product 高级消费品；高消费产品；prestige offices = expensive offices in a good area of the town 高级办事处；有声望的办公处

**presume** v. to suppose something is correct 假设；推定；猜想：I presume the account has been paid. 我想帐已付了。The company is presumed to be still solvent. 相信公司仍有偿付能力。We presume the shipment has been stolen. 我们猜想所发货物已被盗窃。

◇ **presumption** n. thing which is assumed to be correct 推断；假定

**pre - tax or pretax** a. before tax has been deducted or paid 未扣税金；扣税前：pretax profit = profit before tax has been paid 税前利润；The dividend paid is equivalent to one quarter of the pretax profit. 所付股息相当于税前利润的四分之一。

**pretences** pl. n. false pretences = doing or saying something to cheat someone 欺诈(手段)；欺骗；He was sent to prison for obtaining money by false pretences. 他因诈骗钱财而被捕入狱。

**pretend** v. to act like someone else in order to trick or to act as if something is true when it really is not 佯装；伪装：He got in by pretending to be a telephone engineer. 他假装成电话工程师进来的。The chairman pretended he knew the final profit. 董事长假装他知道决算利润。She pretended she had ' flu and asked to have the day off. 他假装得了流感而请一天病假。

**prevent** v. to stop something happening 预防；防止：We must try to prevent the takeover bid. 我们必须尽量阻止兼并出价的发生。The police prevented anyone from leaving the building. 警察阻止任何人离开这座大楼。We have changed the locks on the doors to prevent the former MD from getting into the building. 为防止前任总经理进入大楼,我们已换了所有门上的锁。

◇ **preventive** a. which tries to stop something happening 预防的：to take preventive measures against theft = to try to stop things from being stolen 采取防盗措施

**previous** a. which happens earlier 先前的；以前的：He could not accept the invitation because he had a previous engagement. = because he had earlier accepted another invitation to go somewhere. 他不能接受这个邀请,因为他已有约。

◇ **previously** ad. happening earlier 先

前地;以前地

**price** 1. n. money which has to be paid to buy something 价格;价钱: agreed price = price which has been accepted by both the buyer and seller 议定价格; all－in price = price which covers all items in a purchase ( goods, insurance, delivery, etc. ) 全部在内的价格(包括所购之物、保险费及运费等); asking price = price which the seller is hoping to be paid for the item when it is sold 要价;索价; bargain price = very cheap price 廉价; catalogue price or list price = price as marked in a catalogue or list 商品目录价格;价目表的价格; competitive price = low price aimed to compete with a rival product 竞争性价格;低价; cost price = selling price which is the same as the price which the seller paid for the item ( either the manufacturing price or the wholesale price)原价;成本价格; cut price = very cheap price 削价;减价;廉价; discount price = full price less a discount 打折扣价; factory price or price ex factory = price not including transport from the maker's factory 出厂价; fair price = good price for both buyer and seller 公平价格;好价钱; firm price = price which will not change 稳定的价格; They are quoting a firm price of $ 1.23 a unit. 他们所开的稳定价格为每件 1.23 美元。 going price or current price or usual price = the price which is being charged now 现行价格;市价; to sell goods off at half price = to sell goods at half the price at which they were being sold before 以半价出售; market price = price at which a product can be sold 市场价格; net price = price which cannot be reduced by a discount 实价;净价; retail price = price at which the retailer sells to the final customer 零售价; retail price index = index which shows how prices of consumer goods have increased or decreased over a period of time 零售价格指数; spot price = price for immediate delivery of a commodity 现货价格;现金售价; the spot price of oil on the commodity markets 商品市场上石油的现货价格; price ceiling = highest price which can be reached 最高价;价格上限; price control = legal measures to stop prices rising too fast 价格管制;物价控制; price cutting = sudden lowering of prices 大削价;大减价; price war or price－cutting war = competition between companies to get a larger market share by cutting prices 价格战;削价战; price differential = difference in price between products in a range 价格差异;差价; price fixing = illegal agreement between companies to charge the same price for competing products 固定价格;限价; price label or price tag = label which shows a price 价格标签;标价条: The takeover bid put a $2m price tag on the company. 为兼并那家公司的投标价为 2,000,000 美元。 price list = sheet giving prices of goods for sale 价格表;价目单; price range = series of prices for similar products from different suppliers 价格幅度;物价幅度; cars in the £6－7,000 price range = cars of different makes, selling for between £6,000 and £7,000 汽车的价格幅度为 6,000 英镑到 7,000 英镑(汽车价格从 6,000 英镑到 7,000 英镑不等); price－sensitive product = product which will not sell if the price is increased 价格敏感的商品(价格一旦上涨,立即引起滞销的商品); (b) to increase in price = to become more expensive 涨价: Petrol has increased in price or the price of petrol has increased. 汽油涨价了。 to increase prices or to raise prices = to make items more expensive 提价;涨价: We will try to meet your price. = We will try to offer a price which is acceptable to you. 我们会尽量

满足您的要价。to cut prices = to reduceprices suddenly 削价；减价；to lower prices or to reduce prices = to make items cheaper 降价；减价；(c)(on the Stock Exchange) asking price = price which sellers are asking for shares(证券交易用语)要价；索价；closing price = price at the end of a day's trading 收盘价格；opening price = price at the start of a day's trading 开盘价格；price/earnings ratio = ratio between the market price of a share and the current earnings it produces 价格/收益比率(股票市价和以每股现行收益之间比例) 2. v. to give a price to a product 给…定价；给…标价：car priced at £5,000 标价为5,000英磅的汽车；competitively priced = sold at a low price which competes with that of similar goods from other companies 以竞争性价格出售的；The company has priced itself out of the market. = The company has raised its prices so high that its products do not sell. 这家公司抬价过高而断了自己的销路。

◇ **pricing** n. giving a price to a product 定价；标价：pricing policy = a company's policy in giving prices to its products 定价政策；Our pricing policy aims at producing a 35% gross margin. 我们的定价政策目的在于赢得35%的毛利润。common pricing = illegal fixing of prices by several businesses so that they all charge the same price 共同定价；competitive pricing = putting a low price on a product so that it competes with similar products from other companies 竞争性定价；marginal pricing = making the selling price the same as the cost of a single extra unit above the number already planned 边际定价

NOTE: no plural

**primary** a. basic 初级的；基本的：Primary commodities = raw materials or food 初级产品；primary industry = industry dealing with basic raw materials (such as coal, wood, farm produce)第一工业；主要工业；primary products = products (such as wood, milk, fish) which are basic raw materials 初级产品；农产品

◇ **primarily** ad. mainly 主要地

**prime** a. (a) most important 首要的；头等重要的：prime time = most expensive advertising time for TV commercials. 收视率最高时间(指商业电视广告黄金时间)；We are putting out a series of prime-time commercials. 我们播出了一系列黄金时间商业广告。(b) basic 基本的；原始的；最初的：prime bills = bills of exchange which do not involve any risk 无风险票据；优等汇票；prime cost = cost involved in producing a product, excluding overheads 主要成本；直接成本；prime rate or prime = best rate of interest at which a bank lends to its customers 主要利率；最优惠利率

◇ **Prime Minister** n. head of a government 首相；总理：the Australian Prime Minister or the Prime Minister of Australia 澳大利亚总理

◇ **priming** n. see PUMP PRIMING

**principal** 1. n. (a) person or company which is represented by an agent 委托人；委托公司：The agent has come to London to see his principals. 代理人已到伦敦见他的委托人。(b) money invested or borrowed on which interest is paid 投资额；本金：to repay principal and interest 偿还本息(本金与利息) 2. a. most important 首要的；最重要的：The principal shareholders asked for a meeting. 主要股东们要求召开会议。The country's principal products are paper and wood. 该国主要产品为纸和木材。

**principle** n. basic point or general rule 原则；原理：in principle = in agreement with a general rule 原则上;大体上;a-greementin principle = agreement with the basic conditions of a proposal 原则一致的协议

**print** 1. n. words made (on paper) with a machine(印刷)字体; to read the small print or the fine print on a contract = to read the conditions of a contract which are often printed very small so that people will not be able to read them easily 阅读合同中的小字体 2. v. (a) to make letters on paper with a machine 印刷;刊印: printed agreement 打印好的协定; printed regulations 打印好的规定 (b) to write in capital letters 用印刷体写: Please print your name and address on the top of the form. 请用印刷体将你的名字与地址写在表格的开头。

◇ **printer** n. machine which prints 打印机;印刷机: computer printer or line printer = machine which prints information from a computer, printing one line at a time 计算机打印机; dot - matrix printer = machine which prints by forming letters from many tiny dots 点阵字符打印机

◇ **print out** v. to print information from a computer through a printer 打印出(信息)

◇ **printout** n. computer printout = printed copy of information from a computer 计算机打印出的信息: The sales director asked for a printout of the agents' commissions. 销售主任要求得到一张由计算机打印的代理人佣金表。

**prior** a. earlier 以前的;先前的: prior agreement = agreement which was reached earlier 先前协定; without prior knowledge = without knowing before 预先未知; prior charge = security (such as a preference share) which is repaid before other securities when a company goes into liquidation 优先债权

◇ **priority** n. to have priority = to have the right to be first 享有优先权; to have priority over or to take priority over something = to be more important than something 比 … 更加优先; Reducing overheads takes priority over increasing turnover. 与增加营业额相比,应优先考虑降低间接费用。Debenture holders have priority over ordinary shareholders. 债券持有人比普通股东享有优先权。to give something top priority = to make something the most important item 给予最优先权;使……成为最优先的事项

**private** a. (a) belonging to a single person, not a company or the state 私有的;私人的: letter marked "Private and Confidential" = letter which must not be opened by anyone other than the person it is addressed to 信件上标有"机密亲启"; private client or private customer = client dealt with by a salesman as a person, not as a company 个人客户; private income = income from dividends or interest or rents which is not part of a salary 个人工资外收入; private investor = ordinary person with money to invest 个人投资者;私人投资者; private property = property which belongs to a private person, not to the public 私有财产 (b) in private = away from other people 私下地;私密地: He asked to see the managing director in private. 他要求私下会见总经理。In public he said the company would break even soon, but in private he was less optimistic. 在公众场合他说公司很快收支相抵,但私下里,他并不乐观。(c) private limited company = company with a small number of shareholders whose shares are not traded on the Stock Exchange 私营有限公司 (d) private enterprise = businesses which are owned by private shareholders, not by the state 私人企业;私营企业; The project is funded by private enterprise. 这项工程是由私人企业提供资金的。the private sector = all companies which are owned by private shareholders, not by the state(国民经济的)私营部门经济；私营企业部分

◇ **privately** ad. away from other people 私下地：The deal was negotiated privately. 这笔交易是在私下商定的。

◇ **privatization** n. selling a nationalized industry to private owners 私有化（国营工业出售给私有者）

◇ **privatize** v. to sell a nationalized industry to private owners 使…私有化

**pro** prep. for 为了：pro tem = for the time being or temporarily 暂时；临时；per pro = with the authority of 由…代表：The secretary signed per pro the manager. 由秘书代经理签字。pro forma = invoice sent to a buyer before the goods are sent, so that payment can be made in advance or that business documents can be produced 估价单；预开发票；pro rata. = at a rate which varies according to the size or importance of something 按比例的；Dividends are paid pro rata = Dividends are paid according to the number of shares held. 红利按比例支付

**probable** a. likely to happen 可能的：He is trying to prevent the probable collapse of the company. 他在尽力防止公司可能的破产。

◇ **probably** ad. likely 很可能地：The MD is probably going to retire next year. 总经理很可能明年退休。This shop is probably the best in town for service. 这个商店的服务可能是城里最好的。

**probate** n. proving legally that a document, especially a will, is valid. 遗嘱认证：The executor was granted probate. = The executor was told officially that the will was valid. 遗嘱执行人被告知遗嘱已认证。probate court = court which examines wills to see if they are valid 遗嘱认证法庭

NOTE: no plural

◇ **probation** n. period when a new worker is being tested before getting a permanent job 试用期；见习期. He is on three months' probation. 他正在三个月的试用期。to take someone on probation 使某人见习

NOTE: no plural

◇ **probationary** a. while someone is being tested 试用的；见习的：a probationary period of three months 三个月的试用期；After the probationary period the company decided to offer him a full-time contract. 经过试用期，公司已决定给他订一个全日工作的合同

**problem** n. thing to which it is difficult to find an answer 问题：The company suffers from cash flow problems or staff problems. 公司深受现金流转问题的困扰或公司对职工问题深感头痛。to solve a problem = to find an answer to a problem 解决问题；Problem solving is a test of a good manager. 解决问题是对一个好经理的检验。problem area = area of a company's work which is difficult to run 有问题的地方；Overseas sales is one of our biggest problem areas. 海外销售是我们问题最大的地方(领域)之一。

**procedure** n. way in which something is done 过程；步骤；程序：to follow the proper procedure 遵循适当程序；This procedure is very irregular. = This is not the set way to do something. 这个程序很不合常规。accounting procedures = set ways of doing the accounts of a company 会计程序；disciplinary procedure = way of warning a worker that he is breaking the rules of a company 惩诫办法；complaints procedure or grievance procedure = way of presenting complaints formally from a trade union to a management 投诉程序；The trade union has followed the correct complaints procedure. 工会遵循了正确的投诉程序。dismissal procedures = correct way to dismiss someone, following the rules inthe contract of employment 解雇程序

**proceed** v. to go on or to continue 进行;继续: The negotiations are proceeding slowly. 谈判正在缓慢进行。to proceed against someone = to start a legal action against someone 对某人起诉; to proceed with something = to go on doing something 续续做某事; Shall we proceed with the committee meeting? 我们将继续委员会会议吗?

◇ **proceedings** pl. n. (a) conference proceedings = written report of what has taken place at a conference 会议记录;会议报告 (b) legal proceedings = legal action or lawsuit 法律程序;诉讼程序; to take proceedings against someone 对某人起诉; The court proceedings were adjourned. 法庭诉讼暂停了。to institute proceedings against someone = to start a legal action against someone 对某人起诉

◇ **proceeds** pl. n. the proceeds of a sale = money received from a sale after deducting expenses 销售收入(扣除开支): He sold his shop and invested the proceeds in a computer repair business. 他卖掉了他的商店,并将这笔收入投资于计算机修理业。

**process** 1. n. (a) industrial processes = processes involved in manufacturing products in factories 工艺流程;工业加工; decision - making processes = ways in which decisions are reached 决策程序 (b) the due processes of the law = the formal work of a legal action 法律正常程序 2. v. (a) to process figures = to sort out information to make it easily understood 处理数据; The sales figures are being processed by our accounts department. 销售金额正由财务处分类处理。Data is being processed by our computer. 数据正由我们的计算机分类处理。(b) to deal with something in the

usual routine way(按常规)处理: to process an insurance claim 处理保险索赔; Orders are processed in our warehouse. 订货由我们的库房处理。

◇ **processing** n. (a) sorting of information 处理(有关信息): processing of information or of statistics 信息处理或统计资料处理; batch processing = computer system, where information is collected into batches before being loaded into the computer 信息成批处理; data processing or information processing = selecting and examining data in a computer to produceinformation in a special form 数据处理;信息处理; word processing or text processing = working with words, using a computer to produce, check and change texts, reports, letters, etc. 文字处理 (b) the processing of a claim for insurance = putting a claim for insurance through the usual office routine in the insurance company 处理保险索赔; order processing = dealing with orders 订货处理

NOTE: no plural

◇ **processor** n. word processor = small computer which is used for working with words, to produce texts, reports, letters, etc. 文字处理机;信息处理机

**produce** 1. n. foodstuffs grown on the land 农产品: home produce 国内土特产品; agricultural produce or farm produce 农产品

NOTE: no plural

2. v. (a) to bring out 拿出;提出;出示: He produced documents to prove his claim. 他出示文件来证明他的要求权。The negotiators produced a new set of figures. 谈判者们提出了一组新数字。The customs officer asked him to produce the relevant documents. 海关官员请他出示有关证件。(b) to make or to manufacture 制造;生产: to produce cars or engines or books 制造汽车或引擎;出版

书; to mass produce = to make large quantitiesof a product 大量生产 (c) to give an interest 生息; 产生利息: investments which produce about 10% per annum 每年产生 10% 的利息的投资

◇ **producer** n. person or company or country which manufactures 制造商; 生产者: country which is a producer of high quality watches 优质手表的生产国; The company is a major car producer. 这个公司是一个大的汽车制造(生产)厂商。

◇ **producing** a. which produces 生产的: producing capacity = capacity to produce 生产能力; oil – producing country = country which produces oil 产油国

**product** n. (a) thing which is made or manufactured 产品; 产物: basic product = main product made from a raw material 基本产品; 主要产品; by – product = secondary product made as a raw material is being processed 副产品; end product or final product or finished product = product made at the end of a production process 最终产品; 成品 (b) manufactured item for sale 商品; 产品: product advertising = advertising a particular named product, not the company which makes it 产品广告; 商品广告; product analysis = examining each separate product in a company's range to see why it sells or who buys it, etc. 产品分析; product design = design of consumer products 产品设计; product development = improving an existing product line to meet the needs of the market 产品开发; product engineer = engineer in charge of the equipment for making a product 产品机械工程师; product line or product range = series of different products made by the same company which form a group (such as cars in different models, pens in different colours, etc.) 产品系列; 系列产品;

product management = directing the making and selling of a product as an independent item 产品管理; product mix = group of quite different products made by the same company 产品组合; 产品搭配 (c) gross domestic product = annual value of goods sold and services paid for inside a country 国内生产总值; 国内总产值; gross national product = annual value of goods and services in a country, including income from other countries 国民生产总值

◇ **production** n. (a) showing something 出示; 提供; 拿出: on production of = when something is shown 出示; 拿出: The case will be released by the customs on production of the relevant documents. 只要提供有关文件, 这个诉讼案可以撤诉。Goods can be exchanged only on production of the sales slip 只要出示销售单(小票)就可以换货。(b) making or manufacturing of goods for sale 生产; 制造: Production will probably be held up by industrial action. 生产可能会受到工业行动的阻碍。We are hoping to speed up production by installing new machinery. 我们希望安装新机器从而加快生产速度。batch production = production in batches 分批生产; 成批生产: domestic production = production of goods in the home market 国内产品; 国货; mass production = manufacturing of large quantities of goods 大批生产; 大量生产; mass production of cars or of calculators 大量生产汽车; 大批生产计算机; rate of production or production rate = speed at which items are made 生产率; 生产速度; production cost = cost of making a product 生产成本; production department = section of a company which deals with the making of the company's products 生产部门; 制造部门; production line = system of making a product, where each item (such as a car) moves

slowly through the factory with new sec-tionsadded to it asit goes along 生产流水线；生产作业线；He works on the pro-duction line. 他在生产流水线上干活。She is a production line worker. 她是生产流水线上的一名工人。production manager = person in charge of the pro-duction department 生产经理；produc-tion unit = separate small group of workers producing a certain product 生产单位
NOTE: no plural

◇ **productive** a. which produces 生产性的；生产的：productive capital = cap-ital which is invested to give interest 生产资金；生产资本；productive discus-sions = useful discussions which lead to an agreement or decision 有效的讨论；有成效的讨论

◇ **productively** ad. in a productive way 有结果地；有成效地

◇ **productivity** n. rate of output per worker or per machine in a factory 生产率；生产能力：Bonus payments are linked to productivity. 奖金与生产率挂钩。The company is aiming to increase productivity. 该公司的目的在于提高生产率。Productivity has fallen or risen since the company was taken over. 自从公司兼并管后，生产率降低了(或提高了)。productivity agreement = agree-ment to pay a productivity bonus 劳动生产率协议；支付生产率奖金的协议；productivity bonus = extra payments made to workers because of increased production 生产率；奖金 productivity drive = extra effort to increase produc-tivity 提高生产率运动；生产竞赛
NOTE: no plural

**profession** n. (a) work which needs special skills learnt over a period of time 职业：The managing director is an ac-countant by profession. 总经理是职业会计师。(b) group of specialized workers 同行；同事：the legal profession = all lawyers 法律界同行；the medical pro-fession = all doctors 医务界同行；医生同行

◇ **professional** 1. a. (a) referring to one of the professions 职业的；专业的：The accountant sent in his bill for profes-sional services. 作为专门服务，会计师呈报了他的票据。We had to ask our lawyer for professional advice on the contract. 对于这个合同，我们必须请教我们的律师的专业指点。a professional man = man who works in one of the professions (such as a lawyer, doctor, accountant) 专业人员；专门职业者；professional qualifications = documents showing that someone has successfully finished acourse of study which allows him to work in one of the professions 专业文凭；职业资格 (b) expert or skilled 专业的；技术的：His work is very professional. 他的工作专业性很强。They did a very professional job in de-signing the new office. 他们在设计新办公室的过程中做了专业性很强的工作。(c) doing work for money 职业的：a professional tennis player 职业网球手；He is a professional troubleshooter. = He makes his living by helping companies to sort out their problems. 他是一位排解纠纷的专家(能手)。2. n. skilled person or person who does skilled work for money 专业人员；职业选手；专门职业者

**proficiency** n. skill or being capable of doing something 熟炼；精通：She has a certificate of proficiency in English. 她有英语专长程度的证书。To get the job he had to pass a proficiency test. 要想得到这份工作，他必须通过水平测试。
NOTE: no plural

◇ **proficient** a. capable of doing some-thing well 精通的；熟练的：She is quite proficient in English. 她很精通英语。

**profile** n. brief description 简介；传略：

He asked for a company profile of the possiblepartners in the joint venture. 他要一份可能参加合资企业的公司简介。The customer profile shows our average buyer to be male, aged 25 – 30, and employed in the service industries. 顾客简介表明我们的普通买主是在服务业工作的, 年龄在 25—30 岁的男性

**profit** n. money gained from a sale which is more than the money spent 利润；赢利：clear profit = profit after all expenses have been paid 纯利润；净利；We made ＄6,000 clear profit on the deal. 这笔买卖我们净利 6,000 美元；gross profit = profit calculated as sales income less the cost of the goods sold 总利润；总收益；毛利；net profit = result where income from sales is larger than all expenditure 净利；纯利；利润净额；operating profit = result where sales from normal business activities are higher than the costs 营业利润；trading profit = result where the company's receipts are higher than its expenditure 贸易利润；营业利润；profit and loss account = accounts for a company which show expenditure and income balanced to show a final profit or loss 损益帐户；profit margin = percentage difference between sales income and the cost of sales 利润幅度；profits tax or tax on profits = tax to be paid on profits 利润税；profit before tax or pretax profit = profit before any tax has been paid 税前利润；profit after tax = profit after tax has been paid 税后利润；to take one's profit = to sell shares at a higher price than was paid for them, rather than to keep them as an investment 以高价出售股票获利；抄股票获利；to show a profit = to make a profit and state it in the company accounts 说明利润；We are showing a small profit for the first quarter. 我们将表明第一季度会小有利润。to make a profit = to have more money as a result of a deal 获得利润；to move into profit = to start to make a profit 开始获利；The company is breaking even now, and expects to move into profit within the next two months. 公司现在收支相抵；期待下两个月开始获利。to sell at a profit = to sell at a price which gives you a profit 获利出售；赚钱出售；excess profit = profit which is higher than what is thought to be normal 超额利润；excess profits tax = tax on excess profits 超额利润税；healthy profit = quite a large profit 重利；高利润；paper profit = profit on an asset which has increased in price but has not been sold 帐面利润；帐面盈余；He is showing a paper profit of £25,000 on his investment. 他将表明其投资 25,000 英磅帐面盈余。

◇ **profit centre** n. person or department which is considered separately for the purposes of calculating a profit 利润中心(个人或独立部门分别进行利润核算工作)

◇ **profit – making** a. which makes a profit 营利的；获利的：The whole project was expected to be profit – making by 1985. 全部工程预期 1985 年营利。non profit – making = (organization, such as a club) which is not allowed by law to make a profit 非营利的；Non profit – making organizations are exempt from tax. 非营利组织免税。

◇ **profit – sharing** n. arrangement where workers get a share of the profits of the company they work for 利润分成，分红制：The company runs a profit – sharing scheme. 这个公司实行分红制。

NOTE: no plural

◇ **profit – taking** n. selling investments to realize the profit, rather than keeping them 获取利润；实现利润；Share prices fell under continued profit – taking. 在持续高价出售股票中, 股价下

跌了。

NOTE: no plural

◇ **profitability** n. (a) ability to make a profit 营利能力；可获利润能力（b）amount of profit made as a percentage of costs 可获利润率；measurement of profitability = way of calculating how profitable something is 可获利润率计算

NOTE: no plural

◇ **profitable** a. which makes a profit 营利的；获利的；有益的

◇ **profitably** ad. making a profit 营利地；获利地；有益地

◇ **profiteer** n. person who makes too much profit, especially when goods are rationed or in short supply 牟取暴利者；投机商人；奸商

◇ **profiteering** n. making too much profit 牟取暴利；投机营利

**pro forma** n. pro forma (invoice) = invoice sent to a buyer before the goods are sent , so that payment can be made or that business documents can be produced 预开发票；估价单：They sent us a pro forma。他们寄给我们一张预开发票。

**program** 1 n. computer program = instructions to a computer telling it to do a particular piece of work 计算机程序；to buy a word-processing program 购买文字处理机程序；The accounts department is running a new payroll program. 财务处正在操作一项新的工资处理程序。2. v. to write a program for a computer 编制程序：to program a computer = to install a program in a computer 编制计算机程序；The computer is programmed to print labels. 这台计算机编有打印标签的程序。

NOTE: programming – programmed

◇ **programme or** US **program** n. plan of things which will be done 计划；方案：development programme 发展计划；research programme 研究方案；training programme 培训计划；to draw up a programme of investment or an investment programme 拟订一项投资计划

◇ **programmable** a. which can be programmed 可计划的；可规划的

◇ **programmer** n. computer programmer = person who writes computer programs 计算机编制程序者

◇ **programming** n. computer programming = writing programs for computers 计算机程序编制；programming engineer = engineer in charge of programming a computer system 计算机程序编制工程师；programming language = system of signs, letters and words used to instruct a computer 计算机程序语言

**progress** 1 n. movement of work forward 进展；进度；进步；to report on the progress of the work or of the negotiations 汇报工作进展情况；汇报谈判进展情况；to make a progress report = to report how work is going 做工作进度报告；in progress = which is being done but is not finished 正在进行中；negotiations in progress 正在进行中的谈判；work in progress 正在进展中的工作；progress payments = payments made as each stage of a contract is completed 按进度付款；The fifth progress payment is due in March. 第五期按进度付款于五月到期。

NOTE: no plural

2. v. to move forward or to go ahead 进步；前进；进行：The contract is progressing through various departments. 这个合同正在各部门取得进展。

◇ **progress chaser** n. person whose job is to check that work is being carried out on schedule or that orders are being fulfilled on time, etc. 进度监督员；工作监察员

◇ **progressive** a. which moves forward in stages 渐进的；逐渐的；累进的：progressive taxation 累进税

**prohibitive** a. with a price so high that you cannot afford to pay it 高昂的；抑制性的：The cost of redeveloping the product is prohibitive. 重新研制此产品的成本高得使人不敢问津。

**project** n. (a) plan 计算；规划：He has drawn up a project for developing new markets in Europe. 他起草了一个开发欧洲新市场的计划。(b) particular job of work which follows a plan 项目；工程：We are just completing an engineering project in North Africa. 我们就要完成北非的一项工程项目。The company will start work on the project next month. 公司将于下月开始这个项目的工作。project analysis = examining all costs or problems of a project before work on itis started 项目分析；项目评估；project engineer = engineer in charge of a project 负责(承担)项目工程师；project manager = manager in charge of a project 项目经理

◇ **projected** a. planned or expected 预定的；预计的；projected sales = forecast of sales 预计销售；Projected sales in Europe next year should be over £1m. 明年在欧洲预计的销售额应超过100万英磅。

◇ **projection** n. forecast of something which will happen in the future 预测；估计；设想；projection of profits for the next three years 今后三年的利润预测；The sales manager was asked to draw up sales projections for the next three years. 要求销售经理草拟出今后三年的销售预测。

**promise** 1. n. saying that you will do something 诺言；承诺：to keep a promise = to do what you said you would do 遵守诺言；He says he will pay next week, but he never keeps his promises. 他说他下星期还钱，可他从来不遵守诺言。to go back on a promise = not to do what you said you would do 不守诺言；The management went back on its promise to increase salaries across the board 资方不遵守全面增加工资的承诺。a promise to pay = a promissory note 付款允诺 2. v. to say that you will do something 许诺；允诺：They promised to pay the last instalment next week. 他们答应下周支付最后一次的分期付款。The personnel manager promised he would look into the grievances of the office staff. 人事经理答应他将调查公司职员的疾苦。

◇ **promissory note** n. document stating that someone promises to pay an amount of money on a certain date 本票；期票(许诺在某日支付金额的票据)

**promote** v. (a) to give someone a more important job 提升；晋升；提级：He was promoted from salesman to sales manager. 他从售货员晋升为销售经理。(b) to advertise 做广告(促销)：to promote a new product = to increase the sales of a new product by a sales campaign or TV commercials or free gifts 做广告促销一项新产品 (c) to promote a new company = to organize the setting up of a new company 创办一个新公司

◇ **promoter** n. company promoter = person who organizes the setting up of a new company 公司创办人；公司发起人

◇ **promotion** n. (a) moving up to a more important job 提升；晋升：promotion chances or promotion prospects 晋升机会；He ruined his chances of promotion when he argued with the managing director. 由于他与总经理争执，而失去了晋升的机会。to earn promotion = to work hard and efficiently and so be promoted 获得提升 (b) promotion of a company = setting up a new company 创办公司 (c) promotion of a product = selling a new product by publicity or sales campaign or TV commercials or free gifts

登广告促销一项产品；promotion budget广告促销预算；promotion team 广告促销组；sales promotion 促进销售活动；special promotion 特殊促销

◇ **promotional** a. used in an advertising campaign 促销的：The admen are using balloons as promotional material. 广告员用汽球作为广告促销品。promotional budget = forecast cost of promoting a new product 促销预算

**prompt** a. rapid or done immediately 立即的；即时的；迅速的：prompt service 迅速服务，即时服务；prompt reply to a letter 立即复信；prompt payment = payment made rapidly 立即付款；即时付款；prompt supplier = supplier who delivers orders rapidly 及时供货商

◇ **promptly** ad. rapidly 即时地；迅速地；立即地：He replied to my letter very promptly. 他很快给我复了信。

**proof** n. thing which shows that something is true 证明；证据；documentary proof = proof in the form of a document 文件证明

◇ **-proof** suffix which prevents something getting in or getting out or harming 保护；防…的，抗…的；dustproof cover 防尘盖；inflation-proof pension 不受通货膨胀影响的养老金（抚恤金）；soundproof studio 隔音演播室

**property** n. (a) personal property = things which belong to a person 私人财产；动产：The storm caused considerable damage to personal property. 暴雨给私人财产造成相当大的损失。The management is not responsible for property left in the hotel rooms. 管理部门对遗忘在客房的个人财产不负责任。(b) land and buildings 房地产：property tax 房地产税；damage to property or property damage 房地产损失；The commercial property market is booming. 商业房地产市场日益繁荣。The office has been bought by a property company. = by a company which buys buildings to lease them 这个事务所被一家房地产公司收购了。property developer = person who buys old buildings or empty land and builds new buildings for sale or rent 房地产开发者；private property = property which belongs to a private person and not to the public 私人房地产（c) a building 楼房：We have several properties for sale in the centre of the town. 我们在市中心有几幢楼房等待出售

NOTE: no plural for (a) or (b)

**proportion** n. part (of a total)部分：A proportion of the pre-tax profit is set aside for contingencies. 为预防万一，应留出部分税前利润。Only a small proportion of our sales comes from retail shops. 只有一小部分销售额来自零售商店。in proportion to = showing how something is related to something else 与……成比例：Profits went up in proportion to the fall in overhead costs. 利润上升与间接费用成本下降有关（成比例）。Sales in Europe are small in proportion to those in the USA. 与美国销售额比欧洲销售额小。

◇ **proportional** a. directly related 直接有关的；成比例的：The increase in profit is proportional to reduction in overheads.利润的增加与间接费用成本的削减成比例

◇ **proportionately** ad. in proportion 成比例地

**proposal** n. (a) suggestion or thing suggested 建议；提议：to make a proposal or to put forward a proposal to the board 向董事会提出建议；The committee turned down the proposal. = The committee refused to accept what was suggested. 委员会拒绝了这个建议。(b) official document with details of a property or person to be insured which is sent to the insurance company when asking for an insurance 投保单（要求保险

时向保险公司呈交个人或财产详情正式文件）

◇ **propose** v. (a) to suggest that something should be done 建议；提议：to propose a motion = to ask a meeting to vote for a motion and explain the reasons for this 提出一项动议；to propose someone as president = to ask a group to vote for someone to become president 提议某人当总裁 (b) to propose to = to say that you intend to do something 打算；计划；I propose to repay the loan at £20 a month. 我打算每月偿还贷款 20 英磅。

◇ **proposer** n. person who proposes a motion at a meeting 提议者；提出者

◇ **proposition** n. commercial deal which is suggested 生意；买卖：It will never be a commercial proposition. = It is not likely to make a profit. 它根本不可能是赚钱的买卖

**proprietary** a. (a) product (such as a medicine) which is made and owned by a company 专有的；专利的 proprietary drug = drug which is made by a particular company and marketed undera brand name 专利药品 (b) (in South Africa and Australia) proprietary company = private limited company 私人有限公司（在南非和澳大利亚）；不上市的有限公司

◇ **proprietor** n. owner 所有者；业主；老板：the proprietor of a hotel or a hotel proprietor 旅馆老板

◇ **proprietress** n. woman owner 女业主；女老板：the proprietress of an advertising consultancy 广告咨询业务公司的女老板

**pro rata** a. & ad. at an amount which varies according to the rate applied 按比例分配：a pro rata payment 按比例付款；to pay someone pro rata 按比例给某人付款

**prosecute** v. to bring (someone) to

court to answer a criminal charge 对…起诉；检举：He was prosecuted for embezzlement. 他因贪污而被起诉

◇ **prosecution** n. (a) act of bringing someone to court to answer a charge 起诉；检举；告发：his prosecution for embezzlement 因贪污起诉他 (b) people who have prosecuted someone 原告：The costs of the case will be borne by the prosecution. 此案费用由原告承担。 prosecution counsel or counsel for the prosecution = lawyer acting for the prosecution 原告律师（原告辩护人） NOTE: no plural for (b)

**prospect** n. (a) prospects = possibilities for the future 机会；期望；希望：His job prospects are good. = He is very likely to find a job. 他的就业机会很大。 Prospects for the market or market prospects are worse than those of last year. = Sales in the market are likely to be lower than they were last year. 预期市场销售将低于去年。 (b) possibility that something will happen 可能性；可能：There is no prospect of negotiations coming to an end soon. 谈判不可能很快结束。 (c) person who may become a customer 可能的客户；可能的买主：The salesmen were looking out for possible prospects. 推销员们正在寻找可能的客户

◇ **prospective** a. which may happen in the future 预期的；未来的；可能的：a prospective buyer = someone who may buy in the future 可能的买主；预期客户：There is no shortage of prospective buyers for the computer. 这种计算机不会缺少未来的买主。

◇ **prospectus** n. (a) document which gives information to attract buyers or customers 说明书：The restaurant has girls handing out prospectuses in the street. 饭店请姑娘们在街上散发说明书。 (b) document which gives information about a company whose shares are beingsold to the public for the first time 招股说明书

NOTE: plural is prospectuses

**prosperous** a. rich 富有的；繁荣的；昌盛的：a prosperous shopkeeper 富有的店主；a prosperous town 繁荣的城镇

◇ **prosperity** n. being rich 富裕；繁荣；昌盛：in times of prosperity = when people are rich 繁荣昌盛时期，繁荣期

NOTE: no plural

**protect** v. to defend something against harm 保护；防护：The workers are protected from unfair dismissal by government legislation. 工人们受政府立法保护，以免受不公平的解雇。The computer is protected by a plastic cover. 这台计算机由一个塑料防护罩盖着。The cover is supposed to protect the machine from dust. 这个外壳用来给机器防尘的。to protect an industry by imposing tariff barriers = to stop a local industry from being hit by foreign competition by stopping foreign products from being imported 采取关税壁垒政策来保护工业

◇ **protection** n. thing which protects 保护；保护物：The legislation offers no protection to part - time workers. 立法不保护临时工。consumer protection = protecting consumers against unfair or illegal traders 消费者保护

NOTE: no plural

◇ **protective** a. which protects 保护的；防护的：protective tariff = tariff which tries to ban imports to stop them competing withlocal products 保护关税；protective cover = cover which protects a machine 防护罩；保护套

**pro tem** ad. temporarily or for a time 暂时；目前

**protest** 1. n. (a) statement or action to show that you do not approve of something 反对；抗议：to make a protest against high prices 反对高价；sit - down

protest = action by members of the staff who occupy their place of workand refuse to leave 静坐示威；静坐抗议；in protest at = showing that you do not approve of something 对…抗议：The staff occupied the offices in protest at the low pay offer. 公司职员占据了办公室以抗议工资太低。to do something under protest = to do something, but say that you do not approve of it 不情愿做某事；不服地做某事（b）official document which proves that a bill of exchange hasnot been paid 拒付证书；抗议书 2. v.（a）to protest against something = to say that you do not approve of something 抗议某事；反对某事：The importers are protesting against the ban on luxury goods. 进口商抗议奢侈品进口的禁令。（NOTE: GB English is to protest against something, but US English is to protest something）

（b）to protest a bill = to draw up a document to prove that a bill of exchange has not been paid 开拒付汇票

**prototype** n. first model of a new machine before it goes into production 原型：prototype car or prototype plane 汽车原型；飞机原型：The company is showing the prototype of the new model at the exhibition. 公司在展览会上展示了这种新模型的原型。

**provide** v.（a）to provide for = to allow for something which may happen in the future 预先约定；规定：The contract provides for an annual increase in charges. 合同约定每年都要增加收费。£ 10,000 of expenses have been provided for in the budget. 预算中已经规定了开支费用为 10,000 英磅。（b）to put money aside in accounts to cover expenditure or loss in the future 留出金以作备用：£ 25,000 is provided against bad debts. 留出资金 25,000 英磅以偿付呆帐。（c）to provide someone with something = to supply something to someone

供给；给…提供：Each rep is provided with a company car. 每位推销员都备有一辆公司的汽车。Staff uniforms are provided by the hotel. 职员制服由旅馆提供。

◇ **provided that or providing** conj. on condition that 假如；倘使；如果：The goods will be delivered next week provided or providing the drivers are not on strike. 如果司机们不罢工的话，下星期将可交货。

◇ **provident** a. which provides benefits in case of illness or old age, etc. 福利性的(为老人或疾病)：a provident fund 福利基金；a provident society 福利社会

**province** n. (a) large division of a country 省，州：the provinces of Canada 加拿大各省 (b) the provinces = parts of any country away from the main capital town 外省(首都以外的)：There are fewer retail outlets in the provinces than in the capital. 外省的零售批发商店比首都的少。

◇ **provincial** a. referring to a province or to the provinces 省的：a provincial government 省政府；a provincial branch of a national bank 国家银行的省分行

**provision** n. (a) to make provision for = to see that something is allowed for in the future 预备；防备；准备：There is no provision for or no provision has been made for car parking in the plans for the office block. = The plans do not include space for cars to park. 计划中没有为办公区准备停车场。(b) money put aside in accounts in case it is needed in the future 提供抵充资金：The bank has made a £2m provision for bad debts. 银行提供200万英磅作为坏帐准备。(c) legal condition 条款；规定：We have made provision to this effect = We have put into the contract terms which will make this work. 我们做了这样意思的规定。(d) provisions = food 食物；食品；粮食

◇ **provisional** a. temporary or not final or permanent 临时的；暂时的：provisional forecast of sales 销售暂时预测；provisional budget 临时预算：They telexed their provisional acceptance of the contract. 他们拍出电传表示暂时接受合同。

◇ **provisionally** ad. not finally 临时地；暂时地：The contract has been accepted provisionally. 合同暂时被接受了。

**proviso** n. condition in a contract 条件：We are signing the contract with the proviso that the terms can be discussed again after six months. 我们将签署这个合同，附加条件是六个月后其中的条款将重新讨论。

**proxy** n. (a) document which gives someone the power to act on behalf of someone else 委托书；委任状：to sign by proxy 委托签字；proxy vote = votes made by proxy 委托投票选举；The proxy votes were all in favour of the board's recommendation. 委托选举一致同意董事会的推荐。(b) person who acts on behalf of someone else 代理人；代表人：to act as proxy for someone 做某人的代理人

**P.S.** n. = POST SCRIPTUM additional note at the end of a letter 附笔；再者；又及：Did you read the P.S. at the end of the letter? 你看了信末的附笔没有？

**PSBR** = PUBLIC SECTOR BORROWING REQUIREMENT 公营部门借贷需求

**pt** = PINT 品脱

**ptas** = PESETAS 比塞塔(西班牙货币名称)

**Pty** = PROPRIETARY COMPANY 私人有限公司；不上市有限公司

**public** 1. a. (a) referring to all the people in general 公众的；公共的：public holiday = day when all workers rest and enjoy themselves instead of working 公共例假;公定假日; **public image** = idea which the people have of a company or a person 公众形象; The minister is trying to improve his public image. 部长正在努力提高他自己的公众形象。**public transport** = transport (such as buses, trains) which is used by any memberof the public 公共运输(交通)(b) referring to the government or the state 政府的;国家的: **public expenditure** = spending of money by the local or central government 财政开支;公共开支; **public finance** = the raising of money by governments (by taxes or borrowing)and the spending of it 政府财政(金融); **public funds** = government money available for expenditure 公共基金: **public ownership** = situation where an industry is nationalized 公有制;公有产权 (c) **Public Limited Company** = company whose shares can be bought on the Stock Exchange 大众有限公司;公开上市有限公司; The company is going public. = The company is going to place some of its shares for sale on the stock market so that anyone can buy them. 这家公司的股票即将上市。 2. n. the public or the general public = the people 公众;民众;大众; **in public** = in front of everyone 公开地;当众; In public he said that the company would soon be in profit, but in private he was less optimistic. 他公开场合说公司将很快会赢利,但私下里他对此并非乐观。

NOTE: no plural

◇ **public relations** pl. n. keeping good relations between a company or a group and the public so that people know what the company is doing and can approve of it 公共关系(保持企业或集团与公众之间的良好关系,以使公众了解公司的所为并得到赞同): a public relations man 公关先生; He works in public relations. 他的工作是搞公共关系的。 A public relations firm handles all our publicity. 一家公共关系公司负责处理我们的全部广告宣传工作。a public relations exercise = a campaign to improve public relations 公关运动

◇ **public sector** n. nationalized industries and services 国营经济部分;国营工业和服务业: a report on wage rises in the public sector or on public sector wage settlements 国营经济部门的工资增长报告; **public sector borrowing requirement** = amount of money which a government has to borrow to pay forits own spending 公营部门借款要求

**publication** n. (a) making something public 发表;公布: the publication of the latest trade figures 公布最新贸易数字 (b) printed document which is to be sold or given to the public 出版物;发行物: He asked the library for a list of government publications. 他向图书馆索取政府出版物目录。 The company has six business publications. = The company publishes six magazines or newspapers referring to business. 这个公司发行了六种商业刊物。

NOTE: no plural for (a)

**publicity** n. attracting the attention of the public to products or services by mentioning them in the media 宣传;广告: **publicity agency** or **publicity bureau** = office which organizes publicity for companies who do not have publicity departments 广告公司; **publicity budget** = money allowed for expenditure on publicity 广告预算; **publicity campaign** = period when planned publicity takes place 宣传运动;广告宣传运动; **publicity copy** = text of an advertisement before it is printed 广告宣传底稿; **publicity department** = section of a company which organizes the company's publicity 广告宣传部; **publicity expenditure** = money spent on publicity 广告宣传费用; **publicity manager** = person in charge of a publicity department 广告部经理; publicity matter = sheets or posters or leaflets used for publicity 广告宣传品

NOTE: no plural

◇ **publicize** v. to attract people's attention to a product for sale or a service or an entertainment 做宣传; 做广告: The campaign is intended to publicize the services of the tourist board. 这次宣传运动目的在于为旅游部门的服务做广告。We are trying to publicize our products by advertisements on buses. 我们正试图在公共汽车上做广告来宣传我们的产品。

**publish** v. to have a document (such as a catalogue or book or magazine or newspaper) written and printed and then sell or give it to thepublic 发行; 公布; 出版: The society publishes its list of members annually. 这个协会每年都发行会员册。The government has not published the figures on which its proposals are based. 政府尚未公布作为其建议根据的数据。The company publishes six magazines for the business market. 该公司为商业市场出版六种刊物。

◇ **publisher** n. person or company which publishes 出版商; 发行人; 出版社

**pull off** v. infml. to succeed in negotiating a deal (生意谈判)成功

◇ **pull out** v. to stop being part of a deal or agreement 退出: Our Australian partners pulled out of the contract. 我们澳大利亚合伙人退出了合同

**pump priming** n. government investment in new projects which it hopes will benefit the economy 促进经济发展政府的投资

**punched card** n. card with holes in it which a computer can read and store as information 打孔资料卡(用于计算机认读和储存信息)

**punt** 1. n. money used in the Republic of Ireland 爱尔兰共和国货币 2. v. to gamble or to bet (on something)赌博; 下赌注

◇ **punter** n. person who gambles or who hopes to make money on the Stock Exchange 赌徒; 赌棍

**purchase** 1. n. thing which has been bought 所购物; 进货; 购货: to make a purchase = to buy something 购物; 购买; purchase book = records of purchases 购货帐本; 购货记录; purchase ledger = book in which expenditure is noted 购物分类帐; purchase order = official order made out by a purchasing department for goods which a company wants to buy 购货订单; 订购单; We cannot supply you without a purchase order number. 无购货订单号我们不能供货。purchase price = price paid for something 购进价格; 买价; 进价; purchase tax = tax paid on things which are bought 购买税; bulk purchase or quantity purchase = buying of large quantities of goods at low prices 大宗购买; cash purchase = purchase made in cash 现金购买; hire purchase = system of buying something by paying a sum regularly each month 租购; 分期付款购买: He is buying a refrigerator on hire purchase. 他以分期付款方式购买电冰箱。hire purchase agreement = contract to pay for something by instalments 租购协议; 分期付款协议 2. v. to buy 买; 购买; to purchase something for cash = to pay cash for something 现金购买

◇ **purchaser** n. person or company which purchases 买主; 购买者: The company is looking for a purchaser. = The company is trying to find someone who will buy it. 公司正在寻找买主。The company has found a purchaser for its warehouse. 公司已经找到了愿意购

买其仓库的买主。

◇ **purchasing** n. buying 购买：purchasing department = section of a company which deals with buying of stock, raw materials, equipment, etc. 采购部门；进货部门；购货部门；purchasing manager = head of a purchasing department 购货部经理；purchasing officer = person in a company or organization who is responsible for buying stock, raw materials, equipment, etc.购货员；采购员；purchasing power = quantity of goods which can be bought by a group of people or with an amount of money 购买力；the decline in the purchasing power of the pound 英镑购买力下降；central purchasing = purchasing organized by the main office for all departments or branches 集中购买

NOTE: no plural

**purpose** n. aim or plan 目的；宗旨；计划：We need the invoice for tax purposes or for the purpose of declaration to the tax authorities. = in order for it to be declared to the tax authorities 我们需要发票报税。

**put** 1. n. put option = right to sell shares at a certain price at a certain date 出售选择权 2. v. (a) to place or to fix 标价：The accounts put the stock value at £10,000. = The accounts state that the value of the stock is £10,000.帐目存货的标价为 10,000 英磅。(b)to test something by using the stated means 以某种方式试验某事：to put a proposal to the vote = to ask a meeting to vote for or against the proposal 提议投票表决；to put a proposal to the board = to ask the board to consider a suggestion 向董事会提出建议

NOTE: putting – put

◇ **put down** v. (a) to make a deposit 付定金；付押金：to put down money on a house 支付房屋押金（定金）(b) to write an item in a ledger or an account book 入帐；记在帐上：to put down a figure for expenses 将开支数字入帐

◇ **put in** v. to put an ad in a paper = to have an ad printed in a newspaper 在报上登广告；to put in a bid for something = to offer (usually in writing) to buy something 出价；投标；to put in an estimate for something = to give someone a written calculation of the probable costs of carrying out a job 呈交估算；to put in a claim for damage = to ask an insurance company to pay for damage 要求赔偿损失；The union put in a 6% wage claim. = The union asked for a 6% increase in wages.工会提出工资增加 6% 的要求

◇ **put into** v. to put money into a business = to invest money in a business 对企业投资

◇ **put off** v. to arrange for something to take place later than planned 延期；推迟：The meeting was put off for two weeks. 会议推迟两星期后召开。He asked if we could put the visit off until tomorrow. 他问我是否可以将访问推迟到明天。

◇ **put on** v. to put an item on the agenda = to list an item for discussion at a meeting 列入议事日程；to put an embargo on trade = to forbid trade 禁止通商；Property shares put on gains of 10% – 15%. = Shares in property companies increased in value by 10% – 15%. 房地产股票上扬 10%～15%

◇ **put out** v. to send out 送出去；发放出：to put work out to freelancers 把工作分给自由职业者去做；We put all our typing out to a bureau. 我们把所有打印材料送到打字行去打。to put work out to contract = to decide that work should be done by a company on a contract, rather than employ members of staff to do it 将工作包出去

◇ **put up** v. (a) Who put up the moneyfor the shop? = Who provided the investment money for the shop to start? 谁为商店开业出资? to put something up for sale = to advertise that something is for sale. 做广告推销(出售); When he retired he decided to put his town flat up for sale. 退休后,他决定登广告出售他在城里的公寓。(b) to increase or to make higher 增加;提高: The shop has put up all its prices by 5%. 这个商店将价格全部提高了5%。

# Qq

**quadruplicate** n. in quadruplicate = with the original and three copies 一式四份: The invoices are printed in quadruplicate 这些发票按一式四份打印。
NOTE: no plural

**qualification** n. (a) proof that you have completed a specialized course of study 资格;合格证明: to have the right qualifications for the job 有资格做这项工作; professional qualifications = documents which show that someone has successfully finished a course of study which allows him to work in one of the professions 专业资格证明 (b) period of qualification = time which has to pass before someone qualifies for something 资格获得期

◇ **qualify** v. (a) to qualify for = to be in the right position for or to be entitled to 使合格;使具有资格: The company does not qualify for a government grant. 这家公司没有资格要求政府补助金。She qualifies for unemployment pay. 她有资格领取失业津贴(救济金)。(b) to qualify as = to follow a specialized course and pass examinations so that you can do a certain job 有资格当: she has qualified as an accountant. 她有资格当会计。He will qualify as a solicitor next year. 他明年就有资格当小律师了。(c)

The auditors have qualified the accounts. = The auditors have found something in the accounts of the company which they do not agree with, and have noted it. 审计员们对帐目有保留意见审查。

◇ **qualified** a. (a) having passed special examinations in a subject 有资格的;合格的: She is a qualified accountant. 她是一位合格的会计。We have appointed a qualified designer to supervise the new factory project. 我们任命一位合格的设计师来监督工厂的这项新项目。highly qualified = with very good results in examinations 非常合格的; All our staff are highly qualified. 我们的所有职员都非常合格。They employ twenty – six highly qualified engineers. 他们聘用了26位十分合格的工程师。(b) with some reservations or conditions 有条件的,有限度的: qualified acceptance of a contract 有条件的接受合同; The plan received qualified approval from the board. 董事会有条件地同意了这项计划。(c) qualified accounts = accounts which have been noted by the auditors because they contain something with which the auditors do not agree 有保留意见的帐目

◇ **qualifying** a. (a) qualifying period = time which has to pass before something qualifies for a grant or subsidy, etc. 试用期;资格审定期: There is a six – month qualifying period before you can get a grant from the local authority. 你在得到地方当局的津贴前有6个月的资格审定期。(b) qualifying shares = number of shares which you need to earn to get a bonus issue or to be a director of the company, etc. 附有限制条件的股

票;入围的股票(指需有一定量股票才能得到发 行红股或才能成为公司的董事。)

**quality** n. (a) what something is like or how good or bad something is 质量: good quality or bad quality 优质或劣质; We sell only quality farm produce. = We sell only farm produce of the best quality 我们只销售优质农产品。There is a market for good quality secondhand computers. 出售优质的旧计算机有市场。high quality or top quality = very best quality 优质;高质量; The store specializes in high quality imported items. 这个商店专售优质进口货。(b) quality control = checking that the quality of a product is good 质量管理 NOTE: no plural

**quango** n. official body, set up by a government to investigate or deal with a special problem 专门委员会;特别工作部门(指政府为调查或处理特殊问题的官方机构)

**quantify** v. to quantify the effect of something = to show the effect of something in figures 以数字表示某事的影响(作用): It is impossible to quantify the effect of the new legislation on our turnover. 以数字表示新立法对我们的营业额的影响是不可能的。

◇ **quantifiable** a. which can be quantified 可用数量表示的: The effect of the change in the discount structure is not quantifiable. 贴现率结构的变化结果是不可用数量表示的。

**quantity** n. (a) amount or number of items 数量: a small quantity of illegal drugs 少量违法药品; He bought a large quantity of spare parts. 他买了许多零件。(b) large amount 大量;许多;大宗: The company offers a discount for quantity purchase. 公司对大批购买提供折扣。quantity discount = discount given to a customer who buys large quantities

of goods 大宗交易折扣;数量折扣 (c) to carry out a quantity survey = to estimate the amount of materials and the cost of the labour required for a construction project 数量预测(指对建筑工程所需材料量和劳动成本的估算): quantity surveyor = person who carries out a quantity survey 估算师;估料师;数量鉴定人

**quart** n. old measure of liquids or of loose goods, such as seeds ( = 1. 136 litres)夸脱(计算液体与松散货物如种子的单位, =1.13 升)

**quarter** n. (a) one of four equal parts 四分之一;四等分: a quarter of a litre or a quarter litre = 250 millilitres 四分之一升或 250 毫升; a quarter of an hour = 15 minutes 四分之一小时; three quarters = 75% 四分之三; Three quarters of the staff are less than thirty years old. 四分之三职员不到 30 岁。He paid only a quarter of the list price. 他只付了四分之一价目表的定价。(b) period of three months 季度: first quarter or second quarter or third quarter or fourth quarter or last quarter = periods of three months from January to the end of March or from April to the end of June or from July to the end of September or from October to the end of the year 第一季度;第二季度;第三季度;第四季度;最后一个季度: The instalments are payable at the end of each quarter. 这笔分期付款应在每季度末支付。The first quarter's rent is payable in advance. 第一季度租金应预付。quarter day = day at the end of a quarter, when rents or fees, etc. should be paid 季度付款日 (c) US infml. 25 cent coin(美)二十五美分硬币。

◇ **quarterly** a. & ad. happening every three months or happening four times a year 季度地;按季的: There is a quarterly charge for electricity. 电费按季度收。The bank sends us a quarterly statement. 银行给我们每个季度寄财务报表。We agreed to pay the rent quarterly or on a quarterly basis. 我们同意按季度支付租金。

**quartile** n. one of three figures below which 25％, 50％ or 75％ of a total falls 四分位数

**quasi －** prefix almost or which seems like 类似；准；几乎像；a quasi － official body 准官方机构

**quay** n. place in a harbour where ships tie up 码头；price ex quay ＝ price of goods after they have been unloaded, not including transport from the harbour 码头交货价

**QC** ＝ QUEEN'S COUNSEL 英国王室法律顾问

**query** 1 n. question 问题；疑问：The chief accountant had to answer a mass of queries from the auditors. 总会计师必须回答审计员们提出的众多问题。2 v. to ask a question about something or to suggest that something may be wrong 询问；质问；疑问；The shareholders queried the payments to the chairman's son. 股东们对向董事长之子付款一事表示怀疑。

**question** 1 n. (a) words which need an answer 发问；问题；询问；The managing director refused to answer questions about redundancies. 总经理拒绝回答有关人员精简的问题。The market research team prepared a series of questions to test the public's reactions to colour and price. 市场研究小组为了检测公众对于颜色和价格的反应，准备了一系列的问题。(b) problem 问题：He raised the question of moving to less expensive offices. 他题出要搬到不太贵的办公室这个问题。The main question is that of cost. 主要问题是成本问题。The board discussed the question of redundancy payments. 董事会讨论了裁员补贴的问题。2 v. (a) to ask questions 询问；审问；讯问；The police questioned the accounts staff for four hours. 警察讯问了这位财会人员四个小时。She questioned the chairman on the company's investment policy. 她询问董事长有关公司投资政策问题。(b) to query or to suggest that something may be wrong 疑问；提出异议；We all question how accurate the computer printout is. 我们全体对计算机打印结果的准确性提出异议。

◇ **questionnaire** n. printed list of questions, especially used in market research 调查表；问卷（常用于市场研究）：to send out a questionnaire to test the opinions of users of the system 发出调查表以检查这种系统用户的意见；to answer or to fill in a questionnaire about holidays abroad 填写国外度假调查表

**queue** 1 n. (a) line of people waiting one behind the other 排队；长队；队列：to form a queue or to join a queue 排队；Queues formed at the doors of the bank when the news spread about its possible collapse. 当消息传出这家银行有可能倒闭时，人们在银行门口排起了长队。dole queue ＝ line of people waiting to collect their unemployment money 为领取失业救济金而排的长队 (b) series of documents (such as orders, application forms) which are dealt with in order 一系列票据（如订单，申请表）按顺序处理；His order went to the end of the queue. ＝ His order was dealt with last. 他的订单排在最后。mortgage queue ＝ list of people waiting for mortgages 抵押贷款排序表 2 v. to form a line one after the other for something 排队；站队等候：When food was rationed, people had to queue for bread. 当食物定量配给时，人们只好排队买面包。We queued for hours to get tickets. 我们为买票排了好几个小时的队。a list of companies queueing to be launched on the Stock Exchange 一份排队等待在证券交易所上

市的公司名录

**quick** a. fast or not taking any time 迅速的；快的；急速的：The company made a quick recovery. 公司很快复元。He is looking for a quick return on his investments. 他正在寻找快速回收投资得利的方法。We are hoping for a quick sale. 我们正希望快销。

◇ **quickly** ad. without taking much time 迅速地；快速地：The sale of the company went through quickly. 公司的销售额很快完成了。The accountant quickly looked through the pile of invoices. 会计迅速地审核了这堆发票。

**quiet** a. calm or not excited 平静的；疲软的：The market is very quiet. 市场是疲软的。Currency exchanges were quieter after the government's statement on exchange rates. 货币兑换在政府公布汇率后更疲软了。on the quiet = in secret 秘密地；He transferred his bank account to Switzerland on the quiet. 他把银行存款秘密地转到瑞士。

**quit** v. to resign or to leave (a job) 退出；离去：He quit after an argument with the managing director. 在和总经理发生争论后，他离去(辞职)。Several of the managers are quitting to set up their own company. 几位经理准备辞职开办自己的公司。

NOTE: quitting – quit

**quite** adverb (a) more or less 颇，有几分；相当；多多少少：He is quite a good salesman 他是一个相当不错的推销员。She can type quite fast. 她打字相当快。Sales are quite satisfactory in the first quarter. 第一季度的销售颇令人满意。(b) very or completely 非常；完全地；彻底地：He is quite capable of running the department alone. 他完全能够独立管理这个部门。The company is quite possibly going to be sold. 这个公司完全很有可能被出售。(c) quite a few or quite a lot = many 相当多；许多：Quite a few

of our sales staff are women. 我们相当多的销售人员是妇女。Quite a lot of orders come in the pre – Christmas period. 许多订货是圣诞节前来的。

**quorum** n. number of people who have to be present at a meeting to make it valid 法定人数：to have a quorum = to have enough people present for a meeting to go ahead 具有法定人数；Do we have a quorum? 我们有法定人数吗？

**quota** n. fixed amount of something which is allowed 配额；份额；定额：import quota = fixed quantity of a particular type of goods which the government allows to be imported 进口配额；The government has imposed a quota on the importation of cars. 政府已经定了进口汽车的配额。The quota on imported cars has been lifted. 进口汽车的配额已取消了。quota system = system where imports or supplies are regulated by fixing maximum amounts 配额制；限额进出口制；to arrange distribution through a quota system = to arrange distribution by allowing each distributor only a certain number of items 通过配额制安排销售

**quote** 1 v. (a) to repeat words used by someone else; to repeat a reference number 引述；复述；引用：He quoted figures from the annual report. 他引用年度报告中的数字。In reply please quote this number. 作为答复，请重复这个数字。When making a complaint please quote the batch number printed on the box. 当投诉时，请引用盒子上的批号。He replied, quoting the number of the account. 他回答时引述了这个帐号。(b) to estimate or to say what costs may be 估价；报价：to quote a price for supplying stationery 对文具供货进行报价；Their prices are always quoted in dollars。他们(的价格)总是以美元报价。He quoted me a price of £1,026. 他给我的报价是 1,026 英磅。Can you quote for supplying 20,000 envelopes? 你能否对2万个信封供货报价吗? 2 n. informal estimate of how much something will cost 估价; to give someone a quote for supplying computers 对计算计供货为某人估价; We have asked for quotes for refitting the shop. 我们要求对整修商店估价。His quote was the lowest of three. 他的估价是三者中最低的。We accepted the lowest quote. 我们接受最低估价。

◇ **quotation** n. (a) estimate of how much something will cost 估价; 报价: They sent in their quotation for the job. 他们送来了对这项工作的估价。to ask for quotations for refitting the shop 要求对整修商店做出估价; His quotation was much lower than all the others. 他的报价比其它所有人的都低得多。We accepted the lowest quotation. 我们接受最低报价。(b) quotation on the Stock Exchange or Stock Exchange quotation = listing of the price of a share on the Stock Exchange 股票交易报价; The company is going for a quotation on the Stock Exchange. = The company has applied to the Stock Exchange to have its shares listed. 这公司已经申请让其股票在证券交易所挂牌。We are seeking a stock market quotation. 我们正在寻求证券市场报价。

◇ **quoted** a. quoted company = company whose shares can be bought or sold on the Stock Exchange 上市公司(指公司的股票可在证券市场上进行买卖) quoted shares = shares which can be bought or sold on the Stock Exchange 上市股票;在证券交易所挂牌

**qty = QUANTITY** 数量

**qwerty or QWERTY** n. qwerty keyboard = English language keyboard for a typewriter or computer, where the first letters are Q - W - E - R - T - Y(打字机或计算机上)标准的英文键: The computer has a normal qwerty keyboard. 这台计算机有标准的英文键盘。

# Rr

**R&D** = RESEARCH AND DEVELOPMENT 研究与发展;开发规划: the R&D department 研究与发展部; The company spends millions on R&D. 公司花费数百万元用于研究与发展。

**rack** n. (a) frame to hold items for display 货架;装物架: card rack 卡片架; display rack 展览架; magazine rack 杂志架; rack jobber = wholesaler who sells goods by putting them on racks in retail shops 高价批发商;高价经纪人; (b) rack rent = (i) very high rent 高额租金;与地产年产值相等的租金; (ii) full yearly rent of a property let on a normal lease 按常年地租出租的全年租金

**racket** n. illegal deal which makes a lot of money 非法买卖(生意): He runs a cut - price ticket racket. 他干的是削价票(证)的非法买卖。

◇ **racketeer** n. person who runs a racket 非法买卖者;非法经营者

**raid** n. dawn raid = buying large numbers of shares in a company at the beginning of a day's trading 开盘抢购(开盘时买下某公司的大宗股票): bear raid = selling large numbers of shares to try to bring down prices 卖空浪潮(抛出大宗股票使股价暴跌)

◇ **raider** n. company which buys shares in another company before making a takeover bid 抢购者(公司)(在另一家公司还未做出合并出价前就抢先购买其股票)

**rail** n. railway or system of travel using

trains 铁路: Six million commuters travelto work by rail each day. 每天有 600 万乘客(通勤人员)乘火车上班。We ship all our goods by rail. 我们用火车托运全部货物。Rail travellers are complaining about rising fares. 铁路乘客抱怨车票涨价。Rail travel is cheaper than air travel. 铁路旅行比飞机旅行便宜。free on rail = price including all the seller's costs until the goods are delivered to the railway for shipment 铁路上的交货价

◇ **railhead** n. end of a railway line 铁路终站;铁路线的终点: The goods will be sent to the railhead by lorry. 货物将由货车运送到铁路终点。

◇ **railroad** n. US system using trains to carry passengers and goods 铁路;(美)铁路系统

◇ **railway** n. system using trains to carry passengers and goods 铁路;铁道: a railway station 火车站; a railway line 铁道线; the British railway network 英国铁路网

**raise** 1 n. US increase in salary 长工资;加薪(美): He asked the boss for a raise. 他向老板要求加薪。She is pleased - she has had her raise. 她很高兴——她长工资了。

NOTE: GB English is rise 2 v. (a) to ask a meeting to discuss a question 提出: to raise a question or a point at a meeting 在会上提出问题或提出一个要点; in answer to thequestions raised by Mr Smith 回答由史密斯先生提出的问题; The chairman tried to prevent the question of redundancies being raised. 董事长试图阻止提出精简人员的问题。(b) to raise an invoice = to write out an invoice 开发票 (c) to increase or to make higher 增加;提高: The government has raised the tax levels. 政府提高了税收水准。Air fares will be raised on June 1st. 空运收费将于 6 月 1 日提价。The company

raised its dividend by 10%. 公司提高股息 10%。When the company raised its prices, it lost half of its share of the market. 当公司提高价格时,它失去了 50% 的市场份额。( d ) to obtain ( money ) or to organize ( a loan ) 集资;筹措(款;资金): The company is trying to raise the capital to fund its expansion programme. 公司正在尽力集资以为扩建项目提供资金。The government raises more money by indirect taxation than by direct. 政府间接税收集资比直接税收集资更多。Where will he raise the money from to start up his business? 他将从哪里筹措资金去开办他的企业?

**rake in** v. to gather together 收集: to rake in cash or to rake it in = to make a lot of money 挣到大钱;赚大钱

◇ **rake - off** n. commission 佣金;回扣: The group gets a rake - off on all the company's sales. 这个小组从公司的所有销售中拿回扣。He got a £100,000 rake - off for introducing the new business. 他因介绍了新业务而得到 100,000 英磅的回扣。

NOTE: plural is rake - offs

**rally** 1 n. rise in price when the trend has been downwards 价格止跌;回升: Shares staged a rally on the Stock Exchange. 证券市场的股价有了回升。After a brief rally shares fell back to a new low. 股票经过一次短暂回升后回落到一个新的低点。2 v. to rise in price, when the trend has been downwards 价格止跌;回升: Shares rallied on the news of the latest government figures. 政府最新数字的消息传出后,股价回升了。

**ramp** n. loading ramp = raised platform which makes it easier to load goods onto alorry 装货用的可升起平台

**random** a. done without making any special choice 随意选择的;任意的: random check = check on items taken from a group without any special choice 随意检查；任意抽查；random error = computer error which has no special reason 随机误差；random sample = sample for testing taken without any choice random sampling = choosing samples for testing without any special selection 随机抽取样品；at random = without special choice 随便地；任意地：The chairman picked out two salesmen's reports at random. 董事长随便选出两个销售员的报告。

**range** 1 n. (a) series of items from which the customer can choose 系列；范围：We offer a wide range of sizes or range of styles. 我们提供广泛系列型号和款式。Their rangeof products or product range is too narrow. 他们系列产品范围太窄。We have the mostmodern range of models or model range on the market. 在市场上我们有最现代化模型系列。(b) variation from small to large 变动范围：I am looking for something in the £2 - £3 price range. 我正在寻找价格幅度为 2—3 英磅的东西。We make shoes in a wide range of prices. 我们制鞋的价格幅度很宽。(c) type of variety 种类：This falls within the company's range of activities. 这属于公司多种业务活动之一。2 v. to vary or to be different 变化；不同：The company sells products ranging from the cheap down - market pens to imported luxury items. 公司销售的产品范围从廉价的低档市场上的钢笔到进口的高级奢侈品，应有尽有。The company's salary scale ranges from £5,000 for a trainee to £50,000 for the managing director. 公司工资的等级从学徒工的 5,000 英磅到总经理的 50,000 英磅，级别不等。Our activities range from mining in the USA to computer servicing in Scotland. 我们的业务活动范围涉及到美国的采矿及苏格兰的计算机服务。

**rank** 1 n. position in a company or an organization 等级；地位：All managers are of equal rank. 所有经理的地位同等。in rank order = in order according to position of importance 按地位(级别)顺序 2 v. (a) to classify in order of importance 按…分类：Candidates are ranked in order of appearance. 侯选人按外貌分类(分等级)。(b) to be in a certain position 处于…地位：The non - voting shares rank equally with the voting shares. 无表决权的股票与有投票权的股票地位同等。All managers rank equally. = All managers have the same status in the company. 所有经理的地位同等。

◇ **rank and file** n. ordinary members of a trade union 商会(工会)的普通会员：the rank and file of the trade union membership 工会普通会员；The decision was not liked by the rank and file. 工会普通会员不喜欢这个决定。rank - and - file members = ordinary members 普通成员

◇ **ranking** a. in a certain position 地位的；等级的：high - ranking official 高级官员；He is the top - ranking or the senior - ranking official in the delegation. = The member of the delegation who occupies the highest official post. 他是代表团的首席代表(最高级官员)。

**rapid** a. fast or quick 快的；迅速的；敏捷的：We offer 5% discount for rapid settlement. = We take 5% off the price if the customer pays quickly. 我们提供 5%折扣为了迅速结帐

◇ **rapidly** ad. quickly or fast: The company rapidly ran up debts of over £1m. 公司的债务迅速上升超过 100 万英磅。The new clothes shop rapidly increased sales. 新开张的服装店销售量迅速增加。

**rare** a. not common 少见的；不常有的；罕见的：Experienced salesmen are rare these days. 有经验的销售人员现在不多见。It is rare to find a small business with good cash flow. 很难找到现金流动状况好的小企业。

◇ **rarely** ad. not often 不经常地；罕见地：The company's shares are rarely sold on the Stock Exchange. 这个公司的股票很少上市（证券交易所出售）。The chairman is rarely in his office on Friday afternoons. 周五下午董事长很少在办公室。

**rata** see PRO RATA(按比例的)

**rate** 1 n. (a) money charged for time worked or work completed 费用；收费：all - in rate = price which covers all items in a purchase (such as delivery, tax and insurance, as well as the goods themselves)全部在内的价格；fixed rate = charge which cannot be changed 固定收费；固定价格；flat rate = charge which always stays the same 统一价格；统一收费；a flat - rate increase of 10% 统一价格增加 10%；We pay a flat rate for electricity each quarter. 我们每季度交统一的电费。He is paid a flat rate of £2 per thousand. 按 2‰ 英镑的统一价格给他付款。full rate = full charge, with no reductions 全价；足价；the going rate = the usual or the current rate of payment 现行价；现价；the market rate = normal price in the market 市场价格；We pay the going rate or the market rate for typists. 我们按现价或市场价支付打字员。The going rate for offices is £10 per square foot. 办公室现价为每平方英尺 10 英磅。reduced rate = specially cheap charge 降价；降低的价格 (b) discount rate = percentage taken by a bank when it buys bills 贴现率；折扣率；insurance rates = amount of premium which has to be paid per £1000 of insurance 保险费率；贴水率；interest rate or rate of interest = percentage charge for borrowing money 利率；rate of return = amount of interest or dividend which comes from an investment, shown as a percentage of the

money invested 收益率；回报率（c）bank base rates = basic rate of interest which a bank uses to calculate the actual rate of interest on loans to customers 银行基本利率；cross rate = exchange rate between two currencies expressed in a third currency 交叉汇率；套汇汇率；exchange rate or rate of exchange = rate at which one currency is exchanged for another 汇率；What is today's rate or the current rate for the dollar? 今天的美元的汇率是多少？to calculate costs on a fixed exchange rate = to calculate costs on an exchange rate which does not change 按固定汇率计算成本；forward rate = rate for purchase of foreign currency at a fixed price for delivery at a later date 期货汇率；freight rates = charges for transporting goods 运费率；运价；letter rate or parcel rate = postage (calculated by weight) for sending a letter or a parcel 信件邮资；包裹邮资；It is more expensive to send a packet letter rate but it will get there quicker. 小件邮寄的信件邮资虽贵点儿，但到得快。night rate = cheap telephone calls at night 夜间收费率；夜间电话费（d）amount or number or speed compared with something else 对比数；对比率；快慢增长率：the rate of increase in redundancies 裁员增长数；The rate of absenteeism or the absenteeism rate always increases in fine weather. 好天气时缺勤人数总是增加。birth rate = number of children born per 1,000 of the population 出生率；call rate = number of calls (per day or per week) which a salesman makes on customers 拜访率；或次数；depreciation rate = rate at which an asset is depreciated each year in the company accounts 折旧率；error rate = number of mistakes per thousand entries or per page 误差率；rate of sales = speed at which units are sold 销售率；销售速度（e）GB local taxes on property(英)地

方财产税;地方房地产税: The local authority has fixed or has set the rate for next year. 地方当局已经规定了明年的房地产税。Our rates have gone up by 25% this year. 今年我们的地方财产税增长了25%。2 v. (a) to rate someone highly = to value someone or to think someone is very good 对某人评价很高;高度评价某人 (b) highly – rated part of London = part of London with high local taxes 伦敦高税区

◇ **rateable** a. rateable value = value of a property as a basis for calculating local taxes 征税价值;估税价值

◇ **ratepayer** n. domestic ratepayer = person who pays local taxes on a house or flat 地方房地产税纳税人; business ratepayer = business which pays local taxes on a shop or factory, etc. 企业纳税人

**ratify** v. to approve officially 正式批准;正式认可: The agreement has to be ratified by the board. 这个协定必须经过董事会的正式批准。

◇ **ratification** n. official approval 正式批准;正式认可: The agreement has to go to the board for ratification. 这个协定必须经董事会的正式批准。

**rating** n. (a) valuing of property 财产估价;财产评估: rating officer = official in a local authority who decides the rateable value of a house 估价员 (b) credit rating = amount which a credit agency feels a customer will be able to repay 信誉评估;信用程度; merit rating = judging how well a worker does his work, so that he can be paid according to merit 人事考核;工作评定; performance rating = judging how well a share or a company has performed 业绩评定;成绩评定 (c) ratings = estimated number of people who watch TV programmes 收视率; The show is high in the ratings, which means it will attract good publicity. 演出收视率很高,这就是说吸引了很多观众。

**ratio** n. proportion or quantity of something compared to something else 比率;比例;比: the ratio of successes to failures 成功与失败之比例; Our product outsells theirs by a ratio of two to one. 我们的产品比他们的畅销,销售量为他们的二倍。price/earnings ratio ( P/E ratio) = comparison between the market price of a share and the current dividend it produces 价格收益比率; The shares sell at a P/E ratio of 7. 这些股票以7的价格收益比率售出。

**ration** v. to allow someone only a certain amount (of food or money) 定量;限额;分配: to ration investment capital or to ration funds for investment 定额分配投资资本;限定投资资金; to ration mortgages = to make only a certain amount of money available for house mortgages, and so restrict the number of mortgages which can be given 定额抵押;抵押限额; Mortgages are rationed for first – time buyers. 抵押只限给初次购买者。

◇ **rationing** n. allowing only a certain amount of something to be sold 限额配给;定量分配: There may be a period of food rationing this winter. 今年冬天可能定量配给食物。Building societies are warning of mortgage rationing. 住宅互助协会警告说要限额分配抵押借款。
NOTE: no plural

**rationale** n. set of reasons for doing something 根据;原因;理由: I do not understand the rationale behind the decision to sell the warehouse. 我不明白在出售仓库的决定后面有什么原由。

**rationalization** n. streamlining or making more efficient 合理化

◇ **rationalize** v. to streamline or to make more efficient 使合理;使合理化: The rail company is trying to rationalize its freight services. 铁路运输公司正在努力使其货运服务合理化。

**rat race** n. competition for success in business or in a career 商业竞争；职业竞争；事业上竞争： He decided to get out of the rat race and buy a small farm. 他决定退出商业竞争而去买一个小农场。 NOTE: no plural

**raw** a. in the original state or not processed 未加工的；自然的；原始的： raw data = data as it is put into a computer, without being analyzed 原始数据； raw materials = substances which have not been manufactured ( such as wool, wood, sand)原料；原材料

**re** prep. about or concerning or referring to 关于： re your inquiry of May 29th 关于你在 5 月 29 日的询价； re: Smith's memo of yesterday 关于：史密斯先生昨天的备忘录； re: the agenda for the AGM 关于：年度股东大会的议事日程

**re -** prefix again 又；再；重新

**reach** v. (a) to arrive at a place or at a point 到达；抵达；达到： The plane reaches Hong Kong at midday. 飞机中午到达香港。 Sales reached £1m in the first four months of the year. 今年前 4 个月的销售额达到 100 万英磅。 I did not reply because your letter never reached me. 我没有复信，因为你的信从未到我手里。 (b) to come to 得到…结果： to reach an agreement = to agree 达成协议； to reach an accommodation with creditors = to agree terms for a settlement with creditors 与债权人达成和解； to reach a decision = to decide 做出决定(决策)； The two parties reached an agreement over the terms for the contract. 双方对此合同中的条款达成一致意见。 The board reached a decision about closing the factory. 董事会做出关闭工厂的决定。

**react** v. to react to = to do or to say something in reply to what someone has done or said 对…反应： Shares reacted sharply to the fall in the exchange rate. 股票对汇率的下降反应十分敏感。 How will the chairman react when we tell him the news? 当我们告诉董事长这个消息时，他反应如何？

◇ **reaction** n. change or action in reply to something said or done 反应： the reaction of the shares to the news of the takeover bid 股票对兼并出价的消息反应

**read** v. to look at printed words and understand them 阅读；读懂；读： The terms and conditions are printed in very small letters so that they are difficult to read. 条款与条件是用很小的字体印刷的，以致难以阅读。 Has the managing director read your report on sales in India? 总经理看了我们有关印度销售的报告吗？ Can the computer read this information? = Can the computer take in this information and understand it or analyze it? 计算机能够认读这个信息吗？

◇ **readable** a. which can be read 可读的；可看懂的： machine - readable codes = sets of signs or letters (such as bar codes, post codes) which can be read and understood by a computer 机器认读码； The data has to be presented in computer - readable form. = in a form which a computer can read 这个数据必须用计算机可认读的形式呈现。

**readjust** v. to adjust again 再调整；重新调整： to readjust prices to take account of the rise in the costs of raw materials 考虑到原料成本的涨价要重新调整价格； Shares prices readjusted quickly to the news of the devaluation. 货币贬值的消息一传出，股票价格就迅速重新调整了。

◇ **readjustment** n. act of readjusting 重新调整： a readjustment in pricing 重新调整定价； After the devaluation there

was a period of readjustment in the ex-
changerates. 货币贬值后,是重新调整
汇率的周期。

**readvertise** v. to advertise again 再次
做广告;又做广告: to readvertise a post
= to put in a second advertisement for a
vacant post 再做招聘广告; All the candidates failed the test, so we will just
have to readvertise. 所有侯选人都未通
过考试,所以我们不得不再次做广告。
◇ **readvertisement** n. second advertisement for a vacant post 再次作招聘广
告

**ready** a. (a) fit to be used or to be sold
准备好的;现成的;现货的: The order
will be ready for delivery next week. 这
批货将于下周备好待发。The driver
had to wait because the shipment was not
ready. 因为装运未完,司机只好等侯。
make – ready time = time to get a machine ready to start production 准备时间
(b) ready cash = money which is immediately available for payment 现金;现
款;现钞: These items find a ready sale
in the Middle East. = These items sell
rapidly or easily in the Middle East. 这些
东西在中东很畅销。
◇ **ready – made or ready – to –
wear** a. (clothes) which are mass –
produced, not made for each customer
personally 现成的;成衣的: The ready
– to – wear trade has suffered from foreign competition. 成衣贸易因国外竞争
而蒙受损害。

**real** a. (a) true or not an imitation 真
的;真实的;实在的: His case is made of
real leather or he has a real leather case.
他的皮箱是真皮制的。That car is a real
bargain at ￡300. 那辆汽车 300 英磅,
真便宜。real income or real wages = income which is available for spending after
tax, etc. has been deducted 实际收入;
实际工资; in real terms = actually or
really 实际上; Prices have gone up by

3% but with inflation running at 5%
that is a fall in real terms. 价格上扬
3%,但由于通货膨胀率为5%,所以实
际上还是下降了。(b) real time = time
when a computer is working on the processing of data while the problem to
which the data refers is actually taking
place 实时: real – time system = computer system where data is inputted directly into the computer which automatically processes it to produce information
which can be used immediately 实时系统
(这是一种计算机系统,即将数据直接
输入计算机并进行自动处理以产生可
立即使用的信息) (c) real estate =
property (land or buildings) 不动产;房
地产: He made his money from real estate deals in the 1970s. 他七十年代做房
地产生意发了财。US real estate agent
= person who sells property for cus-
tomers(美)房地产经纪人;房地产代理
人
◇ **really** ad. in fact 实际地;事实上:
The company is really making an acceptable profit. 这个公司实际上盈利可被
人接受的。The office building really belongs to the chairman's father. 这座办公
大楼实际上属于董事长父亲的。The
shop is really a general store, though it
does carry some books. 这个商店实际上
是个百货店,虽然它的确出售些书籍。
◇ **realtor** n. US estate agent or person
who sells real estate for customers(美)房
地产经纪人;房地产代理商
◇ **realty** n. property or real estate 财
产;不动产;房地产

**realize** v. (a) to understand clearly 明
白;认清;认识到: He soon realized the
meeting was going to vote against his
proposal. 他很快就明白了这次会议将
投票反对他的提议。The small shop-
keepers realized that the hypermarket
would take away some of their trade. 这
些小店主们很清楚那个超级市场将会

抢走他们的部分生意。When she went intothe manager's office she did not realize she was going to be promoted. 当她走进经理办公室时, 她不明白她将得到提升。(b) to make something become real 实现: to realize a project or a plan = to put a project or a plan into action 实施计划 (c) to sell for money 变卖; 净得; 赚得: to realize property or assets 变卖财产 (资产); The sale realized £100,000. 这次销售净得了 100,000 英磅。

◇ **realizable** a. realizable assets = assets which can be sold for money 可变卖的资产

◇ **realization** n. (a) gradual understanding 察觉; 意识: The chairman's realization that he was going to be outvoted. 董事长意识到他的得票将被别人超过 (b) making real 实现; 成功现实: the realization of a project = putting a project into action 项目的实施; The plan moved a stage nearer realization when the contracts were signed. 合同签订后, 就向实现这项计划迈近了一步。(c) realization of assets = selling of assets for money 变卖资产

**reapply** v. to apply again 再申请: When he saw that the job had still not been filled, he reapplied for it. 当他发现这个职位依然空缺, 他再次提出申请。

◇ **reapplication** n. second application 再申请; 再运用

**reappoint** v. to appoint someone again 再任命; 再委派; 再指定: He was reappointed chairman for a further three-year period. 他被再次任命的董事长任期为三年。

◇ **reappointment** n. being reappointed 再任命; 再委派; 再指定

**reason** n. thing which explains why something has happened 原因; 理由: The airline gave no reason for the plane's late arrival. 航空公司对于飞机的晚点

没有说明任何原因。The personnel officer asked him for the reason why he was late again. 负责人事的官员要求他说明再次迟到的原因。The chairman was asked for his reasons for closing the factory. 要求董事长解释关闭工厂的原因。

◇ **reasonable** a. (a) sensible or not annoyed 合理的; 通情达理的; 合情合理的: The manager of the shop was very reasonable when she tried to explain that she had left her credit cards at home. 当她试图说明她把信用卡留在家里时, 商店经理很通情达理。No reasonable offer refused. = We will accept any offer which is not extremely low. 不合理的报价才被拒绝 (b) moderate or not expensive. 公道的; 不贵的: The restaurant offers good food at reasonable prices. 这家饭店的饭菜好, 价格也很公道。

**reassess** v. to assess again 再估价; 再确定

◇ **reassessment** n. new assessment 再分派; 再确定

**reassign** v. to assign again 再分派; 再委派; 再指定

◇ **reassignment** n. new assignment 再分派; 再委派; 再指定

**reassure** v. (a) to make someone calm or less worried 使安心; 使放心; 使消除疑虑: The markets were reassured by the government statement on import controls. 由于政府对进口控制的声明, 市场重新恢复了稳定。The manager tried to reassure her that she would not lose her job. 经理试图使她解除疑虑, 她是不会失去工作。(b) to reinsure or to spread the risk of an insurance by asking another insurance company to cover part of it and receive part of the premium 再保险 (请求另一家保险公司保险一部分并获得保险金)

◇ **reassurance** n. making someone

calm 使放心；使安心；再保险
NOTE: no plural

**rebate** n. (a) reduction in the amount of money to be paid 折扣；回扣；折让：to offer a 10％ rebate on selected goods 对精选品提供 10％ 的回扣 (b) money returned to someone because he has paid too much 退款：He got a tax rebate at the end of the year. 他在年底得到了一笔退回的税款。

**rebound** v. to go back up again quickly 迅速返回；弹回；反弹；振作起来：The market rebounded on the news of the government's decision. 当政府所做的决定消息传开，市场迅速反弹。

**recd** = RECEIVED 收讫，收到

**receipt** 1 n. (a) paper showing that money has been paid or that something has been received 收据：customs receipt 海关收据；rent receipt 租金收据；receipt for items purchased 购物收据；Please produce your receipt if you want to exchange items. 如果你想换货，请拿出收据。receipt book or book of receipts = book of blank receipts to be filled in when purchases are made 收据薄 (b) act of receiving something 收到：to acknowledge receipt of a letter = to write to say that you have received a letter 表示(承认)收到一封信；We acknowledge receipt of your letter of the 15th. 我们收到您 15 日的来信。Goods will be supplied within thirty days of receipt of order. 收到定单后 30 天之内交货。Invoices are payable within thirty days of receipt. 在收到发票后 30 天内付款。On receipt of the notification, the company lodged an appeal. 公司一接到通知就提出上诉。(c) receipts = money taken in sales to itemize receipts and expenditure 详细列明收入与支出；收入与支出分类：Receipts are down against the same period of last year. 收入低于去年同一时期。

NOTE: no pl. for (b) 2 v. to stamp or to sign a document to show that it has beenreceived or to stamp an invoice to show that it has been paid 收讫；付讫 (在票据上注明)

**receive** v. to get something which has been delivered 收到；接到：We received the payment ten days ago. 十天前我们收到了支付款项。The workers have not received any salary for six months. 工人们已经 6 个月未领到工资了。The goods were received in good condition. 货物收到时完好无损。"Received with thanks" = words put on an invoice to show that a sum has been paid "谢谢付讫""谢谢收讫"

◇ **receivable** a. which can be received 应收的；可收的：accounts receivable = money owed to a company 应收帐款；bills receivable = bills which a creditor will receive 应收票据

◇ **receivables** pl. n. money which is owed to a company 应收款项；应收帐款

◇ **receiver** n. (a) person who receives something 收件人；收受者：the receiver of the shipment 收货人 (b) official receiver = government official who is appointed to run a company which is in financial difficulties, to pay off its debts as far as possible, and to close it down 官方破产事务官(受政府指派管理陷入经济困境的公司，并清算其债务，或令其关闭的官员)：The court appointed a receiver for the company. 法院向那个公司派去一位破产事务官。The company is in the hands of the receiver. 公司的命运掌握在这位破产事务官手中。

◇ **receivership** n. The company went into receivership. = The company was put into the hands of a receiver. 这个公司由破产事务官的接管。

◇ **receiving** n. (a) act of getting something which has been delivered 接收；收受：receiving clerk = official who works in a receiving office 收料员；receivingdepartment = section of a company which deals with incoming goods or payments 收货（料）部；receiving office = office where goods or payments are received 收货处；收款处（b）receiving order = order from a court appointing a receiver to a company 接受命令（法院发出的派往公司破产事务官的命令）

NOTE: no plural

**recent** a. which happened not very long ago 不久前的；新近的；最近的：the company's recent acquisition of a chain of shoe shops 公司最近收购的连锁鞋店；his recent appointment to the board 他成为董事会成员的最新任命；We will mail you our most recent catalogue. 我们将寄给你我们的最新目录。

◇ **recently** ad. not very long ago 最近地；最新地；近来：The company recently started on an expansion programme. 这个公司最近开始了一项扩建计划。They recently decided to close the branch office in Australia. 他们最近决定关闭澳大利亚分公司。

**reception** n. place (in a hotel or office) where visitors register or say who they have come to see 接待处；注册处：reception clerk = person who works at the reception desk 接待员；招待员；reception desk = desk where customers or visitors check in 注册处；报到处；登记处

◇ **receptionist** n. person in a hotel or office who meets guests or clients, answers the phone, etc. 接待员；招待员

**recession** n. fall in trade or in the economy 不景气；经济衰退：The recession has reduced profits in many companies. 经济衰退降低了许多公司的利润。Several firms have closed factories because of the recession. 由于经济衰退，好几家企业都关闭了他们的工厂。

**recipient** n. person who receives 接收者；收受者：the recipient of an allowance from the company 从公司领取津贴者

**reciprocal** a. applying from one country or person or company to another and vice versa 相互的；互惠的：reciprocal agreement 互惠协定；互惠待遇；reciprocal contract 互惠合同；reciprocal holdings = situation where two companies own shares in each other to prevent takeover bids 相互持控股；reciprocal trade = trade between two countries 互惠贸易

◇ **reciprocate** v. to do the same thing to someone as he has just done to you 回报；酬答：They offered us an exclusive agency for their cars and we reciprocated with an offer of the agency for our buses. 他们向我们主动提供独家代理经营他们的汽车，做为回报我们也请他们代理经营我们的客车。

**reckon** v. (a) to calculate 计算；算帐；结算：to reckon the costs at £25,000 计算成本为 25,000 英磅；We reckon the loss to be over £1m. 我们估计损失超过 100 英磅。They reckon the insurance costs to be too high. 他们计算保险费用太高。(b) to reckon on = to depend on or to expect something to happen 依赖；期望：They reckon on being awarded the contract. 他们期待被授予合同。He can reckon on the support of the managing director. 他能够依赖总经理的支持。

**recognize** v. (a) to know someone or something because you have seen or heard them before 认出；确认；辨认：I recognized his voice before he said who he was. 在他告诉我他是谁之前，我就辨认出他的声音了。Do you recognize the handwriting on the letter? 你认出信上的笔迹了吗？(b) to recognize a union = to accept that a union can act on behalf of staff 承认工会：Although all the staff had joined the union, the manage-

ment refused to recognize it. 虽然全体职工都参加了工会, 但资方拒绝承认。
recognized agent = agent who is approved by the company for which he acts 认可代理人;认可代理商;认可经纪人

◇ **recognition** n. act of recognizing 承认;认可;确定: to grant a trade union recognition = to recognize a trade union 对工会给予承认

**recommend** v. (a) to suggest that something should be done 建议;提议: The investment adviser recommended buying shares in aircraft companies. 投资顾问建议购买航空公司的股票。We do not recommend bank shares as a safe investment. 我们不会建议银行股票作为安全投资。manufacturer's recommended price (MRP) or recommended retail price (RRP) = price which a manufacturer suggests the product should be sold at on the retail market, though often reduced by the retailer 制造商提议价格;制造商提议的零售价; "all typewriters - 20% off MRP""所有打字机低于厂商提议价格的 20% (b) to say that someone or something is good 推荐;举荐;介绍: He recommended a shop in the High Street for shoes. 他推荐去大马路的一家商店买鞋。I certainly would not recommend Miss Smith for the job. 我当然不会推荐史密斯小姐来做这个工作。The board meeting recommended a dividend of 10p a share. 董事会会上推荐股息数每股 10 便士。Can you recommend a good hotel in Amsterdam? 你能推荐一家阿姆斯特丹的好旅馆吗?

◇ **recommendation** n. saying that someone or something is good 推荐;介绍: We appointed him on the recommendation of his former employer. 我们是根据他前雇主介绍委派他的。

**reconcile** v. to make two accounts or statements agree 对帐;使一致;调整;to reconcile one account with another 核对帐目;对帐帐; to reconcile the accounts 调整帐目

◇ **reconciliation** n. making two accounts or statements agree 对帐;使一致;调整: reconciliation statement = statement which explains why two accounts do not agree 对帐报表;对帐表

**reconstruction** n. building again 重建;再建: the economic reconstruction of an area after a disaster 灾难后的对一地区的经济重建

**record** 1 n. (a) report of something which has happened 记录;记载: The chairman signed the minutes as a true record of the last meeting. 董事长在会议记录上签了字作为上次会议的一个真实记载。for the record or to keep the record straight = to note something which has been done 作为记载;留有记录: For the record, I would like these sales figures to be noted in the minutes. 作为记载,我要把这些销售数字记在会议记录里。on record = correctly reported 记录在案;有案可查: The chairman is on record as saying that profits are set to rise. 董事长说的利润开始上升这句话已经记录在案。off the record = unofficially or in private 非正式地;私下地: He made some remarks off the record about the disastrous home sales figures. 他私下里谈到过国内销售损失的数字。(b) records = documents which give information 案卷;档案: The names of customers are kept in the company's records. 客户的姓名都在公司存档。We find from our records that our invoice number 1234 has not been paid. 我们从档案中发现其中一张 1234 号发票没有付讫。(c) description of what has happened in the past 经历;履历: the salesman's record of service or service record 这个推销员的工作履历;the company's record in industrial relations 公司的劳资关系的状况;track record = success or failure of a company or salesman in the past 业绩履历；工作经历：He has a good track record as a salesman. 作为推销员，他有很好的工作履历。The company has no track record in the computer market. 这家公司没有在计算机市场上经营的经历。(d) success which is better than anything before 最高纪录；最佳业绩：record sales or record losses or record profits = sales or losses or profits which are higher than ever before 最高销售；最大损失；最大利润：1985 was a record year for the company. 1985 年是公司的最佳年度。Sales for 1983 equalled the record of 1980. 1983 年的销售与 1980 年的最高记录持平。Our top salesman has set a new record for sales per call. 我们的尖子推销员每次出访中都刷新销售记录。We broke our record for June. = We sold more than we have ever sold before in June. 我们六月份的销售打破了记录。2 v. to note or to report 记录；报告：The company has recorded another year of increased sales. 公司记录下又一个销售增加年。Your complaint has been recorded and will be investigated. 你的投诉已记录下来，并将得到调查。recorded delivery = mail service where the letters are signed for by the person receiving them 回执邮递

◇ **record – breaking** a. which is better than anything which has happened before 破记录的：We are proud of our record – breaking profits in 1984. 我们为 1984 年的破记录的利润而感到骄傲。

◇ **recording** n. making of a note 记录：the recording of an order or of a complaint 订货记录；投诉记录

**recoup** v. to recoup one's losses = to get back money which you thought you had lost 补偿损失；偿还损失

**recourse** n. to decide to have recourse to the courts = to decide in the end to sue someone 决定诉诸法律

**recover** v. (a) to get back something which has been lost 恢复；取回；找回：He never recovered his money. 他根本没有取回那笔钱。The initial investment was never recovered. 初期投资根本未收回。to recover damages from the driver of the car 由汽车司机赔偿损失；to start a court action to recover property 提出法律诉讼追回财产 (b) to get better or to rise 恢复；涨价；上升：The market has not recovered from the rise in oil prices. 市场还未从石油价格上涨中恢复过来。The stock market fell in the morning, but recovered during the afternoon. 股票市场上午下跌了，而下午回升了。

◇ **recoverable** a. which can be got back 可收回的；可补偿的

◇ **recovery** n. (a) getting back something which has been lost 取回；收回；复原：We are aiming for the complete recovery of the money invested. 我们的目的在于重新收回全部投资的款项。to start an action for recovery of property 提出起诉要求收回财产产权 (b) movement upwards of shares or of the economy 回升；复苏(股票或经济方面)：The economy staged a recovery. 经济处于回升期。the recovery of the economy after a slump 不景气后的经济复苏；recovery shares = shares which are likely to go up in value because the company's performance is improving 回升的股票；上扬的股票

**recruit** v. to recruit new staff = to get new staff to join a company 招收新职员：We are recruiting staff for our new store. 我们正在为新商店招收职员。

◇ **recruitment or recruiting** n. the recruitment of new staff = looking for new staff to join a company 招收新职员

**rectify** v. to correct something or to

make something right 纠正；校正：to rectifyan entry 校正入帐

◇ **rectification** n. correction 校正；改正

**recurrent** n. which happens again and again 再发的；复发的；周期性发作的：a recurrent item of expenditure 一项经常性支出(费用)

**recycle** v. to take waste material and process it so that it can be used again 回收应用；回收利用(指废料加工再用)：recycled paper = paper made from waste paper 再生纸

**red** n. in the red = showing a debit or loss 赤字；负债亏损：My bank account is in the red. 我的银行存款已出现赤字。The company went into the red in 1984. 这家公司 1984 年出现亏损。The company is out of the red for the first time since 1950. 这个公司自 1950 年以来第一次不再亏损。
NOTE: no plural

◇ **red tape** n. official paperwork which takes a long time to complete 官样文章；文牍主义；繁文缛节：The Australian joint venture has been held up by government red tape. 澳大利亚的合资企业由于政府的繁文缛节而被耽搁。
NOTE; no plural

**redeem** v. (a) to pay off a loan or a debt 还清；赎回：To redeem a mortgage 赎回抵押品；to redeem a debt 还清债务 (b) to redeem a bond = to sell a bond for cash 兑换债券；

◇ **redeemable** a. which can be sold for cash 可兑换成现金的

**redemption** n. (a) repayment of a loan 偿还；赎回：redemption date = date on which a loan, etc., is due to be repaid 偿还日期；付还日期；赎回日期；redemption before due date = paying back a loan before the date when repayment is due 到期前偿还；满期前赎回；redemption value = value of a security when re-deemed 偿还价值；赎回价值；redemption yield = yield on a security including interest and its redemption value 赎还收益率 (b) repayment of a debt 偿还债务；redemption of a mortgage 赎回抵押品；偿还抵押债务
NOTE: no plural

**redeploy** v. to move workers from one place to another or to give workers totally different jobs to do 重新布置；调配；重新调整：We closed the design department and redeployed the workforce in the publicity and sales departments. 我们关闭了设计部门并重新布置了广告宣传部和销售部的劳动力。

◇ **redeployment** n. moving workers from one place to another 重新布置；调配；重新调整

**redevelop** v. to knock down the buildings on a site, and build new ones 重建(房屋)

◇ **redevelopment** n. knocking down of existing buildings to replace them with new ones 重建：The redevelopment plan was rejected by the planning committee. 重建计划被计划委员会否决了。

**redistribute** v. to move items or work or money to different areas or people 再分配；重新分配；The government aims to redistribute wealth by taxing the rich and giving grants to the poor. 政府通过向有钱人征税来补助穷人的办法达到重新分配财富的目的。The orders have been redistributed among the company's factories. 这些订货(单)已在公司的诸多工厂间重新分配了了。

◇ **redistribution** n. redistribution of wealth = sharing wealth among the whole population 重新分配财富；分享财富

**redraft** v. to draft again 重新起草；再起草：The whole contract had to be redrafted to take in the objections from the chairman. 为了接受董事长的异议，整

个合同都必须重新起草。

**reduce** v. to make smaller or lower 减少；降低: to reduce expenditure 减少支出；降低费用；to reduce a price 降价；to reduce taxes 减税；We have made some staff redundant to reduce overmanning. 为了削减过多的人员，我们精减了一些职员。Prices have been reduced by 15％. 价格已降低15％。Carpets are reduced from £100 to £50. 地毯的价格由 100 英磅降到 50 英磅。The company reduced output because of a fall in demand. 由于需求量下降，公司削减了产量。The government's policy is to reduce inflation to 5％. 政府的政策是将通货膨帐降低到 5％。to reduce staff = to sack employees in order to have a smaller number of staff 裁减雇员

◇ **reduced** a. lower 降低的: Reduced prices have increased unit sales. 降价增加了单位销售额。Prices have fallen due to a reduced demand for the goods. 价格由于货物需求量的减少而降低了。

**reduction** n. lowering (of prices, etc.) 降低: price reductions 降价；tax reductions 减税；staff reductions 削减开支；reduction of expenditure 削减开支；reduction in demand 需求减少；销路减少；The company was forced to make job reductions. 公司被迫减少就业机会。

**redundancy** n. (a) being no longer employed, because the job is no longer necessary 解雇；裁员: redundancy payment = payment made to a worker to compensate for losing his job 裁员补贴；精减人员补助费；voluntary redundancy = situation where the worker asks to be made redundant, usually in return for a large payment 自愿退职 (b) person who has lost a job because he is not needed any more 被裁减人员；多余的人: The takeover caused 250 redundancies. 接管移交造成 250 人的裁员。

◇ **redundant** a. (a) more than is needed or useless 多余的；过多的；丰富的: redundant capital 充足的资金；redundant clause in a contract 合同中多余的款项；The new legislation has made clause 6 redundant. 新立法使第六条款为多余的。(b) to make someone redundant = to decide that a worker is not needed any more 裁减某人；将某人解聘: redundant staff = staff who have lost their jobs because they are not needed any more 多余的职员；被裁减的人员

**re - elect** v. to elect again 重选；再选: He was re - elected chairman. 他再次当选主席。

◇ **re - election** n. being elected again 重新选举；再选: She is eligible to stand for re - election. = It is possible for her to be re - elected if she wants. 她是有资格再次被当选。

**re - employ** v. to employ someone again 再次雇用

◇ **re - employment** n. employing someone again 再度雇用

**re - engage** v. to re - engage staff = to employ staff again 再次雇用

**re - entry** n. coming back in again 再进入；重新入场: re - entry visa or permit = visa which allows someone to leave a country and go back in again 重返签证；重返许可证

**re - examine** v. to examine something again 再检查；再审查；再调查

◇ **re - examination** n. examining something which has already been examined before 再检查；再审查；再调查

**re - export** 1 n. exporting of goods which have been imported(进口货物的) 再出口；转口: re - export trade 转口贸易；We import wool for re - export. 我们进口羊毛是为了再出口。The value of re - exports has increased. 转口额增加了。2 v. to export something which has been imported 再出口；转口

◇ **re – exportation** n. exporting goodswhich have been imported 再出口；再输出

**ref** = REFERENCE 证明人；介绍信；介绍人；参考；查询

**refer** v. (a) to mention or to deal with or to write about something 提到；涉及；有关: We refer to your estimate of May 26th. 我们提到您 5 月 26 日的估价。He referred to an article which he had seen in "The Times". 他提起他曾在"泰晤士报"上看见过的一篇文章。referring to your letter of June 4th 关于您 6 月 4 日的来函 (b) to pass a problem on to someone else to decide 提交；呈交: to refer a question to a committee 把问题提交给委员会; We have referred your complaint to our supplier. 我们已将您的投诉送交给我们的供货人。(c) The bank referred the cheque to drawer. = The bank returned the cheque to person who wrote it because there was not enough money in the account to pay it. 银行将支票退给开票人。"refer to drawer" = words written on a cheque which a bank refuses to pay"退出票人"; NOTE: referring – referred

◇ **referee** n. person who can give a report on someone's character or ability or speed of work, etc. 介绍人；证明人；推荐人: to give someone's name as referee 说出介绍人的姓名; She gave the name of her boss as a referee. 她说出她老板的姓名，作为她的介绍人。When applying please give the names of three referees. 申请时请写出三个证明人的姓名。

◇ **reference** n. (a) terms of reference = areas which a committee or an inspector can deal with 受权范围: Under the terms of reference of the committee, it cannot investigate complaints from the public. 在委员会授权范围之内，它无法调查公众的投诉。The committee's terms of reference do not cover exports. 委员会的授权范围不包括出口事宜。(b) mentioning or dealing with 提及；关于: with reference to your letter of May 25th 关于你的 5 月 25 日的亚函 (c) numbers or letters which make it possible to find a document which has been filed 参与书目；参照；出处: Our reference: PC/MS 1234. 我们的参考书目为：PC/MS1234。Thank you for your letter (reference 1234). 感谢你的来信(参见：1234)。Please quote this reference in all correspondence. 请在所有通信中将此引文出处用括号括起来。When replying please quote reference 1234. 复信时，请将引文出处书为 1234 用括号括上。(d) written report on someone's character or ability, etc. 介绍信；证明书；证明信: to write someone a reference or to give someone a reference 给某人开介绍信; to ask applicants to supply references to ask a company for trade references or for bank references = to ask for reports from traders or a bank on the company's financial status and reputation 要求公司提供商业信誉证明材料及银行担保证书; letter of reference = letter in which an employer or former employer recommends someone for a job 介绍信；证明信；推荐信: He enclosed letters of reference from his two previous employers. 他附上了他的两位前雇主的推荐信。(e) person who reports on someone's character or ability, etc 介绍人；证明人: to give someone's name as reference 说出介绍人的姓名; Please use me as a reference if you wish. 如果你愿意，请让我做你的介绍人。

**refinancing** n. refinancing of a loan = floating a new loan to pay back a previous loan 重新筹措一笔贷款；再融资

**refit** v. to fit out (a shop or factory or office) again 整修；重新装配(商店，工厂或办公室)
NOTE: refitting – refitted

◇ **refitting** n. fitting out (of a shop or factory or office) again 重新装修;重新装配

**reflate** v. to reflate the economy = to stimulate the economy by increasing the money supply or by reducing taxes, leading to increased inflation(增加钱币供应或减少税收)使通货再膨胀来刺激经济: The government's attempts to reflate the economy were not successful. 政府使通货再膨胀来刺激经济的偿试失败了。

◇ **reflation** n. act of stimulating the economy by increasing the money supply or by reducing taxes 使通货再膨胀来刺激经济(以增加货币供应或减少税收来刺激经济)

NOTE: no plural

◇ **reflationary** a. reflationary measures = acts which are likely to stimulate the economy 通货再膨胀促使经济发展措施

**refresher course** n. course of study to make you practise your skills again in order to improve them 在职进修课程: He went on a refresher course in bookkeeping. 他继续学习簿记进修课程。

**refund** 1 n. money paid back 退款: to ask for a refund 要求退款; She got a refund after she had complained to the manager. 她向经理投诉后得到了退款。 full refund or refund in full = refund of all the money paid 全部退款;全额退款: He got a full refund when he complained about the service. 当他抱怨服务不佳,他得了全额退款。 2 v. to pay back money 退款;还款;偿还: to refund the cost of postage 退还邮资; All money will be refunded if the goods are not satisfactory. 如果货物不满意,可以全部退款。

◇ **refundable** a. which can be paid back 可退款的;可偿还的: refundable deposit 可退还的保证金;可退定金; The entrance fee is refundable if you purchase £5 worth of goods. 如果购买价值5英磅的货物,入场费可退还。

**refuse** v. to say that you will not do something or will not accept something 不同意;拒绝;谢绝; They refused to pay. 他们拒绝付款。The bank refused to lend the company any more money. 这家银行拒绝再给那家公司款项。He asked for a rise but it was refused. 他要求提薪,但被拒绝了。The loan was refused by the bank. 银行拒绝了这笔贷款。The customer refused the goods or refused to accept the goods. 客户拒绝接受这些货物。

NOTE: You refuse to do something or refuse something.

◇ **refusal** n. saying no 拒绝;不同意: His request met with a refusal. = His request was refused. 他的要求遭到拒绝。to give someone first refusal of something = to allow someone to be the first to decide if they want something or not 给予某人第一取舍权;给某人优先决定权;给某人先买权; blanket refusal = refusal to accept many different items 综合否决权;总括否决权

**regard** n. with regard to = concerning or dealing with 关于: with regard to your request for unpaid leave 关于你对停薪休假的请求

◇ **regarding** prep. concerning or dealing with 关于: instructions regarding the shipment of goods to Africa 关于运往非洲货物的装运指示

◇ **regardless** a. regardless of = in spite of 不在乎;不顾;不管: The chairman furnished his office regardless of expense. = without thinking of how much it would cost 董事长不惜花费地布置了他的办公室。

**region** n. large area of a country 地区;区域; in the region of = about or approximately 大约；在 … 左右：He was earninga salary in the region of ￡25,000.他当时的薪金在 25,000 英磅左右。The house was sold for a price in the region of ￡100,000.这所房子售价大约是 100,000 英磅。

◇ **regional** a. referring to a region 地区的；地方的；区域的：regional planning = planning the industrial development of a region 区域性计划

**register** 1 n. (a) official list 正式名单；登记入册：to enter something in a register；将某事登记入册；to keep a register up to date 使名单保持最新的；companies' register or register of companies = list of companies, showing their directors and registered addresses 公司正式名册；register of debentures or debenture register = list of debenture holders of a company 公司债券名册；register of directors = official list of the directors of a company which has to be sent to the registrar of companies 董事名册；land register = list of pieces of land, showing who owns it and what buildings are on it 地产注册；Lloyd's Register = classified list showing details of all the ships in the world(英)劳合船级社年鉴；register of shareholders or share register = list of shareholders in a company with their addresses 股东名册 (b) large book for recording details (as in a hotel, where guests sign in, or in a registry where deaths are recorded)登记簿；注册簿；花名册 (c) cash register = machine which shows and adds the prices of items bought in a shop, with a drawer for keeping the cash received 现金出纳机；现金收入记录机 2 v. (a) to write something in an official list 登记；注册：to register a company 注册一个公司；to register a sale 登记销售额；to register a property 注册房地产；to register a trademark 注册商标 (b) to arrive at a hotel or at a conference, sign your name and write your address on a list 登记；报到：They registered at the hotel under the name of Macdonald. 他们以麦克唐纳(卖当劳)的名义在旅馆登记的。(c) to send (a letter) by registered post 挂号(邮寄)：I registered the letter, because it contained some money. 我把那封信挂号寄出了，因为里面有钱。

◇ **registered** a. (a) which has been noted on an official list 已注册的；已登记的：registered share transactio 已登记的证券交易；registered trademark 注册商标；the company's registered office = the head office of the company as noted in the register of companies 办理公司注册办公所在地；公司的法定总公司办公地 (b) registered letter or registered parcel = letter or parcel which is noted by the post office before it is sent, so that compensation can be claimed if it is lost 挂号信；挂号邮件：to send documents by registered mail or registered post 挂号邮寄文件

◇ **registrar** n. person who keeps official records 登记员；注册员：registrar of companies or the company registrar 公司注册员

◇ **registration** n. (a) act of having something noted on an official list 登记；注册：registration of a trademark or of a share transaction 商标注册；股票交易注册；certificate of registration or registration certificate = document showing that an item has been registered 注册证书；registration fee = money paid to have something registered or money paid to attend a conference 注册费；报到费；登记费；挂号费：registration number = official number (such as the number of a car)注册号码；登记号码 (b) land registration = system of registering land and its owners 地产注册；土地注册

◇ **registry** n. (a) place where official records are kept 注册处；登记处；挂号

处: GB land registry = government officewhere details of land are kept(英)土地注册处; registry office = office where records of births, marriages and deaths are kept(出生结婚, 死亡)登记处 (b) port of registry = port where a ship is registered 船舶登记处

**regret** v. to be sorry 悔恨;懊悔;抱歉;遗憾: I regret having to make so many staff redundant. 我很遗憾不得不裁减这么多职员。We regret the delay in answering your letter. 我们很抱歉没有及时给你回信。We regret to inform you of the death of the chairman. 我们遗憾地通知你,董事长已去世。

NOTE: You regret doing something or regret to do something or regret something. Note also: regretting - regretted

**regular** a. (a) which happens or comes at the same time each day or each week or each month or each year 有规律的;有规则的;定期的: His regular train is the 12.45. 他乘坐的定点火车是 12 时 45 分的。The regular flight to Athens leaves at 06.00. 飞往雅典的定期航班 6 时起飞。regular customer = customer who always buys from the same shop 常客;老主额;老客户; regular income = income which comes in every week or month 固定收入; She works freelance so she does not have a regular income. 她是自由职业者,所以她没有固定收入。regular staff = full - time staff 固定职员;正式职员;专职职员 (b) ordinary or standard 平常的;普通的;标准的: The regular price is $1.25, but we are offering them at 99c. 标准价为 1.25 英磅,但是我们可以按 99 美分出售。regular size = ordinary size (smaller than economy size, family size, etc.) 普通型号;标准尺寸

◇ **regularly** adv. happening often each day or week or /month or year 有规律地;有规则地;经常地: The first train in the morning is regularly late. 早晨头班火车经常晚点。

◇ **regulate** v. (a) to adjust something so that it works well or is correct 调整;调节;校准 (b) to change or maintain something by law 管理;控制;制定;管制: Prices are regulated by supply and demand. = Prices are increased or lowered according to supply and demand. 价格受供求关系的控制。government - regulated price = price which is imposed by the government 政府规定价格

◇ **regulation** n. (a) act of making sure that something will work well 管理;控制: the regulation of trading practices 贸易贯例管理;贸易操作管理 (b) regulations = laws or rules 条例;法规;规章制度: the new government regulations on housing standards 政府关于住宅建筑标准的新规定; fire regulations or safety regulations 安全条例;防火安全制度; regulations concerning imports and exports 关于进出口商品规定

NOTE: no plural for (a)

**reimburse** v. to reimburse someone his expenses = to pay someone back for money which he has spent 偿还某人的花费: You will be reimbursed for your expenses or your expenses will be reimbursed. 你的花费将得到偿还。

◇ **reimbursement** n. paying back money 还钱;偿还: reimbursement of expenses 偿付费用;费用偿还

**reimport** 1 n. importing of goods which have been exported from the same country(对进口的产品)再进口; 2 v. to import goods which have been exported 再进口

◇ **reimportation** n. importing goods which have been exported 再进口;

**reinstate** v. to put someone back into a job from which he was dismissed 使恢复(原职): The union demanded that the sacked workers should be reinstated. 工

会要求给解雇的工人们复职。

◇ **reinstatement** n. putting someone back into a job from which he was dismissed 恢复原职;复职

**reinsure** v. to spread the risk of an insurance, by asking another insurance company to cover part of it and receive part of the premium 再保险;转保;分保 (请求其他保险公司共同分担风险并共享保险金。)

◇ **reinsurance** n. act of reinsuring 再保险;转保;分保

◇ **reinsurer** n. insurance company which accepts to insure part of the risk for another insurer 再保险的公司;转保险的公司(同意与其他保险公司共同分担保险风险的) **reinvest** v. to invest again 再投资: He reinvested the money in government stocks. 他再次投资于政府的证券。

◇ **reinvestment** n. investing again in the same securities; investing a company's earnings in its own business by using them to create new products for sale 再投资(同一证券);对本公司再投资(将本公司收益投资用于企业生产供出售的新产品)

**reissue** 1 n. issue of something again 再发行 2 v. to issue something again 再发行: The company reissued its catalogue with a new price list. 这个公司重新发行了带有新价格表的商品目录。

**reject** 1 n. thing which has been thrown out because it is not of the usual standard 废品;次品;不合格物品: sale of rejects or of reject items 次品销售; to sell off reject stock 廉价出清次品库存; reject shop = shop which specializes in the sale of rejects 次品商店 2 v. to refuse to accept or to say that something is not satisfactory 拒绝;抵制;否决;驳回: The union rejected the management's proposals. 工会否决了管理部门的提议。The company rejected the takeover

bid. = The directors recommended that the shareholders should not accept the bid. 公司否决这个兼并的出价。

◇ **rejection** n. refusal to accept 拒绝;否决

**related** a. connected or linked 相关的;有联系的;有关系的: related items on the agenda 备忘录中有关事项; related company = company which is partly owned by another company 联号公司; earnings - related pension = pension which is linked to the size of the salary 与工资有关的养老金(抚恤金)

◇ **relating to** adv. referring to or connected with 与……有关: documents relating to the agreement 与协定有关的文件

◇ **relation** n. (a) in relation to = referring to or connected with 关于;有关: documents in relation to the agreement 有关这个协定的文件 (b) relations = links (with other people or other companies)关系;联系: We try to maintain good relations with our customers. 我们努力与客户保持良好的关系。to enter into relations with a company = to start discussing a business deal with a company 与某一公司建立业务关系; To break off relations with someone = to stop dealing with someone 与某人断交; industrial relations or labour relations = relations between management and workers 劳资关系; The company has a history of bad labour relations. 这个公司的劳资关系一直不好。(c) public relations (PR) = keeping good links between a company or a group and the public so that people know what the company is doing and approve of it 公共关系: public relations department = section of a company which deals with relations with the public 公共关系部; public relations officer = official who deals with relations with the public 公关人员

◇ **relatively** adv. more or less 相对地;比较地: We have appointed a relatively new PR firm to handle our publicity. 我们委派一家比较新的公共关系公司来处理我们的宣传广告事务。

**release** 1 n. (a) setting free 解除;豁免: release from a contract 解除合同义务; release of goods from customs 免关放行的货物; (b) day release = arrangement where a company allows a worker to go to college to study for one day each week 在职学习日: The junior sales manager is attending a day release course. 这位资历浅的销售经理正在参加一个在职学习日的课程。(c) press release = sheet giving news about something which is sent to newspapers and TV and radio stations so that they can use the information in it 新闻发布稿: The company sent out or issued a press release about the launch of the new car. 这家公司发布新闻说这种新型汽车将投放市场。(d) new releases = new records put on the market 上市的新唱片

NOTE: no plural for (a) 2 v. (a) to free 放行;免除;解除: to release goods from customs 免关放行货物; The customs released the goods against payment of a fine. 交付罚款后,海关放行这批货物。to release someone from a debt 豁免某人债务;免除某人欠款 (b) to make something public 发表;公布: The company released information about the new mine in Australia. 公司发表了关于澳大利亚新铁矿砂的消息。The government has refused to release figures for the number of unemployed women. 政府已经拒绝公布失业妇女的数字。(c) to put on the market 投放市场;上市: to release a new record 上市新唱片;投放新唱片; to release dues = to send off orders which had been piling up while a product was out of stock 发送到期的定货

**relevant** a. which has to do with what is being discussed 有关的;相关的: Which is the relevant government department? 哪个是有关政府部门? Can you give me the relevant papers? 你能给我有关的文件吗?

**reliable** a. which can be trusted 可靠的;可信赖的: reliable company 可信赖公司; The sales manager is completely reliable. 这位销售经理完全可以信赖(绝对可靠)。We have reliable information about our rival's sales. 我们有竞争对手销售的可靠信息。The company makes a very reliable product. 这个公司生产的产品非常可靠的。

◇ **reliability** n. being reliable 可靠性;可依赖性: The product has passed its reliability tests. 这种产品已经通过了可靠性检测。

NOTE: no plural

◇ **rely on** v. to depend on or to trust 依靠;信赖;信任: The chairman relies on the finance department for information on sales. 董事长依靠财务部提供销售情况。We rely on part-time staff for most of our mail-order business. 我们依靠上半班的职员完成大部分邮递订购业务。Do not rely on the agents for accurate market reports. 不要信赖代理人会提供准确的市场报告。

**relief** n. help 救济;减免;换班: tax relief = allowing someone to pay less tax 减税; There is full tax relief on mortgage interest payments. = No tax is payable on income used to pay interest on a mortgage. 抵押借款利息全部免税。mortgage relief = allowing someone to pay no tax on mortgage interest payments 抵押借款利息免税; relief shift = shift which comes to take the place of another shift, usually the shift between the day shift and the night shift 换班;轮班

NOTE: no plural

**remain** v. (a) to be left 剩下；余留：Half the stock remained unsold. 还剩一半库存未售出。We will sell off the old stock at half price and anything remaining will be thrown away. 我们将以半价出售全部陈货(库存)，若仍有剩余就都扔掉。(b) to stay 逗留；留下：She remained behind at the office after 6.30 to finish her work. 六点半以后她仍留在办公室干完她的工作。

◇ **remainder** 1 n. (a) things left behind 剩余物；剩下的东西：The remainder of the stock will be sold off at half price. 全部剩余库存将以半价出售。(b) remainders = new books sold cheaply 廉价新书；削价新书：remainder merchant = book dealer who buys unsold new books from publishers at a very low price 出售廉价剩余新书的商人 NOTE: in (a) remainder is usually singular and is written with the 2 v. to remainder books = to sell new books off cheaply 廉价出售新书；削价出售新书：The shop was full of piles of remaindered books. 这个商店堆满了廉价卖不出的新书。

**remember** v. to bring back into your mind something which you have seen or heard or read before 记住；想起；记得：Do you remember the name of the Managing Director of Smith Ltd? 你还记得史密斯有限公司总经理的姓名吗？I cannot remember the make of photocopier which he said was so good. 我想不起他说过的那种相当好的影印机的牌子。Did you remember to ask the switchboard to put my calls through to the boardroom? 你记住请总机把我的电话接到董事会的会议室？She remembered seeing the item in a supplier's catalogue. 她记得在供货人目录中看到这种商品。NOTE: You remember doing something which you did in the past. You remember to do something in the future.

**remind** v. to make someone remember 提醒；使想起：I must remind my secretary to book the flight for New York. 我必须提醒我的秘书预定去纽约的班机。He reminded the chairman that the meeting had to finish at 6.30. 他提醒董事长会议应在6时半结束。

◇ **reminder** n. letter to remind a customer that he has not paid an invoice 催付单：to send someone a reminder 寄给某人一张催付单

**remission** n. remission of taxes = refund of taxes which have been overpaid 税收退还

**remit** v. to send (money) 汇款：to remit by cheque 支票汇款 NOTE: remitting – remitted

◇ **remittance** n. money which is sent 汇款；寄款：Please send remittances to the treasurer. 请把汇款寄给财务主任。The family lives on a weekly remittance from their father in the USA. 这个家庭靠他们在美国的父亲每周汇款生活。

**remnant** n. odd piece of a large item sold separately 零料；零头(可单独出售的大宗货的零头)：remnant sale or sale of remnants 零料出售；零头出售

**remove** v. to take something away 拿走；除去；解除；免职：We can remove his name from the mailing list. 我们可以从通讯录上将他的名字除掉。The government has removed the ban on imports from Japan. 政府已经解除了从日本进口货物的禁令。The minister has removed the embargo on the sale of computer equipment. 部长解除了销售计算机设备的禁令。Two directors were removed from the board at the AGM. = Two directors were dismissed from the board. 两位经理在年度股东大会上被免除董事会职务。

◇ **removal** n. (a) moving to a new house or office 搬迁；搬家：removal or removals company = company which specializes in moving the contents of a houseor an office to a new building 搬家公司 (b) sacking someone (usually a director) from a job 免职；解雇：The removal of the managing director is going to be very difficult. 总经理的免职将是非常困难的。

**remunerate** v. to pay someone for doing something 报酬；酬劳：to remunerate someone for their services 对某人的服务给以报酬

◇ **remuneration** n. payment for services 酬劳；报酬；薪水：She has a monthly remuneration of £400. 她每月薪水为 400 英镑。

NOTE: no plural

◇ **remunerative** a. (job) which pays well 报酬很好的；薪金高的：He is in a very remunerative job. 他有个报酬高的工作。

**render** v. to render an account = to send in an account 开出帐单；结帐：payment for account rendered 支付开出的帐单；Please find enclosed payment per account rendered. 请查收按开出帐单付款。

**renew** v. to continue something for a further period of time 续期；展期；继续：to renew a bill of exchange or to renew a lease 汇票展期或租展期；to renew a subscription = to pay a subscription for another year 续订；to renew an insurance policy = to pay the premium for another year's insurance 继续投保

◇ **renewal** n. act of renewing 续期；展期；继续：renewal of a lease or of a subscription or of a bill 租赁展期；续订或汇票展期；The lease is up for renewal next month. 租约于下月展期。When is the renewal date of the bill? 什么时侯是这张汇票的展期? renewal notice = note sent by an insurance company asking the insured person to renew the insurance 展期通知书；转期通知书；renewal premi-

um = premium to be paid to renew an insurance 展期保险费；续保保险费

NOTE: no plural

**rent** 1 n. money paid to use an office or house or factory for a period of time 租金：high rent or low rent = expensive or cheap rent 高租金；低租金；Rents are high in the centre of the town. 市中心的租金贵。We cannot afford to pay High Street rents. 我们付不起大马路上的租金。to pay three months' rent in advance 余付三个月的租金；back rent = rent owed 欠租；The flat is let at an economic rent . = at a rent which covers all costs to the landlord. 这个单元房以经济租金价格出租。ground rent = rent paid by the main tenant to the ground landlord 地租；nominal rent = very small rent 象征性租金；rent control = government regulation of rents 租金管理(控制)；income from rents or rent income = income from letting offices or houses, etc. 租金收益 2 v. (a) to pay money to hire an office or house or factory or piece of equipment for a period of time 租用；to rent an office or a car 租用办公室或租用汽车；He rents an office in the centre of town. 他在市中心租用了一个办公室。They were driving a rented car when they were stopped by the police. 他们正驾驶着一辆租来的汽车，突然警察拦住他们。(b) to rent (out) = to own a car or office, etc. and let it to someone for money 出租；租出：We rented part of the building to an American company. 我们将这座大楼的一部分出租给一家美国公司。

◇ **rental** n. money paid to use an office or house or factory or car or piece of equipment, etc., for a period of time 租金；租费：The telephone rental bill comes to over £500 a quarter. 租用电话收费帐单每季度超过 500 英镑。rental income or income from rentals = income from letting offices or houses, etc. 租金

收益；car rental firm = company which specializes in offering cars for rent 出租汽车公司；fleet rental = renting all a company's cars from the same company at a special price 车队的租金(公司按特价)

**renunciation** n. act of giving up ownership of shares 放弃股权：letter of renunciation = form sent with new shares, which allows the person who has been allotted the shares to refuse to accept them and so sell them to someone else 放弃股权声明信

NOTE: no plural

**reopen** v. to open again 再开业；重开：The office will reopen soon after its refit. 事务所重新装修后将再次开张。

◇ **reopening** n. opening again 再开业；重开：the reopening of the store after refitting 整修后重新开业的商店

**reorder** 1 n. further order for something which has been ordered before 再订购：The product has only been on the market ten days and we are already getting reorders. 这种产品上市仅十天，而我们已不断收到再订购单。reorder level = minimum amount of stock of an item which must be reordered when stock falls to this amount 再订购的水准 2 v. to place a new order for something 再订购；再订货：We must reorder these items because stock is getting low. 我们必须再订购这些物品，因为库存越来越少了。

**reorganize** v. to organize in a new way 改组；改编；重新组织

◇ **reorganization** n. new way of organizing 改组；改编；重新组织：His job was downgraded in the office reorganization or in the reorganization of the office. 在公司改组中他的工作被降级了。the reorganization of a company or a company reorganization = restructuring the finances of a company 公司改组；公司重新组织

**rep** 1 n. = REPRESENTATIVE 代表；推销员；销售代表：to hold a reps' meeting 召开销售代表会议；Our reps make on average six calls a day. 我们的销售代表平均每天打六次电话。commission rep = representative who is not paid a salary but receives a commission on sales 拿佣金的销售代表 2 v. infml. = REPRESENT 代表；He reps for two firms on commission. 他收两家公司佣金的销售代表。

NOTE: repping – repped

**repack** v. to pack again 重新打包；再打包；重新包装；改装

◇ **repacking** n. packing again 重新打包；再打包；重新包装；改装

**repair** 1 n. mending or making good something which was broken 修理；修补：to carry out repairs to the machinery 对这部机械进行修理；His car is in the garage for repair. 他的汽车在修理厂等待修理。2 v. to mend or to make good something which is broken 修理；修补：The photocopier is being repaired. 这台影印机正在修理。repairing lease = lease where the tenant is responsible for repairs to the building which he is renting 维修组赁

◇ **repairer or repair man** n. person who carries out repairs 修理者；修理工：The repair man has come to mend the photocopier. 修理工已经来修理这台影印机了。

**repay** v. to pay back 偿还；还钱；偿付：to repay money owed 偿还欠款；The company had to cut back on expenditure in order to repay its debts. 这个公司只好削减开支以偿还债务。He repaid me in full. = He paid me back all the money he owed me. 他偿还了欠我的全部款项。

NOTE: repaying – repaid

◇ **repayable** a. which can be paid back

可偿还的：loan which is repayable over tenyears 十年可偿还的贷款

◇ **repayment** n. paying back; money which is paid back 偿还；偿还款项：The loan is due for repayment next year. 这笔贷款明年到期偿还。He fell behind with his mortgage repayments. = He was late in paying back the instalments on his mortgage. 他拖欠了抵押借款的偿还。

**repeat** v. (a) to say something again 重复；复述：He repeated his address slowly so that the salesgirl could write it down. 他慢慢地重复他的地址，以便售货员小姐能把它记下来。When asked what the company planned to do, the chairman repeated "Nothing". 当询问公司计划做什么时，董事长重复道："无可奉告"。(b) to repeat an order = to order something again 再次订购；再订货

◇ **repeat order** n. new order for something which has been ordered before 重新订购：The product has been on the market only ten days and we are already flooded with repeat orders. 这种产品刚上市十天，而我们就已经收到源源涌来的重购订货单。

**replace** v. to put someone or something in the place of something else 代替；替换；取代：The cost of replacing damaged stock is very high. 替换破损存货的费用很高。The photocopier needs replacing. 这台影印机需更换了。The company will replace any defective item free of charge. 这个公司将免费更换次品。We are replacing all our salaried staff with freelancers. 我们正在将所有领薪金职员换成自由职业者。

◇ **replacement** n. (a) replacement cost or cost of replacement = cost of an item to replace an existing asset 重置成本；replacement value = value of something for insurance purposes if it were to be replaced 更新价值；更新保险价值；The computer is insured at its replace-

ment value. 这台计算机按更新价值投保。(b) item which replaces something 替换物；代替物：We are out of stock and are waiting for replacements. 我们现无存货而正等待进新货。(c) person who replaces someone 代替者；替代者：My secretary leaves us next week, so we are advertising for a replacement. 我的秘书下星期要走，所以我们现在正登广告招聘一位替代者。

NOTE: no plural for (a)

**reply** 1 n. answer 回答；答复：There was no reply to my letter or to my phone call. 没有复信给我。或：没有给我回电话。I am writing in reply to your letter of the 24th. 我正在给你 24 日的来信写回信。The company's reply to the takeover bid. 公司对兼并出价的答复. reply coupon = form attached to a coupon ad which has to be filled in and returned to the advertiser 回联单；international postal reply coupon = coupon which can be used in another country to pay the postage of replying to a letter 国际信件邮资回复单；He enclosed an international reply coupon with his letter. 他在信中附了一张国际信件(邮资)回复单。reply paid card or letter = card or letter to be sent back to the sender with a reply, the sender having already paid for the return postage 邮资已付的明信片或信 2 v. to answer 回答；答复；to reply to a letter 回信；复函；The company has replied to the takeover bid by offering the shareholders higher dividends. 公司以给股东们的更高股息来作为对兼并发价的答复。

**report** 1 n. (a) statement describing what has happened or describing a state of affairs 汇报，报告：to draft a report 起草一份报告；to make a report or to present a report or to send in a report 做报告或提交一份报告；The sales manager reads all the reports from the sales team. 销售经理看了销售组的全部报

告。The chairman has received a report from the insurance company. 董事长收到了这个保险公司的一份报告。The company's annual report or the chairman's report or the directors' report = document sent each year by the chairman of a company or the directors to the shareholders, explaining what the company has done during the year 公司的年度报告；董事长的报告；经理的报告；confidential report = secret document which must not be shown to other people 机密报告；feasibility report = document which says if something can be done 可行性报告；financial report = document which gives the financial position of a company or of a club, etc. 财务报告；progress report = document which describes what progress has been made 进度报告；the treasurer's report = document from the honorary treasurer of a society to explain the financial state of the society to its members 财务主任报告 (b) a report in a newspaper or a newspaper report = article or news item 新闻报导；报纸上的报导：Can you confirm the report that the company is planning to close the factory? 你能证实这个公司正在计划关闭那家工厂的传说吗？(c) official document from a government committee 正式报告：The government has issued a report on the credit problems of exporters. 政府发布了一个关于出口商信誉问题的报告。2 v. (a) to make a statement describing something 叙述；汇报：The salesmen reported an increased demand for the product. 推销员们汇报此产品的需求增加了。He reported the damage to the insurance company. 他向保险公司汇报了损失情况。We asked the bank to report on his financial status. 我们要求银行汇报它的财务状况。He reported seeing the absentee in a shop. 他说他在商店里看见那个旷工的人。(b) to report to some-

one = to be responsible to or to be under someone 向 … 负责；受 … 领导；He reports direct to the managing director. 他直接向总经理负责。The salesmen report to the sales director. 推销员们受销售经理领导。(c) to go to a place or to attend 去；前往；参加；to report for an interview 参加会晤；Please report to our London office for training. 请前往我们的伦敦办事处参加培训。

NOTE: for (a), you report something or report on something or report doing something

**repossess** v. to take back an item which someone is buying under a hire - purchase agreement, because the purchaser cannot continue the payments 收回已售出商品(因为购货人不能继续支付，租购的物品而被收回)

**represent** v. (a) to work for a company, showing goods or services to possible buyers 代表；代理：He represents an American car firm in Europe. 他代表驻欧洲的一家美国汽车公司。Our French distributor represents several other competing firms. 我们在法国的销售店代表几家其它竞争的公司。(b) to act for someone 代表(某人做)；he sent his solicitor and accountant to represent him at the meeting: 他派出他的律师和会计代表他出席会议。Three managers represent the workforce in discussions with the directors. 三位经理代表职工与董事们商谈。

◇ **re - present** v. to present something again 再呈交：He re - presented the cheque two weeks later to try to get payment from the bank. 为从银行得到付款，两星期后他再次向银行呈交支票。

◇ **representation** n. (a) act of selling goods for a company 代理；代销：We offered them exclusive representation in Europe. 我们向他们提供在欧洲的独家

经销代理权。They have no representation in the USA. 他们在美国没有代理。(b) having someone to act on your behalf 代表：The minority shareholders want representation on the board. 少数股东要求在董事会中有代表。(c) complaint made on behalf of someone 申述；陈情；说明：The managers made representations to the board on behalf of the hourly – paid members of staff. 经理们代表职工中的"小时工"向董事会陈述情况。

◇ **representative** 1 a. which is an example of what all others are like 代表性的；典型的：We displayed a representative selection of our product range. 我们展出了我们的产品系列的典型精品。The sample chosen was not representative of the whole batch. 抽出的样品不能代表整批产品。2 n. (a) sales representative = person who works for a company, showing goods or services for sale 销售代表；代销人：We have six representatives in Europe. 我们在欧洲有六位销售代表。They have vacancies for representatives to call on accounts in the north of the country. 他们在该国北部访问客户销售代表空缺。(b) company which works for another company, selling their goods 代销公司；代理公司：We have appointed Smith & Co our exclusive representatives in Europe. 我们已经指定史密斯公司作为我们在欧洲的独家代销公司。(c) person who acts on someone's behalf 代表；代理人：He sent his solicitor and accountant to act as his representatives at the meeting. 他派他的律师和会计代表他出席会议。The board refused to meet the representatives of the workforce. 董事会拒绝接见职工的代表们。

**repudiate** v. to refuse to accept 拒绝；：to repudiate an agreement = to refuse to continue with an agreement 拒绝履行协议

◇ **repudiation** n. refusal to accept 拒绝

**reputable** a. with a good reputation 声誉好的；名声好的：We only use reputable carriers. 我们只用信誉好的承运人。a reputable firm of accountants 享有盛名的会计公司

◇ **reputation** n. opinion of someone or something held by other people 名声；名誉；威望：company with a reputation for quality; 以质量闻名的公司；He has a reputation for being difficult to negotiate with. 他以难以谈判而出名。

**request** 1 n. asking for something 请求；要求；恳求：They put in a request for a government subsidy. 他们请求政府补贴。His request for a loan was turned down by the bank. 银行拒绝了他的贷款要求。on request = if asked for 承索；索要；We will send samples on request or "Samples available on request. 样品承索即寄。2 v. to ask for 请求；要求：to request assistance from the government 请求政府帮助；I am sending a catalogue as requested. 我将目录按要求寄出。

**require** v. (a) to ask for or to demand something 要求；命令：to require a full explanation of expenditure 要求详尽说明开支情况；The law requires you to submit all income to the tax authorities. 法律要求你将全部收入向税务当局汇报。(b) to need 需要：the document requires careful study. 这个文件需要仔细研究。To write the program requires a computer specialist. 编写程序需要计算机专家。

◇ **requirement** n. what is needed 需要；要求：public sector borrowing requirement = amount of money which a government has to borrow to pay for its own spending 公营部门借款要求

◇ **requirements** pl. n. things which are needed 需要物；必要品：to meet a customer's requirements 满足客户的要

求; If you will supply us with a list of yourrequirements, we shall see if we can meet them. 如果你能向我们提供要求货物单，我们一定设法能满足你们所要的货物。the requirements of a market or market requirements = things which are needed by the market 市场需求品; budgetary requirements = spending or income needed to meet the budget forecasts 预算要求；预算收支要求; manpower requirements = number of workers needed 人力需求

**requisition** 1 n. official order for something 正式订购; 订购单: What is the number of your latest requisition? 你最近一次订购单的号码是多少? cheque requisition = official note from a department to the company accounts staff asking for a cheque to be written 支票申请单 2 v. to put in an official order for something 征用; to ask for supplies to be sent 要求提供

**resale** n. selling goods which have been bought 再卖; 转卖(将买进货物再次出售): to purchase something for resale 为转卖而购买杂物; The contract forbids resale of the goods to the USA. 合同禁止转卖这些产品到美国。
NOTE: no plural

◇ **resale price maintenance** n. system where the price for an item is fixed by the manufacturer and the retailer is not allowed to sell it for a lower price 维持转卖价格(由制造商对某项产品所定价格，禁止零售商低价出售的一种价格维持制度)

**rescind** v. to annul or to cancel 取消; 废除: to rescind a contract or an agreement 取消合同或协议

**rescue** 1 n. saving someone or something from danger 解救; 挽救; 救援: rescue operation = arrangement by a group of people to save a company from collapse 挽救措施; The banks planned a rescue operation for the company. 银行计划对这个公司采取挽救措施。2 v. to save someone or something from danger 营救; 救援; 挽救: The company nearly collapsed, but was rescued by the banks. 这个公司濒临倒闭，但得到了银行的救助。

**research** 1 n. trying to find out facts or information 研究; 探索; 调查: consumer research = research into why consumers buy goods and what goods they may want to buy 消费者调查; market research = examining the possible sales of a product and the possible customers for it before it is put on the market 市场研究; research and development = scientific investigation which leads to making new products or improving existing products 研究与开发; The company spends millions on research and development. 这个公司以数百万资金用于研究与开发。scientific research = study to try to find out information 科学研究; He is engaged in research into the packaging of the new product line. 他从事于新产品系列包装的研究。The company is carrying out research into finding a medicine to cure colds. 这家公司正在研究寻找治疗感冒的新药。research department = section of a company which does research 科研部; a research institute or organization = place which exists only to carry out research 研究院; 研究机构; research unit = separate small group of research workers 研究单位; 研究小组; research worker = person who works in a research department 2 v. to study or to try to find out information about something 研究; 探索; 调查: to research the market for a product 对某项产品市场进行调查

◇ **researcher** n. person who carries out research 研究者; 调查者

**reservation** n. booking a seat or table or room 预定(座位; 饭桌; 房间): I want to make a reservation on the train to Plymouthtomorrow evening. 我想预订明晚去普利茅斯的火车票。room reservations = department in a hotel which deals with bookings for rooms 客房预订部; Can you put me through to reservations? 你可以给我接通客房预订部吗?

**reserve** 1 n. (a) money from profits not paid as dividend, but kept back by a company in case it is needed for a special purpose 储备(部分利润不作红利分配,而由公司储存以应付特别紧急需要): bank reserves = cash and securities held by a bank to cover deposits 银行储备金; capital reserves = money from profits, which forms part of the capital of a company and can be used for distribution to shareholders only when a company is wound up 资本储备;资本公积; capitalization of reserves = issuing free bonus shares to shareholders 准备金资本化; cash reserves = a company's reserves in cash deposits or bills kept in case of urgent need 现金储备;现金准备; The company was forced to fall back on its cash reserves. 这个公司被迫求助于它自己的现金储备。to have to draw on reserves to pay the dividend 不得不动用储备金支付股息; contingency reserve or emergency reserves = money set aside in case it is needed urgently 应急准备; 紧急储备; reserve for bad debts = money kept by a company to cover debts which may not be paid 坏帐准备金,呆帐储备金; hidden reserves = illegal reserves which are not declared in the company's balance sheet 秘密准备金; 隐蔽公积金; sums chargeable to the reserve = sums which can be debited to a company's reserves 可记入储备的金额; reserve fund = profits in a business which have not been paid out as dividend but have been ploughed back into the business 储备资金;准备基金 (b) reserve currency = strong currency held by other countries to support their own weaker currencies 储备货币: currency reserves = foreign money held by a government to support its own currency and to pay its debts 外汇储备; a country's foreign currency reserves = a country's reserves in currencies of other countries 国家外汇储备; The UK's gold and dollar reserves fell by $200 million during the quarter. 英国国家黄金与美元的储备在这个季度下降了2亿美元。(c) in reserve = kept to be used at a later date 后备的;储存的;保留的: to keep something in reserve 将某物储存; We are keeping our new product in reserve until the launch date. 我们将我们的新产品保留到投放市场日。(d) reserves = supplies kept in case of need 储备;贮存: Our reserves of fuel fell during the winter. 我们的燃料储备今年冬天减少了。The country's reserves of gas or gas reserves are very large. 这个国家天然气储存量很大。(e) reserve price = lowest price which a seller will accept at an auction 最低价格;保留价格: The painting was withdrawn when it did not reach its reserve. 这幅画当未达到保留价格时就撤回了。2 v. to reserve a room or a table or a seat = to book a room or table or seat or to ask for a room or table or seat to be kept free for you 预订客房(餐桌;座位); I want to reserve a table for four people. 我想预订一张四人餐桌。Can your secretary reserve a seat for me on the train to Glasgow? 你的秘书能为我预订一张去格拉斯哥的火车票吗?

**residence** n. (a) house or flat where someone lives 住宅;住处: He has a country residence where he spends his weekends. 他有一座乡村住宅,在那里可以度周末。(b) act of living or operating officially in a country 居住;居留; residence permit = official document allowing a foreigner to live in a country 居住许可证; He has applied for a residence permit. 他已经申请了居住许可证。She was granted a residence permit for one year. 她已得到一年居住许可证。

NOTE: no plural for (b)

◇ **resident** n. person or company living or operating in a country 居民;在一国营业的公司: The company is resident in France. 这个公司常在法国营业。non‐resident = person or company which is not officially resident in a country 非居民;非居住者; He has a non‐resident account with a French bank. 他在一家法国银行中有非居民帐户。She was granted a non‐resident visa. 她得到了一张非居民签证。

**residue** n. money left over 余款;剩余财产: After paying various bequests the residue of his estate was split between his children. 当偿付各种遗赠物后, 他的剩余财产分给了他的孩子们。

◇ **residual** a. remaining after everything else has gone 剩余的;残留的

**resign** v. to give up a job 辞职;放弃: He resigned from his post as treasurer. 他辞去财务主任职务。He has resigned with effect from July 1st. 他的辞职从7月1日生效。She resigned as finance director. 她辞去财务主任职务。

◇ **resignation** n. act of giving up a job 辞职;放弃: He wrote his letter of resignation to the chairman. 他向董事长写了辞职书。to hand in or to give in or to send in one's resignation = to resign from a job 递交辞呈;提出辞职

**resist** v. to fight against something or not to give in to something 抵制;对抗;不屈服: The chairman resisted all attempts to make him resign. 董事长抵制一切要他辞职的企图。The company is resisting the takeover bid. 公司拒绝接受兼并的出价。

◇ **resistance** n. showing that people are opposed to something 反对;抵制: There was a lot of resistance from the shareholders to the new plan. 股东们强烈反对这项新计划。The chairman's proposal met with strong resistance from the banks. 董事长的提议遭到银行的强烈反对。consumer resistance = lack of interest by consumers in buying a new product 消费者抵制; The new product met no consumer resistance even though the price was high. 新产品虽然价格高, 但是却有人问津。

NOTE: no plural

**resolution** n. decision to be reached at a meeting 决议;决定: to put a resolution to a meeting = to ask a meeting to vote on a proposal 将提案送交会议通过; The meeting passed or carried or adopted a resolution to go on strike. 会议通过了罢工的决议。The meeting rejected the resolution or the resolution was defeated by ten votes to twenty. 这次会议以20:10的票数否决了这个议案。**resolve** v. to decide to do something 决定: The meeting resolved that a dividend should not be paid. 会议决定不付股息。

**resources** pl. n. (a) source of supply of something 资源: natural resources = supplies of gas, oil, coal, etc. which are available in the ground 自然资源; The country is rich in natural resources. 这个国家的自然资源很丰富。We are looking for a site with good water resources. = a site with plenty of water available 我们正在寻找有良好水资源的地方。(b) financial resources = supply of money for something 财政资源: The costs of the London office are a drain on the company's financial resources. 伦敦事务所的花费使这公司的财源的耗竭。The company's financial resources are not strong enough to support the cost of the research programme. 公司的财政资源不足以支付研究项目的费用。The cost of the new project is easily within our resources. = We have enough money to pay for the new project. 我们有充足的财源支付这项新项目的费用。

**respect** 1 n. with respect to = concerning 关于 2 v. to pay attention to 重视；考虑；to respect a clause in an agreement 考虑协定中某一项条款；The company has not respected the terms of the contract. 该公司没有注意到合同条款。

◇ **respectively** adv. referring to each one separately 各自地；分别地：Mr Smith and Mr Jones are respectively MD and Sales Director of Smith Ltd. 史密斯先生与琼斯先生分别是史密斯有限公司的总经理和销售主任。

**response** n. reply or reaction 回答；反应：There was no response to our mailing shot. 对我们的邮寄的广告单无反应。We got very little response to our complaints. 我们的投诉几乎未得到什么反应。

**responsibility** n. (a) being responsible 对…负责：There is no responsibility on the company's part for loss of customers' property. 公司方面对客户财产损失不负责任。The management accepts no responsibility for loss of goods in storage. 管理部门对库存货物损失不承担责任。(b) responsibilities = duties 责任；义务：He finds the responsibilities of being managing director too heavy. 他发觉总经理的责任太重了。

NOTE: no plural for (a)

◇ **responsible** adjective (a) responsible for = directing or being in charge of 对…负责：He is responsible for all sales. 他负责全面销售。(b) responsible to someone = being under someone's authority 向某人负责；He is directly responsible to the managing director. 他直接对总经理负责。(c) a responsible job = job where important decisions have to be taken or where the employee has

many responsibilities 负责任的工作；He is looking for a responsible job in marketing. 他正在寻找一个负责任的推销的工作。

**rest** n. what is left 其余的；剩下的：The chairman went home, but the rest of the directors stayed in the boardroom. 董事长回家了，而其余的董事们留在董事会会议室里。We sold most of the stock before Christmas and hope to clear the rest in a sale. 圣诞节前我们卖出了大批存货，并希望一次出清剩余的货物。The rest of the money is invested in gilts. 其余的钱投资于金边证券。

NOTE: usually singular, written with the

**restaurant** n. place where you can buy a meal 餐馆；饭店：He runs a French restaurant in New York. 他在纽约开了一个法国餐馆。

◇ **restaurateur** n. person who runs a restaurant 餐馆主人；饭店老板

**restitution** n. (a) giving back (property) 偿还；归还：The court ordered the restitution of assets to the company. 法院判决将资产归还给那个公司。(b) compensation or payment for damage or loss 赔偿；补偿（损失）(c) (in the EEC) export restitution = subsidies to European food exporters 出口补贴；外销津贴（欧共体）

NOTE: no plural

**restock** v. to order more stock 重新进货；再储存；再进货：to restock after the Christmas sales 圣诞节销售后重新进货

◇ **restocking** n. ordering more stock 重新进货；再储存；再进货

NOTE: no plural

**restraint** n. control 控制；约束；抑制；克制：pay restraint or wage restraint = keeping increases in wages under control 工资约束；restraint of trade = (i) situation where a worker is not allowed to use his knowledge in another company if he changes jobs 业务限制；业务约束（雇员若变换工作后，不可将他的业务知识用于其它公司）(ii) attempt by companies to fix prices or create monopolies or reduce competition, which could affect free trade 贸易约束；贸易管制（某些公司企图固定价格，制造垄断或减少竞争的这些都会影响自由贸易的行为）

**restrict** v. to limit or to impose controls on 限制；限定；约束：to restrict credit 限制信贷；We are restricted to twenty staff by the size of our offices. 因办公室规模有限，我们只能有 20 名职员。to restrict the flow of trade or to restrict imports 限制贸易流量；限制进口产品；to sell into a restricted market = to sell goods into a market where the supplier has agreed to limit sales to avoid competition 销售打入控制的市场

◇ **restriction** n. limit or controlling 限制；控制：import restrictions or restrictions on imports 进口限制；to impose restrictions on imports or on credit = to start limiting imports or credit 限制进口货；限制信贷；to lift credit restrictions = to allow credit to be given freely 解除信贷控制

◇ **restrictive** a. which limits 限制的；限制性的；约束性的：restrictive trade practices = arrangement between companies to fix prices or to share the market, etc. 限制性贸易贯例；限制性贸易常规

**restructure** v. to reorganize the financial basis of a company 重新调整；重新组织；重新安排

◇ **restructuring** n. the restructuring of the company = reorganizing the financial basis of a company 公司的改组
NOTE: no plural

**result** 1 n. (a) profit or loss account for a company at the end of a trading period 损益帐户：The company's results for 1984. 公司的 1984 年损益帐户 (b) something which happens because of something else 结果；成果；效果：What was the result of the price investigation? 价格调查结果怎样? The company doubled its sales force with the result that the sales rose by 26%. 公司对其销售人员不太相信，结果是销售额增加 26%。The expansion programme has produced results. = has produced increased sales. 这个扩建计划已经产生效果。payment by results = being paid for profits or increased sales 按劳付酬 2 v. (a) to result in = to produce as a result 导致；造成 (b) to result from = to happen because of something 起因于…；由…造成：The increase in debt resulted from the expansion programme. 由于扩建计划造成债务的增加。The doubling of the sales force resulted in increased sales. 双倍的销售力量导致增加了销售额。The extra orders resulted in overtime work for all the factory staff. 额外的订购造成全厂人员加班加点。

**resume** v. to start again 重新开始：The discussions resumed after a two hour break. 经过二个小时休息后，讨论重新开始。

**resume** n. US summary of a person's life story with details of education and work experience(美)个人简历；履历
NOTE: GB English is curriculum vitae

**resumption** n. starting again 重新开始；恢复：We expect an early resumption of negotiations. = We expect negotiations will start again soon. 我们期望尽快恢复谈判。
NOTE: no plural

**retail** 1 n. sale of small quantities of goods to ordinary customers 零售：retail dealer = person who sells to the general public 零售商；retail price = full price paid by a customer in a shop 零售价格；retail price index = index showing how prices of retail goods have risen over a period of time 零售价格指数；retail shop或 retail outlet = shop which sells goods to the general public 零售商店；the retail trade = all people or businesses selling goods retail 零售业务；The goods in stock have a retail value of £1m. = The value of the goods if sold to the public is £1m, before discounts etc. are taken into account. 库中存货的零售价值为 100 万英磅。2 ad. He sells retail and buys wholesale = He buys goods in bulk at a wholesale discount and sells in small quantities to the public. 他批发买入而零售卖出。3 v. (a) to retail goods = to sell goods direct to the public 零售货物 (b) to sell for a price 以⋯⋯价格出售：These items retail at or for 25p. = The retail price of these items is 25p. 这些物品的零售价为 25 便士

◇ **retailer** n. person who runs a retail business, selling goods direct to the public 零售商

◇ **retailing** n. selling of full price goods to the public 零售：From car retailing the company branched out into car leasing. 公司的业务从汽车零售扩大到汽车出租。
NOTE: no plural

**retain** v. (a) to keep 保留；留存：Out of the profits, the company has retained £50,000 as provision against bad debts. 公司从利润中留出 50,000 英磅以对付呆(坏)帐。retained income = profit not distributed to the shareholders as dividend 保留收益；留存收益；The balance sheet has £50,000 in retained income. 资产负债表上有 50,000 英磅的留存收益。(b) to retain a lawyer to act for a company = to agree with a lawyer that he will act for you (and pay him a fee in advance) 预付聘金请律师为公司代理法律事务

◇ **retainer** n. money paid in advance to someone so that he will work for you,

and not for someone else 聘请费(预先支付)：We pay him a retainer of £1,000. 我们预先支付给他聘请费 1.000 英磅。

**retire** v. (a) to stop work and take a pension 退休：She retired with a £6,000 pension. 她退休领取 6,000 英磅养老金。The founder of the company retired at the age of 85. 这位公司创始人于 85 岁退休。The shop is owned by a retired policeman. 这个商店是由一个退休警察拥有的。(b) to make a worker stop work and take a pension 使⋯⋯退休；They decided to retire all staff over 50. 他们决定让所有超过 50 岁的职员退休。(c) to come to the end of an elected term of office 期满离任；退役；退职：The treasurer retires from the council after six years. 财务主任六年后期满退出理事会。Two retiring directors offer themselves for re - election. 两位离任的董事提出他们将参加下届竞选。

◇ **retiral** n. US = RETIREMENT

◇ **retirement** n. act of retiring from work 退休；to take early retirement = to leave work before the usual age 提前退休：retirement age = age at which people retire (in the UK usually 65 for men and 60 for women) 退休年令；retirement pension = pension which someone receives when he retires 退休金
NOTE: no plural

**retrain** v. to train someone for a new job, or to do the same job in a more modern way 再培训

◇ **retraining** n. act of training again 再培训：The shop is closed for staff retraining. 为了职员再培训，这家商店关门歇业了。He had to attend a retraining session. 他不得不参加一期的再培训。
NOTE: no plural

**retrenchment** n. reduction of expenditure or of new plans 减少支出；削减费用：The company is in for a period of retrenchment. 公司目前正值削减开支阶段。

**retrieve** v. to get back (something) which has been lost; to get back (information) which is stored in a computer 寻回；取回(物)；回收(计算机信息)：The company is fighting to retrieve its market share. 这个公司正在为恢复其市场分额(占有率)而奋斗。All of the information was accidentally wiped off the computer so we cannot retrieve our sales figures for the last month. 全部信息被计算机意外地抹掉了，所以我们无法得到上个月的销售数字。

◇ **retrieval** n. getting back 回收：data retrieval or information retrieval = getting information from the data stored in a computer 数据检索；数据或信息回收；retrieval system = system which allows information to be retrieved 回收系统；检索系统

NOTE: no plural

**retroactive** a. which takes effect from a time in the past 有追溯效力的：retroactive pay rise 补发增加的工资：They got a pay rise retroactive to last January. 他们得到了去年一月补发的加薪。

◇ **retroactively** adv. going back to a time in the past 有追溯效力地；追溯既往地

**return** 1 n. (a) going back or coming back 返回；回来：return journey = journey back to where you came from 归程；a return ticket or a return = a ticket for a journey to a place and back again 来回票；往返票；I want two returns to Edinburgh. 我要两张爱丁堡的往返票。return fare = fare for a journey from one place to another and back again 往返费用 (b) sending back 寄还；送还：He replied by return of post. = He replied by the next post service back. 他在复函中作了回答。return address = address to send back something 退信地址；

These goods are all on sale or return. = If the retailer does not sell them, he sends them back to the supplier, and pays only for the items sold. 所有这些货物准许退还。(c) profit or income from money invested 利润；收益：to bring in a quick return 产生快速收益；What is the gross return on this line? 这笔生意的毛利是多少呢？return on investment (ROI) or on capital = profit shown as a percentage of money invested 投资利润率；报酬率；rate of return = amount of interest or dividend produced by an investment, shown as a percentage 收益率 (d) official return = official report 正式申报；to make a return to the tax office or to make an income tax return = to send a statement of income to the tax office 呈交所得税申报表；to fill in a VAT return = to complete the form showing VAT receipts and expenditure 填写增值税申报表；nil return = report showing no sales or income or tax etc. 无收益报表；无赢利申报；daily or weekly or quarterly sales return = report of sales made each day or week or quarter 日销售报表；周销售报表；季度销售报表 2 v. (a) to send back 送回；退回：to return unsold stock to the wholesaler 将未出售的货退给批发商；to return a letter to sender 将信退给寄信人；returned empties = empty bottles or containers which are sent back to a supplier 退回空瓶子(空箱子) (b) to make a statement 说明；申报：to return income of £15,000 to the tax authorities 向税务部门申报 15,000 英磅的所得

◇ **returnable** a. which can be returned 可退还的；允许可退回的：These bottles are not returnable. 这些瓶子不可退还。

◇ **returns** pl. n. (a) profits or income from investment 收益；利润(指投资)：The company is looking for quick returns on its investment. 这个公司正在寻求投

资快速收益。law of diminishing returns = general rule that as more factors of production (land, labour and capital) are added to the existing factors, so the amount they produce is proportionately smaller 利润（或收益）递减法则；报酬递减法则 (b) unsold goods, especially books or newspapers or magazines sent back to the supplier 退货（特指退还给发货人未售出的书和报刊）

**revalue** v. to value something again (at a higher value than before)再估价；重新估价（通常比原价高）: The company's properties have been revalued. 这个公司的财产已重新估价了。The dollar has been revalued against all world currencies. 美元对所有国际货币价比，做了重新调整。

◇ **revaluation** n. act of revaluing 再估价；重新估价；The balance sheet takes into account the revaluation of the company's properties. 资产负债表考虑到了公司财产的重新估价计算的。the revaluation of the dollar against the franc 美元对法郎的比价重新调整

**revenue** n. (a) money received 收入；收益: revenue from advertising or advertising revenue 广告收入； Oil revenues have risen with the rise in the dollar. 石油收益因美元增值而增加。revenue accounts = accounts of a business which record money received as sales, commission etc. 营业收入帐户 (b) money received by a government in tax 税收: Inland Revenue or US Internal Revenue Service = government department which deals with tax 国内税收；(美)国内税务局； revenue officer = person working in the government tax offices 税务员

**reversal** n. change from being profitable to unprofitable 倒利（从赢利到非赢利的变化）: The company suffered a reversal in the Far East. 这个公司在远东倒利了。

**reverse** 1 a. opposite or in the opposite direction 相反的；反向的: reverse takeover = takeover of a large company by a small company 反向兼并；倒转接收（由小公司接收大公司）； reverse charge call = telephone call where the person receiving the call agrees to pay for it 对方付费电话 2 v. (a) to change a decision to the opposite 改变；取消: The committee reversed its decision on import quotas. 委员会取消了对进口货物的配额的决定。(b) to reverse the charges = to make a phone call, asking the person receiving it to pay for it 对方付费（电话）

**reversion** n. return of property to an original owner（财产）复归: He has the reversion of the estate . = He will receive the estate when the present lease ends. 他享有财产复归权。

◇ **reversionary** a. (property) which passes to another owner on the death of the present one 可继承的: reversionary annuity = annuity paid to someone on the death of another person 可继承的年金（养老金）

**review** 1 n. (a) general examination 检查；审查；考核: to conduct a review of distributors 对经销商进行检查； financial review = examination of an organization's finances 财务检查； wage review or salary review = examination of salaries or wages in a company to see if the workers should earn more 工资调整. She had a salary review last April. = Her salary was examined (and increased) in April. 去年 4 月她有一次工资调整。(b) magazine or monthly or weekly journal 刊志；月刊；周刊 2 v. to examine something generally 检查；审查；审核: to review salaries = to look at all salaries in a company to decide on increases 调整工资； His salary will be reviewed at the end of the year. 他的工资

将在年底调整。The company has decided to review freelance payments in the light of the rising cost of living. 根据生活费用的提高,公司已决定调整自由职业者的酬金。to review discounts = to look at discounts offered to decide whether to change them 折扣调整

**revise** v. to change something which has been calculated or planned 修改;修订;订正: Sales forecasts are revised annually. 销售预测每年都修订。The chairman is revising his speech to the AGM. 董事长正在修改他在年度股东大会上的讲话。

**revive** v. to make more lively; to increase (after a recession) 复兴;振兴;重振: The government is introducing measures to revive trade. 政府正在引用某些措施来振兴贸易。Industry is reviving after the recession. 经济衰退后,工业正在复兴。

◇ **revival** n. revival of trade = increase in trade after a recession 贸易复兴

**revoke** v. to cancel 取销;废弃;撤销: to revoke a clause in an agreement 取消协定中某一条款; The quota on luxury items has been revoked. 奢侈品限额已被撤销了。

**revolving** a. revolving credit = system where someone can borrow money at any time up to an agreed amount, and continue to borrow while still paying off the original loan 循环贷款(一种贷款的制度,贷款人可以随时借贷商定的数额,并可边偿还原始贷款,边继续借贷)

**rich** a. (a) having a lot of money 富的;有钱的;富裕的: a rich stockbroker 富有的证券经纪人; a rich oil company 富有石油公司 (b) having a lot of natural resources 丰富的: The country is rich in minerals. 这个国家矿产资源丰富。oil-rich territory 石油资源丰富地区

**rid** v. to get rid of something = to throw something away because it is useless 去掉;除去: The company is trying to get rid of all its old stock. 这个公司正在设法处理掉存货。Our department has been told to get rid of twenty staff. 我们的部门被告知裁员 20 名。
NOTE: getting rid – got rid

**rider** n. additional clause 附加条款;追加条款: to add a rider to a contract 合同中追加一项条款

**rig** 1 n. oil rig = platform which holds the equipment for taking oil out of the earth 石油井架;石油平台(装有采油设备) 2 v. to arrange for a result to be changed 操纵;控制: They tried to rig the election of officers 他们企图操纵官员们的选举。to rig the market = to make share prices go up or down so as to make a profit 操纵市场;控制(股票)市场; rigging of ballots or ballot – rigging = trying to change the result of an election by altering or destroying voting papers 投票选举舞弊
NOTE: rigging – rigged

**right** 1 a. (a) good or correct 正确的;对的;好的: The chairman was right when he said the figures did not add up. 当董事长说到数字没加在一起时,他是对的。This is not the right plane for Paris. 这不是去巴黎的合适飞机。(b) not left The credits are on the right side of the page. 贷方在这页的右方。2 n. (a) legal title to something 权利: right of renewal of a contract 合同展期权; She has a right to the property. 她享有这笔财产权所有权。He has no right to the patent. 他没有这项专利权。The staff have a right to know how the company is doing. 职员有权知道公司的经营情况。foreign rights = legal title to sell something (especially a book) in a foreign country 国外销售权; right to strike = legal title for workers to stop working if they have a good reason for it 罢工权利; right of way = legal title to go across someone's property 路权;通行权;地段权 (b) rights issue = giving shareholders the right to buy more shares at a lower price 股权发行

◇ **rightful** a. legally correct 合法的: rightful claimant = person who has a legal claim to something 合法索赔人;合法债权人; rightful owner = legal owner 合法业主;合法所有者

◇ **right-hand** a. belonging to the right side 右边的;右手的;右方的: The credit side is the right-hand column in the accounts. 贷方是在帐目的右栏里。He keeps the address list in the right-hand drawer of his desk. 他把通讯录放在他桌子的右边抽屉里。right-hand man = main assistant 最得力的助手

**ring** 1 n. group of people who try to fix prices so as not to compete with each other and still make a large profit 价格联盟(指为获得更大的利益不相互竞争共同确定价的集团) 2 v. to call using the telephone 打电话: He rang (up) his stockbroker. 他给他的股票经纪人打了个电话。

NOTE: ringing - rang - has rung

◇ **ring back** v. to telephone in reply to a phone call 回电话: The managing director rang - can you ring him back? 总经理来过电话,你能给他回个电话吗?

**rise** 1 n. (a) increase or growing high 增加;上涨: rise in the price of raw materials 原材料价格的上涨; Oil price rises brought about a recession in world trade. 原油价格的上涨造成了世界贸易的衰退。There is a rise in sales of 10% or sales show a rise of 10%. 销售量增加了10%. Salaries are increasing to keep up with the rises in the cost of living. 工资正在增加以跟上生活费用的上涨。The recent rise in interest rates has made mortgages dearer. 最近利率的上涨使得抵押贷款利率更高了。(b)

increase in salary 增加工资: She asked her boss for a rise. 她向老板要求增加工资。He had a 6% rise in January. 一月份他的工资增加了6%。

NOTE: US English for (b) is raise 2 v. to move upwards or to become higher 涨;增长: prices are rising faster than inflation. 价格的上涨比通货膨胀还快。Interest rates have risen to 15%. 利率已增长到15%。

NOTE: rising - rose - has risen

**risk** n. (a) possible harm or chance of danger 风险;危险: to run a risk = to be likely to suffer harm 冒风险; to take a risk = to do something which may make you lose money or suffer harm 冒风险; financial risk = possibility of losing money 财务风险(指亏本的可能性): There is no financial risk in selling to East European countries on credit. 向东欧国家赊销没有财务风险。He is running the risk of overspending his promotion budget. 他将冒推销预算超支的风险。The company is taking a considerable risk in manufacturing 25m units without doing any market research. 在没有做任何市场调查的情况下,生产25m的元件,公司要冒相当大的风险。(b) risk capital = capital for investment which may easily be lost in risky projects, but which can also provide high returns 风险资本(指用于投资的资本可能轻易地在冒险项目中受到损失,但也可能带来高利润) (c) at owner's risk = situation where goods shipped or stored are insured by the owner, not by the transport company or the storage company 损失由物主负责: Goods left here are at owner's risk. 留在这里的货物由货主承担损失。The shipment was sent at owner's risk. 这批货的发运由货主承担风险。(d) loss or damage against which you are insured……险(保险业用词);保险对象: fire risk = situation or goods which could start a fire 火险;火灾

风险：That warehouse full of paper is a firerisk. 那间堆满纸的仓库有火灾危险。(e) He is a good or bad risk = It is not likely or it is very likely that the insurance company will have to pay out against claims where he is concerned. 他是个条件很好(风险很大)的保险对象。

◇ **risk－free** a. with no risk involved 无风险：a risk－free investment 无风险投资

◇ **risky** a. dangerous or which may cause harm 危险的；冒险的：He lost all his money in some risky ventures in South America. 在南美的一些风险投机中他损失了所有钱财。

**rival** n. person or company which competes in the same market 竞争者：a rival company 竞争公司；to undercut a rival 削价与竞争者抢生意；We are analyzing the rival brands on the market. 我们正在分析市场上我们产品竞争的品牌。

**road** n. (a) way used by cars or lorries, etc. to move from one place to another 道路；公路：to send or to ship goods by road 用公路运输货物；Eoad transport costs have risen. 公路运输的费用已经上涨。The main office is in London Road. 总办事处设在伦敦街。Use the Park Road entrance to get to the buying department. 从公园大道入口进入采购部。(b) on the road = travelling 在旅途中：The salesmen are on the road thirty weeks a year. 销售人员一年有 30 周是在旅途中度过的。We have twenty salesmen on the road. 我们有 20 名销售人员在外面出差。

**robot** n. machine which can be programmed to work like a person 机器人：The car is made by robots. 这辆汽车是机器人造的。

◇ **robotics** n. study of robots or making of robots 机器人的研制或制作。
NOTE: takes a singular v.

**rock** n. large stone 巨石；The company

is on the rocks. = The company is in great financial difficulties. 公司隐陷入了严重的财政困境。

◇ **rock bottom** n. rock－bottom prices = the lowest prices possible 最低价格：Sales have reached rock bottom. = Sales have reached the lowest point possible. 销售额已达最低点。

**rocket** v. to rise fast 飞速上升：rocketing prices 飞速上涨的价格；Prices have rocketed. 价格已飞速上涨。

**ROI** = RETURN ON INVESTMENT 投资收益率(报酬率)；报资利润率

**roll** 1 n. something which has been turned over and over to wrap round itself 卷状物；卷：The desk calculator uses a roll of paper. 这台台式计算机使用卷纸。2 v. to make something go forward by turning it over 滚动：They rolled the computer into position. 他们用滚动方式将计算机滚到位。

◇ **roll on/roll off** a. (ferry) where lorries and cars can drive straight into or off the boat(渡口)滚装式的(指车辆直接开上、开下)

◇ **roll over** v. to roll over credit or a debt = to make credit available over a continuing period or to allow a debt to stand after the repayment date 延期；到期转期(指将已到期的信贷延期使用，或允许已到偿还期限的债务们继续有效)

◇ **rolling plan** n. plan which runs for a period of time and is updated regularly for the same period 滚进计划；逐年延展计划(指要一段时间的计划，并在此期限内对计划进行定期更新)

◇ **rolling stock** n. wagons, etc., used on the railway 铁路运输设备(铁路车辆等)

**room** n. (a) part of a building, divided off from other parts by walls 房间：The chairman's room is at the end of the corridor. 董事长的房间在走廊的尽头。

conference room = room where a small meetingcan take place 会议室；mail room = section of a building where incoming letters are sorted and distributed to departments 邮件房；收发室；（b）bedroom in a hotel 饭店的客房：I want a room with bath for two nights. 我要一个带卫生间的房间，住两晚。double room = room with two beds, for two people 双人房间；room service = arrangement in a hotel where food or drink can be served in a guest's bedroom 送酒菜到旅客房间的饭店服务（c）space 空间，地位：The filing cabinets take up a lot of room. 文件柜占了房间很大一块地方。There is no more room in the computer file. 计算机文件里没有空间了。

NOTE: no plural for（c）

**rotation** n. taking turns 循环；轮流；交替：to fill the post of chairman by rotation = each member of the group is chairman for a period then gives the post to another member 轮流当董事长；Two directors retire by rotation . = Two directors retire because they have been directors longer than any others, but can offer themselves for re‐election. 按轮流制，两位董事退出董事会（但他们还可重新参加选举）。

NOTE: no plural

**rouble** n. money used in Russia 卢布（前苏联和俄罗斯货币）

**rough** a.（a）approximate or not very accurate 大约的；大概的：rough calculation or rough estimate = approximate answer 粗略估计；概算：I made some rough calculations on the back of an envelope. 我在信封背面大概算了一下。（b）not finished 来加工的；粗制的：rough copy = draft of a document which will have changes made to it before it is complete 草稿：He made a rough draft of the new design. 他画了一个新设计粗稿。

◇ **roughly** ad. more or less 大约地；约略地：The turnover is roughly twice last year's. 营业额大约是去年的两倍。The development cost of the project will be roughly £ 25,000. 该项目的开发费用大约是 25,000 英磅。

◇ **rough out** v. to make a draft or a general design 作出草案；草拟设计方案：The finance director roughed out a plan of investment. 财务主任草拟了一个投资计划。

**round** 1 a.（a）in round figures = not totally accurate, but correct to the nearest 10 or 100 以概数表示（以十、百整数表示而不计小数目）大概的；约略的（b）round trip = journey from one place to another and back again 往返旅行：round‐trip ticket 来回票；round‐trip fare 往返费用

◇ **round down** v. to decrease to the nearest full figure 以四舍五入简化

◇ **round up** v. to increase to the nearest full figure 以四舍五入计算：to round up the figures to the nearest pound 将数按英磅的四舍五入计算

**route** n.（a）way which is regularly taken 路线；路程：bus route = normal way taken by a bus from one place to another 公共汽车的路线；Companies were warned that normal shipping routes were dangerous because of the war. 公司得到警告说，因为战争，正常的运输路线变得危险了。（b）en route = on the way 在途中：The tanker sank when she was en route to the Gulf. 在油船去海湾的途中她沉了。

**routine** 1 n. normal or regular way of doing something 惯例；常规：He follows a daily routine. – he takes the 8.15 train to London, then the bus to his office, and returns by the same route in the evening. 他按照惯例——坐 8:15 的火车去伦敦，然后乘汽车到办公室，晚上原路线返回。Refitting the conference room has disturbed the office routine. 重新装修会议室,打乱了办公室的日常工作。2 a. normal or which happens regularly 例行的;惯例的: routine work 日常工作; routine call 例行访问; a routine check of the fire equipment 对消防器材的例行检查

**royalty** n. money paid to an inventor or writer or the owner of land for the right to use his property (usually a certain percentage of sales, or a certain amount per sale) 专利权税(付给发明者款项);版税(付给作者的款项);土地使用费(付给土地所有者,以得到使用其土地的权利): oil royalties 石油产地使用费; He is receiving royalties from his invention. 他获得发明专利权。

**RPM** = RESALE PRICE MAINTENANCE 维持转卖价格

**RRP** = RECOMMENDED RETAIL PRICE 建议的零售价格

**RSVP** = REPONDEZ S' IL VOUS PLAIT letters on an invitation showing the person to whom replies should be sent(请贴等用语)请答复

**rubber** n. elastic material from the juice of a tree 橡胶;橡皮: US rubber check = cheque which cannot be cashed because the person writing it does not have enough money in the account to pay it (美)空头支票;(由于开票人帐户上存款不足银行拒付的支票)

◇ **rubber stamp** 1 n. stamp with rubber letters or figures on it to put the date or a note on a document 橡皮图章: He stamped the invoice with the rubber stamp "Paid". 他用橡皮图章在发票上盖了"付讫"字样。2 v. to agree to something without discussing it 不加讨论即予批准或赞同某事: The board simply rubber stamped the agreement. 董事会未经讨论地就批准此协议(合同)。

**rule** 1 n. (a) general way of conduct 规则;常规: As a rule = usually 通常地;

照例地: As a rule, we do not give discounts over 20%. 通常我们给的折扣不超过20%。company rules = general way of working in a company 公司惯例;公司规定(公司工作的一般方式): It is a company rule that smoking is not allowed in the offices. 办公室里不许吸烟是公司的规定。(b) to work to rule = to work strictly according to the rules agreed by the company and union, and therefore to work very slowly 墨守成规地工作(指严格按照公司和工会的规定工作,因此工作效率不高); 2 v. (a) to give an official decision 裁决;裁定: The commission of inquiry ruled that the company was in breach of contract. 调查委员会裁定该公司违反了合同。The judge ruled that the documents had to be deposited with the court. 法官裁决这份文件须寄存在法院。(b) to be in force or to be current 有效的;现行的(价格): prices which are ruling at the moment 此刻的现行价格

◇ **ruling** 1 a. in operation at the moment or current 现行的: We will invoice at ruling prices. 我们会以现行价格开发票。2 n. decision 裁决: The inquiry gave a ruling on the case. 经过调查,已对此案作出裁决。According to the ruling of the court, the contract was illegal. 根据法院的判决,这份合同是非法的。

**run** 1 n. (a) making a machine work (机器的)运转;运行: a cheque run = series of cheques processed through a computer(通过计算机处理的一系列支票)支票运转 a computer run = period of work of a computer 计算机运行(工作)期; test run = trial made on a machine(在机器上进行的)试验;测试 (b) rush to buy something 争购;抢购;挤兑: The Post Office reported a run on the new stamps. 邮局对大家争购新邮票作了报道。a run on the bank = rush by customers to take deposits out of a bank which they think may close down

（银行）挤兑（指由于存户认为银行可能倒闭，而从银行挤兑存款）; a run on the pound = rush to sell pounds and buy other currencies 抛售英镑（争购其它货币）(c) regular route (of a plane or bus) 路线 2 v. (a) to be in force 生效; 有效: The lease runs for twenty years. 租期长达 20 年。 The lease has only six months to run. 租赁有效期只有 6 个月。(b) to amount to（累积而）达到共计; 合计: The costs ran into thousands of pounds. 费用达几千英镑。(c) to manage or to organize 管理; 经营: she runs a mail-order business from home. 她在家经营邮购业务。 They run a staff sports club. 他们管理看一个职工体育俱乐部。 He is running a multimillion-pound company 他经营着一个资金达数百万英镑的公司。(d) to work on a machine 开动（机器）: Do not run the photocopier for more than four hours at a time. 每次使用复印机不得超过 4 小时。 The computer was running invoices all night. 计算机整夜处理发票。(e) (of buses, trains etc.) to be working 行驶中（公共汽车、火车等）: There is an evening plane running between Manchester and Paris. 有一架晚班飞机来往于曼彻斯特和巴黎之间。 This train runs on weekdays. 这班火车除周未外天天有。 NOTE: running – ran – has run

◇ **runaway** a. runaway inflation = very rapid inflation, which is almost impossible to reduce 恶性通货膨胀

◇ **run down** v. (a) to reduce a quantity gradually 逐渐减少: to run down stocks or to let stocks run down 逐步减少存货 (b) to slow down the business activities of a company before it is going to be closed 逐渐停止; 逐渐减少（在公司行将关闭之前，对其商务活动采取逐步停业）: The company is being run down. 公司的业务正在逐渐减少。

◇ **run into** v. (a) to run into debt = to start to have debts（开始）负债 (b) to amount to 总计: Costs have run into thousands of pounds. 费用共计已达数千英磅。 He has an income running into five figures . = He earns more than ￡10,000. 他的收入达五位数。

◇ **running** n. (a) running total = total carried from one column of figures to the next 从一行数延伸到下行的总数 (b) running costs or running expenses or costs of running a business = money spent on the day-to-day cost of keeping a business going 运行成本; 日常费用; 经营费用 (c) The company has made a profit for six years running. = The company has made a profit for six years one after the other. 此公司已连续六年盈利。

◇ **run out of** v. to have nothing left or to use up all the stock 用光; 耗尽: We have run out of headed notepaper. 我们已用完了有抬头的信纸。 The printer has run out of paper. 打印机没纸了。

◇ **run up** v. to make debts go up quickly（债款）迅速积累（增加）: He quickly ran up a bill for ￡250. 他很快地使帐单上的欠款增加到 250 英镑。

**rupee** n. money used in India and some other countries 卢比（印度和其他一些国家的货币）

**rush** 1 n. doing something fast 忙碌; 急速: rush hour = time when traffic is worst or when everyone is trying to travel to work or from work back home 高峰时间: The taxi was delayed in the rush hour traffic. 出租车因高峰期交通拥挤而延误了时间。 rush job = job which has to be done fast 需尽快做的工作; 突击性工作; rush order = order which has to be supplied fast 紧急订单 2 v. to make something go fast 使匆忙地做（某事）: to rush an order through the factory 催工厂赶快完成订单; to rush a shipment to Africa 赶快向非洲发一批货

# Ss

**sack** 1. n. (a) large bag made of strong cloth or plastic 袋(由结实的布或塑料制成的): a sack of potatoes 一袋土豆; We sell onions by the sack. 我们按袋出售洋葱。(b) to get the sack = to be dismissed from a job 被解雇 NOTE: no plural for (b)
2. v. to sack someone = to dismiss someone from a job 解雇某人: He was sacked after being late for work. 他因上班迟到而被解雇。

◇ **sacking** n. dismissal from a job 解雇; 革职: The union protested against the sackings. 工会抗议解雇工人

**SAE or s. a. e.** = STAMPED ADDRESSED ENVELOPE 贴有邮票和具有本人地址的回邮信封

**safe** 1. n. heavy metal box which cannot be opened easily, in which valuable documents, money, etc. can be kept put the documents in the safe 保险箱; 保险柜: We keep the petty cash in the safe. 我们把零用现金放在保险箱里。fire-proof safe = safe which cannot be harmed by fire 耐火保险箱; night safe = safe in the outside wall of a bank, where money and documents can be deposited at night, using a special door 夜间保险箱(装在银行外墙上的保险箱, 用的是一种特殊的门, 人们可在夜晚将钱和文件存在里面); wall safe = safe installed in a wall 墙上的保险箱 2. a. (a) out of danger 安全的: keep the documents in a safe place = in a place where they cannot be stolen or destroyed 将文件放在安全地方。safe keeping = being looked after carefully 妥善保管, 妥善保护: We put the documents into the bank for safe keeping. 我们把文件放在银行妥善保管。(b) safe investments = shares, etc., which are not likely to fall in value 保值投资; 安全投资

◇ **safe deposit** n. bank safe where you can leave jewellery or documents 保险库; 保管库(指可存放宝石或文件的银行保管库)

◇ **safe deposit box** n. small box which you can rent to keep jewellery or documents in a bank's safe(银行)保险箱(指一种小箱子, 可租用来存放宝石或文件, 并将此放在银行的保险仓库内)

◇ **safely** adv. without being harmed 安全地: The cargo was unloaded safely from the sinking ship. 货物被安全地从沉船上卸下。

◇ **safeguard** v. to protect 保护; 维护: to safeguard the interests of the shareholders 保护股东的利益

◇ **safety** n. (a) being free from danger or risk 安全; 保险: safety margin = time or space allowed for something to be safe 安全边际; 安全界限; margin of safety = sales which are above the breakeven point 安全边际; 安全系数(指超过保本点销量的销售); to take safety precautions or safety measures = to act to make sure something is safe 采取预防措施; 采取安全措施; safety regulations = rules to make a place of work safe for the workers 安全规则. (b) fire safety = making a place of work safe for the workers in case of fire 防火措施; fire safety officer = person in a company responsible for seeing that the workers are safe if a fire breaks out 防火员. (c) for safety = to make something safe or to be safe. 使…保险(安全); 为保险(安全): Put the documents in the cupboard for safety; 为了安全起见, 将文件放在小柜里。to take a copy of the disk for safety 为安全起见, 将磁盘做一份拷贝

NOTE: no plural

**sail** v. to travel on water or to leave harbour 航行 ( 于水面 ); 起航: The ship sails at 12:00. 这艘船 12 时起航。

◇ **sailing** n. departure (of a ship) 航行; 开航: There are no sailings to France because of the strike. 由于罢工, 没有开往法国的船。

**salary** n. payment for work, made to an employee usually as a cheque atthe end of each month 工资; 薪水; 薪金: She got a salary increase in June. 6 月份她增加了工资。 The company froze all salaries for a six-month period. 公司使所有工资冻结了 6 个月。 basic salary = normal salary without extra payments 基本工资; gross salary = salary before tax is deducted. 薪资总额 ( 指扣除税前的工资 ); net salary = salary which is left after deducting tax and national insurance contributions. 净工资 ( 指征所得税和国家保险摊款, 剩下的工资 ); starting salary = amount of payment for an employee when starting work. 起点工资: He was appointed at a starting salary of £10,000. 他的起始工资定为 10,000 英磅。 salary cut = sudden reduction in salary 薪水削减; salary cheque = monthly cheque by which an employee is paid 工资支票; salary deductions = money which a company removes from salaries to give to the government as tax, national insurance contributions, etc. 薪水扣除 ( 款 ); salary review = examination of salaries in a company to see if workers should earn more 工资调整: She had a salary review last April or her salary was reviewed last April. 去年 4 月份对她的工资进行了调整。 scale of salaries or salary scale = list of salaries showing different levels of pay in different jobs in the same company 工资表; 薪资表; the company's salary structure = organization of salaries in a company, with different rates for different types of job 公司工资结构

◇ **salaried** a. earning a salary 有薪金的; 拿薪金的: The company has 250 salaried staff. 公司有 250 名拿工资的职员。

**sale** n. (a) act of selling or of giving an item in exchange for money 出售; 销售; 卖: cash sale = selling something for cash 现金销售; 现销业务; credit card sale = selling something for credit, using a credit card 信用卡销售; forced sale = selling something because a court orders it or because it isthe only thing to do to avoid a financial crisis 强制销售 ( 因法院命令而出售某物或因这是唯一能避免财政危机的做法 ); sale and lease-back = situation where a company sells a property to raise cash and then leases it back from the purchaser 出售回租 ( 指公司为筹集现款将房产售出, 然后再从买主那将里其租回 ); sale or return = system where the retailer sends goods back if they are not sold, and pays the supplier only for goods sold 剩货保退 ( 指如果货物未售出, 零售商可将其退回, 并只付给供应商已售货物的款 ): We have taken 4,000 items on sale or return. 我们已进了 4,000 种剩货保退商品。 bill of sale = document which the seller gives to the buyer to show that a sale has taken place 出货单; 买卖契约; conditions of sale = agreed ways in which a sale takes place (such as discounts and credit terms) 销售条件 (b) for sale = ready to be sold 待售; 出售: to offer something for sale or to put something up for sale = to announce that something is ready to be sold 将某物出售: They put the factory up for sale. 他们要卖掉工厂。 His shop is for sale. 他的商店要出售。 These items are not for sale to the general public. 这些商品不向公众出售。 (c) on sale = ready to be sold in a shop 出售；上市的(指货物在商店出售)：These items are on sale in most chemists. 这些商品在大多数药店里均有出售。(d) sales = money received for selling something or number of items sold 销售额；销售量：Sales have risen over the first quarter. 销售额第一季度已有增加。sales analysis = examining the reports of sales to see why items have or have not sold well 销售分析(指审查商品已售出或未售出的销售原因的报告)；sales appeal = quality which makes customers want to buy 销售感染力(指可使顾客想购买的产品质量)；sales book = record of sales 销售簿；book sales = sales as recorded in the sales book 帐面销售额；sales budget = plan of probable sales 销售额预算；sales campaign = planned work to achieve higher sales 推销运动；sales conference or sales meeting = meeting of sales managers, representatives, publicity staff, etc., to discuss results and future sales plans 销售会议；cost of sales = all the costs of a product sold, including manufacturingcosts and the staff costs of the production department 销售成本；sales department = section of a company which deals in selling the company's sproducts or services 销售部门；domestic sales or home sales = sales in the home market 国内销售；sales drive = vigorous work to increase sales 促销运动；sales executive = person in a company in charge of sales 销售经理；sales figures = total sales, or sales broken down by category 销售金额(指总的销售额或按种类分类的销售额)；sales force = group of salesmen 推销人员；销售力量；sales forecast = calculation of future sales 销售预测；forward sales = sales (of shares, commodities, foreign exchange) for delivery at a later date 期货销售；预售(指股票、商品和外汇交易可在以后交货) sales ledger = book in

which income from sales is recorded 销货客户分户帐；sales ledger clerk = office worker who deals with the sales ledger 销售客户分户帐的记帐员；sales literature = printed information (such as leaflets, prospectuses) which help sales 促销印刷品(广告)；sales manager = person in charge of a sales department 销售经理；monthly sales report = report made showing the number of items or amount of money received for selling stock 月销售表报；In the sales reports all the European countries are bracketed together. 在销售报告中所有的欧洲国家归为一类。sales revenue = money received from sales 销货收益；销售收入；sales tax = tax to be paid on each item sold 营业税；销售税；sales volume or volume of sales = number of units sold 销售量；(e) selling of goods at specially low prices 大贱卖；(特价)廉售：The shop is having a sale to clear old stock. 这家商店正在进行特价廉售以清除旧存货。The sale price is 50% of the normal price. 大贱卖售价是通常价格的 50%。bargain sale = sale of all goods in a store at cheap prices 大减价；大廉价；clearance sale = sale of items at low prices to get rid of the stock 清仓大甩卖；half - price sale = sale of items at half the usual price 半价出售；jumble sale = sale of old used household goods 旧货廉卖；the sales = period when major stores sell many items at specially low prices 降价期(指主要商店的许多商品以特低价出售的时间)：I bought this in the sales or at the sales or in the January sales. 我是在降价期间(一月降价期内)买这件物品的。

◇ **saleability** n. quality of an item which makes it easy to sell 可销售性
NOTE: no plural

◇ **saleable** a. which can easily be sold 易出售的

◇ **saleroom** n. room where an auction

takes place 拍卖场

◇ **salesclerk** n. US person who sells goods to customers in a store(美)售货员

◇ **salesgirl** n. girl who sells goods to customers in a store 女售货员；女营业员

◇ **saleslady** n. woman who sells goods to customers in a store 女售货员

◇ **salesman** n. (a) man who sells goods or services to members of the public 推销员(指向公众界推销商品或服务的人): He is the head salesman in the carpet department. 他是地毯部的首席推销员。a used car salesman 旧车推销员; door - to - door salesman = man who goes from one house to the next, asking people to buysomething 挨户推销员(指挨家挨户推销其商品的人); insurance salesman = man who encourages clients to take out insurance policies 保险推销员 (b) person who represents a company, selling its products or services to retail shops 销售代表(指代表公司向零售店推销其产品或服务的人): We have six salesmen calling on accounts in central London. 我们有 6 名销售代表在伦敦市中心巡访客户。
NOTE: plural is salesmen

◇ **salesmanship** n. art of selling or of persuading customers to buy 推销术；销售术
NOTE: no plural

◇ **saleswoman** n. woman in a shop who sells goods to customers 商店女售货员
NOTE: plural is saleswomen

**salvage** 1. n. (a) saving a ship or a cargo from being destroyed 遇难船只及货物的打捞: salvage money = payment made by the owner of a ship or a cargo to the person who has saved it 救援报酬；打捞费；救助费; salvage vessel = ship which specializes in saving other ships and their cargoes 救援船；打捞船 (b) goods saved from a wrecked ship or from a fire, etc.(从遇难船只或火灾中)抢救出来的物资: a sale of flood salvage items 出售从水灾中打捞的物品
NOTE: no plural 2. v. (a) to save goods or a ship from being wrecked 打捞: We are selling off a warehouse full of salvaged goods. 我们正在廉价出售一个仓库，里面堆满了打捞的货物。(b) to save something from loss 挽救…；免受损失: The company is trying to salvage its reputation after the managing director was sent to prison for fraud. 在总经理因诈骗罪入狱后，公司正设法挽回其名誉。The receiver managed to salvage something from the collapse of the company. 破产事务管设法从公司的倒闭中挽回一些东西。

**sample** 1. n. (a) specimen or a small part of an item which is used to show whatthe whole item is like 样本；样品: a sample of the cloth or a cloth sample 一块布样; check sample = sample to be used to see if a whole consignment is acceptable 验货的样品; free sample = sample given free to advertise a product 免费样品; sample book or book of samples = book showing samples of different types of cloth or paper, etc. 样本册 (b) small group taken to show what a larger group is like 抽样: We interviewed a sample of potential customers. 我们与有可能成为客户的代表进行了面谈。a random sample = a sample taken without any selection 随机抽样；随意抽样(指不加选择地抽取样品) 2. v. (a) to test or to try something by taking a small amount 抽样试验；抽样检验: to sample a product before buying it 在买某一产品以前，先进行抽样检查 (b) to ask a representative group of people questions to find out what the reactions of a much larger group would be 抽样调查(指向具有代表性的人提问题从而知道更多人的反应): They sampled 2,

000 people at random to test the new drink. 他们随意请来了 2,000 人来试尝这种新饮料。

◇ **sampling** n. (a) testing a product by taking a small amount 抽样检验: sampling of Common Market produce 对欧洲共同市场的农产品进行抽样检验; acceptance sampling = testing a small sample of a batch to see if the whole batchis good enough to be accepted 验收抽样; 承认货样 (b) testing the reactions of a small group of people to find outthe reactions of a larger group of consumers 抽样调查: random sampling 随意调查 (取样)

**sanction** 1. n. (a) permission 批准; 认可: You will need the sanction of the local authorities before you can knock down the office block. 在拆除办公大楼之前, 你必须得到地方当局的批准。(b) economic sanctions = restrictions on trade with a country in order to influenceits political situation or in order to make its government changeits policy 经济制裁: to impose sanctions on a country or to lift sanctions 对一个国家进行制裁或撤消制裁。2. v. to approve 批准; 认可: The board sanctioned the expenditure of £1.2m on the development project. 董事会批准了该开发项目 120 万英磅的费用

**sandwich** n. two pieces of bread with meat or cheese, etc. between them 三明治

◇ **sandwich boards** n. boards carried in front of and behind a person to carry advertisements 三明治式广告 (挂在人身体胸前和背后的广告牌)

◇ **sandwich course** n. course of study where students spend a period of time working in a factory or office as part of a college course 三明治式课程; 工读交替制课程 (指将学生在工厂或办公室实习一段时间作为大学课程一部分的学习课程)

◇ **sandwich man** n. man who carries sandwich boards 挂着广告牌的人

**satisfaction** n. feeling of being happy or good feeling 满意; 满足: customer satisfaction = making a customer pleased with what he has bought 顾客满意; job satisfaction = a worker's feeling that he is happy in his place of work and pleased with the work he does 工作满意
NOTE: no plural

◇ **satisfy** v. (a) to satisfy a client = to make a client pleased with what he has purchased 让顾客(对所购商品)满意: a satisfied customer = a customer who has got what he wanted 已满足需求的顾客 (b) to satisfy a demand = to fill a demand 满足需求: We cannot produce enough to satisfy the demand for the product. 我们的生产量无法满足顾客对该产品的需求。

**saturation** n. filling completely 饱和: saturation of the market or market saturation = situation where the market has taken as much of the product as it can buy 市场饱和; The market has reached saturation point. = The market is at a point where it cannot buy any more of the product. 市场已达饱和点。
NOTE: no plural

◇ **saturate** v. to fill something completely 使饱和: to saturate the market 使市场饱和; The market for home computers is saturated. 家用计算机市场已经饱和了。

**save** v. (a) to keep (money) or not to spend (money) 省钱; 不花钱: He is trying to save money by walking to work. 他为了省钱步行去上班。She is saving to buy a house. 她正在存钱买房子。(b) not to waste or to use less 节省: To save time, let us continue the discussion in the taxi to the airport. 为了节省时间, 让我们在去机场的出租车上继续讨论。The government is encouraging companies to saveenergy. 政府正鼓励各公司节约能源。(c) to store data on a computer disk 存贮(指将数据贮存在计算机的磁盘上): Do not forget to save your files when you have finished keyboarding them. 在你输入完文件后，别忘了把它存盘。

◇ **save – as – you – earn** n. GB save – as – you – earn scheme = scheme where workers can save money regularly by having it deducted automatically from their wages and invested in National Savings 定期储蓄计划(指工人可通过从其工资中自动扣除并投资于国民储蓄进行定期储蓄)

◇ **save on** v. not to waste or to use less 节省；节约: By introducing shift work we find we can save on fuel. 我们发现引入轮班工作制可以节省燃料。

◇ **saver** n. person who saves money 节俭的人

◇ **save up** v. to put money aside for a special purpose 储蓄；存钱(指为某一特殊目的的存款): They are saving up for a holiday in the USA. 他们正为去美国度假存钱。

◇ **saving** 1. n. using less 节省；节约: We are aiming for a 10% saving in fuel. 我们的目标是节省10％的燃料。2. suffix which uses less(后缀)节省的；节约的: an energy – saving or labour – saving device = machine which saves energy or labour 能源节省设备；节省劳力设备；time – saving = which takes less time 省时的

◇ **savings** pl. n. money saved 储蓄(金)存款: He put all his savings into a deposit account. 他把所有的积蓄存入帐户。GB National Savings = scheme run by the Post Office, where small investors caninvest in government savings certificates, premium bonds, etc. (英)国民储蓄计划(该计划由邮局执行，按

所计划小额投资者可对政府储蓄债券、溢价债券等进行投资) savings certificate or US savings bond = document showing that you have invested money in a governmentsavings scheme 储蓄存单；(美)储蓄公债(指该证券已表明你已在政府储蓄计划中投了资) savings account = bank account where you can put money in regularly and which pays interest, often at a higher rate than a deposit account 储蓄帐户

◇ **savings bank** n. bank where you can deposit money and receive interest on it 储蓄银行

◇ **savings and loan** ( association ) n. US financial association which accepts and pays interest on deposits from investors and lends money to people who are buying property 储蓄与贷款社；储蓄贷款协会(指吸收投资者存款并付利息，而且借钱给要购置房地产的人的金融机构)

**SAYE** = SAVE – AS – YOU – EARN 定期储蓄计划

**scab** n. infml. worker who goes on working when there is a strike(非正式)工贼；破坏罢工的人

**scale** 1. n. (a) system which is graded into various levels 等级；比例: scale of charges or scale of prices = list showing various prices 收费表；价格表; fixed scale of charges = rate of charging which does not change 固定收费比例; scale of salaries or salary scale = list of salaries showing different levels of pay in differentjobs in the same company 工资等级(比例)；工资级别表: He was appointed at the top end of the salary scale 他的工资级别最高。incremental scale = salary scale with regular annual salary increases 常规增薪幅度或等级 (b) large scale or small scale = working with large or small amounts of investment or staff, etc. 大规模；小规模: to start in business on a small scale = to start in businesswith a small staff or few products or little investments 开始小规模营业(指用少数人员，极少产品投资开始营业)；economies of scale = making a product more economical by manufacturing it or buying it in larger quantities 规模经济(指采取大批量生产或购买，使产品更经济)(c) scales = machine for weighing 秤(指称重量的机器) 2. v. to scale down or to scale up = to lower or to increase in proportion(按比例)缩减；(按比例)增加

**scam** n. US infml. case of fraud(美)(非正式诡计；骗局)

**scarce** a. not easily found or not common 稀有的；缺乏的；不足的：scarce raw material 稀有原料。Reliable trained staff are scarce. 可靠的受过培训的职员太少了。

◇ **scarceness or scarcity** n. lack being scarce 缺乏；不足：the scarceness of trained staff 受过培训的人员不足。There is a scarcity of trained staff. 缺乏受过训练的人员。scarcity value = value of something because it is rare and there is a large demand for it 缺货价格；稀货价格(价值)
NOTE: no plural

**schedule** 1. n. (a) timetable or plan of time drawn up in advance 时间表；计划表：to be ahead of schedule = to be early 提前；to be on schedule = to be on time 准时；to be behind schedule = to be late 延误：The project is on schedule. 这个项目按时进行。The building was completed ahead of schedule. 这座楼提前完工了。I am sorry to say that we are three months behind schedule. 很抱歉，我们比计划落后了 3 个月。The managing director has a busy schedule of appointments. 总经理的整个日程排得很紧。His secretary tried to fit me into his schedule. 他的秘书试图使我适合于

他的日程安排。(b) list (especially additional documents attached to a contract)附件(指特别附在合同上的文件)：Please find enclosed our schedule of charges. 兹随信附上的我们的收费表。schedule of territories to which a contract applies 合同适用领域队件。see the attached schedule or as per the attached schedule 见附表；按附件 (c) GB tax schedules = six types of income as classified for tax(英)税率表(指按税分类的六种收入) 2. v. (a) to list officially 正式列出：scheduled prices or scheduled charges 正式列出的价格 (b) to plan the time when something will happen 计划；安排；排定：The building is scheduled for completion in May. 该大楼计划五月完工。scheduled flight = regular flight which is in the airline timetable 定期航班：He left for Helsinki on a scheduled flight. 他乘定期航班去了赫尔辛基。

◇ **scheduling** n. drawing up a plan or a timetable 作计划；订时间表
NOTE: no plural

**scheme** n. plan or arrangement or way of working 计划；规划；方案：bonus scheme 奖金方案；pension scheme 养老金方案；profit - sharing scheme 利润分享方案

**science** n. study or knowledge based on observing and testing 科学：business science or management science = the study of business or management techniques 商业学；管理学：He has a master's degree in business science. 他获得了商业学硕士学位。science park = area near a town or university set aside for technological industries 科技园(指为科技工业留出的,靠近城镇或大学的地方)

**scope** n. opportunity or possibility 机会；可能性：There is scope for improvement in our sales performance. = The sales performance could be improved. 我们的销售工作有改进的可能。There is considerable scope for expansion into the exportmarket. 很有可能扩展到出口市场。

**scrap** 1. n. waste material or pieces of metal to be melted down to makenew metal ingots 废料；废金属：to sell a ship for scrap 把船当废金属卖掉。Its scrap value is £2,500. 它的报废价值是 2,500 英磅。scrap dealer or scrap merchant = person who deals in scrap 买卖废品的商人 2. v. (a) to give up or to stop working on 废弃；放弃：to scrap plans for expansion 废弃扩展计划 (b) to throw (something) away as useless 丢弃：They had to scrap 10,000 spare parts. 他们不得不丢弃 10,000 个备件 NOTE: scrapping – scrapped

**screen** 1. n. glass surface on which computer information or TV pictures, etc., can be shown 屏幕：a TV screen 电视屏幕。He brought up the information on the screen. 他将信息在屏幕上显示出来。2. v. to screen candidates = to examine candidates to see if they are completely suitable 选拔（挑选）候选人

◇ **screening** n. the screening of candidates = examining candidates to see if they are suitable 选拔候选人

**scrip** n. scrip issue = new shares given free to shareholders 发行红利股

**sea** n. area of salt water 海；海洋：to send a shipment by sea 由海上运送货物；by sea mail = sent by post abroad, using a ship, not by air 海外邮寄（用船，而不是空邮）

◇ **seaport** n. port by the sea 海港

**seal** 1. n. (a) common seal or company's seal = metal stamp for stamping documents with the name of thecompany to show they have been approved officially 公章；公司印章（指将带有公司名称的图章盖在文件上，表明他们已正式批准了）：to attach the company's seal to a document 正文件上盖上公司的章；contract under seal = contract which has been legally approved with the seal of the company 盖印合同 (b) piece of paper or metal or wax attached to close something, so that it can be opened only if the paper or metal or wax is removedor broken 封条；封铅；封蜡；封印（指将一条纸、铅、蜡等贴在要封的物品上，只有将封条、封铅或封蜡除去，才能打开它）：customs seal = seal attached by customs office to a box, to show that the contents have not passed through the customs 海关封条 2. v. (a) to close something tightly 密封：The computer disks were sent in a sealed container. 计算机的磁盘是放在一个密封的容器里寄出的。sealed envelope = envelope where the back has been stuck down to close it 封口信封 The information was sent in a sealed envelope. 信息是放在一个封口信封里发走的。sealed tenders = tenders sent in sealed envelopes, which will all be opened ata certain time 密封投标书（指投标书是放在密封信封里送出的，只能在一定时间内可启封）：The company has asked for sealed bids for the warehouse. 公司已要求对仓库进行密封投标。(b) to attach a seal or to stamp something with a seal 盖印；盖章于…：The customs sealed the shipment. 海关；盖章确认了了这批货运。

**search** n. examination of records by the lawyer acting for someone who wants to buy a property, to make sure that the vendor has the right to sell it 调查（指律师代表买主对出售房地产的卖主进行调查，确认该买主是否有权出售）

**season** n. (a) one of four parts which a year is divided into (spring, summer, autumn, winter)季；季节 (b) a period of time when something usually takes place 时机；时令：low season or high season = period when there are few travellers or lots of travellers 旅游淡季

或旺季: Air fares are cheaper in the low season. 飞机票价在旅游淡季较便宜。 tourist season or holiday season = period when there are many people on holiday 旅游旺季; busy season or slack season = period when a company is busy or not very busy 旺季或淡季(公司); dead season = time of year when there are few tourists about 旅游淡季; end of season sale = selling goods cheaply when the season in which they would be used is over (such as summer clothes sold cheaply in the autumn)季末销售

◇ **seasonal** a. which lasts for a season or which only happens during a particular season 季节的;季节性的;随季节而变化的: The demand for this item is very seasonal. 对该物品的需求非常有季节性。 seasonal variations in sales patterns 销售模式中的季节性变化; seasonal adjustments = changes made to figures to take account of seasonal variations 季节调整(根据季节变化而对数字进行更改); seasonal demand = demand which exists only during the high season 季节性需求; seasonal unemployment = unemployment which rises and falls according to the season 季节性失业

◇ **seasonally** ad. seasonally adjusted figures = statistics which are adjusted to take account of seasonal variations 季节性调整数字

◇ **season ticket** n. rail or bus ticket which can be used for any number of journeys over a period (normally 1, 3, 6 or 12 months) 月票;定期票(指一段时间内可用于许多次旅行的火车或公共汽车票)

**sec** = SECRETARY 秘书 hon sec = honorary secretary 名誉秘书

**second** 1. a. (thing) which comes after the first 第二的;次要的;次等的: second half – year = six month period from July to the end of December 后半年;下

半年; second mortgage = further mortgage on a property which is already mortgaged 第二次抵押(指对已抵押的财产做再次抵押); second quarter = three month period from April to the end of June 第二季度 2. v. (a) to second a motion = to be the first person to support a proposal put forward by someone else 附议;支持提议: Mrs Smith seconded the motion or the motion was seconded byMrs Smith. 史密斯女士支持这个提议。(b) to lend a member of staff to another company or to a government department, etc., for a fixed period of time 调动;调派(人员);借调: He was seconded to the Department of Trade for two years. 他借调到贸易部工作两年。

◇ **secondary** a. second in importance 次要的;第二的: secondary banks = companies which provide money for hire – purchase deals 二级银行(指向租购业务提供资金的公司); secondary industry = industry which uses basic raw materials to make manufacturedgoods 第二产业(指用基本原材料制作工业制成品的产业); secondary picketing = picketing of a second factory, which is not directly connected with a strike, to prevent it supplying a striking factory or receiving supplies from it 二线纠察队

◇ **second – class** a. & adv. less expensive or less comfortable way of travelling 次等的(地);二等的(地);便宜的(地): to travel second – class 乘二等车(或舱)旅行: The price of a second – class ticket is half that of a first class. 二等票的价格是一等票的一半。I find second – class hotels are just as comfortable as the best ones. 我发现二流饭店和一流的一样舒适。second – class mail = (i) GB less expensive, slower, mail service(英)(便宜的,但较慢的邮递服务)二等邮递 (ii) US mail service for sending newspapers and magazines(美)(报纸、杂志等的)邮递服务: A second

– class letter is slower than a first – class. 二等信件比一等慢点。Send itsecond – class if it is not urgent. 如不急的话, 就按二等邮件寄。

◇ **seconder** n. person who seconds a proposal 附议者 (指赞同某项提议的人): There was no seconder for the motion so it was not put to the vote 因此动议无附议者, 所以该动议不再交付表决

◇ **second half** n. period of six months from 1st July to end of December 下半年: The figures for the second half are up on those for the first part of the year. 下半年的数字高于上半年的数字

◇ **secondhand** a. & ad. used or not new or which has been owned by someone before 用过的(地);旧的(地);二手的(地): a secondhand car salesman 二手汽车推销员; the secondhand computer market or the market in secondhand computers 二手计算机市场;旧计算机市场; to buy something secondhand 购买二手货;Look at the prices of secondhand cars or look at secondhand carprices. 看看旧(二手)汽车的价格。secondhand dealer = dealer who buys and sells secondhand items 二手货交易商

◇ **secondment** n. being seconded to another job for a period 借调(被调派做另一工作一段时间): He is on three years' secondment to an Australian college. 他被借调到一所澳大利亚学院工作三年。

◇ **second – rate** a. not of good quality 次等的;二流的: never buy anything second – rate 从不买二流东西

◇ **seconds** pl. n. items which have been turned down by the quality controller as not being top quality 次品: The shop has a sale of seconds. 这个商店有次品出售。

**secret** n. & a. (something) hidden or not known by many people 秘密(的);机密(的): The MD kept the contract secret from the rest of the board. 总经理没有将这个合同告诉董事会的其他董事。They signed a secret deal with their main rivals. 他们与其主要竞争者签了一份秘密协议。to keep a secret = not to tell someone a secret which you know 保守秘密

◇ **secretary** n. (a) person who helps to organize work or types letters or files documents or arranges meetings, etc. for someone 秘书: secretary and personal assistant 秘书和个人助手; My secretary deals withincoming orders. 我的秘书处理新来的订货单。His secretary phoned to say he would be late. 他的秘书打电话讲他将迟到。(b) official of a company or society(公司或团体的)官员;行政人员;高级职员: company secretary = person who is responsible for a company's legal and financial affairs 公司的高级职员(负责公司法律和财务事务的人); honorary secretary = person who keeps the minutes and official documents of a committee or club, but is not paid a salary 名誉秘书: He was elected secretary of the committee or committee secretary. 他被选为该委员会的名誉秘书。membership secretary = committee member who deals with the ordinary members of a society 委员秘书 (c) GB member of the government in charge of a department(英)部长;大臣(负责政府某一部门的官员): Education Secretary 教育大臣。Foreign Secretary 外交部长(大臣); US Secretary of the Treasury = senior member of the government in charge of financial affairs(美)财政部长

◇ **Secretary of State** n. (a) GB member of the government in charge of a department(英)国务大臣 (b) US senior member of the government in charge of foreign affairs(美)国务卿

◇ **secretarial** a. referring to the work of a secretary 秘书的;有关秘书事务

的：She is taking a secretarial course. 她正在上文秘课程。He is looking for secretarial work. 他在寻找文秘工作。We need extra secretarial help to deal with the mailings. 我们需要额外的文秘助手来处理邮件。secretarial college = college which teaches typing, shorthand and word - processing 文秘学院；文法学院

◇ **secretariat** n. important office and the officials who work in it 秘书处；书记处；the United Nations secretariat 联合国秘书处

**section** n. part of something 部分；部门：legal section = department in a company dealing with legal matters 法律部门；司法部门

**sector** n. part of the economy or the business organization of a country 经济部门；国家商务组织：All sectors of the economy suffered from the fall in the exchange rate. 所有经济部门都遭受到这次汇率下跌带来损失。Technology is a booming sector of the economy. 技术是一个迅速发展的经济部门。public sector = nationalized industries and public services 公共部门；公营部门；public sector borrowing requirement = amount of money which a government has to borrow to pay for its own spending 公营部门借款要求（指政府不得不借款支付其自身开支的金额）；private sector = all companies which are owned by private shareholders, not by the state 私营部门：The expansion is funded completely by the private sector. 此项发展是完全由私营部门出资的。Salaries in the private sector have increased faster than in the public. 私营部门的工资比公营增加的快。

**secure** 1. a. safe or which cannot change 安全的；可靠的：secure job = job from which you are not likely to be made redundant 牢靠的工作；secure investment = investment where you are not likely to lose money 可靠的投资 2. v.（a）to secure a loan = to pledge a property as a security for a loan 为贷款作抵押（指抵押财产作为贷款担保）（b）to get（something）safely into your control 取得；获得；促成：to secure funds 获得资金；He secured the backing of an Australian group. 他得到了一个澳大利亚集团的资助。

◇ **secured** a. secured loan = loan which is guaranteed by the borrower giving valuable property as security 抵押贷款；（指借款人出示有价值财产作为抵押所获贷款：secured creditor = person who is owed money by someone, and can legally claim the same amount of the borrower's property if he fails to pay back the money owed 有担保的债权人；secured debts = debts which are guaranteed by assets 以资产担保的债务

◇ **securities** pl. n. investments in stocks and shares；certificates to show that someone owns stock 证券：gilt - edged securities or government securities = investments in British government stock 金边证券；头等债券；政府有价证券；公债券（指英国政府债券）；listed securities = shares which can be bought or sold on the Stock Exchange or shares which appear on the official Stock Exchange list 挂牌上市证券；the securities market = Stock Exchange or place where stocks and shares can be bought or sold 证券市场；股票交易所；securities trader = person whose business is buying and selling stocks and shares 证券交易人；

◇ **security** n. （a）job security = feeling which a worker has that he has a right to keep his job or that his job will never end 工作保障：security of employment = feeling by a worker that he has the right to keep his job until he retires 就业保障；security of tenure = right to keep a job or rented accommodation, provided that certain conditions are met 使用期保障; (b) being protected 安全; 保护: airport security = actions taken to protect aircraft and passengers again-stattack 机场安全措施; security guard = person who protects an office or factory against burglars 保安人员; 安全保卫人员; office security = protecting an office against theft(办公室的)防盗措施 (c) being secret 保密; 保险: Security in this office is nil. = Nothing can be kept secret in this office. 此办公室保密等于零。 security printer = printer who prints paper money, secret government documents, etc. 保密印刷工人(印制纸币, 政府保密文件等的印刷工) (d) social security = money or help provided by the government to people who need it 社会保障; 社会保险: He lives on social security payments. 他靠社会保险的付款生活。(e) guarantee that someone will repay money borrowed 担保; 保证: to stand security for someone = to guarantee that if the person does not repay a loan, you will repay it for him 为某人提供担保; to give something as security for a debt 使某物作为债务担保; to use a house assecurity for a loan 用房子作为贷款担保; The bank lent him £20,000 without security 在无担保的情况下, 银行借给他 20,000 英磅。

NOTE: no plural

**see – safe** n. agreement where a supplier will give credit for unsold goods at the end of a period 货物赊售协议(在某一期限末没卖出的货物, 供应商给予销售商信贷): We bought the stock see – safe. 我们按货物赊售协议买这批货。

**seek** v. to ask for 请求: They are seeking damages for loss of revenue. 他们一直在要求获得收入损失赔偿金。to seek an interview = to ask if you can see someone 请求会见: She sought an interview with the minister. 她请求与部长会面。

NOTE: seeking – sought

**seize** v. to take hold of something or to take possession of something 抓住; 拥有; 查封; 没收: The customs seized the shipment of books. 海关查封了这批书。The court ordered the company's funds to be seized. 法院下令依法没收该公司的资金。

◇ **seizure** n. taking possession of something 没收; 占有; 抵押: The court ordered the seizure of the shipment or of the company's funds. 法院下命没收这批货或该公司的资金。

**select** 1. a. of top quality or specially chosen 优等的; 精选的: Our customers are very select. 我们的顾客是精选者。a select range of merchandise 商品的精选系列 2. v. to choose 选择; 挑选: Selected items are reduced by 25%. = Some items have been reduced by 25%. (挑选了)有些商品降价 25%

◇ **selection** n. choice; thing which has been chosen 选择; 挑选: a selection of our product line 我们的生产线选择; selection board or selection committee = committee which chooses a candidate for a job 选拔董事会; 选拔委员会(指挑选某项工作候选人的委员会); selection procedure = general method of choosing a candidate for a job 选拔程序(指挑选某项工作候选人的一般方法)

◇ **selective** a. which chooses 选择的; 选择性的: selective strikes = strikes in certain areas or at certain factories, but not everywhere 选择性罢工

**self** pron. your own person 自己; 本身: (on cheques) "pay self" = pay the person who has signed the cheque(支票上的)"向自己支付"

◇ **self –** prefix referring to oneself(前缀)…"自"; "自身"

◇ **self – contained office** n. office which has all facilities inside it, and its own entrance, so that it is separate from other offices in the same building 设备齐全独门独产的办公室(指办公室里拥有所有设备并有自身的入口,所以它与同一建筑物里的其它办公室是分开的)

◇ **self - employed** 1. a. working for yourself or not on the payroll of a company 个体经营的;不受雇于别人的: a self - employed engineer 一位个体经营工程师。He worked for a bank for ten years but now is self - employed. 他为银行工作了十年,但现在他是一名个体经营者。2. n. the self - employed = people who work for themselves 个体经营者
NOTE: can be followed by a verb in the plural

◇ **self - financed** a. The project is completely self - financed. = The project pays its development costs out of its ownrevenue, with no subsidies. 此项目完全是自筹资金。

◇ **self - financing** 1. n. the financing of development costs, purchase of capital assets etc., of a company from its own resources 自筹资金;资金自给; NOTE: no plural 2. a. the company is completely self - financing. = The company finances its development costs or capital assets, etc. from its own resources. 这个公司完全是自筹资金。

◇ **self - made man** n. man who is rich and successful because of his work, not because he inherited money or position 自力成功的人;白手起家的人(指因自身工作而富有和成功,而不是因他继承了财产和地位的人)

◇ **self - regulation** n. regulating by a body (such as the Stock Exchange) of its own members 自已管理(证券交易所)

◇ **self - regulatory** a. (group) which regulates itself(群体)自己管理的

◇ **self - service** a. a self - service store = shop where customers take goods from the shelves and pay for them at the checkout 自助商店: self - service petrol station = petrol station where the customers put the petrol in their cars themselves 自助加油站

◇ **self - sufficiency** n. being self - sufficient 自给自足
NOTE: no plural

◇ **self - sufficient** a. producing enough food or raw materials for its own needs 自给自足的(指生产足够的食品或原材料用于自身需求): The country is self - sufficient in oil. 这个国家石油自给自足。

◇ **self - supporting** a. which finances itself from its own resources, with no subsidies 自立的;自给的(指其财政来自于自身资源,没有补助)

**sell** 1. n. act of selling 卖: to give a product the hard sell = to make great efforts to persuade customers to buy it 对某种产品进行强行推销; He tried to give me the hard sell. = He put a lot of effort into trying to persuade me to buy his product. 他试图对我进行强行推销。soft sell = persuading people to buy, by encouraging and not forcing them to do so 软式推销(指使用诱劝等而不是强迫人购买)
NOTE: no plural

2. v. (a) to give goods in exchange for money 卖: to sell cars or to sell refrigerators 卖汽车或出售冰箱 They have decided to sell their house. 他们已决定卖房子。They tried to sell their house for £100,000. 他们试图以 100,000 英磅卖掉他们的房子。to sell something on credit 赊售某物: Her house is difficult to sell. 他们的房子难以出售。Their products are easy to sell. 他们的产品易卖(好卖)。to sell forward = to sell foreign currency, commodities, etc., for delivery ata later date 出售期货 (b) to be bought 售出;卖出: These items sell well in the pre - Christmas period. 这些

商品圣诞节前销路好。Those packs sell for £ 25 a dozen. 那些小包售价 25 英磅一打。

NOTE: selling – sold

◇ **sell – by date** n. date on a food packet which is the last date on which the food is guaranteed to be good 有效期；使用期限（指食品包装上标明的保证食品质量的最后日期）

◇ **seller** n. (a) person who sells 卖方：There were few sellers in the market, so prices remained high. 因市场上没有什么卖主，所以价格仍较高。seller's market = market where the seller can ask high prices because there is a large demand for the product 卖方市场（指因对此产品需求量大，所以卖方可要高价的市场）(b) thing which sells 畅销货：This book is a steady seller. 这本书是一本稳定的畅销书。best – seller = item (especially a book) which sells very well 最为畅销的物品

◇ **selling** 1. n. direct selling = selling a product direct to the customer without going through a shop 直接销售：mail – order selling = selling by taking orders and supplying a product by post 邮售；selling costs = amount of money to be paid for advertising, reps' commissions, etc., involved in selling something 推销成本；销售费用；selling price = price at which someone is willing to sell 售价；卖价 2. suffix 后缀 fast – selling items = items which sell quickly 畅销商品；best – selling car = car which sells better than other models 畅销车

◇ **sell off** v. to sell goods quickly to get rid of them 廉价出清（存货）；减价销完

◇ **sell out** v. (a) to sell all stock 卖出；售完；卖光：to sell out of a product line 卖掉生产线。We have sold out of electronictypewriters. 我们已将所有电动打字机售完。This item has been sold

out. 这种商品已卖完。(b) to sell out = to sell one's business 抛售；脱售（企业）；结束：He sold out and retired to the seaside 他卖掉了自己的企业，退休后到海滨去了。

◇ **sellout** n. This item has been a sellout. = All the stock of the item has been sold. 此种商品已售完

◇ **sell up** v. to sell a business and all the stock（企业和所有存货）完全卖出

**semi –** prefix half（前缀）半

◇ **semi – finished** a. semi – finished products = products which are partly finished 半（制）成品

◇ **semi – skilled** a. semi – skilled workers = workers who have had some training 半熟练工人

**send** v. to make someone or something go from one place to another 送；寄；派遣：to send a letter or an order or a shipment；寄信；发订单；The company is sending him to Australia to be general manager of the Sydney office. 公司正准备派他去澳大利亚担任悉尼办事处的总经理。Send the letter airmail if you want it to arrive nextweek. 假如你想要信下周到，就发航空信。The shipment was sent by rail. 这批货由钱路发运的。

NOTE: sending – sent

◇ **send away for** v. to write asking for something to be sent to you 去函索取；致函索要：We sent away for the new catalogue. 我们去函要新目录。

◇ **sender** n. person who sends 发送人；发货人："return to sender" = words on an envelope or parcel to show that it is to be sentback to the person who sent it"退回发货（信）人"（写在信封或包裹上）

◇ **send in** v. to send（a letter）递送（信等）：He sent in his resignation. 他递交了辞呈现。to send in an application 递交申请书

◇ **send off** v. to put（a letter）in the

post 邮寄

◇ **send off for** v. to write asking for something to be sent to you 去函索取；致函索要：We sent off for the new catalogue. 我们去函索要了新目录。

◇ **send on** v. to post a letter which you have received, and address it to someone else 转寄；转送(书信)：He sent the letter on to his brother. 他将那封信转寄给他兄弟了。

**senior** a. older；more important；(worker) who has been employed longer than another 年长的；主要的；资格较老的；较高的：senior manager or senior executive = manager or director who has a higher rank than others 高级管理(主管)人员；senior partner = most important partner in a firm of solicitors or accountants 高级合伙人；；John Smith, Senior = the older John Smith (i.e. the father of John Smith, Junior) 老约翰·史密斯(小约翰·史密斯的父亲)

◇ **seniority** n. being older；being an employee of the company longer 年长；资历深：The managers were listed in order of seniority. = The manager who had been an employee the longest was put at the top of the list. 按资历顺序，列出经理们的名单。

NOTE: no plural

**sensitive** a. able to feel something sharply 敏感的；洞察力强的：The market is very sensitive to the result of the elections. 市场对选举的结果非常敏感。price – sensitive product = product which will sell less if the price is increased. 价格敏感的产品。

**separate** 1. a. not together 独自的；分离的：to send something under separate cover = to send something in a different envelope 将某物另函寄出。2. v. to divide 区分；分开：The personnel are separated into part – timers and full – time staff. 全体职工分为非全日工制和全日

工制工作人员。

◇ **separately** ad. not together 个别地；分离地；独立地：Each job was invoiced separately. 每个工种分别开发票。

◇ **separation** n. US leaving a job (resigning, retiring, or being fired or made redundant) (美)离职(因辞职、退休、被解雇等)

**sequester or sequestrate** v. to take and keep (property) because a court has ordered it 没收；没收；扣押(财产)

◇ **sequestration** n. taking and keeping of property on the order of a court 扣押；没收(财产)

◇ **sequestrator** n. person who takes and keeps property on the order of a court 没收财产的保管人

**serial number** n. number in a series 序列号；连续偏号：This batch of shoes has the serial number 25 – 02. 这批鞋的编号是 25—02。

**series** n. group of items following one after the other 系列；连续：A series of successful takeovers made the company one of the largest in the trade. 连续不断的成功的兼并使该公司成为商界最大的公司之一。

NOTE: plural is series

**serious** a. bad or important 严重的；重大的：The storm caused serious damage. 暴风雨造成了重大损失。The management is making serious attempts to improve working conditions. 管理部门正努力尝试改善工作条件。The damage to the computer was not very serious. 这台计算机的损坏不太严重。

◇ **seriously** ad. badly 严重地：The cargo was seriously damaged by water. 船货被水严重损坏。

**servant** n. person who is paid to work in someone's house 仆人；佣人：civil servant = person who works for the government 文官；公务员

**serve** v. to deal with (a customer)服务：to serve a customer = to take a customer's order and provide what he wants 为顾客服务; to serve in a shop or in a restaurant = to deal with customers' orders 接待顾客; to serve someone with a writ or to serve a writ on someone = to give someone a writ officially, so that he has to obey it 将传票送交给某人

**service** 1. n. (a) working for a company or in a shop, etc.服务；工作：length of service = number of years someone has worked 工作(服务)年限; service agreement or service contract = contract between a company and a director showing allconditions of work 劳动合同 (b) the work of dealing with customers or payment for help for the customer 服务；服务费：The service in that restaurant is extremely slow. 此餐馆的服务极差。to add on 10% for service 另收 10%的服务费; The bill includes service. = Includes a charge added for the work involved 帐单包含服务费。Is the service included? 包括服务费吗? service charge = charge added to the bill in a restaurant to pay for service oramount paid by tenants in a block of flats for general cleaning(餐馆、客房的)服务费 (c) keeping a machine in good working order 维修；保养；检修：The machine has been sent in for service. 这台机器已送来检修。the routine service of equipment 设备日常的维修(定期维修); service contract = contract by which a company keeps a piece of equipment in good working order 维修合同; after-sales service = service of a machine carried out by the seller for the buyer 售后服务; service centre = office or workshop which specializes in keeping machines ingood working order 维修服务中心; service department = section of a company which keeps customers' ma-chines in goodworking order 维修服务部门; service engineer = engineer who specializes in keeping machines in good workingorder 维修工程师; service handbook or service manual = book which shows how to service a machine 维修手册; service station = garage where you can buy petrol and have small repairs doneto a car(汽车)加油站；修理站 (d) business or office which gives help when it is needed 服务部门(机构)：answering service = office which answers the telephone and takes messages for a company 代接电话服务站; 24 - hour service = help which is available for the whole day24 小时服务; 全天提供服务; service bureau = office which specializes in helping other offices 服务处; 后勤处; service department = department of a company which does not deal with production or sales (accounts, personnel, etc.)后勤服务部门(如财务、人事等) service industry = industry which does not make products, but offers a service (such as banking, insurance, transport)服务行业(不生产产品提供服务的行业如：银行、保险公司、交通运输等) (e) to put a machine into service = to start using a machine 机器投入使用 (f) regular working of a public organization(公用事业的)公共设施：The postal service is efficient. 邮政服务效率很高。The bus service is very irregular. 公共汽车非常无规律。We have a good train service to London. 我们有一班很好的开往伦敦的火车。the civil service = the administration of a country 行政机构：He has a job in the civil service. 他在行政机构工作。Civil service pensions are index - linked. 文职人员退休金是与生活指数挂钩。2. v. (a) to keep a machine in good working order 维修；保养；检修：The car needs to be serviced every six months. 这辆汽车需每六个月检修一次。The computer has gone back to the manufacturer for servicing. 这台计算机已送回厂家进行检修。(b) to service a debt = to pay interest on a debt 支付债务利息: The company is having problems in servicing its debts. 该公司在支付债息方面有问题。

**session** n. meeting or period when a group of people meets 会议;会期;一届会议: The morning session or the afternoon session will be held in the conference room. 上午会议或下午会议都将在会议室召开。 opening session or closing session = first part or last part of a conference 会议开幕时间或闭幕时间

**set** 1. n. group of items which go together or which are used together or which are sold together 一套;一批;一副;一组: set of tools or set of equipment 一套工具;一套设备; boxed set = set of items sold together in a box 一套盒装商品 2. a. fixed or which cannot be changed 固定的;不变的: set price 固定价格; set menu = cheaper menu in a restaurant where there are only a few choices(餐馆里较便宜,但选择较少的)套餐 3. v. to fix or to arrange 设定;安排: We have to set a price for the new computer. 我们要为这台新计算机定价。 The price of the calculator has been set low, so as to achieve maximum unit sales. 为了达到最大单位销售量,此种计算器的价格定得较低。 The auction set a record for high prices. = the prices at the auction were the highest ever reached. 这次拍卖的价格创了最高记录。

NOTE: setting – set

◇ **set against** v. to balance one group of figures against another group to try to make them cancel each other out 从…扣除;用…抵消: to set the costs against the invoice 以从发票中减去成本。 Can you set the expenses against tax? 你能从税额中扣除花费吗?

◇ **set aside** v. to decide not to apply a decision 把…置于一旁;使…无效: The arbitrator's award was set aside on appeal. 上诉后仲裁人的裁决就无效了。

◇ **set back** v. to make something late 推迟: The project was set back six weeks by bad weather. 因恶劣的天气,该工程推迟了六周。

◇ **setback** n. stopping progress 挫折;失败: The company suffered a series of setbacks in 1984. 1984年这个公司遭受了连续不断的挫折。 The shares had a setback on the Stock Exchange. 股票交易所的股票下跌。

◇ **set out** v. to put clearly in writing 表明;陈述: to set out the details in a report 在报告中陈述细节

◇ **set up** v. (a) to begin (something) or to organize (something) new 开办;创立;建立: to set up an inquiry or a working party 设立间讯处或工作组; to set up a company = to start a company legally 创办一家公司 (b) to set up in business = to start a new business 开办新企业: He set up in business as an insurance broker. 他开始从事保险经纪人的职业。 He set himself up as a freelance engineer. 他开始从事自由职业工程师的工作。

◇ **setting up costs** or **setup costs** pl. n. costs of getting a machine or a factory ready to make a new product after finishing work on another one 准备成本;开办费

◇ **setup** n. (a) arrangement or organization 机构;组织体系;体制: the setup in the office = the way the office is organized 办公室的体制 (b) commercial firm 商业公司: He works for a PR setup. 他为公关公司工作。

**settle** v. (a) to settle an account = to pay what is owed 结算;结帐 (b) to settle a claim = to agree to pay what is asked for 清算债务;解决索赔: The insurance company refused to settle his claim for storm damage. 保险公司拒付暴风雨损失的索赔费。The two parties settled out of court. = The two parties reached an agreement privately without continuing the court case. 双方私下和解。

◇ **settlement** n. (a) payment of an account 结帐；清算；付帐：settlement day = day when accounts have to be settled 清算日；交割日；结算日：Our basic discount is 20% but we offer an extra 5% for rapid settlement. = We take a further 5% off the price if the customer pays quickly. 我们的基本折扣是20%，但如客户马上结算的话，我们可另外再给5%的折扣。settlement in cash or cash settlement = payment of an invoice in cash, not by cheque 现金结算 (b) agreement after an argument 和解：to effect a settlement between two parties = to bring two parties together to make them agree 促使双方和解

◇ **settle on** v. to leave property to someone when you die 赠与；转让：He settled his property on his children. 他决定(死后)将财产赠给他的孩子们

**several** a. more than a few or some 一些；数个：Several managers are retiring this year. 今年有几个经理要退体。Several of our products sell well in Japan. 我们的几种产品在日本畅销。

◇ **severally** ad. separately or not jointly 分别地；各自地；单独地：They are jointly and severally liable. = They are liable both as a group and as individuals. 作为集体和个人他们都有责任。

**severance pay** n. money paid as compensation to someone who is losing his job 解雇费；遣散费

**severe** a. bad or serious 严劣的；严重的：The company suffered severe losses in the European market. 该公司在欧洲市场上遭受了严重损失。The government imposed severe financial restrictions. 政府实行了严格的财务限制。

◇ **severely** ad. badly or in a serious way 严重的；严峻地：Train services have been severely affected by snow. 由于下雪，火车的运转受到严重影响。

**shady** a. not honest 可疑的；靠不住的；shady deal 不正当的交易；可疑的交易

**shake** v. (a) to move something quickly from side to side 摇动；震动 (b) to surprise or to shock 震惊；使惊奇：The markets were shaken by the company's results. 该公司的获胜震惊了市场。

NOTE: shaking – shook – has shaken

◇ **shakeout** n. reorganization, where some people are left, but others go 人员改组：a shakeout in the top management 最高管理层的人员改组；Only three companies were left after the shakeout in the computer market. 计算机市场重新调整之后，只剩下了三家公司。

◇ **shakeup** n. total reorganization 大改组(人员等)：The managing director ordered a shakeup of the sales departments. 总经理命令(下令)销售部门进行人员大改组

◇ **shaky** a. not very sure or not very reliable 不稳的；不可靠的：The year got off to a shaky start. 今年有不稳定的开始。

**share** 1. n. (a) to have a share in = to take part in or to contribute to 参与；出份力：to have a share in management decisions 参与管理决策；market share or share of the market = percentage of a total market which the sales of a company cover 市场份额；市场享有额；The company hopes to boost its market share. 该公司希望增加其市场份额。Their share of the market has gone up by 10%. 他们的市场份额已上升了10%。(b) one of many parts into which a company's capital is divided 股份；He bought a block of shares in Marks and

Spencer. 他买了马克——斯潘塞公司的大宗股票。Shares fell on the London market. 伦敦市场的股票下跌。The company offered 1. 8m shares on the market. 该公司在市场上出售了 180 万的股票。"A" shares = ordinary shares with limited voting rights A 股(有限制投票权的普通股); "B" shares = ordinary shares with special voting rights (often owned bythe founder of the company and his family)B 股(有特殊投票权的普通股,通常是公司创始人和其家属持有); bonus share = extra share given to an existing shareholder 红股;红利股(公司按比例无偿分给现有股东的股份); deferred shares = shares which receive a dividend only after all other dividends have been paid 递延付息股票(份);后派的股利; founder's shares = special shares issued to the person who starts a company 创始人股份; ordinary shares = normal shares in a company, which have no special benefits or restrictions 普通股; preference shares = shares (often with no voting rights) which receive their dividend before all other shares and are repaid first (at facevalue) if the company goes into liquidation 优先股; share allocation or share allotment = sharing of a small number of shares among a large number ofpeople who have applied to buy them 股票分配; to allot shares = to give a certain number of shares to people who have appliedto buy them 分配股票; share capital = value of the assets of a company held as shares 股本;股份资本; share certificate = document proving that someone owns shares 股票; share issue = selling new shares in a company to the public 股票发行 2. v. (a) to own or use something together with someone else 分享;共同使用;共同具有; to share a telephone 共用一部电话; to share an office 合用一个办公室 (b) to divide

something up among several people 均分;分摊;分配: Three companies share the market. 三个公司瓜分市场。to share computer time 共享计算机时间; to share the profits among the senior executives 在高级主管人员间分享利润; to share information or to share data = to give someone information which you have 共享信息或数据

◇ **shareholder** n. person who owns shares in a company 股东;股票持有人: to call a shareholders' meeting 召开股东大会; shareholders' equity = ordinary shares owned by shareholders in a company 股东的股本;股东权益; majority or minority shareholder = person who owns more or less than half the shares in a company 占多数(少数)股权的股东; the solicitor acting on behalf of the minority shareholders 代表持少数股分股东的律师

◇ **shareholding** n. group of shares in a company owned by one person 股份持有股东: a majority shareholding or a minority shareholding = group of shares which are more or less than half the total "多数"股份持有;"少数"股份持有: He acquired a minority shareholding in the company. 他得到了公司的"少数"持有股份。She has sold all her shareholdings. 她已将所有持有股份卖掉。dilution of shareholding = situation where the ordinary share capital of a company has been increased, but without an increase in the assets so that each share is worth less than before 股份产权削弱;股票价值耗减(指股份资本已经增加,但所对应的公司资产并未增加,因而每股实际价值已经下降)

◇ **shareout** n. dividing something among many people 分摊;分配: a shareout of the profits 利润分配

◇ **sharing** n. dividing up 分配;分享: profit sharing = dividing profits among workers 分红（制）；利润分享：The companyoperates a profit - sharing scheme. 公司施行利润分享计划。time - sharing = (i) owning a property in part, with the right to use it for aperiod each year；时间分享（拥有一部分房地产，每年有权使用一段时间）(ii) sharing a computer system with differentusers using different terminals 时间分享：(指用不同终端和不同的用户分享一个计算机操作系统)

NOTE: no plural

**shark** n. loan shark = person who lends money at a very high interest rate 高利贷者

**sharp** a. (a) sudden 突然的；急剧的：sharp rally on the stock market 股市上的突然跌后复升；sharp drop in prices 价格暴跌 (b) sharp practice = way of doing business which is not honest, but not illegal 骗局；不择手段做生意的行为

◇ **sharply** ad. suddenly 突然地；急剧地：Shares dipped sharply in yesterday's trading. 在昨天交易中，股票价格突然下跌。

**sheet** n. (a) sheet of paper = piece of paper 纸张；一张纸：sheet feed = device which puts one sheet at a time into a computer printeror photocopier 进纸器；sales sheet = paper which gives details of a product and explains why it is good 介绍产品小报；time sheet = paper showing when a worker starts work and when he leaveswork in the evening 工作时间记录表（记录工人上、下班时间）(b) balance sheet = statement of the financial position of a company at the end of a financial year or at the end of a period 资产负债表：the company's balance sheet for 1984 公司 1984 年的资产负债表；The accountants prepared a balance sheet for the first half - year. 会计已准备好上半年的资产负债表。

**shelf** n. flat surface attached to a wall or in a cupboard on which items for sale are displayed 货架：The shelves in the supermarket were full of items before the Christmas rush. 圣诞争购热潮前超级市场的货架堆满了商品。shelf filler = person whose job it is to make sure that the shelves in ashop are kept full of items for sale 货架装填人（负责保证货架上摆满商品的工作人员）；shelf life of a product = number of days or weeks when the product will stay on the shelf in the shop and still be good to use 产品储存期限；shelf space = amount of space on shelves in a shop(商店的)货架空间

NOTE: plural is shelves

**shell company** n. company which does not trade, but exists only as a name to be used to hold shares in other companies 空壳公司(本身不做买卖，只是名义上存在以便持有其他公司股票)

**shelter** n. protected place 掩蔽场所；保护(庇护)处：tax shelter = financial arrangement (such as a pension scheme) whereinvestments can be made without tax 逃税(将收益用于投资等用途以逃避纳税的财务安排,如：养老金计划)

**shelve** v. to postpone or to put back to another date 延期；推迟：The project was shelved. 这项工程延期了。Discussion of the problem has been shelved. 这个问题的讨论被搁置。

◇ **shelving** n. (a) rows of shelves or space on shelves 成排的货架；架上的空间：We installed metal shelving in the household goods department. 我们在日用品部安装了成排的金属货架。(b) postponing 延期；推迟：The shelving of the project has resulted in six redundancies. 此项工程的搁置已导致了 6 人被解雇。

**shift** 1. n. (a) group of workers who work for a period, and then are replacedby another group period of time worked by a group of workers 轮班；day shift = shift worked during the daylight hours (from early morning to late afternoon)白班；日 班；night shift = shift worked during the night 夜班；There are 150 men on the day shift. 有 150 人上白班。 He works the day shift or night shift. 他 上白班或夜班。We work an 8 - hour shift. 我们每班工作 8 小时。The management is introducing a shift system or shift working.管理部门将采用轮班工 作制。They work double shifts. = Two groups of workers are working shifts together 他们双班制工作。(b) movement or change 转换；转变；移动：a shift in the company's marketing strategy 公司 销售战略上的转变；The company is taking advantage of a shift in the market towards higher priced goods. 公司正 在利用市场向高价商品转换的有利时机。 2. v. to move or to sell 移动；售出：we shifted 20,000 items in one week. 我们 一周内售出了 20,000 件商品

◇ **shift key** n. key on a typewriter or computer which makes capital letters(打 字机的)大写字母按键

◇ **shift work** n. system of work in a factory with shifts 轮班工作制

**shilling** n. money used in Kenya 先令 (肯尼亚货币)

**ship** 1. n. large boat for carrying passengers and cargo on the sea(用于载客 和运货的）船舶：cargo ship = ship which carries cargo, not passengers 货 轮；container ship = ship made specially to carry containers 集装箱船；ship chandler = person who supplies goods (such as food) to ships 船需用品供应商；to jump ship = to leave the ship on which you are working and not come back 私自 离船；未经许可离船而去 2. v. to send (goods), but not always on a ship 发货 (并不仅限于用船运)：to ship goods to the USA 向美国发货；We ship all our

goods by rail. 我们由铁路发运所有货 物。The consignment of cars was shipped abroad last week. 寄售的小汽车于上周 装船发往国外。to drop ship = to deliver a large order direct to a customer's shop or warehouse, without going through an agent 直接发运(不经代理商 之手,直接将货物运交客户商店或他的 仓库)

NOTE: shipping - shipped

◇ **ship broker** n. person who arranges shipping or transport of goods for customers on behalf of ship owners 船舶经 纪人(代表船主安排为顾客运输货物的 人)

◇ **shipment** n. goods sent 发运货物； 装运的货物；Two shipments were lost in the fire. 两批货物遭了火灾。A shipment of computers was damaged. 一批装 运计算机受损。We make two shipments a week to France. 我们一周向法 国发运两批货。bulk shipment = shipments of large quantities of goods 大批货 物运输；consolidated shipment = goods from different companies grouped together into a single shipment 合并装运；drop shipment = delivery of a large order from a manufacturer direct to a customer's shop or warehouse, without going through an agent 直接发运

◇ **shipper** n. person who sends goods or who organizes the sending of goods for other customers 发货人；装货人

◇ **shipping** n. sending of goods 装运； 运送；海运：shipping charges or shipping costs 运输费用；shipping agent = company which specializes in the sending of goods 货运代理商；海运业者 shipping clerk = clerk who deals with shipping documents 运输业务办事员；shipping company or shipping line = company which owns ships 航运公司；船运公 司(指拥有船只的公司)；shipping instructions = details of how goods are to be shipped and delivered 装船须知；装货指示；shipping note = note which gives details of goods being shipped 装运通知单

NOTE: no plural. Note also that shipping does not always mean using a ship

◇ **shipyard** n. factory where ships are built 造船厂

**shoot up** v. to go up fast 急升；(价格等)暴涨：Prices have shot up during the strike. 罢工期间价格已暴涨。

NOTE: shooting – shot

**shop** 1. n. oun (a) place where goods are stored and sold 商店；店铺：bookshop 书店；computer shop 计算机店；electrical goods shop 电器商店；He has bought a shoe shop in the centre of town. 他在市中心买下了一家鞋店。She opened a women's wearshop. 她开了一家妇女服装店。All the shops in the centre of town close on Sundays. 星期日市中心的所有商店都不开门。retail shop = shop where goods are sold only to the public 零售商店；the corner shop = small privately owned general store 小杂货店；shop assistant = person who serves customers in a shop 店员；shop front = part of a shop which faces the street, including the entrance and windows 店面；商店临街部分(包括入口和窗户)；shop window = window in a shop where goods are displayed so that customers can see them or place where goods or services can be exhibited 橱窗；(NOTE: US English usually uses store) (b) place where goods are made or workshop 工厂；工场；车间：machine shop = place where working machines are kept 机械工场；机械车间；repair shop = small factory where machines are repaired 修理厂；on the shop floor = in the factory or in the works or among the ordinary workers 在工厂；在普通工人中：The feeling on the shop floor is that the manager does not know his job. 普通

工人的感觉就是这个经理不懂业务。(c) closed shop = system where a company agrees to employ only union members in certain jobs 闭锁工厂（在某项工作中公司同意只雇佣工会会员的制度）：The union is asking the management to agree to a closed shop. 工会正要求资方同意闭锁工厂制度。2. v. to shop (for) = to look for things in shops (在商店)购物

NOTE: shopping – shopped

◇ **shop around** v. to go to various shops or offices and compare prices before making a purchase or before placing an order 逐店选购：You should shop around before getting your car serviced. 在将车送去修理之前，你应该多方参考，比较。He is shopping around for a new computer. 为购买一台新计算机，他正逐店选购。It pays to shop around when you are planning to ask for a mortgage. 当你正打算申请抵押贷款时，应多方参考，比较，这样做是值得的。

◇ **shopkeeper** n. person who owns or runs a shop 店主

◇ **shoplifter** n. person who steals goods from shops 在商店行窃的扒手

◇ **shoplifting** n. stealing goods from shops 在商店行窃

NOTE: no plural

◇ **shopper** n. person who buys goods in a shop 购物者；顾客：The store stays open to midnight to cater for late – night shoppers. 为照顾夜晚购物的顾客，该店一直开到午夜。shoppers' charter = law which protects the rights of shoppers against shopkeepers who are not honest 保护顾客权益的章程

◇ **shopping** n. (a) buying goods in a shop；goods bought in a shop 买东西；购物：to go shopping 去买东西；to buy one's shopping or to do one's shopping in the local supermarket 去当地超级市

场买东西（购物）（b）shopping basket = basket for carrying shopping 购物篮（筐）；shopping centre = group of shops linked together with car parks and restaurants 购物中心；US shopping mall = enclosed covered area for shopping, with shops, restaurants, banks and other facilities（美）购物中心（通常是围封起来的用于购物的地方，有商店、餐馆、银行和其他设施）；shopping precinct = part of town which is closed to traffic so that people can walk about and shop 商业区；购物区 window shopping = looking at goods in shop windows, without buying anything 浏览商店橱窗；逛商店（只看看橱窗，而不买东西）shopping around = looking at prices in various shops before buying what you want 逐店选购

NOTE: no plural

◇ **shop - soiled** a. dirty because of having been on display in a shop（在商店里）摆久了的；陈旧的

◇ **shop steward** n. elected trade union representative of workers who reports their complaints to the management 工人代表（工会中代表工人向资方反映意见的）

◇ **shopwalker** n. employee of a department store who advises the customers and supervises the shop assistants in a department 大商店的巡视员；铺面巡视员

**short** 1. a. (a) for a small period of time 短期的；短暂的；短促的：short credit = terms which allow the customer only a little time to pay 短期信用；短期赊帐（顾客必须在短期内付款）；in the short term = in the near future or quite soon 短期；不久的未来 (b) not as much as should be 短缺的；不足的：The shipment was three items short. 这批货物缺了三种。When we cashed up we were £10 short = We had £10 less than we

should have had 当我们结算一天营业额时，我们少了10英磅。to give short weight = to sell something which is lighter than it should be 缺斤少两（卖主出售货物时给的量不足）；(c) short of = with less than needed or with not enough of 短缺的；不足的：we are short of staff or short of money. 我们的人手不足 或缺钱。The company is short of new ideas. 这个公司缺乏新观念（思想）(d) to sell short = to agree to sell something (such as shares) which you do not possess, but which you think you will be able to buy for less 卖空（出售自身没有,但认为能低价买入的期货,如:股票）short selling or selling short = arranging to sell something in the future which you think you can buy for less than the agreed selling price 卖空行为；to borrow short = to borrow for a short period 短期借用 2. n. shorts = government stocks which mature in less than five years' time 短期债券（期限低于5年的政府债券）

◇ **shortage** n. lack or not having enough 缺少；缺额；不足: a chronic shortage of skilled staff 长期缺乏熟练工,熟练工长期不足；We employ part - timers to make up for staff shortages. 我们雇佣临时工以弥补人员不足（短缺）。The import controls have resulted in the shortage of spare parts. 进口控制已导致了备件不足（短缺）。manpower shortage or shortage of manpower = lack of workers 人力短缺；There is no shortage of investment advice. = There are plenty of people who want to give advice on investments. 有大量提供投资的忠告。

◇ **short change** v. to give a customer less change than is right, hoping that he will not notice 故意少找（钱给顾客）

◇ **short - dated** a. short - dated bills = bills which are payable within a few days 短期票据 short - dated securities

= government stocks which mature in less than five years time 短期证券；短期债券（期限少于 5 年的政府债券）

◇ **shorten** v. to make shorter 变短；缩短：to shorten credit terms 缩短信用期

◇ **shortfall** n. amount which is missing which would make the total expected sum 不足量；缺额；缺少：We had to borrow money to cover the shortfall between expenditure and revenue. 我们不得不借钱以弥补收支间的差额。

◇ **shorthand** n. rapid way of writing using a system of signs 速记：shorthand secretary = secretary who takes dictation in shorthand 速记员；shorthand typist = typist who can take dictation in shorthand and then type it 速记打字员（用速记把谈话记录下来，然后将其打成文字的人）；to take shorthand = to write using shorthand 速记：He took down the minutes in shorthand. 他将会议记录速记下来。

◇ **shorthanded** a. without enough staff 缺少人手的；人手不足：We are rather shorthanded at the moment. 此刻我们有点人手不足。

◇ **short - haul** a. short - haul flight = flight over a short distance (up to 1,000 km) 短距离飞行

◇ **shortlist** 1. n. list of some of the better people who have applied for a job, who can be asked to come for a test or an interview（供最后挑选谋职业用的）候选人名单：to draw up a shortlist 拟一份决选候选人名单；He is on the shortlist for the job. 他列入了谋职者的决选人名单上。2. v. to make a shortlist 把…列入决选名单上。Four candidates have been shortlisted. 四位候选人已列入决选名单。Shortlisted candidates will be asked for an interview. 入决选名单的候选人将要进行面试。

◇ **short - range** a. short - range forecast = forecast which covers a period of a few months 近期预测的

◇ **short - staffed** a. with not enough staff 人手不足地；缺乏人手地：we are rather short - staffed at the moment. 此刻我们相当缺人手

◇ **short - term** a. for a short period 短期的：to place money on short - term deposit 将钱存入短期存款；short - term contract 短期合同；on a short - term basis = for a short period 短期地，不久；short - term debts = debts which have to be repaid within a few weeks 短期债款（须在几周内偿还的）；short - term forecast = forecast which covers a period of a few months 短期预测；short - term gains = gains made over a short period (less than 12 months) 短期收益（不足 12 个月）；short - term loan = loan which has to be repaid within a few weeks 短期贷款（偿还期限为几周）

◇ **short time** n. shorter working hours than usual 短工时；不足的工时：to be on short time 工时不足；以部分时间开工：The company has had to introduce short - time working because of lack of orders. 因缺少订货，公司已采用减少工作时间的方法。

**shot** n. mail shot or mailing shot = leaflets sent by post to possible customers 广告品投寄

**show** 1. n. (a) exhibition or display of goods or services for sale 展览，展销：motor show 汽车展销；computer show 计算机展览；show house or show flat = house or flat built and furnished so that possible buyers can see what similar houses could be like 住房展示（指备有家具的房子或公寓。供买主以此作为比较的样品）(b) show of hands = vote where people show how they vote by raising their hands 举手表决：The motion was carried on a show of hands. 此项提议举手表决通过了。2. v. to make something be seen 显示；显出；出示：to

show a gain or a fall 呈上升或下降趋势；to show a profit or a loss 显示出盈利或亏本
NOTE: showing – showed – has shown

◇ **showcard** n. piece of cardboard with advertising material, put near an item for sale 广告；招贴；海报

◇ **showcase** n. cupboard with a glass front or top to display items 陈列柜；橱窗

◇ **showroom** n. room where goods are displayed for sale 陈列室；展览室：car showroom 汽车陈列室

**shrink** v. to get smaller 缩小；减少；收缩：The market has shrunk by 20%. 市场已收缩了 20%。The company is having difficulty selling into a shrinking market. 该公司要打入范围正在缩小的市场是有困难的。
NOTE: shrinking – shrank – has shrunk

◇ **shrinkage** n. (a) amount by which something gets smaller 收缩量；收缩程度：to allow for shrinkage 考虑到收缩量 (b) infml. losses of stock through theft (especially by members of the staff of the shop)(非正式)存货损耗(商店存货因被窃而减少，尤其由于本店职员的偷窃)

◇ **shrink – wrapped** a. covered in tight plastic protective cover 收缩薄膜包装的

◇ **shrink – wrapping** n. act of covering (a book, fruit, record etc.) in a tight plastic cover 收缩薄膜包装

**shut** 1. a. closed or not open 关上的；闭上的；关闭的：The office is shut on Saturdays. 星期六办公室打烊。2. v. to close 关闭；封闭：to shut a shop or a warehouse 关闭商店或仓库
NOTE: shutting – shut

◇ **shut down** v. to shut down a factory = to make a factory stop working for a time 关闭工厂(指临时性的)：The offices will shut down for Christmas. 圣诞节办公室将关闭。Six factories have shut down this month. 这个月六个工厂停工

◇ **shutdown** n. shutting of a factory (工厂等之)停工；关闭

◇ **shutout** n. locking of the door of a factory or office to stop the staff getting in 闭厂；办公室关闭

**sick** a. ill or not well 患病的；有病的：sick leave = time when a worker is away from work because of illness 病假；sick pay = pay paid to a worker who is sick, even if he cannot work 病假工资

◇ **sickness** n. being ill 生病；疾病：sickness benefit = payment paid by the government or private insurance to someone who is ill and cannot work 疾病津贴(尤指政府或私营保险公司发给因病不能工作者的补贴) The sickness benefit is paid monthly. 按月支付疾病津贴。

**side** n. (a) part of something near the edge 边；侧面；一方：credit side = right – hand side of accounts showing money received 贷方；debit side = left – hand side of accounts showing money owed or paid 借方 (b) one of the surfaces of a flat object 一面：Please write on one side of the paper only. 请只写在这张纸的一面上。(c) on the side = separate from your normal work, and hidden from your employer 作为兼职；正业之外的：He works in an accountant's office, but he runs a construction company on the side. 他在会计事务所工作，但正业之外他又经营一家建筑公司。Her salary is too small to live on, so the family lives on what she can make on the side. 她的工资太少以致不能维持生活，所以全家要靠她兼职收入生活。

◇ **sideline** n. business which is extra to your normal work 副业；兼职：He runs a profitable sideline selling postcards to tourists. 他在干一个有收益的副业——向游客出售明信片。

**sight** n. seeing 看；观看；见：bill payable at sight = bill which must be paid when it is presented 见票即付的汇票；即期汇票；sight bill or sight draft = bill of exchange which is payable at sight 即期汇票；见票即付的汇票；to buy something sight unseen = to buy something without having inspected it 未看现货就买

NOTE: no plural

**sign** 1. n. advertising board or notice which advertises something 广告板；招牌：They have asked for planning permission to put up a large red shop sign 他们已请求计划部门允许立一块红色的商店大招牌。Advertising signs cover most of the buildings in the centre of the town. 城市中心的大部分建筑物上都被广告牌覆盖。2. v. to write your name in a special way on a document to showthat you have written it or approved it 签名；签字(在文件上)：to sign a letter or a contract or a document or a cheque 签署信件；签合同；在文件上签字；在支票上签字；The letter is signed by the managing director. 这封信要由总经理签署的。The cheque is not valid if it has not been signed by the finance director. 如果财务主任没有在上面签字,该支票无效。The warehouse manager signed for the goods = The manager signed a receipt to show that the goods had been received. 仓库经理签字表明货已收到。He signed the goods in or he signed the goods out. = He signed the stock report to show that the goods had arrivedor had been dispatched. 他签字表明货已收到或发走。

◇ **signatory** n. person who signs a contract, etc. 签名者：You have to get the permission of all the signatories to the agreement if you want to change the terms. 你要修改条款的话,你须得到此合同所有签名人的许可。

◇ **signature** n. name written in a special way by someone 签名；签字：a pile of letters waiting for the managing director's signature. 一堆等着总经理签名的信；He found a pile of cheques on his desk waiting for signature. 他发现他桌上有一堆等着签字的支票。All cheques need two signatures. 所有支票都需两人签字。

◇ **sign on** v. to start work, by signing your name in the personnel office 签约受雇；(在人事部门登记,然后开始工作)：to sign on for the dole = to register as unemployed 登记领取失业救济金

**silent** a. not speaking 沉默的；不作声的：silent partner = partner who has a share of the business but does not work init 不参加经营的合伙人(拥有该企业的股票,但不参与具体经营的合伙人)

**simple interest** n. interest calculated on the capital only, and not added to it 单利(利息不并入本金内,仅按本金计算的利息)

**sincerely** ad. Yours sincerely or US Sincerely yours = words used as an ending to a business letter addressed to a named person 你的忠诚的；谨上；敬启(商务信函未署名前的客套语)

**sine die** phr. to adjourn a case sine die = to postpone the hearing of a case without fixing a new date for it 使一个案子无限期地延期审理

**single** a. one alone 单一的：(a) single fare or single ticket or a single = fare or ticket for one journey from one place to another 单程票：I want two singles to London. 我要两张去伦敦的单程票。(b) single premium policy = insurance policy where only one premium is paid rather than regular annual premiums 一次付清保险费的保险单。single-entry bookkeeping = method of bookkeeping where payments or sales are noted with-only one entry 单式簿记；in single fig- ures = less than ten 少于十的数：Sales are down to single figures. 销售额下降 到不足十(十以下)。Inflation is now in single figures. 通货膨胀现在是单位数。 single – figure inflation = inflation rising at less than 10% per annum 单位数通货 膨胀的

**sink** v. (a) to go to the bottom of the water 下沉；沉没：The ship sank in the storm and all the cargo was lost. 这艘船 沉没在暴风雨中，所有的货物都毁了。 (b) to go down suddenly 下降；降低(突 然地)：Prices sank at the news of the closure of the factory. 听到这个工厂关 闭的消息，价格突然下跌。(c) to invest money (into something) 投资于：He sank all his savings into a car – hire business. 他将所有的积蓄投入了出租 汽车生意。 NOTE: sinking – sank – sunk

◇ **sinking fund** n. fund built up out of amounts of money put aside regularly to meet a future need 累积基金；偿债基金 (定期从储存备用金中提存一定金额， 作为偿还的基金，以满足将来需求)

**sir** n. Dear Sir = way of addressing a letter to a man whom you do not know or to a limited company 亲爱的先生(致不 认识的人或某一个有限公司等信件中 的称呼) Dear Sirs = way of addressing a letter to a firm 诸位先生(致某企业的 信件中的称谓)

**sister** a. sister company = one of sever- al companies which are part of the same group 姐妹公司(同一集团所属的几家 公司中的一家) sister ship = ship which is of the same design and belongs to the samecompany as another ship 姐妹 船(与另一船式样相同，属同一公司所 有的船)

**sit – down** a. sit – down protest or sit – down strike = strike where the work- ers stay in their place of work and refuse to work or to leave 静坐抗议或静坐罢 工(指工人呆在工作地，拒绝工作和离 开的罢工)

◇ **sit – in** n. strike where the workers stay in their place of work and refuse to work or leave 静坐罢工 NOTE: plural is sit – ins

**site** 1. n. place where something is built (建造房屋等的)地皮；地基：We have chosen a site for the new factory. 我们已 为这座新工厂选好了一块地皮。The supermarket is to be built on a site near the station. 这个超级市场将建在车站 附近的一个地皮上。building site or construction site = place where a build- ing is being constructed 工地：All visi- tors to the site must wear safety helmets. 到工地的所有参观者必须带上安全帽。 green field site = site for a factory which is in the country, and not surrounded by other buildings 工厂的绿色田野工地 (通常在农村，周围无其他建筑)；site engineer = engineer in charge of a build- ing being constructed 现场工程师(负责 在建的建筑物的工程师) 2. v. to be sited = to be placed 建在……：The fac- tory will be sited near the motorway. 这 个工厂将建在高速公路附近。

**situated** a. placed 位于…；坐落在… 的：The factory is situated on the edge of the town. 这座工厂坐落在该城的边 上。The office is situated near the rail- way station. 该办公室(代表处)位于火 车站附近。

◇ **situation** n. (a) state of affairs 处 境；形势；情况：financial situation of a company 公司的财务状况；the general situation of the economy 总的经济形势 (b) job 工作；职位：situations vacant or situations wanted = list in a newspaper of vacancies for workers or of people- wanting work(报纸上的)招聘和求职 广告 (c) place where something is 位 置；地点：The factory is in a very pleasant situation by the sea. 这个工厂坐落在海边一个宜人的地方。

**size** n. measurements of something or how big something is or how manythere are of something 大小；体积；规模；尺寸: What is the size of the container? 这个集装箱的体积是多大? The size of the staff has doubled in the last two years. 在过去两年里职工人数已增加了一倍。This packet is the maximum size allowed by the post office. 这个包是邮局允许的最大尺寸。

**skeleton** n. skeleton staff = few staff left to carry on essential work while most of theworkforce is away 基干人员（骨干）

**skill** n. ability to do something because you have been trained 技能；技巧；She has acquired some very useful office management skills. 她已学到一些很有用的办公管理技能。He will have to learn some new skills if he is going to direct the factory. 如果他要领导这个工厂，他就必须学一些新技术。

◇ **skilled** a. having learnt certain skills 熟练的；有技能的；skilled workers or skilled labour = workers who have special skills or who have had long training 熟练工人

**slack** a. not busy 萧条的；呆滞的；Business is slack at the end of the week. 这周末生意不景气（萧条）。January is always a slack period. 一月份总是萧条时期。

◇ **slacken off** v. to become less busy 呆滞；萧条；Trade has slackened off. 贸易已呆滞

**slander** 1. n. untrue spoken statement which damages someone's character 诽谤；中伤；底毁；action for slander or slander action = case in a law court where someone says that another personhad slandered him(法律上)诽谤诉讼案 2. v. to slander someone = to damage someone's character by saying untrue things abouthim 诽谤某人；造谣中伤某人

NOTE: compare LIBEL

**slash** v. to cut or to reduce sharply(大幅度地)削减；减低: to slash prices or credit terms 杀价；削减信贷条件；Prices have been slashed in all departments. 所有部门的价格已大幅度削减了。The bank has been forced to slash interest rates. 银行已被迫大幅度降低利率。

**sleeper** n. share which has not risen in value for some time, but which may suddenly do so in the future 爆冷门的股票；潜在股(指时价并不高，但能在将来某个时间突然上升的股票)

◇ **sleeping** a. sleeping partner = partner who has a share in the business but does not work in it 隐名合伙人；隐名股东(拥有该企业的股票，但不参与具体经营的合伙人)

**slide** v. to move down steadily(不停地)下滑；滑动: Prices slid after the company reported a loss. 这个公司报亏损之后，价格就下滑。

NOTE: sliding - slid

◇ **sliding** a. which rises in steps 累进的: a sliding scale of charges = list of charges which rises gradually according to value orquantity or time, etc. 累进收费(费用可按价值、数量或时间等变动而逐步增加)

**slight** a. not very large or not very important 微小的；不大的: There was a slight improvement in the balance of trade. 贸易差额方面有所改善。We saw a slight increase in sales in February. 我们看到二月份的销售额略有增加

◇ **slightly** ad. not very much 不大地；有点: Sales fell slightly in the second quarter. 第二季度的销售量有所下降。The Swiss bank is offering slightly better terms. 瑞士银行将提供稍微优惠些的

条件。

**slip** 1. n. (a) small piece of paper 纸条: compliments slip = piece of paper with the name of the company printed on it, sent with documents, gifts, etc., instead of a letter 礼贴；问侯的便条; deposit slip = piece of paper stamped by the cashier to prove that you have paid money into your account 存款单；解缴款存根; distribution slip = paper attached to a document or to a magazine, showing all the people in an office who should read it 供传阅的名单; pay slip = piece of paper showing the full amount of a worker's pay, and the money deducted as tax, pension and insurance contributions 工资单(标明某工人应得的工资和应扣除的税金、养老金和保险费等); paying-in slip = printed form which is filled in when money is being deposited in a bank 存款单；激款凭单(在银行存款时填写的表格); sales slip = paper showing that an article was bought at a certain shop 销货单；销售发票(证明某件商品是在某个商店购买的): Goods can be exchanged only on production of a sales slip 货物只能以出示销售发票兑换。(b) mistake 疏忽；错误: He made a couple of slips in calculating the discount. 在计算折扣时, 他出了几个差错。2. v. to go down and back 下减; 下跌: Profits slipped to £1.5m. 利润(率)降到了150万英磅。Shares slipped back at the close. 收盘时, 股票回升了。
NOTE: slipping - slipped

◇ **slip up** v. to make a mistake 犯错误；疏忽: We slipped up badly in not signing the agreement with the Chinese company. 我们犯了严重错误, 没有和那个中国公司签约。

◇ **slip-up** n. mistake 错误；过失
NOTE: plural is slip-ups

**slogan** n. publicity slogan = group of words which can be easily remembered, and which is used in publicity for a product 广告用语(标语)(一种简洁, 吸引人且容易记住的广告用语): We are using the slogan "Smiths can make it" on all our publicity. 我们在所有广有广告上使用了"史密斯公司能成功"的口号:

**slot machine** n. machine which provides drinks or cigarettes, plays music, etc., when a coin is put in it(投币式)自动售货机(投入一枚硬币, 就会提供饮料、香烟、奏出音乐等的机器)

**slow** 1. a. not going fast 慢的: a slow start to the day's trading 该交易日的开局清淡; The sales got off to a slow start, but picked up later. 买卖开始清淡, 但后来有所好转(有了起色)。Business is always slow afterChristmas. 圣诞节过后, 生意总是清淡。They were slow to reply or slow at replying to the customer's complaints. 他们对顾客的投诉答复迟缓。The board is slow to come to a decision. 董事会是缓慢地作出决定。There was a slow improvement in sales in the first half of the year. 今年上半年销售情况有所改善(好转)。2. ad. to go slow = to protest against management by working slowly 怠工(以抗议资方)

◇ **slow down** v. to stop rising or moving or falling 使慢下来；降低；减速: Inflation is slowing down. 通货膨胀的速度在放慢。The fall in the exchange rate is slowing down. 汇率下跌的速度在放慢。The management decided to slow down production. 资方决定放慢生产速度

◇ **slowdown** n. becoming less busy 放慢；减缓: a slowdown in the company's expansion 公司扩展业务放慢

◇ **slowly** ad. not fast 缓慢地；慢慢地: The company's sales slowly improved. 该公司的销售情况在慢慢地好转。We are slowly increasing our market share. 我们正在逐步增加我们的市场份额。

**slump** 1. n. (a) rapid fall 暴跌：slump insales 销售量急剧下跌；slump in profits 利润下降；slump in the value of the pound 英磅迅速贬值；the pound's slump on the foreign exchange markets 外汇市场上英磅暴跌。(b) period of economic collapse with high unemployment and loss of trade 经济衰退期(伴随着高失业率和贸易亏损的经济衰退时期)：We are experiencing slump conditions. 我们正经历着经济衰退。the Slump = the world economic crisis of 1929 – 1933 (1929 年到 1933 年的)世界经济危机。2. v. to fall fast 下降；暴跌：Profits have slumped. 利润已急剧下降。The pound slumped on the foreign exchange markets. 英磅在外汇市场上暴跌。

**slush fund** n. money kept to one side to give to people to persuade them to do what you want 行贿基金

**small** a. not large 小的；不大的：small ads = short private advertisements in a newspaper ( selling smallitems, asking for jobs, etc.)小广告；small businesses = little companies with low turnover and few employees 小企业；small businessman = man who runs a small business 经营小企业者；small change = loose coins 零钱；找头；GB small claims court = court which deals with disputes over small amounts of money (英)处理小额索赔的法院(庭)；the small investor = person who has a small amount of money to invest 小额投资者；small shopkeepers = owners of small shops 小店主；小业主

◇ **small – scale** a. working in a small way, with few staff and not much money 小规模的：a small – scale enterprise = a small business 小型企业

**smash** v. to break ( a record ) or to do better than ( a record )打破(记录)；超过(记录)：to smash all production records 打破所有生产记录。Sales have smashed all records for the first half of the year. 销售量已突破了今年上半年的所有记录。

**smuggle** v. to take goods into a country without declaring them to thecustoms 私运；走私(指未向海关申报就将货物运入国境)：They had to smuggle the spare parts into the country. 他们不得不向这个国家走私备件。

◇ **smuggler** n. person who smuggles 走私者

◇ **smuggling** n. taking goods illegally into a country 走私：He made his money in arms smuggling. 他的钱是在军火走私中赚的。

NOTE: no plural

**snap** a. rapid or sudden 仓促的；突然的：The board came to a snap decision. 该董事会作出了仓促的决定。They carried out a snap check or a snap inspection of the expense accounts. 他们对费用帐户进行了突然的审查。

◇ **snap up** v. to buy something quickly 抢购；争购：to snap up a bargain 抢购便宜货(廉价商品)；He snapped up 15% of the company's shares. 他抢购了该公司 15%的股票。

NOTE: snapping – snapped

**snip** n. infml bargain(非正式)廉价品，便宜货：These typewriters are a snip at £50 这些打字机是 50 英磅一台的便宜货

**soar** v. to go up rapidly 剧增；猛涨：Food prices soared during the cold weather. 这个冬季食品价格猛涨。Share prices soared on the news of the takeover bid or the news of the takeover bid sent share prices soaring. 兼并出价的消息使得股票价格飞涨。

**social** a. referring to society in general 社会的：social costs = ways in which something will affect people 社会成本：The report examines the social costs of building the factoryin the middle of the town. 这个报告对在城市中部建厂的社会成本进行了审查。 social security = money from contributions paid to the National Insurance provided by the government to people who need·it 社会保障;社会保险: He gets weekly social security payments. 他按周领取社会保险金。 the social system = the way society is organized 社会制度;

◇ **society** n. (a) way in which people in a country are organized 社会: consumer society = type of society where consumers are encouraged to buy goods 消费社会; the affluent society = type of society where most people are rich 富人社会 (b) club or group of people with the same interests 俱乐部;协会;团体;会;社: He has joined a computer society. 他加入了计算机协会。 building society = financial institution which accepts and pays interest on deposits, and lends money to people who are buying property 房屋互助会(吸收存款,支付利息并贷款给要购买房地产的人的一种金融机构); cooperative society = organization where customers and workers are partners andshare the profits 合作社; friendly society = group of people who pay regular subscriptions to a fund whichis used to help members who are ill or in financial trouble 互助会(该会会员要定期缴纳捐助基金,以用于帮助患病的或经济有困难的会员)

◇ **socio－economic** a. referring to social and economic conditions 社会经济的: the socio－economic system in capitalist countries 资本主义国家的社会经济体制; socio－economic groups = groups in society divided according to income and position 社会—经济集团(按收入和地位进行)

**soft** a. not hard 软的: soft currency = currency of a country with a weak economy, which is cheap to buy and dif-

ficult to exchange for other currencies 软通货; soft loan = loan (from a company to an employee or from a government toanother government) at very low or nil interest 软贷款;低息贷款; to take the soft option = to decide to do something which involves least risk, effort or problems 做无风险,不费力的事; soft sell = persuading people to buy by encouraging them, but not forcingthem to do so 软推销;劝诱推销术

◇ **software** n. computer programs (as opposed to machines) 软件(计算机程序)
NOTE: no plural

**sole** a. only 唯一的;独一无二的: sole agency = agreement to be the only person to represent a company or to sell a product in a certain area. 独家代理;独家代理权: He has the sole agency for Ford cars 他有福特汽车的独家代理权。 sole agent = person who has the sole agency for a product in an area sole distributor = retailer who is the only one in an area who is allowed tosell a certain product 独家代理商; sole owner = person who owns a business on his own, with no partners 独家经营(属有)者; sole trader = person who runs a business by himself but has not registered it as a company 个体经营者;个体商人

**solemn** a. solemn and binding agreement = agreement which is not legally binding, but which all parties are supposed to obey 正式的有拘束力的合同(该合同法律上无拘束力,但各方都该遵守)

**solicit** v. to solicit orders = to ask for orders or to try to get people to order goods 请求顾客订货

◇ **solicitor** n. GB lawyer who gives advice to members of the public and acts for them legally(英)小律师: to instruct a solicitor = to give orders to a solicitor to start legal proceedings on your behalf 指定一位律师(代表你起诉)

**solus** (**advertisement**) n. advertisement which does not appear near other advertisements for similar products 单独刊登的广告(不出现在其他类似产品广告附近的商品广告)

**solution** n. answer to a problem 解决(办法);解答;解释: to look for a solution to the financial problems 寻求解决财政困难的办法。The programmer came up with a solution to the systems problem;程序员想出了一个解决系统问题的办法。We think we have found a solution to the problem of getting skilled staff. 我们认为, 我们已找到了解决获得熟练工问题的办法。

**solve** v. to solve a problem = to find an answer to a problem 解决问题: The loan will solve some of our short - term problems. 这笔贷款将解决我们一些短期问题

**solvent** a. having enough money to pay debts 有偿还能力的: When he bought the company it was barely solvent. 他买下这个公司时,该公司几乎没有偿还能力
◇ **solvency** n. being able to pay all debts 有偿还能力
NOTE: no plural

**sort** v. to put (a lot of things) in order 整理;整顿;把…分类: She is sorting index cards into alphabetical order. 她在按字母顺序整理索引卡。
◇ **sort out** v. to put into order; to settle (a problem) 整理;解决(问题);处理: Did you sort out the accounts problem with the auditors? 你和审计员一起把帐目上的问题解决了吗?

**sound** a. reasonable or which can be trusted 合理的;稳妥的: The company's financial situation is very sound. 该公司的财务状况很好。He gave us some very sound advice. 他给了我们一些非常合理的忠告。
◇ **soundness** n. being reasonable 合理
NOTE: no plural

**source** n. place where something comes from 来源;出处: source of income 收入来源; You must declare income from all sources to the tax office. 你必须将所有收入来源向税务局申报。income which is taxed at source = where the tax is removed before the income is paid 已纳过税的收入。

**space** n. empty place or empty area 空间;空地 advertising space = space in a newspaper set aside for advertisements 广告栏(在报纸上为广告留出的空位); to take advertising space in a newspaper = to place a large advertisement in a newspaper 在报纸上登载大幅广告; floor space = area of the floor in an office 办公楼面面积; office space = area available for offices or used by offices 办公使用面积: We are looking for extra office space for our new accounts department. 我们正在为我们的新财务部寻找另外的办公地方。
◇ **space bar** n. key on a typewriter or computer which makes a single space between letters 空行键(打字机上或计算机上一按即跳一格的)
◇ **space out** v. to place things with spaces between them 隔开;留间隔: The company name is written in spaced - out letters. 公司的名称是以隔开字母的形式书写的。Payments can be spaced out over a period of ten years. 在十年内分期付款。

**spare** a. extra or not being used 多余的;备用的: He has invested his spare capital in a computer shop. 他已将其闲置资金投资于一个计算机商店。to use up spare capacity = to make use of time or space which has not been fully used 利用空闲生产能力(指利用未得到充分利用的时间或空间); spare part = small piece of machinery used to replace part of a machine which is broken 备件；备用件：The photocopier will not work — it needs a spare part. 复印机要停止工作——它需要一个备件。spare time = time when you are not at work 余暇；空闲时间；工余时间：He built himself a car in his spare time. 他在工余时间自己组装了一辆汽车。

**spec** n. to buy something on spec = to buy something as a speculation, without being sure of its value 冒险，投机购买某物(不了解其价值)

◇ **specs** pl. n. = SPECIFICATIONS (复数名词)规格；说明书

**special** ad. different or not normal or referring to one particular thing 特殊的；专门的：He offered us special terms. 他给我们提供了特惠条件。The car is being offered at aspecial price. 这辆车正以特价出售。special deposits = large sums of money which banks have to deposit with the Bank of England 特别存款；专用存款(大数额款项，银行必须将其存入英格兰银行行)

◇ **specialist** n. person or company which deals with one particular type of product or one subject 专家；行家；专营店：You should go to a specialist in computers or to a computer specialist for advice. 你应去计算机专营店或去找一个计算机专家咨询。

◇ **speciality or specialty** n. particular interest or special type of product which a company deals in 专业；特制品；特长：Their speciality is computer programs. 他们的专业(特长)是计算机程序。US specialty store = shop selling a limited range of items of good quality (美)名牌货商店；特色商品店

◇ **specialization** n. study of one particular thing or dealing with one particular type of product 专门研究(某学科)；专营(某种产品)：The company's area of specialization is accounts packages for small businesses. 该公司的专营产品是小企业用的记帐组合程序。

◇ **specialize** v. to trade in one particular type of product or service 专营(某种产品和服务)：The company specializes in electronic components. 这个公司专卖电子元件。They have a specialized product line. 他们拥有一条专用生产线。He sells very specialized equipment for the electronics industry. 他经销用于电子工业的专用设备。

**specie** pl. n. coins(复名词)硬币

**specify** v. to state clearly what is needed 详细说明；具体指定：to specify full details of the goods ordered 详细说明所订货物的细目；Do not include VAT on the invoice unless specified. 发票上不要包括增值税，除非有明确细说明。

◇ **specification** n. detailed information about what is needed or about a product to be supplied 详细说明书；规范；规格：to detail the specifications of a computer system 详述计算机系统的说明书；job specification = very detailed description of what is involved in a job 工作规范；工作细则；to work to standard specifications = to work to specifications which are acceptable anywhere in the industry 按标准规范工作：The work is not up to specification or does not meet our specifications. = The product is not made in the way which was detailed. 产品不符合规格要求。

**specimen** n. thing which is given as a sample 样品；样本：to give specimen signatures on a bank mandate = to write the signatures of all people who can sign cheques for an account so that the bank can recognize them 在银行委托书上样签

**speculate** v. to take a risk in business which you hope will bring you profits 投机，冒险：to speculate on the Stock Exchange = to buy shares which you hope willrise in value 在证券交易所上进行投机买卖

◇ **speculation** n. risky deal which may produce a short - term profit 投机买卖 (生意)：He bought the company as a speculation. 他冒险（投机）购买了这家公司。She lost all hermoney in Stock Exchange speculations. 她将所有的钱赔进了股票投机生意。

◇ **speculative** a. speculative builder = builder who builds houses in the hope that someone will want to buy them 投机建房者 speculative share = share which may go up or down in value 投机性股票（价值波动较大的股票）

◇ **speculator** n. person who buys goods or shares or foreign currency in the hope that they will rise in value 投机者；投机商：a property speculator 房地产投机商；a currency speculator 外汇投机商；a speculator on the Stock Exchange or a Stock Exchange speculator 证券（股票）投机者

**speed** n. rate at which something moves 速度：dictation speed = number of words per minute which a secretary can write down in shorthand 听写速度(指秘书用速记每分钟记下的字数)；typing speed = number of words per minute which a typist can type 打字速度

◇ **speed up** v. to make something go faster(使)加速；增速：We are aiming to speed up our delivery times. 我们正力争加快交货时间

**spend** v. (a) to pay money 花费；花钱：They spent all their savings on buying the shop. 他们花了所有的积储（存款）购买这家商店。The company spends thousands of pounds on research. 这个公司在研究方面要花成千上万英磅。(b) to use time 度过；消磨（时间)：The company spends hundreds of man - hours on meetings. 这个公司开会就要耗掉几

百个工时。The chairman spent yesterday afternoon with the auditors. 昨天下午，董事长跟审计人员们一起度过的。

NOTE: spending - spent

◇ **spending** n. paying money 开支；开销；经费：cash spending or credit card spending 现金开支或信用卡开支；consumer spending = spending by consumers 消费开支；spending money = money for ordinary personal expenses 零用钱；spending power = having money to spend on goods；amount of goods which can be bought for a certain sum of money 购买力；消费能力；The spending power of the pound has fallen over the last ten years. 在过去十年里，英磅的购买力已下跌。the spending power of the student market 学生市场的购买力

NOTE: no plural

**sphere** n. area 范围；领域：sphere of activity 活动范围；sphere of influence 影响范围；势力范围

**spin off** v. to spin off a subsidiary company = to take a part of a large company and make a smaller subsidiary from it 派生出子公司(母公司收回子公司全部股本，使之脱离成为更小的子公司)

NOTE: spinning - span - spun

◇ **spinoff** n. useful product developed as a secondary product from a mainitem 副产品：One of the spinoffs of the research programme has been the development of the electric car. 研究项目的副产品之一是开发电动汽车。

**spiral** 1. n. thing which twists round and round getting higher all the time 螺旋上升；(物价)不断加剧地上升：The economy is in an inflationary spiral or wage - price spiral = The economy is in a situation where price rises encourage higher wage demands which in turn make prices rise. 经济处在螺旋上升的通货膨胀状态下或处在工资与价格的螺旋上升状态下。2. v. to twist round and round, getting higher all the time (物价)螺旋式上升;不断加剧上升: a period of spiralling prices 物价螺旋上升时期; spiralling inflation = inflation where price rises make workers ask for higher wageswhich then increase prices again 螺旋式上升的通货膨胀(指由于物价上涨使得工人要求提高工资,由于工资增加又引起了物价上涨)

NOTE: spiralling - spiralled but US English spiraling - spiraled

**split** 1. n. (a) dividing up 分开;分裂: share split = dividing of shares into smaller denominations the company is proposing a five for one split 拆股;分股(将一股分为面额较小的): The company is proposing that each existing share should be divided into five smaller shares. 公司打算将每一现行股拆成五个小面额股。(b) lack of agreement 不一致;分歧: a split in the family shareholders 家庭股东意见不一致(分歧) 2. v. (a) to split shares = to divide shares into smaller denominations 分股。The shares were split five for one. = Five new shares were given for each existing share held. 每股拆成五个小面额股。(b) to split the difference = to come to an agreement over a price by dividing the difference between the amount the seller is asking and amount the buyer wants to pay and agreeing on a price between the two 折衷;彼此将就(同意将价格差额由买卖双方分担)

NOTE: splitting - split

**spoil** v. to ruin or to make something bad 损坏: Half the shipment was spoiled by water. 这批货的一半被水损坏。The company's results were spoiled by a disastrous last quarter. 公司的成果被灾难性的上季度给毁了。

**sponsor** 1. n. (a) person who pays money to help research or to pay for a business venture; company which pays to help a sport, in return for advertising rights 赞助人(者)(出资帮助某项研究,商务活动或赞助某项体育运动以获得广告权)(b) company which advertises on TV 广告客户(在电视上作广告的公司) 2. v. to pay money to help research or business development 赞助: to sponsor a television programme 赞助某个电视节目。The company has sponsored the football match. 该公司已为这场足球赛提供了赞助。Government - sponsored trade exhibition 政府主办贸易展览会

◇ **sponsorship** n. act of sponsoring 主办;发起;赞助: government sponsorship of overseas selling missions 政府赞助的海外推销团

**spot** n. (a) buying something for immediate delivery 现场交易: spot cash = cash paid for something bought immediately 现金;现款;现款支付; the spot market in oil = the market for buying oil for immediate delivery 石油现货市场; spot price or spot rate = price or rate for something which is delivered immediately 现货价格;现货汇率 (b) place 场所;地点: to be on the spot = to be at a certain place 在场;在某地: We have a man on the spot to deal with any problems which happen on the building site. 我们有一个人在现场,处理工地上发生的问题。(c) TV spot = period on TV which is used for commercials 电视上插广告时间: We are running a series of TV spots over the next three weeks. 我们要在以后三周时间里插播出一系列电视广告节目。

**spread** 1. n. (a) range 范围;幅度: He has a wide spread of investments or of interests. = He has shares in many different types of companies. 他拥有范围广的投资或权益。(b) (on the Stock Exchange) difference between buying and selling prices(证券交易所中的)买价与售价差额; 2. v. to space out over a period of time 分开(一段时间);分期:

to spread payments over several months 几个月内分期支付(分几个月支付); to spread a risk = to make the risk of insurance less great by asking othercompanies to help cover it 分散风险 NOTE: spreading – spread

◇ **spreadsheet** n. computer printout showing a series of columns of figures(计算机打印机打出的)棋盘式对照表

**square** n. (a) shape with four equal sides and four right angles 正方形;方形物: Graph paper is drawn with a series of small squares. 座表纸是用一系列小方格绘制而成的。(b) way of measuring area, by multiplying the length by the width 平方;二次幂(计算面积的方法,将长宽相乘): The office is ten metres by twelve – its area is one hundred and twenty square metres. 这个办公室是 10 米乘 12 米——其面积是 120 平方米。square measure = area in square feet or metres 平方单位制;面积量度 NOTE: written with figures as$^2$: 10ft$^2$ = ten square feet; 6m$^2$ = six square metres

◇ **squared paper** n. graph paper or paper printed with a series of small squares 座标纸;划有方格的纸

**squeeze** 1. n. government control carried out by reducing amounts available 收缩;紧缩;压缩: credit squeeze = period when lending by the banks is restricted by thegovernment 信贷紧缩; profit squeeze = control of the amount of profits which companies can pay outas dividend 利润压缩(缩减) 2. v. to crush or to press; to make smaller 挤;压榨;减少: to squeeze margins or profits or credit 缩减利润率;缩减利润;紧缩信贷; Our margins have been squeezed by the competition. = Profits have been reduced because our margins have to be smaller for us to stay competitive. 我们的利润率已被竞争所压缩。

**stability** n. being steady or not moving up or down 稳定;稳定性: price stability 价格稳定性; a period of economic stability 经济稳定时期; the stability of the currency markets 货币市场的稳定性 NOTE: no plural

◇ **stabilization** n. making stable or preventing sudden changes in prices, etc. 稳定;平衡: stabilization of the economy = keeping the economy stable by preventing inflation from rising, cutting high interest rates and excess money supply 经济稳定

◇ **stabilize** v. to make steady 使稳定: Prices have stabilized. = Prices have stopped moving up or down. 价格已稳定下来。to have a stabilizing effect on the economy = to make the economy more stable 使经济产生稳定影响

◇ **stable** a. steady or not moving up or down 稳定的;稳固的: stable prices 稳定的价格; stable exchange rate 稳定的汇率; stable currency 稳定的货币; stable economy 稳定的经济

**stack** 1. n. pile or heap of things on top of each other 堆;垛: There is a stack of replies to our advertisement. 有一堆对我们广告的答复信件。2. v. to pile things on top of each other 堆放;成堆: The boxes are stacked in the warehouse. 这些箱(盒)子堆放在仓库里。

**staff** 1. n. people who work for a company or for an organization(某公司或机构的)工作人员;职员: to be on the staff or a member of staff or a staff member = to be employed permanently by a company 永久职员之一(被公司永久雇佣的); staff agency = agency which looks for office staff for companies 参谋机构;为公司寻找工作人员的代理机构; staff appointment = a job on the staff 职员委派; staff association = society formed by members of staff of a company to representthem to the management and to organize entertainments 职工联谊会; accounts staff = people who work in the accounts department 财会人员; clerical staff or office staff = people who work in offices 职员; 行政人员; counter staff = sales staff who work behind counters 站柜台的售货员; senior staff or junior staff = older or younger members of staff; people in more important orless important positions in a company 年长(年轻)职员; 高(低)级职员 NOTE: staff refers to a group of people and so is often followed by averb in the plural 2. v. to employ workers 雇佣(工人); 招聘人员: to be staffed with skilled part‐timers; 配备熟练的非全日工。to have difficulty in staffing the factory 为这个工厂配备工人有困难

◇ **staffer** n. US member of the permanent staff(美)永久职员

◇ **staffing** n. providing workers for a company(为公司)提供人员: staffing levels = numbers of members of staff required in a department of a company for it to work efficiently 配备人员水平(标准); the company's staffing policy = the company's views on staff‐how many are needed for eachdepartment or if they should be full‐time or part‐time or what thesalaries should be, etc. 公司的人事政策; NOTE: no plural

**stag** 1. n. person who buys new issues of shares and sells them immediately to make a profit 炒买炒卖股票者; 股票投机商(认购新上市股票并立即脱售以赚取利润者)2. v. to stag an issue = to buy a new issue of shares not as an investment, but to sell immediately at a profit 投机性认购; 炒买炒卖股票(认购新上市股票, 不作为投资, 而是立即脱售以赚取利润)NOTE: stagging‐stagged

**stage** 1. n. period or one of several points of development 阶段; 时期: the different stages of the production process 生产过程中的不同阶段; The contract is still in the drafting stage. = The contract is still being drafted. 该合同仍在起草阶段。in stages = in different steps 在不同阶段; 分期: The company has agreed to repay the loan in stages. 公司已同意分期偿还贷款。2. v. (a) to put on or to organize (a show) 安排; 举办(展览会): The exhibition is being staged in the conference centre. 展览会正在会议中心举办。to stage a recovery = to recover 恢复; 复苏: The company has staged a strong recovery from a point of near bankruptcy 该公司已从濒临破产的状态中强劲地恢复过来。(b) staged payments = payments made in stages 分期支付

**stagflation** n. inflation and stagnation of an economy 滞胀(经济的通货膨胀和停滞伴随发生)

**stagger** v. to arrange (holidays, working hours) so that they do not all begin and end at the same time 使错开(工作时间、假日): Staggered holidays help the tourist industry. 错开假期帮了旅游业的忙。We have to stagger the lunch hour so that there is always someone on the switchboard 我们必须错开午饭时间, 以便电话总机一直有人(值)。

**stagnant** a. not active or not increasing 停滞的; 萧条的: Turnover was stagnant for the first half of the year. 今年上半年营业额是停滞的。astagnant economy 停滞的经济

◇ **stagnate** v. not to increase or not to make progress (使)停滞; (使)呆滞: The economy is stagnating. 经济正在停滞。After six hours the talks were stagnating. 六个小时后, 会谈就停滞了。

◇ **stagnation** n. not increasing or not making any progress 停滞; 呆滞: The

country entered a period of stagnation. 这个国家进入了经济停滞时期。economic stagnation = lack of expansion in the economy 经济停滞
NOTE: no plural

**stake** 1. n. money invested 投资本金: to have a stake in a business = to have money invested in a business 拥有某公司的股份。to acquire a stake in a business = to buy shares in a business 购买某公司的股票: He acquired a 25% stake in the business 他认购了这个公司25%的股票。2. v. to stake money on something = to risk money on something 拿…冒风险

**stamp** 1. n. (a) device for making marks on documents; mark made in this way 印章; 图章; 戳记: The invoice has the stamp "Received with thanks" on it. 发票上印有"收到, 谢谢"的戳记。The customs officer looked at the stamps in his passport. 海关人员看了看他护照上的盖印。date stamp = stamp with rubber figures which can be moved, used formarking the date on documents 日期戳; rubber stamp = stamp made of hard rubber cut to form words 橡皮图章; stamp pad = soft pad of cloth with ink on which a stamp is pressed, before marking the paper 印泥; 印油 (b) small piece of gummed paper which you buy from a post office and stick on a letter or parcel to pay for the postage 邮票: a postage stamp; 邮票; a £1 stamp 面值1英磅的邮票 (c) stamp duty = tax on legal documents (such as the conveyance of a property to a new owner) 印花税 (对法律文书征收的税, 如: 财产转让证书) 2 v. (a) to mark a document with a stamp 盖章 (于); 盖戳 (于): to stamp an invoice "Paid"; 在发票上盖上"付讫"字样。The documents were stamped by the customs officials. 海关官员在文件上盖了章。(b) to put a postage stamp on (an envelope, etc.) 贴邮票于: stamped ad-

dressed envelope = envelope with your own address written on it and a stamp stuck on it to pay for the return postage 附有回复地址和邮资已付的信封: Send a stamped addressed envelope for further details andcatalogue. 寄去附有回复地址和邮资的信封以索取更详细的资料和目录。

**stand** 1. n. arrangement of shelves or tables, etc. at an exhibition for showing a company's products 台; 架: display stand = special stand for displaying goods for sale 展览摊位; 展台: exhibition stand = separate section of an exhibition where a company exhibitsits products or services 展区; news stand = small wooden shop on a pavement, for selling newspapers 报刊亭; 2. v. to be or to stay to stand liable for damages = to be liable to pay damages 有赔偿损失的责任 The company's balance stands at £24,000. = The balance is £24,000. 公司的余额是 24,000 英磅。
NOTE: standing – stood
◇ **stand down** v. to withdraw your name from an election 退出竞选
◇ **stand in for** v. to take someone's place 代替; Mr Smith is standing in for the chairman, who is ill. 董事长病了, 史密斯先生代替他。

**standard** 1. n. normal quality or normal conditions which other things arejudged against 标准; 水准: standard of living or living standards = quality of personal home life (such as amount of food orclothes bought, size of family car, etc.) 生活水平 (准) production standards = quality of production 生产标准; up to standard = of acceptable quality 达到标准: This batch is not up to standard or does not meet ourstandards. 这批货 (产品) 没有达到标准。gold standard = linking of the value of a currency to value of a quantity ofgold 金本

位制 2 . a. normal or usual 普通的；标准：a standard model car 普通型式的汽车；We have a standard charge of £ 25 for a thirty - minute session. 30 分钟的课时我们收取的标准费是 25 英磅。 standard agreement or standard contract = normal printed contract form 标准协议；标准合同；standard letter = letter which is sent without any change to various correspondents 标准信（向不同的通讯者发同一内容的信）；standard rate = basic rate of income tax which is paid by most taxpayers 标准税率

◇ **standardization** n. making sure that everything fits a standard or is produced inthe same way 标准化；合标准：standardization of design 设计标准化；standardization of measurements 测量标准化；standardization of products = reducing a large number of different products to a serieswhich have the same measurements or design or packaging, etc. 产品标准化
NOTE: no plural

◇ **standardize** v. to make sure that everything fits a standard or is produced inthe same way（使）标准化；（使）合标准

**standby** n. (a) standby ticket = cheap air ticket which allows the passenger to wait until the last moment to see if there is an empty seat on the plane 临时出售的机票（一种允许乘客在飞机起飞前有空位子时乘机的机票，通常较为便宜）standby fare = cheap fare for a standby ticket 临时出售机票的价格 (b) standby arrangements = plans for what should be done if an emergency happens, especially money held in reserve in the International Monetary Fund for use by a country in financial difficulties 备用协定（指国际货币基金组织特为会员国的备用信贷，以备一国出现金融危机时使用）standby credit = credit which is available if a company needs it 备用信贷

**standing** 1 . a. standing order = order written by a customer asking a bank to pay money regularly to an account 长期订单；定期支付单：I pay my subscription by standing order. 我用长期订单支付认缴款项。2 . n. (a) long - standing customer or customer of long standing = person who has been a customer for many years 长期客户 (b) good reputation 名望；地位：the financial standing of a company 某公司的财务信誉；company of good standing = very reputable company 信誉好的公司
NOTE: no plural

**standstill** n. situation where work has stopped 停顿；停滞；Production is at a standstill. 生产处于停滞状态。The strike brought the factory to a standstill. 罢工使工厂停工。

**staple** 1 . a. (a) staple commodity = basic food or raw material 主要商品（指基本食品或原材料）；staple industry = main industry in a country（国家的）主要工业；staple product = main product 主要产品 (b) small piece of bent metal for attaching papers together 订书钉：He used a pair of scissors to take the staples out of the documents 他用剪刀将订书钉从文件上取了出来。2 . v. to staple papers together = to attach papers with staples 用订书钉将文件钉在一起。He could not take away separate pages, because the documents were stapled together 他无法将单页拿走，因为文件钉在一起了。

◇ **stapler** n. small device used to attach papers together with staples 订书机

**start** 1 . n. beginning 开始；开端：cold start = beginning a new business or opening a new shop with no previous turnover to base it on 冷开张（指在无前期销售额为基础开办一个新企业或商店）；house starts US housing starts = number of new private houses or flats of which constructionhas been started duringa year 新建的住宅 2. v. to start a business from cold or from scratch = to begin a new business, with no previous turnover to base iton 冷开张(在无前期销售额的情况下,开办一家新企业)

◇ **starting** n. beginning 开始;起点: starting date = date on which something starts 开工日期; starting salary = salary for an employee when he starts work with a company 起始(起点)薪金

◇ **start - up** n. beginning of a new company or new product 开办;创办;开始生产(新产品): start - up costs 起动成本;初期成本

NOTE: plural is start - ups

**state** 1. n. (a) independent country; semi - independent section of a federal-country (such as the USA) 国家;州: (b) government of a country 政府: state enterprise = company run by the state 国营企业; The bosses of state industries are appointed by the government. 国营企业的老板是由政府任命的。state ownership = situation where an industry is nationalized 国家所有制(工业) 2. v. to say clearly 说明;陈述;阐明: The document states that all revenue has to be declared to the tax office. 文件阐明所有的收入必须向税务局申报。

◇ **state - controlled** a. run by the state 国家控制的;国家管理的: state - controlled television 国家控制的电视业

◇ **state - of - the - art** a. technically as advanced as possible(技术上)最先进的;现代化的

◇ **state - owned** a. owned by the state or by a state 国营的;国有的

**statement** n. saying something clearly 陈述;声明: to make a false statement = to give wrong details 作不真实陈述; statement of expenses = detailed list of money spent 费用清单; bank statement = written document from a bank show-ing the balance of an account 银行结单;银行对帐单(指银行表明帐户余额的书面文件); monthly or quarterly statement = statement which is sent every month or every quarter by thebank 月(季)结单(报表)(b) financial statement = document which shows the financial situation of a company 财务报表; The accounts department have prepared a financial statement for the shareholders. 财务部已为股东们准备了一份财务报表。(c) statement of account = list of invoices and credits and debits sent by a supplier toa customer at the end of each month 帐单;帐目表

**station** n. (a) place where trains stop for passengers 车站(火车): The train leaves the Central Station at 14.15. 火车14点15分离开中央车站 (b) TV station or radio station = building where TV or radio programmes are produced 电视台;广播电台

**stationery** n. office supplies for writing, such as paper, carbons, pens, etc 文具;办公用品: stationery supplier 文具供应商; office stationery 办公用品; continuous stationery = paper made as a long sheet used in computer printers (计算机打印机用的)连在一起不分开打印纸

NOTE: no plural

**statistics** pl. n. study of facts in the form of figures(复数名词)统计;统计数字(资料): to examine the sales statistics for the previous six months 对前三个月的销售统计数字进行审核;Government trade statistics show an increase in imports.政府贸易统计数字表明进口在增长。

◇ **statistical** a. based on figures 统计的: statistical analysis 统计分析; statistical information 统计情报(资料); statistical discrepancy = amount by which sets of figures differ 统计差异

◇ **statistician** n. person who analyzes statistics统计员;统计学家

**status** n. (a) importance or position in society 重要地位;社会地位;要人身份: The chairman's car is a status symbol. = The size of the car shows how important the company is.董事长的汽车是表明其社会地位的象征。loss of status = becoming less important in a group 地位下降;降低职位; status inquiry = checking on a customer's credit rating 情况查询(指对客户的信用等级进行调查)(b) legal status = legal position 法律地位
NOTE: no plural

◇ **status quo** n. state of things as they are now 现状: The contract does not alter the status quo. 该合同改变不了现状。

**statute** n. law made by parliament(议会制定的)法令;成文法规: statute book = list of laws passed by parliament 法令全书; statute of limitations = law which allows only a certain amount of time (a few years)for someone to claim damages or property 时效法规;限制法规(指对有关要求损害赔偿,财产所有权等所规定的有时间限制的法律)

◇ **statutory** a. fixed by law 法定的: There is a statutory period of probation of thirteen weeks. 有13周的法定试用期。statutory holiday = holiday which is fixed by law 法定节(假)日

**stay** 1. n. (a) length of time spent in one place 逗留;停留: The tourists were in town only for a short stay. 游客们在城里只作了短暂停留。short - stay guests = customers who spend only a few nights at a hotel 暂住旅客(指在宾馆里只住几夜的旅客)(b) stay of execution = temporary stopping of a legal order(法律上)缓期执行: The court granted the company a two - week stay of execution 法庭准予该公司为期两周

的缓期执行。2. v. to stop at a place 住;逗留;停留: The chairman is staying at the Hotel London. 董事长下榻在伦敦酒店。Profits have stayed below 10% for two years. 两年来利润一直停留在10%以下。Inflation has stayed high in spite of the government's efforts to bring it down.尽管政府努力降低通货膨胀,但它仍居高不下。

**STD** = SUBSCRIBER TRUNK DIALLING 国际直拨电话系统

**steady** 1. a. continuing in a regular way 稳定的;平稳的: steady increase in profits 利润稳定增长; The market stayed steady. 市场稳定。There is a steady demand for computers. 对计算机有稳定的需求。2. v. to become firm or to stop fluctuating(使)稳定;(使)稳固: The markets steadied after last week's fluctuations. 继上周的波动之后,市场稳定下来了。Prices steadied on the commodity markets.商品市场上的价格稳定下来了。The government's figures had a steadying influence on the exchange rate. 政府的数字对外汇汇率有稳定影响。

◇ **steadily** ad. in a regular or continuous way 稳定地;稳固地: Output increased steadily over the last two quarters. 在上两个季度里产量稳步增长。The company has steadily increased its market share.该公司稳步地增加了其市场份额。

◇ **steadiness** n. being firm or not fluctuating 稳定;稳固: The steadiness of the markets is due to the government's intervention 市场的稳定应归功于政府的干预。
NOTE: no plural

**steal** v. to take something which does not belong to you 窃取;偷: The rival company stole our best clients. 竞争对手公司抢走了我们最大的客户。One of our biggest problems is stealing in the wine department. 我们最大的问题之一是酒品部发生失窃。

NOTE: stealing – stole – has stolen

**steep** a. very sharp or very high (price) 过高的；急剧上升的: a steep increase in interest charges 利率费用急剧增长；a steep decline in overseas sales 海外销售额急剧下降

**stencil** n. sheet of special paper which can be written or typed on, and used in a duplicating machine(油印用的)蜡纸

**stenographer** n. official person who can write in shorthand 速记员

**step** n. (a) type of action 步骤；措施: The first step taken by the new MD was to analyse all the expenses. 新总经理采取的第一步是对所有费用进行分析。to take steps to prevent something happening = to act to stop something happening 采取措施防止某事发生。(b) movement 活动；移动 becoming assistant to the MD is a step up the promotion ladder 给总经理当助手是登上晋升的梯子。in step with = moving at the same rate as 与…步调一致: The pound rose in step with the dollar. 英磅与美元同步上升。out of step with = not moving at the same rate as 与…步调不一致: The pound was out of step with other European currencies. 英磅与其它的欧洲货币步调不一致。Wages are out of step with the cost of living. 工资与生活费不成正比。

◇ **step up** v. to increase 增加: to step up industrial action 增加(扩大)罢工；The company has stepped up production of the latest models. 公司已增加了最新型产品的生产

NOTE: stepping – stepped

**sterling** n. standard currency used in the United Kingdom 英磅(英国使用的标准货币): to quote prices in sterling or to quote sterling prices 用英磅报价；pound sterling = official term for the British currency 英磅；sterling area = area of the world where the pound sterling is the main trading currency 英磅区(拍世界上以英磅为主要贸易货币的地区)；sterling balances = a country's trade balances expressed in pounds sterling 英磅结存；英磅收支差额(指一国的贸易差额是以英磅表示的)；sterling crisis = fall in the exchange rate of the pound sterling 英磅危机

NOTE: no plural

**stevedore** n. person who works in a port, loading or unloading ships 码头装卸工人

**steward** n. (a) man who serves drinks or food on a ship or plane(轮船)飞机上的)男乘务员 (b) shop steward = elected union representative of workers, who represents their complaints to the management 工人代表(指选出的代表工人向资方反映意见的工会工人代表)

◇ **stewardess** n. woman who serves drinks or food on a ship or plane(轮船、飞机上的)女乘务员

**stick** v. (a) to attach with glue 粘贴: to stick a stamp on a letter 将邮票贴在信上；They stuck a poster on the door. 他们将一张广告贴在这扇门上。(b) to stay still or not to move 停留；不动: Sales have stuck at £2m for the last two years. 前两年销售额一直停留在200万英磅。

NOTE: sticking – stuck

◇ **sticker** 1. n. small piece of gummed paper or plastic to be stuck on something as an advertisement or to indicate a price 背面有粘胶的广告，标签，招贴等: air-mail sticker = blue sticker with the words "By air mail" which can be stuck on an envelope or parcel to show that it is being sent by air 航空邮件标签 2. v. to put a price sticker on an article for sale 贴价格标签(商品上): We had to sticker all the stock. 我们必须在所有货物

上贴上价格标签。

**stiff** a. strong or difficult 强硬的；艰难的：stiff competition 激烈的竞争；He had to take a stiff test before he qualified. 在取得资格之前,他必须通过一次严格的考试。

**stimulate** v. to encourage or to make (something) become more active 刺激；鼓励；促进：to stimulate the economy 刺激经济；to stimulate trade with the Middle East 促进与中东之间的贸易

◇ **stimulus** n. thing which encourages activity 刺激物；促进因系

NOTE: plural is stimuli

**stipulate** v. to demand that a condition be put into a contract 订定；规定；约定：to stipulate that the contract should run for five years 规定该合同有效期为五年 to pay the stipulated charges 支付规定的费用；The company failed to pay on the date stipulated in the contract. 该公司没有按合同中规定的日期付款。The contract stipulates that the seller pays the buyer's legal costs. 合同规定卖方要支付买方的诉讼费。

◇ **stipulation** n. condition in a contract(合同的)条款；项目

**stock** 1. n. (a) quantity of raw materials 原料；储存量：We have large stocks of oil or coal. 我们有大量石油或煤的储备。the country's stocks of butter or sugar 国家黄油或糖的储存量 (b) quantity of goods for sale(供出售的)商品量：opening stock = details of stock at the beginning of an accounting period 初期储备；期初存货(会计期初存货细目)；closing stock = details of stock at the end of an accounting period 期末存货；stock code = number and letters which indicate an item of stock 存货编码；stock control = making sure that enough stock is kept and that quantities and movements of stock are noted 存货控制(指保证足够的库存,核实存货的

数量和变动情况)；stock depreciation = reduction in value of stock which is held in a warehouse for some time 存货折旧(指货物因在仓库存放一段时间而引起的存货价值下降)；stock figures = details of how many goods are in the warehouse or store etc. 存货数；存货清单；stock level = quantity of goods kept in stock 库存水平：We try to keep stock levels low during the summer. 夏天我们尽量使库存水平低些。stock turn or stock turnround or stock turnover = total value of stock sold in a year divided by the average value of goods in stock 存货周转率；stock valuation = estimating the value of stock at the end of an accountingperiod 存货估价：to buy a shop with stock at valuation = to pay for the stock the same amount as its value asetimated by the valuer 按存货估价价值买下一个商店。stock in hand = stock held in a shop or warehouse 现有存货(品)；to purchase stock at valuation = to pay for stock the price it is valued at 按估价购买存货 (c) in stock or out of stock = available or not available in the warehouse or store 有存货或无存货：to hold 2,000 lines in stock 有 2,000 种存货；The item went out of stock just before Christmas but came back into stock in the first week of January. 这种商品圣诞节前刚售完,但一月份的第一周来了货。We are out of stock of this item. 这种商品我们无存货。to take stock = to count the items in a warehouse 清查存货；盘点 (d) stocks and shares = shares in ordinary companies 股票；股份；stock certificate = document proving that someone owns stock in a company 股票；debenture stock = capital borrowed by a company, using its fixed assets as security 借款股份；dollar stocks = shares in American companies 美元股票；government stock = government securities 政府证券；loan stock = money lent to a company at a fixed rate of interest 债券借贷股票; convertible loan stock = money lent to a company which can be converted into shares ata later date 可兑换的债券; US common stock = ordinary shares in a company giving the shareholders theright to vote at meetings and receive a dividend (美) 普通股 (e) the stock market = place where shares are bought and sold 股票市场: stock market price or price on the stock market 股市价格; stock market valuation = value of shares based on the current market price 股市估价 (f) normal or usually kept in stock 常备货; 库存品: Butter is a stock item for any good grocer. 黄油对任何会经营的食品商来讲是常备商品。stock size = normal size 普通号码; 标准尺寸; 一般号码: We only carry stock sizes of shoes. 我们只出售标准尺寸的鞋子。2. v. to hold goods for sale in a warehouse or store 存货; 库存; 备货: to stock 200 lines 备有 200 种商品的货

◇ **stockbroker** n. person who buys or sells shares for clients 股票 (证券) 经纪人 (措代客户买卖股票的人): stockbroker's commission = payment to a broker for a deal carried out on behalf of aclient 股票经纪人佣金

◇ **stockbroking** n. trade of dealing in shares for clients 代客买卖股票 (证券) 业务; 股票 (证券) 经纪业务: a stockbroking firm 股票 (证券) 交易公司 NOTE: no plural

◇ **stock controller** n. person who notes movements of stock 存货控制员

◇ **Stock Exchange** n. place where stocks and shares are bought and sold 证券交易所: He works on the Stock Exchange. 他在证券交易所工作。Shares in the company are traded on the Stock Exchange. 该公司的股票在证券交易所进行交易。Stock Exchange listing = official list of shares which can be

bought or sold on theStock Exchange 证券交易所挂牌

◇ **stockholder** n. person who holds shares in a company 持股人; 股东

◇ **stockholding** n. shares in a company held by someone 股金; 股份

◇ **stock − in − trade** n. goods held by a business for sale 商品存货 NOTE: no plural

◇ **stockist** n. person or shop which stocks a certain item 存货商

◇ **stock jobber** n. person who buys and sells shares from other traders on theStock Exchange (以经纪人为对象的证券批发商) 证券经纪人; 证券商

◇ **stock jobbing** n. buying and selling shares from other traders on the Stock-Exchange 证券股票买卖 NOTE: no plural

◇ **stocklist** n. list of items carried in stock 存货单

◇ **stockpile** 1. n. supplies kept by a country or a company in case of need (国家、企业应急用的存货) 囤贮; 贮存; 积存: a stockpile of raw materials 原料囤贮 (储备) 2. v. to buy items and keep them in case of need 贮存; 堆放: to stockpile raw materials 储存原材料

◇ **stockroom** n. room where stores are kept 贮藏室; 库房

◇ **stocktaking** n. counting of goods in stock at the end of an accounting period 存货盘点 (会计期未清点存货): The warehouse is closed for the annual stocktaking. 仓库关门进行年度存货盘点。stocktaking sale = sale of goods cheaply to clear a warehouse before stocktaking 清仓甩卖 NOTE: no plural

◇ **stock up** v. to buy supplies of something which you will need in the future 办货; 贮备: They stocked up with computer paper. 他们贮备了一些计算机打印纸。

**stop 1.** n. (a) end of an action 停止；中止；结束；终止：Work came to a stop when the company could not pay the workers' wages. 公司不能支付工人工资时，工作就停了。The new finance director put a stop to the reps' expense claims 新财务主任停止了推销员的费用赔偿要求。(b) not supplying 中止 (供给)：account on stop = account which is not supplied because it has not paid its latest invoices 帐户停用；停止供货 (对一客户)；to put an account on stop 中止帐户；to put a stop on a cheque = to tell the bank not to pay a cheque which you have written 停止付支票。2. v. (a) to make (something) not to move any more 停止；阻止：The shipment was stopped by the customs. 这批货被海关扣留了。The government has stopped the import of cars. 政府已停止进口汽车。(b) not to do anything any more 停止；中止：The work force stopped work when the company could not pay their wages. 公司不能支付工作人员工资时，他们就停工了。The office staff stop work at 5.30. 办公室工作人员 5 点半下班。We have stopped supplying Smith & Co. 我们已停止供货给史密斯公司。(c) to stop an account = not to supply an account any more on credit because bills have not been paid 中止帐户；中止向客户供货；to stop a cheque = to ask a bank not to pay a cheque you have written 停止支付支票；to stop payments = not to make any further payments 停止支付 (d) to stop someone's wages = to take money out of someone's wages 从某人工资中扣钱：We stopped £25 from his pay because he was late. 因他迟到，我们从他薪金中扣了 25 英镑。

NOTE: stopping – stopped

◇ **stop over** v. to stay for a short time in a place on a long journey (在旅程中) 中途停留：We stopped over in Hong Kong on the way to Australia. 在去澳大利亚途中我们在香港停留了一下。

◇ **stopover** n. staying for a short time in a place on a long journey (旅程) 中途停留：The ticket allows you two stopovers between London and Tokyo. 该票允许你在伦敦和东京之间作两次停留。

◇ **stoppage** n. (a) act of stopping 停止；中止：stoppage of deliveries 停止交货；stoppage of payments 停止支付；Deliveries will be late because of stoppages on the production line. 因生产线故障，交货要推迟。(b) money take from a worker's wage packet for insurance, tax, etc. (从工资中) 扣除；扣留 (保险费，税款等)

**storage** n. (a) keeping in store or in a warehouse 贮藏；保管；仓库：We put our furniture into storage. 我们将家具存放在仓库里。storage capacity = space available for storage 存储量；仓容量；storage company = company which keeps items for customers 储存公司；storage facilities = equipment and buildings suitable for storage 仓储设施；storage unit = device attached to a computer for storing information on disk or tape 存储器；cold storage = keeping food, etc., in a cold store to prevent it going bad 冷藏；to put a plan into cold storage = to postpone work on a plan, usually for a very long time 推迟执行工作计划 (通常时间很长) (b) cost of keeping goods in store 仓储费；保管费：Storage was 10% of value, so we scrapped the stock. 因仓储费是货物价值的 10%，所以我们就废弃了这批存货。(c) facility for storing data in a computer (计算机的) 存储器：disk with a storage capacity of 10Mb 存储容量为 10 兆字节的磁盘

NOTE: no plural

◇ **store 1.** n. (a) place where goods are kept 仓库；货栈：cold store = warehouse or room where food can be kept cold冷藏仓库 (b) quantity of items or materials kept because they will be needed 存货量；仓储量：I always keep a store of envelopes ready in my desk. 我总是在写字台里备一些信封。(c) large shop(大的)商店：a furniture store；家具店；a big clothing store 一家大服装店；chain store = one store in a number of stores 连锁店；department store = large store with sections for different types of goods 百货商店；discount store = shop which specializes in cheap goods sold at a high discount 减价商店；廉价商店 general stores = small country shop which sells a wide range of products 杂货店；普通商店 2. v. (a) to keep in a warehouse 储存；贮藏；to store goods for six months 货物贮存六个月 (b) to keep for future use 备用；储备：We store our pay records on computer. 我们将工资记录储存在计算机里。

◇ **storekeeper or storeman** n. person in charge of a storeroom 仓库保管员

◇ **storeroom** n. room where stock can be kept or small warehouse attached to afactory 贮藏室；(工厂旁的)库房

**straight line** n. straight line depreciation = depreciation calculated by dividing the cost of an asset bythe number of years it is likely to be used 直线折旧法 (指用可能使用年限以资产费用计算出的折旧)

**strategy** n. plan of future action 策略；战略：business strategy 经营战略；企业策略；company strategy 公司策略；marketing strategy 市场战略；销售方针；financial strategy 财政战略

◇ **strategic** a. based on a plan of action 战略的；策略的：strategic planning = planning the future work of a company 战略计划(指计划一公司的未来工作)

**stream** n. mass of people or traffic, all going in the same direction(人、车辆汇成的)流；流动：We had a stream of customers on the first day of the sale. 我们开业的第一天顾客就川流不息。to come on stream = to start production 投入生产；开始生产

◇ **streamer** n. device for attaching a tape storage unit to a computer 磁带机控制器(用于连接磁带机和计算机的)

◇ **streamline** v. to make (something) more efficient or more simple 使简化…；使…效率更高：to streamline the accounting system 简化会计制度；to streamline distribution services 精简销售部门

◇ **streamlined** a. efficient or rapid 有效的；速成的：streamlined production 流线型生产；The company introduced a streamlined system of distribution. 公司采用了有效的销售系统

◇ **streamlining** n. making efficient 效率高；精简
NOTE: no plural

**street** n. road in a town 街；街道：High Street = main shopping street in a British town 大马路(英国城镇里的主要商业街)；the High Street banks = main British banks which accept deposits from individual customers 大马路上银行(吸收个人存款的主要英国银行)；street directory = (i) list of people living in a street 姓名地址录；通讯录 (ii) map of a town with all the streets listed in alphabetical order in an index 城市交通图(附有所有街道的城市地图，这些街道是按字母顺序列在索引上的)

**strength** n. being strong or at a high level 实力；力量：The company took advantage of the strength of the demand for home computers. 该公司利用了人们家庭电脑的强烈需求。The strength of the pound increases the possibility of high interest rates. 英磅的实力增加了高利率的可能性。

**stretch** v. to pull out or make longer 使

过度伸展；过度紧张：The investment programmehas stretched the company's resources. 该投资项目已使公司财源相当紧张。He is not fully stretched. = His job does not make him work as hard as he could. 他的工作不是非常紧张。

**strict** a. exact 严格地；in strict order of seniority 论资排辈（严格按照资历排列）

◇ **strictly** ad. exactly 严格地；精确地：The company asks all staff to follow strictly the buying procedures. 公司要求所有职员严格遵循购买卖程序。

**strike** 1. n. (a) stopping of work by the workers（because of lack of agreement with management or because of orders from a union）罢工（因未与资方达成协议或工会命令等）：all – out strike = complete strike by all workers 全体工人罢工；general strike = strike of all the workers in a country 总罢工；official strike = strike which has been approved by the main office of a union 正式罢工；protest strike = strike in protest at a particular grievance 抗议性罢工（指由于一些特殊不满，而举行的抗议性罢工）；sit – down strike = strike where workers stay in their place of work and refuse to work or leave 静坐罢工；就地罢工；sympathy strike = strike to show that workers agree with another group ofworkers who are on strike 声援性罢工；token strike = short strike to show that workers have a grievance 象征性罢工；unofficial strike = strike by local workers, which has not been approved by themain union 非官方性罢工；非正式罢工（指未经工会批准的罢工）；wildcat strike = strike organized by workers without the main union office-knowing about it 自发性罢工（b）to take strike action = to go on strike 举行罢工；进行罢工：strike call = demand by a union for a strike 罢工号召；no – strike agreement or no – strike clause =

(clause in an) agreement where the workers say that they will never strike 永不罢工的协议或条款；strike fund = money collected by a trade union from its members, used topay strike pay 罢工基金；strike pay = wages paid to striking workers by their trade union 罢工津贴；strike ballot or strike vote = vote by workers to decide if a strike should be held 罢工表决（c）to come out on strike or to go on strike = to stop workl 罢工：The office workers are on strike for higher pay. 职员们举行罢工要求增加工资。to call the workforce out on strike = to tell the workers to stop work 号召工人罢工：The union called its members out on strike. 工会号召其会员罢工。2. v. (a) to stop working because there is no agreement with management 罢工（因未与资方达成协议）：to strike for higher wages or for shorter working hours 举行罢工（要求增加工资或缩短工作时间）。to strike in protest against bad working conditions 为抗议恶劣的工作条件而罢工 to strike in sympathy with the postal workers = to strike to show that you agree with the postal workers whoare on strike 为声援邮政工人举行罢工。(b) to strike a bargain with someone = to come to an agreement 与某人达成协议：A deal was struck at £25 a unit. = We agreed the price of £25 a unit. 买卖以25英磅一件成交。

NOTE: striking – struck

◇ **strikebound** a. not able to work or to move because of a strike 因罢工而停顿的：Six ships are strikebound in the docks. 六艘船因罢工而停在码头上。

◇ **strikebreaker** n. worker who goes on working while everyone else is on strike 罢工破坏者

◇ **striker** n. worker who is on strike 罢工者

**stripper** n. asset stripper = person who

buys a company to sell its assets 资产兼并者(指购买一公司是为出售其资产的人)

◇ **stripping** n. asset stripping = buying a company in order to sell its assets 资产兼并(购买一公司是为出售其资产)

**strong** a. with a lot of force or strength 强烈的；强壮的：a strong demand for home computers 对家庭电脑的强劲需求。The company needs a strong chairman.该公司需要一个强有力的董事长。strong pound = pound which is high against other currencies 坚挺的英镑

◇ **strongbox** n. safe or heavy metal box which cannot be opened easily, inwhich valuable documents, money, etc., can be kept 保险箱(柜)

◇ **strongroom** n. special room (in a bank) where valuable documents, money, golds, etc., can be kept 保险库(存放重要文件、金钱、黄金等的)

**structure** 1. n. way in which something is organized 结构；构造；组织：The paper gives a diagram of the company's organizational structure. 该文件提供了该公司组织结构的简图。the price structure in the small car market. 小轿车市场的价格结构。the career structure within a corporation；一公司内部的职业结构。The company is reorganizing its discount structure.该公司正在重新制定其折扣结构。capital structure of a company = way in which a company's capital is set up 一公司的资本结构；the company's salary structure = organization of salaries in a company with different rates ofpay for different types of job 该公司的薪水结构 2. v. to arrange in a certain way 组织；构造：to structure a meeting 组织会议

◇ **structural** a. referring to a structure 结构上的；组织上的：to make struc-

tural changes in a company 对公司的组织结构进行调整；structural unemployment = unemployment caused by the changing structure of an industry or society 结构性失业(指由于社会或产业结构调整而引起的失业)

**stub** n. cheque stub = piece of paper left in a cheque book after a cheque has been written and taken out 支票存根

**studio** n. place where designers, film producers, artists, etc., work(设计者、电影制片人、艺术家等的)工作室：design studio = independent firm which specializes in creating designs for companies 设计公司(指专门为其他公司进行设计的独立公司)

**study** 1. n. examining something carefully 学习；研究：The company has asked the consultants to prepare a study of new production techniques.公司已请顾问们准备研究新的生产工艺。He has read the government study on sales opportunities.他已阅读了有关销售时机的政府研究报告。to carry out a feasibility study on a project = to examine the costs and possible profits to see if the project should be started 对一项目进行可行性研究(对成本和可能利润进行调查从而知道这个项目是否上马)。2. v. to examine (something) carefully 学习；研究：We are studying the possibility of setting up an office in New York. 我们正在研究在纽约开设办事处的可能性。The government studied the committee's proposals for two months. 政府对该委员会的建议研究了两个月。You will need to study the market carefully before deciding on the design of the product.在确定该产品的设计方案之前,你需仔细研究一下市场。

**stuff** v. to put papers, etc., into envelopes 把…装入,把…装满；填、塞：We pay casual workers £2 an hour for stuffing envelopes or for envelope stuffing. 我们付装信封的临时工一小时2英磅。

◇ **stuffer** n. US advertising paper to be put in an envelope for mailing(美)装入信封邮寄的广告的材料

**style** n. way of doing or making something 式样；方式：a new style of product. 一种新式产品；old - style management techniques 老式的管理技术

**sub** n. (a) wages paid in advance 预支薪水(工资)(b) = SUBSCRIPTION 捐助；认购

**sub -** prefix under or less important(前缀)表示"在…之下"；"次；低；付"

◇ **sub - agency** n. small agency which is part of a large agency 分代理处；分销处

◇ **sub - agent** n. person who is in charge of a sub - agency 分部代理人；分代理

◇ **subcommittee** n. small committee which is part of or set up by a main committee(委员会下的)小组委员会；附属委员会：The next item on the agenda is the report of the finance subcommittee. 议事日程上的下一个项目是财政小组委员会的报告。

◇ **subcontract** 1. n. contract between the main contractor for a whole project and another firm who will do part of the work 转包合同；分包合同；分契；转契：They have been awarded the subcontract for all the electrical work in the new building. 他们已拿到了这座新建筑物所有电气工作的转包合同。We will put the electrical work out to subcontract. 我们将把电气工作转包出去。2. v. to agree with a company that they will do part of the work for a project 分包；转包：The electrical work has been subcontracted to Smith Ltd. 电气工作已转包给史密斯有限公司。

◇ **subcontractor** n. company which

has a contract to do work for a main contractor 转包公司；分包公司

◇ **subdivision** n. US piece of empty land to be used for building new houses (美)小块空地(用于建房

**subject to** a. (a) depending on 有待于…；须经…：The contract is subject to government approval. = The contract will be valid only if it is approved by the government. 该合同须经政府批准。agreement or sale subject to contract = agreement or sale which is not legal until a proper contract has been signed 以合同为准的协议或出售(指合同签定后协议或买卖才合法)；offer subject to availability = the offer is valid only if the goods are available 以有货可供为准的报价 (b) These articles are subject to import tax. = Import tax has to be paid on these articles. 这些物品须付进口税。

**sub judice** a. being considered by a court (and so not to be mentioned in the media)(法庭的案件)正在审理中(而不许在报纸等上面提及的)：The papers cannot report the case because it is still sub judice. 报纸不能报道这个案件，因此案仍在审理之中。

**sublease** 1. n. lease from a tenant to another tenant 分租；转租 2. v. to lease a leased property from another tenant 分租；转租：They subleased a small office in the centre of town. 他们将市中心的一间小办公室转租出去了。

◇ **sublessee** n. person or company which takes a property on a sublease 转租人(公司)

◇ **sublessor** n. tenant who lets a leased property to another tenant 转租出的人；分租出的人

◇ **sublet** v. to let a leased property to another tenant 转租；分租：We have sublet part of our office to a financial consultancy. 我们已将部分办公室转租给一个财务咨询机构。

NOTE: subletting – sublet

**submit** v. to put (something) forward to be examined 提交；呈送；提出：to submit a proposal to the committee 向委员会提交提案。He submitted a claim to the insurers 他向承保人提出了索赔。The reps are asked to submit their expenses claims once a month. 要求推销员每月提交一次他们的支出需要。

NOTE: submitting – submitted

**subordinate** 1. a. less important 次要的；从属的：subordinate to = governed by or which depends on 从属…；依靠… 2. n. member of staff who is directed by someone 部下；部属；下级人员：His subordinates find him difficult to work with. 他的部下发现难于和他一起工作。

**subpoena** 1. n. order telling someone to appear in court as a witness 传票（告诉某人作为证人出庭的命令）2. v. to order someone to appear in court（以传票）传讯某人：The finance director was subpoenaed by the prosecution. 财务经理被检察机关传讯。

**subscribe** v. (a) to subscribe to a magazine = to pay for a series of issues of a magazine 订阅杂志 (b) to subscribe for shares = to apply for shares in a new company 认购股票

◇ **subscriber** n. (a) subscriber to a magazine or magazine subscriber = person who has paid in advance for a series of issues of a magazine 杂志订户：The extra issue is sent free to subscribers. 增刊免费送给订户 (b) subscriber to a share issue = person who has applied for shares in a new company 股票认购者 (c) telephone subscriber = person who has a telephone 电话用户：subscriber trunk dialling = telephone system where you can dial international numbers direct from your own telephone without going through the operator 国际直拨电话系统

◇ **subscription** n. (a) money paid in advance for a series of issues of a magazine or for membership of a society（杂志）预定金；（社团）会员费：Did you remember to pay the subscription to the computer magazine? 你记住要付计算机杂志的预定金了吗? He forgot to renew his club subscription. 他忘了续交俱乐部会员费。to take out a subscription to a magazine = to start paying for a series of issues of a magazine 开始缴杂志预订金 to cancel a subscription to a magazine = to stop paying for a magazine 取消订杂志；subscription rates = amount of money to be paid for a series of issues of a magazine（杂志等的）预订费标准 (b) subscription to a new share issue = offering shares in a new company for sale 认购新发行的股票；subscription list = list of subscribers to a new share issue 认股清册；认购清册（新股认购者名单）：The subscription lists close at 10.00 on September 24th. = No new applicants will be allowed to subscribe for the share issue after that date. 到9月24日10点钟停止认购新股。

**subsidiary** 1. adj. (thing) which is less important 辅助的；补充的；次要的；附属的：They agreed to most of the conditions in the contract but queried one or two subsidiary items. 他们同意了该合同中大多数条款，但一、二项辅助条款有疑问。subsidiary company = company which is owned by a parent company 附属公司；子公司 2. n. company which is owned by a parent company 附属公司；子公司：Most of the group profit was contributed by the subsidiaries in the Far East. 集团的大部分利润是由远东的子公司缴纳。

**subsidize** v. to help by giving money 资助；给…补助金；补贴：The government has refused to subsidize the car industry. 政府已拒绝给汽车工业补贴。subsidized accommodation = cheap accommodation which is partly paid for by an employer or a local authority, etc. 膳宿补贴 (由雇主或当地政府支付一部分的便宜食宿)

◇ **subsidy** n. (a) money given to help something which is not profitable 补助金;补贴(指给予帮助不盈利企业的款项): The industry exists on government subsidies. 该工业(产业)靠政府补助生存。The government has increased its subsidy to the car industry. 政府已增加了对汽车工业的补贴。(b) money given by a government to make something cheaper 补贴(指为使某物便宜,政府给的款额): the subsidy on butter or the butter subsidy 黄油补贴

**subsistence** n. minimum amount of food, money, housing, etc., which a person needs 最低维持生活标准(食物,钱,住房等): subsistence allowance = money paid by a company to cover the cost of hotels, meals, etc., for a member of staff who is travelling on business 差旅补贴; to live at subsistence level = to have only just enough money to live on 以最低维持生活水平生活;勉强糊口 NOTE: no plural

**substantial** a. large or important 大的;重要的 She was awarded substantial damages. = She received a large sum of money as damages. 获得了一大笔损害赔偿金。to acquire a substantial interest in a company = to buy a large number of shares in a company 获得一公司的重要权益(购进了一公司的大量股票)

**substitute** 1. n. person or thing which takes the place of someone or something else 代理人;代替物: 2. v. to take the place of something else 代替(某物)

**subtenancy** n. agreement to sublet a property 财产转租(分租)协议

◇ **subtenant** n. person or company to which a property has been sublet(财产)转租人(公司);次承租人

**subtotal** n. total of one section of a complete set of figures 小计;部分和

**subtract** v. to take away (something) from a total 减;减去;去掉: If the profits from the Far Eastern operations are subtracted, you will see that the group has not been profitable in the European market. 如果除去远东营业利润,你将看到该集团在欧洲市场已无利可图。

**subvention** n. subsidy 津贴;补助金

**succeed** v. (a) to do well or to be profitable 成功;获利: The company has succeeded best in the overseas markets. 该公司在海外市场获得巨大成功。His business has succeeded more than he had expected. 他的企业比预期的成功。(b) to do what was planned 成功;完成: She succeeded in passing her shorthand test. 她通过了速记考试。They succeeded in putting their rivals out of business. 他们成功地将竞争对手挤出商界。(c) to follow (someone)继承;接替: Mr Smith was succeeded as chairman by Mr Jones. 由琼斯先生接替史密斯先生作董事长

◇ **success** n. (a) doing something well 成功;成就: The launch of the new model was a great success. 新型号产品投放市场是巨大成功。The company has had great success in the Japanese market. 该公司已在日本市场取得了巨大成就。(b) doing what was intended 成功;成就: We had no success in trying to sell the lease. 我们在出售租赁权方面没有成功。He has been looking for a job for six months, but with no success. 他寻找工作已6个月,但没有成功。

◇ **successful** ad. which does well 成功地: a successful businessman 一位成功的商人; a successful selling trip to Germany 一次成功的德国销售旅行

◇ **successfully** ad. done well 成功地: he successfully negotiated a new contract with the unions. 他成功地与工会商定了一项新契约。The new model was successfully launched last month. 上月成功地将新型产品投方市场。

◇ **successor** n. person who takes over from someone 继承人；继任者：Mr Smith's successor as chairman will be Mr Jones. 史密斯先生的董事长继任者将是琼斯先生。

**sue** v. to take someone to court or to start legal proceedings against someone to get money as compensation 起诉(在法庭上)：to sue someone for damages 起诉某人要求获得损失赔偿金：He is suing the company for $50,000 compensation. 他在控告这个公司并要求5万美元的赔偿费。

**suffer** v. to be in a bad situation or to do badly 遭受；蒙受：Exports have suffered during the last six months. 前6个月内,出口已蒙受损失。to suffer from something = to do badly because of something 遭受…：The company's products suffer from bad design. 该公司的产品因设计不佳而受损。The group suffers from bad management. 该集团因经营不善而受损。

**sufficient** a. enough 足够的：The company has sufficient funds to pay for its expansion programme. 该公司有足够的资金支付其发展计划。

**suggest** v. to put forward a proposal 提议；建议(意见等)：The chairman suggested (that) the next meeting should be held in October. 董事长建议下次会议应在10月份召开。We suggested Mr Smith for the post of treasurer. 我们提议史密斯先生担任出纳员。

◇ **suggestion** n. proposal or idea which is put forward 建议；意见：suggestion box = place in a company where members of staff can put forward their ideas for making the company more efficient and profitable 意见箱

**suitable** a. convenient or which fits 合适的；适宜的；适当的：Wednesday is the most suitable day for board meetings 星期三召开董事会会议是最合适的日子。We had to readvertise the job because there were no suitable candidates. 因无合适人选,我们不得不对这个工作重新登广告招聘。

**suitcase** n. box with a handle for carrying clothes and personal belongings when travelling 手提箱：The customs officer made him open his three suitcases. 海关官员要他打开他的三个手提箱。

**sum** n. (a) quantity of money 金额：A sum of money was stolen from the personnel office. 人事处的一笔钱被窃。He lost large sums on the Stock Exchange. 他在证券交易所损失了一大笔钱。She received the sum of £500 in compensation. 她得到了一笔五百英磅的赔偿费 the sum insured = the largest amount which an insurer will pay under the terms of an insurance 保险金额；lump sum = money paid in one payment, not in several small payments 一次付清；总付 (b) total of a series of figures added together 总数；总和

**summary** n. short account of what has happened or of what has been written 摘要；总结；提要：The chairman gave a summary of his discussions with the German trade delegation. 董事长对与德国贸易代表团的洽谈进行了总结。The sales department has given a summary of sales in Europe for the first six months. 销售部门对上半年欧洲的销售情况进行了总结。

**summons** n. official order to appear in court to be tried (法律上) 传唤；传票：He threw away the summons and went on holiday to Spain. 他仍掉传票,并去西班牙度假。

**sundry** a. & n. various 各式各样的；各种的：sundry items or sundries = small items which are not listed in detail 杂货

**superannuation** n. pension paid to someonewho is too old or ill to work any more 退休金；养老金(指付给不再工作的老人或病人的养老金或退休金) superannuation plan or scheme = pension plan or scheme 退休金制(计划)
NOTE: no plural

**superintend** v. to be in charge of 负责；主管：He superintends the company's overseas sales. 他负责该公司海外销售业务。

◇ **superintendent** n. person in charge 负责人；主管人

**superior** 1. a. better or of better quality 优越的；优良的；品质优良的：Our product is superior to all competing products. 我们的产品优于所有竞争产品。Their sales are higher because of their superior distribution service 他们的销售额较高，因为他们的推销服务是优质的。2. n. more important person 上级 Each manager is responsible to his superior for accurate reporting of sales. 每位经理向其上级负责做销售情况的精确报告。

**supermarket** n. large store, usually selling food, where customers serve themselves and pay at a checkout. 超级市场：Sales in supermarkets or supermarket sales account for half the company's turnover 超级市场的销售额占公司营业额的一半。

**superstore** n. very large self - service store which sells a wide range of goods 超级市场

**supertanker** n. very large oil tanker 超级油轮

**supervise** v. to watch work carefully to see if it is well done 监督；管理：The move to the new offices was supervised by the administrative manager. 搬入新办公室由总务处长监管。She supervises six girls in the accounts department. 她在财会部门管六个女孩。

◇ **supervision** n. being supervised 监督；管理：New staff work under supervision for the first three months. 前三个月新职员在指导下进行工作。She is very experienced and can be left to work without any supervision. 她很有经验，不用指导就可胜任工作。The cash was counted under the supervision of the finance manager. 在财务经理的监督下清点现金。
NOTE: no plural

◇ **supervisor** n. person who supervises 管理人；监督人

◇ **supervisory** a. as a supervisor 监督的；管理的：supervisory staff 管理人员。He works in a supervisory capacity. 他在做管理工作。

**supplement** 1. n. thing which is added 增补；补充：The company gives him a supplement to his pension. 公司给他增补了退休金。2. v. to add 增补；增加：We will supplement the warehouse staff with six part - timers during the Christmas rush. 圣诞节繁争购期间我们将增加六个临时仓库工作人员

◇ **supplementary** a. in addition to 增补的；辅助的；补充的：supplementary benefit = payments from the government to people with very low incomes 辅助福利(指政府给予收入低的人的补助)

**supply** 1. n. (a) providing something which is needed 供给(量)；供应(量)；补给：money supply = amount of money which exists in a country(一国的)货币供应量；supply price = price at which something is provided 供应价格；供给价格；supply and demand = amount of a product which is available and the amount which is wanted by customers 供求；供与求；the law of supply and demand = general rule that the amount of a product which is available is related to the needs of the possible customer 供需法则（指一产品的可供量与顾客需求量相关的总法则）(b) in short supply = not available in large enough quantities to meet the demand 供应不足: Spare parts are in short supply because of the strike. 因罢工, 备件供应不足。(c) stock of something which is needed 补给的; 存货; The factory is running short of supplies of coal. 这个工厂煤储备不足。Supplies of coal have been reduced. 煤的供应已减少。office supplies = goods needed to run an office (such as paper, pens, typewriters)办公用品（如纸、笔、打字机等）2. v. to provide something which is needed 供给; 供应; 提供: to supply a factory with spare parts 向一工厂提供备件; The finance department supplied the committee with the figures. 财务部向委员会提供数字。Details of staff addresses and phone numbers can be supplied by the personnel staff. 管人事的人员能提供职员的详细地址和电话号码。

◇ **supply side economics** n. economic theory, that governments should encourage producers and suppliers of goods by cutting taxes, rather than encourage demand by making more money available in the economy 供应学派经济学（指一种经济学理论, 主张政府应该通过减税来鼓励商品的生产厂和供应商, 而不是通过增发更多的货币来鼓励需求）

◇ **supplier** n. person or company which supplies or sells goods or services 供应者; 供应(厂商): office equipment supplier 办公设备供应商; They are major suppliers of spare parts to the car industry. 他们是汽车工业备件的主要供应商。

**support** 1. n. (a) giving money to help 援助; 资助: The government has provided support to the electronics industry. 政府已向电子工业提供了资助。We have no financial support from the banks. 我们没有银行的财政资助。(b)

agreement or encouragement 支持; 鼓励: The chairman has the support of the committee. 董事长得到了委员会的支持。

**support price** = price (in the EEC) at which a government will buy agricultural produce to stop the price falling 支持价格; 维持价格（指在欧洲共同体内, 政府收购农产品以阻止其价格下跌）

NOTE: no plural

2. v. (a) to give money to help 资助; 支援: The government is supporting the electronics industry to the tune of $2m per annum. 政府每年向电子工业提供的资助总共达 200 万美元。We hope the banks will support us during the expansion period. 在发展时期我们希望银行会给我们以资助。(b) to encourage or to agree with 拥护; 支持: She hopes the other members of the committee will support her. 她希望该委员会的其他成员会支持她。The market will not support another price increase. 市场不会允许另一次提价。

**surcharge** n. extra charge 额外费: import surcharge = extra duty charged on imported goods, to try to stop them from being imported and to encourage local manufacture 进口附加税

**surety** n. (a) person who guarantees that someone will do something 保证人: to stand surety for someone 为某人作保 (b) deeds or share certificates, etc., deposited as security for a loan (贷款抵押的)契约或股票的证书

**surface** n. top part of the earth 外层; 外观; 表面: to send a package by surface mail = to send it by land or sea, but not by air 平信方式邮寄包裹（以水陆方式邮寄包裹, 而不是空邮）; surface transport = transport on land or sea 水陆运输

NOTE: no plural

**surplus** n. extra stock or something

which is more than is needed 多余；过剩；剩余（多余的库存或某些超出实际需要的东西）：surplus government equipment 多余的政府设施；Surplus butter is on sale in the shops. 商店里正廉价在出售过剩的黄油。We are holding a sale of surplus stock. 我们正在廉价出售剩余存货。Governments are trying to find ways of reducing the agricultural surpluses in the Common Market. 各国政府正在试图寻找减少欧洲共同体市场上剩余农产品的方法。We are trying to let surplus capacity in the warehouse. 我们正试着出租仓库的过剩的储存能力。a budget surplus = more revenue than was planned for in the budget 预算盈余；预算结余（指超出预算中计划部份的收入）These items are surplus to our requirements. = We do not need these items. 这些商品对我们的需求是多余的。to absorb a surplus = to take a surplus into a larger amount 吸收盈余

**surrender** 1. n. giving up of an insurance policy before the contracted date for maturity 交出；放弃（指在合同期满之前放弃保险单）：surrender value = money which an insurer will pay if an insurance policy is given up 退保金额 2. v. to surrender a policy = to give up an insurance 放弃保险

**surtax** n. extra tax on high income（对高收入征收的）附加税；超额累进所得税

**survey** 1. n. (a) general report on a problem（调查）报告；（审查）报告：The government has published a survey of population trends. 政府发布了关于人口趋势的调查报告。We have asked the sales department to produce a survey of competing products. 我们已经要求销售部门提供一份关于各种竞争产品的调查报告。(b) examining something to see if it is in good condition 调查；审查：We have asked for a survey of the house be-fore buying it. 我们要求在购买房子前先进行一些调查。The insurance company is carrying out a survey of the damage. 保险公司正对损失进行调查。damage survey = survey of damage done 损失调查；损坏鉴定 (c) measuring exactly 估量；测量：quantity survey = calculating the amount of materials and cost of labour needed for a construction project 数量估计（指对建筑项目中劳力成本以及所需材料进行计算）2. v. to examine (something) to see if it is in good condition 检查

◇ **surveyor** n. person who examines buildings to see if they are in good condition 检验员；鉴定人：quantity surveyor = person who calculates the amount of materials and cost of labour needed for a construction project 数量检验员（指负责计算建筑项目中所需材料及劳力成本的人）

**suspend** v. (a) to stop (something) for a time 暂停：We have suspended payments while we are waiting for news from our agent. 在等待代理商消息期间，我们暂停付款。Sailings have been suspended until the weather gets better. 天气好转之前，航渡暂停。Work on the construction project has been suspended. 该建筑项目的工作已暂停。The management decided to suspend negotiations. 经理们决定暂停谈判。(b) to stop (someone) working for a time 暂停：He was suspended on full pay while the police investigations were going on. 在警方调查期间，他的工资被暂时停发。

◇ **suspension** n. stopping something for a time 暂停：suspension of payments 暂停支付；suspension of deliveries 暂停发货

**swap** 1. n. exchange of one thing for another 交换；交易 2. v. to exchange one thing for another 交换；交流；用…作交易：He swapped his old car for a new motorcycle. 他以他的旧汽车换了一辆新摩托车。They swapped jobs. = Each of them took the other's job. 他们互相交换了工作。

NOTE: swapping – swapped

**swatch** n. small sample 小块样品: colour swatch = small sample of colour which the finished product must look like 小块颜色样品

**sweat** n. drops of liquid which come through your skin when you are hot 汗珠;汗

◇ **sweated labour** n. (a) people who work hard for very little money 血汗劳工(指工作卖力而报酬很少的劳动者): Of course the firm makes a profit – it employs sweated labour. 当然该企业能盈利,因雇佣了廉价的血汗劳工。(b) hard work which is very badly paid 血汗劳动(指报酬少而又艰苦的工作)

◇ **sweatshop** n. factory using sweated labour 血汗工厂(使用廉价劳动力的工厂);

**switch** v. to change from one thing to another 转换;改变;转移: to switch funds from one investment to another 将资金从一项投资转到另一项; The job was switched from our British factory to the States. 这项工作从我们英国的工厂转到了美国。

◇ **switchboard** n. central point in a telephone system, where all lines meet 电话交换台;电话总机: switchboard operator = person who works the central telephone system(电话总机)接线员

◇ **switch over to** v. to change to something quite different 转换或变换到完全不同的方面; We have switched over to a French supplier. 我们已经转向一家法国供应商。The factory has switched over to gas for heating. 这个工厂已采用煤气来供暖。

**swop** = SWAP 交换

**symbol** n. sign or picture or object which represents something(代表某一事物的)象征;图象;符号: They use a bear as their advertising symbol. 他们用熊来作他们的广告标志。

**sympathy** n. feeling sorry because someone else has problems 同情;同情心: The manager had no sympathy for his secretary who complained of being overworked. 经理对他秘书抱怨工作时间过长一点也不表示同情。sympathy strike = strike to show that workers agree with another group of workers who are on strike 声援性罢工;同情性罢工; to strike in sympathy = to stop work to show that you agree with another group of workers who are on strike 声援罢工; The postal workers went on strike and the telephone engineers came out in sympathy. 邮政工人罢工,电话工程师也举行罢工表示声援。

◇ **sympathetic** a. showing sympathy 同情的: sympathetic strike = sympathy strike 声援性罢工;同情性罢工

**syndicate** 1. n. group of people or companies working together to make money 联合企业;集团;辛迪加: a German finance syndicate 德国金融辛迪加 arbitrage syndicate = group of people who together raise the capital to invest in arbitrage deals 套利辛迪加;套汇辛迪加(指共同筹集资金从事套利或套汇交易的人) underwriting syndicate = group of underwriters who insure a large risk 保险辛迪加(集团)(指共同承保巨大风险的承保人) 2. v. to produce an article, drawing, etc., which is published in several newspapers or magazines 报业辛迪加(在多家报纸或杂志上同时发表文章、漫画等)

◇ **syndicated** a. published in several newspapers or magazines 报业辛迪加的(在多家报刊或杂志上发表的): He writes a syndicated column on personal finance. 他为有关个人财务的辛迪加专

栏写稿

**synergy** n. producing greater effects by joining forces than by acting separately (企业合并后的协力优势或协合作用) 协同作用；协同效果

**synthetic** adj. artificial or made by man 人造的；合成的：synthetic fibres or synthetic materials = materials made as products of a chemical process 合成纤维；合成材料

**system** n. (a) arrangement or organization of things which work together 系统；制度：Our accounting system has worked well in spite of the large increase in orders. 尽管订货大量增加，我们的财会系统仍运行良好。decimal system = system of mathematics based on the number 10 十进制（指以十为进制的数字系统）；filing system = way of putting documents in order for easy reference 档案制度；归档系统（指为易于查找而按顺序放置文件的方式）；to operate a quota system = to regulate supplies by fixing quantities which are allowed 实行配额制度：We arrange our distribution using a quota system – each agent is allowed only a certain number of units. 我们用配额制度安排推销——每个代理商只容许一定的单位数量。(b) computer system = set of programs, commands, etc., which run a computer 计算机系统 (c) systems analysis = using a computer to suggest how a company should work by analyzing the way in which it works at present 系统分析 systems analyst = person who specializes in systems analysis 系统分析员

◇ **systematic** adj. in order or using method 有系统的；有秩序的；有组织的：He ordered a systematic report on the distribution service. 他命令对推销服务情况作系统的报告。

# Tt

**tab** n. = TABULATOR 制表键

**table** 1. n. (a) piece of furniture with a flat top and legs 桌子：typing table = table for a typewriter 打字机桌 (b) list of figures or facts set out in columns table of contents = list of contents in a book （书的）目录 actuarial tables = lists showing how long people of certain ages are likely to live 保险统计表 2. v. to put items of information on the table before a meeting 把…列入议程；提出建议：The report of the finance committee was tabled. 财政委员会的报告被列入了议事日程。to table a motion = to put forward a proposal for discussion by putting details of it on the table at a meeting 提出动议

◇ **tabular** a. in tabular form = arranged in a table 列成表格的；制成表的

◇ **tabulate** v. to set out in a table 把…制成表；列表

◇ **tabulation** n. arrangement of figures in a table 制表；列表；表

◇ **tabulator** n. part of a typewriter or computer which sets words or figures automatically in columns（打字机，计算机的）制表键

**tachograph** n. device in a lorry, which shows details of distance travelled and time of journeys 计程表；速度表

**tacit** a. agreed but not stated 心照不宣的；不言而喻的：tacit approval 默认；默许；tacit agreement to a proposal 对一项提议的默契

**tactic** n. way of doing things so as to be at an advantage 战术；策略：His usual tactic is to buy shares in a company, then mount a takeover bid, and sell out at a profit. 他通常的战术是购买一公司的

股票,然后进行兼并出价,出售这些股票而获利. The directors planned their tactics before going into the meeting with the union representatives. 在和工会代表会面之前,董事们事先计划了他们的战术。

**tag** n. label 标签: price tag 价目标签; name tag 名字标签。

**take** 1. n. money received in a shop 收入(商店的) 2. v. (a) to receive or to get 得到; 获得: The shop takes £2, 000 a week. = The shop receives £2, 000 a week in cash sales. 该店每周的现金销售额为 2,000 英镑。 He takes home £250 a week. = His salary, after deductions for tax, etc., is £250 a week. 他拿回家的工资一周是 250 英镑。(b) to do a certain action 采取: to take action = to do something. 采取行动; You must take immediate action if you want to stop thefts. 如果想制止偷窃,你必须立即采取行动。 to take a call = to answer the telephone 接电话; to take the chair = to be chairman of a meeting 担任会议主席; In the absence of the chairman his deputy took the chair。 在主席缺席的情况下,由他的副手任会议主席。 to take dictation = to write down what someone is saying 听写;记录口授(指记下某人说的话); The secretary was taking dictation from the managing director. 秘书正在记录总经理的话。 to take stock = to count the items in a warehouse 点清存货;盘货; to take stock of a situation = to examine the state of things before deciding what to do 观察;审度 (c) to need (a time or a quantity)需要;花费;占用: It took the factory six weeks or the factory took six weeks to clear the backlog of orders. 该厂用了六周时间清点积压的订单。 It will take her all morning to do my letters. 给我写信,将占用她整个上午时间。 It took six men and a crane to get the computer into the office. 将这台计算机搬进办公室用了六个人和一台起重机。

NOTE: taking – took – has taken

◇ **take away** v. (a) to remove one figure from a total 减去: If you take away the home sales, the total turnover is down. 如果你将国内销售额去掉,那么总营业业是下降的。(b) to remove 除去;搬开;退回: We had to take the work away from the supplier because the quality was so bad. 因质量太差,我们不得不从供应商那里撤回这项业务。 The police took away piles of documents from the office. 警方将成堆的文件从办公室拿走。 sales of food to take away = cooked food sold by a shop to be eaten at some other place 供应外卖食物

◇ **takeaway** n. shop which sells food to be eaten at some other place 外卖餐馆: a takeaway meal 从外卖餐馆买回来的一餐饭; a Chinese takeaway 一个外卖的中国餐馆

◇ **take back** v. (a) to return with something 收回;带回;拿回: When the watch went wrong, he took it back to the shop。 表坏时,他将它送回那家商店. If you do not like the colour, you can take it back to change it. 如果不喜欢这种颜色,你可以拿回来换。(b) to take back dismissed workers = to allow former workers to join the company again 允许解雇的工人再回来工作。

◇ **take – home pay** n. amount of money received in wages, after tax, etc., has been deducted(扣除税后的)实得工资

NOTE: no plural

◇ **take into** v. to take inside 收进;装入: to take items into stock or into the warehouse 把货物搬进仓库

◇ **take off** v. (a) to remove or to deduct 减去;扣除;除去: He took £25 off the price. 他将价格降了 25 英镑。(b) to start to rise fast 开始快速(迅速)

上升：Sales took off after the TV commercials. 电视广告之后，销售量猛增。(c) She took the day off. = She decided not to work for the day. 她决定这天休假。

◇ **take on** v. to agree to employ someone or to agree to do something 聘用；同意做某事；承担：She took on the job of preparing the VAT returns. 她承担了准备增值税申报的工作。to take on more staff 聘用更多人员；He has taken on a lot of extra work. 他承担许多额外的工作。

◇ **take out** v. to remove 扣除；剔出：to take out a patent for an invention = to apply for and receive a patent 得到一项发明的专利权；to take out insurance against theft = to pay a premium to an insurance company, so that if a theft takes place the company will pay compensation 投被盗险；办理偷窃险

◇ **take over** v. (a) to start to do something in place of someone else 接任；Miss Black took over from Mr Jones on May 1st. 布莱克小姐5月1日接替了琼斯先生。The new chairman takes over on July 1st. 新董事长7月1日上任。The take - over period is always difficult. = the period when one person is taking over work from another 接任期间总是困难的。(b) to take over a company = to buy (a business) by offering to buy most of its shares 兼并公司：The buyer takes over the company's liabilities. 买主接收了公司的所有债务。The company was taken over by a large multinational. 该公司被一家大跨国公司兼并。

◇ **takeover** n. buying a business 兼并；接收：takeover bid = offer to buy all or most of the shares in a company so as to control it 收购竞争；合并递价；兼并；to make a takeover bid for a company = to offer to buy most of the shares in a company 出价盘进一个公司；兼并一个公司出价(指表示愿意购买一公司的大部分股票)；to withdraw a takeover bid = to say that you no longer offer to buy the shares in a company 撤回兼并递价(就是说你不再愿意购买某公司的股票)；The company rejected the takeover bid. = The directors recommended that the shareholders should not accept the offer. 公司拒绝了兼并递价。The disclosure of the takeover bid raised share prices. 兼并递价消息的泄漏使得股票价格上涨。contested takeover = takeover where the board of the company being bought do not recommend it, and try to fight it 有争议的兼并(指要被收购的公司董事会不欢迎收购,并要反收购)

◇ **taker** n. buyer or person who wants to buy 买主：There were no takers for the new shares. 新股票没有买主。

◇ **take up** v. to take up an option = to accept an option which has been offered and put into action 接受选择权(表示可接受该选择权)；Half the rights issue was not taken up by the shareholders. 一半的增股没有被股东接受。take up rate = percentage of acceptances for a rights issue 接受承兑(增股)比率

◇ **takings** pl. n. money received in a shop or a business(复数名词)收入；进款：The week's takings were stolen from the cash desk. 这周的销售款从收款台中被盗了。

**tally** 1. n. note of things counted or recorded 点数；记帐：to keep a tally of stock movements or of expenses 记录股市的变动或费用。tally clerk = person whose job is to note quantities of cargo 理货员；点数员；tally sheet = sheet on which quantities are noted 计数单；理货单 2. v. to agree or to be the same 一致；符合：The invoices do not tally. 发票不符。The accounts department tried to make the figures tally. 财会部门设法让

数字相符合。

**tangible** a. tangible assets = assets which are solid ( such as furniture, jewellery, etc.)有形资产

**tanker** n. special ship for carrying liquids (especially oil)油轮；油船

**tap** n. GB government stocks issued direct to the Bank of England(英)直接向英国银行发行的政府债券

◇ **tap stock** n. issue of government securities 政府债券的

**tape** n. long, flat, narrow piece of plastic 磁带；尺子：magnetic tape = sensitive tape for recording information 录音磁带；computer tape = magnetic tape used in computers 计算机磁带；measuring tape or tape measure = long tape with centimetres or inches marked on it for measuring how long something is 带尺；卷尺。

**tare** n. (allowance made for the) weight of a container and packingwhich is deducted from the total weight；(allowance made for the)weight of a vehicle in calculating transport costs 包装重量；毛重；皮重：to allow for tare 考虑到皮重。

**target** 1. n. thing to aim for 目标：production targets = amount of units a factory is expected to produce 生产指标；sales targets = amount of sales a representative is expected to achieve 产品销售指标；target market = market in which a company is planning to sell its goods 目标市场(指某家公司计划出售其商品的市场)；to set targets = to fix amounts or quantities which workers have to produce or reach 订指标；to meet a target = to produce the quantity of goods or sales which are expected 完成指标；to miss a target = not to produce the amount of goods or sales which are expected 未达到指标：They missed the target figure of £2m turnover. 他们未达到 200 万英磅营业额的指标数。

2. v. to aim to sell 把(销售)作为目标：to target a market = to plan to sell goods in a certain market 瞄准一市场

**tariff** n. (a) customs tariffs = tax to be paid for importing or exporting goods 关税：tariff barriers = customs duty intended to make imports more difficult 关税壁垒 to impose tariff barriers on or to lift tariff barriers from a product 对某种产品强行实施或解除关税壁垒 differential tariffs = different duties for different types of goods 差别税则；General Agreement on Tariffs and Trade = international agreement to try to reduce restrictions in trade between countries 关税及贸易总协定 (b) rate of charging for electricity, hotel rooms, train tickets, etc.价目表；收费表(如电,旅馆房间,火车票等的收费)

**task** n. (a) work which has to be done 工作；任务：to list task processes = to make a list of various parts of a job which have to be done 列工作程序表 (b) task force = special group of workers or managers who are chosen to carryout a special job or to deal with a special problem 特别工作小组；特别任务小组

**tax** 1. n. (a) money taken by the government or by an official body to pay for government services 税；airport tax = tax added to the price of an air ticket to cover the cost of running an airport 机场税；capital gains tax = tax on capital gains 资本所得税；capital transfer tax = tax on gifts or bequests of money or property 资本转移税；corporation tax = tax on profits made by companies 公司税；excess profits tax = tax on profits which are higher than what is thought to be normal 超额利润税；income tax = tax on salaries and wages 所得税；land tax = tax on the amount of land owned 土地税；sales tax = tax on the price of goods sold 销售税；营业税；turnover tax = tax on company turnover 周转税；营

业税;交易税; value added tax = tax on goods and services, added as a percentage to the invoiced sales price 增值税;(b) ad valorem tax = tax calculated according to the value of the goods taxed 从价税(指按课税商品价格计算的税); back tax = tax which is owed 退税;拖欠税款; basic tax = tax paid at the normal rate 主税;基本税; direct tax = tax paid directly to the government (such as income tax)直接税 indirect tax = tax paid to someone who then pays it to the government (such as VAT)间接税; to levy a tax or to impose a tax = to make a tax payable 征税:The government has imposed a 15% tax on petrol. 政府已对汽油征收了 15% 的税。to lift a tax = to remove a tax 取消税收: The tax on company profits has been lifted. 取消征收公司盈利部分的税。exclusive of tax = not including tax 税除外; tax abatement = reduction of tax 减税; tax adjustments = changes made to tax 税收调整; tax adviser or tax consultant = person who gives advice on tax problems 税务顾问; tax allowance or allowances against tax = part of the income which a person is allowed to earn and not pay tax on 免税额; tax avoidance = trying (legally) to minimize the amount of tax to be paid 避税;合法避税; in the top tax bracket = paying the highest level of tax 按最高税级纳税; tax code = number given to indicate the amount of tax allowances a person has 税收法规; tax concession = allowing less tax to be paid 税收减让; tax credit = part of a dividend on which the company has already paid tax, so that the shareholder is not taxed on it again 税额减免;纳税额的扣除;税收抵免; tax deductions = (i) money removed from a salary to pay tax 课税扣除(指从薪金中扣钱纳税)(ii) US business expenses which can be claimed against tax(美)税额减免(指能

减免税的营业费用); tax deducted at source = tax which is removed from a salary or interest before the money is paid out 从源扣缴的税款(指在付钱之前,从薪金或利息中扣除的税款); tax evasion = trying illegally not to pay tax 逃税;偷税漏税; tax exemption = (i) being free from payment of tax 免税(ii) US part of income which a person is allowed to earn and not pay tax on(美)收入的部份免税; tax form = blank form to be filled in with details of income and allowances and sent to the tax office each year 纳税申报表格; tax haven = country where taxes are low, encouraging companies to set up their main offices there 低税国; tax holiday = period when a new company pays no tax 免税期; tax inspector or inspector of taxes = official of the Inland Revenue who examines tax returns anddecides how much tax someone should pay 税务稽查员; tax loophole = legal means of not paying tax 税法漏洞; tax relief = allowing someone not to pay tax on certain parts of his income 税款减免; tax return or tax declaration = completed tax form, with details of income and allowances 报税单;税单;纳税申报单; tax shelter = financial arrangement (such as a pensi on scheme) where investments can be made without tax 避税手段;纳税隐蔽所(指把收益用于投资等用途,如:养老金计划,以逃避纳税的财务安排) tax year = twelve month period on which taxes are calculated (in the UK, 6th April to 5th April of the following year 纳税年度;征税年度; 2. v. to make someone pay a tax or to impose a tax on something 要(人)付税;对(某物)征税: to tax businesses at 50% 对企业征收 50% 的税; Income is taxed at 35%. 所得税率为 35%。 Luxury items are heavily taxed. 对奢侈品征收的税很重。

◇ **taxable** a. which can be taxed 可征

税的;应纳税的: taxable items = items onwhich a tax has to be paid 应纳税的商品; taxable income = income on which a person has to pay tax 须纳税的收入; 应税收入

◇ **taxation** n. act of taxing 征税; 纳税; direct taxation = taxes (such as income tax) which are paid direct to the government 直接税; indirect taxation = taxes (such as sales tax) which are not paid direct to the government 间接征税; The government raises more money by indirect taxation than by direct. 政府由间接征税所得的款项比直接征税多。 double taxation = taxing the same income twice 双重征税; double taxation agreement = agreement between two countries that a person living in one country will not be taxed in both countries on the income earned in the other country 双重税协议(协定)
NOTE: no plural

◇ **tax – deductible** a. which can be deducted from an income before tax is calculated 可减免课税的(指在计算税之前可予以收入中扣除的): These expenses are not tax – deductible. = Tax has to be paid on these expenses. 这些费用是不可减免课税的。

◇ **tax – exempt** a. not required to pay tax; (income or goods) which are not subject to tax 免税的(如:个人收入,商品)

◇ **tax – free** a. on which tax does not have to be paid 免税的;无税的

◇ **taxpayer** n. person or company which has to pay tax 纳税人(或公司): basic taxpayer or taxpayer at the basic rate 基本纳税人; corporate taxpayers 公司纳税人

**taxi** n. car which takes people from one place to another for money 出租汽车; He took a taxi to the airport. 他乘出租汽车去机场。Taxi fares are very high in New York. 纽约的出租汽车费非常高。

**team** n. group of people who work together 队(组(指一起工作的一群人): management team = group of all the managers working in the same company 管理班子;管理层; sales team = all representatives, salesmen and sales managers working in a company 销售队伍

◇ **teamster** n. US truck driver(美)卡车司机。

◇ **teamwork** n. being able to work together as a group 协同;配合;合作(指有能力作为一个群体在一起工作)
NOTE: no plural

**technical** a. (a) referring to a particular machine or process 技术的;工艺的: The document gives all the technical details on the new computer. 文件提供了有关新型计算机的全部技术资料。(b) technical correction = situation where a share price or a currency moves up or down because it was previously too low or too high 技术性的纠正(股票或某种货币以前价格过高或过低而引起现在的价格下降或上升的形势)

◇ **technician** n. person who is specialized in industrial work 技术员;技师;技工 computer technician 计算机专业人员; laboratory technician = person who deals with practical work in a laboratory 实验员

◇ technique n. skilled way of doing a job 技术;技能;技巧; The company has developed a new technique for processing steel. 公司开发了一种加工钢的新技术。He has a special technique for answering complaints from customers. 他有一种答复客户抱怨的特殊技巧。management techniques = skill in managing a business 管理技术(技巧); marketing techniques = skill in marketing a product 销售技术

◇ **technology** n. applying scientific knowledge to industrial processes 工业技

术;工艺学 information technology = workingwith data stored on computers 情报技术; the introduction of new technology = putting new electronic equipment into a business or industry 新技术引进

◇ **technological** a. referring to technology 技术的;工艺的: the technological revolution = changing of industry by introducing new technology 科技革命

**tel** = TELEPHONE 电话

**telecommunications** pl. n. systems of passing messages over long distances (by cable, radio, etc.)电讯;远程通讯系统

**telegram** n. message sent to another country by telegraph 电报; to send an international telegram 发国际电报

◇ **telegraph** 1. n. system of sending messages along wires 电报: to send a message by telegraph 发电报; telegraph office = office from which telegrams can be sent 电报局 2. v. to send a message by telegraph 发电报; to telegraph an order 用电报订货

◇ **telegraphic** a. referring to a telegraph system 电报的;电报传送的; telegraphic address = short address used for sending telegrams 电报挂号

◇ **telemessage** n. GB message sent by telephone, and delivered as a card(英)电话传送信息

**telephone** 1. n. machine used for speaking to someone over a long distance 电话机;电话: We had a new telephone system installed last week. 上周我们装了一套新的电话系统。 to be on the telephone = to be speaking to someone using the telephone(给某人)打电话;通电话: The managing director is on the telephone to Hong Kong. 总经理正在给香港通电话。 She has been on the telephone all day. 她一整天都在打电话。 by telephone = using the telephone 用电话: to place an order by telephone 电话订货; to reserve a room by telephone 电话预订房间; house telephone or internal telephone = telephone for calling from one room to another in an office or hotel 内线电话; telephone book or telephone directory = book which lists all people and businesses in alphabetical order with their telephone numbers 电话号码薄;电话薄; He looked up the number of the company in the telephone book. 他在电话薄上查寻那家公司的电话号码。 telephone call = speaking to someone on the telephone 通电话; to make a telephone call = to speak to someone on the telephone 给某人打电话; to answer the telephone or to take a telephone call = to speak in reply to a call on the telephone 接电话; telephone exchange = central office where the telephones of a whole district are linked 电话局;电话交换台; telephone number = set of figures for a particular telephone subscriber 电话号码; Can you give me your telephone number? 你能将你的电话号码给我吗? telephone operator = person who operates a telephone switchboard 电话接线员;话务员; telephone orders = orders received by telephone 电话订货: Since we mailed the catalogue we have received a large number of telephone orders. 自我们寄出目录后,我们收到了大量的电话订货。 telephone subscriber = person who has a telephone 电话用户。 telephone switchboard = central point in a telephone system where all internal and external lines meet 电话交换台;总机 2. v. to telephone a place or a person = to call a place or someone by telephone 打电话: His secretary telephoned to say he would be late. 他的秘书打电话说他可能会晚到。 He telephoned the order through to the warehouse. = He telephoned the warehouse to place an order. 他打电话直接向仓库订货。 to telephone about something = to make a telephone call to speakabout something 关于某事打电话：He telephoned about the January invoice. 他打电话谈了一月份的发票。to telephone for something = to make a telephone call to ask for something 打电话要某物：He telephoned for a taxi. 他打电话叫出租车。

◇ **telephonist** n. person who works a telephone switchboard 电话接线员；话务员。

◇ **teleprinter** n. machine like a typewriter, which can send messages by telegraph and print incoming messages 电传打字机：teleprinter operator 电传打字员

◇ **telesales** pl. n. sales made by telephone 电话销售

◇ **teletypewriter** n. US = TELEPRINTER 电传打字机

**telex** 1. n. (a) system of sending messages by teleprinter 电传：to send information by telex 用电传发消息。The order came by telex. 来电传订货。telex line = wire linking a telex machine to the telex system 电传线；We cannot communicate with our Nigerian office because of the breakdown of the telex lines. 由于电传线路中断，我们无法和我们在尼日利亚的办事处取得联系。telex operator = person who operates a telex machine 电传接线员；telex subscriber = company which has a telex 电传用户 (b) a telex = (i) a machine for sending and receiving telex messages 电传机 (ii) message sent by telex 电传：He sent a telex to his head office. 他给总部发了一份电传。We received his telex this morning. 今天早上我们收到了他的电传。2. v. to send a message using a teleprinter 发电传：Can you telex the Canadian office before they open? 你能在加拿大办事处上班前给他们发电传吗？He telexed the details of the con-

tract to New York. 他把该合同的细节电传给了纽约。

**teller** n. person who takes cash or pays cash to customers at a bank (银行等的) 出纳员

**tem** see PRO TEM

**temp** 1. n. temporary secretary 临时秘书：We have had two temps working in the office this week to clear the backlog of letters. 这周我们有两位临时秘书在办公室工作清理积压的信件。temp agency = office which deals with finding temporary secretaries for offices 专为公司招收临时秘书的部门 2. v. to work as a temporary secretary 做临时秘书工作

◇ **temping** n. working as a temporary secretary 做临时秘书工作；She can earn more money temping than from a full-time job. 她做临时秘书比一份全日工作挣钱多。NOTE: no plural

**temporary** a. which only lasts a short time 暂时的；临时的：He was granted a temporary export licence. 他得到了临时出口许可证。to take temporary measures 采取临时措施；He has a temporary post with a construction company. 他在一家建筑公司获得了一个临时职位。He has a temporary job as a filing clerk or He has a job as a temporary filing clerk. 他有一份临时工作做档案管理员。temporary employment = full-time work which does not last for more than a few days or months 临时雇用；短期雇用；temporary staff = staff who are appointed for a short time 临时职员。

◇ **temporarily** ad. lasting only for a short time 暂时地；临时地

**tenancy** n. (i) agreement by which a tenant can occupy a property 租赁协议；租用合同 (ii) period during which a tenant has an agreement to occupy aproperty 租期

◇ **tenant** n. person or company which rents a house or flat or office to live or work in 房客；承租人；租户：The tenant is liable for repairs. 租户负责维修. sitting tenant = tenant who is living in a house when the freehold or lease is sold 有居住权的承租人。

**tend** v. to be likely to do something 趋势；倾向于：He tends to appoint young girls to his staff. 他倾向于派年轻女孩当职员。

◇ **tendency** n. being likely to do something 趋势；趋向：The market showed an upward tendency. 市场呈现出上涨的趋势（或市场看涨）。There has been a downward tendency in the market for several days. 这几天市场呈下跌趋势。The market showed a tendency to stagnate. = The market seemed to stagnate rather than advance. 市场呈现出呆滞的趋势。

**tender** 1. n. (a) offer to work for a certain price 报价；投标：a successful tender or an unsuccessful tender 成功的投标或不成功的投标；to put a project out to tender or to ask for or to invite tenders for a project = to ask contractors to give written estimates for a job 投标承包一项目(指要求承包商出示项目的书面估算)；to put in a tender or to submit a tender = to make an estimate for a job 投标(指为一项工作造估算)；to sell shares by tender = to ask people to offer in writing a price for shares 以招标的方式出售股票；sealed tenders = tenders sent in sealed envelopes which will all be opened together at a certain time 密封标书 (b) legal tender = coins or notes which can be legally used to pay a debt ( small denominations cannot be used to pay large debts)法定货币；合法货币 2. v. (a) to tender for a contract = to put forward an estimate of cost for work to be carried out under contract 投

标订合同：to tender for the construction of a hospital 投标承建一家医院 (b) to tender one's resignation = to give in one's resignation 提出辞职

◇ **tenderer** n. person or company which tenders for work 投标人；投标公司：The company was the successful tenderer for the project. 这家公司是这个项目的成功投标人。

◇ **tendering** n. act of putting forward an estimate of cost 投标；报价：To be successful, you must follow the tendering procedure as laid out in the documents. 要成功，你就必须遵循该文件表明的投标手续。

**tentative** a. not certain 尝试的；暂定的：They reached a tentative agreement over the proposal. 他们就这项建议达成了临时协议。We suggested Wednesday May 10th as a tentative date for the next meeting. 我们建议 5 月 10 日星期三作为下次会议的暂定日期。

◇ **tentatively** ad. not sure 暂定地；尝试地：We tentatively suggested Wednesday as the date for our next meeting. 我们建议暂定星期三为我们下次会议的日期。

**tenure** n. (a) right to hold property or position(财产、职位等的)占有；占有权：security of tenure = right to keep a job or rented accommodation provided certain conditions are met 占有权的保障；使用权保证 (b) time when a position is held 占有期；使用期：during his tenure of the office of chairman 在他任董事长期间

**term** n. (a) period of time when something is legally valid(法律)有效期；期限：the term of a lease 租赁期；The term of the loan is fifteen years. 这笔贷款期限为 15 年. to have a loan for a term of fifteen years 有一笔期限为 15 年的贷款；during his term of office as chairman 在他任董事长期间。term deposit = money invested for a fixed period at a higher rate of interest 定期存款; term insurance = life assurance which covers a person's life for a period of time 定期保险: He took out a ten-year term insurance. 他投了 10 年的定期保险. term loan = loan for a fixed period of time 定期贷款; 定期放款; term shares = type of building society deposit for a fixed period of time at a higher rate of interest 定期股票; short-term = for a period of months 短期; long-term = for a long period of time 长期; medium-term = for a period of one or two years 中期 (一到两年)(b) terms = conditions or duties which have to be carried out as part of a contract or arrangements which have to be agreed before a contract is valid(合同, 契约的)条件; 条款; He refused to agree to some of the terms of the contract. 他不同意该合同中的某些条款. By or under the terms of the contract, the company is responsible for all damage to the property. 按合同规定, 该公司要对所有的财产损失负责. to negotiate for better terms 为获得更好的条件进行协商; terms of payment or payment terms = conditions for paying something 支付条件; terms of sale = conditions attached to a sale 销售条件; cash terms = lower terms which apply if the customer pays cash 现金支付优惠条件; "Terms: cash with order" = terms of sale showing that payment has to be made in cash when the order is placed "条款; 订货付现". easy terms = terms which are not difficult to accept or price which is easy to pay 易接受条件; 优惠价格: The shop is let on very easy terms. 这家商店以极易接受条件出租. to pay for something on easy terms 按优惠价购买某物; on favourable terms = on especially good terms 按优惠条件: The shop is let on very favourable terms 这家商店以极优惠条件出租. trade

terms = special discount for people in the same trade 贸易条件; 贸易条款(对同行业人的特殊折扣)(c) part of a legal or university year(法庭)开庭期; 学期 (d) terms of employment = conditions set out in a contract of employment (合同中的)雇用条款

**terminal** 1. n. (a) computer terminal = keyboard and screen, by which information can be put into a computer or can be called up from a database 计算机终端: computer system consisting of a microprocessor and six terminals 包括一个微处理机和六个终端的计算机系统 (b) air terminal = building in a town where passengers meet to be taken by bus to an airport outside the town 终点航站; 机场大厦; airport terminal or terminal building = main building at an airport where passengers arrive and leave 机场的候机大厅; container terminal = area of a harbour where container ships are loaded or unloaded 集装箱码头; ocean terminal = building at a port where passengers arrive and depart 港口的候船大厅; 2. a. at the end 末端的; 终点的; terminal bonus = bonus received when an insurance comes to an end 保险到期时得到的红利

**terminate** v. to end (something) or to bring (something) to an end 终止; 结束: to terminate an agreement 终止合同; His employment was terminated. 他的雇用期到了. The offer terminates on July 31st. 报盘于 7 月 31 日截止. The flight from Paris terminates in New York. 来自巴黎的航班的终点是纽约.

◇ **terminable** a. which can be terminated 可终止的; 有限期的

◇ **termination** n. (a) bringing to an end 终止; 终点: termination clause = clause which explains how and when a contract can be terminated(合同中的)终止条款 (b) US leaving a job (resigning, retiring, or being fired or maderedundant)(美)离职(包括辞职、退休、解雇、裁员)

**territory** n. area visited by a salesman (销售员访问)区域: a rep's territory 销售代表的访问区域; His territory covers all the north of thecountry. 他的推销访问区域遍及整个北部国土。

**tertiary** a. tertiary industry = service industry or industry which does not produce or manufacture but offers a service (such as banking, retailing or accountancy)第三产业(指服务行业,或不从事商品生产或制造的行业如:银行业,零售业,会计工作); tertiary sector = section of the economy containing the service industries 第三产业部门(指经济部门中的服务性行业)

**test** 1. n. (a) examination to see if something works well or is possible 测试;考试: test certificate = certificate to show that something has passed a test 考试合格证书; driving test = examination to see if someone is able to drive a car 驾驶考试; feasibility test = test to see if something is possible 可行性试验; market test = examination to see if a sample of a product will sell in a market 市场测试 (b) test case = legal action where the decision will fix a principle which other cases can follow 判例 2. v. to examine something to see if it is working well 测试;试验: to test a computer system 对计算机系统进行测试。 to test the market for a product or to test market a product = to show samples of a product in a market to see if it will sell well 试销一种新产品(对一种产品进行试销); We are test marketing the toothpaste in Scotland. 我们正在苏格兰试销这种牙膏。

◇ **test－drive** v. to test－drive a car = to drive a car (before buying it) to see if it works well(在买之前)试车

◇ **testing** n. examining something to see if it works well 检测;测试: During the testing of the system several defects were corrected 在系统的检测期间,纠正了几个错误。

**testimonial** n. written report about someone's character or ability(能力;品德等的)证明书;签定书: to write someone's testimonial 给某人写鉴定; unsolicited testimonial = letter praising someone or a product, without the writer having been asked to write it 主动送来的表扬信

**text** n. written part of something 正文;本文;原文: He wrote notes at the side of the text of the agreement. 他在协议正文的旁边写了注解。 text processing = working with words, using a computer to produce, check and change documents, reports, letters, etc. (用计算机进行)文本处理

**thank** v. to show someone that you are grateful for what has been done 感谢: The committee thanked the retiring chairman for his work. 委员会对离任的董事长的工作表示感谢。 "Thank you for your letter of June 25th". 谢谢你6月25日的来信。

◇ **thanks** pl. n. word showing that someone is grateful 感谢之辞;感谢: "Many thanks for your letter of June 25th". 非常感谢你6月25日的来信。 vote of thanks = official vote at a meeting to show that the meeting is grateful for what someone has done 通过表决;表示感谢;公开鸣谢: The meeting passed a vote of thanks to the organizing committee for their work in setting up the international conference. 大会通过表决对这次国际会议的组织委员会所做的工作表示感谢。

◇ **thanks to** ad. because of 由于;因为: The company was able to continue trading thanks to a loan from the bank.

由于得到了银行的贷款,这家公司才得以继续经营。It was no thanks to the bank that we avoided making a loss. = We avoided making a loss in spite of the bank's actions. 并非由于银行我们才免遭了损失。

**theft** n. stealing 偷盗: We have brought in security guards to protect the store against theft. 我们聘请了保安人员以防商店被盗。They are trying to cut their losses by theft. 他们正试图减少因偷窃造成的损失。to take out insurance against theft 投防盗保险。

**theory** n. statement of the general principle of how something should work 学说;理论;原理: In theory the plan should work. = The plan may work, but it has not been tried in practice. 从理论上讲,这个计划是可行的。

**think tank** n. group of experts who advise or put forward plans 智囊团

**third** n. part of something which is divided into three 第三级的;第三的: to sell everything at one third off = to sell everything at a discount of 33% 以 33% 的折扣出售物品; The company has two thirds of the total market. = The company has 66% of the total market. 这家公司的产品占总市场的三分之二 (66%)。

◇ **third party** n. any person other than the two main parties involved in a contract(合同主要双方之外的)第三方: third - party insurance = insurance to cover damage to any person who is not one of the people named in the insurance contract 第三方保险;第三者责任保险。The case is in the hands of a third party. = The case is being dealt with by someone who is not one of the main interested parties. 第三方正在着手处理这个案子。

◇ **third quarter** n. three months periods from July to September 第三季度 (指从七月到九月)

◇ **Third World** n. countries of Africa, Asia and South America which do not have highly developed industries 第三世界: We sell tractors into the Third World or to Third World countries. 我们向第三世界或第三世界国家出售拖拉机。

**threshold** n. limit or point at which something changes 最低限度;临界(值、点): threshold agreement = contract which says that if the cost of living goes up by more than a certain amount, pay will go up to match it 级限协定;临界协议(指合同规定如生活费用上升到一定指数,工资自动随之上涨) threshold price = in the EEC, the lowest price at which farm produce imported into the EEC can be sold 临界价格;最低限价(指欧州共同市场内销售进口农产品所制定的最低限价); pay threshold = point at which pay increases because of a threshold agreement 工资增加起点; tax threshold = point at which another percentage of tax is payable 税收起征限度: The government has raised the minimum tax threshold from £6,000 to £6,500. 政府已将最低税收起征限度税由6,000英磅增加到6,500英磅。

**thrift** n. (a) saving money by spending carefully 节约;节俭 (b) US private local bank or savings and loan association or creditunion, which accepts and pays interest on deposits from small investors (美)私人地方银行;储蓄和借贷协会;信用合作社

NOTE: no plural for (a)

◇ **thrifty** a. careful not to spend too much money 节俭的;节约的

**thrive** v. to grow well or to be profitable 旺盛;繁荣; a thriving economy 繁荣的经济。thriving black market in car radios 汽车用收音机的黑市猖獗; The company is thriving in spite of the recession.

尽管处于经济衰退期,但这家公司依然生意兴隆。

**throughput** n. amount of work done or of goods produced in a certain time 生产量;生产能力; We hope to increase our throughput by putting in two new machines. 我们希望通过使用两台新机器来提高我们的生产能力。The invoice department has a throughput of 6,000 invoices a day. 发票部门每天能处理 6,000 张。

**throw out** v. (a) to reject or to refuse to accept 拒绝;不接收: The proposal was thrown out by the planning committee. 这项建议被计划委员会否决了。The board threw out the draft contract submitted by the union. 董事会否决了工会提交的合同草案。(b) to get rid of (something which is not wanted) 扔掉;抛出(无用之物): We threw out the old telephones and installed a computerized system. 我们扔掉了旧电话,装了一部电脑系统。The AGM threw out the old board of directors. 年度股东大会解雇(撵走)了老的董事会。NOTE: throwing – threw – has thrown

**tick** 1. n. (a) infml. credit(非正式)信用;赊欠: All the furniture in the house is bought on tick. 这所房子里的所有家具都是赊购的 (b) mark on paper to show that something is correct or that something is approved(核对某物用的)记号: Put a tick in the box marked "R". 在标有"R"的方框内上标上记号。NOTE: no plural for (a). Note also US English for (b) is check = 2. v. to mark with a sign to show that something is correct 对…标以记号: Tick the box marked "R" if you require a receipt. 如需要收据,请在标"R"的方框内标上记号

◇ **ticker** n. US machine (operated by telegraph) which prints details of share prices and transactions rapidly on paper tape(股市行情)自动收录器

**ticket** n. (a) piece of paper or card which allows you to do something 票;券: entrance ticket or admission ticket = ticket which allows you to go in 入场券; theatre ticket = ticket which allows you a seat in a theatre 戏票 (b) piece of paper or card which allows you to travel 车票: train ticket or bus ticket or plane ticket 火车票;汽车票;飞机票; season ticket = train or bus ticket which can be used for any number of journeys over a period (usually one, three, six or twelve months) 月票, 定期票;长期票; single ticket or US one - way ticket = ticket for one journey from one place to another 单程车票 return ticket or US round - trip ticket = ticket for a journey from one place to another and back again 往返票;来回票 (c) ticket agency = shop which sells tickets to theatres(戏院等的)售票代理处 ticket counter = counter where tickets are sold 售票台 (d) paper which shows something(货物上的)票签;标签: baggage ticket = paper showing that you have left a piece of baggage with someone 行李标签; price ticket = piece of paper showing a price 价格标签

**tie** v. to attach or to fasten (with string, wire, etc.)(用带、绳、线)系;扎;捆: He tied the parcel with thick string. 他用粗绳子将行李捆起来。She tied two labels on to the parcel. 她把两个标签系挂在这件包裹上。NOTE: tying – tied

◇ **tie - on label** n. label with a piece of string attached so that it can be tied to an item 系挂标签

◇ **tie up** v. (a) to attach or to fasten tightly 系紧;拴住(船只)停泊处: The parcel is tied up with string. 行李用绳捆紧了。The ship was tied up to the quay.

这艘船停泊在码头上。He is rather tied up at the moment. = He is very busy. 他现在很忙。(b) to invest money in one way, so that it cannot be used for other investments 使搁死在: He has £ 100,000 tied up in long - dated gilts. 他已将 10 万英镑投资拴死在长期的金边证券。The company has £ 250,000 tied up in stock which no one wants to buy. 这家公司已将 25 万英磅投资搁死在无人要买的股票。

◇ **tie - up** n. link or connection 连结;联系: The company has a tie - up with a German distributor. 这家公司与德国一家经销商有联系。

NOTE: plural is tie - ups

**tight** a. which is controlled or which does not allow any movement 紧的;牢固的: The manager has a very tight schedule today - he cannot fit in any more appointments. 经理今天的日程已经安排得很紧了,无法再安插更多的会面了. Expenses are kept under tight control. 费用处于严格控制下。tight money = money which is borrowed at a high interest rate 银根紧缩;银根紧; tight money policy = government policy to restrict money supply 紧缩银根政策

◇ **- tight** suffix which prevents something getting in(后缀)密封的;不漏的: The computer is packed in a watertight case. 计算机是用不透水箱子包装的。Send the films in an airtight container. 用密封容器运送胶片。

◇ **tighten** v. to make ( something ) tight or to control ( something )(使)绷紧;(使)变紧;控制 …: The accounts department is tightening its control over departmental budgets. 会计部门将严格控制其部门预算。

◇ **tighten up on** v. to control ( something ) more(使)…控制更紧(更严) The government is tightening up on tax evasion. 政府正逐步更严格控制偷

税漏税。We must tighten up on the reps' expenses. 我们必须严加控制业务代表的开销。

**till** n. drawer for keeping cash in a shop (店铺中)装钱的抽屉;钱柜: cash till = cash register or machine which shows and adds prices of items bought, with a drawer for keeping the cash received 现金柜; There was not much money in the till at the end of the day. 一天下来,钱柜里没有多少现金。

**time** n. ( a ) period when something takes place (such as one hour, two days, fifty minutes, etc. )时间: computer time = time when a computer is being used (paid for at an hourly rate)计算机机时; real time = time when a computer is working on the processing of data while the problem to which the data refers is actually taking place 实时系统(指计算机对涉及的数据处理和问题进行数据处理的时间); time and motion study = study in an office or factory of how long it takes to do certain jobs and the movements workers have to make to do them 工时与动作研究(指对办公室、工厂做某项工作所用的时间和对工人操作过程的动作进行的研究) time and motion expert = person who analyzes time and motion studies and suggests changes in the way work is done 工时与动作研究专家 (b) hour of the day (such as 9:00, 12:15, ten o'clock at night, etc. )点钟;时刻: The time of arrival or the arrival time is indicated on the screen. 到达时刻在屏幕上显示。Departure times are delayed by up to fifteen minutes because of the volume of traffic. 因交通流量之原因, 出发时间耽搁了 15 分钟。on time = at the right time 准时;按时; The plane was on time. 这架飞机是准时的。You will have to hurry if you want to get to the meeting on time or if you want to be on time for the meeting. 如果你想准时到会,你要快一点。opening time or closing time = time when a shop or office starts or stops work(商店办公室等的)开门或关门时间（c）system of hours on the clock(钟表的)计时方式: Summer Time or Daylight Saving Time = system where clocks are set back one hour in the summer to take advantage of the longer hours of daylight 夏令时间，夏时制; Standard Time = normal time as in the winter months 标准时间（d）hours worked 工作时间; 工时: He is paid time and a half on Sundays. = He is paid the normal rate plus 50% extra when he works on Sundays. 他星期日工作的时候工资加半。full – time = working for the whole normal working day 全日制; overtime = hours worked more than the normal working time 加班时间; 额外工作时间; part – time = not working for a whole working day 非全日的; 兼职的; (e) period before something happens 时期: time deposit = deposit of money for a fixed period, during which it cannot be touched 定期存款; delivery time = number of days before something will be delivered 交货时间; lead time = time between placing an order and receiving the goods 订货至接货时间; time limit = period during which something should be done 期限; 时限: to keep within the time limits or within the time schedule = to complete work by the time stated 在规定期限内完成任务 NOTE: no plural for (a), (c) and (d)

◇ **time – card or** US **time – clock card** n. card which is put into a timing machine when a worker clocks in or clocks out, and records the time when he starts and stops work 计时卡(指记录工人上、下班时间的卡片)

◇ **time – keeping** n. being on time for work 准时工作; He was warned for bad time – keeping. 他因工作不守时受到警告。 NOTE: no plural

◇ **time rate** n. rate for work which is calculated as money per hour or per week, and not money for work completed 计时工资制

◇ **time saving** 1. a. which saves time 省时的: a time – saving device 一台省时的设备 2. n. trying to save time 节省时间: The management is keen on time saving. 管理人员力求节省时间。

◇ **time scale** n. time which will be taken to complete work 时间限度: Our time scale is that all work should be completed by the end of August. 我们的时间限度是所有的工作应到8月底完成。 He is working to a strict time scale. 他正严格按时间限度进行工作。

◇ **time share** n. system where several people each own part of a property (such as a holiday flat), each being able to use it for a certain period each year(财产的)时间分享;

◇ **time – sharing** n. (a) = TIME SHARE 时间分享;分时 (b) sharing a computer system, with different users using different terminals(用不同的终端,不同的用户共同使用一计算机系统)分时;时间分划 NOTE: no plural

◇ **time sheet** n. paper showing when a worker starts work in the morning and leaves work in the evening(指记录工人上、下班时间)时间表

◇ **timetable** 1. n. (a) list showing times of arrivals or departures of buses or trains or planes, etc.(汽车、火车、飞机)时刻表: According to the timetable, there should be a train to London at 10:22. 根据时刻表,10点22分应有一列开往伦敦的火车。 The bus company has brought out its winter timetable. 汽车公司已经公布了冬运时刻表。(b) list of appointments or events 工作日程表: The manager has a very full timetable, so I doubt if he will be able to see you today. 经理的日程已经排满, 所以我不能肯定今天能否见你。conference timetable = list of speakers or events at a conference 会议日程表 2. v. to make a list of times 列表; 安排; 部署

◇ **time work** n. work which is paid for at a rate per hour or per day, not per piece of work completed 计时 (工资) 工作, 按时计酬的工作

◇ **timing** n. way in which something happens at a particular time 时间安排; 时间选择: The timing of the conference is very convenient, as it comes just before my annual holiday. 会议的时间安排很合适, 因正好在我年度休假之前。His arrival ten minutes after the meeting finished was very bad timing. 他选择的到达时间不好, 正好在散会后十分钟。NOTE: no plural

**tip** 1. n. (a) money given to someone who has helped you 小费: I gave the taxi driver a 10 cent tip. 我给了那位出租司机十美分小费。The staff are not allowed to accept tips. 职员不允许收小费。(b) advice on something to buy or to do which could be profitable (能带来收益的) 忠告; 提示: a stock market tip 股市告诫; He gave me a tip about a share which was likely to rise because of a takeover bid. 他提醒我由于兼并递价, 那种股票可能上涨。tip sheet = newspaper which gives information about shares which should be bought or sold (有关股票买卖的) 内情通报 2. v. (a) to give money to someone who has helped you 给小费: He tipped the receptionist £5. 他给了接待员 5 英磅小费。(b) to say that something is likely to happen or that something might be profitable 暗示; 提示 (指某事可能发生或有利可图): Two shares were tipped in the business section of the paper. 报纸上的商业版暗示两种股票将升值。He is tipped to become the next chairman. 据透露, 他将出任下届董事长。

NOTE: tipping – tipped

**TIR** = TRANSPORT INTERNATIONAL ROUTIER 国际陆路运输协定

**title** n. (a) right to own a property. 所有权: She has no title to the property. 对这笔财产她无所有权。He has a good title to the property. 他享有这笔财产有效所有权。title deeds = document showing who is the owner of a property 地契; 所有权凭证; 契据 (b) name given to a person in a certain job 头衔; 称号: He has the title "Chief Executive". 他的头衔是总裁。(c) name of a book or film, etc. (书籍, 电影等的) 书名; 片名

**token** n. (a) thing which acts as a sign or symbol 标志; 标号; 象征: token charge = small charge which does not cover the real costs 象征性费用: A token charge is made for heating. 对取暖进行象征性收费。token payment = small payment to show that a payment is being made 象征性付款; token rent = very low rent payment to show that a rent is being asked 象征性租金; token strike = short strike to show that workers have a grievance 象征性罢工 (b) book token or flower token or gift token = card bought in a store which is given as a present and which must be exchanged in that store for goods 书籍礼券; 花束礼券或礼券: We gave her a gift token for her birthday. 我们给了她一张生日礼券。

**toll** n. payment for using a service (usually a bridge or a ferry) (使用桥梁、渡口等需付的) 通行费: We had to cross a toll bridge to get to the island. 我们必须通过一座收费桥到达该岛。You have to pay a toll to cross the bridge. 你过桥必须付通行费。

◇ **toll call** n. US long - distance telephone call (美) 长途电话

◇ **toll free** ad. US without having to paya charge for a long – distance telephone(美)(长途电话)免费地: to call someone toll free 免费给某人打长途电话; toll free number 免费长途电话号码

**tombstone** n. infml. official announcement in a newspaper showing that a loan has been subscribed 报纸上的证券发行广告(非正式)。

**ton** n. measure of weight 吨: GB long ton = measure of weight ( = 1016 kilos)(英重量单位)长吨 = 1016 公斤。US short ton = measure of weight ( = 907 kilos)(美)短吨 = 907 公斤 metric ton = 1,000 kilos 公吨 =1000 公斤

◇ **tonne** n. metric ton or 1,000 kilos 公吨

◇ **tonnage** n. space for cargo in a ship, measured in tons(船舶的)吨位; 吨数: gross tonnage = amount of total space in a ship 总吨位(数); deadweight tonnage = largest amount of cargo which a ship can carry safely 载重吨位

NOTE: no plural

**tone** n. dialling tone = noise made by a telephone to show that it is ready for you to dial a number 拨号音

**tool** n. instrument used for doing manual work (such as a hammer, screwdriver) 工具;器具;用具(指用手操作的,如:锤子、螺丝刀等): machine tools = tools worked by motors, used to work on wood or metal 机床

◇ **tool up** v. to put machinery into a factory 用机械器具装备工厂

**top** 1. a. & n. (a) upper surface or upper part 上面;顶部: Do not put coffee cups on top of the computer. 不要把咖啡杯放在计算机上。top copy = first sheet of a document which is typed with several carbon copies or photocopies(打字的文件复印本、照相复制本的)首页。(b) highest point or most important place 顶点;关键点: The company is in

the top six exporters. 这家公司是六家最大进口商之一。top flight or top – ranking = in the most important position 最高级的;第一流的;最好的: Top – flight managers can earn very high salaries. 一流的管理人员挣得工资很高。He is the top – ranking official in the delegation. 他是这个个代表团的最高级别官员。top – grade = most important or of the best quality 最高级的;优质的: The car only runs on top – grade petrol. 这辆轿车上只能用优质的汽油。top management = the main directors of a company(公司的)上层管理人员; to give something top priority = to make something the most important item, so that it is done very fast 使…绝对优先; top quality = very best quality 最优质的: We specialize in top quality imported goods. 我们主要经营最优质的进口商品。2. v. to go higher than 高于;超过;胜过: Sales topped ₤1m in the first quarter. 一季度销售额超过了 100 万英磅。

NOTE: topping – topped

◇ **top – hat pension** n. special extra pension for senior managers(高层管理人员的)要人养老金

◇ **top – selling** a. which sells better than all other products(比其他产品)畅销的: top – selling brands of toothpaste 几种畅销牌子的牙膏

◇ **top up** v. to fill up something which is not full 装满;加满: to top up stocks before the Christmas rush 在圣诞节购物高峰之前将货备足

**tort** n. harm done to someone or property which can be the basis of a lawsuit(法律上)民事侵权行为

**total** 1. a. complete or with everything added together 全部的;总共的: total amount 总额; total assets 总资产; total cost 总成本,成本总额; total expenditure 总支出; total income 总收入; total output 总产量；total revenue 收入总额；The cargo was written off as a total loss. = The cargo was so badly damaged that the insurers said it had no value.(因严重损害）这批货以全损注销。2. n. amount which is complete or with everything added up 总数；总共；总计：The total of the charges comes to more than £1,000. 费用总额达 1,000 英磅。grand total = final total made by adding several subtotals 总计；共计 3. v. to add up to 合计；总共；总计：costs totalling more than £25,000 总计为 2.5 万英磅的成本（费用）

NOTE: totalling – totalled but US English totaling – totaled

◇ **totally** ad. completely 完全地；总共地：The factory was totally destroyed in the fire. 这座工厂完全毁于火灾。The cargo was totally ruined by water. 货物全被水毁了。

**tour** n. (holiday) journey to various places, coming back in the end to the place the journey started from 旅行；旅游；巡视：The group went on a tour of Italy. 这批人去意大利旅行。The minister went on a fact‐finding tour of the region. 那位部长对这一地区进行实地调查的巡视。conducted tour = tour with a guide who shows places to the tourists 有导游的旅行；package tour = tour where the hotel, travel, and meals are all arranged in advance and paid for in one payment 由旅行社代办的旅行；tour operator = person or company which organizes tours 旅游经营者或公司；to carry out a tour of inspection = to visit various places or offices or factories to inspect them 进行巡视

◇ **tourism** n. business of providing travel, hotel rooms, food, entertainment, etc., for tourists 旅游业
NOTE: no plural

◇ **tourist** n. person who goes on holi‐ day to visit places away from his home 旅游者；观光客：tourist bureau or tourist information office = office which gives information to tourists about the place where it is situated(指为旅游者提供咨询服务的部门）旅行社；tourist class = lower quality or less expensive way of travelling(指质量和价格较低的）经济舱位；二等舱；He always travels first class, because he says tourist class is too uncomfortable. 他总是坐头等舱旅行，他说经济舱太不舒服。tourist visa = visa which allows a person to visit a country for a short time on holiday 旅游签证

**tout** 1. n. person who sells tickets (to games or shows) for more than the price printed on them 票贩子 2. v. to tout for custom = to try to attract customers 招徕顾客；拉生意

**track record** n. success or failure of a company or salesman in the past(公司、推销员的）履历；经历：He has a good track record as a secondhand car salesman. 作为旧车销售商他有良好的经历。The company has no track record in the computer market. 这家公司在计算机市场中没有什么成绩记载。

**trade** 1. n. (a) business of buying and selling 贸易；交易：export trade or import trade = the business of selling to other countries or buying from other countries 出口贸易或进口贸易；foreign trade or overseas trade or external trade = trade with other countries 对外贸易；home trade = trade in the country where a company is based 国内贸易；trade cycle = period during which trade expands, then slows down, then expands again 贸易周期；商业循环(指从繁荣到萧条的经常性波动）；balance of trade or trade balance = international trading position of a country, excluding invisible trade 贸易差额；贸易平衡：The country had an adverse balance of trade for the second month running. 这个国家已连续两个月对外贸易逆差。 favourable balance of trade = situation where a country's exports are larger than its imports 贸易顺差(指出口大于进口) (b) to do a good trade in a range of products = to sell a large number of the range of products 某类产品销路好; fair trade = international business system where countries agree not to charge import duties on certain items imported from their trading partners 互惠贸易;公平贸易; free trade = system where goods can go from one country to another without any restrictions 自由贸易; free trade area = group of countries practising free trade 自由贸易区; trade agreement = international agreement between countries over general terms of trade 贸易协定; trade bureau = office which specializes in commercial enquiries 商业咨询处; to impose trade barriers on = to restrict the import of certain goods by charging high duty 实行贸易壁垒; trade deficit or trade gap = difference in value between a country's high imports and low exports 贸易赤字(逆差); trade description = description of a product to attract customers 产品说明书;商品说明; GB Trade Descriptions Act = act which limits the way in which products can be described so as to protect customers from wrong descriptions made by manufacturers (英)商品说明法; trade directory = book which lists all the businesses and business people in a town 企业名录; trade mission = visit to a country by a group of foreign businessmen to discuss trade. 贸易代表团; to ask a company to supply trade references = to ask a company to give names of traders who can report on the company's financial situation and reputation 要求某公司提供贸易查询资料 (c) people or companies dealing in the same type of product 行业;生意: He is in the secondhand car trade. 他从事旧车生意。 She is very well known in the clothing trade. 他在服装业很有名气。 trade association = group which links together companies in the same trade 同业协会(工会); trade counter = shop in a factory or warehouse where goods are sold to retailers 批发店; trade discount or trade terms = reduction in price given to a customer in the same trade 商业折扣;同行折扣; trade fair = large exhibition and meeting for advertising and selling a certain type of product 贸易展览会;商品交易会: There were two trade fairs running in London at the same time. 在伦敦两个商品交易会同时举行。 to organize or to run a trade fair 组织或操办贸易展览会; trade journal or trade magazine or trade paper or trade publication = magazine or newspaper produced for people and companies in a certain trade 行业杂志;行业报刊; trade press = all magazines produced for people working in a certain trade 行业杂志(总称) trade price = special wholesale price paid by a retailer to the manufacturer or wholesaler 批发价

NOTE: no plural for (a) or (b)

2. v. to buy and sell or to carry on a business 交易;经商: to trade with another country 与另一国家进行贸易; to trade on the Stock Exchange 在证券交易所内进行交易; The company has stopped trading. 这家公司已经停止经营。 The company trades under the name "Eeziphitt". 这家公司以"Eeziphitt"的名称进行经营。

◇ **trade in** v. (a) to buy and sell certain items 买卖;贸易;经营: The company trades in imported goods 这家公司经营进口商品。 He trades in French wine 他经营法国酒。 (b) to give in an old item as part of the payment for a new one 以(旧物)折价换取(同类新物);贴

换：The chairman traded in his old Rolls Royce for a new model. 董事长将他的旧罗尔斯—罗伊斯轿车贴换了一辆新型号的轿车。

◇ **trade - in** n. old item (such as a car or washing machine) given as part of the payment for a new one 以（旧物）折价（换新物）；折价物：to give the old car as a trade - in 将这辆旧车进行折价；trade - in price = amount allowed by the seller for an old item being traded in for a new one 折价物价格

◇ **trademark or trade name** n. particular name, design, etc., which has been registered by the manufacturer and which cannot be used by other manufacturers 商标；商品名称（指厂家已注册的，其它厂家不能用的商品名称或图案设计）：You cannot call your beds "Softn' kumfi" – it is a registered trademark. 你们生产的床不能叫"Softn'kumfi"的名称——它是一个已注册商标。

◇ **trade - off** n. exchanging one thing for another as part of a business deal 交易；交换；以货易货

◇ **trader** n. person who does business 商人；贸易商：commodity trader = person whose business is buying and selling commodities 商品贸易商；free trader = person who is in favour of free trade 自由贸易商；sole trader = person who runs a business, usually by himself, but has not registered it as a company 个体商人；独家贸易商。

◇ **tradesman** n. shopkeeper or person who runs a shop 店主；零售商；商人 NOTE: plural is tradesmen

◇ **tradespeople** pl. n. shopkeepers（复数名词）商人

◇ **trade union or trades union** n. organization which represents workers who are its members in discussions with employers about wages and conditions of

employment 行业工会（指代表工人利益，就工资和就业条件同资方进行交涉的工人组织）：They are members of a trades union or they are trade union members. 他们是某工会会员。He has applied for trade union membership or he has applied to join a trades union. 他已申请加入工会组织。Trades Union Congress = organization linking all British trade unions（英）英国工会联盟 NOTE: although Trades Union Congress is the official name for the organization, trade union is commoner than trades union in GB English. US English is labor union

◇ **trade unionist** n. member of a trade union 工会会员

◇ **trading** n. business of buying and selling 交易；买卖；贸易：trading account = account of a company's gross profit 营业帐户；trading area = group of countries which trade with each other 贸易区；商业区；trading company = company which specializes in buying and selling goods 贸易公司；adverse trading conditions = bad conditions for trade 贸易逆境；trading estate = area of land near a town specially for factories and warehouses 工商业区；trading loss = situation where a company's receipts are less than its expenditure 贸易亏损；trading partner = company or country which trades with another 贸易伙伴；trading profit = situation where a company's gross receipts are more than its gross expenditure 营业利润；销售利润；trading stamp = special stamp given away by a shop, which the customer can collect and exchange later for free goods 赠券；fair trading = way of doing business which is reasonable and does not harm the customer 公平交易；公平买卖；GB Office of Fair Trading = government department which protects consumers against unfair or illegal business

(英)保护消费者权益局; insider trading= illegal buying or selling of shares by staff of a company who have secret information about the company's plans(股市中的)内幕交易(指了解发股公司内幕情况的员工所做的不合法股票交易) NOTE: no plural

**traffic** n. (a) movement of cars or lorries or trains or planes; movement of people or goods in vehicles 交通;运输;货运量;客运量: There is an increase in commuter traffic or goods traffic on the motorway. 高速公路上的通勤人员客运量或货运量有所增加。Passenger traffic on the commuter lines has decreased during the summer. 夏季这条通勤人员线上的客运量已减少。air traffic controller = person who controls the landing and taking off of planes at an airport 机场调度人员 (b) illegal trade 非法交易(买卖): drugs traffic or traffic in drugs 毒品交易 NOTE: no plural

**train** 1. n. set of coaches or wagons pulled by an engine along railway lines 火车;列车: a passenger train or a goods train 客车;货车; to take the 9:30 train to London 乘九点半的火车去伦敦。He caught his train or he missed his train. 他赶上火车或他没赶上火车。to ship goods by train 用火车运货; freight train or goods train = train used for carrying goods 货车 2. v. to teach (someone) to do something; to learn how to do something 培养;训练;培训: He trained as an accountant. 他受训当会计。The company has appointed a trained lawyer as its managing director. 这家公司已任命一位专门律师任其总经理。

◇ **trainee** n. person who is learning how to do something 受训员;实习生: We employ a trainee accountant to help in the office at peak periods. 高峰时期我们将雇用一位实习会计在办公室帮忙。Graduate trainees come to work in the laboratory when they have finished their courses at university. 那些毕业实习生当完成其大学课程时, 就到实验室工作。management trainee = young member of staff being trained to be a manager 管理实习人员

◇ **traineeship** n. post of trainee 学员身份

◇ **training** n. being taught how to do something 训练;培养: There is a ten-week training period for new staff. 新职工有一个为期十周的培训期。The shop is closed for staff training. 商店停业进行职工培训。industrial training = training of new workers to work in an industry 工业培训(指对新工人进行培训); management training = training staff to be managers, by making them study problems and work out solutions to them 管理培训; on-the-job training = training given to workers at their place of work 在职培训; off-the-job training = training given to workers away from their place of work (such as at a college or school)脱产培训; training levy = tax to be paid by companies to fund the government's training schemes 训练征税(指向为政府训练计划提供资金的公司征收的税); training officer = person who deals with the training of staff 负责职员培训的官员; training unit = special group of teachers who organize training for companies 从事培训单位 NOTE: no plural

**transact** v. to transact business = to carry out a piece of business 经营业务;做交易

◇ **transaction** n. business transaction = piece of business or buying or selling 商品交易; cash transaction = transaction paid for in cash 现金交易: a transaction on the Stock Exchange = purchase or sale of shares on the Stock Exchange 证券交易所交易: The paper publishesa daily list of Stock Exchange transactions. 这家报纸公布每天在证券交易所上市证券交易一览表。exchange transaction = purchase or sale of foreign currency 外汇交易；fraudulent transaction = transaction which aims to cheat someone 欺诈性交易

**transfer** 1. n. moving someone or something to a new place 职务调动；转移；移动；转让: He applied for a transfer to our branch in Scotland. 他申请调到我们设在苏格兰的分支机构。transfer of property or transfer of shares = moving the ownership of property or shares from one person to another 财产转让；股票过户（转让）；airmail transfer = sending money from one bank to another by airmail 航空汇款；bank transfer = moving money from a bank account to an account in another country 银行间转帐；银行汇款；credit transfer or transfer of funds = moving money from one account to another 信用转帐（转让）；资金转让；stock transfer form = form to be signed by the person transferring shares 股票转让（过户）表格 2. v. (a) to move someone or something to a new place 调动；转移；移动: The accountant was transferred to our Scottish branch. 那位会计被调到我们在苏格兰的分支机构。He transferred his shares to a family trust. 他将他的股票转让给了一家私人信托社。She transferred her money to a deposit account. 她将她的钱转入存款帐户。transferred charge call = phone call where the person receiving the call agrees to pay for it 由接电话人付款的电话 (b) to change from one type of travel to another 换乘: When you get to London airport, you have to transfer onto an internal flight. 当你到达伦敦机场时，你必须换乘国内航班。

NOTE: transferring – transferred

◇ **transferable** a. which can be passed to someone else 可转让的: The season ticket is not transferable. = The ticket cannot be given or lent to someone else to use. 本月票不可转让。

**tranship** v. to move cargo from one ship to another(货物)转船运输；转运

NOTE: transhipping – transhipped

**transit** n. (a) movement of passengers or goods on the way to a destination 运输；运送(人；货物等): to pay compensation for damage suffered in transit or for loss in transit 支付运输过程中所受损失的赔偿金；Some of the goods were damaged in transit. 在运输过程中有些货物损坏了。goods in transit = goods being transported from warehouse to customer 在运输途中的货物 (b) transit lounge = room in an airport where passengers wait for connecting flights(机场的)候机厅；transit visa or transit permit = document which allows someone to spend a short time in one country while travelling to another country 过境签证

NOTE: no plural

**translate** v. to put something which is said or written in one language into another language 翻译: He asked his secretary to translate the letter from the German agent. 他要秘书将德国代理商的那封信翻译出来。We have had the contract translated from French into Japanese. 我们已请人将此合同由法文译成日文。

◇ **translation** n. something which has been translated 译文；译本: She passed the translation of the letter to the accounts department. 她把这封信的译文送到了财会部。translation bureau = office which translates documents for companies 翻译社(指为公司翻译文件的机构)

◇ **translator** n. person who translates 翻译者；译员。

**transmission** n. sending 传递；传送:

transmission of a message 传递消息

◇ **transmit** v. to send ( a message )传递;传送( 消息等)

NOTE: transmitting – transmitted

**transport** 1. n. moving of goods or people 运输;运送: air transport or transport by air 航空运输;rail transport or transport by rail 铁路运输;road transport or transport by road 公路运输;passenger transport or the transport of passengers 客运;旅客运输;the passenger transport services of British Rail 英国铁路旅客运输服务;What means of transport will you use to get to the factory? 你乘什么交通工具去工厂? The visitors will be using public transport or private transport. = The visitors will be coming by bus or train, etc., or in their own cars 游客将乘公共交通工具或私人交通工具来。public transport system = system of trains, buses, etc., used by the general public 公共运输系统

NOTE: no plural

2. v. to move goods or people from one place to another in a vehicle 运送;运输: The company transports millions of tons of goods by rail each year. 这家公司每年由铁路运输成百万吨的货物。The visitors will be transported to the factory by air or by helicopter or by taxi. 参观者将乘飞机或直升飞机或出租汽车到这家工厂。

◇ **transportable** a. which can be moved 可运输的;可运送的。

◇ **transportation** n. ( a ) moving goods or people from one place to another 货运;客运 ( b ) vehicles used to move goods or people from one place to another 交通工具: The company will provide transportation to the airport. 该公司将提供去机场的交通工具。ground transportation = buses, taxis, etc., available to take passengers from an airport to the

town 地面交通工具

NOTE: no plural

◇ **transporter** n. company which transports goods( 货物等的)运输公司

◇ **Transport International Routier** n. system with international documents which allows dutiable goods to cross several European countries by road without paying duty until they reach their final destination 国际陆路货运协定(指允许征税货物由公路运输通过数个欧洲国家直至其目的地,才需交税的制度)

**travel** 1. n. moving of people from one place to another or from one country to another 旅行;旅游: Business travel is a very important part of our overhead expenditure.商务旅行是我们经常开支的一个极重要部分。travel agent = person in charge of a travel agency 旅行社代理人;travel agency = office which arranges travel for customers 旅行社;travel allowance = money which an employee is allowed to spend on travelling 差旅津贴;travel magazine = magazine with articles on holidays and travel 旅游杂志;the travel trade = all businesses which organize travel for people 旅游业

NOTE: no plural

2. v. (a) to move from one place to another or from one country to another 旅行;旅游: He travels to the States on business twice a year. 他每年去美国出差两次。In her new job, she has to travel abroad at least ten times a year. 在新工作岗位上,她每年至少要出国旅行十次。(b) to go from one place to another, showing a company's goods to buyers and taking orders from them 旅行推销货物: He travels in the north of the country for an insurance company. 他在该国的北部地区为一家保险公司做旅行推销。

NOTE: travelling – travelled 但 ( 美 ) traveling – traveled

◇ **traveller or US traveler** n. ( a )

person who travels 旅客；旅行者：businesstraveller = person who is travelling on business 出差者；旅行推销员；traveller's cheques or US traveler's checks = cheques taken by a traveller which can be cashed in a foreign country 旅行支票（b）commercial traveller = salesman who travels round an area visiting customers on behalf of his company 商务旅行者(指代表其公司在一地区旅行,巡回访问顾客的商人)

◇ **travelling** n. travelling expenses = money spent on travelling and hotels for business purposes 差旅费

**tray** n. filing tray = container kept on a desk for documents which have to be filed(放在书桌上存放文件的)文件筐：in tray = basket on a desk for letters or memos which have been received and are waiting to be dealt with(放在书桌上存放来函或待办文件的)收入文件筐；out tray = basket on a desk for letters or memos which have been dealt with and are ready to be sent out(放在书桌上存放办毕并待发的文件的)待发文件筐；pending tray = basket on a desk for papers which cannot be dealt with immediately(放在书桌上存放未能及时处理的文件的)待处理文件筐

**treasurer** n. (a) person who looks after the money or finances of a club or society, etc.司库；出纳员；掌管财政的人：honorary treasurer = treasurer who does not receive any fee 义务（名誉）司库（b）US main financial officer of a company(美)(公司的)财务主管

**treasury** n. the Treasury = government department which deals with the country's finance 财政部；treasury bill = bill of exchange which does not give any interest and is sold by the government at a discount 国库券；treasury bonds = bonds issued by the Treasury of the USA(美)国库债券(指美国财政部

发行的债券)

**treaty** n. (a) agreement between countries(国家之间的)条约：commercial treaty 通商条约；商约（b）agreement between individual persons(人与人之间的)协议；协定：to sell a house by private treaty = to sell a home to another person not by auction 按私下成交契约出售房屋

**treble** v. to increase three times 使成三倍；使增加两倍：The company's borrowings have trebled. 这家公司的借贷已增加了两倍。

**trend** n. general way things are going 倾向；趋势：There is a trend away from old-established food stores. 有一种运离老字号的食品店趋势。a downward trend in investment 投资呈下降趋势；We notice a general trend to sell to the student market. 我们注意到向学生市场出售的总趋势。The report points to inflationary trends in the economy. 该报告说明经济方面有通货膨胀的趋势. an upward trend in sales 销售量呈上升趋向。economic trends = way in which a country's economy is moving 经济趋向；market trends = gradual changes taking place in a market 市场趋向；市场走势

**trial** n. (a) court case to judge a person accused of a crime(法庭)审判：He is on trial or is standing trial for embezzlement. 他因贪污而受审。(b) test to see if something is good 测验；测试：on trial = being tested 在试验中；在测试中：The product is on trial in our laboratories. 该产品正在实验室进行测试。trial period = time when a customer can test a product before buying it 试用期；trial sample = small piece of a product used for testing 试验样品；测试样品。free trial = testing of a machine or product with no payment involved 免费试用（c）trial balance = draft adding of debits and credits to see if they balance 试算表(指核查帐户借方与贷方是否平衡的一种财务表)。

◇ **tribunal** n. official court which examines special problems and makes judgements 法庭(常指特种法庭)：adjudication tribunal = group which adjudicates in industrial disputes 裁决法庭(指裁决产业争端的机构) industrial tribunal = court which can decide in disputes about employment 产业法庭(指解决劳资纠纷的法庭) rent tribunal = court which can decide if a rent is too high or low(裁定租价过高或过低的)有关租价的法庭

**trick** n. clever act to make someone believe something which is not true 欺骗、诡计：confidence trick = business where someone gains another person's confidence and then tricks him 骗局、欺诈(指在商业中利用对方的信任来进行欺诈)

◇ **trickster** n. confidence trickster = person who carries out a confidence trick on someone 设法让人相信的骗子(指利用别人的信任来进行欺诈活动的人)

**trip** n. journey 旅行：business trip = journey to discuss business matters with people who live along way away or overseas 商务旅行

**triple** 1. v. to multiply three times(使)三倍于；使增至三倍；增加两倍：The company's debts tripled in twelve months. 12个月内这家公司的债务增加了两倍。The acquisition of the chain of stores has tripled the group's turnover. 这家连锁店的收购已使该集团的营业额增至三倍。2. a. three times as much 三倍的：The cost of air-freighting the goods is triple their manufacturing cost. 这批货物的空运费是其制造费的三倍。

**triplicate** n. in triplicate = with an original and two copies 一式三份：to print an invoice in triplicate 将发票印成一式三份；invoicing in triplicate = preparing three copies of invoices 发票一式三份

**trouble** n. problem or difficult situation 麻烦；困难：We are having some computer trouble or some trouble with the computer. 我们的计算机出了点毛病。There was some trouble in the warehouse after the manager was fired. 那位经理被解雇后，这家仓库有些麻烦。

◇ **troubleshooter** n. person whose job is to solve problems in a company(公司里)解决问题的人；排解纠纷者

**trough** n. low point in the economic cycle 商业周期的低潮

**truck** n. (a) large motor vehicle for carrying goods 卡车；运货车：fork-lift truck = type of small tractor with two metal arms in front, used for lifting and moving pallets 铲车；叉式升降装卸机 (b) open railway wagon for carrying goods 铁路散逢货车

◇ **trucker** n. person who drives a truck 卡车驾驶员

◇ **trucking** n. carrying goods in trucks 货运；载货汽车运输：trucking firm 载货汽车运输公司 NOTE: no plural

**true** a. correct or accurate 真实的；正确的；准确的：true copy = exact copy 真实的副本：I certify that this is a true copy. 我证明这是真正的副本。certified as a true copy 证明为真正的副本

**truly** ad. Yours truly or US Truly yours = ending to a formal business letter where you do not know the person you are writing to 您的忠实的(指正式商务信函末尾的客套语)

**trunk call** n. telephone call to a number which is in a different area 长途电话

**trust** 1. n. (a) being confident that something is correct, will work, etc. 信任；信用；信赖：We took his statement on trust. = We accepted his statement withoutexamining it to see if it was correct. 我们盲目地相信了他的话。(b) passing goods or money or secrets to someone who will look after them well 托管;信托: He left his property in trust for his grandchildren. 他将其给孙子们财产让人保管。He was guilty of a breach of trust. = He did not act correctly or honestly when people expected him to. 他犯了背信的错误。He has a position of trust. = His job shows that people believe he will act correctly and honestly. 他有着被人信赖的职位。(c) management of money or property for someone 受委托保管;管理某人的财产: They set up a family trust for their grandchildren. 他们为孙辈们办理了家庭信托. US trust company = organization which supervises the financial affairs of private trusts, executes wills, and acts as a bank to a limited number of customers (美) 信托公司; trust deed = document which sets out the details of a private trust 信托契据;委托书; trust fund = assets (money, securities, property) held in trust for someone 信托基金; investment trust = company whose shares can be bought on the Stock Exchange and whose business is to make money by buying and selling stocks and shares 投资信托公司; unit trust = organization which takes money from investors and invests it in stocks and shares for them under a trust deed 单元信托;互惠投资公司(指根据信托契据向小额投资人收集资金,并将其投资于证券的组织) (d) US small group of companies which control the supply of a product (美) 托拉斯;联合企业

NOTE: no plural for (a) and (b)

2. v. to trust someone with something = to give something to someone to look after 把某物交给某人保管: Can he be trusted with all that cash? 能将那些现金交给他保管吗?

◇ **trustbusting** n. US breaking up monopolies to encourage competition 取缔垄断;反托拉斯

◇ **trustee** n. person who has charge of money in trust or person who is responsible for a family trust 受托管理人;受托人;托管人(指受委托管理某人财产的人): the trustees of the pension fund 养老基金的受托管理人; Trustee Savings Bank = bank which takes savings from small savers, and is guaranteed by the government 信托储蓄银行

◇ **trustworthy** a. (person) who can be trusted 值得信任的;可靠的;可信赖的: Our cashiers are completely trustworthy. 我们的出纳员都是完全可靠的。

**TUC** = TRADES UNION CONGRESS 英国工会联盟

**tune** n. piece of music 调子;曲调: The bank is backing him to the tune of £10,000. = The bank is helping him with a loan of £10,000. 银行将贷款总数达约一万英镑之多支持他。

**turn** 1. n. (a) movement in a circle or change of direction 旋转;转变 (b) profit or commission 利润;佣金: jobber's turn = profit made by a stock jobber 股票中间人的赢利(赚头) (c) stock turn = total value of stocks sold in a year divided by the average value of goods in stock 存货周转率(指用库存货物的平均值除以年售出货物的总值): The company has a stock turn of 6.7. 这家公司的存货周转率为6.7。2. v. to change direction or to go round in a circle 改变方向;旋转

◇ **turn down** v. to refuse 拒绝: The board turned down their takeover bid. 董事会拒绝了他们的兼并递价。The bank turned down their request for a loan. 银行拒绝了他们的贷款请求。The application for a licence was turned down. 申请执照的请求被拒绝了。

◇ **turnkey** n. turnkey operation = dealwhere a company takes all responsibility for constructing, fitting and staffing a building (such as a school or hospital or factory) so that it is completely ready for the purchaser to take over 整套承包合同(指一建筑物从土建,安装到人员配备都由一家公司统包直至最终完工交给买方使用)

◇ **turn out** v. to produce 生产;出产: The factory turns out fifty units per day. 这家工厂每天生产五十件。

◇ **turn over** v. to have a certain amount of sales 营业额达到…: We turn over £2,000 a week. 我们一周的营业额为 2,000 英磅。

◇ **turnover** n. (a) GB amount of sales (英)营业额;销售额: The company's turnover has increased by 235%. 这家公司的营业额已增长了。We based our calculations on the forecast turnover. 我们是按预测的营业额来计算的。stock turnover = total value of stock sold in a year divided by the average value of goods held in stock 库存周转率;存货周转率 (b) changes in staff, when some leave and others join 人员调整: staff turnover or turnover of staff 职员调整 (c) US number of times something is used or sold in a period (usually one year), expressed as a percentage of a total(美)(一年内)某物使用和出售次数(用百分数表示)

◇ **turn round** v. to make (a company) change from making a loss to become profitable (使公司)扭亏为盈: He turned the company round in less than a year. = He made the company profitable in less than a year. 在不到一年时间内他使这家公司扭亏为盈。

◇ **turnround** n. (a) value of goods sold during a year divided by the average value of goods held in stock 商品周转率;存货周转率 (b) action of emptying a ship, plane, etc., and getting it ready for another commercial journey 转港过程 (c) making a company profitable again(公司)扭亏为盈。

**two - part** n. paper (for computers or typewriters) with a top sheet for the original and a second sheet for a copy(用于计算机,打印机)双联纸(上面的一张为原件,第二张为复印件): two - part invoices 双联发票 two - part stationery 双联文件纸

**tycoon** n. important businessman 企业界巨头;

**type** v. to write with a typewriter 打字: He can type quite fast. 他打字打得相当快。All his reports are typed on his portable typewriter. 他所有的报告都是在便携式打字机上打的。

◇ **typewriter** n. machine which prints letters or figures on a piece of paper when a key is pressed 打字机: portable typewriter 便携式打字机;手提式打字机 electronic typewriter 电动打字机

◇ **typewritten** a. written on a typewriter 打字的;用打字机打的: He sent in a typewritten job application. 他呈递了一份用打字机打的职业申请书。

◇ **typing** n. writing letters with a typewriter 打字: typing error = mistake made when using a typewriter 打字错误: The secretary must have made a typing error. 这位秘书一定是出了打字错误。typing pool = group of typists, working together in a company, offering a secretarial service to several departments 打字组(指在公司一起工作, 为几个部门提供秘书服务的打字员们) copy typing = typing documents from hand written originals, not from dictation 手写原稿的打字(不是口授的打字)
NOTE: no plural

◇ **typist** n. person whose job is to write letters using a typewriter 打字员:

copy typist = person who types documentsfrom hand written originals not from dictation 手写原稿打字员 shorthand typist = typist who takes dictation in shorthand and then types it 速记打字员

# Uu

**ultimate** a. last or final 最后的;最终的; ultimate consumer = the person who actually uses the product 最后消费者;用户

◇ **ultimately** ad. in the end 最后;最终地: Ultimately, the management had to agree to the demands of the union. 最后,管理部门还是同意了工会的要求。

◇ **ultimatum** n. statement to a someone that unless he does something within a period of time, action will be taken against him 最后通牒: The union officials argued among themselves over the best way to deal with the ultimatum from the management. 工会官员间进行争论以谋求对付管理部门最后通牒的最好方法。 NOTE: plural is ultimatums or ultimata

**umbrella** n. umbrella organization = large organization which includes several smaller ones 伞式组织

**UN** = THE UNITED NATIONS 联合国

**unable** a. not able 不可能的: The chairman was unable to come to the meeting. 董事长不能到会。

**unacceptable** a. which cannot be accepted. 不能接受的: The terms of the contract are quite unacceptable. 此合同的条款的确无法接受。

**unaccounted for** a. lost, without any

explanation 未说明的;未计入的: Several thousand units are unaccounted for in the stocktaking. 几千件货物未计入存货盘点。

**unanimous** a. where everyone votes in the same way 一致同意的;无异议的: There was a unanimous vote against the proposal 全票反对该提议。 They reached unanimous agreement. 他们达成了一致协议。

◇ **unanimously** ad. with everyone agreeing 毫无异议地;众口一词地: The proposals were adopted unanimously. 该提议毫无异议地被采纳了。

**unaudited** a. which has not been audited 未审核(计)的: unaudited accounts 未审计的帐户

**unauthorized** a. not permitted 未经授权的;未批准的: unauthorized access to the company's records 未经批准接触公司的档案; unauthorized expenditure 未被授权的开支;No unauthorized persons are allowed into the laboratory. 任何人未经许可不得进入该实验室。

**unavailable** a. not available 得不到的;无效的;不能利用的: The following items on your order are temporarily unavailable. 订货单的下列货物暂时不能得到。

◇ **unavailability** n. not being available 不可得到的; NOTE: no plural

**unavoidable** a. which cannot be avoided 无法避免的: Planes are subject to unavoidable delays. 飞机常有不可避免的耽搁。

**unbalanced** a. (budget) which does not balance or which is in deficit(预算)不平衡的;存在赤字的

**uncalled** a. (capital) which a company is authorized to raise and has been issued but is not fully paid 未缴的;未收的(资本)

**uncashed** a. which has not been cashed

未兑现的：uncashed cheques 未兑现支票

**unchanged** a. which has not changed 未改变的；没有变动的

**unchecked** a. which has not been checked 未经核对的；未经检查的：unchecked figures 未经核对的数字

**unclaimed** a. which has not been claimed 无人领取的：unclaimed baggage = cases which have been left with someone and have not been claimed by their owners 无人认领的行李；Unclaimed property or unclaimed baggage will be sold by auction after six months. 无人认领的财产或行李六个月后就将被拍卖。

**uncollected** a. which has not been collected 未收款的：uncollected subscriptions 未收的认股款；uncollected taxes 未收的税款

**unconditional** a. with no conditions 无条件的；无保留的：unconditional acceptance of the offer by the board 董事会无条件接受了这个报价；The offer went unconditional last Thursday. = The takeover bid was accepted by the majority of the shareholders and therefore the conditions attached to it no longer apply. 上周四该兼并递价被无条件接受(指多数股东接受了这个兼并递价，因此，有关的条件就无用了)。

◇ **unconditionally** ad. without imposing any conditions 无条件地：The offer was accepted unconditionally by the trade union. 工会无条件地接受了这项提议。

**unconfirmed** a. which has not been confirmed 未确认的；未认可的：There are unconfirmed reports that our agent has been arrested. 没有证实报道的说我们的代理已被拘留。

**unconstitutional** a. not allowed by the rules or laws of a country or organization 不合宪法的；不合规定的：The chairman ruled that the meeting was unconstitutional. 会议主席裁定该会议

是不符合章程规定的。

**uncontrollable** a. which cannot be controlled 无法控制的；无法抑制的：uncontrollable inflation 无法控制的通货膨胀

**uncrossed cheque** n. cheque which can be cashed anywhere 非划线支票(指在任何地方都可兑换现金的支票)

**undated** a. with no date written 未注日期的；无定期的：He tried to cash an undated cheque. 他试图兑现未注日期的支票。

undated bond = bond with no maturity date 无偿还日期限的债券；无日期债券

**under** prep. (a) lower than or less than 低于；少于：The interest rate is under 10%. 利率低于 10%。Under half of the shareholders accepted the offer. 半数以下的股东接受了此提议。(b) controlled by or according to 按照；根据；依照：Under the terms of the agreement, the goods should be delivered in October. 根据此协议规定，应在十月份交货。He is acting under rule 23 of the unionconstitution. 他在按工会章程 23 条行事。

◇ **under -** prefix less important than or lower than 次于…；低于…

◇ **underbid** v. to bid less than someone 出价低于(某人)

NOTE：underbidding - underbid

◇ **underbidder** n. person who bids less than the person who buys at an auction(拍卖中)出价较低者

◇ **undercapitalized** a. without enough capital 投资不足的；资金短缺的：The company is severely undercapitalized. 这家公司资金严重短缺。

◇ **undercharge** v. to ask for too little money 少收费；少要价；定价过低；索价过低：He undercharged us by £25. 他少收我们 25 英磅。

◇ **undercut** v. to offer something at a

lower price than someone else 削价出售;削低价格;廉价供应

◇ **underdeveloped** a. which has not been developed 不发达的;未开发的: Japan is an underdeveloped market for our products. 对我们的产品来讲,日本是一个未开发的市场。underdeveloped countries = countries which are not fully industrialized 不发达国家

◇ **underemployed** a. with not enough work 就业不足的;不充分就业的: The staff is underemployed because of the cutback in production. 因生产减少,职员未被充分利用。underemployed capital = capital which is not producing enough interest 不产生足够利息的资本

◇ **underemployment** n. (a) situation where workers in a company do not have enough work to do 不充分就业(公司) (b) situation where there is not enough work for all the workers in a country 就业不充分(国家)
NOTE: no plural

◇ **underequipped** a. with not enough equipment 设备不足的;设施不足的

◇ **underestimate** 1. n. estimate which is less than the actual figure 估价过低;低估: The figure of £50,000 in turnover was a considerable underestimate. 营业额50,000英磅这个数字是过低的估计。2. v. to think that something is smaller or not as bad as it really is 对…估价过低;低估;看轻: They underestimated the effects of the strike on their sales. 他们低估了这次罢工对销售的影响。He underestimated the amount of time needed to finish the work. 他低估了完成这项工作所需的时间量

◇ **underlease** n. lease from a tenant to another tenant 转租;分租

◇ **undermanned** a. with not enough staff to do the work 人员配备不足的;缺少人员的

◇ **undermanning** n. having too few workers than are needed to do the company's work 人员配备不足: The company's production is affected by undermanning on the assembly line. 因该装配线人员配备不足,所以该公司的生产受到了影响。
NOTE: no plural

◇ **undermentioned** a. mentioned lower down in a document 下述的

◇ **underpaid** a. not paid enough 工资过低的;少付工资的: Our staff say that they are underpaid and overworked. 我们的职员讲,他们工作过量,却工资过低。

◇ **underrate** v. to value less highly than should be 低估…的价值;低估;对…评价过低: Do not underrate the strength of the competition in the European market. 不要低估了欧州市场的竞争实力。The power of the yen is underrated. 低估了日元的实力。

◇ **undersell** v. to sell more cheaply than 售价比…低;低价出售: to undersell a competitor 以低于竞争者的价格出售; The company is never undersold. = No other company sells goods as cheaply as this one. 无其他公司商品售价比这家公司低或这家公司商品售价比其他公司低。
NOTE: underselling – undersold

◇ **undersigned** n. person who has signed a letter (文件未尾的) 签名者: We, the undersigned: = We, the people who have signed below:我们,本文件签署人:
NOTE: can be followed by a plural verb

◇ **underspend** v. to spend less 少花费;花费得少: He has underspent his budget. = He has spent less than was allowed in the budget. 他的开销低于其预算。
NOTE: underspending – underspent

◇ **understaffed** a. with not enough staff to do the company's work 人员不

足的;人手不够的;劳动力不足的

◇ **understand** v. to know or to see what something means 理解;谅解;明白 NOTE: understanding – understood

◇ **understanding** n. private agreement(非正式的)协议;协定: to come to an understanding about the divisions of the market 就市场的划分达成非正式协议; on the understanding that = on condition that or provided that 如果;在…条件下: We accept the terms of the contract, on the understanding that it has to be ratified by our main board. 如果我们的主要部门批准了此合同,那么该合同的条款我们就接受。

◇ **understate** v. to make something seem less than it really is 打折扣地报道;不如实地陈述: The company accounts understate the real profit. 公司的帐面不如实地陈述了实际利润。

◇ **undertake** v. to agree to do something 同意;接受;承担: to undertake an investigation of the market 接受市场调查; They have undertaken not to sell into our territory. 他们已同意不向我们的推销区推销。 NOTE: undertaking – undertook – has undertaken

◇ **undertaking** n. (a) business 事业;企业: commercial undertaking 商业机构 (b) (legally binding) promise(具有法律效力的)承诺;保证: They have given us a written undertaking not to sell their products in competition with ours. 他们已向我们作了书面保证,不出售与我们有竞争的产品。

◇ **underutilized** a. not used enough 未充分利用的

◇ **undervalued** a. not valued highly enough 低估的;定值过低的: The properties are undervalued on the balance sheet. 资产负债表上的资产定值偏低。 The dollar is undervalued on the foreign exchanges. 外汇市场上,美元定价偏低。

◇ **undervaluation** n. being valued at a lower worth than should be 估价过低;低估价值

◇ **underweight** a. The pack is twenty grams underweight. = The pack weighs twenty grams less than it should. 此包重量少了 20 克。

◇ **underworked** a. not given enough work to do 工作量不足的: The directors think our staff are overpaid and underworked. 董事们认为我们的职员所得的工资太高,工作量却不足。

◇ **underwrite** v. (a) to accept responsibility for 同意 承担…责任;保证: to underwrite a share issue = to guarantee that a share issue will be sold by agreeing to buy all shares which are not subscribed 包销新发行股票; The issue was underwritten by three underwriting companies. 此次证券发行由三家证券包销公司包销。 (b) to insure or to cover (a risk)保险;承保: to underwrite an insurance policy 签署保险单 (c) to agree to pay for costs 同意支付…费用: The government has underwritten the development costs of the project. 政府已同意承担该项目的开发费用。 NOTE: underwriting – underwrote – has underwritten

◇ **underwriter** n. person who underwrites a share issue or an insurance(新股票的)包销者;承购者;保险商: Lloyd's underwriter = member of an insurance group at Lloyd's who accepts to underwrite insurances 劳合社保险人; marine underwriter = person who insures ships and their cargoes 海上保险(海险)承保人

**undischarged bankrupt** n. person who has been declared bankrupt and has not been released from that state 未解除债务的破产者

**undistributed profit** n. profit which has not been distributed as dividends to shareholders 未分配利润；未分盈利（指企业利润中未向持股者分配的红利）

**unearned income** n. money received from interest or dividends, not from salary or profits of one's business 非营业收益；份外收益（指非薪津或企业利润所得，而来自于利息或股息）

**uneconomic** a. which does not make a commercial profit 不经济的；不实用的：It is an uneconomic proposition. = It will not be commercially profitable. 不赚钱的生意（无商业利润）。uneconomic rent = rent which is not enough to cover costs 不经济的租金（指租金不抵成本）

**unemployed** a. not employed or without any work 失业的；闲置的：unemployed office workers = office workers with no jobs 无工作职员；the unemployed = the people without any jobs 失业者

◇ **unemployment** n. lack of work 失业：mass unemployment = unemployment of large numbers of workers 大量工人失业；unemployment benefit or US unemployment compensation = payment made to someone who is unemployed 失业津贴；失业救济金
NOTE: no plural

**unfair** a. unfair competition = trying to do better than another company by using techniques such as importing foreign goods at very low prices or by wrongly criticizing a competitor's products 不正当（不公平）竞争：unfair dismissal = removing someone from a job for reasons which are not fair 不合理解雇

**unfavourable** a. not favourable 不利的；不适宜的：unfavourable balance of trade = situation where a country imports more than it exports 贸易逆差；unfavourable exchange rate = exchange rate which gives an amount of foreign currency for the home currency which is not good for trade 不利的外汇汇率：

The unfavourable exchange rate hit the country's exports. 不利的汇率打击了这个国家的出口。

**unfulfilled** a. (order) which has not yet been supplied 未履行的；未满足的

**ungeared** a. with no borrowings 无借款的；无货款的；未举债

**unilateral** a. on one side only or done by one party only 单方面的；一方的：They took the unilateral decision to cancel the contract. 他们单方面决定取消了这份合同。

◇ **unilaterally** ad. by one party only 单方面地：They cancelled the contract unilaterally. 他们单方面取消了合同。

**uninsured** ad. not insured 未保过险的

**union** n. (a) trade union or trades union or US labor union = organization which represents workers who are its members in discussions with management about wages and conditions of work 工会：union agreement = agreement between a management and a trade union over wages and conditions of work 管理部门与工会之间的协议；union dues or union subscription = payment made by workers to belong to a union 工会会费；union officials = paid organizers of a union 工会官员；union recognition = act of agreeing that a union can act on behalf of staff in a company 工会认可 (b) customs union = agreement between several countries that goods can go between them without paying duty, while goods from other countries have special duties charged on them 关税同盟（指几个国家间缔结的建立统一关税，彼此间的商品无需缴纳进出口关税，而对来自其他国家的商品则实行进出口关税）

◇ **unionist** n. member of a trade union 工会成员（会员）

◇ **unionized** a. (company) where the members of staff belong to a trade union (公司)组织成工会的；成立工会的

**unique** a. special or with nothing like it 特别的；独一无二的：unique selling proposition = special quality of a product which makes it different from other goods and therefore attractive to customers 独一无二的销售买卖

**unissued capital** n. capital which a company is authorized to issue but has not issued as shares 未发行股本(指允许发行但尚未发行的股票)

**unit** n. (a) single product for sale 单位，单件：unit cost = the cost of one item (i. e total product costs divided by the number of units produced)单位成本；unit price = the price of one item 单价 (b) separate piece of equipment or furniture(设备或家具的)件；套：display unit = special stand for showing goods for sale 陈列台；visual display unit = screen attached to a computer which shows the information stored in the computer 视觉显示屏；(c) factory unit = single building on an industrial estate(工业区的)单个建筑物 (d) production unit = separate small group of workers which produces a certain product 生产单位：research unit = separate small group of research workers 研究单位 (e) monetary unit or unit of currency = main item of currency of a country (a dollar, pound, yen etc.) 货币单位(美元；英磅，日元等)：unit of account = currency used for calculating the EEC budget and farm prices 记帐单位；计价单位(指用于计算欧共体各成员国预算和农产品价格的货币) (f) single share in a unit trust(单位信托中的)单股

**unit trust** n. organization which takes money from small investors and invests it in stocks and shares for them under a trust deed, the investment being in the form of shares (or units) in the trust 单位信托；互惠投资公司(指按信托契据向小额投资人收集资金，并代投资人投资于股票和债券的组织)

**unite** v. to join together 联合；团结：The directors united with the managers to reject the takeover bid. 董事们联合经理们一起抵制兼并通价。United Nations = organization which links the countries of the world to promote good relations between them 联合国

**unladen** a. empty or without a cargo 空的；未载货的

**unlawful** a. against the law or not legal 非法的；不合法的

**unlimited** a. with no limits 无限的：The bank offered him unlimited credit. 银行向他提供了无限期信贷。unlimited liability = situation where a sole trader or each partner is responsible for all the firm's debts with no limit at the amount each may have to pay 无限责任

**unlined** a. unlined paper = paper with no lines printed on it 无线条纸

**unlisted** a. unlisted securities = shares which are not listed on the Stock Exchange 未上市证券；非挂牌证券(指未在证券交易所登记挂牌的证券)：unlisted securities market = market for buying and selling shares which are not listed on the Stock Exchange 未在证券交易所挂牌价上市证券市场

**unload** v. (a) to take goods off (a ship, etc.)(从船等交通工具上)卸货：The ship is unloading at Hamburg. 这艘船正在汉堡港卸货。We need a fork - lift truck to unload the lorry. 我们需要一辆铲车从卡车上卸货。We unloaded the spare parts at Lagos. 我们把备件卸在拉各斯。There are six unloading facilities for container ships. 有六台用于集装箱船的卸载设备。(b) to sell (shares which do not seem attractive) 倾销；抛售；脱手(似乎不走俏的股票)：We tried to unload our shareholding as soon as the company published its accounts. 公司一公布其帐目，我们就设法将我们的

股票抛售出去。

**unobtainable** a. which cannot be obtained 无法获得的；不能得到的

**unofficial** a. not official 非正式的；非官方的：unofficial strike = strike by local workers which has not been approved by the main union 非官方性罢工

◇ **unofficially** a. not officially 非正式地；非官方地：The tax office told the company unofficially that it would be prosecuted. 税务局非正式地通知这家公司，它可能会被起诉。

**unpaid** a. not paid 未付的；无报酬的；未缴纳的：unpaid holiday = holiday where the worker does not receive any pay 无工资假期（日）（指休假期间，工人拿不到工资）；unpaid invoices = invoices which have not been paid 尚未付款的发票

**unprofitable** a. which is not profitable 无利益的；赚不到钱的

**unquoted shares** pl. n. shares which have no Stock Exchange quotation 未挂牌股票；未报价的股票

**unredeemed pledge** n. pledge which the borrower has not claimed back by paying back his loan 未赎回的抵押；未收回抵押

**unregistered** a. (company) which has not been registered 未注册的；未登记的

**unreliable** a. which cannot be relied on 不可靠的；靠不住的：The postal service is very unreliable. 该邮政服务是很不可靠的。

**unsealed envelope** n. envelope where the flap has been pushed into the back of the envelope, not stuck down（未封口的）信封

**unsecured** a. unsecured creditor = creditor who is owed money, but has no security from the debtor for it 无担保债权人：unsecured debt = debt which is not guaranteed by assets 无担保债务；unsecured loan = loan made with no security 无担保贷款；信用放款

**unseen** a. not seen 未看见地；未被注意地：to buy something sight unseen = to buy something without having inspected it 未经仔细查看购买某物

**unsettled** a. which changes often or which is upset 不安定的；易变的：The market was unsettled by the news of the failure of the takeover bid. 由于兼并递价失败的消息，市场不稳定。

**unskilled** a. without any particular skill 不熟练的；没有经验的；不灵巧的：unskilled labour or unskilled workforce or unskilled workers 非熟练劳动力（工作人员，工人）

**unsocial** a. to work unsocial hours = to work at times (i. e. in the evening or at night or during public holidays) when most people are not at work 在休息时间工作（如：傍晚，夜里或公共假日）

**unsold** a. not sold 未售出的；未出售的：Unsold items will be scrapped. 未售出的商品将被废弃。

**unsolicited** a. which has not been asked for 未经请求的；主动提供的：an unsolicited gift 主动提供的礼物；unsolicited testimonial = letter praising someone or a product without the writer having been asked to write it(顾客)主动送来的表扬信

**unstable** a. not stable, or changing frequently 不稳定的；易变的；反复无常的：unstable exchange rates 不稳定汇率

**unsubsidized** a. with no subsidy 无补贴金的

**unsuccessful** a. not successful 不成功的；失败的：an unsuccessful businessman 一位不成功的商人；The project was expensive and unsuccessful. 这个项目造价高，又不成功。

◇ **unsuccessfully** ad. with no success 不成功的；失败地：The company unsuccessfully tried to break into the South American market. 这家公司试图打入南

美市场是失败的。

**untrue** a. not true 不真实的;虚假的

**unused** a. which has not been used 未用的;新的: We are trying to sell off six unused typewriters. 我们正设法廉价出售六台未用过的打字机。

**unwaged** a. the unwaged = people with no jobs 失业者
NOTE: is followed by a plural verb

**unwritten** a. unwritten agreement = agreement which has been reached in speaking ( such as in a telephone conversation) but has not been written down 非书面协议

**up** ad. & prep. in a higher position or to a higher position 在上(面、部);向(朝)上;在…以上: The inflation rate is going up steadily. 通货膨胀正逐步上升。Shares were up slightly at the end of the day. 今天收盘时股票有些上升。

**up to** ad. as far as or as high as 到远;直到;最多到;高达: We will buy at prices up to £25. 我们购物的价格最多到25英磅。

◇ **up to date** a. current or recent or modern 现代的;最新的: an up - to - date computer system 最新的计算机系统; to bring something up to date = to add the latest information or equipment to something 使某物现代化(最新)(如:信息,设备等); to keep something up to date = to keep adding information to something so that it always has the latest information in it 使…保持最新内容: We spend a lot of time keeping our mailing list up to date. 我们花费了许多时间,使我们的通讯录保持最新内容。

**update** 1. n. information added to something to make it up to date 现代化;(关于…的)最新资料 2. v. to revise something so that it is always up to date 更新;使不过时;使现代化: The figures are updated annually. 这些数字每年都要更新。

**up front** ad. in advance 预先;事先: money up front = payment in advance 预付款; They are asking for £100,000 up front before they will consider the deal. 他们要预付10万英磅之后才考虑这笔买卖。He had to put money up front before he could clinch the deal. 他必须预付定金才能达成这笔交易。

**upgrade** v. to increase the importance of someone or of a job 升级;提高;增加(某人或某项工作的重要性): His job has been upgraded to senior manager level. 他已被提升到高级管理人员层。

**upkeep** n. cost of keeping a building or machine in good order(房屋,设备等的)维修费;保养费
NOTE: no plural

**uplift** n. increase 增加: The contract provides for an annual uplift of charges. 本合同规定费用要逐年增加。

**up market** ad. more expensive or appealing to a wealthy section of the population 昂贵地;高消费地: The company has decided to move up market. = The company has decided to start to produce more luxury items. 公司已决定走向高档品市场。

**upset price** n. lowest price which the seller will accept at an auction 最低拍卖限价;开拍价格;拍卖底价

**upturn** n. movement towards higher sales or profits 好转;上升;提高: an upturn in the economy 经济形势好转; an upturn in the market 市场情况好转

**upward** a. towards a higher position 向上的;上升的: an upward movement 向上移动

◇ **upwards** ad. towards a higher position The market moved upwards after the news of the budget. 这项预算公布之后,市场价格上涨了。
NOTE: US English uses upward as both a. and ad.

**urgent** a. which has to be done quickly

紧急的;急迫的:

◇ **urgently** ad. immediately 急切地; 马上;立刻

**usage** n. how something is used 用法; 用途

NOTE: no plural

**use** 1. n. way in which something can be used 使用;用法;利用: directions for use = instructions on how to run a machine(机器) 使用说明(指南); to make use of something = to use something 利用;使用; in use = being worked 在使用着: The computer is in use twenty-four hours a day. 这台计算机一天 24 小时都在用。 items for personal use = items which a person will use for himself, not on behalf of the company 个人用品; He has the use of a company car. = He has a company car which he uses privately. 他能用公司的车(公车私用)。 land zoned for industrial use = land where planning permission has been given to build factories 准予建造工厂的用地。 2. v. to take a machine, a company, a process, etc., and work with it 使用;操作: We use airmail for all our overseas correspondence. 我们所有的海外通信都使用航空邮件。 The photocopier is being used all the time. 这台影印机一直在用。 They use free-lancers for most of their work. 他们的大部分工作都由自由职业者来做。

◇ **useful** a. which can help 有用的;有帮助的

◇ **user** n. person who uses something 用户;使用者: end user = person who actually uses a product 最终用户;直接用户(指实际使用某一产品的人); user's guide or handbook = book showing someone how to use something 用户指南;使用说明

◇ **user – friendly** a. which a user finds easy to work(用户)易于操作的; 易于使用的: These programs are really user – friendly. 这些程序确实易于用户使用。

**USM** = UNLISTED SECURITIES MARKET 无牌价证券市场;未上市证券交易市场

**USP** = UNIQUE SELLING PROPOSITION 独一无二的销售买卖

**usual** a. normal or ordinary 平常的;普通的;通常的: Our usual terms or usual conditions are thirty days' credit. 我们的通常条件是三十天的信贷。 The usual practice is to have the contract signed by the MD. 通常惯例是合同要由总经理签字。 The usual hours of work are from 9:30 to 5:30. 正常的工作时间是上午 9:30 到下午 5:30。

**usury** n. lending money at high interest 高利贷;重利

NOTE: no plural

**utilize** v. to use 使用;利用

◇ **utilization** n. making use of something 使用;利用: capacity utilization = using something as much as possible 生产能力的利用

NOTE: no plural

**vacancy** n. empty place or room; job which is not filled 空位;空房;空缺: We advertised a vacancy in the local press. 我们在当地报纸上登了一则空缺招聘广告。 We have been unable to fill the vacancy for a skilled machinist. 我们一直无法填补一位熟练机工的空缺。 They have a vacancy for a secretary. 他们有一个秘书的空缺。 job vacancies = jobs which are empty and need people to do them 职务空缺; vacancy rate = average number of rooms empty in a hotel over a period of time, shown as a percentage of the total number of rooms 客房率 ( 旅馆、饭店在一定时期的房间 )

◇ **vacant** a. empty or not occupied 空的；未被占用的： vacant possession = being able to occupy a property immediately after buying itbecause it is empty 空屋出卖 ( 广告用语 )： The house is for sale with vacant possession. 此房以空屋出卖方式出售。 situations vacant or appointments vacant = list ( in a newspaper ) of jobs which are available ( 报纸上的 ) 招聘广告

**vacate** v. to vacate the premises = to leave premises, so that they become empty 腾出房屋

◇ **vacation** n. (a) GB period when the law courts are closed ( 英 )( 法庭的 ) 休庭期 (b) US holiday or period when people are not working ( 美 ) 假日；度假期： The CEO is on vacation in Florida. 总经理首席业务代表去佛罗里达度假了。

**valid** a. (a) which is acceptable because it is true 正当的；正确的： That is not a valid argument or excuse. 那是不正确的论点。 (b) which can be used lawfully 有效的；有法律效力的： The contract is not valid if it has not been witnessed. 如这份合同没有人作证签名就无效。 Ticket which is valid for three months。 有效期为三个月的票。 He was carrying a valid passport. 他带的是一本有效的护照。

◇ **validate** v. (a) to check to see if something is correct 证实；确认： The document was validated by the bank. 此单据得到了银行确认。 (b) to make ( something ) valid 使生效；使合法化

◇ **validation** n. act of making something valid 使生效；批准；确认
NOTE： no plural

◇ **validity** n. being valid 有效性；合法化 period of validity = length of time for which a document is valid 有效期

NOTE： no plural

**valorem** see AD VALOREM 按价；照价

**valuable** a. which is worth a lot of money 贵重的；有价值的 valuable property or valuables = personal items which are worth a lot of money ( 私人的 ) 贵重物品

◇ **valuation** n. estimate of how much something is worth 估价；计价；评价： to ask for a valuation of a property before making an offer for it 在发价之前，要对财产进行估价； stock valuation = estimating the value of stock at the end of an accounting period 股票估价； to buy a shop with stock at valuation = to pay for the stock the same amount as its value asestimated by a valuer 按存货的估价购买商店

◇ **value** 1. n. amount of money which something is worth 价值： He imported goods to the value of £ 250. 他进口了价值为 250 英磅的货物。 the fall in the value of sterling 英镑的币值下降；The valuer put the value of the stock at £ 25,000. 估价人估算的存货价值为 25,000 英镑。 good value ( for money ) = a bargain or something which is worth the price paid for it 物有所值；优良价值；等值 ( 指与所付价钱相称的产品 )： That restaurant gives value for money. 这家餐馆货真价实。 Buy that computer now - it is very good value. 现在买那台计算机真是很值的。 Holidays in Italy are good value because of the exchange rate. 因汇率的缘故，在意大利度假是值得的。 to rise in value or to fall in value = to be worth more or less 价值升高或下跌； asset value = value of a company calculated by adding together all itsassets 资产价值； book value = value as recorded in the company＇s accounts 帐面价值； "Sample only - of no commercial value" = not worth anything if sold "只是样品——无商业价值" declared value = value of goods entered on a customs declaration form 设定价值；申报价值；discounted value = difference between the face value of a share and its lower market price 贴现价值；face value = value written on a coin or banknote or share 票面价值；面额；market value = value of an asset or of a product or of a company, if sold today 市场价值；par value = value written on a share certificate 票面价值；面值；scarcity value = value of something which is worth a lot because it is rare and there is a large demand for it 稀货价值；surrender value = money which an insurer will pay if an insurance policy is given up before maturity date 退保金额（指被保险人在偿还日前放弃保险单时，保险人应付给被保险人的金额）2. v. to estimate how much money something is worth 估价：He valued the stock at £25,000. 他估计这批货物价值 25,000。英镑。We are having the jewellery valued for insurance. 我们正为入保险的珠宝请人估价。

◇ **Value Added Tax** n. tax imposed as a percentage of the invoice value of goods and services 增值税（指按商品发票面值征收一定百分比的间接税）

◇ **valuer** n. person who estimates how much money something is worth 估价者；评估人

**van** n. small goods vehicle 小型货车：delivery van = van for delivering goods to customers（为顾客送货的）小型货车

**variable** a. which changes 可变的；变换的：variable costs = money paid to produce a product which increases with the quantity made（such as wages, raw materials）可变成本；直接成本（指生产一种产品所付的钱，可随产量的增加而变动，如：工资，原材料等）

◇ **variability** n. being variable 可变性
NOTE: no plural

◇ **variance** n. difference 变化；差异；

不同：budget variance = difference between the cost as estimated for the budget, and the actual cost 预算差异（指预算金额与实际金额之间的差额）；at variance with = which does not agree with 与…不一致；与…不和：The actual sales are at variance with the sales reported by the reps. 实际销售额与销售代表所报的（销售额）不一致。

◇ **variation** n. amount by which something changes 变动；差异：seasonal variations = changes which take place because of the seasons 季节变动；季节波动；seasonal variations in buying patterns 购买的模式随季节变动

**variety** n. different types of things 变化，多样性；多种：The shop stocks a variety of goods. 这家商店备有各种商品。We had a variety of visitors at the office today. 今天我们办公室有各种各样的来访者。US variety store = shop selling a wide range of usually cheap items（美）杂货店（指出售多种廉价商品的商店）

◇ **vary** v. to change or to differ 变化；使变动；不同；改变：The gross margin varies from quarter to quarter. 毛利随季变动。We try to prevent the flow of production from varying in the factory. 我们试图阻止改变该厂的生产流程。

**VAT** = VALUE ADDED TAX 增值税：The invoice includes VAT at 15%. 此发票含 15% 增值税。The government is proposing to increase VAT to 17.5%. 政府计划将增值税增加到 17.5%。Some items（such as books）are zero-rated for VAT. 有些商品（如：书籍）是免增值税的。He does not charge VAT because he asks for payment in cash. 因他要求用现金支付，所以不征增值税。VAT declaration = statement declaring VAT income to the VAT office 增值税申报；VAT invoicing = sending of an invoice including VAT 开出的含增值税发票；VAT invoice = invoice which shows VAT separately(单独显示增值税的)增值税发票；VAT inspector = government official who examines VAT returns and checks that VAT is being paid 增值税稽查员；VAT office = government office dealing with the collection of VAT in an area(某一地区)负责征收增值税的办事处

◇ **VAT man or vatman** n. VAT inspector 增值税税务员

**VDU or VDT** = VISUAL DISPLAY UNIT or VISUAL DISPLAY TERMINAL 视觉显示装置；视觉显示终端

**vehicle** n. machine with wheels, used to carry goods or passengers on a road 交通工具；运输工具；机动车(指用于载客或运货的带轮车辆)：commercial vehicle or goods vehicle = van or truck used for business purposes 商用货车；heavy goods vehicle = very large lorry 大型载货车；Goods vehicles can park in the loading bay. 货车可停在装卸货物场道里。

**vending** n. selling 出售：(automatic) vending machine = machine which provides drinks, cigarettes, etc., when a coin is put in(自动的)售货机

◇ **vendor** n. (a) person who sells (a property)卖主；小贩：the solicitor acting on behalf of the vendor 代表卖主的律师。(b) street vendor = person who sells food or small items in the street 街头摊贩

**venture** 1. n. business or commercial deal which involves a risk 商业冒险；投机：He lost money on several import ventures. 在几宗进口冒险生意中他亏了本。She has started a new venture – a computer shop. 她已开办了一个新的冒险企业——一家计算机商店。joint venture = very large business project where two or more companies, often from different countries, join together 合营企业；合资公司；venture capital =

capital for investment which may easily be lost in risky projects, but can also provide high returns 投机资本；风险资本(指可带来高利润，但风险又大的资金或投资) 2. v. to risk (money)投机；冒险

**venue** n. place where a meeting is to be held 会场；集会地点：We have changed the venue for the conference. 我们已改换了会议地点。What is the venue for the exhibition? 展览会的地点在哪里？

**verbal** a. using spoken words, not writing 口头的；非书面的：verbal agreement = agreement which is spoken (such as over the telephone)(如：通过电话)口头协议

◇ **verbally** ad. using spoken words, not writing 以口头方式；口头地；非书面地：They agreed to the terms verbally, and then started to draft the contract. 他们口头上同意了那些条件，然后开始起草合同。

**verify** v. to check to see if something is correct 证明；检查；核实

◇ **verification** n. checking if something is correct 证明；审核；核对：The shipment was allowed into the country after verification of the documents by the customs. 海关核实完单据后，那批货才被允许进入这个国家。

**vertical** a. upright or straight up or down 垂直的；纵的；直立的：vertical communication = communication between senior managers via the middle management to the workers 纵向联络(指高层经理们与工人之间通过中层经理人员进行联络)；vertical integration = joining two businesses together which deal with different stages in the production or sale of a product 纵向一体化(指企业联合对某一产品的生产或销售的不同阶段)

**vessel** n. ship 船舶：merchant vessel = commercial ship which carries a cargo 商

船

**vested** a. vested interest = special interest in keeping an existing state of affairs 既得利益；占有权益（指用于维持现有有事态的特别权益）：She has a vested interest in keeping the business working. = She wants to keep the business working because she will make more money if it does. 她在维持企业运转方面，她才有既得利益。

**vet** v. to examine something carefully 仔细观察（检查）：All candidates have to be vetted by the managing director. 所有的候选人都必须由总经理仔细审查。The contract has been sent to the legal department for vetting. 这份合同已送法律部门进行审查。
NOTE: vetting – vetted

**via** prep. using (a means or a route) 经由（路线）；通过（方式；渠道等）：The shipment is going via the Suez Canal. 这批货将经过苏伊士运河。We are sending the cheque via our office in New York. 我们将通过我们在纽约的办事处转交这张支票。They sent the message via the telex line. 他们通过电传发送这个信息。

**viable** a. which can work in practice 可行的；有实用性的：not commercially viable = not likely to make a profit 无商业利润（价值）的（指不可能获利）
◇ **viability** n. being viable or being able to make a profit 可行性；获利性
NOTE: no plural

**vice -** prefix deputy or second in command 代理；次；副：He is the vice - chairman of an industrial group. 他是一家产业集团的副董事长。She was appointed to the vice - chairmanship of the committee. 她被任命为该委员会的副主席。
◇ **vice - president** n. US one of the executive directors of a company（美）副总裁：senior vice - president = one of a few main executive directors of a company (公司)资深副总裁之一

**view** n. way of thinking about something 看法；意见；见解：We asked the sales manager for his views on the reorganization of the reps' territories. 我们征求了销售经理对调整推销员的区域的意见。The chairman takes the view that credit should never be longer than thirty days. 董事长认为信用证决不能超过三十天。to take the long view = to plan for a long period before your current investment will become profitable 从长远观点来看；in view of = because of 由于…；鉴于…；考虑到… In view of the falling exchange rate, we have redrafted oursales forecasts. 由于汇率不断下跌，我们已重新起草销售预测。

**vigorous** a. energetic or very active 有力的；活跃的：We are planning a vigorous publicity campaign. 我们打算进行一次强有力的宣传运动。

**VIP** = VERY IMPORTANT PERSON 要人；大人物：VIP lounge = special room at an airport for important travellers 要人休息室（指机场专为重要旅客设立的接待室）；We laid on VIP treatment for our visitors or we gave our visitors a VIP reception . = We arranged for our visitors to be looked after and entertained well. 我们为来访者提供了要人级侍遇（指我们好好款待了客人们）。

**visa** n. special document or special stamp in a passport which allows someone to enter a country（护照等上的）签证：You will need a visa before you go to the USA. 去美国之前，你需要签证。He filled in his visa application form. 他填写了证证申请表。entry visa = visa allowing some one to enter a country 入境签证 multiple entry visa = visa allowing someone to enter a country many times（可多次使用的）入境签证；tourist visa = visa which allows a person to visit a country for a short time on holiday 旅游签证; transit visa = visa which allows someone to spend a short time in one country while travelling to another country 过境签证;

**visible** a. which can be seen visible imports or exports = real products which are imported or exported 有形进口或出口(指实际产品进或出口)

**visit** 1. n. short stay in a place 短期逗留: We are expecting a visit from our German agents. 我们期望我们的德国代理来此短期逗留。He is on a business visit to London. 他短期出差去伦敦了。We had a visit from the VAT inspector。增值税税务员来过我们这儿了。2. v. to go to a place or to see someone for a short time 访问;拜访;游览: He spent a week in Scotland, visiting clients in Edinburghand Glasgow. 他在苏格兰呆了一周,访问了爱丁堡和格拉斯哥的客户。The trade delegation visited the Ministry of Commerce. 这个贸易代表团参观了商业部。

◇ **visitor** n. person who visits 访问者;参观者: The chairman showed the Japanese visitors round the factory. 董事长领日本客人参观了这家工厂。visitors' bureau = office which deals with visitors' questions 旅客问讯处

**visual** a. which can be seen 视觉的;看得见的; visual display terminal or visual display unit = screen attached to a computer which shows the information stored in the computer 视觉显示装置(终端)

**vivos** n. gift inter vivos = present given to another living person 生前的赠与

**vocation** n. type of job which you feel you want to do; wanting to be in a certain type of job 职业;行业;业务: He followed his vocation and became an accountant. 他按着他的专业学,并成了一名会计。

◇ **vocational** a. referring to a choice of job 职业上的;行业的: vocational guidance = helping young people to choose a suitable job 就业指导;职业指南; vocational training = training for a particular job 职业培训;业务培训

**void** 1. a. not legally valid 无效的;作废的: The contract was declared null and void. = The contract was said to be no longer valid. 此合同被宣布无效。2. v. to void a contract = to make a contract invalid 使合同无效

**volume** n. quantity of items 数量;产量;容量: volume discount = discount given to customer who buys a large quantity of goods 多买折扣;大批量折扣(指给购买商品数量大的顾客的折扣); volume of output = number of items produced 产量; volume of sales or sales volume = number of items sold 销售额; low or high volume of sales = small or large number of items sold 销售额大或小; volume of trade or volume of business = number of items sold or number of shares sold on the Stock Exchange during a day's trading 贸易量;营业数量;(股票)成交额: The company has maintained the same volume of business in spite of the recession. 尽管经济衰退,这家公司仍保持了相同的贸易额。

**voluntary** a. (a) done without being forced 自愿的: voluntary liquidation = situation where a company itself decides it must close and sell its assets 自愿清理;自原清偿(指公司自身决定关闭并出售其资产); voluntary redundancy = situation where a worker asks to be made redundant 自愿裁员 (b) done without being paid 义务的;无偿的;志愿的: voluntary organization = organization which has no paid staff 义务组织(团体)(此团体的工作人员不拿报酬,都是义务工)

◇ **voluntarily** ad. without being forced or paid 自愿地;自发地

**vote** 1. n. marking a paper, holding up yourhand, etc. , to show your opinion or to show who you want to be elected 投票;表决;选举(写条,举手等,表示自己的意见或选择): to take a vote on a proposal or to put a proposal to the vote = to ask people present at a meeting to say if they do or do not agree with the proposal 就某项提议投票表决; block vote = casting of a large number of votes (such as of a trade union delegation) all together in the same way 集体投票表决; casting vote = vote used by the chairman in the case where the votes for and against a proposal are equal 决定权;决定性一票: The chairman has the casting vote. 董事长有决定性一票. He used his casting vote to block the motion. 他用决定性一票反对此项动议. postal vote = election where the voters send in their voting papers by post 邮政选举(指选举人通过邮寄其选票进行投票表决) 2. v. to show an opinion by marking a paper or by holding up your hand at a meeting 投票: The meeting voted to close the factory. 会议投票决定关闭这家工厂. 52% of the members voted for Mr Smith as chairman. 52%委员们投票选举史密斯先生为主席. to vote for a proposal or to vote against a proposal = to say that you agree or do not agree with a proposal 投票赞成(反对)某项议案; Two directors were voted off the board at the AGM. The AGM voted to dismiss two directors. 年终股东大会上投票罢免了两位董事。 She was voted on to the committee. = She was elected a member of the committee. 她被选为该委员会的委员。

◇ **voter** n. person who votes 选举人;投票人

◇ **voting** n. act of making a vote 投票: voting paper = paper on which the voter puts a cross to show for whom he wants to vote 选票; voting rights = rights of shareholders to voting at company meetings 投票权;表决权(指股东在公司会议上的投票权); non – voting shares = shares which do not allow the shareholder to vote at company meetings 无投票权的股票

NOTE: no plural

**voucher** n. (a) paper which is given instead of money 代金券;代用券(可代替现金使用的票券): cash voucher = paper which can be exchanged for cash 现金凭单;现金代用券(指可兑换现金的凭单); With every £20 of purchases, the customer gets a cash voucher to the value of £2. 每购买20英镑的物品,顾客可得到价值为2英镑的现金代用券一张. gift voucher = card, bought in a store, which is given as a present and which must be exchanged in that store for goods 赠与券;礼品券(一种商店作为礼物赠送的代用券,凭此券可在该店内兑换商品); luncheon voucher = ticket, given by an employer to a worker, which can be exchanged in a restaurant for food 赠与午餐券(一种由雇主发给工人的票证,凭此票证工人们可在某个餐馆内免费就餐) (b) written document from an auditor to show that the accounts are correct or that money has really been paid 收据;证书;证明

**voyage** n. long journey by ship(乘船)长途旅行

# Ww

**wage** n. money paid (usually in cash each week) to a worker for work done 工资;工钱(通常按周以现金支付给工人): She is earning a good wage or good wages in the supermarket. 她在超级市场挣着优厚的工资。basic wage = normal pay without any extra payments 基本工资：The basic wage is £110 a week, but you can expect to earn more than that with overtime. 基本工资一周是 110 英镑, 但你可加班多挣。hourly wage or wage per hour = amount of money paid for an hour's work 小时工资；minimum wage = lowest hourly wage which a company can legally pay its workers 最低限度工资；wage adjustments = changes made to wages 工资调整；wage claim = asking for an increase in wages 提高工资的要求；wages clerk = office worker who deals with the pay of other workers 负责工资工作的职员；wage differentials = differences in salary between workers in similar types of jobs 工资差别；工资差额；wage freeze or freeze on wages = period when wages are not allowed to increase 工资冻结；wage levels = rates of pay for different types of work 工资水平；工资标准；wage negotiations = discussions between management and workers about pay 工资谈判；wage packet = envelope containing money and pay slip 工资袋；wages policy = government policy on what percentage increases should be paid to workers 工资政策；wage - price spiral = situation where price rises encourage higher wage demands which in turn make prices rise 工资物价螺旋式上升；wage scale = list of wages, showing different rates of pay for different jobs in the same company 工资等级；工资级差 NOTE: wages is more usual when referring to money earned, but wage is used before other nouns

◇ **wage - earner** n. person who earns money paid weekly in a job 靠工资生活者；雇拥劳动者；

◇ **wage - earning** a. the wage - earning population = people who have jobs and earn money 工薪阶层(指靠工资收入生活的阶层)

**wagon** n. goods truck used on the railway(铁路上的)货车

**waive** v. to give up (a right)放弃(权利、要求等)；弃权：He waived his claim to the estate. 他放弃了他对该财产要求权。to waive a payment = to say that payment is not necessary 不需报酬；无偿

◇ **waiver** n. giving up (a right) or removing the conditions (of a rule)弃放(权利、要求)；免除(制度；规定等)：If you want to work without a permit, you will have to apply for a waiver. 如你想在未经许可的情况下工作的话, 你必须申请豁免。waiver clause = clause in a contract giving the conditions under which the rights in the contract can be given up 弃权条款(指合同中的一条款,规定订约方可放弃合同权利的条件)

**walk** v. to go on foot 步行：He walks to the office every morning. 每天早晨他都步行去办公室。The visitors walked round the factory. 参观者们在工厂各处走了走。

◇ **walk off** v. to go on strike or to stop working and leave an office or factory 罢工；停止工作：The builders walked off the site because they said it was too dangerous. 因他们讲太危险了, 所以建筑工人们都离开了工地。

◇ **walk out** v. to go on strike or to stop working and leave an office or factory 罢工；停止工作：The whole workforce walked out in protest. 全体工作人员退席以示抗议。

◇ **walk - out** n. strike or stopping work 罢工；停业：Production has been held up by the walk - out of the workers. 因工人罢工, 生产已停顿。 NOTE: plural is walk - outs

**Wall Street** n. street in New York

where the Stock Exchange is situated; theAmerican financial centre 华尔街(美国纽约市一条街道的名称,著名的证券交易所所在地,是美国的金融中心): a Wall Street analyst 华尔街分析家; She writes the Wall Street column in the newspaper. 在报纸上她编写华尔街专栏。

**want** n. thing which is needed 需求;需要: want ads = advertisements listed in a newspaper under special headings(such as "property for sale", or "jobs wanted")求物广告;招聘广告; to draw up a wants list = to make a list of things which you need 开列所需物品的清单

**war** n. fighting or argument between countries or companies 战争;竞争(公司间的): price war 价格战; tariff war 关税战

**warehouse** 1. n. large building where goods are stored 仓库;货栈: bonded warehouse = warehouse where goods are stored until excise duty has been paid 保税仓库;保税关栈; warehouse capacity = space available in a warehouse 仓库容量; price ex warehouse = price for a product which is to be collected from the manufacturer's or agent's warehouse and so does not include delivery 卖方仓库交货价 2. v. to store (goods) in a warehouse(将…(货物)存放在仓库里

◇ **warehousing** n. act of storing goods 存货;存货栈 NOTE: no plural

◇ **warehouseman** n. person who works in a warehouse 仓库工作人员;仓库员

**warn** v. to say that there is a possible danger 警告;告诫: He warned the shareholders that the dividend might be cut. 他提醒股东红利可能削减。The government warned of possible import duties. 政府告诫了可能要征的进口税。NOTE: you warn someone of something, or that something may happen

◇ **warning** n. notice of possible danger 警告;告诫: to issue a warning 发出警告;给予警告; Warning notices were put up around the construction site. 工地周围贴满了警告通知。

**warrant** 1. n. official document which allows someone to do something 保证;证明;许可证: dividend warrant = cheque which makes payment of a dividend 股息单;股息证书; share warrant = document which says that someone has the right to a number ofshares in a company 股份保证书;认股权 2. v. (a) to guarantee 担保;保证(货物)的质量: All the spare parts are warranted. 所有的备件都是保证质量的。(b) to show that something is reasonable 证明…是正确的;使…合理: The company's volume of trade with the USA does not warrant six trips a year to New York by the sales director. 这家公司与美国的贸易额不能证明销售经理一年六次去纽约是合理的。

◇ **warrantee** n. person who is given a warranty 被保证人

◇ **warrantor** n. person who gives a warranty 保证人

◇ **warranty** n. (a) guarantee or legal document which promises that a machine willwork properly or that an item is of good quality 保证;担保;保证书;担保书: The car is sold with a twelve-month warranty. 这车售出,保修期为12个月。The warranty covers spare parts but not labour costs. 此保证单包括备件,但不包括劳务费。(b) promise in a contract(合同中的)保证;允诺: breach of warranty = failing to do something which is a part of a contract(合同中的)违反保证 (c) statement made by an insured person which declares that the facts stated by him are true(由被保人所做的)担保;保证

**wastage** n. amount lost by being wasted 商品损耗率;消耗量: Allow 10% extra material for wastage. 允许 10% 的额外材料损耗。 natural wastage = losing workers because they resign or retire, not because they are made redundant or are sacked 自然减员(指减员是因辞职或退休,而不是因为人员过剩而裁员或被解雇)

NOTE: no plural

◇ **waste** 1. n. rubbish or things which are not used 废料;废物;垃圾;浪费: The company was fined for putting industrial waste into the river. 公司因向河中倾倒工业废料而被罚款。 It is a waste of time asking the chairman for a rise. 向董事长要求增加工资是浪费时间。 That computer is a waste of money – there are plenty of cheaper models which would do the work just as well. 那台计算机是浪费钱——有好多较便宜的机型也可做好这项工作。

NOTE: no plural

2. a. not used 无用的;多余的;废弃的: waste materials 废料; Cardboard is made from recycled waste paper. 硬纸板是利用回收的废纸制成的。 waste paper basket = container near an office desk into which pieces of rubbish can be put 废纸篓 3. v. to use more than is needed 浪费: to waste money or paper or electricity or time 浪费钱(纸,电和时间); The MD does not like people wasting his time with minor details. 总经理不喜欢人们因琐碎小事浪费他的时间。 We turned off all the heating so as not to waste energy. 为了不浪费能源,我们关掉了所有的暖气。

◇ **wasteful** a. which wastes a lot of something 浪费的;挥霍的;不经济的: This photocopier is very wasteful of paper. 这台影印机非常费纸。

**waterproof** a. which will not let water through 不透水的;防水的: The parts are sent in waterproof packing. 部件用防水材料包装发送。

**waybill** n. list of goods carried, made out by the carrier 运货单(由承运人开出的)

**weak** a. not strong or not active 弱的;疲软的: weak market = share market where prices tend to fall because there are no buyers 疲软的市场; Share prices remained weak. = Share prices did not rise. 股价持续疲软(指股价仍无回升)。

◇ **weaken** v. to become weak 削弱;减弱;疲软: The market weakened. = Share prices fell. 市场疲软(指股票价格下跌)

◇ **weakness** n. being weak 疲软

**wealth** n. large quantity of money owned by someone 财富;财产: wealth tax = tax on money or property or investments owned by someone 财产税(指对个人拥有的钱,财产或投资所征收的税)

NOTE: no plural

◇ **wealthy** a. very rich 富有的;富裕的

**wear and tear** n. fair wear and tear = acceptable damage caused by normal use 合理磨损;正常磨损(指日常使用造成的合理损耗): The insurance policy covers most damage but not fair wear and tear to the machine. 保险单保大多数损耗,但不保机器的正常磨损。

NOTE: no plural

**week** n. period of seven days (from Monday to Sunday)周;星期(从星期一到星期日): to be paid by the week = to be paid a certain amount of money each week 按周付酬; He earns £500 a week or per week. 他每周挣 500 英镑。 She works thirty – five hours per week or she works a thirty – five – hour week. 每周工作 35 个小时。

◇ **weekday** n. normal working day (not Saturday or Sunday)工作日;平日

（除星期六或星期日）

◇ **weekly** a. done every week 按周的；每周的：The weekly rate for the job is £250.这项工作的周工资为 250 英镑。a weekly magazine or a weekly = magazine which is published each week 周刊

**weigh** v. (a) to measure how heavy something is 称…重量；称：He weighed the packet at the post office. 在邮局里他称了称这个包裹的重量。(b) to have a certain weight 有…重量；重（若干）：The packet weighs twenty – five grams. 这包重 25 克。

◇ **weighbridge** n. platform for weighing a lorry and its load（称车和其载量的）台秤；桥秤

◇ **weighing machine** n. machine which measures how heavy a thing or a person is 称量机；衡器

◇ **weight** n. measurement of how heavy something is 重量：to sell fruit by weight = the price is per pound or per kilo of the fruit 按重量出售水果（指以磅，千克为单位出售水果）；false weight = weight on a shop scales which is wrong and so cheats customers 假重量；不足的分量；gross weight = weight of both the container and its contents 毛（总）重；net weight = weight of goods after deducting the packing material and container 净重；to give short weight = to give less than you should 缺斤少两；克扣分量；缺分量；inspector of weights and measures = government official who inspects goods sold in shops to see if the quantities and weights are correct 度量衡检查员（指监督和检查商店所出售商品计量是否正确的政府官员）

◇ **weighted** a. weighted average = average which is calculated taking several factors into account, giving some more value than others 加权平均数；加权平均值（见 average）；weighted index = index where some important items are given more value than less important ones 加权指数

◇ **weighting** n. additional salary or wages paid to compensate for living in anexpensive part of the country 工资补贴（指一个国家某地区因生活费用高而给予的额外工资）：salary plus a London weighting 工资加伦敦地区工资补贴

**welfare** n. (a) looking after people 福利；福利事业：The chairman is interested in the welfare of the workers' families. 董事长关心体力工人家庭的福利事业。welfare state = country which looks after the health, education, etc., of the people 福利国家 (b) money paid by the government to people who need it 福利费
NOTE: no plural

**well – known** a. known by many people 知名的；有名的

◇ **well – paid** a. earning a high salary 报酬优厚的；高工资的

**wharf** n. place in a dock where a ship can tie up to load or unload 码头；停泊处
NOTE: plural is wharfs or wharves

◇ **wharfage** n. charge for tying up at a wharf 码头费；停泊费（指停泊于码头所缴纳的费用）
NOTE: no plural

◇ **wharfinger** n. person who works on a wharf 码头管理人

**wheeler – dealer** n. person who lives on money from a series of profitable business deals 从事多种商业的人

**whereof** ad. fml. In witness whereof I sign my hand. = I sign as a witness that this is correct. 作为证人我的签字，这是正确的。

**white** a. & n. the colour of snow 白色的：white sale = sale of sheets or towels, etc. (被单，毛巾等的)出售

◇ **white – collar union** n. trade union formed of white – collar workers 白领工人工会

◇ **white - collar worker** n. worker inan office, not in a factory 白领工人；职员；白领阶层（指在办公室而不去工厂工作的人员）

◇ **white goods** pl. n. (a) machines ( such as refrigerators, washing machines) which are used in the kitchen 家用电器(指厨房用的如：冰箱,洗衣机等) (b) sheets or towels, etc. 被单；毛巾等

◇ **white knight** n. person or company which rescues a firm in financial difficulties, especially which saves a firm from being taken over by an unacceptable purchaser 救星；事业捍卫者；救援者（指挽救一家陷入财政危机的公司,尤其是使其避免被无法接受的买主收买的人或公司）

◇ **White Paper** n. GB report from the government on a particular problem 白皮书(指英国政府就某问题所做的正式报告)

**whole - life insurance** n. insurance where the insured person pays a fixed premium each year and the insurance company pays a sum when he dies 终身人寿保险(指被保人每年付固定保险费,到其死时,保险公司可支付一笔钱)

**wholesale** n. & ad. buying goods from manufacturers and selling in large quantities to traders who then sell in smaller quantities to the general public 批发；批发地；大批地：wholesale discount 批发折扣；wholesale shop 批发商店；wholesale dealer = person who buys in bulk from manufacturers and sells to retailers 批发商；wholesale price index = index showing the rises and falls of prices of manufactured goods as they leave the factory 批发价格指数；He buys wholesale and sells retail. = He buys goods in bulk at a wholesale discount and then sells in small quantities to the public. 他整批购买商品,然后零散出售。

NOTE: no plural

◇ **wholesaler** n. person who buys goods in bulk from manufacturers and sells them to retailers 批发商

**wholly - owned subsidiary** n. company which is owned completely by another company 附属公司,独家开设的分号（子公司）

**wildcat strike** n. strike organized suddenly by workers without the main union office knowing about it 工人自发性罢工

**will** n. legal document where someone says what should happen to his property when he dies 遗嘱：He wrote his will in 1964. 1964 年他立了遗嘱。According to her will, all her property is left to her children. 根据她的遗嘱,她所有的财产留给她的儿女们。

**win** v. to be successful 获胜；取得成功：to win a contract = to be successful in tendering for a contract 赢得合同；中标；The company announced that it had won a contract worth £25m to supply buses and trucks. 这家公司宣布已赢得了价值 2500 万英镑供应公共汽车和卡车的合同。

NOTE: winning - won

**windfall** n. sudden winning of money or sudden profit which is not expected 意外的收获；横财：windfall tax = tax on sudden profits 暴利税

**wind up** v. (a) to end (a meeting)结束（会议）：He wound up the meeting with a vote of thanks to the committee. 他以投票感谢该委员会结束了这次会议。(b) to wind up a company = to put a company into liquidation 停业；关闭公司（以清算）：The court ordered the company to be wound up. 法院令这家公司停业清理。

NOTE: winding - wound

◇ **winding up** n. liquidation or closing of a company and selling its assets(企业的)停业清理：a compulsory winding up order = order from a court saying that a company must be wound up(法院的)强制性清算;强制关闭

**window** n. opening in a wall, with glass in it 窗户: shop window = large window in a shop front, where customers can see goods displayed 橱窗; window display = display of goods in a shop window 橱窗陈设; window envelope = envelope with a hole in it covered with plastic like a window, so that the address on the letter inside can be seen 开窗信封; window shopping = looking at goods in shop windows, without buying anything 逛商店;

◇ **window dressing** n. (a) putting goods on display in a shop window, so that they attract customers 橱窗装饰;橱窗陈列(以吸引顾客)(b) putting on a display to make a business seem better or more profitable or more efficient than it really is 粉饰门面;弄虚作假;

**wire** 1. n. telegram 电报: to send someone a wire 给某人发电报 2. v. to send a telegram to (someone)打电报(给某人): He wired the head office to say that the deal had been signed. 他打电报告诉总公司那笔买卖已签署。

**withdraw** v. (a) to take (money) out of an account(从银行)提款: to withdraw money from the bank or from your account 从银行(帐户)中提款; You can withdraw up to £50 from any bank on presentation of a banker's card. 出示一张银行卡你能从银行提不超过50英镑的钱。(b) to take back (an offer)撤回;收回: One of the company's backers has withdrawn. = He stopped supporting the company financially. 该公司的一位支持者已撤出(指他停止了在财政上对公司的支持)。to withdraw a takeover bid 撤回兼并递价; The chairman asked him to withdraw the remarks he has made about the finance director. 董事长

要他撤回他对财务主任的评论。

NOTE: withdrawing - withdrew - has withdrawn

◇ **withdrawal** n. removing money from an account 提款;撤回: withdrawal without penalty at seven days' notice = money can be taken out of a deposit account, without losing any interest, provided that seven days' notice has been given 无罚金提前7天通知提款; to give seven days' notice of withdrawal 提前7天通知提款

**withholding tax** n. (i) tax which takes money away from interest or dividend before it is paid to the investor 预扣税款(指在支付投资者之前,从利息,红利中的税款)(ii) US income tax deducted from the paycheck of a worker before he is paid(美)预扣所得税(指雇主在付给工人薪金之前,扣的所得税)

**within** prep. inside 在…里面;在…内

**witness 1.** n. person who sees something happen 证人;连署人: to act as a witness to a document or a signature = to sign a document to show that you have watched the main signatory sign it 作为文件或签字的证人; The MD signed as a witness. 总经理作为证人签了名。The contract has to be signed in front of two witnesses. 此合同必须当着两位证人的面签署。2. v. to sign (a document) to show that you guarantee that the other signatures on it are genuine 证明;作证: to witness an agreement or a signature 在协议上签名作证

**wording** n. series of words 措词;字句: Did you read the wording on the contract? 你看了此合同的措词吗?

NOTE: no plural

**word - processing** n. working with words, using a computer to produce, check and change texts, reports, letters, etc. 文字处理: Load the word - processing program before you start keyboarding. 在你开始用键盘操作之前, 必须装上文字处理程序。word - processing bureau = office which specializes in word - processing for other companies 文字处理社 (指专门为其他公司进行文字处理的机构)

NOTE: no plural

◇ **word - processor** n. small computer or typewriter with a computer in it, used for working with words to produce texts, reports, letters, etc. 文字处理机

**work** 1. n. (a) things done using the hands or brain 劳动; 工作; 作业: casual work = work where the workers are hired for a short period 临时工作; clerical work = work done in an office 文书工作; manual work = heavy work done by hand 手工劳动; 体力劳动; work in progress = value of goods being manufactured which are not complete at the end of the accounting period 未完工程; 在制品 (b) job or something done to earn money 做事; 工作: He goes to work by bus. 他乘公共汽车上班。She never gets home from work before 8 p. m.. 她从没有晚上 8 点以前下班回家。His work involves a lot of travelling. 他的工作有许多旅行的机会。He is still looking for work. 他仍在找工作。She has been out of work for six months. 她已失业 6 个月。work permit = official document which allows someone who is not a citizen to work in a country 工作许可证 (指允许非公民在一个国家工作的官方证件)

NOTE: no plural

2. v. (a) to do things with your hands or brain, for money 工作; 劳动; 干活: The factory is working hard to complete the order. 为完成订单, 这家工厂一直在苦干。She works better now that she has been promoted. 即然她被提升了, 所以干得更好。to work a machine = to make a machine function 开机器; to work to rule = to work strictly according to rules agreed between the company and the trade union, and therefore work very slowly 按章工作, (指严格地按照公司与工会的规定工作, 因此工作速度极慢) (b) to have a paid job 从事某种职业; 工作: She works in an office. 她在办公室工作。He works at Smith's. 他在史密斯公司工作。He is working as a cashier in a supermarket. 他在超级市场做出纳员。

◇ **worker** n. (a) person who is employed 雇员; 工人: blue - collar worker = manual worker in a factory 蓝领工人; casual worker = worker who can be hired for a short period 临时工; 短工; clerical worker = person who works in an office 办公室工作人员; 文书工作者; factory worker = person who works in a factory 工厂工人; manual worker = worker who works with his hands 体力劳动者; white - collar worker = office worker 白领工人; 白领阶层; 脑力劳动者; worker director = director of a company who is a representative of the workforce 工人董事; worker representation on the board = having a representative of the workers as a director of the company (董事会的) 职工代表 (b) person who works hard 辛勤劳动者: she's a real worker. 她是一位真正的辛勤劳动者。

◇ **working** a. (a) (person) who works 工作的; 劳动的: the working population of a country 一国家的劳动人口; working partner = partner who works in a partnership 经营合伙人; working party = group of experts who study a problem 特派组; 工作组; The government set up a working party to examine the problem of computers in schools. 政府设立了一个专家工作组检查学校计算机问题。(b) referring to work 工作的; 运转的; 运用的: working capital = capital in cash and stocks needed for a company to be able to work 流动

资金；周转资金；营运资金；working conditions= general state of the place where people work (if it is hot, noisy, dark, dangerous, etc.)工作条件；生产条件(如：热、噪声、暗、危险等)；the normal working week = the usual number of hours worked per week 正常工作周时间：Even though he is a freelance, he works a normal working week. 既使他是自由职业者，他仍按正常工作周时间上班。

◇ **workforce** n. all the workers (in an office or factory)劳动力；工作人员

◇ **workload** n. amount of work which a person has to do 工作量；工作负担：He has difficulty in coping with his heavy workload. 应付繁重的工作量他有困难。

◇ **workman** n. man who works with his hands 工作；劳动者；工匠
NOTE: plural is workmen

◇ **work out** v. (a) to calculate 计算；算出：He worked out the costs on the back of an envelope. 他在信封的背面计算费用。He worked out the discount at 15%. 他算出折扣为 15%。She worked out the discount on her calculator. 她在计算器上算出了折扣。(b) He is working out his notice. = He is working during the time between resigning and actually leaving the company. 在提出辞职这段时间，他一直在工作。

◇ **workplace** n. place where you work 工作场所；车间；工厂

◇ **works** n. factory 工厂：an industrial works 一家工厂；an engineering works 一家制造厂；The steel works is expanding. 这家钢铁厂正在扩建。 works committee or works council = committee of workers and management which discusses the organization of work in a factory 劳资协议会；price ex works = price not including transport from the manufacturer's factory 工厂交货价格

(不包运输费)；the works manager = person in charge of a works 厂务经理；厂长
NOTE: not plural, and takes a singular verb

◇ **work - sharing** n. system where two part - timers share one job 工作分担(指两位兼职者共担一项工作)

◇ **workshop** n. small factory 车间；作坊；工场

◇ **workspace** n. memory or space available on a computer for temporary work 工作空间；贮存空间(计算机的)

◇ **workstation** n. desk with a computer terminal, printer, telephone, etc., where a word - processing operator works 工作台；控制台(指放置计算机终端、打印机、电话等的文字处理机工作人员工作台面)

◇ **work - to - rule** n. working strictly according to the rules agreed between the union and management and therefore very slowly, as a protest 按章工作；怠工(指作为抗议，严格按照工会和资方的规定工作，因此极慢)

**world** n. (a) the earth 地球；世界：the world market for steel = the possible sales of steel in the whole world. 世界钢材市场；He has world rights to a product = he has the right to sell the product anywhere in the world. 他具有某一产品的世界经销权。(b) people in a particular business or people with a special interest···界；···领域：the world of big business 商界；the world of publishing or the publishing world 出版界；the world of lawyers or the legal world 法律界

◇ **World Bank** n. central bank, controlled by the United Nations, whose funds come from the member states of the UN and which lends money to member states 世界银行(也称中央银行，由联合国控制，其资金来自联合国的各成员国，并给各成员国提供贷款)

◇ **worldwide** a. & ad. everywhere in theworld 全世界的；世界范围的：The company has a worldwide network of distributors. 这家公司具有世界范围的经销店网络。Worldwide sales or sales worldwide have topped two million units. 全世界的销售量已高于 200 万件。This make of computer is available worldwide. 这种牌名的计算机是世界各地都能买到。

**worth** 1. a. having a value or a price 值…的；相当于…价值的：Do not get it repaired – it is worth only £25. 不要修理了，它才值 25 英镑。The car is worth £6,000 on the secondhand market. 这辆汽车在旧货市场值 6,000 英镑。He is worth £10m. = His property or investments, etc. would sell for £10m. 他拥有价值 1000 万英磅的财产。What are ten pounds worth in dollars? = What is the equivalent of ♯10 in dollars? 10 英镑值多少美元？NOTE: always follows the verb to be 2. n. value 价值：give me ten pounds' worth of petrol = give me as much petrol as £10 will buy 给我价值 10 英镑的汽油。

◇ **worthless** a. having no value 不值钱的；无价值的；无用的：The cheque is worthless if it is not signed. 如这张支票没签名，是无用的。

**wrap (up)** v. to cover something all over (in paper)(用纸)包；裹；捆：He wrapped (up) the parcel in green paper. 他用绿色的纸将此包包起来了。to gift – wrap a present = to wrap a present in special coloured paper 用礼品包装纸将礼品包起来

◇ **wrapper** n. material which wraps something 包装物；包皮：The biscuits are packed in plastic wrappers. 饼干是用塑料包皮包装的。

◇ **wrapping** n. wrapping paper = special coloured paper for wrapping pre-sents 包装纸(彩色的)；gift – wrapping = (i) service in a store for wrapping presents for customers 商店为顾客提供的包装礼品服务(ii) coloured paper for wrapping presents 彩色的礼品包装纸

**wreck** 1. n. (a) ship which has sunk or which has been badly damaged and cannotfloat(船只等)失事；遇难：They saved the cargo from the wreck. 他们从遇难船上的救出了货物。Oil poured out of the wreck of the tanker. 原油从那艘遇难的油轮中滚滚流出来。(b) company which has collapsed(公司等)破产；倒闭：He managed to save some of his investment from the wreck of the company. 他设法从这家倒闭的公司中挽救出一些他的投资。Investors lost thousands of pounds in the wreck of the investment company. 这家投资公司倒闭时投资者们损失了数千英镑。2. v. to damage badly or to ruin 严重损害；毁灭：They are trying to salvage the wrecked tanker. 他们正设法营救那艘遇难油轮。The negotiations were wrecked by the unions. 谈判遭到了工会严重破坏。

**writ** n. legal document ordering someone to do something or not to do something(法院等的)命令；令状；传票：The court issued a writ to prevent the trade union from going on strike. 法院发出命令阻止工会举行罢工。to serve someone with a writ or to serve a writ on someone = to give someone a writ officially, so that he has to obey it 将传票送交给某人

**write** v. to put words or figures on to paper 书写；写下：She wrote a letter of complaint to the manager. 她给经理写了封投诉信。The telephone number is written at the bottom of the notepaper. 电话号码写在那张信纸的底部。NOTE: writing – wrote – has written

◇ **write down** v. to note an asset at a

lower value than previously 减记（价值）；划减；降低帐面价值：written down value 减记资产价值；The car is written down in the company's books. 这辆车减记在公司的帐簿上。

◇ **writedown** n. noting of an asset at a lower value 减记（资产价值）；划减

◇ **write off** v. to cancel (a debt) or to remove an asset from the accounts as having no value 销帐；注销（指将资产从帐上注销）：to write off bad debts 注销坏帐；Two cars were written off after the accident. = The insurance company considered that both cars were a total loss.事故发生后，两辆车都报废了（指保险公司认为这两辆车是彻底损坏）。The cargo was written off as a total loss. = The cargo was so badly damaged that the insurers said it had no value.这批船货作为全损报废。

◇ **write - off** n. total loss or cancellation of a bad debt or removal of an asset's value in a company's accounts 损失总额；注销坏帐；删除帐面值：The car was a write - off.这辆车报废了。to allow for write - offs in the yearly accounts 要考虑到年终帐面注销坏帐的问题

◇ **write out** v. to write in full 写完；写好：She wrote out the minutes of the meeting from her notes. 她按她的笔记将这次会议的记录整理好。to write out a cheque = to write the words and figures on a cheque and then sign it 开支票（指在空白支票上填上数额、日期并签上字）

◇ **writing** n. something which has been written 书写；书面形式：to put the agreement in writing 将此协议写下来；He has difficulty in reading my writing. 他看我的书写有困难。

NOTE: no plural

**wrong** a. not right or not correct 错误的；不正确的：The total in the last column is wrong. 最后一栏的总额是错误

的。The sales director reported the wrong figures to the meeting. 销售经理向会议报告的数字是错的。I tried to phone, but I got the wrong number. 我试着打过电话，但我的号码是错的。

◇ **wrongful** a. unlawful 非法的；不正当的：wrongful dismissal = removing someone from a job for reasons which are wrong 非法解雇

◇ **wrongly** ad. not correctly or badly 错误地；不正确地：He wrongly invoiced Smith Ltd for £250, when he should have credited them with the same amount. 当他应把同样金额记入史密斯有限公司贷方时，他错误地给该公司开了 250 英镑的发票。

**X = EXTENSION** 延长；延期；展期

**Xerox** 1. n. (a) trade mark for a type of photocopier 施乐（一种复印机的商标）：to make a xerox copy of a letter 将信件用施乐机复制一份；We must order some more xerox paper for the copier. 我们必须为这台复印机多订购一些施乐牌复印纸。We are having a new xerox machine installed tomorrow. 明天我们要安装一台新的施乐复印机。(b) photocopy made with a xerox machine 复印件（用施乐复印机复印的）：to send the other party a xerox of the contract 发给另一方一份这个合同的复印件；We have sent xeroxes to each of the agents. 我们已将复印本送给每位代理商了。2. v. to make a photocopy with a xerox machine（用施乐复印机）复印；影印：to xerox a document 复印

一份文件；She xeroxed all the file. 她将这份文件全部复印了。

# Yy

**yard** n. (a) measure of length ( = 0.91 metres)(长度单位)码(1 码 = 0.91 米) (NOTE: can be written yd after figures: 10yd) (b) factory which builds ships 造船厂

**yd** = YARD 码

**year** n. period of twelve months 年；年度：calendar year = year from January 1st to December 31st 历年(12 个月, 从 1 月 1 日到 12 月 31 日)；financial year = the twelve month period for a firm's accounts 财政年度；会计年度(一个企业财政年度为 12 个月)；fiscal year = twelve month period on which taxes are calculated (in the UK it is April 6th to April 5th of the following year)财政年度(在英国是从本年的 4 月 6 日到第二年的 4 月 5 日)；year end = the end of the financial year, when a company's accounts are prepared 年终(指财政年度结束)：The accounts department has started work on the year - end accounts. 财务部门已开始进行年终帐的结算。

◇ **yearbook** n. reference book which is published each year with updated or new information 年监；年报

◇ **yearly** a. happening once a year 每年的；一年一次的：yearly payment 年支付费用；yearly premium of £250 年保险金为 250 英镑

**yellow pages** pl. n. section of a telephone directory (printed on yellow paper) which lists businesses under various headings (such as computer shops or newsagents, etc.)黄色封面电话查号簿(指各商业部门的电话号码都在此部分, 如：计算机商店, 报刊经售人等)

**yen** n. money used in Japan 日元(日本的货币)
NOTE: usually written Y before a figure: Y2,700 (say "two thousand seven hundred yen")

**yield** 1. n. money produced as a return on an investment(投资等的)收益：current yield = dividend calculated as a percentage of the price paid per share 本期收益(指按每股所付的价格的百分比算出的股息)；share with a current yield of 5% 本期股票的收益为 5%。dividend yield = dividend expressed as a percentage of the price of a share 股息收益；earnings yield = money earned in dividends per share as a percentage of the market price of the share 净收益；effective yield = actual yield shown as a percentage of the price paid 实际收入；fixed yield = fixed percentage return which does not change 固定收益；gross yield = profit from investments before tax is deducted 毛收益 2. v. to produce (as interest or dividend, etc.)产生；产出(利息, 股息等)：government stocks which yield a small interest 利息少的政府债券；shares which yield 10% 收益为 10%的股票

# Zz

**zero** n. nought or number 0 零：The code for international calls is zero one zero (010). 国际电话的区域号是 010. zero inflation = inflation at 0% 通货膨胀指数为零

NOTE: nought is more common in GB English

◇ **zero – rated** a. (item) which has a VAT rate of 0%(商品)增值税率为零

◇ **zero – coupon bond** n. bond which does not carry any interest or where the interestis contained in the capital gain 零息债券(指利息为零或利率包含在资本收益里的债券)

◇ **zero – rating** n. rating of an item at 0% VAT 增值税率为零的商品

**zip code** n. US letters and numbers used to indicate a town or street in an address on an envelope(美)邮政编码

NOTE: the GB English for this is postcode

**zone** 1. n. area of a town or country (for administrative purposes)(城市等的)区;地区(以便管理): development zone or enterprise zone = area which has been given special help from the government to encourage businesses and factories to set up there 开发区; free trade zone = area where there are no customs duties 自由贸易区(免税区) 2. v. to divide (a town) into different areas for planning purposes(将城镇)划分(成若干区域以便规划): land zoned for light industrial use = land where planning permission has been given to build small factories for light industry 此地划作建轻工业厂房用

# DATE DUE

| | | | |
|---|---|---|---|
| | | | |
| | | | |
| | | | |
| | | | |
| | | | |
| | | | |
| | | | |
| | | | |
| | | | |
| | | | |
| | | | |
| | | | |
| | | | |
| | | | |
| | | | |
| | | | |
| | | | |
| | | | |
| | | | |
| | | | |
| | | | |
| GAYLORD | | | PRINTED IN U.S.A. |